Praise for
Understanding the War Industry

"To an ever-increasing extent, the business of America is the business of war. But although Americans live in the shadow of a war economy, few understand the full extent of its power and influence. Thanks to Christian Sorensen's deeply researched book into the military-industrial complex that envelops our society, such ignorance can no longer be an excuse."

—ANDREW COCKBURN, author of *Kill Chain: The Rise of the High Tech Assassins*

"A devastating account of American militarism, brilliantly depicted, and exhaustively researched in an authoritative manner. Sorensen's book is urgent, fascinating reading for anyone who wants to save the country and the world from political, economic, and ecological disaster. Its message is so convincingly delivered that it will change many open minds forever and for the better."

—RICHARD FALK

"Have you ever wondered why the United States is always at war? This meticulously researched book lays out in painstaking detail exactly how our nation has been captured by a war industry that profits from endless conflict and pursues profit at all costs. It will shock you, infuriate you, and hopeful inspire you to help dismantle the grotesque killing machine that steals our resources, wreaks havoc around the world, and leaves the merchants of death laughing all the way to the bank."

—MEDEA BENJAMIN, codirector, CODEPINK for Peace

"I'm adding Christian Sorensen's new book, *Understanding the War Industry,* to the list of books I think will convince you to help abolish war and militaries… [It is] not so much analysis as an effort to persuade through the repetition of examples, countless examples, naming names and laid out over hundreds of pages. The author admits that he's only scratching the surface. But he's scratching it in lots of different places, and the result ought to be persuasive for most people."

—DAVID SWANSON, World Beyond War

More Praise for *Understanding the War Industry*

"Christian Sorensen is the Seymour Melman of the 21st century, dissecting the military-industrial-congressional complex and providing us a way to understand this convoluted machine which exploits and oppresses the entire world…"

—WILL GRIFFIN, founder and director of The Peace Report.

"It has long been obvious that America's numerous, hugely expensive and destructive and seemingly perpetual wars of choice have not been intended to serve any interests of the vast majority of the American people. In *Understanding the War Industry,* Christian Sorensen presents detailed and thoroughly documented evidence to convincingly support his conviction that the dominant force among those seeking war for the sake of war is the pursuit of profit maximization by the corporate 'war industry.' He concludes: 'There will be no escape from interminable wars until this reality is recognized and resisted.' This book offers a major contribution to that struggle."

—JOHN V. WHITBECK, International Laywer

UNDERSTANDING THE WAR INDUSTRY

Christian Sorensen

Clarity Press, Inc.

© 2020 Christian Sorensen
ISBN: 978-1-949762-22-8
ebook: 978-1-949762-23-5

Cover design: R. Jordan Santos
Cover photo credit: Guy Corbishley / Alamy Stock Photo
In-house editor: Diana G. Collier

ALL RIGHTS RESERVED: Except for purposes of review, this book may not be copied, or stored in any information retrieval system, in whole or in part, without permission in writing from the publisher.

Library of Congress Control Number: 2020935492

Clarity Press, Inc.
2625 Piedmont Rd. NE, Suite 56
Atlanta, GA. 30324
https://www.claritypress.com

Table of Contents

PREFACE ix

CHAPTER 1: THE BIG PICTURE 1
    Trillions. 1
    Carnage. 1
    Pollution 3
    Occupying Afghanistan, Destroying Iraq. 8
    BOSS 13
    Bombing. 18
    Industry Locations 20
    Justifications. 24
    Futures Command 27
    Endnotes. 30

CHAPTER 2: MAGNIFYING INFLUENCE 46
    Pulling In Military Retirees 47
    Stacking the Pentagon Deck. 50
    Shattering the Glass Ceiling. 52
    Campaign Finance 54
    Lobbying. 61
    Pressure Groups 66
    Banking and Investment Firm Stakeholders. 68
    Corporate Media & Think Tanks 70
    Endnotes. 76

CHAPTER 3: FINANCIALS AND LEGALESE 92
    Contract Types 92
    Multifarious Funding/Incessant Purchasing. 93
    Weaseling the Contracts 97
    Inculpating Small Business 99
    Seducing Native Americans 101
    The (Failed) Audit 103
    Offices & Administration 106
    Ensuring Legal Impunity 107
    Propagandizing Recruitment 113
    Endnotes. 117

CHAPTER 4: THE TRICKS OF THE TRADE 133
Cooperation 133
Memes 134
Threat Fabrication 138
Ruses. 143
Built-In Obsolescence 146
Euphemisms 148
Endnotes 153

CHAPTER 5: FOREIGN MILITARY SALES 164
Rationalizations 164
The MQ-4C Triton 165
A Single Month's Sales 166
Zionism, an Industry Perspective 168
A Tale of Two Regimes: D.C. and the House of Saud 173
Selling to Countries Within Central Command 176
Selling to the U.S. for Operations Within Central Command 177
Outposts, Death, and Airwars 181
Gotta Get That Cash 186
The Key to Military Policy 187
Endnotes 190

CHAPTER 6: THE ACADEMY 207
Beantown & Beyond 207
Stanford University 212
Computing, Colonization, and Language Capacity 214
Johns Hopkins, the Star 218
Higher Education 221
Labs & Centers 223
Militarizing Education 224
Brain Drain 228
Endnotes 230

CHAPTER 7: INFORMATION TECHNOLOGY 241
Information Takeover 241
Intel 244
Managing Data Overload 248

    Cloudy with a Chance of Fleecing..........................249
        Amazon...250
        Microsoft.......................................252
        Google..253
    A Taste of C4ISR & CACI.....................................255
    Cyber...259
    DMT and Special Relationships...............................261
    Endnotes..265

CHAPTER 8: "OUR" HEMISPHERE........................277

    SOUTHCOM..277
    Brazil..281
    Honduras..282
    Colombia..283
    Mexico..286
    Special Marketing Ops.......................................287
    The Puerto Rican Colony....................................289
    Guantánamo: Occupied Territory............................295
    Endemic Tunnel Vision.....................................296
    Endnotes..299

CHAPTER 9: THE NUCLEAR ARSENAL.....................313

    Ogden..313
    Beyond Reckless..314
    MDA..316
    The Modernization Scam.....................................321
    Endnotes..326

CHAPTER 10: REMOTELY PILOTED VEHICLES
AND SPACE ASSETS....................................336

    Unmanned Aerial Vehicles...................................336
    In Your FACE (Fairs, Air Shows, Conferences, Exhibits).........338
    Variations on a Theme......................................340
    Death Toll..342
    One Season...343
    Space: The Final Profiteer...................................345
    Space Force..351
    Endnotes..353

CHAPTER 11: TWO, THREE, MANY SPECIAL OPERATIONS 366

    The Status Quo 366
    Superheroes or Super Profit? 368
    Provisioning Hyper-Enabled Operators 372
    SOFIC 2019 and MARSOF 2030 375
    SOF Construction for Nonstop War 378
    Seeking New Enemies 379
    Endnotes 380

CHAPTER 12: TRANSITIONING 389

    Education and Organizing 389
    Elections and Legislation 390
    Demobilization 391
    Disobedience 391
    The Draft 392
    Demilitarizing Industry 392
    International Solidarity 395
    Prosecutions 396
    Redirecting Funding 397
    Endnotes 398

ACRONYMS & INITIALISMS . . . .

INDEX . . . .

Preface

1970 was a year of shocks.

In January, as the globe was still coping with the My Lai Massacre, Christopher Pyle revealed how U.S. Army Intelligence Command had been running an enormous domestic surveillance and infiltration program against progressives, radicals, environmental campaigners, racial justice advocates, and anti-war activists. D.C. and Moscow tested nuclear weapons in March. In April, the Israeli Air Force bombed the *Bahr al-Baqar* school in Egypt, killing dozens of children and staff. In the same month, D.C. initiated an invasion of Cambodia. The National Campus Strike kicked off in May. May also saw the Ohio National Guard shoot protestors at Kent State University. Ten days later, police killed two more at Jackson State University in Mississippi. The rest of 1970 wasn't much better.

One positive event in 1970 was the publication of Seymour Melman's seminal work, *Pentagon Capitalism: The Political Economy of War.* In that book, Melman analyzed how the headquarters of the U.S. Armed Forces coordinated and administered the businesses that make weapons of war. This book does not attempt to refute Melman's argument. Rather, it contends that, in the fifty years since *Pentagon Capitalism* hit the press, the playing field has changed.

President Dwight D. Eisenhower warned us about the military-industrial-congressional triangle (MIC) in his famous farewell address in January 1961. He referred to it as the military-industrial complex, omitting the congressional side, which had been present in earlier drafts of his address. Eisenhower warned:

> We must never let the weight of this combination [the military-industrial-congressional complex] endanger our liberties or democratic processes. ... Only an alert and knowledgeable citizenry can compel the proper meshing of the huge industrial and military machinery of defense with our peaceful methods and goals.

Clearly, the warning has gone unheeded. Today, in the twenty-first century, the MIC, rather than being curtailed, has demonstrably further penetrated the institutions of U.S. government. The MIC may be viewed as an insulated war-promoting configuration comprised of the Pentagon, the headquarters of the U.S. Armed Forces; industry, the corporations that develop and sell goods and services to the U.S. and allied governments; and the U.S. Congress, which implements policies and authorizes the funding for the Pentagon.

The change from Melman's time is this: war corporations—the industrial part of the MIC—now hold the most power in the trifecta. The Pentagon no longer controls the U.S. war industry. Industry runs the show. Industry employs expansive, sometimes pernicious, operations in order to dominate political processes and military functions.

What has happened in the Department of Defense has happened across the U.S. government. Corporatization of government functions is taking place everywhere. A few recent examples include the Environmental Protection Agency colluding with chemical corporations, the Food & Drug Administration aiding giant agri-businesses, and the Federal Communications Commission working to repeal net neutrality. Corporations that break the law are less and less likely to face punishment.[1] The U.S. government serves corporate interests. And the raison d'être of corporations is to maximize profit. Nowhere is this more evident than in the Department of Defense, which will be referred to herein by its former, more accurate name: the Department of War. An honest acknowledgment of reality is the first step to understanding the war industry.

This book proceeds on the basis of a few foundational facts: (1) The United States of America is no longer a republic, but an oligarchy.[2] (2) Capital is concentrated in very few hands.[3] (3) The Department of War is not the predominant decision-maker on matters of war and peace. The boardrooms of U.S. corporations are. This unelected bureaucracy has attained war-making authority without democratic debate, let alone democratic support.

The information provided here regarding corporations comes from the Pentagon's daily contract announcements,[4] unless otherwise cited. Individually, these daily announcements seem of little import. But years of cataloguing and arranging the contracts have yielded significant details, patterns, and themes, documented here. As a hero of mine once said, "A lot of tape and a little patience make all the difference." The reporting of journalists, brochures and press releases issued by corporations, interviews, and my own independent experiences supplement my research.

As this book confirms, the wars the U.S. government wages do not cater to the needs of the U.S. citizenry. Today's wars are propelled by the need of corporate behemoths to accrue ever greater profits. U.S. public opinion has no effect on decisions of war and peace. The public may feel free to comment, but the path had already been chosen.

This book is neither an official account nor a specialist military history. Many battles, events, and turning points are omitted. Units of the U.S. Armed Forces are only mentioned when it is illustrative of the goods and services sold by corporations or of a significant pattern of behavior within the war industry as a whole. This book gives the industry point of view. It does not intend to imply that industry is omnipotent or that the Pentagon doesn't eagerly gobble up goods and services for its own narrow purposes. But, despite the extent of documentation provided here, this is not a comprehensive review. The U.S. war industry is far too massive to thoroughly capture or map within a single volume. The focus instead is on the ways the industry operates, on its overall structure and patterns.

I tried to steer clear of foreign war corporations, like the Canadian Commercial Corporation (Ottawa, Canada), which operates on behalf of Canadian industries. In practice, CCC is an adjunct to the U.S. war industry, supporting a variety of U.S. war products, including land vehicles. CCC's board of directors is a who's-who of Canadian capitalists. Some foreign corporations (e.g. the U.K.'s BAE Systems, Italy's Leonardo DRS) play a strong role in the U.S. war industry and are therefore included here and there.

This book is intended as a thorough introduction to the issue. In a nutshell, it lays out how the U.S. war industry operates. The Power Rankings of U.S. war corporations are, as of autumn 2019:

1. Lockheed Martin
2. Boeing "Defense, Space, and Security"
3. Raytheon Technologies (Raytheon + United Technologies; they're merging)
4. General Dynamics
5. Northrop Grumman
6. L3 Harris (L3 and Harris Corp. just merged)
7. Textron
8. Huntington Ingalls
9. SAIC
10. AECOM
11. Booz Allen Hamilton
12. Leidos
13. CACI
14. Honeywell
15. PAE
16. General Electric
17. Accenture
18. DynCorp
19. KBRWyle
20. Jacobs

The Power Rankings introduce you to the main players in the game. Intended as a measure of a corporation's strength, the Rankings are based on public contracts (frequency and dollars received from the War Department), expenditures (political lobbying and campaign contributions), industrial footprint, and recent, major contract wins. These corporations will become familiar to you over the course of this work.

A note on the terms I use. The **war industry** refers specifically to the corporations that design, market, and sell goods and services (including war and "intelligence" products) to the U.S. government and allied governments and regimes around the world. Calling themselves "defense contractors," war corporations do more than design and pitch products. They also plot, plan, fabricate, test, qualify, assemble, produce, inspect, package, deliver, sustain, maintain, upgrade, and redesign products. They are focused on maximizing profit.[5]

The headquarters of the U.S. Armed Forces is a building known as the **Pentagon,** which sits in Arlington, Virginia, overlooking the Potomac River. The word "Pentagon" is used as a metonym for the entire U.S. Department of War. Most soldiers, sailors, airmen, and Marines are *not* part of the MIC. Only the high-ranking generals and admirals are. Enlisted troops join the U.S. Armed Forces largely for economic reasons (though it can be comfortable for them to couch their participation in traditionally patriotic terms), as the uniform is one of the few well-paying jobs remaining in an economy that Wall Street and D.C. have systematically gutted using neoliberal economic policies.

I refer to neoliberal economic policies throughout this book. These policies decrease government monitoring and regulation of corporate activity; allow free movement of corporate goods and services across borders; cut spending on healthcare, education, and public infrastructure; export and automate jobs; and sell off such government assets and services as schools, transportation, and utilities. The U.S. war industry thrives in D.C.'s embrace of neoliberalism.

Once in a while I use the term **war machine.** This term encompasses the entire beast: the war industry, the uniformed troops who fight the wars, the Pentagon officials (generals, admirals, and senior civilians), and Capitol Hill.

References to **"D.C."** and the **"D.C. regime"** are used as a metonym for the elites who have flocked to the greater metropolitan D.C. area. These terms reflect the bipartisan pro-war consensus that festers on Capitol Hill and the surrounding municipal enclaves of the oligarchy.

Once in a while I reference **U.S. Empire** or **U.S. imperialism.** I do so in accordance with the following definition:

U.S. imperialism (*noun*)—the attempt of the major capitalist state (armed, aided, and abetted by the U.S. war industry) to impose its will on the world, particularly the global south.

War profiteering is the primary motivator of D.C.'s wars. Other motivating factors—like the Zionist lobby and D.C.'s desire to control the world's remaining oil reserves—align well with or overlap with U.S. war profiteering.

The word **mercenary,** as used here, refers to personnel who work for war corporations, nominally under the U.S. flag, while receiving greater financial pay than their uniformed peers. Therefore, a mercenary is not just someone who is paid well to pick up a weapon, but also those who are paid well to do tasks (e.g. logistics, IT, cyber, maintenance) that were traditionally carried out by uniformed U.S. Armed Forces personnel. The war industry prefers the term "contractor." I use mercenary.

Finally, I often use the verb **corporatize** instead of "privatize," because I believe it best captures the visceral power grab associated with privatization of government activities.

A note on naming. I write the *New York Times* as *The New York Times,* in the same way people refer to OSU as *The* Ohio State University. It fits the self-assured temperament of the newspaper of record. I omit the exclamation point from the independent news organization *DemocracyNow* to avoid confusion regarding emphasis. When referencing war corporations, particularly smaller or more obscure ones, I provide the location where the war corporation produces the specific good or service in question. For example, Booz Allen Hamilton is headquartered in McLean, Virginia, but Booz Allen Hamilton (Lexington Park, MD) sells services to the Naval Air Warfare Center Aircraft Division's Special Communications Mission Solutions Division in St. Inigoes, Maryland. Since the Lexington Park branch is where the particular services are developed or sold, Lexington Park is the location I credit.

The Pentagon is constantly renaming organizations it controls. While I was writing this monograph, the Space and Naval Warfare Systems Center Pacific became the Naval Information Warfare Center Pacific, and the Evolved Expendable Launch Vehicle program became the National Security Space Launch program. For simplicity, I use the old names. My transliteration of Arabic to English sometimes favors popular representation: al-Qaeda, instead of al-Qa'ida. Finally, in citations I keep others' Arabic transliteration choices without the pedantic "sic."

I sent many questions and requests for explanation to U.S. corporations during the course of my research. Most corporations did not respond. Instead of repeatedly stating "[corporation] did not answer my question" or "[corporation] declined to comment" throughout this research, I tend to note only when a corporation replied with helpful information.

Any mistakes herein are mine alone, and not the fault of any editors, associates, peers, or the publisher. The views expressed herein are my own, certainly not the official stance of the Department of War or any war corporation.

Chapter One lays out the foundation and costs of war. Chapter Two demonstrates how the war industry gains influence and propels the military-industrial-congressional triangle. Chapter Three covers the financial and legal foundations enabling war. Chapter Four explores some tricks the war industry employs. Chapter Five explores foreign military sales. Chapter Six analyzes academic institutions that are part of the war industry. Chapter Seven explores perhaps the most profitable sector: information technology. Chapter Eight demonstrates how industry views the hemisphere. Chapters Nine through Eleven tackle a few salient sectors of profit: nuclear weaponry, drones, space-based technology, and special operations.

A people must be informed in order to keep their democracy healthy and functioning. It is my hope that this book contributes, even slightly, to the full awakening of the U.S. public—citizenry and residents together—so they can confront those who have turned the United States into a nation of permanent warfare at their expense. Peacefully, of course. We're all in this together.

ENDNOTES

1 "Penalties for Corporate Violations Plummet by Double Digits Under Trump." *Public Citizen.* 25 July 2018: <www.citizen.org/media/press-releases/penalties-corporate-violations-plummet-double-digits-under-trump>. The study examines 12 federal agencies. Punishment of corporate criminality fell by an average of over 50%. EPA fines against corporate polluters, for instance, dropped around 95%. This isn't a Trump-only phenomenon; the Obama administration didn't prosecute the Wall Street criminals who crashed the global economy in 2008-9. See also "Justice Department Data Reveal 29 Percent Drop in Criminal Prosecutions of Corporations." Syracuse University Transactional Records Access Clearinghouse (TRAC). 13 October 2015: <https://trac.syr.edu/tracreports/crim/406/>.

2 Martin Gilens and Benjamin I. Page. 2014. "Testing Theories of American Politics: Elites, Interest Groups, and Average Citizens." *Perspectives on Politics* 12(3): 564-581. Merriam-Webster provides us with a strong, practical definition of *oligarchy:* a government in which a small group exercises control especially for corrupt and selfish purposes.

3 Frank, Robert. "Richest 1% now owns half the world's wealth." *CNBC.* 14 November 2017. Kirsch, Noah. "The 3 Richest Americans Hold More Wealth Than Bottom 50% Of The Country, Study Finds." *Forbes.* 9 November 2017. For analysis of the state of global capital, see "The Global Power Elite: A Transnational Class" (*The Real News Network,* 26 December 2018).

4 Prior to the summer of 2018, these contracts were available at <defense.gov/News/Contracts>. From summer 2018 through summer 2019, daily contract listings were available at <dod.defense.gov/News/Contracts>. They're now available at <defense.gov/Newsroom/Contracts>. The contracts I cite here are generally drawn from a period spanning the summer of 2014 through 30 Sept 2018,

the end of that fiscal year. These contract announcements provide such valuable information as the type of good or service sold, the production location, the contract number, the awardee (sometimes a country, sometimes a branch of the U.S. Armed Forces), the date of award, and the size of the contract. Sometimes these bits of information are omitted. Sometimes this information is modified or amended in a later listing. I use the date of the contract announcement as the date of sale.

5 I did my best to capture and attribute war goods & matériel accurately. However, the scribes within the Dept. of War did not make it easy: their daily contract lists are rife with errors, including misspelled names of war corporations ("Vectrul" instead of Vectrus) and places (the South American country of "Columbia," instead of Colombia). The Dept. of War also often credits corporations under defunct or former names.

The history of the present D.C. regime is a history of repeated injuries and usurpations, all having in direct object the establishment of an absolute tyranny over these States.

To prove this, let facts be submitted to a candid world.

1

The Big Picture

TRILLIONS

At least $6.4 trillion has been allocated to post-9.11 U.S. "homeland security" and wars in Iraq, Afghanistan, Pakistan, and Syria through to fiscal year 2020.[1] Capitol Hill spent roughly $1.25 trillion in 2019 on war-related costs.[2] The Department asks for and receives an enormous budget every year while simultaneously cooking the books.[3]

Many war corporations receiving money from the Pentagon do not pay their fair share of taxes.[4] The tax burden falls on the working class. The working class in the United States pays high taxes relative to those in other industrialized nations but is not granted the social safety net that usually comes with high taxation.[5] And, of those taxes that workers pay, far more tax dollars go to war corporations than to the troops.[6]

To spend trillions on war is morally criminal, since rigorous estimates indicate that it would take roughly a mere $70 billion yearly to lift the poorest above the poverty line.[7] The money D.C. spends on war harms government ledgers[8] and leads to rising inequality.[9]

Other costs loom large. These costs are measured in lives and pollution.

CARNAGE

The war on Iraq began with the 1991 U.S. invasion, which was followed by U.S-led sanctions against that country. Such sanctions prevented crucial medical supplies and daily necessities from entering Iraq. "Undisputed UN figures show that 1.7 million Iraqi civilians died due to the West's brutal sanctions regime, half of whom were children," British author Dr. Nafeez Ahmed accurately states.[10] *The Lancet*, a peer-reviewed medical journal, estimates roughly 655,000 humans lost their lives in Iraq from the 2003 U.S. invasion through July 2006.[11] Physicians for Social Responsibility estimates that U.S. wars, 2001-11, have led to the death of at least 1.3 million humans[12] in Iraq, Afghanistan, and Pakistan. The Pentagon's battlefield is global.[13] Journalist Nick Turse reports U.S. special operations forces are present in 149 countries.[14] Most of the deaths attributable to the U.S. military, as a result of these elective global wars, will never come to light. "Total deaths from Western interventions in Iraq and Afghanistan since the 1990s—from direct killings and the longer-term impact of war-imposed deprivation—likely constitute around 4 million… and could be as high as 6-8 million people when accounting for higher avoidable death estimates in Afghanistan."[15]

War corporations sell armed mercenaries to the War Department. These mercenaries die, too. Why use armed mercenaries? The war industry knows it needs to keep the deaths of uniformed troops at a minimum. Too many soldiers, sailors, airmen, and Marines dying (in the optional wars pushed by the war industry) would draw unnecessary attention to the racket. Mercenaries die in warzones. They absorb deaths that would otherwise bloody the military ranks. This allows the War Department and Capitol Hill to cite low casualty figures. Additionally, using mercenaries keeps conscription off the table. Conscription would expand the burden of war into the upper-middle and upper classes of society, dragging in the sons and daughters of the ruling elite. That would be unacceptable to industry executives and the D.C. regime. Mercenaries keep the war machine firing on all cylinders.

Over 6,960 U.S. Armed Forces personnel (uniformed troops and some War Department civilians) and 7,250 mercenaries have died in the post-9.11 wars.[16] Nearly one million veterans have filed disability claims with the Department of Veterans Affairs.[17] The common human fights[18] while the rich human profits.

These morbidity statistics do not account for the veterans who return to the United States and subsequently commit suicide. The suicide rate among veterans increased thirty-five percent from 2001 to 2016.[19] That means over twenty veterans per day commit suicide, with the highest suicide rates in rural areas like New Mexico, Nevada, and Montana.[20] 2018 saw the highest number of suicides among active-duty personnel since 2012: 321 active-duty troops killed themselves.[21] In a symposium hosted by a war industry pressure group, the National Defense Industrial Association, Michael Lumpkin, former Assistant Secretary of War for Special Operations & Low Intensity Conflict and at the time a senior executive at the corporation Leidos, suggested that the Pentagon collect data about the troops[22] in order to monitor them and prevent suicide. Fortunately, Leidos has the technology to do that.

No statistic or prose can accurately convey the grief felt in families—Iraqi, U.S., Afghan, or any nationality—that have been torn apart by these elective wars. Nor is there an official count of the rapes committed by U.S. troops.[23] Nor are there public figures regarding the pallets of cash D.C. flew into Iraq and then lost track of.[24] Nor are there tallies regarding the degradation and humiliation suffered by people detained in Iraq without judicial process.[25]

POLLUTION

The U.S. Department of War is one of the world's worst polluters. But there are no statistics available that calculate how much pollution the U.S. Armed Forces operating fossil-fuel-intensive weapons platforms have released into the natural world during post-9.11 wars.

One aspect of the War Department's pollution that goes unreported is its construction. Construction is a very common type of military purchase. The Department of War relies on hundreds of construction corporations to build and repair military installations of all sizes. Corporations such as AECOM, Jacobs, Parsons, Tetra Tech, and Whiting-Turner are among the Pentagon's go-to construction firms. The Department of War is the single largest employer of construction workers inside the United States, according to my calculations. It has hundreds of projects going on at any given time. Hiring so many construction workers effectively co-opts part of the working class, clouding workers' minds with mainstream "patriotic" sentiment, while simultaneously binding construction workers economically to nonstop war. Many within the working class feel good about their labor without cognizing their complicity in the global slaughter, to say nothing of their subservient position within a society that withholds and diverts socio-economic benefits from their class. Ambitious capitalists who flock to lucrative war funding come up with traditionally patriotic names for their construction companies. Many firms titled *American*, *Patriot*, and *Veteran* dot the landscape.[26] Construction is not the only field to adopt traditionally patriotic names.[27]

Military construction physically lays the foundation that lengthens the wars. A single construction contract can cover a large area, focusing on military bases in different states or more broadly across a whole region of the U.S. Sometimes the locations are not disclosed. This mostly happens because the Pentagon has yet to finalize the task orders within the overall contract. Occasionally it is because the project details are classified. The Pentagon does not require construction firms to reuse, repurpose, and recycle materials.

Military construction is unsustainable infrastructure. Environmentally friendly, or "green," descriptions are no more than marketing gimmicks. You cannot green a massive, polluting array of hundreds of installations whose primary purpose (aside from profiting industry) is to use fossil-fuel-based platforms to eavesdrop, coerce, kill people, destroy others' infrastructure, and acquire others' riches.

Nonetheless, the MIC employs "green" visions as a popular misdirection. On 15 May 2019, U.S. Senator Elizabeth Warren tweeted, "We don't have to choose between a green military and an effective one. My plan will improve our service members' readiness and safety, and achieve cost savings for American taxpayers. Together, we can flight climate change—and win." Her plan to green the military ("Our military can help lead the fight in combating climate change," available at *Medium*.com) strove, in the name of military readiness, for "net zero carbon emissions" for all "non-combat bases and infrastructure by 2030." Knowingly or through sheer ignorance, Senator Warren did the old bait and switch: falsely advertising the possibility of greening the Pentagon, thereby reconciling green-minded people to military spending despite the reality that energy consumption reduction runs counter to the underlying MIC agenda.

Two military contracts, of many such, show the Pentagon's true cards.

On 20 March 2019, the Pentagon issued a contract to build fuel facilities at Shaw Air Force Base, South Carolina. Home to fighter aircraft and the Air Force's main unit overseeing operations in the Middle East, Shaw is a major consumer of fossil fuels. The construction at Shaw will include a new 2,400 gallon per minute (gpm) pump house facility, four new 600 gpm truck fillstands, a new concrete parking area for refueler trucks, and many other oil-based bells and whistles. Such fossil fuel infrastructure only perpetuates the U.S. military's polluting, carbon-intensive expanse.

On 16 May (and 31 July) 2019, the Pentagon allocated millions to implement energy conservation measures at Camp Lejeune, a Marine Corps facility in North Carolina. The conservation measures to be put in place include installing new automatic meters, meter data software, lighting systems, and HVAC systems. Pollution is a consistent byproduct of the manufacture and installation of this technology and equipment. Though the contract announcement declared the "primary goal of the project is to reduce energy consumption and provide more resilient and sustainable facility infrastructure," no emphasis is placed on the Armed Forces adjusting daily behavior to significantly reduce energy demands. No emphasis is placed on reusing or repurposing infrastructure. Severe reduction and reuse crash head-on with the war industry's polluting essence and profit-generating raison-d'être, as well as capitalism's demand for infinite growth. Keeping radical change off the table is a corporate priority. Corporate America is in charge when it comes to energy. Peerless Technologies Corp. runs much of the Air Force's energy policy. CDM Federal Programs Corp. leads the Navy's public works "business line," including utility privatization and energy management.[28] Comparable corporate interests run the energy files of other branches of the Armed Forces.

The 20 March and 16 May contracts show the direction in which the U.S. military is headed: building more fossil fuel infrastructure while implementing expensive measures, promoted as "energy efficient," which do nothing to alter the military's overall polluting nature, but look great to politicians and image-conscious officers.

Notably, throughout 2019 the Pentagon continued to purchase polluting platforms, like fighter aircraft and diesel-powered expeditionary fast transport ships.

A green-ish empire is still an empire.[29] Building more and more military infrastructure keeps U.S. society headed in the wrong direction. If addressing pollution is to be taken seriously, then demilitarization of U.S. society and demobilization of the war industry are the only healthy, non-polluting ways forward.

The construction boom discloses the twisted priorities of the military-industrial-congressional triangle. The National Museum of the Army at Fort Belvoir gets millions for costly exhibits[30] as the U.S. government imposes austerity measures on the hard-luck masses. Military bases from Hawaiʻi to Virginia get new living quarters[31] as public housing crumbles. The U.S. Air Force Academy gets a new golf clubhouse[32] as D.C. defunds public education. These projects show how detached the MIC is from the ailing U.S. society.

Fossil fuels power all military construction—from cranes to backhoes to bulldozers to dump trucks to private vehicles commuting to and from the work sites to fossil-fuel-intensive manufacture of concrete and steel. Not a single structure is erected without immense, unmeasured fossil fuel pollution.

Even if we don't include military construction, the War Department uses more fossil fuel products than any other institution and emits more carbon dioxide than many nations.[33] Here's a typical fuel contract from March 11, 2019: Sixteen different corporations sold a total $2,817,799,719 of fuel to the War Department. The contract featured Big Oil majors (e.g. BP, Shell, Exxon Mobil) and smaller names (e.g. Wynnewood Energy of Texas). Fuel contracts like this are a monthly occurrence.

Any calculation of the MIC's total fossil fuel consumption must include the fossil fuels the war industry uses in manufacture and shipping of goods and services, in addition to the War Department's fossil fuel consumption. Corporate opacity prevents such an accounting.

The biggest polluter in the world has no legal obligation to reduce its massive carbon footprint, let alone account for its global pollution: Due to industry pressure and the Pentagon's intransigence, the U.S. Armed Forces are exempt from the Kyoto Protocol of 1998 (and were exempt from the Paris climate agreement of 2016 prior to U.S. withdrawal). Indeed, the MIC carbon footprint remains unmentioned in climate activism, which focuses instead on "what *you* can do to prevent climate change."

The War Department's total polluting output is stunning. Pollutants contaminate soil and groundwater at military sites across the United States. These pollutants can include radioactive waste, rocket fuel, components of buried chemical and conventional weaponry, exploded ordnance, degreasers and other chemical solvents, petroleum products, aircraft coatings, and fire retardants. One-time military sites across the U.S. are riddled with pollutants, from the Aleutian Islands to the Atlantic seaboard.[34] The U.S. government's "overall estimated environmental liability was $577 billion" during fiscal year 2018, according to a U.S. Senator[35]—an underestimate, as this figure does not include any of its overseas pollution. Many polluted sites, home and abroad, are located in or around populated areas.

Capitalism—the incessant, rapacious transformation of the natural world into goods and services[36]—is inherently destructive, exploitative, and polluting. U.S.-based capital is particularly vicious in this regard, and the U.S. Department of War is the tip of the spear. How does the Pentagon clean up its pollution? By turning to Corporate America, of course.

Many corporations tackle the Pentagon's pollution. The bigger ones, such as Jacobs and Tetra Tech, are best known for their engineering and construction prowess. Corporate America conducts studies and environmental assessments, prepares plans, drafts documents, and issues reports; surveys sites, oversees wetlands, and supervises land use; writes up Comprehensive Environmental Response, Compensation, and Liability Act documentation; administers and monitors compliance with laws (e.g. Safe Water Drinking Act, Clean Water Act); estimates costs; dredges muck; peruses Executive Orders; plots basing patterns; reviews the National Environmental Policy Act; removes contaminated soil; excavates, characterizes, separates, and transports waste; studies socio-economic issues and demographics; drafts emergency response preparedness; disposes of radioactive material; and runs community outreach and strategic engagement.[37] Public relations are often packaged as part of a corporation's environmental remit, ensuring that total honesty regarding the polluting footprint of the military and industry will not come to light.

There are at least 39,000 contaminated military sites across the U.S. About 900 of the roughly 1,200 Superfund sites in the U.S. are military-related facilities.[38] A Superfund site is a site so polluted that even the U.S. federal government cannot ignore it. The Comprehensive Environmental Response, Compensation, and Liability Act of 1980, a.k.a. SuperFund, provides federal money to clean up hazardous-waste sites, including pollution that the Pentagon has left behind. SuperFund money can address formerly used defense sites (FUDS), places the War Department possessed and polluted.[39] A distinct effort, the formerly utilized sites remedial action program (FUSRAP) identifies and cleans up sites polluted by decades of U.S. atomic energy activities. The U.S. Army Corps of Engineers (USACE) is in charge of both FUDS and FUSRAP. And USACE hands off these programs to Corporate America. Potential paydays can total hundreds of millions of dollars.

Often, corporations are grouped together when cleaning up the mess. Groupings indicate the extent of the pollution. On 19 April 2016, a group of corporations including AECOM and Booz Allen Hamilton were allocated a potential $122.5 million to support the NDCEE. The full name, National Defense Center for Environmental Excellence, is misleading. Instead of prioritizing the environment, NDCEE works to get military technology into the hands of the War Department *while avoiding pitfalls presented by environmental and safety regulations.* On 14 July 2015, nine corporations including AECOM and Tetra Tech were allocated up to $240 million for military munitions response at multiple sites. The military munitions response program (MMRP) addresses exploded and unexploded ordnance. Geographical distance is no obstacle. One environmental contract can cover a continent.[40]

All U.S. military bases are contaminated to some extent. The land under and around an air force base, for example, can suffer from the polluting remnants of munitions and the carcinogenic coatings used on aircraft. Coatings like hexavalent chromium are used in protecting missiles, aircraft, and certain land vehicles from corrosion. The substances used to put out aircraft fires are highly toxic.[41] Pollution damages the soil and water in and around a military installation. Men and women in uniform can get poisoned. Rashes, vomiting, cancer, memory loss, nosebleeds, and miscarriages can ensue.

The U.S. Armed Forces and the corporations running U.S. military bases in Iraq and Afghanistan burned trash in open-air pits. Anything and everything went into these pits, including the occasional body.[42] Routinely incinerated were appliances, batteries, fecal matter, medical waste, paint thinner, vehicle parts, and a variety of plastics. Jet fuel, itself a carcinogen, was often used to ignite the blaze. Severe medical problems afflicted anyone who crossed paths with the black clouds and the particulates spewing from these burn pits. The Pentagon bureaucracy dragged its feet, refusing to concede any correlation between burn pits and pulmonary disease in its troops and veterans. More than 230 U.S. military bases in Afghanistan and Iraq used burn pits before the War Department started limiting use in 2009.[43] Despite mounting pressure from veterans and their families, 42 burn pits in Iraq and 184 burn pits in Afghanistan were still operating as of May 2010.[44] Pentagon public affairs did not reply to my requests for a precise number of U.S. burn pits in use today.

In early 2015, the Special Inspector General for Afghanistan Reconstruction (SIGAR) reported that the Pentagon had not planned properly for waste disposal prior to its invasion of Afghanistan. SIGAR said the War Department did not even follow its own guidelines regarding solid waste disposal. SIGAR said continued use of burn pits puts troops in harm's way.[45] Some generals who spent time in Afghanistan pushed back against those who opposed the use of burn pits, griping about the "difficult" "operational environment" in which commanders had to make decisions regarding waste disposal.[46] U.S. generals, mind you, live in relatively posh conditions whenever in Afghanistan.

In October 2014, the Department of Veterans Affairs finally established a registry to track veterans who believed they were exposed to burn pits during their time in Afghanistan or Iraq. Over 30,000 people had enrolled in the registry by the end of January 2015.[47] The War Department's Congressionally Directed Medical Research Program gives funding to study sickness and treatments for diseases related to military service. Research into exposure to burn pits was added to this list in 2015. It was then dropped in 2016.[48] In autumn 2016, the Government Accountability Office affirmed that the Pentagon needed to study exposure to burn pits and the long-term health problems that may result. The GAO accused the Pentagon of taking too long to study the problem.[49] (It took the Pentagon decades to compensate the veterans exposed to Agent Orange, the toxic herbicide made by U.S. corporations and used as a weapon and defoliant in Southeast Asia in the 1960s.)

In January 2018, a judge ruled that burn pits could be linked to lung disease.[50] The ruling might help mercenaries and troops who were exposed to burn pits, who now suffer from respiratory or pulmonary ailments, and who are currently denied coverage by the Department of Veteran Affairs. U.S. troops still suffer. In November 2018, a Brigadier General with the Vermont National Guard died "from an aggressive cancer linked to his three tours of duty in Afghanistan."[51] Data indicates a rise in certain types of cancers among veterans over the past two decades of war.[52]

The Pentagon has no plans to help Iraqis or Afghans who were exposed to its burn pits.

OCCUPYING AFGHANISTAN, DESTROYING IRAQ

The attacks of 11 September 2001 killed 2,973 victims in New York, Pennsylvania, and D.C. By 22 September 2006, the 2,974th member of the U.S. Armed Forces had died in post-9.11 conflict.[53] Another milestone was hit in 2006: At the end of the Cold War, the U.S. military budget was $298.9 billion, but by 2006 the military budget was double this number.[54]

How did we get to that point? A Marxist party took power in the Afghan capital of Kabul in 1978. Trying to agitate against Moscow and foment a coup against the Soviet-backed government in Kabul, the Central Intelligence Agency (CIA) funneled money and weaponry to allies inside Afghanistan before Moscow invaded the country in December 1979.[55] After Moscow invaded Afghanistan, CIA's efforts blossomed into deep coordination with Pakistan's Inter-Services Intelligence (on-the-ground logistics) and the House of Saud (finance). U.S. Presidents Jimmy Carter and Ronald Reagan supported CIA's work in Afghanistan as they ignited, coalesced, and armed jihadists as a tool of U.S. foreign policy. After Moscow withdrew from Afghanistan following the Geneva Accords of 1988, CIA continued to support some Afghan warlords during Afghanistan's civil wars (1989-2001), while the D.C. regime mostly ignored Afghanistan (aside from politically opportune missile strikes like those President William J. Clinton launched in summer 1998). The 9.11 Commission Report, known formally as the *National Commission on Terrorist Attacks Upon the United States*, claimed that al-Qaeda had perpetrated the 2001 attack, and used Afghanistan as a location from which to plot it. Proponents of war argued that this was sufficient reason for the U.S. War Department to invade Afghanistan (a largely illiterate society in which ninety-two percent of the population does not even understand what "9.11" means, according to the *International Council on Security & Development*[56]). The Taliban, whose rule extended over some population centers of Afghanistan at the time of the 9.11 attacks, had offered after September 2001 to work to hand over Usama Bin Laden if the U.S. government would furnish proof of his involvement in the attacks.[57] The White House declined, preferring to bomb Afghanistan. The Pentagon sent troops to mineral-rich Afghanistan[58] to project power and seize territory close to central Asian energy resources. The war in Afghanistan was initially billed as an "anti-terrorism" war, a linguistic sleight that granted it a certain cachet in the eyes of U.S. Congress. As new military operations in Iraq sustained an increasingly greater number of U.S. casualties, many D.C. liberals contended loudly that the war in Iraq was bad, but the war in Afghanistan was just.

Corporations began selling weaponry to the Afghan government shortly after Hamid Karzai assumed presidential authority in December 2001. The longer the war lasted, the better U.S. weapons brokers became at dealing. Sales to Afghanistan have been thorough and broad.[59] Corporations have even managed Afghanistan intelligence operations. One such program cost $457 million and didn't meet a bare minimum of standards.[60]

Notably, sales have included avionics maintenance equipment for "counter narcotic activities."[61] (Opium production skyrocketed after the U.S. Armed Forces began occupying the country, though the Taliban government had nearly eliminated it.[62])

There are many unreported instances of profiteering specific to the Afghanistan War (2001-present). One particularly grueling and expensive industry dream that the Pentagon is pursuing is to create an Air Force for Afghanistan. The U.S. war industry and its think tanks cleverly pretend that building an Afghan Air Force would allow the Pentagon to withdraw with dignity from the country—with a strong Air Force, the Afghan military would be able to hold ground against the Taliban, so the argument goes. In 2019 *The New York Times* phrased the reality thusly: "Eleven years after the United States began building an air force for Afghanistan at a cost now nearing $8 billion, it remains a frustrating work in progress, with no end in sight. Some aviation experts say the Afghans will rely on American maintenance and other support for years."[63] That's the whole point. Building a modern air force—in an impoverished country amid nonstop war involving numerous factions—is a limitless endeavor, by its very nature. Notable corporations involved in building the Afghan Air Force are AAR, Sierra Nevada Corp., and Lockheed Martin. AAR has sold maintenance and maintenance training on Lockheed Martin cargo aircraft. Sierra Nevada Corp. has sold modified light attack aircraft to Afghanistan. Billable categories include support equipment, transportation, repair, and sustainment.[64] U.S.-directed plans for the Afghan Air Force aim for 80 Lockheed Martin UH-60 helicopters in Afghan possession by 2030.[65]

Reality hurts. Here's how a typical battle goes down: Taliban fighters overrun territory (usually an outpost, sometimes a whole city) held by the U.S. military coalition. U.S. military units summon aircraft to strafe or bomb the Taliban with U.S.-made ordnance. Civilians die. Then the whole process is repeated—and has been, effectively since the Taliban started regaining ground in 2002.[66] U.S. war corporations are the primary winners in this vicious cycle. Corporate goods and services form the bulk of the U.S. presence in Afghanistan. The corporate occupation force in Afghanistan has included Boeing, PAE, SAIC, and others.[67] For a pretty penny, such corporations as AAR and Columbia Helicopters transport U.S. military forces, cargo, or casualties across the country. War industry officials and their think tank affiliates routinely insist that "progress" is being made,[68] regardless of objective levels of violence, narcotics exports, or territory held.

In the first half of 2019, sixty-two percent of civilian casualties in Afghanistan were caused by the U.S., NATO, and allied Afghan forces, according to the United Nations.[69] It cannot be claimed, and never has been, that Afghanistan attacked the United States, yet this is what happened to the country.

Nor did Iraq attack the United States. D.C.'s assault on Iraq has been lengthy and is ongoing. During the first Gulf War (1980-88) between Iran and Iraq, CIA and the Pentagon supported both countries (helping whichever side was losing), aiming to lengthen the war and devastate Arabs and Persians alike. Shortly after the first Gulf War ended, Iraq accused Kuwait of drilling horizontally along the Iraq-Kuwait border and stealing Iraq's oil. Iraq raised diplomatic protests to no avail, then invaded Kuwait in 1990, after the U.S. Ambassador to Iraq advised Saddam Hussein that the U.S. took no side in the dispute.[70] Public relations firms marketed the ensuing war. In October 1990, a Kuwaiti girl testified before U.S. Congress. Her testimony was one big lie, prefabricated with a public relations firm, Hill & Knowlton.[71] Another firm, The Rendon Group, reportedly managed public relations for the Kuwaiti government before and during wartime. The War Department invaded Iraq in early 1991, pummeling the Iraqi Army. Low estimates indicate over 100,000 Iraqi military personnel died during the war. The Pentagon demolished Iraq's civilian infrastructure. This included bridges, civilian factories, electricity power stations, oil refineries, railways, roads, shopping markets, and telephone exchanges and lines. On 13 February 1991, the War Department bombed a civilian shelter, according to the BBC.[72] The U.S. Air Force and Navy dropped well over 80,000 tons of bombs on the country during 17 January–28 February 1991. The War Department's military offensive left Iraqi society in ruins. The ground war ended in 1991, but D.C.'s military forces—wielding U.S. corporate products, like cruise missiles and fighter jets[73]—remained in control of much of Iraq's airspace. D.C. bombed Iraq regularly during 1991-2003 and imposed brutal sanctions on the country, leading to hundreds of thousands, perhaps millions, of preventable deaths.[74]

The re-invasion of Iraq in the spring of 2003 was the culmination of an alliance of the three most powerful forces in D.C.: the war industry,[75] Big Oil, and the Zionist lobby. These groups overrode any democratic decision-making that U.S. citizens might have thought they enjoyed. Aligning like ominous asteroids they peppered a compliant Capitol Hill with pretexts for launching an illegal war[76] against a sovereign people. The U.S. war industry and ideologically aligned entities inundated D.C. with propaganda in order to bring Iraq into the post-9.11 wars.[77] Allegations began with Saddam Hussein's alleged links to al-Qaeda. He had none.[78] They progressed to Saddam's alleged possession of Weapons of Mass Destruction. He had none.[79] Propagandists settled on the need to topple Saddam because he was a dictator, plain and simple. This propaganda campaign was aimed mostly at the U.S. Congress and other oligarchs, not the U.S. citizenry, whose views were deemed irrelevant. The people do not matter to the U.S. oligarchy or its war industry. The people are numbers to be crunched—records, digits, and figures which enable profit—and a source of taxes to syphon. Despite that, the U.S. public voiced their opinion clearly. Hundreds of thousands of people demonstrated in New York City.[80] Over 50,000 people protested in D.C.[81] At least 500,000 people protested nationwide, and 10-15 million people protested worldwide.[82]

It is now commonplace to frame the 2003 invasion of Iraq as a "mistake." This is not accurate. The war industry achieved what it intended. The scholar Michael Parenti elaborates: D.C. destroyed a country that "had the audacity to retain control of its own oil supply, kept its entire economy under state control (rather than private corporate ownership)," and not allow in the International Monetary Fund or giant foreign corporations.

[Iraq] charted an independent course under a dictator who originally had served the CIA, and had destroyed the left progressive democracy that existed in Iraq since the 1958 revolution. But Saddam then retained control of the country's resources instead of throwing everything wide open to western investors. Saddam also got out of line on oil quotas (wanting an equitable share of the international market). And he decided to drop the U.S. dollar as the reserve currency and use the Euro instead. So he and his country have been correctly destroyed in keeping with the interests of the U.S.-led global empire. Everything is now privatized, deregulated, devastated.[83]

One result of the U.S. military occupation will outlast the shattered streets and buildings, the power grids and sewer systems, the U.S.-designed constitution and imposed politico-economic system that still might be restructured, if Iraqi sovereignty should be regained: the U.S. military's use of depleted uranium (used in armor and ordnance due to its density). This will poison Iraq's very soil over untold generations, long after the immediate public health emergency in Iraq subsides. Detonation of DU dispersed radioactive particles and carcinogenic material left Iraq's soil and water contaminated from al-Basrah to Babil to al-Anbar. Congenital birth defects are rampant. Children are born with cancers, cleft palates, elongated heads, extra fingers and toes, heart abnormalities, missing or stunted limbs, multiple heads, and severe brain damage, among other ailments. Many children are born premature, others not at all; mothers across Iraq miscarry at very elevated rates. Other afflictions in the general population include anemia, nervous system problems, immune system collapse, infertility, kidney disease, leukemia, and sterility. Experts assert there is a direct correlation between rises in cancer rates and the number of times U.S. forces dropped ordnance on a particular area. Assaults against the city of Fallujah destroyed civilian infrastructure and killed and displaced residents. Cancer rates skyrocketed in the city's children since the U.S. attacks. In parts of Iraq, the rate of birth defects surpasses *by ten times* the rate Hiroshima witnessed while suffering from the effects of the U.S. atomic bomb. Particles and traces of DU will remain radioactive in Iraq long after the U.S. is eventually forced to completely withdraw.[84]

No matter. Once established in the cradle of civilization, the U.S. war industry began selling goods and services to the new Iraqi government now amenable to Western corporate interests, which bought them even as it underfunded utilities and public services. Recent sales from the U.S. war industry to Iraq include small arms, tanks and vehicles, aircraft (crewed and remotely piloted), training, maintenance, base operations, and missiles, rockets, and bombs.

Today's analysis is brought to you by the letter T: Textron vehicles and aircraft and Trace Systems satellite service—all sold to the Iraqi government. Headquartered in Providence, Rhode Island, Textron is one of New England's biggest war corporations. Textron makes drones, surveillance aircraft, attack helicopters, and armored vehicles. Two other major New England war corporations—Raytheon of Massachusetts and United Technologies of Connecticut—are merging. Raytheon produces radar, communication systems, sensors, and weaponry. Missiles are its bread and butter. United Technologies makes aircraft engines (via its Pratt & Whitney brand), surveillance pods, and aircraft parts. You can catch such corporations at Mohammed Ali Air Base, Balad Air Base, and across Iraq. U.S. industry knew that sales to the post-Saddam Iraqi government would be lucrative. Invasion and occupation pay dividends.

BOSS

If other countries' public services are to be opened for profit, why should the U.S. military be exempt? Once upon a time, the military ran its own services. The latrines need to be cleaned in the training squadron? Get Airman Snuffy to do it. The front windows of a command & control facility at Fort Campbell need to be cleaned? Sergeant Moody knows where the ladders are. An oven needs to be scrubbed at Naval Station Pearl Harbor? Get Seaman Caterina on it. The vehicles need to be fueled at Fort Benning. No worries. We're soldiers. We can do it. The trash needs to be taken out aboard Little Creek. Freddie the Frog will take it out before lunch. The grass needs to be mowed inside the front gate at Fairchild Air Force Base. Get a couple of the SERE boys over there. They'll mow it before they hit the woods. Efficient and economical, this was how U.S. military installations once ran. Not anymore.[85]

Corporate America is now in charge of these tasks that keep a military installation up and running. They call it base operations support services (BOSS). Corporations selling BOSS usually provide a combination of facility management, fire and emergency services, grounds maintenance, janitorial services, pavement clearance, pest control, and waste management. Dug in, a variety of corporations now perform the most basic duties that used to be done by soldiers, sailors, airmen, and Marines. Airman Snuffy did a good job cleaning the latrines because he had a little pride in the uniform, he was low in the chain of command, and he'd get punished if he didn't do a good job. On-the-ground employees of Corporate America, on the other hand, do it for the dollars, while executives inevitably cut corners in order to squeeze every drop of profit out of the arrangement. EMCOR, IAP, Fluor, Pride, and TRAX International are some of the big names running

BOSS stateside. Of great size and scope, BOSS is a profitable sector of the war industry. Low-wage U.S. citizens and residents carry out most BOSS stateside.

Third-country nationals (TCN)—not locals and not U.S. citizens—carry out a lot of BOSS overseas.[86] (Workers of the world have more in common with one another than they have in common with the ruling class.) The cost of paying a corporation for BOSS is "higher than paying government employees or soldiers" to do it "because of the profit motive involved," *International Business Times* reports.[87] Able to summon immense resources, matériel, and logistics capabilities, corporations selling BOSS often receive non-competitive contracts at high prices for work overseas. Overcharging for BOSS and other services on U.S. installations overseas has been regular practice.[88] A typical confluence of corporate interests is as follows. KBR builds a dining facility on a U.S. base in Iraq where SOS International runs BOSS. TCN, recruited by a Gulf company that is regularly accused of human trafficking, run the facility under subcontract from a U.S. corporation. Generators running on fossil fuel power the facility, which serves thousands of troops and mercenaries at every meal.[89] The plagues of our era intertwine in this unsustainable facility: fossil fuel dependency, Gulf despotism, D.C. imperialism, and corporate domination.

The mere provision of food to U.S. troops deployed overseas illustrates some problems that come with acceding to corporate control, as industry largely dictates terms and conditions under which U.S. troops are fed in a given country. Corporate contracts guiding food services to U.S. troops on U.S. installations across the Middle East regularly stipulate that local businesses are not allowed to prepare or serve food to the U.S. troops. U.S. corporations use shady brokers to hire TCN at relatively paltry wages to prepare and serve the food. And much of that food is shipped into the country in which the U.S. has military installations (not produced locally), which costs even more money. Such deference to U.S. corporations (and their profit motives) goes against the War Department's celebrated Counter Insurgency Field Manual, 3-24, which stresses the need to build trust with the locals. As FM 3-24 states, an important way to earn the trust of the locals is to provide them with jobs and to take measures that show the U.S. military cares about their wellbeing.

Individual contracts do not satisfy. Corporations pursue bigger game. The Air Force Contract Augmentation Program (AFCAP) provides repair, construction, BOSS, and HAZMAT management, among other services. Expansive in operations and narrow in beneficiaries, AFCAP gathers a handful of corporations to cover pretty much any contingency, cause, demand, exercise, operation, or disaster the War Department could be engaged in. Every excuse is fair game for profiting: drug war, NATO missions, war on terror, humanitarian relief, nation building, arms sales. Each AFCAP iteration costs billions of dollars.[90] The U.S.

Army has the Logistics Civil Augmentation Program (LOGCAP) wherein a handful of corporations provides a wide range of goods and services with a focus on amplified BOSS, to the tune of billions of dollars.[91] A corporate employee described LOGCAP honestly: "Almost any position that it would take to run a small city, those are the same positions that we run in small military cities in the Middle East."[92] The Congressional Research Service explained that because "increased costs mean increased fees to the contractor," there is "no incentive for the contractor to limit the government's costs."[93] LOGCAP V is ongoing as I write this. It is worth up to $82 billion.

Lanes beyond AFCAP and LOGCAP exist for other sectors of war. Want to cash in on the Pentagon's reckless spending on complex and redundant software and computer products? Sign up to be part of Network-Centric Solutions, a popular way for the Air Force to acquire IT goods and services. Selling drones? Join the Mid-Endurance Unmanned Aircraft Systems. Crafty at finding and hiring people with language skills? Jump aboard the Defense Language Interpretation & Translation Enterprise. Selling products that can be used for space operations? Think about working through Space Logistics Infrastructure Support Services. Can you gather people who are handy with a wrench? Consider Rapid Disaster Infrastructure Response.[94] Contracting vehicles match each sector of war.

Corporate reach is astonishing. You could find a corporation, IAP, based out of Florida, running BOSS at U.S. military installations in places as diverse as Deveselu, Romania, and Crete, Greece. (Deveselu is home to a missile "defense" site, while Crete, especially Souda Bay, is integral to U.S. monitoring of Mediterranean nations.) Like a burly, inebriated uncle, KBR shows up and acts inappropriately.[95] KBR has run BOSS at U.S. military installations from Kenya to Djibouti to the Persian Gulf and has aided Apartheid Israel in renovating facilities. You could find Vectrus in charge of dining facilities in Kuwait; BOSS in Germany; supplies in Italy; and IT work in Afghanistan, the Persian Gulf, Jordan, the Balkans, and Turkey. These installations are an abbreviated rap sheet documenting military-industry.

The absurdity of BOSS knows no limit. On 30 June 2016 and 16 February 2018, Adept Process Services (National City, CA) was contracted to operate the port at Joint Base Pearl Harbor Hickam, O'ahu, Hawai'i. Who's going to operate the port? Not the U.S. Navy. They're only the Navy! A corporation does it instead.

BOSS cash rolls in: over a six-year period, corporations received $989 million just for landscaping and groundskeeping at military facilities, $910 million for garbage collection, and an overall $2.6 billion for janitorial/custodial services.[96]

Friends and acquaintances of mine who were in Iraq before, during, and after the infamous 2011 U.S. withdrawal educate us as to its profitability: When the White House decided to draw down U.S. forces in Iraq, corporations swooped in and made a lot of money dismantling U.S. military facilities. (These were many of the same corporations that had profited from the earlier invasion and provision of construction and BOSS.) When the White House later decided to ramp up U.S. forces in Iraq, corporations swooped in and rebuilt and reconstructed the installations recently dismantled. More money, no problem. Invade, construct, BOSS, take down, repeat. Accounts by D.C. insiders corroborate the absurd, costly nature of ramping up and down the U.S. military presence overseas.[97]

The ruin and repair of Iraq is manifold. The Mosul Dam suffered from debilitating structural problems, which were exacerbated by the 2003 U.S. invasion, the lengthy U.S. occupation, and subsequent battles with militants. On 29 March 2018, AECOM was contracted to help reinforce the soil and bedrock around the dam. Costing millions, the contract was awarded without an open, competitive bidding process.[98] Whose actions weakened the dam? The MIC. Who is repairing the dam? The U.S. war industry. AECOM's contract to repair the Mosul Dam is a microcosm of the larger destruction of Iraq (1990-present). The U.S. war industry makes a killing destroying a nation and then makes a killing repairing its parts.

During 2011-14, the U.S. military presence in Iraq was reduced, not withdrawn. The occupation continued. A variety of forces remained: U.S. special mission units; U.S. mercenaries from prominent war corporations; a militarized State Department, which, instead of being an advocate of diplomacy, was warlike in rhetoric and posture; a full complement of espionage personnel (from corporatized U.S. intel agencies and war corporations), many working out of the massive U.S. Embassy complex in Baghdad; a small contingent of conventional troops performing non-combat roles, like training Iraqi forces; corporate representatives tending to industry products; and a robust round-the-clock presence of U.S. warplanes (designed, sold, and maintained by U.S. war corporations) flying from U.S. bases (run by war corporations) in such Gulf countries as Qatar, thus accessing Iraqi airspace. The "withdrawal" of U.S. forces from Iraq was a ploy by D.C. politicians looking to varnish their legacy in office. Profiteers won in the end: U.S. forces never left.

In the shredded remains of Iraqi society, many gangs and factions formed and reformed. The most brutal gangs subscribed to the vitriolic Wahhabi ideology spread by Saudi Arabia, D.C.'s close ally. These gangs sometimes overlapped with CIA's support for armed jihadists across the border in Syria. One particularly brutal gang took over some parts of Syria and Iraq. Ratings-obsessed corporate media (often airing ads from war corporations) hyped up this gang as the apocalyptic arrival of an Islamic caliphate. The gang benefitted from the street cred, as this media frenzy accorded it top billing as a "threat" to the U.S. The war industry benefitted, as this media frenzy engendered increased weapon sales. Soon corporate media, the War Department, and war industry think tanks were regularly claiming the gang, known as the "Islamic State," controlled 34,000 square miles (roughly 88,000 square kilometers) of territory across Iraq and Syria. In reality, that "control" was not full or effective, and it existed over non-contiguous territory.

Spurred on by the U.S. war industry's think tanks,[99] the Pentagon decided to deploy more troops en masse to Iraq in 2014. Intervention in Iraqi and Syrian affairs under the guise of fighting terrorism has been a bastion of U.S. mercenary activity.[100] Attempted destabilization of the Syrian government was in full swing, with the Pentagon, CIA, and war industry together arming a wide array of jihadist groups.[101] Armaments that the War Department and CIA purchased and handed over to groups inside Syria included but were not limited to vehicles, anti-armor missiles, night vision devices, mines, and rifles. Many of D.C.'s Gulf allies supported this move, themselves funding and arming various jihadist groups, including more than a few, like al-Nusra, with ties to the previous enemy-of-the-day, al-Qaeda. The MIC's goal was twofold: (1) destroy the Syrian state through the promotion of sectarianism and the arming of violent proxy groups, preventing Shi'a powers from posing a challenge to U.S. military dominance or Israeli hegemony;[102] and (2) establish a small military presence in northeast Syria where oil fields are plentiful, soil is relatively fertile, and the Euphrates River flows. From a bird's-eye view (corporate board's eye view), these goals provided a period of profitable conflict.

The Pentagon, the militarized State Department, and the war industry demonized the "Islamic State" more than any previous enemy-of-the-day. Again and again, ISIS was portrayed as nothing short of a whirlwind of terror. Understanding anything about it or the context in which it arose—or indeed, who was the source of its convoys of shiny new Toyotas in Syria and Libya[103]—would have put a kink in industry's plans and profits. To regard the gang as being comprised of humans was anathema. Humans could be talked to, understood, and negotiated with. Humans could feel anguish and pain. Questions from authentic scholars about rampant illiteracy among ISIS members and socioeconomic motivations for joining (e.g. lack of jobs, population growth, changes in climate, forced conscription, family protection) did not pierce the Beltway propaganda. The greatest concession portions of the Beltway offered was reference to a "mistake"—the fact that shortly after the 2003 aggression, U.S.-enforced de-Baathification and demobilization of the Iraqi army had thrown untold thousands out of work, including military leadership.

With this gang so thoroughly dehumanized, the U.S. War Department was able to loosen the rules of engagement beyond already slack criteria. Loose rules of engagement allowed indiscriminate use of a variety of ordnance when "liberating" areas under ISIS' control. The Syrian city of ar-Raqqah, located on the north bank of the Euphrates River, was once one of the more prosperous cities in the region. With major portions of the city under ISIS' control, the War Department attacked the city, killed countless families, and displaced thousands of residents.[104] Weaponry used against ar-Raqqah was made in Hattiesburg, MS; Scranton, PA; Williston, VT; and Tucson, AZ, among other locales, I note. Once again, munitions fabricated by war corporations left behind hazardous unexploded ordnance and polluting remnants. Ar-Raqqah's cultural heritage was left in ruins, ravaged beyond anything ISIS could have foreseen or hoped for. A similar devastation was wreaked upon Mosul in Iraq.

Neither Afghanistan nor Iraq nor Syria attacked the United States on 9.11, yet products from the U.S. war industry, employed by U.S. military forces, have ravaged these nations. As of spring 2019, D.C. had over five thousand troops in Iraq, according to *The New York Times*.[105] I close this section with a grim milestone: In Afghanistan, 2019, total deaths of Western troops climbed over 3,541,[106] and U.S.-led coalition aircraft carried out a record number of sorties,[107] as "Boeing Defense, Space & Security" broke company records, attaining $23 billion in annual revenue.[108]

BOMBING

Industry successfully achieved an increase in bombing rates across Republican and Democrat administrations. President George W. Bush's ownership and pride in the wars in Afghanistan and Iraq is well known. President Barack H. Obama expanded the wars, targeting seven countries with airstrikes during his tenure. The number of U.S. airstrikes conducted in 2016 topped 26,000.[109] By 2018, under President Donald J. Trump, the airstrike rate had increased to one bomb every twelve minutes by some accounts.[110] U.S. war industry bombers, drones, and fighter planes dropped more corporate weaponry on Afghanistan in 2018 than the previous three years *combined*.[111] Lieutenant General Joseph Guastella, the man in charge of bombing the region (full title: "Combined Forces Air Component Commander"), justified these strikes as having "supported multiple ongoing campaigns, deterred aggression, maintained security, and defended our networks," journalist Oriana Pawlyk quotes.[112] Airstrikes receive bipartisan support.

Many U.S. bombers, like the Boeing B-1 and the Boeing B-52, carrying ordnance from Boeing, General Dynamics, and Raytheon, take off from an atoll in the central Indian Ocean known as Diego Garcia. The U.S. Department of War has regularly stolen people's land. It stole land in Guam, compensating locals with a paltry sum or nothing at all. It took the Enewetak Atoll in the Marshall Islands. It stole Vieques, Puerto Rico. It teamed up with the Danish government to remove the indigenous Inughuit to make way for Thule Air Base in northwest Greenland.

And, the War Department teamed up with the U.K. to remove Chagossians from the Chagos Archipelago in the Indian Ocean in order to set up what is now called Naval Support Facility Diego Garcia. Throughout the late 1960s and early 1970s, the U.S. and U.K. expelled the native population, dumping them in the slums of Mauritius and the Seychelles.[113] The native population has not been allowed back. James Schlesinger, former CIA director and former U.S. Secretary of War, said, "Indeed [Diego Garcia] is one of the wisest investments of government funds that we have seen over the last three or four decades."[114]

The Public Library of U.S. Diplomacy released via *WikiLeaks* disclosed how the U.S. State Department and the Pentagon worked hand-in-hand to prevaricate about the nature of U.S. military facilities on Diego Garcia.[115] With diplomatic support from D.C., London threw money and legal expertise at lawsuits brought by those expelled and their families. The U.K. and U.S. governments have won the legal battle,[116] for now, against the wishes of the world.[117] Maintaining a steady pace in recent years, construction at Diego Garcia has included upgrading seaside refueling capabilities, repairing Receiver Site Building Facility 201, and building a solar power system.[118] A lot of corporate profit—BOSS, bombs, bombers, construction, fuel, maintenance, etc.—runs through Diego Garcia.

Executives adjust their industrial base in order to keep up with existing demand and anticipated sales. Raytheon executives ordered a new $75 million, 6,5000 square-meter factory to be built at one of the core nodes in the U.S. war industry: Redstone Arsenal in Huntsville, Alabama.[119] Huntsville got its start as the center of the Pentagon's post-World War II rocket and ballistic missile programs. Every single major war corporation now has a presence at Redstone. The new Raytheon facility in Huntsville, inaugurated in late 2012, shows how lust for profit trumps the health of the working class. First, Raytheon executives took advantage of advancements in automation in order to minimize the number of jobs at the new facility (lowering what could have been 90-100 jobs to around 50). Then, executives mandated the use of cumbersome software products among the remaining factory workers, controlling and logging every production step. Workers are frustrated with this software and with micromanaging plant supervisors, I am told. These trends—automation and increased monitoring of workers—distress factory employees across the country, from Textron factories in Maryland to General Atomics facilities in California.

The war industry increased its production capacity throughout the first half of 2018.[120] Increased production of offensive and defensive capacity continued over the summer. Relevant missile and bomb contracts during summer 2018 exceeded $3,800,393,000.[121]

Autumn came. Leaves changed color. Industry's supremacy remained. In September, Boeing was contracted to provide satellite-guided bombs. On the same day, Lockheed Martin was contracted to advance engineering and production for air-launched cruise missiles. September ends the fiscal year, and FY2018 was one of the best ever for the U.S. war industry. Already operating at full steam for the past seventeen years, it continued to ramp up production.[122] Constantly. The pursuit and bombing of sundry baddies in the Middle East, which is the backbone of post-9.11 military action, reflects a direct exchange: money from U.S. taxpayers (or from sold Treasury marketable securities) to U.S. war corporations, and bombs and missiles from U.S. war corporations to sovereign land in the Middle East. These are one-way routes, leaving wealthy executives and dead civilians at either end.

The destruction of Iraqi and Syrian cities is tangible evidence of this direct transfer. In 2016 *Fortune* reported, "the business of bombing the Islamic State continues to boom."[123] U.S.-led military operations in Syria killed more than 1,600 civilians in ar-Raqqa during 2017, according to Amnesty International.[124] 2018 was the deadliest year on record for Syrian children, according to UNICEF.[125] In early 2019, the War Department increased its bombing rate in Iraq and Syria, and stopped issuing reports detailing what it was bombing.[126] In May 2019, the War Department said it had killed 1,300 civilians in 34,502 airstrikes during operations in Iraq and Syria since 2014, while the U.K.-based monitoring group *Airwars* put the figure closer to 13,000 civilians.[127] Lives are destroyed daily. Corporations profit hourly.

INDUSTRY LOCATIONS

U.S. war corporations exist across the United States. The top four war industry nodes in the United States are Huntsville, Alabama, which you recently encountered; the corridor stretching from northeast Virginia, through D.C., to Baltimore; the Dallas-Fort Worth region of Texas; and southern California.

War corporations ring D.C. like a slo-mo siege of Leningrad. Northeast Virginia and southwest Maryland are where most major war corporations have their headquarters. Virginian towns—Chantilly, Dulles, Falls Church, Fairfax, Herndon, Manassas, McLean, Reston, Tysons Corner, and Vienna—are home to headquarters (e.g. Northrop Grumman in Falls Church, Booz Allen Hamilton in McLean) and facilities (e.g. Harris Corp. in Herndon). Areas like Hampton Roads, Newport News, Norfolk, and Virginia Beach are other popular spots for war corporations, particularly those contracting heavily with the U.S. Navy.

McLean and Fairfax exemplify industry's infrastructural muscle. McLean is home to branches of Alion Science & Technology, Booz Allen Hamilton, CACI, DynCorp, Iridium Satellite, Northrop Grumman, SAIC, and many smaller war corporations.[128] Journalists Dana Priest and William Arkin of the *Washington*

Post introduce Fairfax in the context of the intelligence sector of the U.S. war industry:

> Six of the 10 richest counties in the United States, according to Census Bureau data, are in these clusters [in and around Washington, D.C.]. Loudoun County, ranked as the wealthiest county in the country, helps supply the workforce of the nearby National Reconnaissance Office headquarters, which manages spy satellites. Fairfax County, the second-wealthiest, is home to the NRO, the CIA and the Office of the Director of National Intelligence. Arlington County, ranked ninth, hosts the Pentagon and major intelligence agencies. Montgomery County, ranked 10th, is home to the National Geospatial-Intelligence Agency. And Howard County, ranked third, is home to 8,000 NSA employees.[129]

The list of war corporations in Fairfax is as tall as an intercontinental ballistic missile. General Dynamics' massive information technology division is based there. ManTech, one of a handful of corporations that runs the corporatized intelligence workload,[130] works in Fairfax on unmanned systems (for use on the sea's surface and below the surface) and space products. Lockheed Martin works in Fairfax on submarine software and firmware, including one product called Integrated Submarine Imaging Systems, a.k.a. ISIS. Lockheed Martin also works on Aegis software there. Aegis is a convoluted web of sensors, software, and hardware that tracks targets for the Navy and guides missiles to destroy them. Many other war corporations have facilities in Fairfax.

The greater D.C. area has the highest median income in the United States.[131] Lockheed Martin's headquarters is in Bethesda, Maryland, immediately northwest of the nation's capital. Maryland towns (e.g. Aberdeen, Annapolis, Beltsville, Germantown, Indian Head, Linthicum Heights, Jessup, Laurel, and Severn) are rife with war corporations. Most war corporations located in the Maryland towns of California, Hollywood, Lexington Park, Patuxent River, and St. Inigoes have deep relationships with Naval Air Station Patuxent River and its associated units. NAS Patuxent River is located on one of Maryland's fingers jutting into the Chesapeake. By no means is war the lone financial stimulant in the greater D.C. area, but it does hog the most federal discretionary spending each year.[132]

Pick any state at random. Mississippi exemplifies the way war corporations dapple the map: In the south, Pascagoula is where Huntington Ingalls builds and maintains naval ships; in the center, Forest is where Raytheon builds radar; up north in Tupelo is where General Atomics works on a new electromagnetic system for launching and arresting aircraft on aircraft carriers; Vertex Aerospace is headquartered in Madison, an hour's drive west; and Vicksburg, farther west, is home to the U.S. Army Corps of Engineers' Engineer Research & Development Center, where war corporations tackle difficult engineering and "national security" problems. Mississippi is average when it comes to war industry infrastructure.

Pick any region of the U.S. at random. New England, you say? War production in New England is diverse: General Dynamics ships and maintenance in Bath, Maine; L3 night vision and range finders in Londonderry and Manchester, New Hampshire; United Technologies electronics and actuators in Vergennes, Vermont, and General Dynamics ordnance in Williston, Vermont, just east of Burlington. Greater Boston, Massachusetts, is home to Raytheon headquarters, Lincoln Lab, Boston Ship Repair LLC, propaganda firms, and private equity firms. Cambridge is home to the Massachusetts Institute of Technology, Draper Lab, and Raytheon BBN. Rhode Island houses Textron's headquarters and plenty of naval technology. Connecticut is home to aircraft engine production (Hartford) and submarine manufacturing (Groton). These are just the main examples of industry in New England. The Midwest, you say? A sample of Midwest corporate topography includes the Ohio towns of Dayton, where R&D corporations sashay before the Air Force Research Lab; Cincinnati, where General Electric produces aircraft engines; and Mason, where L3 makes navigation equipment. Indiana has Indianapolis, a production center of land, sea, and air propulsion. A corporate-controlled arsenal known as Rock Island sits in the middle of the Mississippi River between Illinois and Iowa. Cedar Rapids, Iowa, is home to communications equipment production, and Middletown, Iowa, is home to ammunition production. St. Louis is a site of Boeing weapon production. We now set off for the west coast. It's like the Oregon Trail, except instead of getting dysentery and snakebites you get greed and empire.

The Dallas-Fort Worth region of Texas, a hive of war industry activity, demands a detour. The Hive is comprised of Greenville, Dallas, Grand Prairie, Fort Worth, Richardson, Garland, and McKinney. Looking at a small portion of The Hive's activity educates us about some of industry's goods and services. Greenville is where Boeing refurbishes VIP aircraft and L3 devises eavesdropping and targeting electronics.[133] Dallas is where Lockheed Martin works on a variety of missile programs, and Raytheon works on many destructive products (including a six-barrel rotary cannon, a glide bomb, and a cruise missile). A lot of industry work in Grand Prairie centers around aircraft and projectiles (e.g. surface-to-air and air-to-surface missiles, and mobile rocket artillery systems). Smaller corporations manufacturing parts and repairing engines for aircraft are based out of Grand Prairie.

Fort Worth is home to significant bustle: Boeing electronic warfare, Northrop Grumman drone parts, Textron helicopters (produced under the Bell brand), and PAE maintenance and intelligence products. United Technologies' Rockwell Collins brand and Elbit Systems, an Apartheid Israel corporation, work on pilot helmets. DynCorp manages activities (e.g. aviation maintenance and matériel from Honduras to the Netherlands to Afghanistan). Lockheed Martin in Fort Worth puts together costly aircraft: F-35 and F-22 fighters. Smaller corporations that provide aircraft parts have facilities in Fort Worth.

The Texas towns of McKinney, Richardson, and Garland round out The Hive. Raytheon has a huge presence in McKinney, where it produces targeting systems, forward looking infrared, and radar. In Richardson, Boeing works on high-speed fiber optic networks for ships and Raytheon works on a glide bomb that can be dropped far from target. In Garland, General Dynamics produces bombs, and Raytheon works on components for its PATRIOT missile battery. Multiple corporations work in Garland on the U.S. Army's Distributed Common Ground System, a troubled system that is supposed to aggregate and share information about the global battlefield. Though it isn't home to significant war industry facilities, Southlake, Texas, can be considered part of The Hive. Southlake is where some of the wealthier corporate officials retreat at night. Corporations do a lot more in The Hive. This distillation of Hive activity introduced corporate locations and pursuits.

War corporations love The Hive. Representative Kay Granger of Texas' 12th Federal Congressional District, which includes Fort Worth, is a good example of how war corporations buy elected officials via campaign finance. In 2018, the majority of Granger's top twenty donors were war corporations or PACs with war industry ties. Corporations included Lockheed Martin, Progeny Systems, Northrop Grumman, Boeing, Cubic, General Atomics, General Dynamics, Honeywell, Leidos, Parsons, SAIC, and Textron.[134]

And we're off to the West Coast!

The war industry suffocates San Diego. Corporations such as Colonna's Shipyard West and Epsilon Systems Solutions operate through the Southwest Regional Maintenance Center, while corporations running through the veins of Space & Naval Warfare Systems Center Pacific (SSC Pacific) include Booz Allen Hamilton, Leidos, Northrop Grumman, and SAIC.[135] The town of Carlsbad is located along the southern California coast, roughly halfway between San Diego and Huntington Beach. ViaSat, which makes data links so platforms can communicate, is located in Carlsbad. Other corporations such as RQ Construction and North Star Scientific Corp. operate there. Southeast of Carlsbad is Poway, where General Atomics manufactures an infamous drone, the MQ-9 Reaper. Los Angeles is home to Los Angeles Air Force Base, a key avenue in corporate militarization of space. Regions of Los Angeles with a major war industry presence—including El Segundo, Huntington Beach, Newport Beach, and Redondo Beach—support the space sector. The San Gabriel Mountains run along the northern part of Los Angeles county. The town of Monrovia lies along the southern base of these mountains. A five-hour bike ride to the west is Simi Valley, tucked away in the Santa Susana Mountains. The drone-maker AeroVironment calls Monrovia and Simi Valley home. Up the coast, Silicon Valley vends all manner of surveillance, space, and IT products to the War Department. Sacramento is where Kratos churns out drones.

Our trail ends in Oregon, home to Vigor Marine LLC, Columbia Helicopters, and FLIR Surveillance, for ship maintenance, transportation, and thermal observation, respectively.

The U.S. war industry profits as well through global supply chains—whether setting up subsidiaries in allied countries or using the countries' industrial bases to produce a weapons platform (like the F-35, parts of which are built in locations as diverse as Italy and Japan). War corporations manage global chains by organizing, coordinating, and enforcing a hierarchical command structure upon disparate locations worldwide. Orders flow down the chain and capital flows up, allowing the corporation's executives—not workers who make the products—to harvest enormous amounts of wealth. This exacerbates inequality, not just in Lemont Furnace, Pennsylvania, and Marietta, Georgia, but also Rochester, England, and Aire-sur-l'Adour, France—all locations where U.S. war products are made. War corporations paint these actions as "building lasting capacity."

JUSTIFICATIONS

From east coast to west, the war industry is populated by people performing various jobs, including acquisition specialist, administrative assistant, analyst, armed mercenary, astrophysicist, data officer, engineer, lawyer, lobbyist, linguist, mathematician, public relations specialist, technician, and tradesperson. From the haughtiest academic to the humblest welder, how do people justify working in the war industry?

Money. War is profitable to many people. A mercenary position within the war industry—say, project engineer at Lockheed Martin or information technology guru at SAIC—can bring in a six-figure salary. The psychopaths in executive positions within the war industry can earn over $20 million per year. *It's the money, stupid!*

Civilian use. When cornered, employees of war corporations invoke civilian applications of military technology. Corporate PR specialists point to the internet, the jet engine, radar, and satellite technology as coming from funding war.[136] "Are you saying that the only way to achieve technological breakthroughs is through war?" the masses reply, catching PR specialists off guard. "We can harness the human mind in many ways. So far, by the numbers, the U.S. government has only spent significant money on war. Try throwing that kind of money at unpressured, non-militarized research and development, and see what the sciences produce." Some of today's war corporations (perhaps Honeywell, maker of fire alarms and thermostats, or Boeing, which has a commercial aircraft division) might foreground these peripheral civilian benefits as cover for the bulk of their war-making investments.

Distancing. Lockheed Martin's Director of Communications once said, "The missile has nothing to do with the manufacturer... Lockheed Martin was not the one that was there, firing the missile."[137] That distancing puts the onus on the military. It's no different than the engineer at a U.S. university who justifies her work on nuclear weapons along the lines of, "Well it's not me pushing the button. Surely, there are military professionals in charge of this." Other cogs in the war industry rationalize like so: "I might disagree with the wars, but I'm not the one elected to make such decisions. I'm just doing my job." That distancing puts the onus on policy. Those who resort to distancing focus on their own daily, incremental tasks, blocking out all consequence.

Traditional patriotism. Traditional patriotism rallies a person around the flag and shuns holding authority to account. True patriotism, however, involves questioning government, making government accountable, and changing government when it is polluted and corrupt. Traditional patriotism allows the wars to continue. War typically involves the working class of one country being tricked into fighting the working class of another country, or, as in the cases of Vietnam and Afghanistan, the peasantry of another country.

For the troops. Some people justify working for the war industry by saying they do it for the troops. A Lockheed Martin technician who works on a product used on Boeing AH-64 "Apache" helicopters to target humans, vehicles, and buildings stated, "One of the things that tells me that we have an impact... is when [the soldiers] come back in after re-deployment [a euphemism for returning to the U.S.], they tell how they were so happy to see the Apache come over the horizon when they needed it the most. And once they see that help is on the way, then everything's okay. That's the true measure of success."[138] Journalist Jeffrey Stern describes how one machinist at a missile factory rationalizes his role:

> [T]he thing that he said made him most proud about working at Raytheon was helping to keep American servicemen and women safe. The company makes a point of hiring veterans with combat injuries, which reminds him of whom he's working for and why. He feels it when he sees the gigantic photos of service members that the company hangs in the most prominent parts of the plant. The photos,

he explained, are of relatives of Raytheon workers. When he's at work, the notion of helping American servicemen and women is not abstract. It's almost tactile.[139]

Well played, Raytheon.

The phrase "support the troops" is a clever slogan through which the MIC throws a blanket of patriotism over the underlying issue: supporting the wars. "Support the troops" has been very effective in getting blue-collar workers to line up in favor of war.

Opportunism. Industry lobbyists exemplify this. They make a lot of money pressuring U.S. Congress. Lobbyists repackage war and death as "defense" and "jobs." Sometimes they do this by promoting the cult of "precision" and "state-of-the-art" technology. Aware of exactly what they are promoting due to the need to disguise it, the war industry lobbyist is corrupt beyond rescue. Lobbyists infest Capitol Hill like plague-filled rodents. Congress, in turn, listens to the lobbyist and pushes war upon the jumbled working class that is too busy suffocating under the corporate boot to discern or confront the bigger exploitative picture.

Insouciance. Many smart people are blissfully comfortable with the paycheck and creature comforts that being part of the war industry brings. Consider one plucked at random from the leadership of a war corporation. The man's résumé is impressive: PhD from a prestigious university; over 2,000 flight hours on industry aircraft; awards from industry and the Pentagon; and not one ounce of moral trepidation, even though his participation in the war industry leads directly to the deaths of innocents abroad and perpetuates war.

Power relations. The elites in authority within military, industry, and Capitol Hill don't have to think much about the consequences of their work: the bodies piling up in Africa and the Middle East, the troops maimed, the families destroyed. They don't have to think about this because they have all the means of violence (police, the surveillance state, the prison system, the Armed Forces) and influence (the mass media, think tanks, complicit academe, money, and all the accolades that society confers upon titans of industry) to squash criticism of the pernicious effects of their actions. As Academic David Graeber has pointed out, in structural inequalities the people on top are not obligated to put in the mental labor to try to understand the perspective of the lower classes or those they oppress.

The above cocktail of denial ingredients allows one to justify working in the war industry. A small minority within the industry recognizes the gravity of the situation—that funneling so much money to war corporations has a negative effect on U.S. security because it vaccums up manpower, time, and capital, and forestalls social development and infrastructure maintenance—but is afraid of the consequences of speaking up. Violence and social isolation deter the few within it who push back against the machinery of war. The leaker is fined and jailed, the minor whistleblower demoted, the demonstrator gassed and beaten, and the conscientious hacker locked up for a decade. When a few people push back, the D.C. regime and its industrial sponsors crush them. Violence, hierarchy, compartmentalization, and chain of command enforce the status quo.

FUTURES COMMAND

U.S. war corporations work hard to guide the establishment of military locations. The establishment of Army Futures Command, for example, was a big win in a long string of victories for the war industry. In Futures Command, the war industry achieved an entire Command dedicated to producing new, unnecessary toys for optional wars.

The heart of Futures Command is something called a Cross Functional Team (CFT). CFTs are tasked with upending the ponderous weapons acquisition process. There are eight CFTs. Each CFT works on one of the U.S. Army's "modernization" priorities, which reflect what is important to industry.[140] These priorities are air & missile defense; aircraft; armored vehicles; computer networks; kitting up infantry; long-range artillery; training simulation; and navigation. Ergo, Futures Command will work to replace perfectly capable weapons systems: AH-64 helicopter, Bradley fighting vehicle, M1 Abrams tank, PATRIOT missiles, and UH-60 helicopter. But why would the war industry work to replace some of its most prized items? Money. Corporate executives know they will get more money from developing and producing new, high-tech weaponry than they would from sustaining the perfectly functional weaponry already in the Pentagon's arsenal. Research, development, testing, evaluation, and production costs a lot of money. Modernization lays bare the true nature of the war industry: one corporate hand grabbing newly issued government debt and the other corporate hand reaching into the increasingly infirm guts of the public tax base and wrenching out its wealth.

CFTs are industry magnets, minus the heavy Pentagon bureaucracy. The Secretary of the Army said Futures Command will "establish unity of command and unity of effort by consolidating the Army's entire modernization process under one roof. It will turn ideas into action through experimenting, prototyping, testing."[141] CFTs have direct access to the Department of the Army leadership.[142] This includes former industry executives now working in the top rungs of the Pentagon. CFTs have special transactional authority to play looser and faster with War Department funding.

Under Secretary of the Army Ryan McCarthy helped Secretary of the Army Mark Esper in the selection process that settled on Austin, Texas, as the home for

Futures Command. The Department of the Army cited many reasons for choosing Austin, among them "access to key partners," the city's entrepreneurial spirit, local quality of life, and homegrown talent.¹⁴³ Only one of these is an authentic reason for Austin's selection—Austin's "access to key partners," including war corporations and academia.¹⁴⁴ Generous financial incentives given by the city to corporations also helped.

The U.S. war industry that functionally runs the Pentagon sees Austin as a potential new Silicon Valley, a region with the right blend of finance, corporate infrastructure, and amenities capable of creating military technologies while cushioning spoiled personnel (e.g. industry engineers and mid-to-high-level suits). French political authors writing under the collective pen name The Invisible Committee provide context:

> The agents of capital everywhere are getting down to the business of creating an 'ecosystem' enabling the individual with the right team to develop fully, to 'maximize his talents'... According to this new orthodoxy... value production depends on innovation capability. But, as the planners themselves recognize, an environment favorable to creation and its sharing, a productive atmosphere, can't be invented, it is 'situated,' it sprouts in a place where a history, an identity, can enter into resonance with the spirit of innovation.¹⁴⁵

Every step in the hunt for a city in which to place Futures Command was rife with corporate override. McCarthy, the Army Under Secretary and former Lockheed Martin executive, acknowledged that the Army had worked with a corporation that helps corporations develop formulae to evaluate cities and find the right location for a major headquarters.¹⁴⁶

Esper, the Raytheon executive turned Secretary of the Army, said the Army chose Austin, in part, due to the city's affordable cost of living. Affordable? Austin has suffered widespread gentrification in recent years and is one of many increasingly unaffordable cities in the U.S. One cannot expect a war executive to know anything about thrift or affordability.¹⁴⁷

War industry officials know they've got in their hands the military's acquisition process. Say, for example, Futures Command is developing a replacement for Raytheon's PATRIOT surface-to-air missile system. That's no problem. Actually, it's a welcomed challenge. Futures Command will forward a request for proposals to war corporations. Raytheon will pitch a new system. Northrop Grumman might pitch a system. Lockheed Martin's Grand Prairie, Texas, branch will probably get in on the action, too. By design, program managers within Futures Command will be "hard-lined" to the Army's main acquisition headquarters.¹⁴⁸ And, no matter which corporation wins the hypothetical PATRIOT replacement, many win in the end; the losing corporations will likely end up as subcontractors on the project, perhaps designing key portions of the radar or missiles.

Metropolitan areas tied to the war industry are doing *relatively* well financially—corporate executives overseeing industrial activity make high salaries, raising the median income—while the rest of the United States is in dire straits. Millions are food insecure,[149] poverty is rampant,[150] the infant mortality rate is higher than in other wealthy nations,[151] over 500,000 people are homeless on a given night, including tens of thousands of military veterans,[152] opioids and other hard drugs beat up the populace,[153] and shoddy, polluting infrastructure clogs the transportation landscape. Labor participation and happiness rates are extremely low.[154] D.C.'s neoliberal economic policies have exploited and debased the working class. There is no relief in sight. The Pentagon sends U.S. troops and mercenaries abroad to fight elective, polluting, deadly wars. The wars kill civilians. The wars kill U.S. troops and mercenaries. The wars pollute the soil, the water, and the air. The wars cost trillions and splinter families. The war industry is the monster propelling this institutionalized disaster.

The chiefs of the U.S. war industry and the officials and functionaries seeking fiscal and professional gain across corporate strata have an inherent incentive to look for and promote war. In 1935, retired Marine Major General Smedley Butler famously asserted, "War is a racket!"[155] This is still true. Corporate success is measured in money: In 2018, the top five war corporations made over $16 billion.[156] The costs to the planet and its humans are all too real, but the captains of industry and their allied politicians live insulated from these costs. There is plenty of money to take care of the American people. The D.C. regime chooses not to. Let it be known.

U.S. war corporations and their politicians are responsible for most post-9.11 deaths: Afghan, Colombian, Iraqi, Libyan, Pakistani, Somali, Syrian, U.S., Yemeni. War corporations misdirect us by saying they have "delivered strong operating results, demonstrating the power of our business portfolio."[157] The profiteering behind endless war is a crime against humanity. Studying the war industry, its nature, and the way it operates is crucial if humanity ever wants to rid itself of corporate greed and achieve peace.

ENDNOTES

1 Crawford, Neta C. "United States Budgetary Costs and Obligations of Post-9/11 Wars Through FY2020: $6.4 Trillion." *Watson Institute for International and Public Affairs*. 13 November 2019. Includes "direct war and war-related spending and obligations for future spending on post-9.11 war veterans." The Costs of War Project is updated regularly at <watson.brown.edu/costsofwar>. Congresswoman Barbara Lee points out (*The Nation*, 20 June 2018): "Despite the trillions of dollars spent on the so-called War on Terror—a sum that could have sent every young person in the United States to college—we have invested almost nothing in a peace process to draw down our military operations."

2 $554.1B base budget for U.S. Armed Forces + $173.8B overseas contingency operations + $24.8B nuclear weapons (in the Energy Dept.) + $9B "defense-related" activities like FBI "homeland security" + $216B Veteran Affairs + $69.2B Homeland Security + $51B militarized "international affairs" + $156.3B War share of interest on the national debt. Roughly $80B in "intelligence" spending was not included in this tally because it's too opaque and hard to discern in the overall War budget. See Hartung and Smithberger ("America's Defense Budget Is Bigger Than You Think." *The Nation*. 7 May 2019).

3 Kotlikoff, Laurence. "Has Our Government Spent $21 Trillion of Our Money Without Telling Us?" *Forbes*. 8 December 2017. For supporting documentation, see <missingmoney.solari.com/key-documents>. This $21 trillion is about only monies disclosed in Inspector General reports, which do not cover all Pentagon spending. Michigan State University professor Mark Skidmore and his graduate students analyzed many of the Pentagon's financial statements (1998-2015) discovering that the Pentagon had access to far more money than Congress had ever appropriated. They concluded at least $21 trillion of financial transactions "could not be traced, documented, or explained," as reported by Dave Lindorff (*The Nation*, 27 November 2018). In its annual budget requests to Congress, the Pentagon reports financial statements from the previous fiscal year, which contain numbers that Pentagon staffers completely made up, Lindorff reported. Note: The Government Accountability Office has deemed the War Dept. *high risk* for significant fraud, waste, and abuse.

4 Corporations paying no taxes or getting a tax refund include AECOM, Amazon, Honeywell, and IBM. See Kathryn Kranhold "You paid taxes. These corporations didn't" (*Center for Public Integrity*, 11 April 2019) and Erik Sherman "How These Fortune 500 Companies (Legally) Paid $0 In Taxes Last Year" (*Fortune*, 11 April 2019). The Institute on Taxation & Economic Policy issued a report on 16 Dec 2019, which affirmed that 91 corporations, including Halliburton, did not pay any federal income taxes on their 2018 U.S. income. See Matthew Gardner, et al. ("Corporate Tax Avoidance in the First Year of the Trump Tax Law," <itep.org>). This shirking of responsibility is part of a wider pattern within U.S. elite. The richest 400 families in the U.S. paid a lower share of the tax burden in 2018 than any other income range, according to Emmanuel Saez and Gabriel Zucman in *The Triumph of Injustice* (New York, NY: W. W. Norton & Co., 2019).

5 Bruenig, Matt. "U.S. Workers Are Paying High Taxes. But Without Any of the Benefits." *Jacobin*. 14 April 2019.

6 Lindsay Koshgarian breaks this down in "For Military Contractors, Tax Day Is Pay Day." *Truthout*. 10 April 2019.

7 The U.S. Census Bureau indicates that the 5.7 million very poor families with children would need, on average, $11,400 more to live above the poverty line (as of 2016). The total money needed to help these people out and bring them above the poverty line would be roughly $69.4 billion/year. $1.74 trillion could completely eliminate all poverty in the U.S. West, Rachel. "For the Cost of the Tax Bill, the U.S. Could Eliminate Child Poverty. Twice." *TalkPoverty.org*. 12 December 2017.

8 War is the federal government's largest discretionary spending allocation. U.S. federal government annual deficit—defined as the difference between what the federal government receives, typically in taxes, and the money it spends—reached $779 billion in FY2018, a 17% increase from FY2017. The annual deficit hit roughly $1.1 trillion for FY2020. The U.S. National Debt is passing $22.28 *trillion* as I write this on 11 May 2019, per <usdebtclock.org>.

9 Zielinski, Rosella Cappella. "How Do War Financing Strategies Lead to Inequality? A Brief History from the War of 1812 through the Post-9/11 Wars." Watson Institute for International & Public Affairs. 28 June 2018.

10 "Unworthy victims: Western wars have killed four million Muslims since 1990." Middle East Eye. 18 April 2016.

11 Burnham, Gilbert, Riyadh Lafta, et. al. 2006. "Mortality after the 2003 invasion of Iraq: a cross-sectional cluster sample survey." *The Lancet* 368(9545): 1421-1428.

12 "Body Count: Casualty Figures after 10 Years of the 'War on Terror.'" Physicians for Social Responsibility. March 2015. PSR mobilizes health professionals to advocate for environmental responsibility and a nuclear weapons-free world.

13 The Army alone has about 23,000 soldiers deployed around the world, not including Afghanistan, indicated Gen. Ray Odierno in testimony before the Senate on 13 February 2013. There are around 28,500 U.S. troops (soldiers, sailors, airmen, Marines) just in South Korea. Odierno later retired from the Army and became a senior advisor at the investment bank JPMorgan Chase.

14 Turse, Nick. "A Wider World of War." TomDispatch. 14 December 2017. "That's about 75% of the nations on the planet…"

15 Ahmed, Nafeez. "Unworthy victims: Western wars have killed four million Muslims since 1990."

16 "U.S. & Allied Killed and Wounded." Watson Institute for International and Public Affairs at Brown University. Accessed 30 May 2018: <watson.brown.edu/costsofwar/costs/human/military>. 13 U.S. troops were killed in combat in Afghanistan in 2018. 11 in 2017, per *The New York Times* (Fahim Abed, 26 June 2019). As of the 3rd quarter (April, May, June), FY2019, there were roughly 22,000 U.S.-citizen "contractor personnel" in CENTCOM, according to the War Dept. ("Contractor Support of U.S. Operations in the USCENTCOM Area of Responsibility," June 2019).

17 "U.S. & Allied Killed and Wounded." Watson Institute.

18 Only 17% of dead U.S. troops came from high income level, the *AP* reported (Alfano, Sean. "War Casualties Pass 9/11 Death Toll." 22 September 2006). For a detailed study, see Lutz, Amy. 2008. "Who Joins the Military?: A Look at Race, Class, and Immigration Status." *Journal of Political and Military Sociology* 36(2): 167-188.

19 Philipps, Dave. "Suicide Rate Among Veterans Has Risen Sharply Since 2001." The New York Times. 7 July 2016. Sebastian Junger (Tribe. NY: Hachette Books, 2016, pp. 83-4) provides nuance: It "was only in 2008 that—for the first time in decades—the suicide rate among veterans surpassed the civilian rate in America, and though each death is enormously tragic, the majority of those veterans were over the age of fifty." Tribe offers sound insights regarding the ill condition of U.S. society.

20 Yen, Hope. "Suicide rates among veterans highest in western U.S., rural areas." Associated Press. 16 September 2017.

21 Kime, Patricia. "Active-Duty Military Suicides at Record Highs in 2018." *Military.com*. 30 January 2019. Overall U.S. suicide rates in 2017 reached the highest since World War II, according to a June 2019 Centers for Disease Control & Prevention study cited by *Time* magazine (Jamie Ducharme, 20 June 2019). The Air Force saw an average of 100 suicides/year during 2014-19, according to

Brian Everstine. "USAF Orders Stand-Down to Combat Rising Suicide Rate." *Air Force Magazine*. 1 August 2019.

22 Cox, Matthew. "Retired SEAL: Tracking Special Operators' Performance May Help Prevent Suicides." Military.com. 6 February 2019. Possible categories for inclusion: financial, nutritional, physical, spiritual, spousal. No mention of the brutalities of war.

23 Some rapes were recorded. For example, soldiers from the 4th Infantry Division raped a 15-year-old girl and killed her family, according to the *Washington Post* (Ellen Knickmeyer, 3 July 2006). The case was "at least the fourth American military investigation announced since March of alleged atrocities by U.S. forces in Iraq," the *Post* reported. According to the *AP* ("Killings shattered dreams of rural Iraqi family," 23 May 2009), two of the sons returned home to find their parents shot and their sister's body burning. PFC Steven Green was convicted of conspiracy and murder. He received a life sentence.

24 For over a year after the U.S. invasion, roughly $12 billion in *cash* was flown from the United State to Iraq, "ostensibly as a stopgap measure to help run the Iraqi government and pay for basic services until a new Iraqi currency could be put into people's hands," *Vanity Fair* reported ("Billions Over Baghdad," 1 October 2007). The Pentagon did not track this money well. One planeload—a Lockheed Martin C-130 cargo aircraft—contained $2.4 billion in $100 bills. The cargo weighed 30 tons. "Of the $12 billion in U.S. banknotes delivered to Iraq in 2003 and 2004, at least $9 billion cannot be accounted for."

25 From March 2003 through Sept 2007, the U.S. occupation detained at least 23,500 and co-opted Iraqi security forces detained at least 21,300. Pincus, Walter. "U.S. Expects Iraq Prison Growth." Washington Post. 14 March 2007, as cited in Stephen Graham's Cities Under Siege (London: Verso, 2011).

26 American International Contractors of Arlington, VA, has appeared repeatedly in Pentagon contracts. American Mechanical (Fairbanks AK) and American Scaffold of San Diego, CA, too. Patriot Construction (Dunkirk, MD) is a regular vendor of construction services. Patriot Construction (Stockton, CA) has worked construction for the Defense Logistics Agency. Veterans Construction Coalition (Norfolk, VA) has done construction work at Wright-Patterson AFB, OH. Then there's the Military & Federal Construction Company (Jacksonville, NC), which has repaired living quarters at Camp Lejeune, NC.

27 Patriot Contract Services (Concord, CA) has helped preposition matériel worldwide. American Cyber (Clifton, VA) sells consulting, engineering, cyber security. American Electronics (California, MD) and American Technology Solutions International (Fredericksburg, VA) administer its program executive offices, units of military organization that are in charge of large acquisitions or a major program. American Electronic Warfare Associates (California, MD) sells electronic warfare testing, expertise, and training. American Ordnance (Middletown, IA) makes ammunition. American Petroleum Tankers (Blue Bell, PA) transports fossil fuel products. American President Lines (Scottsdale, AZ) sells ocean transportation. American Systems Corp. (Chantilly, VA) researches non-lethal weapons, ship power systems, and unmanned undersea vehicles.

28 Peerless and CDM contracts issued 1 April 2019 and 27 Aug 2019, respectively.

29 Meyer, Will. "Elizabeth Warren's Green Imperialism Isn't the Answer." *TruthDig*. 30 May 2019. Will Meyer noted, "perhaps the most urgent question facing the country is not 'how fast can we green the military,' as Warren's plan suggests, but who is most threatened by climate change, America's armed forces or the people subjugated by them?" Great point.

30 Issued 28 Sept 2017 and 9 April 2018. These two installments cost over $32 million.

31 Construction on bachelor enlisted quarters, 2016, issued 12 Feb, 8 & 31 Mar, 26 May, 20 June, 12 July, 12 Aug, 20 Sept, 7 Dec.

32 Issued 18 May 2018, 20 Sept 2018, 19 Sept 2018, 26 May 2016. The U.S. Military Academy gets facility upgrades, too.

33 Semova, Dimitrina, et al. "U.S. Department of Defense is the Worst Polluter on the Planet." *Project Censored*. 2 October 2010. Elaine Graham-Leigh ("Why stopping wars is essential for stopping climate change." *Counterfire*. 22 March 2019) puts the War Dept.'s daily fossil fuel use at around 1 million barrels. She writes, "U.S. military personnel on active service make up around 0.0002% of the world's population, but are part of a military system which generates around 5% of the world's greenhouse gas emissions." The U.S. Armed Forces account for 70% of total U.S. carbon emissions, says Robert Shetterly writing in *Common Dreams* ("In the Shadow of Warships and the Climate Emergency: On Getting Arrested at Bath Iron Works," 14 May 2019). For a comprehensive study of the carbon footprint, see Crawford, Neta. "Pentagon Fuel Use, Climate Change, and the Costs of War." Watson Institute for International and Public Affairs. 12 June 2019. For analysis of fossil fuel logistics, see Belcher, Oliver, et al. "Hidden carbon costs of the 'everywhere war': Logistics, geopolitical ecology, and the carbon boot-print of the U.S. military." Durham University Department of Geology and the Lancaster Environmental Center (U.K.). 3 May 2019.

34 E.g., VS2 LLC owns the corporate entity known as CB&I Federal Services. VS2 LLC is a JV between APTIM and VSE Corp. APTIM manages engineering, construction, and environmental projects for Big Oil in addition to the War Dept. VSE is a large War player in the fields of IT, supply chain logistics, and engineering. APTIM and Kemron Environmental Services (Atlanta, GA) have worked on remediating land at Hunters Point Naval Shipyard, southeast San Francisco. APTIM has also remediated soil poisoned with polychlorinated biphenyl (PCB) at Naval Weapons Industrial Reserve Plant, Bethpage, NY, remediated an old naval facility in the Aleutian Islands, and dealt with radioactive and toxic waste on the East Coast. Cape Environmental Management (Overland Park, KS) is remediating parts of the former Sunflower Army Ammunition Plant in De Soto, KS. The JV Sevenson-USA Environmental (Niagara Falls, NY) has also worked there to remove and decontaminate underground structures. The ammunition plant in Kansas produced millions of pounds of propellant for projectiles (that went on to kill and maim humans in Korea and southeast Asia). The U.S. military committed war crimes in Korea (1950-3). The U.S. industrial arsenal—particularly napalm and carpet bombs—destroyed towns and cities, leveled dams and power stations, and killed at least 20% of the North's population, per Harden, Blaine (*Washington Post*, 24 March 2015); Shorrock, Tim (*The Nation*, 30 March 2015); and "Prof. Bruce Cummings: U.S. Bombing in Korea More Destructive Than Damage to Germany, Japan in WWII" on the 12 June 2018 episode of *DemocracyNow*. OTIE (Milwaukee, WI) has tried to remediate pollutants at Plum Brook Ordnance Works near Sandusky, OH. These are just a few examples of hundreds.

35 Quoted in Colgan, Jeff. "Congress worries that climate change will force the U.S. to pay foreign governments millions. Here's why." *Washington Post*. 11 June 2019. Tom Carper (D-DE) is on the Senate Environment & Public Works Committee.

36 This transformation of the natural world is not just the razing of forests or the mining of minerals. One must include the petrochemical industry's transformation of fossil fuels into plastics and other polluting polymers.

37 Corporate America is also in charge of studying/documenting the effect a planned base or weapons range might have on the surrounding community—aircraft noise, potential for mishaps and accidents, and the extent to which land use works with or against local designs—even though Corporate America stands to benefit if the base or range gets established.

38 Nazaryan, Alexander. "The U.S. Department of Defense is one of the world's biggest polluters." *Newsweek*. 17 July 2014.

39 The "scope and magnitude of the FUDS Program are significant, with more than 10,000 properties identified for potential inclusion in the program." Accessed 31 October 2018: <www.usace.army.mil/Missions/Environmental/Formerly-Used-Defense-Sites/>. Relevant FUDS contracts in 2017 issued 22 March, 1 Sept, 26 Sept.

40 For example, a 9 June 2015 environmental contract to 6 U.S. firms covered U.S. military facilities in Germany, Italy, Turkey, Portugal, Spain, and the U.K. Facilities in the U.K. included RAF Alconbury, Fairford, Lakenheath, Croughton, Menwith Hill, and Mildenhall. The latter three have substantial personnel coordinating with NSA.

41 See "Toxic Emissions from Aircraft Firefighter Training." *U.S. Environmental Protection Agency*. Report No. 453-R-93-027. Issued 1993. Accessed 11 April 2019 via <https://nepis.epa.gov>; Hölemann, Hans. "Environmental Problems Caused by Fires and Fire-Fighting Agents." *Fire Safety Science—Proceedings of the Fourth International Symposium*. Available at <www.iafss.org/publications/fss/4/61/view>, pp. 61-77; and Shane, Leo. "Cancer-causing foam could be banned in military training next year, off military bases entirely by 2029." *Military Times*. 4 June 2019.

42 In one burn pit, an Army officer burned the remains of a man he had summarily shot. Cooper, Tackett, and Shah. "Twist in Green Beret's Extraordinary Story: Trump's Intervention After Murder Charges." *The New York Times*. 16 December 2018.

43 Brunswick, Mark. "GAO says Pentagon needs to do more about burn pit exposure." *Star Tribune*. 24 October 2016.

44 Risen, James. "Veterans Sound Alarm Over Burn-Pit Exposure." *The New York Times*. 6 August 2010.

45 "Final Assessment: What We Have Learned from Our Inspections of Incinerators and Use of Burn Pits in Afghanistan." *Special Inspector General for Afghanistan Reconstruction*. February 2015: <www.sigar.mil/pdf/alerts/SIGAR-15-33-AL.pdf>.

46 Kime, Patricia. "IG thrashes DOD in final burn pit report." *Military Times*. 12 February 2015.

47 Kime, Patricia. "IG thrashes DOD in final burn pit report."

48 Jordan, Bryant. "Congress Drops Burn Pit Exposure from Pentagon Research List." *Military.com*. 23 December 2015.

49 Brunswick, Mark. "GAO says Pentagon needs to do more about burn pit exposure." *Star Tribune*. 24 October 2016.

50 Rempfer, Kyle. "Burn pits downrange caused lung disease in service members, court rules." *Army Times*. 15 February 2018.

51 His name was Brigadier General Michael T. Heston. Naylor, Donita. "General's death draws attention to burn pit dangers." *Providence Journal*. 26 November 2018.

52 Copp, Tara, Shirsho Dasgupta, and Ben Wieder. "Exclusive: Veterans want answers as new data shows rise in cancers over two decades of war." McClatchy. 30 October 2019.

53 Alfano, Sean. "War Casualties Pass 9/11 Death Toll." Associated Press. 22 September 2006.

54 FY2001 "defense" budget was $335 billion, roughly $484 billion in 2019 dollars. FY2019 budget is roughly $750 billion (roughly $1.25 trillion if you account for all "national security"-related expenditures, per William Hartung & Mandy Smithberger in *The Nation*, 7 May 2019). For more on military spending doubling, see the *National Priorities Project*, "How Military Spending has Changed Since 9/11." For financial irresponsibility in Afghanistan, see David Francis "The U.S. Government Can't Account for Billions Spent in Afghanistan" (*Financial Times*, 27 Dec 2010) and the Pentagon IG report (No. D-2009-108, 23 Sept 2009).

55 Gates, Robert. From the Shadows. New York: Simon & Schuster, 1996, pp. 145-7.

56 Trofimov, Yaroslav. "Many Afghans Shrug at 'This Event Foreigners Call 9/11.'" *Wall Street Journal*. 8 September 2011.

57 "Bush rejects Taliban offer to hand Bin Laden over." The Guardian. 14 October 2001.

58 Industry is poised to win vis-à-vis Afghanistan's mineral wealth if violence ever subsides there: Risen, James. "U.S. Identifies Vast Mineral Riches in Afghanistan" (The New York Times, 13 June 2010); Pleven, Liam. "Pentagon In Race for Raw Materials" (Wall Street Journal, 3 May 2010); Klare, Michael T. *The Race for What's Left* (New York: Picador, 2012, pp. 138-141, 172); Banco, Erin. "The U.S. Isn't Leaving Afghanistan Anytime Soon" (Daily Beast, 28 January 2019). Winners and users of such wealth could include tech firms, U.S. War Dept. (including its Strategic Materials Security Program), and telecoms.

59 Sales to Afghan forces included Datron World Communications (Vista, CA) and Harris Corp. radios, parts, services; Integrated Microwave Technology (Hackettstown, NJ) handheld ISR devices; MD Helicopters (Mesa, AZ) aircraft, training, and maintenance; Orbital ATK (Fort Worth, TX) reconnaissance aircraft; PAE training & mentoring; General Dynamics rockets; and L3 fuzes. Issued 2016 (6 May, 29 Aug, 16 June, 15 Sept, 6 Oct), 2017 (16 Nov, 24 May, 5 Sept, 1 Sept, 15 Sept, 23 May, 28 Sept, 27 July, 31 Jan). Many U.S. corporations, particularly ones in Puerto Rico (see Chapter Eight), sell uniforms to the Afghan Armed Forces and National Police. Other corporate goods and services sold beyond 2016-17 included AM General, Critical Solutions Int., and Textron vehicles; Capco (Grand Junction, CO) training bombs; CNS Aviation (Pensacola, FL) avionics test sets; Iron Mountain Solutions (Madison, AL) helicopter tech support; Jacobs logistics; ManTech vehicle logistics; Navistar (Lisle, IL) vehicle refuelers; and Tukuh Technologies (Kansas City, MO) training management.

60 McVeigh, Karen. "U.S. plan to improve Afghan intelligence operations branded a $457m failure." *The Guardian*. 2 August 2017.

61 Issued 2 June 2016.

62 Woody, Christopher. "Opium production has set another record in Afghanistan—here's where it increased the most." *Business Insider.* 16 November 2017.

63 Zucchino, David. "The U.S. Spent $8 Billion on Afghanistan's Air Force. It's Still Struggling." *The New York Times*. 10 January 2019. About 265 U.S.-trained Afghan pilots "now fly 118 aircraft" supplied by the U.S. "The fleet is projected to double by 2023." The *Times* goes on: "Aviation experts have criticized a decision to phase out the old workhorses of the Afghan forces—Russian-made Mi-17 helicopters—for American-made UH-60 Black Hawks." One retired U.S. Brigadier General said the "Mi-17 was 'the perfect helicopter' for Afghanistan because it can carry more troops and supplies than the Black Hawk and is less complicated to fly. 'Let's be candid,' he said of the switch. 'That was largely done for political reasons.'"

64 Issued 4 Sept 2018, 4 April 2019, 29 July 2019.

65 Zucchino, David. "The U.S. Spent $8 Billion on Afghanistan's Air Force. It's Still Struggling."

66 This cycle has real, disastrous consequences. For example, in spring 2019 the Taliban was achieving stunning tactical victories. Taliban fighters captured/killed an entire Afghan National Army company on Monday, 11 March 2019, as described by Mohammed Saber and Rod Nordland ("Taliban Wipe Out an Afghan Army Company While Talking Peace With the U.S." *The New York Times*. 11 March 2019). Two days later, U.S. aircraft destroyed an *Afghan* Army base. *The New York Times* ("Afghan Army Base Is Wiped Out by U.S. Airstrikes, Officials Say," 13 March 2019) quoted a military spokesperson, who prevaricated, blamed the fog of war, and then said, "We are operating in a complex environment, Afghans included, where attacks come from fighters who do not wear their uniforms." Later in the week, the Taliban pulled off the biggest capture of Afghan soldiers yet. See Rahim and Nordland. "Taliban Capture About 150 Afghan Soldiers After Chase Into Turkmenistan." *The New York Times*. 17 March 2019.

67 AC First (a JV between construction giant AECOM and software/IT firm CACI) of Germantown, MD, snags funds for logistics support, maintenance, supply, and transportation services in and around Bagram, Afghanistan. Bagram is 55-65 km, depending on the road, north of the international airport in Kabul. BAE Systems (McLean, VA) provides services, presumably on land vehicles, to U.S. Forces at Bagram. Boeing gets money for drones, equipment, and field service representatives. CACI (McLean, VA) makes money off IT and intel ops out of Bagram. Keep in mind, the corporate provision of intel services is largely software-based. These projects support U.S. and NATO troops in Afghanistan; IT and cyber for Afghanistan's intelligence organizations, which work with U.S. forces; and intelligence for the Director of Intelligence of NATO's Resolute Support Mission. CACI has sold similar technical support for U.S. Army intelligence units stationed in Europe, including locations in Germany (e.g. Sembach, Wiesbaden, Kaiserslautern) and Italy. EXP (Chicago, IL) maintains electrical systems in Bagram. EXP has run electrical safety assessments/repairs from Jordan to the UAE. Other products keeping the U.S. occupation going are Jacobs logistics & support services; Mission 1st Group (Arlington, VA) expertise managing projects and running network infrastructure, including some IT work; Newbegin Enterprises (Johnson City, TN) vehicle parts; and Noble Supply & Logistics (Rockland, MA) materials for military installations and U.S. federal agencies throughout the Middle East. PAE maintains military vehicles at Hamid Karzai International Airport. SAIC (Reston, VA) sold its work protecting military assets on Bagram and in Kandahar. Sierra Nevada Corp. (Mary Esther, FL) sells contractor logistic support to U.S. forces in Afghanistan. Multiple corporations work on the Persistent Ground Surveillance System, a blimp deployed above U.S. military installations overseas to keep an eye on things. Relevant contracts include but are not limited to 3 May 2016, 24 June 2016, 1 July 2016, 20 Sept 2017, 17 Nov 2017, 20 Nov 2017, 21 Dec 2017, 28 March 2018, 6 Aug 2018, 8 Aug 2018, 21 Sept 2018. The aforementioned corporations comprise a small sample of the contracts involving U.S. military forces that occupy Afghanistan.

68 Has there been "progress" in Afghanistan? Yes, according to U.S. generals and Secretaries of War. Progress has been made in military training, military operations, and even peace talks. See transcripts: "Department of Defense Press Briefing by General Nicholson via teleconference from Kabul, Afghanistan," 22 August 2018; "Joint Press Conference with Secretary Carter and President Ghani at Presidential Palace in Kabul, Afghanistan," 21 February 2015; "Press Conference by Secretary Hagel at NATO Headquarters, Brussels, Belgium," 5 February 2015; "Department of Defense Press Briefing by Secretary Hagel in the Pentagon Briefing Room," 22 January 2015. Secretaries of State, such as Hillary Clinton, regularly made claims of "progress" in Afghanistan. See "Clinton Highlights Progress in Afghanistan." VOA News. 23 June 2011; Ukman, Jason. "Clinton urges Congress: Don't 'undercut' U.S. progress in Afghanistan and Pakistan." Washington Post. 27 October 2011.

69 Woodyatt and Siad. "More civilians are being killed by Afghan and international forces than by the Taliban and other militants." CNN. 31 July 2019. The Afghans allied to D.C. are also dying, at a rate of about 25/day, according to Afghan President Ashraf Ghani, The New York Times (Azadzoi and Nordland, 27 November 2018) reported.

70 Tyson and Lang (*Accessory to War*, p. 331) point out that "Iraq's oil revenues were crashing while Kuwait was helping to keep world oil prices low through its own overproduction." Professors John Mearsheimer and Stephen Walt note, "U.S. Ambassador April Glaspie told Saddam, '[W]e have no opinion on the Arab-Arab conflicts, like your border disagreement with Kuwait.' The U.S. State Department had earlier told Saddam that Washington 'had no special defense or security commitments to Kuwait.' The United States may not have intended to give Iraq a green light, but that is effectively what it did." In 2011, Walt added, "The more interesting question—and the one that concerned us when we wrote our original 2003 article—was what that meeting tells us about Saddam's calculations. I think the recently released [WikiLeaks] cable describing that meeting is consistent with our interpretation.

Saddam is clearly aggrieved, and most of Glaspie's responses are attempts to mollify him. Nowhere in this cable is there evidence of a clear deterrent warning, or an unambiguous statement of an American security guarantee to Kuwait. She reminds Saddam that we have concerns about his intentions—which was clearly not news to Saddam—but there's not even a hint from her of what Washington would do if he seized Kuwait." See "An Unnecessary War." *Foreign Policy.* Jan/Feb 2003, pp. 51-59. Walt. "WikiLeaks, April Glaspie, and Saddam Hussein." *Foreign Policy.* 9 January 2011.

71 "While I was there I saw the Iraqi soldiers come to the hospital with guns. They took the babies out of the incubators. Took the incubators, and left the children to die on the cold floor," the girl claimed. She was the daughter of the Kuwaiti Ambassador to the U.S., according to *The New York Times* ("Deception on Capitol Hill," 15 January 1992).

72 The total number of humans massacred was over 400. "1991: U.S. bombers strike civilians in Baghdad." *BBC News*: <news.bbc.co.uk/onthisday/hi/dates/stories/february/13/newsid_2541000/2541107.stm>.

73 Writing in *The New York Times*, Steven Lee Myers ("With Little Notice, U.S. Planes Have Been Striking Iraq All Year," 13 August 1999) reported, over the past 8 months, U.S. and U.K. "pilots have fired more than 1,100 missiles against 359 targets." He continued: "With the increase in tempo, the fighting over the zones is costing upwards of $1 billion a year, though Pentagon officials say it is difficult to fix an exact cost." 200+ aircraft, 19 warships, and 22,000 U.S. troops worked on the effort.

74 Iraqi and independent journalists have done an excellent job reporting on the U.S. targeting of utilities, like water purification facilities, the destruction of which led to a surge in preventable diseases after the war. The U.S.-led sanctions against Iraq then blocked medicine (that treat waterborne diseases) from entering Iraq. Writing in the *Guardian,* journalist John Pilger ("Squeezed to death," 3 March 2000) noted, "'Containing' Iraq with sanctions destroys Iraq's capacity to threaten U.S. control of the Middle East's oil while allowing Saddam to maintain internal order. As long as he stays within present limits, he is allowed to rule over a crippled nation." See also Sadiq and Tiller. "The Debate Over U.N. Sanctions." *PBS.* November 2002. Denis Halliday, head of U.N. humanitarian work in Iraq, resigned in protest of the U.S.-led economic siege. He believed the U.N. was underestimating the preventable deaths that sanctions had caused in Iraq. Part of ruining a society is harming its children. For statistics, see Fulwood and Williams Jr. "170,000 Iraqi Children Face Death, Health Study Finds." *LA Times.* 21 May 1991.

75 The U.S. war industry set up front groups to lobby for invasion, including *The Committee for the Liberation of Iraq.* Schulman, Daniel. "The Iraq War, Brought to You by Your Friends at Lockheed Martin." *Mother Jones.* 16 January 2007. Arranged by war industry officials, the Committee featured D.C. insiders, powerful lobbyists, entrenched capitalist policymakers, party bosses, former high-ranking Pentagon officials, war industry consultants, and industry executives.

76 "Iraq war illegal, says Annan." *BBC News.* 16 September 2004. Hirsch, Afua. "Iraq invasion violated international law, Dutch inquiry finds." *The Guardian.* 12 Jan 2010.

77 Some of the strongest propaganda efforts came from the White House and the Pentagon's Office of Special Plans, a den of Zionists and neoconservative ideologues with deep ties to the U.S. war industry. Taking out Saddam Hussein was a strategic interest of the Zionist regime occupying Palestine because Hussein's forces were the main regional power capable of contending militarily with the Zionist occupation. See Julian Borger ("The spies who pushed for war." *The Guardian.* 17 July 2003) and Peter Enav ("Israeli General Derides Findings on Iraq." *AP.* 4 December 2003) for a kinder scrutiny.

78 "Saddam 'had no link to al-Qaeda.'" *BBC.* 9 September 2006. Mount, Mike. "Hussein's Iraq and al Qaeda not linked, Pentagon says." *CNN.* 13 March 2008.

79 Borger, Julian. "There were no weapons of mass destruction in Iraq." *The Guardian*. 7 October 2004.

80 "Cities jammed in worldwide protest of war in Iraq." *CNN*. 16 February 2003.

81 "Global protests against Iraq war." *BBC*. 19 January 2003.

82 Garfield, Leanna. "The 9 biggest marches and protests in American history." *Business Insider*. 20 January 2017.

83 Parenti, Michael. "The Iraq War Is a Smashing Success." 21 September 2011. Available at <www.michaelparenti.org> and an anti-war blog <dandelionsalad.wordpress.com/2011/09/25/the-iraq-war-is-a-smashing-success-by-michael-parenti/>.

84 For outstanding investigative reporting on DU in Iraq, see Jamail, Dahr. "Iraq: War's legacy of cancer." *Al Jazeera*. 15 March 2013; and "Did the U.S. cause Fallujah's birth defects?" *Al Jazeera*. 3 August 2012. For an academic analysis of what has happened to Fallujah, consult Busby, Chris et al. 2010. "Cancer, Infant Mortality, and Birth Sex-Ratio in Fallujah, Iraq 2005-2009." *International Journal of Environmental Research and Public Health* 7(7): 2828-2837. For information on DU use against Syria, see Oakford, Samuel. "The United States Used Depleted Uranium in Syria." *Foreign Policy*. 14 February 2017.

85 The U.S. military began corporatizing its support services in the 1960s. See Phelps, Martha L. "Supporting the Troops: A History of Military Contracting in the United States." *The Routledge Research Companion to Security Outsourcing: The Role of the Market in 21st Century Warfare*, edited by Joakim Berndtsson and Christopher Kinsey, New York: Routledge, 2016. Corporatization accelerated over the decades.

86 War corporations' subcontractors hire recruiters and smugglers to bring TCN from Africa and South Asia to U.S. military facilities overseas, including facilities located in warzones. Smugglers and recruiters engage in devious hiring practices including lying about salaries, charging exorbitant recruitment fees, and rushing recruits out of their home countries. Subcontractors and corporations often confiscate worker passports and identification. Once on U.S. bases, TCN do a variety of jobs. For a pittance, they cook, clean, prepare & serve food, dispose of trash, do the troops' laundry, and ring up sales at checkout counters. TCN report abuse, wage theft, and dismal living conditions. Reported violations of human rights of TCN in U.S. warzones include non-consensual sex, inadequate food, poor water quality, and lack of water access. See Stillman, Sarah. "The Invisible Army" (*New Yorker*, 6 June 2011); "Victims of Complacency: The Ongoing Trafficking and Abuse of Third Country Nationals by U.S. Government Contractors" (*American Civil Liberties Union*, June 2012); "Documents Reveal Details of Alleged Labor Trafficking by KBR Subcontractor" (*Project on Government Oversight*, 14 June 2011); Raz, Guy. "U.S. Contractors in Iraq Rely on Third-World Labor" (*NPR*, 10 October 2007). These journalists did not use the term "war corporations."

87 Young, Angelo. "Cheney's Halliburton Made $39.5 Billion on Iraq War." *International Business Times*. 23 March 2013. Corporations working BOSS in Iraq "received at least $138 billion of U.S. taxpayer money for government contracts" during the first decade of the Occupation. Including base security.

88 "Contracting Abuses in Iraq." C-SPAN. 28 April 2008; Hayes-Greenhouse and Chindeya. "Private, No-Bid Contractors Doing Iraq Jobs." NPR. 15 August 2005; Jehl, Douglas. "Pentagon Finds Halliburton Overcharged on Iraq Contracts." *The New York Times*. 11 December 2003; Linton, Eric. "U.S. Sues KBR Over Iraq War Overcharges." *International Business Times*. 19 November 2012; Minnis, Glenn. "Halliburton: $61M Overcharge?" CBS News. 12 December 2003; "Pentagon: Halliburton Overcharged in Iraq." AP. 12 December 2003; Pincus, Walter. "Audit finds that Iraq contractor overcharged for repair parts." *Washington Post*. 30 October 2009; "Prosecutors investigate

claims U.S. contractor in Afghanistan, Iraq overcharged." AP. 14 August 2010; Vine, David. "Contractors Raked in $385 Billion on Overseas Bases." *Mother Jones.* 14 May 2013.

89 E.g.: One sergeant remarked, "The food is better prepared than at the old facility, and the T-bone steak is definitely great." McCann, Chris. "New Baghdad Area Dining Facility Feeds 9,000 Per Meal." *Army News Service.* 22 March 2007.

90 AFCAP is a "rapid response contingency contract tool" for U.S. government to use for "urgent assistance," by picking from a small group of "pre-qualified vendors." See "Air Force Contract Augmentation Program (AFCAP)." *Air Force Civil Engineer Center.* Accessed 16 July 2018: <www. afcec.af.mil/shared/media/document/AFD-140227-020.pdf>. AFCAP III, issued in 2005, cost up to $10 billion. On 25 June 2015, the Pentagon issued a contract worth up to $5 billion for BOSS as part of AFCAP IV.

91 "Each company may be awarded up to $5 billion annually" with a "maximum annual value of $15 billion… Over the life of LOGCAP IV, the maximum contract value is $150 billion." Bailey Grasso, Valerie. "Defense Logistical Support Contracts in Iraq and Afghanistan: Issues for Congress." *Congressional Research Service.* 20 September 2010. See also <kbr.com/logistics-civil-augmentation-program-(logcap)-iv> & <fluor.com/projects/contingency-operations-logistics-construction>.

92 "Stephen discusses the LOGCAP IV mission and how Fluor's culture instills high performance." *Fluor.* Accessed 3 July 2018: <www.fluor.com/about-fluor/videos?videoid=74>, (00:38).

93 Bailey Grasso, Valerie. "Defense Logistical Support Contracts in Iraq and Afghanistan: Issues for Congress."

94 In 2014 (16 July and 18 Sept), corporations were allocated over $300 million for Rapid Disaster Infrastructure Response, which helps USACE with "time sensitive, emergency construction and debris removal." Distinct from contracting programs like AFCAP or LOGCAP, RDIR reinforces and expands infrastructure. Multiple award construction contract is another way to go. A Coast Guard lieutenant explains, "This contracting vehicle allows an agency to award multiple contracts for a given type of work, in order to have established contractors in place to complete construction work without the need for a full open solicitation." Wimmer, Todd. *The Military Engineer.* Alexandria: The Society of American Military Engineers, 2018.

95 Goldenberg, Suzanne. "Pentagon 'hid' damning Halliburton audit." *The Guardian.* 15 March 2005. "Documents Reveal Details of Alleged Labor Trafficking by KBR Subcontractor." *Project on Government Oversight.* 14 June 2011. Mandak, Joe. "KBR Suit Over GI's Death in Iraq Is Revived." *AP.* 2 August 2013. Paid roughly $32B for work in Iraq and Afghanistan, 2001-9, KBR was involved in "'the vast majority' of war-zone fraud cases and a majority of the $13 billion in 'questioned' or 'unsupported' costs," Scahill reports (*Alternet,* 10 June 2009). Other alleged infractions include shoddy work and overbilling. "Transforming Wartime Contracting: Controlling Costs and Reducing Risks" (*Commission on Wartime Contracting in Iraq and Afghanistan,* August 2011) offers some remedies.

96 Makinson, Larry. "Outsourcing the Pentagon." *Center for Public Integrity.* 29 September 2004. Updated 19 May 2014.

97 In demolishing and deconstructing some of its military infrastructure in Afghanistan in autumn 2014, the U.S. government "handed over to Afghanistan about $900 million of 'foreign excess real property'—military hand-me-downs of various kinds—and destroyed another $46 million worth because the items were too sensitive or impractical to transfer." The "largest single gift" was Camp Leatherneck in Helmand, "valued at $235 million." At a different time and place in Afghanistan, the U.S. bombed its "own machinery so the Taliban could not steal it" and because "it was too much trouble to haul the equipment out." Coll, Steve. *Directorate S.* New York: Penguin Press, 2018, pp. 667, 215. Coll was president of New America (think tank), 2007-12.

98 "We give the people of Iraq a head start to build their engineering capabilities and to the regional economy by supporting efforts to stabilize the Mosul Dam," said the Mosul Dam Task Force project executive (and USACE Civilian of the Year). Macri, Joe. "USACE Employee Awarded Top Honors for Three Separate Assignments." *USACE Middle East District*. 22 August 2019.

99 Industry think tanks pushed analyses supportive of U.S. military action. Think tankers supportive of U.S. military action included but certainly were not limited to Jon Alterman and Anthony Cordesman at CSIS; Richard Fontaine and Ilan Goldenberg at CNAS; Daniel Byman and Peter Mandaville at Brookings; and Kenneth Pollack and Danielle Pletka at AEI.

100 Private contractors and other mercenaries working for the U.S. War Department increased eight-fold in 2015. "The sharp increase, disclosed in a recent Pentagon report to Congress, underscores the military's reliance on civilians even for missions with relatively small troop presence," the publication *Defense One* reports. "In addition to the 2,028 Pentagon contractors, another 5,800 are employed by other agencies" (implied: the U.S. State Department and CIA). Weisgerber, Marcus. "Back to Iraq: U.S. Military Contractors Return In Droves." *Defense One*. 23 February 2016.

101 In Syria, armed groups—some aided by U.S. intelligence agencies, others by the War Department—varied in their military effectiveness and ideologies. Some groups in Syria, for example, received great assistance from CIA. The Pentagon backed others. These groups were known to fight one another. See Hennigan, W.J., Brian Bennett, and Nabih Bulos. "In Syria, militias armed by the Pentagon fight those armed by the CIA." *LA Times*. 27 March 2016.

102 The Zionist regime had long tried to implement this policy of sowing sectarian division across the Middle East, advocating for it with every U.S. administration since President Reagan in 1981. This policy is known informally as the Yinon Plan.

103 Toyota and Japan assert their own bewilderment at the source. See <https://abcnews.go.com/International/us-officials-isis-toyota-trucks/story?id=34266539>. Bukkehave (Fort Lauderdale, FL) acquires Mercedes and Toyota vehicles, mostly trucks, for a variety of governments and fighting forces. Countries Bukkehave sells to include Burkina Faso, Burundi, Chad, Djibouti, Ethiopia, Ghana, Iraq, Kenya, Libya, Mali, Mauritania, Niger, Oman, Tunisia, Uganda. Relevant contracts: 18 Sept 2014, 24 Sept 2014, 5 Aug 2016, 14 Sept 2016, 16 Sept 2016, 28 Sept 2016, 9 Aug 2018. The 9 Aug 2018 sale supported U.S.-backed forces operating inside sovereign Syrian territory under the auspices of Operation Inherent Resolve. There is no immediate evidence that Bukkehave's acquisitions have been transferred directly to ISIS. Bukkehave did not respond for comment.

104 "War of Annihilation: Devastating Toll on Civilians, Raqqa—Syria." Amnesty International. 2018.

105 Wong, Edward and Eric Schmitt. "U.S. Pressures Iraq Over Embrace of Militias Linked to Iran." 19 March 2019.

106 "Afghanistan Fatalities Total: 3542." iCasualties.org. Last updated 22 January 2019. Accessed 1 February 2019: <www.icasualties.org/App/AfghanFatalities>.

107 In 2018, U.S.-led coalition aircraft carried out more than 6,500 sorties in Afghanistan, per David Zucchino ("The U.S. Spent $8 Billion on Afghanistan's Air Force. It's Still Struggling." The New York Times. 10 January 2019).

108 Gregg, Aaron. "Defense business helps Boeing soar past $100 billion revenue mark for the first time." *Washington Post*. 31 January 2019. In FY2019, D.C. sold $55.4 billion of war industry goods and services and the State Dept. cleared $67.9 billion in weapons. See Aaron Mehta's "America sold over $55 billion in weapons in FY19" (*Defense News*, 15 October 2019) and "Here's how many foreign military sales the U.S. State Department OK'd in FY19" (*Defense News*, 4 October 2019). Sales cleared by State are not final. The Defense Security Cooperation Agency sends the cleared

names to U.S. Congress. After congressional approval, the foreign government and U.S. military/industry enter into further negotiation on price, quantity, and quality.

109 The 7 countries were Afghanistan, Iraq, Libya, Pakistan, Somalia, Syria, and Yemen, according to Heather Saul (*The Independent*, 24 September 2014). Investigative journalist Nicolas Davies ("Obama's Bombing Legacy." *Consortium News*. 18 January 2017) put the associated war expenditures in context: Obama "increased U.S. military spending beyond the post-World War II record set by President George W. Bush... The final record is that Obama has spent an average of $653.6 billion per year, outstripping Bush by an average of $18.7 billion per year (in 2016 dollars). In historical terms, after adjusting for inflation, Obama's military spending has been 56 percent higher than Clinton's, 16 percent higher than Reagan's, and 42 percent more than the U.S. Cold War average." In "America dropped 26,171 bombs in 2016. What a bloody end to Obama's reign" (*The Guardian*, 9 January 2017), Medea Benjamin cites calculations of 26,171 made by Micah Zenko. Writing in *Fortune*, Clay Dillow ("U.S. Sold $33 Billion in Weapons to Gulf Countries Last Year," 28 March 2016) reports Lockheed Martin got $18M in 2015 to increase Hellfire missile production from 500 to 650 missiles per month. LM had already increased production of Paveway II laser-guided bombs four-fold. In its FY2017 war budget request, the Pentagon asked for $1.8B so war corporations can produce 45,000 smart bombs to replenish Department of War magazines.

110 Camp, Lee. "Trump's Military Drops a Bomb Every 12 Minutes, and No One Is Talking About It." *Truthdig*. 19 June 2018.

111 "Combined Forces Air Component Commander 2013-2018 Airpower Statistics." *U.S. Air Forces Central Command*. Current as of 31 December 2018. Accessed 14 February 2019.

112 Pawlyk, Oriana. "U.S. Airstrikes Hit Decade-Long High Amid Peace Efforts in Afghanistan." *Military.com*. 11 February 2019.

In 2011, Guastella completed the Senior Executive Fellows program at Harvard University's School of Government.

113 Vine, David. *Island of Shame: The Secret History of the U.S. Military Base on Diego Garcia*. Princeton: Princeton University Press, 2009.

114 Amanpour, Christiane, Rebecca Leung, and Andrew Tkach. "Diego Garcia: Exiles Still Barred." *60 Minutes*. 12 June 2003. Mr. Schlesinger "gained a reputation as someone willing to cut jobs and implement unpopular policies with little regard for what other people thought of him." Smith, Timothy. "James R. Schlesinger, CIA chief and Cabinet member, dies." *Washington Post*. 27 March 2014.

115 Press guidance repeatedly stressed communications, not offensive military capabilities, on the island. Expansive construction in the 1970s was downplayed or referred to in modest terms. Discussion of nuclear weapons on or transiting the base was skirted. Any major weapons platform on Diego Garcia was referred to as "temporary" and emphatically not based there. The ethnically cleansed population was deceitfully referred to as "contract laborers" who were "transferred when the [copra] plantations were closed down." U.S. offensive military capabilities on Diego Garcia were presented as a "limited support facility." This lie is maintained to this day, as the U.S. military facility on Diego Garcia is officially called "Naval Support Facility Diego Garcia." On <www.wikileaks.org>, see "Publicity on Diego Garcia Agreement," 1976 Feb 25 (16:12); "Observation Trip to Diego Garcia," 1974 Oct 22 (21:42); "Diego Garcia Press Guidance," 1974 March 13 (22:57); "Diego Garcia Expansion, Q's and A's," 1974 Feb 1 (23:11); "Journalist Visits to Diego Garcia," 1973 July 26 (05:55).

116 "UK denies Chagos Islanders the right to return home." *Al Jazeera English*. 29 June 2016.

117 The U.N. passed a non-binding resolution in May 2019 demanding the U.K. return control of the Chagos Islands to Mauritius. 116 countries voted in favor, 6 against, 56 abstained. BBC reported that London's Foreign & Commonwealth Office (FCO) "said Britain did not recognise Mauritius'

claim to sovereignty, but would stand by an earlier commitment to hand over control of the islands to Mauritius when they were no longer needed for defence purposes." The FCO stated, "The joint UK-U.S. defence facility on the British Indian Ocean Territory *helps to keep people in Britain and around the world safe from terrorism, organised crime and piracy*" (emphasis mine). "Chagos Islands dispute: UN backs end to UK control." *BBC News*. 22 May 2019.

118 Relevant contracts issued 30 May 2017, 14 April 2017, 30 Aug 2018, 1 April 2019, 7 May 2019, 5 July 2018, 31 Oct 2017.

119 Prior to the corporate yeast known as the Cold War, the U.S. War Department owned and operated military arsenals throughout the country, which produced the weapons needed in the event of war. Some arsenals (e.g. Picatinny, Letterkenny, Rock Island, Watervliet) still exist, though war corporations have taken them over and control most production. In a class of its own, Redstone is more of a massive stronghold of military and industry than an arsenal producing ordnance.

120 On 30 January 2018, Lockheed Martin ramped up its capacity to produce Hellfire missiles, with its goal to produce 11,000 missiles per year. On 6 February, Raytheon continued developing (as part of an earlier contract) its assortment of missiles. On 6 and 19 March 2018, the U.K.'s BAE Systems and Raytheon increased their ability to produce guidance kits (for rockets) and air-to-air missiles, respectively. On 27 April, Raytheon sustained cruise missile production across the U.S.

121 Not included in my tally was a 10 July 2018 contract (worth a potential $4.1 billion) for Lockheed Martin, Northrop Grumman, and Raytheon to provide MDA with autonomous acquisition and precision tracking & discrimination "to optimize the defensive capability of the Ballistic Missile Defense system and counter evolving threats."

122 Small Diameter Bomb and JASSM-XR issued 10 Sept 2018. JASSM-XR issued without open, fair, and free competition. Writing in the *Washington Post* on 26 October 2018, Aaron Gregg reported General Dynamics' annual revenue rose to $28.5 billion. Lockheed Martin sold $14.3 billion in one quarter alone, a 16% jump from the previous year. Raytheon sales jumped 8.3%. Northrop Grumman quarterly sales increased 23% over a year ago, per Jane Edwards ("Kathy Warden: Northrop to Merge Two Tech Service Business Areas Into One Entity." *Executive Mosaic*. 26 October 2018) and Gregg.

123 Dillow, Clay. "U.S. Sold $33 Billion in Weapons to Gulf Countries Last Year." *Fortune*. 28 March 2016. Historian Daniel Immerwahr (*How to Hide an Empire*, p. 207) offers antecedents: The 37th Infantry Division was trying to retake Manila in Feb. 1945. "Rather than engage [Rear Admiral Sanji] Iwabuchi's men in direct combat, it would simply destroy any buildings in which they might be hiding. 'Putting it crudely, we really went to town,' [U.S. General Robert S.] Beightler reported." The principle hasn't changed much today, I note. Except for the underlying motivation: Today, too many dead U.S. troops would draw unwanted attention to nonstop war and potentially jeopardize the whole racket.

124 "Syria: Unprecedented investigation reveals U.S.-led Coalition killed more than 1,600 civilians in Raqqa 'death trap.'" *Amnesty International*. 25 April 2019.

125 "2018 deadliest year yet for Syrian children: UN." *Al-Jazeera*. 11 March 2019.

Unexploded ordnance was the biggest cause of child deaths and injuries.

126 Aaronson, Trevor. "Defense Department abruptly stopped releasing key details on strikes in war against ISIS." *The Intercept*. 9 January 2019.

127 "IS fight: U.S.-led coalition says it killed 1,300 civilians in Syria and Iraq." BBC News. 31 May 2019.

128 Smaller corporations include Advanced Technology Systems Co., DDL OMNI Engineering, Excellus Solutions, Mission Services, Qi Tech, Trowbridge & Trowbridge, TWD & Associates, and Vexterra Group. A favorite of DARPA, Aixxia received funding on 19 April 2017 to help design

an online platform through which war corporations, researchers, and "interested research sponsors" work together to "explore new scientific ideas and concepts." PwC and KPMG, which sell accounting services to the Pentagon, work out of McLean as well.

129 Priest, Dana and William Arkin. "Top Secret America: The secrets next door." 21 July 2010.

130 Like many major war corporations selling signals intelligence (SIGINT) and IT goods and services, ManTech has dedicated executive positions for NSA programs. One focus of ManTech's vice president for NSA programs is "growth opportunities." Hubler, David. "ManTech names its main man for NSA." *Washington Technology*. 11 March 2010. Corporations not focused on SIGINT have comparable positions. Google, for example, has a position known as a "defense and intelligence sales lead," dedicated to cultivating contacts and contracts with the War Dept.

131 Zou, Manyun. "The DC Area Has the Highest Median Income in the U.S. Again." *Washingtonian*. 21 September 2016. Shah, Neil. "Washington Sees Incomes Soar as Most of U.S. Declines. *Wall Street Journal*. 19 September 2013. The 50 highest-paid CEOs in greater D.C. made over $687 million in total compensation in 2018, according to Carolyn Proctor in "The D.C. area's 50 highest-paid public company CEOs may delight, surprise or frustrate you" (*Washington Business Journal*, 1 October 2019).

132 The military budget usually takes up around 61% of annual discretionary spending, depending on how you calculate it (do you add overseas contingency operations funding?). The 2019 NDAA, which was signed into law in the summer of 2018, allocated roughly $716B towards war, preparation for war, and corporate welfare to the war industry.

133 Do not confused Greenville, TX, with Greenville, SC. Some work on the Lockheed Martin F-35 occurs in the latter location. Fluor also has major offices in Greenville, SC. Fluor sells construction services and BOSS.

134 Statements regarding recipients of industry funding were derived from information provided by the Center for Responsive Politics, <www.opensecrets.org>, current as of 2 Aug 2018. U.S branches of foreign war corporations (e.g. Elbit Systems, BAE Systems) give money to campaigns of elected officials.

135 A lot of money is up for grabs. In FY2016, for example, SSC Pacific allocated roughly $1.23 billion on contracts, according to Pritchard, Sharon. "SSC Pacific FY17 Contract States." *SSC Pacific*. 17 October 2017: <www.public.navy.mil/spawar/Pacific/Documents/SSC-Pacific-FY17-Contract-Stats.pdf>, pp. 2-3.

136 If military R&D were indeed extremely beneficial for civilian life, "then the countries with the largest investments and the greatest intensity of military research would be by all odds the countries most advanced in civilian technology… But that is not the case. The star performers in the development of civilian industrial technology, and in allied industrial productivity, since World War II have not been the United States and the Soviet Union [or Russia], but instead Japan and Germany. That difference is to be seen in virtually every class of industrial products." Melman, Seymour. "Special Interdisciplinary Panel—Barriers to Disarmament." *Towards Preventing Nuclear Omnicide*. St. Louis: First International Conference of the International Philosophers for the Prevention of Nuclear Omnicide, 1 May 1986. The same argument can be made today. China's prowess in civilian industrial technology predates and is uncorrelated with its increasing investments in military R&D.

137 Fisk, Robert. "Is This Some Kind of Crusade?" The Independent. 18 May 1997.

138 "Apache Fire Control: Performance Based Logistics (PBL)." *Lockheed Martin*. Published 15 March 2018: <www.youtube.com/watch?v=AYR6AsPO6Wk>, (4:31).

139 "From Arizona to Yemen: The Journey of an American Bomb." The New York Times. 11 December 2018.

140 The Department of the Army—led by a former Raytheon executive and a former Lockheed Martin executive, in the secretary and under secretary slots, respectively—set forth several "modernization priorities." Each priority is fluid enough for war corporations to submit intricate, costly, and endlessly upgradable products. The War Dept. *already* is head and shoulder above any nation in each modernization category; developing more weaponry and matériel is entirely unnecessary. But that's the point. CFTs are the product of and substantially comprised of corporate personnel.

141 Cox, Matthew. "It's Official: Austin Is Home of New Army Futures Command." *Military.com DOD Buzz*. 13 July 2018.

142 Army Futures Command will be the fourth Command within Army bureaucracy. The Army Commands already in existence are Army Forces Command, Army Materiel Command, and Army Training & Doctrine Command.

143 Cox, Matthew. "It's Official: Austin Is Home of New Army Futures Command."

144 Austin was already home to facilities of Lockheed Martin, JJLL LLC (the joint venture between JLL and J&J Worldwide that sells BOSS), Ultra Electronics, BAE Systems, and other industry players. The university presence is integral. Futures Command set up shop in multiple locations in the city: a tower owned by the University of Texas, the "Capital Factory" in the Omni hotel, and the University of Texas' School of Engineering. Personnel also hobnobbed in local cafés and entertained at the South By Southwest festival, according to Jen Judson (Defense News, 17 June 2019). In 2016, the War Dept. established Defense Innovation Unit Experimental (DIUx) offices in Austin to build "bridges between our national security endeavor at the Pentagon and America's wonderfully innovative and open technology community... Austin's commitment to innovation, access to talent and academia, as well as the department's longstanding ties to Texas make this an ideal next location for DIUx," Secretary of War Ash Carter proclaimed (Release No. NR-321-16, 14 September 2016). In Army-speak, Futures Command's "group headquarters will be located near innovative and agile industrial and academic institutions to align with these organizations and in a place where the command will inculcate the culture needed to develop the innovation and synergy required to lead the Army's modernization effort." See "Army Futures Command" (Army Futures Command Task Force, 28 March 2018). As of autumn 2019, Texas A&M University is building a $130 million testing hub for Futures Command.

145 The Invisible Committee. *To Our Friends*. Cambridge: MIT Press, 2014, pp. 176, 180, 179. The great metropolitan areas compete to attract capital and people. "There is no longer a generic 'population.' There is the young 'creative class' that makes its social and relational capital bear fruit in the heart of the smart metropolises, and all those who have so clearly become 'unemployable.' There are lives that count and others that aren't even factored into the accounts. There is a *plurality* of populations, some at risk and others having a substantial purchasing power." Conveniently, one of the War Dept.'s favorite propaganda firms, GSD&M Idea City, is located in Austin, Texas. GSD&M is currently in charge of Air Force recruitment.

146 Judson, Jen. "Army Futures Command taking charge of conjuring up new capability." *Defense News*. 26 March 2018.

147 For a careful analysis of the mentality and pathology of the U.S. oligarchy, listen to Paul Jay and Professor Leo Panitch on *The Real News Network* ("Obama Joins Club of the Super-Rich—Defends Global Capitalism in Lecture," 30 July 2018).

148 The 'headquarters' in this case is Army Acquisition Executive. Judson, Jen. "Army Futures Command taking charge of conjuring up new capability." *Defense News*. 26 March 2018. "Army Futures Command." *Army Futures Command Task Force*. 28 March 2018.

149 Resnikoff, Ned. "Food insecurity is at historic highs and getting worse." *MSNBC*. 41 April 2014.

150 Pilkington, Ed. "UN condemns Trump administration for exacerbating U.S. poverty levels." *The Guardian*. 22 June 2018. Many other studies exist on this topic. A thorough *and* accessible study on the topic is Buchheit, Paul. "The Real Numbers: Half of America Is in Poverty—and It's Creeping Upward." *Alternet*. 20 January 2015.

151 Johnson, David. "American Babies Are Less Likely to See Their First Year Than Babies in Other Countries." *Time*. 9 January 2018.

152 The National Coalition for Homeless Veterans <nchv.org> cites U.S. Dept. of Housing & Urban Development figures: roughly 40,000 homeless veterans sleep on the streets any given night.

153 Glenza, Jessica. "Opioid crisis: overdoses increased by a third across U.S. in 14 months, says CDC." *The Guardian*. 6 March 2018.

154 See Stephen Gandel (*Fortune*, 2 July 2015) and "Happy Planet Index—United States of America," *New Economics Foundation*. Labor participation, happiness rates, and the Job Quality Index (JQI) are more accurate measures of economic wellbeing than the traditional measure, GDP, which mostly reflects the relative success of giant corporations.

155 Butler, Smedley. *War Is a Racket*. 1935. For a history of post-WWII war machine, see James Carroll's House of War (New York: Houghton Mifflin, 2006). Carroll notes, "The Pentagon's business would be the only business that would get the government's full attention" (194).

156 War corporations in 2018 earned $16.09 billion from operations. Net sales were over $170 billion. See <www.gd.com/Articles/2019/01/30/general-dynamics-reports-fourth-quarter-full-year-2018-results>, <investors.boeing.com/investors/investor-news/press-release-details/2019/Boeing-Reports-Record-2018-Results-and-Provides-2019-Guidance/default.aspx>, <investor.raytheon.com/news-releases/news-release-details/raytheon-reports-strong-fourth-quarter-and-full-year-2018>, <www.northropgrumman.com/AboutUs/AnnualReports/Pages/default.aspx>, <www.lockheedmartin.com/content/dam/lockheed-martin/eo/documents/annual-reports/2018-annual-report.pdf>.

157 "Annual Report 2017." *General Dynamics*. March 2018.

2

Magnifying Influence

Corruption is the inducement of dishonest and destructive behavior for professional or financial gain. When corporations target government officials, departments, and agencies, privatization, exploitation, and pollution ensue. No law or regulation can compete with the corrupting tendencies of capitalism. The theoretical physicist Albert Einstein expressed this problem well:

> Private capital tends to become concentrated in few hands, partly because of competition among the capitalists, and partly because technological development and the increasing division of labor encourage the formation of larger units of production at the expense of the smaller ones. The result of these developments is an oligarchy of private capital the enormous power of which cannot be effectively checked even by a democratically organized political society. This is true since the members of legislative bodies are selected by political parties, largely financed or otherwise influenced by private capitalists who, for all practical purposes, separate the electorate from the legislature. The consequence is that the representatives of the people do not in fact sufficiently protect the interests of the underprivileged sections of the population. Moreover, under existing conditions, private capitalists inevitably control, directly or indirectly, the main sources of information (press, radio, education). It is thus extremely difficult, and indeed in most cases quite impossible, for the individual citizen to come to objective conclusions and to make intelligent use of his political rights.[1]

This is the environment in which the war industry operates.

Strategy involves establishing priorities, making choices, and then matching available resources to goals, means to ends. The war industry has a five-step strategy to capture government:

1. Pull retiring military officers into war corporations.
2. Stack the deck by placing ex-industry officials in the Pentagon's leadership.
3. Finance congressional campaigns.
4. Lobby creatively.
5. Fund think tanks and corporate media.

Here's how the strategy plays out.

PULLING IN MILITARY RETIREES

War corporations recruit retired high-ranking military officers. Generals and admirals retire from the U.S. Armed Forces and then join war corporations where they set to work converting their knowledge (about the acquisition process, senior military and civilian leaders, long-term military policy, and how the Pentagon works) and connections into profit. Some military retirees are sent to their old stomping grounds to pitch and sell goods and services. They are received deferentially due to their professional stature and the rank they had recently enjoyed in military uniform. Some retirees work as lobbyists on Capitol Hill. Others spend their time at corporate offices where jobs can include manager, mentor, director, vice president, and private consultant. Many high-ranking retirees—those who excel at networking, credentialism, and posturing—join a corporation's board of directors. Only a small number of 3- and 4-star officers decline this systemic corruption and retire peacefully to pursue hobbies and spend time with family.[2] War corporations have plenty to choose from: there are many more generals and admirals in uniform today than there were at the end of World War II. Mere issuance of a bulletin announcing the hiring of a former high-ranking general or admiral often leads to a boost in stock price.[3]

The nature of U.S. military leadership increases the number of officers taking the military-to-corporation trajectory. U.S. officers ascend to high rank through a combination of factors: (1) loyalty to the existing structure, including the primacy of war corporations within the military-industrial-congressional triangle; (2) support for nonstop, optional global war; and (3) professional deference to pro-war pretexts and jargon coming from industry think tanks and pressure groups. Men and women who make it to the highest military ranks are very good at conforming to the system. I am unaware of a single U.S. general or admiral who comprehends the battlefield, converses fluently in a foreign language with allies and adversaries, and possesses physical and martial dominance. The upper ranks of the U.S. Armed Forces are rife with a poor caliber of officers predisposed to seek out profit and reward upon retirement.

Excuses echo around the Beltway. Some of the unethical retirees who move from the Armed Forces to industry say they're just promoting a "strategic partnership" with a given war corporation. Others assert they're merely matching "private-sector expertise" with the War Department's mission. Still others claim their actions promote U.S. interests and support the nation's defense. A former executive vice president of a major war corporation told the *Baltimore Sun* that the corporation hires government officials just for their expertise, not their influence within Pentagon circles: "We do a much better job for our customers if we have people in the company who really know the customers."[4] That's only half true. The whole truth is that war corporations use eager retired officers to open doors, influence policy, and increase sales. Loopholes allow industry to dodge paltry, lenient laws.[5]

Consider a few examples of the military-to-corporation track.

General James Cartwright finished his military career as Commander of U.S. Strategic Command (STRATCOM) and then Vice Chairman of the Joint Chiefs of Staff. General Cartwright oversaw many Raytheon products while at STRATCOM.[6] As Vice Chairman of the Joint Chiefs, Cartwright helped keep Raytheon's $2.7 billion blimp known as JLENS up and running.[7] Cartwright joined Raytheon's board a little over five months after retiring from the military.[8] Cartwright also became the inaugural Harold Brown Chair at the think tank known as the Center for Strategic & International Studies (CSIS), which annually receives industry money (over $100K from Raytheon; Lockheed Martin and Boeing each donate between $200K and $499K; Northrop Grumman gives $500K or more). One of CSIS' endeavors is the Missile Defense Project, which hypes various "threats" to the United States and promotes products from the U.S. war industry to meet those threats.[9]

Kenneth Todorov used to direct the Missile Defense Agency when he was a Brigadier General. Now he's vice president of Missile Defense Solutions at Northrop Grumman. Lieutenant General William Phillips was the top Army officer in charge of acquiring products from the war industry. He is now a Boeing vice president. General Johnnie Wilson once ran U.S. Army Materiel Command, which keeps track of matériel and manages military installations. He then became a pitchman for Honeywell, peddling the corporation's technology and logistics.[10] Major General Kevin Leonard was in charge of logistics and transportation during his time in the Army. In retirement he has worked on various logistics and warehousing projects for Amazon, Fluor, and Vectrus, the latter being his current employer.[11] Vice Admiral Anthony Winns was the U.S. Navy's Inspector General, a position dedicated to "maintaining the highest level of integrity and public confidence."[12] Winns is now a vice president at Lockheed Martin.

High-ranking intelligence officials also move from government to industry. An associate deputy director at the National Security Agency (NSA) named Harold Smith became a managing director at Accenture, which is a big seller to NSA and government in general. Ira "Gus" Hunt, CIA's former chief technology officer, now works for Accenture, leading its cybersecurity division. General Keith Alexander retired from his position as director of NSA in spring 2014, and two months later established a cyber-security corporation.[13] John Chris Inglis was deputy director at NSA, and now is managing director at Paladin Capital Group, a D.C.-based investment firm focusing on cyber and war corporations. There, he works with managing director (former NSA director) Kenneth Minihan. Stephen Kappes ended his CIA career as deputy director. In early June 2018, Kappes joined the board of the telecom giant Sprint, which sells a lot to the War Department.[14] Teresa Shea moved from director of signals intelligence at NSA to vice president of technology at In-Q-Tel, a venture capital firm founded by U.S. espionage agencies. Shea is now a vice president at Raytheon. Many intel officials take the government-to-corporate path.

Some officials rotate through government and industry repeatedly. This in-and-out is called the revolving door. Ryan McCarthy was a special assistant in the Robert Gates' War Secretariat and worked on acquisition and supply chain matters in the Pentagon, expertise that later proved valuable at Lockheed Martin, where he worked vice president jobs specializing in sustaining and promoting the F-35 (perhaps the most costly, error-ridden weapon in history). McCarthy is now back in government as Under Secretary of the Army. General Dynamics elected former commander of U.S. Central Command General James Mattis to their board of directors, effective August 2013. The CEO of General Dynamics stated, Mattis "is a visionary and an inspiring leader who is renowned for his wisdom, courage, and integrity."[15] During his time at General Dynamics, Mattis accrued roughly $1 million in payment and stock.[16] Sitting on the board of General Dynamics, Mattis swore before Congress that reduced military spending was a threat to U.S. national security.[17] Mattis left General Dynamics to become Secretary of War in January 2017.[18] During his tenure as Secretary, Mattis oversaw global war, increases in the U.S. war budget, and many weapon sales to Australia, Europe, Middle East dictators, and others. Wherever Mattis traveled overseas, he brought the Defense Security Cooperation Agency director (the man in charge of weapon sales to foreign governments).[19] Mattis finished his stint as War Secretary in January 2019 and rejoined the board of General Dynamics in August. "We are honored to have him on our board," the CEO said.[20]

Examples of Pentagon officials heading from the Department of War into industry are legion. War corporations' recruitment of fresh, high-ranking officials is not limited to recently retired generals and admirals. The Project on Government

Oversight (POGO) found hundreds of instances of war corporations hiring former members of Congress, the civil service, legislative staff, and military personnel during one fiscal year.[21] Pulling high-ranking government officials into corporations is one part of the war industry's strategy. Another part is placing industry executives into the War Department's leadership.

STACKING THE PENTAGON DECK

Corporate officials move smoothly from executive offices to the Pentagon. These men and women who run the Pentagon have been raised in an environment of profiteering; they are steeped in corporate thought; their allegiance is to *corporate* success. They bring with them their industry contacts and an exploitative ideology. They naturally turn to corporate products when presented with a military problem. They benefit professionally and financially. The Pentagon is rife with officials who came from the U.S. war industry.[22]

Here are a few examples: the Assistant Secretary of War for Special Operations & Low Intensity Conflict was previously a trader for Goldman Sachs focusing on oil and natural gas cases; the Administrator of the Defense Technical Information Center (DTIC), directing billions of dollars of investment in industry, held multiple war industry directorships and key managerial positions; the Deputy Under Secretary of War for Policy had been a vice president at CACI, one of the major corporations providing software and personnel to the War Department and sundry U.S. intelligence agencies; the Director of Operational Test & Evaluation came from a string of executive positions at organizations that embody the nexus of academia and military-industry (MITRE, SRC,[23] and then Carnegie Mellon's Software Engineering Institute); the Pentagon's Chief Information Officer had been global chief information officer for JPMorgan Chase; the Under Secretary of War in charge of the Pentagon's finances had been a partner at the accounting firm Kearney & Company, which has strong business with the Pentagon;[24] and the Under Secretary of War for Policy had been a senior vice president at Lockheed Martin.[25] Such examples of industry-to-Pentagon abound.

Power hitters from industry enter "public service" and influence programs and policies. This invariably boosts the profits of industry employers, who, thenceforth, capture and direct more of the Pentagon. You will encounter these types—former corporate officials in Pentagon leadership positions—throughout this book.

Some of the most effective highfliers touch all three sides of the military-industrial-congressional triangle during their ascent. David J. Berteau worked in the War Department, proceeded to the war corporation SAIC, then on to the industry think tank CSIS, and then back to the War Department to be Assistant

Secretary of War. He's now in charge of the industry pressure group known as the Professional Services Council, which presents itself as a trade association "advocating for the federal contractor" (particularly in the sectors of IT, logistics, and R&D). John Luddy is currently vice president of National Security Policy at the industry pressure group known as the Aerospace Industries Association, or AIA. He basically plans how AIA is going to "advocate" to (i.e. influence) the military and congressional sides of the MIC. Luddy worked as vice president of Washington Operations for a corporation that makes rocket engines, worked in the Pentagon as special assistant of legislative affairs, and worked in the Senate as a policy advisor and as an aide to the chairperson of the Senate Armed Services Committee (SASC). John Hamre is currently running CSIS, before which he was variously Deputy Secretary of War, Under Secretary of War (comptroller), and chairperson of the Defense Policy Board. Prior to his tenure in the Department of War, Hamre was an SASC staffer overseeing weapons procurement and war budgets and R&D. Touching all sides of the MIC confers knowledge to achieve profit.

A glimpse at the board of directors of General Dynamics[26] demonstrates the two phenomena we've studied thus far: pulling War Department officials into war corporations and placing corporate executives in Department leadership. Rudy deLeon worked for a think tank popular among liberal hawks, the Center for American Progress. He was also a senior vice president at Boeing (2001-6), Deputy Secretary of War (2000-1), and Under Secretary of War for Personnel & Readiness (1997-2000). Lester Lyles, director, was previously commander of Air Force Materiel Command and Vice Chief of Staff of the Air Force. Mark Malcolm was Senior Advisor to Cerberus Capital, a private equity firm that invests heavily in the war industry. Cerberus owns DynCorp and other war corporations. C. Howard Nye, the man in charge of Martin Marietta Materials, which spun off from Martin Marietta during its 1996 merger with Lockheed, is another director. The final director, William Osborn, leads an investment bank with significant assets in the war industry. He is also on the board of Caterpillar, which sells vehicles and equipment to Apartheid Israel and the Pentagon. The boards of other major war corporations are comparably sculpted.

Marillyn Hewson is the Chief Executive Officer of Lockheed Martin. *Fortune*'s most powerful U.S. woman in business for three years in a row, she currently sits on many boards, DuPont and Johnson & Johnson included. Titans of industry cross-populate boards. For example, Wes Bush—no relation to the political dynasty—has been chairman of Northrop Grumman since 2011. He is on the boards of Cisco, General Motors, and Dow. The titans of war corporations schmooze, consult, and plot with the titans of U.S. industry in general.

One study has found that at least one in five CEOs displays "clinically significant levels of psychopathic traits."[27] I would surmise that the percentage is higher among CEOs of war corporations. When trying to determine the extent of a CEO's derangement, weigh their deceit, pretentious misrepresentations, manipulative operations, pomposity, lies, phony charm, and inability to feel remorse.

Hewson is close to the Saudi and UAE regimes, which are major Lockheed Martin customers. She serves on the board of trustees for King Abdullah University in Saudi Arabia and the UAE's Khalifa University for Science and Technology. Hewson gets along well with the Saudi despot Mohammad Bin Salman (MBS) and the Emirati despot Mohammad bin Zayed (MBZ). She has praised the Saudi regime at a time when the regime was persecuting women and leading a military offensive that turned Yemen into the largest man-made humanitarian disaster.[28] Amnesty International recapped the situation: "There is extensive evidence that irresponsible arms flows to the Saudi Arabia-led coalition have resulted in enormous harm to Yemeni civilians. But this has not deterred the USA, the UK, and other states… from continuing transfers of billions of dollars' worth of such arms."[29] The Pentagon around this time equivocated to Congress.[30] *Save the Children* estimated at least 85,000 Yemeni children under five years of age had starved to death by November 2018.[31] Hewson fully supported this war on Yemen.

CEOs shirk accountability craftily. When public outrage spiked after the House of Saud murdered *Washington Post* columnist Jamal Khashoggi, Hewson claimed, "We do business through the U.S. government… We take their lead on what we sell to 70 countries… It's a matter of following the government's lead."[32] The CEO of Raytheon International, John Harris, weaseled in a similar manner, saying, "Our role is not to make policy, our role is to comply with it."[33] Raytheon CEO Thomas Kennedy also said his war corporation would follow D.C.'s lead, affirming, "I'm pretty confident that we will weather this complexity."[34] The head of the industry pressure group NDIA urged Capitol Hill to not overreact.[35]

Hewson has painted her corporate governance as actually serving her country.[36] Hewson is proud of the weaponry she sells around the world, asserting that sales to foreign governments have grown from seventeen to thirty percent of overall sales during her tenure leading the corporation.[37] Hewson's time as Lockheed Martin CEO has "returned 293 percent to shareholders," according to *CNBC*.[38] At the 2018 Conference of the Society of Women Engineers, Hewson used her platform as the keynote speaker to glaze profiteering in a protective coating of gender politics.[39]

SHATTERING THE GLASS CEILING

Joan Dempsey blazed the trail within military-industry. Dempsey now is senior executive advisor at Booz Allen Hamilton. The leaders of some of the nation's most powerful war corporations are now women: Kathy Warden, CEO of

Northrop Grumman; Nazzic Keene, CEO of SAIC; and Eren Ozmen, president and owner of Sierra Nevada Corporation.[40]

Leanne Caret is CEO of Boeing "Defense, Space & Security." According to *Fortune* magazine, Caret's leadership helped make Boeing "the best-performing stock in the Dow Jones industrial average" in 2017. Caret hit for the cycle in October 2018. In baseball, hitting for the cycle involves hitting a single, a double, a triple, and a home run—all in the same game. In war profiteering, hitting for the cycle involves polluting, corrupting academia, schmoozing with oppressive regimes, and selling weapons of war—all in twenty-four hours. In early October 2018, Caret traveled thousands of miles to Doha, where she spoke with engineering students at Qatar University, guided the university to more pro-war posture, met with officials from the Qatari regime, and strengthened the Boeing-Qatari partnership.

Phebe Novakovic is CEO of General Dynamics. After attending Smith College, she became a weapons analyst for a war corporation. She spent time in CIA and then went to Wharton for a Master of Business Administration. *Fortune* reports, "After grad school Novakovic followed a well-trod path through government (purchaser of defense products and services) to private industry (seller of those products and services)." Novakovic worked with the White House Office of Management and Budget overseeing intel and war budgets, and soon became special assistant to the Secretary of War in the Clinton administration.[41] She took all of that knowledge, joined General Dynamics, and never looked back. In her extramural activities, Novakovic is chairperson of the Association of the United States Army, a pressure group led by industry executives that pushes the priorities of corporations and masks this behavior as taking care of the troops.

Women of war converse and do business with others in the larger military-industrial-congressional triangle and complementary structures.[42] CIA director Gina Haspel and her coterie move in these circles. As of January 2019, women led three of the Agency's top directorates.[43]

Ellen Lord was a long-time Textron executive (and vice chairperson of the industry pressure group NDIA) before heading to the War Department, where she became the first Under Secretary of War for Acquisition and Sustainment. She makes appearances at think tanks and industry pressure groups. According to Aaron Mehta of *Defense News,* when she took office, "she made it a priority to begin pushing decision authority on programs down from the [Office of the Secretary of War] level to the individual services, something that was expressly desired by key members of the Congressional defense committees."[44] Forcing this kind of control on individual services will lead to *even less* oversight, something corporations crave; individual branches of the Armed Forces are far easier to influence and corrupt. Facing retired 3- and 4-stars, industry wiles, and images of retirement gigs in war industry paradise, the services' officer corps buckles faster than one can spell M-I-C.

Heather Wilson was recently Secretary of the Air Force. Wilson has claimed that being a mom helps a woman become a high-ranking war official:

> If I ask everyone in this room to think about the most protective person you know in your life, someone who would do anything to keep you safe, half the people in this room would think about their moms... We are the protectors; that's what the military does. We serve to protect the rest of you, and that's a very natural place for a woman to be.[45]

What if these women of war listened to a hero like Sonia Santiago? Sonia informs us:

> Motherhood generates life. War is the antithesis of motherhood. When we have children, we create to live, not to kill. We at Mothers Against War in Puerto Rico have the inescapable historical commitment and responsibility to preserve life, not just of our children's, but of the thousands of innocent victims who we do not know and are killed in war.[46]

The military-industrial-congressional triangle tunes Santiago out. U.S. corporate media heap praise upon female war profiteers and criminals.[47] Industry pressure groups get in on the fun. NDIA has an affiliate, Women in Defense, which works to get more women into the war industry and military leadership. Aside from pulling Pentagon officials into war corporations and placing officials from war corporations in the Pentagon's leadership, financing political campaigns helps the U.S. war industry capture government.

CAMPAIGN FINANCE

Giant corporations finance the campaigns of people running for congressional office. Those people, once in office, help out the corporations. D.C. is so corrupt that they've legalized this process—effectively, they've legalized bribery.

In *Buckley v. Valeo* of 1976, the U.S. Supreme Court ruled that limits on election spending are unconstitutional. In *Citizens United v. Federal Election Commission* of 2010, the Supreme Court distorted the First Amendment's free speech clause, allowing corporations to spend unlimited amounts on political contributions. In *McCutcheon v. Federal Election Commission* of 2014, the Supreme

Court got rid of limits on the total number of political contributions one can give over a two-year period. Now it is perfectly legal for a corporation to give money to congressional campaigns (to bribe Congress) repeatedly, without end.

The Senate Armed Services Committee (SASC) is supposed to exercise oversight of the War Department. It does no such thing. U.S. war corporations corrupt every member of SASC through campaign finance. This ensures bipartisan support for endless war.[48] Senator John McCain's tenure as SASC chairperson is illustrative. The McCain campaign took money from General Atomics, General Electric, Raytheon, investment banks, and private equity firms. Despite a struggle with brain cancer, McCain spent the second full week of September 2017 shepherding the National Defense Authorization Act (NDAA) through the Senate. The NDAA establishes military budget levels and sets some war policy. Arguing for increased military funding, McCain blamed recent military accidents (including a collision involving the USS *John S. McCain*, his family's namesake) on a "strained force with aging equipment and not enough of it." The Senate version of the NDAA included $640 billion for the Pentagon's base budget ($37 billion more than the White House had asked for) and another $60 billion for Overseas Contingency Operations, a slush fund for war.[49] War corporations and war criminals mourned McCain's death.[50] A former McCain staffer and current think tank president, Richard Fontaine, polished McCain's legacy: "To have a meaningful national life, America had to be a force for good for its own people and people around the world, and that's more or less how he organized his approach to foreign policy and national security."[51]

Rhode Island's Jack Reed, the ranking member of the SASC, has taken campaign money from AECOM, General Dynamics, Raytheon, Apollo Global Management (a private equity firm heavy into the industry), and massive investment banks, like Merrill Lynch and Citigroup. Investment banks and/or private equity firms finance every SASC member, so I've largely omitted such entities from the following list, unless the organization excels in war industry investments. Here are campaign donors for the remaining members of the Senate Armed Services Committee:

- Angus King (I-ME)—Boeing, General Dynamics, Lockheed Martin, Raytheon, United Technologies
- Ben Sasse (R-NE)—AEI, Boeing, General Electric, Honeywell, and dark money PACs
- Bill Nelson (D-FL)—Harris, Lockheed Martin (LM), Leonardo SpA, Cerberus Capital, Raytheon
- Claire McCaskill (D-MO)—Boeing, Citigroup, MacAndrews & Forbes (owns AM General)

- Dan Sullivan (R-AK)—Blackstone Group, The Cohen Group, KKR, dark money PACs
- David Perdue (R-GA)—Blackstone Group, LM, SEI Investments, and dark money PACs
- Deb Fischer (R-NE)—Northrop Grumman (NG), Raytheon, and dark money PACs
- Gary Peters (D-MI)—Boeing, Carlyle Group, General Dynamics, General Electric
- James Inhofe (R-OK)—Boeing, General Dynamics, Honeywell, Huntington Ingalls, Orbital ATK
- Jeanne Shaheen (D-NH)—Boeing, General Electric, Google, LM, NG, Raytheon
- Joe Donnelley (D-IN)—General Dynamics, GE, Honeywell, MacAndrews & Forbes, NG, Raytheon
- Joni Ernst (R-IA)—Boeing, Carlyle, and many, many dark money PACs
- Lindsey Graham (R-SC)—Boeing, Cerberus, Fluor, General Electric, LM, Raytheon
- Martin Heinrich (D-NM)—Blackstone Group, General Atomics, Harris, NG, LM
- Mazie Hirono (D-HI)—AECOM, BAE Systems, General Dynamics, Huntington Ingalls, Parsons Corp
- Mike Rounds (R-SD)—Citigroup, Honeywell, NG, and dark money PACs
- Richard Blumenthal (D-CT)—General Dynamics, General Electric, United Technologies
- Roger Wicker (R-MS)—Boeing, General Atomics, Honeywell, Navistar, LM, Raytheon, dark money
- Ted Cruz (R-TX)—Chertoff Group, Halliburton, LM, and plenty of dark money
- Thom Tillis (R-NC)—Honeywell, LM, NG
- Tim Kaine (D-VA)—Boeing, Cerberus Capital, LM, NG
- Tim Scott (R-SC)—Boeing, Blackstone Group, Honeywell, LM, NG, United Tech
- Tom Cotton (R-AR)—Blackstone Group, Carlyle Group, General Electric, KKR, Raytheon

Reading this list, you saw a lot of political action committees, PACs. The war industry finances many of these. PACs are tax-exempt organizations that aggregate donations to fund political campaigns or influence federal elections. A congressperson's Leadership PAC is used to raise money for other members of Congress and candidates running for election.[52] By funding Leadership PACs, war corporations fluff three clients (incumbents, incumbents who are friends with incumbents, and aspiring members of Congress) with one stroke. Super PACs (a.k.a. independent expenditure-only committees) allow *unlimited* contributions.

Funding SASC officials' campaigns pays off. In May 2018, SASC voted 25-2 to advance the NDAA to the Senate floor. A year later, SASC advanced the next NDAA (which included many gifts to the war industry, like $10 billion for 94 Lockheed Martin F-35 fighter jets, "16 more than the Pentagon asked for"[53]).

The above exercise can be repeated for the U.S. House Committee on Armed Services and any congressional appropriation or intelligence committee.

Funding congressional campaigns directly impacts the way U.S. elected officials vote. For example, Representatives in U.S. Congress who voted against reining in NSA's unconstitutional phone-spying operations received "twice as much campaign financing" from war corporations compared to those who voted to rein in NSA's operations.[54]

War corporations back any candidate, regardless of party, who promotes industry talking points and supports corporate designs. Look at the now-retired Congressman Howard "Buck" McKeon (R-CA). Chairperson of the House Armed Services Committee in his prime, Buck represented California's 25th district. Buck was regularly a top recipient of campaign contributions from the war industry.[55] Many war corporations operated in Buck's district. Now look at Adam Schiff (D-CA), the current ranking member of the House Permanent Select Committee on Intelligence. (Reminder: the bulk of the U.S. intelligence workload is done by the war industry, specifically corporations marketing and selling hardware, software, and personnel to civilian and military agencies.) Schiff represents California's 28th district, home to many war corporations. Schiff receives substantial campaign contributions from the war industry.[56] Northrop Grumman was his largest contributor in 2016. Industry targets liberal heroes—people like Kirsten Gillibrand (D-NY) and Elizabeth Warren (D-MA)—as it targets Tom Cotton and Lindsey Graham.[57]

Texas' 23rd Congressional District shows just how harmful Republicans and Democrats can be. In November 2018, voters in Texas' 23rd Congressional District had to choose between two characters that define themselves by their "national security" credentials. The Republican incumbent was a former CIA officer—"On Capitol Hill, he likes to say, 'I was the dude in the back alleys at four in the morning'"—who left CIA and then joined a cybersecurity company (headed by his old CIA boss) before becoming a member of Congress. The Democratic opponent was a career Air Force intelligence officer, unapologetic Iraq War vet, former Booz Allen Hamilton consultant, and senior adviser for Obama's Interagency

Trade Enforcement Center. She also helped set up U.S. Africa Command, abetting the destruction of Libya in 2011.[58] These were the voters' choices.

History molds those aspiring to authority within the MIC. The very narratives of their lives are based in corporate salivation for more profit. Consider the Cold War, formulated and kicked off in the waning years of World War II. The U.S. war industry was riding high. It was the most powerful force on Earth in terms of mechanical and political mobilization. And it was benefitting from the goodwill earned through global victory. Devastated after WWII, the USSR was not the savage beast that U.S. propaganda and media outlets claimed. Positioning the USSR as an aggressive power served U.S. industry's expansionist aims and D.C.'s imperial agenda. The MIC consistently hyped the USSR and downplayed D.C.'s mammoth arsenal, justifying increased U.S. military budgets and investment in war.[59]

Far from being a good versus evil battle against an implacable enemy, the Cold War was initiated by the captains of U.S. industry initially as a means of staving off what they were most terrified of—a movement within the U.S. that opted to put people before profit. The U.S. government in tandem with U.S. industry bushwhacked territorial expansion, all under the guise of the imminent arrival of dreaded communist hordes. From Greece and the Philippines in the 1940s through Panamá in 1989, no country was off-limits. D.C. was far more aggressive globally during the Cold War (and today) than Moscow. A war, when "successful" from the CEO point of view, would open up new markets for U.S. industries to sell their wares or would open up new territory where U.S. industries could extract the resources to manufacture goods and services. Soon, war itself became the means of profit. Endless war for endless profit.

Born in U.S. Empire's smothering embrace, we, the U.S. public, feel nauseated when confronted with D.C.'s true nature. Accordingly, we counter that gut reaction with the mendacious reply, "We had to fight the scourge of communism wherever it was in the world. The militarization of the U.S. economy was an ancillary, unintended result." We are willfully blind to the truth: In order for the war industry (through which Wall Street and Corporate America had become fantastically rich) to survive and thrive, a decision was made to use substantial federal and commercial powers to hype communism as an existential threat to the United States, thereby justifying permanent militarization of the U.S. and expansion of industry. D.C. cannibalized and distorted its economy in the arms race and proxy wars, and forced Moscow to do the same. Moscow's economy buckled first. The Cold War subsided in the early 1990s when popular will for change ascended from within the USSR, and the Soviet economy ran out of steam. (Mikhail Gorbachev had contributed by prying open portions of authority.) When the Soviet Union collapsed, so too did the primary excuse D.C. had used to engage in global war.

U.S.- and U.K.-based finance leapt into action, pillaging the economies of the former USSR, driving the 1990s Russian economy into one of the worst peacetime depressions on record, and reducing the Russian people's longevity by a decade.

Conventional insight says that the end of the Cold War facilitated a lower war budget, forcing the U.S. war industry to consolidate. In fact, industry fought tooth and nail to keep the war budget above $250 billion (roughly $386 billion in 2019 dollars). The war industry's public relations apparatuses, think tanks, and media allies inflated the threat of Saddam Hussein as an excuse for the Pentagon to maintain a constellation of bases across the Persian Gulf. Simultaneously, industry doubled down on the corporatization of the military; jobs once carried out by the troops were delivered to corporate hands. Industry also pushed the militarized War on Drugs, devastating the Western Hemisphere from Latin America to Main Street, USA. War corporations merged and acquired one another to maintain and expand influence. Some of the bigger moves of the 1990s were Boeing merging with McDonnell Douglas, Lockheed merging with Martin Marietta, and Raytheon gobbling up Hughes Aircraft. The Clinton White House, a country club of neoliberal ideology, was fully onboard with the corporatization of the War Department. President William J. Clinton's major triumphs in office were all goals of the ruling class: expanding sanctions against Iran's oil sector in 1995; the Financial Services Modernization Act of 1999, which deregulated the banks; increasing military spending; launching ordnance at Afghanistan, the Balkans, Iraq, and Sudan; and the Telecommunications Act of 1996, which deregulated the telecoms and allowed cross-ownership in corporate media.[60] Support for neoliberal economic policies, including the corporatization of war, is one of many traits that both factions in the D.C. regime share.

When the dust settled at the end of the 1990s, three corporations held about two-thirds of the U.S. war industry: Boeing, Lockheed Martin, and Raytheon set out to please shareholders and insatiable investment firms. The Pentagon had less leverage over industry because, in part, these three giants were almost the only game in town. War corporations stepped up their game, influencing Capitol Hill with greater ferocity and creativity. Campaign contributions and lobbying expenditures increased. And more and more titans of capital cycled from corporate suites through the Pentagon's leadership ranks. Simultaneously, industry pursued more sales overseas, including increased sales to brutal regimes like Mubarak's Egypt, the House of Saud, and Apartheid Israel. Why is this history and context so important? Because the 2010s saw new mergers and acquisitions: AECOM buying URS; AMEC buying Foster Wheeler; PAE acquiring A-T Solutions; Northrop Grumman buying Orbital ATK; General Dynamics buying the IT corporation CSRA; and United Technologies absorbing Rockwell Collins. Most recently, SAIC purchased the IT powerhouse Engility, Parsons bought the geospatial corporation OGSystems, and Textron bought Howe & Howe Technologies, a maker of combat vehicles. Two new mergers are happening as I write: Harris and L3, and Raytheon and United Technologies. Together Harris and L3 sell a variety of goods and services, including satellite communications, radios, signals intelligence products, radar, submarine and drone sensors, and aircraft maintenance. Together Raytheon and United Technologies sell everything from missiles, bombs, and radar to pilot helmets, targeting systems, and engines.

The years between the Cold War and the War on Terror saw U.S. capitalists obtain obscene riches. Through promotion of neoliberal economic policies and aggressive globalization, U.S. capital conquered more markets and gathered more natural resources than at any point since 1945. Corporate America as a whole was also corrupting hearts and minds, numbing the public with entertainment and deluging them with consumerism. As we, the people, largely allowed more and more of the globe to fall under the purview of U.S. industry and its Pentagon abettors, it became more and more necessary for industry to schematize U.S. society in order to maintain and sustain its hegemonic designs. Crises that could be handled diplomatically, like Saddam Hussein's invasion of Kuwait, are seized upon to further military aspirations. High-ranking U.S. military officers (eying jobs in industry) assess enemy capabilities based on the procurement wish list of their respective branch of the Armed Forces, while the war industry hypes enemies based on sales and marketing strategies.

Enter 9.11. Under the guise of needing to combat terrorists and "deny them safe haven"—an endeavor backed up with a barrage of Arab stereotypes and Muslim savagery on corporate media—the U.S. government and the U.S. war industry trod a familiar path: torrential territorial expansion, with war itself increasingly the means of profit. Endless war for endless profit was back in the saddle. The post-9.11 conflict glut removed any remaining restraints on corporate authority, and Corporate America put the finishing touches on the wholesale corporatization of jobs once done by uniformed troops.

Many interlocking allies of the war industry inflate the threat of terrorism. Corporate media inflate terrorism because it raises ratings. High ratings attract advertising revenue. According to the logic divvied out on corporate media, the United States is in an existential battle against vicious, global terrorists; anyone who asks for nuance in discerning the grievances voiced by "terrorist" groups is aiding and abetting the enemy. Appeals to pride, fear, greed, and hate flood corporate media. Corporate media play a crucial role in propagandizing the domestic U.S. audience and people abroad who defer to U.S. media. There is no better bad guy than the Arab, about which the U.S. public knows little. The Arab terrorist is a powerful, long-standing trope within U.S. corporate and Zionist-dominated Hollywood culture. Terrorism can be a more effective boogeyman than communism. A rational person can make an economic or social argument in favor of communism. A rational person can do no such thing for terrorism. Everyone is against terrorism, though people might disagree what distinguishes a terrorist from, say, a freedom fighter. The emergence of experts, terrorism studies, and academic disciplines corrals the public's understanding of terrorism.[61] Now, people who don't understand foreign languages, culture and history or the grievances of oppressed populations are able to brand themselves as counterterrorism experts.[62]

The terrorism meme enhances many agendas. Zionists and neoconservatives demonize Arabs and Persians, some wanting the U.S. to fight Israel's wars. Christian Zionists are on board with a view to advancing the rapture. And, by demonizing others as terrorists, Zionists juxtapose themselves as the good guys, the friends, the enlightened non-terrorists, even though Zionists pioneered terrorism, using everything from ethnic cleansing to assassination when trying to establish their ethnocracy in Palestine prior to "successes" in 1948 and 1967. Make no mistake: There are actual terrorists out there, but to what extent does the war industry acknowledge or the public realize that their ranks especially include the jihadists used by CIA to destabilize recalcitrant governments, Mossad operatives setting off car bombs in Arab capitals in order to sow social strife, and U.S. military operations that carry out violence against civilians to achieve political goals? The war industry cannot embrace such a clear understanding. Doing so would alienate its primary customers: the U.S. government and allied regimes.

Corporations have mastered D.C.'s preferred influencer: bribery. War corporations divvy out millions in campaign contributions to Congress. War corporations gave around $30 million in 2012, $25.5 million in 2014, and nearly $30 million in 2016.[63] Much of this money has gone to appropriation and armed services committees. This bribery has many benefits. The most obvious benefit is the continuation of global war, but subtler benefits exist. With Congress in their pocket, U.S. war corporations avoid paying costs for which they should otherwise be responsible: environmental cleanup; compensation to families whose loved ones were killed in optional wars for which the war industry lobbied; and full medical care and housing for all veterans who fought in these wars.

This brings us to lobbying.

LOBBYING

War corporations hire professional lobbying firms in order to influence federal policy. War corporations regularly spend millions on lobbying Capitol Hill.[64] This is an effective, straightforward method for corporations to get their way. But war corporations are more creative in their lobbying: they carefully select the footprint of their industrial base in order to put maximum pressure across congressional districts. Politicians and their war industry bosses are proficient at claiming the "defense" industry creates jobs, not because of "jobs"—that's just a talking point—but because it ingratiates the corporations with politicians. All major war corporations rig the terrain in the same fashion. Rigging the terrain before a single lobbyist even arrives on Capitol Hill ensures congressional compliance with war industry directives. They've been doing it for decades,[65] honing their skills.

The aircraft, missile, and ship sectors of the war industry demonstrate the strategic layout of corporate facilities. Over 1,000 suppliers produce roughly 300,000 parts for the Lockheed Martin F-35 jet. Lockheed Martin's supply chain covers most U.S. states and many countries whose capitalist governments have agreed to purchase the aircraft.[66] Northrop Grumman spreads work on its MQ-4C drone across at least fourteen stateside locations.[67] One contract for Boeing F/A-18 fighter jets was spread across sixteen declared U.S. locations, Ottawa, and various undeclared locations outside the contiguous U.S.[68] One contract for Bell-Boeing tiltrotor aircraft was spread over twenty declared locations, from New York to California.[69] Raytheon spreads work on its Standard Missile-6 across more than thirty locations,[70] and spreads work on Tomahawk missiles across 40 locations.[71] The "defense" industry supports over 2.4 million U.S. jobs, Raytheon's CEO tells Capitol Hill.[72]

How about boats? The LPD (landing platform, dock) is a new ship being built by Huntington Ingalls. As of this writing, the LPD is over budget by hundreds of millions of dollars. Huntington Ingalls spreads LPD work across the U.S. and beyond.[73] Lockheed Martin spreads work on one littoral combat ship—a surface ship loaded with gizmos and designed to operate close to shore—across 45 locations.[74] The Multi Mission Surface Combatant (MMSC) is a new Lockheed Martin product, marketed as being able to maneuver adeptly close to shore as well as on open ocean. D.C. and Riyadh are purchasing MMSC. Stateside, Lockheed Martin divvies out MMSC work from Baltimore, Maryland, to Carson, California.[75] Some parts are produced or assembled in Canada, Germany, Sweden, and the U.K., a maneuver to play the "jobs" card with European leaders and to further economically imbricate Europe with the United States. European elites, in turn, can pull the "jobs" trick on their respective populaces. "Jobs, jobs, jobs," the corrupt U.S. politicians say. Meanwhile, they formulate policies and enact laws that gut the U.S. manufacturing base, export jobs, and automate the rest.

Industry is positioned well. Lockheed Martin's CEO sits on the Executive Branch's American Workforce Policy Advisory Board, which establishes strategies to finesse the working class into the global economy during increased automation, outsourcing, war, and austerity measures.[76] On 13 February 2019, U.S. Commerce Secretary and former private equity magnate Wilbur Ross (net worth roughly $700 million) announced the Advisory Board's members—a who's who of entrenched and rising capitalists: The CEOs of Apple, Visa, Walmart, Home Depot, IBM, and the U.S. Chamber of Commerce; and leaders of the Kentucky Community & Technical College System and the American Association of Community Colleges who can help carve out a pliant workforce.

Lockheed Martin is a master of playing the jobs card. Recent written boasts include "Lockheed Martin Meets 1,800 Employee Hiring Commitment; Plans to Add 400 More Jobs in Fort Worth," "F-35 Program Creates 26,000 Jobs in California," and "Lockheed Martin Could Add 2,400 Jobs in Six Years." Lockheed Martin regularly claims the F-35 program "supports 194,000 direct and indirect jobs nationwide."[77] A report from the Center for International Policy looked at 2012-18: Lockheed Martin actually cut 15,000 jobs from its workforce while it was *the top corporate recipient of tax dollars* (a peak of $50.6 billion received in 2017). "In short, since 2012 the number of taxpayer dollars going to Lockheed has expanded by billions, the value of its stock has nearly quadrupled, and its CEO's salary went up 32%, even as it cut 14% of its American work force. Yet Lockheed continues to use job creation, as well as its employees' present jobs to get yet more taxpayer money."[78]

Industry tickles state officials with "jobs." Maryland governor Larry Hogan spoke at the inauguration of a new cybersecurity training facility in Baltimore: "With our skilled workforce, world-class academic community, and proximity to the federal government, Maryland has truly become the cyber capital of the world... This state-of-art center will help ensure that even more Marylanders are fully trained and prepared to meet the demands of 21st century jobs." The training facility is run by Cyberbit, a subsidiary of an Israeli war corporation, Elbit Systems.[79] Whether headquartered in the U.S. or Apartheid Israel, corporations and governments play the jobs card expertly.

Take caution when a war corporation throws the word "jobs" around. Many of these jobs are part-time, temporary, or menial (e.g. painters, welders, roustabout), parsed out to an increasingly desperate workforce. Some are construction jobs that vanish in a year or so. Blue-collar jobs in the war industry are often in difficult working conditions[80] and typically lack such labor rights as hardy collective bargaining powers and lengthy maternity / paternity leave.[81] Industry jobs that pay very well require advanced degrees, which the majority of the population does not have. Some jobs within the tallies that corporations throw around are non-U.S. jobs (e.g. microchips manufactured overseas). Other jobs are induced, i.e. allegedly stimulated by the mere presence of war industry activity (e.g. the mom making less-than-minimum wage on a ridesharing app driving an industry executive from work to a pub, or the waiter at a Tucson restaurant where a missile engineer dines). Industry inflates job tallies.

In its fraudulently amplified jobs tallies, corporations might even include jobs that are already ongoing in production elsewhere. A war corporation might include in its tally people already producing, for example, a wire that happens to be used in a weapon of war. The wire is being produced regardless of whether or not a war corporation is purchasing it, yet the war corporation includes this in its job counts. This fudging of the numbers—counting a job that already exists and happens to produce something a war corporation can use—happens regularly. A war corporation might include in its tallies jobs that are barely tangential to the product at hand, such as third-party manufacturers. This is like saying, "Kevin Bacon worked with 94,000 people on his last project," by including workers who never arrived on set: employees of the timber company from which the movie's producers purchased wood, and employees of the cosmetics company, even though only two of them sold products to Hair & Makeup. So, the next time a major war corporation claims it is creating jobs, take the number it gives with a few grains of salt.

The playing field favors the war industry before any lobbying takes place on Capitol Hill. The terrain is fixed, rigged decisively in favor of war corporations, which tell Congress, "Look at all these jobs we've got in your district." Congress buys it—hook, line, and sinker. The claim that the "defense" industry brings jobs is a stale public relations ploy. It hides the truth that needs to be repeated: spending on healthcare, education, or clean energy can create more jobs than spending on war.[82]

The money that D.C. funnels to war corporations ultimately loses jobs because that money could have otherwise supported public services. The jobs lost in the public realm include teachers educating our youth, manual laborers improving public transportation, residents establishing urban permaculture, scientists tackling the energy crisis, public servants re-wilding our environment, and specialists helping humans acquire affordable housing. Jobs are lost when federal monies are funneled into the commerce of nonstop war. Starved governmental services are sacrificed in order to support a brutal industry. Professor Seymour Melman pointed out a related fact: The "size of military expenditures and expenditures for military research are systematically, but negatively, correlated with productivity growth." And, unlike other products, you can't eat, consume, play with, learn from, or interact with most goods and services sold by the war industry.[83] The war industry blatantly lies about jobs, hurts the public, and builds products that the public cannot use or benefit from.

The war industry can inflate job numbers because there is no accountability: Capitol Hill is largely content letting Corporate America police itself. You are likely familiar with cases where corporations get to inspect their own product (from the airline industry[84] to the pork industry[85]) instead of government inspectors doing the job. Corporations policing corporations is rampant in the war industry, like when the advertising agency GSD&M measures the effectiveness of its military recruiting efforts. Sometimes one corporation polices part of industry, like when Calibre Systems conducts "cost and economic analysis of major weapons system programs and associated acquisition/financial management policies and procedures."[86] Customers of the war industry police themselves. The Saudi-UAE coalition that is destroying Yemen with U.S. weaponry polices itself with regard to civilian deaths. It says it's doing a good job.[87] The Israeli military investigated the Israeli military's 1 August 2014 murder of 135 Palestinians in Rafah, Gaza. The investigation exonerated all of the Israeli troops involved. (Since Israel's 1967 expansion, no Israeli military member has ever been convicted of murdering a Palestinian.[88]) CIA assesses its own murder-by-drone program,[89] feeding positive reports to Capitol Hill.

War corporations spread production and operation of weaponry and big-ticket items across congressional districts as one way of pressuring elected officials, then professional lobbyists take it from there. A former D.C. lobbyist explains the system:

> Years of legalized bribery had exposed me to the worst elements of our country's political workings. Not even my half-million-a-year salary could outweigh my conscience... Today, most lobbyists are engaged in a system of bribery but it's the legal kind, the kind that runs rampant in the corridors of Washington...[90]

The U.S. war industry hires the best lobbying groups,[91] many packed with MIC players. Retired military officers and D.C. insiders, for example, lead the Spectrum Group. The Spectrum Group's five partners all have deep experience in, or dealings with, the war industry. It draws its members largely from Pentagon retirees. A former high-ranking Pentagon official now working as a lobbyist can shirk registering as a lobbyist by carefully documenting that they spend less than twenty percent of their time talking to or petitioning Congress.[92] Wily staffers on Capitol Hill regularly become lobbyists for the war industry.[93]

Seemingly benign traditions must be considered forms of political persuasion. Tours of war corporations (e.g. Senator Gary Peters visiting BAE Systems, Senator Jeanne Shaheen visiting L3) happen all the time. Elected officials are regaled with job tallies and bold claims about economic impact. Tours of military installations supplement industry's tales and lies. The military gives Congress technological demonstrations of industry goods, batters Congress with refined talking points, and touts an installation's economic benefits and contributions to the wars. The economic benefits are often unsubstantiated and the contributions to the wars are inflated. No stone is left unturned—whether it's Senator Martin Heinrich at a drone squadron on Holloman Air Force Base in New Mexico, Senator Tim Kaine at naval bases in Hampton Roads, Virginia, or Senator Joni Ernst at an air refueling wing in Sioux City, Iowa. Members of Congress tour military installations overseas as well. Tingling with the thrill of being in or around a warzone, elected officials tour installations, Potemkin villages in terms of efficacy and necessity. They talk about "intelligence," a word batted about with patent fraudulence and seductive glamor. All costs of war—financial, physical, and emotional—are tucked out of sight. (Congressional staffers, too, tour such installations.) Elected officials are led on tours, get fed inaccuracies and misrepresentations, and then depart without imbibing accuracy or candor.

Lobbying, you see, is not confined to the formal pay-as-you-go model.

PRESSURE GROUPS

Industry operates pressure groups. Pressure groups are emphatically not lobbying firms, but they influence the military and Capitol Hill with consistency and weight. The National Defense Industrial Association (NDIA) calls itself the "trusted leader in defense and national security associations." NDIA postures as a mere "platform through which leaders in government, industry and academia can collaborate and provide solutions to advance the national security and defense needs of the nation."[94] NDIA has roughly 1,600 individual and corporate members. With a name like a late-nineties internet chat room, the Aerospace Industries Association (AIA) is "the nation's biggest trade association, representing more than 340 U.S. aerospace and defense companies and suppliers," according to Raytheon.[95] AIA advocates effectively for "industry-developed" regulation and gigantic military budgets. The Association of the United States Army (AUSA) comes across as a benevolent organization because it gives scholarships to children in military families, but AUSA exists to benefit industry. AUSA produces an Industry Guide in order to help you, the war corporation, "place your company in front of your customers."[96] Additionally, a corporation can sponsor AUSA in order to get better positioning and visibility at AUSA's many events.[97]

Pressure groups work well through regional chapters. Some pressure groups arrange congressional testimony. Pressure groups also put out fact sheets, policy packets, and educational initiatives. NDIA, AIA, and AUSA are headquartered in Arlington, Virginia, close to the Pentagon. Pressure groups sponsor and support industry displays (e.g. NDIA, Air Armaments Symposium; AIA, Dubai Air Show; and AUSA, Global Force Symposium & Exposition in Huntsville). Such displays are where corporate representatives schmooze with military honchos (officer and civilian), pitching goods, services, and recommendations to those directing the wars. A pressure group can state it was "founded to educate its constituencies on all aspects of national security." This is one way to lobby without lobbying. Many industry pressure groups adopt this "educating constituencies" character. Some pressure groups are charities or social welfare groups—501(c)3 or 501(c)4, respectively. Donations to such groups are not subject to campaign contribution limits. A 501(c)6 designation allows great leeway for influencing legislation and the allocation of corporate money. Retired flag officers and corporate titans lead pressure groups.[98] The director of the Defense Security Cooperation Agency (the government unit in charge of abetting industry sales to allied governments) regularly talks to and collaborates with pressure groups.[99] Pressure groups create favorable seas in the Pentagon and legislatures. Pressure groups are conduits of industry desires.

Industry has crafted pressure groups of all shapes, sizes, and dispositions. There's BENS, Business Executives for National Security, a non-profit "comprised of over 450 senior business and industry executives who volunteer their time and expertise to address the national security community's most pressing challenges."[100] BENS is "comprised of senior business and industry executives who apply best business practices" to advocate for pro-war, pro-corporate policies, admitting "We aim to be discreet."[101] Indeed. There's AOC, the Association of Old Crows. Posturing more like a sociable brotherhood of affable electronic warfare veterans than an industry-dominated pressure group, AOC has a board of directors packed with war industry officials, including those from AECOM, Engility, Raytheon, and some of the Pentagon's main fiber optics and engineering providers.[102] There's AIAA, the American Institute of Aeronautics & Astronautics, a pro-industry publisher and matchmaker, organizing conferences, catering to industry officials, and acting as the "voice of the aerospace profession" when it comes to reaching Capitol Hill on policy matters.[103] The list of pressure groups is as long as the industry is creative.

Wherever there's a concentration of military installations in a given area of the United States, there's typically an associated pressure group. For example, the Tidewater Association of Service Contractors focuses on military units in and around Hampton Roads, Virginia, "in order to improve the productivity of contracting and the quality of the end product for the mutual benefit of the Government and industry," holding industry days and facilitating liaising opportunities between government and war corporations.[104] The Patuxent Partnership focuses on military units around southern Maryland on the Chesapeake Bay. Big money is at stake.[105] Local economic groups, such as the Arizona Commerce Authority or the Economic Development Corporation of Fayetteville and Cumberland County, North Carolina, support industry aims.

Some industry pressure groups are organized by function. Corporations looking to promote drones can join the Association for Unmanned Vehicle Systems International. For corporations looking to promote expensive radar and anti-ballistic missile technology, there's the Missile Defense Advocacy Alliance of Alexandria, Virginia. For corporations eying the intelligence budget, there's the Intelligence & National Security Alliance. For corporations with significant business in mapping and geospatial technology, there's the U.S. Geospatial Intelligence Foundation. Corporations specializing in electronic gizmos can organize through the Armed Forces Communications & Electronics Association. There are many more of these function-based pressure groups.

Government boards and committees are a way for industry to influence the posture and behavior of the War Department from the inside.[106] The National Security Resources Board was convened in the early Cold War as a way to mobilize industry to support (and in practice outpace) the needs of the War Department. Since then, all kinds of boards have infected the Pentagon. Consider the War Department's Defense Policy Board. The DPB is presented as a way for the Pentagon to take advantage of the expertise of business professionals. In reality, it is a way for corporate executives to put another hand on the Pentagon's rudder. Incumbent DPB members lead the way with corporate allegiances.[107] Boards are ubiquitous in the interlaced halls of military and industry. The Defense Business Board complements the Defense Policy Board. DBB's motto is "Business Excellence in Defense of the Nation," though the corporate allegiance could be characterized as "Business Profit at the Nation's Expense." Industry academics, like those from Johns Hopkins University and MIT, regularly appear on war boards. Federal Advisory Committees (FACs) work in parallel to boards. FACs exist across the U.S. government, many focusing on foreign policy and "defense" in addition to specific industry sectors like "intelligence," "space," "homeland security," and "cyber." With over 900 active as of 2009,[108] FACs are a superb way for war industry officials and elites with longstanding industry ties to influence policy and steer the ship. Boards, committees, and other assemblages influence government from all angles.

BANKING AND INVESTMENT FIRM STAKEHOLDERS

The big banks and investment firms are in actuality the foremost propellants of the war industry's influence. Some firms raise money, invest in a war corporation, and later sell the corporation or take it public. The *Washington Post* cites figures stating that private equity firms invested over $30 billion in 358 war corporations ("aerospace and defense companies") during 2004-13.[109] And accordingly, private equity firms have their own lobbying organizations,[110] as they, too, expect a return on their investment. For example, the top aide of former speaker of the House John Boehner (R-OH) went on to become a lobbyist for Private Equity Growth Capital Council (PEGCC). The lobbying organization announced that Boehner's former chief of staff, Mike Sommers, will be PEGCC's new CEO. Sommers vowed, "Our member firms can be assured that they will have the support they need in Washington to create value and move our economy forward." War corporations must maximize profit—by maximizing the numbers of weapons they sell and the wars they are involved in—under this model.

CEOs of war corporations regularly network with investment firms. CEOs and CFOs from across the war industry (e.g. Leidos CFO Reagan, Raytheon CEO Kennedy, Parsons CEO Harrington) participated in the 2019 Morgan Stanley Laguna Conference, held at the Ritz-Carlton, Dana Point, CA. Lockheed Martin CEO Marillyn Hewson spoke 29 May 2019 at the annual Strategic Decisions Conference, put on by Alliance Bernstein. Huntington Ingalls, General Dynamics, Northrop Grumman, and other war corporations regularly attend these conferences (alongside reps from the most powerful U.S. tech, entertainment, and consumer-goods corporations). Executives work hard arranging, implementing, and utilizing all of their resources to achieve record profits.

When war corporations are merging or acquiring other corporations, banks like Goldman Sachs and Morgan Stanley serve as financial advisors. The top five investors in shares of Lockheed Martin are giant financial firms. They call themselves financial services, investment advisors, or global investment firms. They are State Street Corp., Vanguard Group, BlackRock, Capital World Investors, and Wellington Management Group.[111] They know war production is a reliable, steady investment.

Pressure groups, financial giants, and formal lobbyists represent a powerful combined strike force.

Lobbying pays off. D.C. slashed spending on social programs while applauding the John S. McCain National Defense Authorization Act of fiscal year 2019. At $717 billion, the FY2019 NDAA gave the Department of War an *increase* of $82 billion from the previous year.[112] This increase alone was larger than Russia's annual military budget, larger than the total budget of the U.S. Department of Education. Industry had every right to be elated. War corporations had worked very hard funding congressional campaigns, lobbying creatively, and sustaining pro-war narratives in think tanks and media. The FY2019 NDAA became Public Law 115-232, and the FY2019 DOD Appropriations Act became Public Law 115-245. The resulting war budget catered to corporate wish lists: new submarines,[113] new guided missile destroyers, a new $10 billion+ aircraft carrier, development of the new Northrop Grumman B-21 bomber, and plenty more. (War budgets reflect industry wants, sometimes in opposition to what the military brass asks for.)

The National Defense Industrial Association applauded passage of the FY2019 NDAA.[114] Icing the cake, the Pentagon closed out FY2018 by allocating $7.54 billion to industry in one day.[115]

Let's put the $717 billion in perspective. It is estimated that less than $300 billion could end world hunger.[116] Roughly a third of the budget, or $239 billion, "could provide primary and early secondary education for the entire world population," as pointed out by a prominent working-class website.[117]

The war industry frames its lobbying in kindly terms: "Defense companies" are merely assisting policymakers in understanding a complex world; defense companies are making sure that government is able to hear industry's concerns. You see, regulations just stifle development. We in industry are good at identifying emerging market opportunities. The United States shouldn't be left behind. Our businesses need to be competitive on the global stage. (These machinations often include euphemisms like "harmonizing investor protection provisions," "voicing opinions of the business community with regards to investment," "working to minimize trade barriers and encourage privatization so businesses can grow," and "informing government about teamwork and community.") War corporations pull military retirees into their organizations, place executives within the Pentagon's leadership, fund congressional campaigns, and lobby Capitol Hill. They've got all bases covered. The only move left is to control the narrative.

CORPORATE MEDIA AND THINK TANKS

John Brennan was director of CIA during 2013-17. Brennan left two big imprints on the Agency. He revamped its entire bureaucratic structure. (In doing so he created the Directorate of Digital Innovation, where U.S. war corporations scarfed up a lot of the workload.) Brennan's other imprint happened with less fanfare: exploit ethnic diversity to achieve espionage victories. Brennan pushed hard to diversify the Agency's workforce. CIA's chief of talent acquisition concedes, "As we look at diversity and inclusion, with our global mission, we need diversity... We need to be inclusive across the board. Because when we're working with other cultures and engaging people of other cultures, that is a part of diversity."[118] Gina Haspel, who officially took charge of CIA in May 2018, also emphasized "efforts to recruit a more diverse workforce," the *Washington Post* reports.[119] The U.K.'s MI6 took the same steps.[120] Diversity is encouraged insofar as it helps Langley and Vauxhall Cross achieve espionage victories, not because it is inherently good or valuable.

John Brennan illustrates the finessing of corporate media. In early 2018, he joined MSNBC as a paid contributor. Brennan is at MSNBC for a reason. Though MSNBC is pro-war in its content and production, progressive thought is able to sneak through once in a while. Brennan's appointment keeps such thought out of the center-left portion of corporate media vis-à-vis war and peace. Comparable career intel professionals (like former Deputy Director of CIA Mike Morrell as a CBS News national security contributor) handle other corporate media. Their carefully cultivated cachet prescribes the boundaries of acceptable thought when it comes to D.C.'s foreign policy. John Brennan occupies media like Paul Bremer occupied Iraq. (Both personify greed: Brennan as the former director of the Agency in charge of protecting and promoting U.S. capitalism, and Bremer as the corporate apotheosis—a Kissinger & Associates, Marsh & McLennan veteran—privatizing Iraq's public assets.[121]) Continuity is the name of the game.

Retired generals and admirals regularly contribute to corporate media. Without disclosing his existing ties to war corporations and think tanks, retired Air Force general T. Michael Moseley wrote in *Defense News* in April 2019 that the Air Force is woefully underequipped: "Now, nearly the entire Air Force demands aircraft recapitalization, or entire missions will sunset for want of viable aircraft... The only way to address these concurrent shortfalls is to buy modern replacements in sufficient numbers as fast as possible."[122] He cited the typical bevy of threats—Iran, North Korea, Russia, and China. For all intents and purposes, retired officers writing in corporate media without disclosing corporate ties continues the infamous TV analyst program in which the Pentagon hired retired military officers to advocate on behalf of military action in the Middle East.[123]

A handful of business interests owns media outlets in the United States.[124] Profit drives corporate media. U.S. corporate media (CNN, MSNBC, FoxNews, et al.) share the same business model: air what attracts the highest ratings in order to get more advertising revenue. Corporate media entertain and distract the masses while reaping profit selling advertisement. Corporate media do not air news. They air info-tainment, designed not to inform or foster critical thinking about the world. Informing the public is not a priority. Maintaining the existing economic order is. To the extent that corporate media air any information at all, the information reflects the opinions of the ruling class and the dogma of Corporate America. There is no room to firmly address domestic issues (e.g. unemployment, capitalist exploitation of the working class, poor public education, over-dependency on petroleum, the corrupt political party duopoly, government subsidies of harmful industries, GMOs and plastics in our food chain, war). Politically conditioning the U.S. public, corporate media never blame the D.C. regime for problems in the world. Aiming for high ratings and lucrative advertising revenue, corporate media self-censor and taper the spectrum of acceptable foreign policy debate. War corporations purchase advertisements on news shows to further confine the debate. (Why do you think General Dynamics advertises on Sunday morning news shows? Because Joe Schmoe watching at home might purchase a Virginia-class submarine, an Abrams tank, or a Stryker fighting vehicle? Or because General Dynamics wants corporate media to never question the root causes of nonstop war?[125]) Corporate pundits and newscasters do not speak out against advertisers. This business model restricts freedom of speech.[126] Pro-war is as pro-war does. The Smith-Mundt Modernization Act of 2012 allowed even greater government propaganda on U.S. corporate media. In addition to promoting wars, corporate media help protect individuals who sell the wars.[127] Drawing funding from the wealthy donor class and large corporate interests, National Public Radio is similarly confined. NPR's new CEO as of September 2019 is John Lansing, a political operator who recently led U.S. propaganda at the U.S. Agency for Global Media.

Private equity dominates other media through which people learn about war. Sightline Media Group's products include most of the major military-focused periodicals: *Air Force Times*, *Army Times*, *C4ISRNET*, *Defense News*, *Federal Times*, *Marine Corps Times*, and *Navy Times*. Regent Equity Partners owns Sightline Media Group. Private equity prioritizes profit. And when war is profit, earnest questions are sacrilege.

The official social media accounts of the U.S. Armed Forces market and promote corporate weaponry. On 24 May 2019, the U.S. Air Force tweeted in celebration of the MQ-9 drone reaching four million flying hours (with no mention of the manufacturer, General Atomics). On 23 May 2019, the U.S. Army tweeted in praise of a pint-sized drone called the Black Hornet (with no mention of the manufacturer, FLIR). Tweets like these happen all the time. Lauding industry goods and services without mentioning industry is sly at best, and devious at worst, especially considering how corporate personnel, not uniformed personnel, are reported to run the Armed Forces' Twitter accounts for recruiting and PR purposes. Sometimes tweets go too far, even by military standards. On New Year's Eve 2018, U.S. Strategic Command (@USStratcom) tweeted, "#TimesSquare tradition rings in the #NewYear by dropping the big ball...if ever needed, we are #ready to drop something much, much bigger." A video of a [Northrop Grumman] B-2 bomber dropping ordnance accompanied the tweet. As nuclear expert, Joe Cirincione, remarked, "At first, I did not believe this could be real. But it is. It is an industry ad doubling as a sick, bragging joke by our Strategic Command. Disgraceful."[128]

The Pentagon runs its own media empire. The Assistant to the Secretary of War for Public Affairs is responsible for most Department media. The Defense Media Activity (DMA) produces multimedia content "to inform, educate, and entertain" U.S. military audiences worldwide.[129] One can claim that DMA contributes to the propagandizing of the troops, though in today's interconnected world DMA content is available online for all to consume. The American Forces Press Service is a news organization operating under DMA. The Defense Video & Imagery

Distribution System (DVIDS) is another way DMA distributes content. DVIDS liaises with non-government media to show the U.S. military's friendly face. Some of DVIDS' finer pieces about the U.S. military in Africa include "Cake boss contributes to quality-of-life in Djibouti" and "Camp Lemonnier hosts Djiboutian Bazaar."[130] A subtle DVIDS outlet is the Joint Hometown News Service, based in Fort Meade, Maryland. It works to get pro-military stories in newspapers across the country.[131] DMA and DVIDS are highly dependent on corporations.

Corporate media and Hollywood popularize pro-war aims. Tapping into today's saturated, media-savvy consumer requires a robust, cooperative effort, replete with celebrity, humor, and flattery. Seth Meyers, host of NBC's *Late Night*, was happy to produce a skit inside the Pentagon.[132] Meyers sets the stage by framing those in uniform as "our nation's armed forces," when in reality they are the war industry's military workers whose task is to keep the oil flowing, take out regional competitors of Israel, and fight for corporate interests. Members of the U.S. military are anything but "our" nation's armed forces. Meyers effectively portrays the Secretary of War, a position occupied at the time by Ashton Carter, as an avuncular soul. Carter performs well. He switches fluidly between grinning buffoon and goodhearted protector. Carter spent most of his life in service of the MIC, using his formidable brainpower for military-academic research and policy analysis. There is no mention of corporate profiteers, let alone environmental destruction, dead civilians, dead U.S. troops and mercenaries, the co-opting of Silicon Valley, support for dictatorships, or promotion of neoliberal policy. Jokes abound. They're well placed, obviating any criticism of Pentagon policy. Meyers turns serious topics (invading sovereign nations and weak nuclear security) into wisecracks. Meyers frequently reminds the viewer that the Pentagon is home to 284 bathrooms, but omits the fact that extra bathrooms were included in the building's original design in order to comply with racist segregation laws.

Meyers remarks, "One of the great things about the Pentagon are all the interesting items they have on display." He then shows trophy cases including the personal property of Saddam Hussein, whose country the Pentagon and war industry destroyed. Any reference to the actual realities of what took place "over there" is absent here: no images of the corpses of Iraqis whose deaths were "collateral damage"; no splintered shells of U.S. ordnance launched from drones against populations throughout the Middle East and Africa; no samples of the poisoned soil and water from towns the war industry polluted in the U.S. and overseas; no flag-draped coffins of U.S. troops who died overseas, images of which the Pentagon conceals unless families of the deceased request an exemption; no pictures of the thousands of veterans who have taken their own lives after being used and discarded. After the comedy sketch, Secretary Carter appears live on the talk show for questions and answers. He admits that he wants to appeal to the 18-24 age group. He calls the U.S. military the "finest fighting force the world has ever known," yet the Pentagon hasn't won a single war in their lifetime. Hats off to Carter and Meyers. Their deception worked, judging by the live audience's reactions and the enthusiastic comment section below the video. The Pentagon and industry personnel dictated the terms, and the U.S. populace largely swallowed them.

Hollywood cooperates fully with the push for war. If, for example, you are a producer wanting to make a movie involving military or paramilitary operations, you're going to want assistance from the Pentagon or CIA in acquiring matériel. This realism is an important part of producing a convincing film. The Pentagon and CIA are happy to help, but at a price: they must approve your movie's script. If the script questions the accepted benevolence of U.S. foreign policy, the movie won't receive support from the Pentagon or industry. It will be sunk before it starts. Dedicated offices in Arlington and McLean liaise with Hollywood.[133] Today, this occurs in films ranging from the latest comic book blockbuster to the acclaimed 1960s historical drama. In general, Hollywood has demonized, slandered, and stereotyped Middle Easterners for decades,[134] priming the U.S. public to already loathe them by the time 9.11 rolled around. Even when Hollywood films don't demonize enemies, the war industry can find a way to benefit. In 2017, a Boston-area high school screened the film Hidden Figures, which chronicles pioneering female engineers of color. Raytheon personnel were there to guide the event and plant the seeds for future recruitment.[135]

Collectively, think tanks guide the discourse inside the Beltway. Think tanks promote views advantageous to their funders. They are designed with one purpose: issuing information that endorses and advances the ideological viewpoints and profits of their benefactors. They have abandoned any pretense of objective scholarship and become PACs. Big Oil leads the way. Big Oil, coincidentally a major war industry ally, funds think tanks. We, supposedly Homo sapiens, are facing a do-or-die climate situation,[136] yet since policymakers in D.C. rely on research funded by the fossil fuel industry,[137] Capitol Hill does not take the necessary measures.

Think tanks promote industry products. Boeing makes Joint Direct Attack Munitions (JDAM) kits that use GPS to guide bombs on or near a target. So Boeing funds a think tank, whose chief operating officer then writes a fawning piece in *Forbes* about how delightful, inexpensive, and revolutionary JDAMs are.[138] That's your average Wednesday.

Overall, U.S. war corporations fund major D.C. think tanks to invent, hype, and promote new threats and new rationalizations for why the United States must continue fighting war.[139] D.C's legal system doesn't require think tanks to publicly disclose their donors.[140] In this environment you get report after report about Iran's "malign activities," China's "destabilizing influence," Russian "aggression," and the Arabs' "terrorism." Corporate media amplify this disinformation.

Pick three prominent think tanks. Look up their leadership and senior personnel. You'll find war corporations all over the place, like a family of T-Rex stomping down K Street. Consider CSIS, the Brookings Institution, and the Heritage Foundation. All accept war industry funding. Leadership comes from big business (including Big Oil and the war industry), Wall Street, and corporate media. Prominent personalities on CSIS' board include a former Boeing CEO, a chairperson of the Bechtel Group (which helps run the U.S. Navy's nuclear propulsion program and builds war infrastructure), and a former Secretary of War. Prominent personalities on Brookings' board include David Rubenstein, co-leader of The Carlyle Group; academics from Georgetown and Harvard; and investment tycoon Haim Saban ("I'm a one-issue guy, and my issue is Israel," as stated in *The New Yorker*, 10 May 2010). The President of Brookings is John Allen, a retired general who led U.S. Forces in Afghanistan and never pushed back against MIC prescriptions of "progress" and "increasing stability" during his time in government. Heritage is great at spreading fear. Starting off every fiscal year, Heritage issues its Index of U.S. Military Strength. In 2019, it warned that the U.S. military would struggle fighting two major conflicts at the same time. The report called for a 400-ship Navy, a 1,200 fighter/attack aircraft Air Force, a 50-brigade combat team Army, and a 36 battalion Marine Corp—a lot of platforms and vessels. The report, which also highlighted an array of threats (Middle East Terrorism, North Korea, Russia, Af-Pak Terrorism, China, Iran—you know the drill) benefits industry first and foremost. MIC leaders point to such purportedly authoritative reports to push for more funding, a greater expanse of military operations, and increased use of the military as the preferred tool even for diplomatic or humanitarian issues.[141]

No need for a congressperson to check out the Congressional Budget Office reports when a think tank (that takes money from the same war corporations your campaign takes money from) will promptly provide a silky-smooth, pro-war validation. Many think tanks even draft legislation for congresspeople who receive campaign funding from the war industry. Professor Rodrigue Tremblay educates us about an additional purpose of think tanks: they "serve as incubators for government departments, supplying them with already trained personnel and providing employment for public officials who are out of office." The same revolving door that exists between the War Department and war corporations takes place between think tanks and federal agencies and departments.[142]

A Pentagon has five sides. Well, so does the war industry's strategy to influence government. This strategy pulls military retirees into war corporations, places industry executives in the Pentagon, bribes officials through campaign finance, lobbies creatively, and manipulates the narrative. The U.S. war industry exerts this influence in a society that is already molded by decades of corporate propaganda. We live in an era of mass consumption, and we've been conditioned to turn to corporate commodities to meet all of our needs. This suits industry executives, salespeople, and personnel well. The war industry's influence kills U.S. democracy, and even people's capacity for independent thought. A dumbed-down, compliant population is *how* the war industry thrives.

ENDNOTES

1 Albert Einstein's essay titled "Why Socialism?" was originally published in *Monthly Review* in May 1949. It is accessible at <https://monthlyreview.org/2009/05/01/why-socialism>.

2 The numbers tell us we should be worried. The *Boston Globe* concluded that during 2004-8, 80% of retiring 3- and 4-star officers—high-ranking officers are known as 3- and 4- stars, in reference to the rank displayed on their epaulets—went to work as industry consultants or corporate executives, compared to less than 50% during 1994-8. Roughly 90% of 3- and 4-stars who retired in 2007 went on to work for war corporations. A 2012 report from *Citizens for Responsibility & Ethics in Washington* (CREW) found that over 3 years, 70% of 3- and 4-star retirees "took jobs with defense contractors or consultants." Many were also appointed to Pentagon advisory boards. CREW cited the *Swiss Economic Institute*, which concluded that war corporations expect retirees to increase company profits. Bender, Bryan. "From the Pentagon to the private sector." *Boston Globe*. 26 December 2010. Smith, R. Jeffrey. "Generals no longer retire to Vermont—they lobby for contractors in Washington." *Center for Public Integrity*. 21 November 2012.

3 Smith, R. Jeffrey. "Generals no longer retire to Vermont—they lobby for contractors in Washington."

4 Gorman, Siobhan. "Little-known contractor has close ties with staff of NSA." *Baltimore Sun*. 29 January 2006.

5 Retired officers are supposed to wait a year before promoting war industry products to their former military branch, but that doesn't stop them from informing others at their corporation about the best approach. In some instances, retirees are not allowed to immediately lobby in favor of the weapon system they used to be in charge of. They can, however, lobby on behalf of newfangled versions of the weapon system. *USA Today* instructs us about another loophole. A loophole in federal ethics laws allowed the Army to hire military retirees as "mentors," effectively sidestepping any rules regarding a 1-year cooling off period. One of the retirees who benefitted from the loophole invoked the troops, insisting, "The cooling off period doesn't seem to make a lot of sense when we have soldiers' lives at stake." According to *USA Today* ("Army mentoring deals bypass ethics law," 7 December 2009), "of the 158 retired generals and admirals identified as senior mentors, 80% had financial ties to defense contractors. These retired officers, when hired as contractors, are not subject to the ethics and disclosure rules that would apply if they were part-time federal employees. Their pay and identities as senior mentors are shielded from public view because most of them are hired as subcontractors."

6 At the Institute for Foreign Policy Analysis, General Cartwright effectively promoted ballistic missile interceptors, Raytheon's latest Tomahawk missile, and THAAD, a Lockheed Martin product that uses Raytheon radar. "IFPA Fletcher Conference." *U.S. Strategic Command*. Accessed 14 June 2018: <www.stratcom.mil/Media/Speeches/Article/986455/ifpa-fletcher-conference/>.

7 Some within the U.S. Army suggested getting rid of the costly blimp in order to save money, but Cartwright said no, vouching for its potential. Cartwright won. Raytheon's product stayed.

Willman, David. "How a $2.7 billion air-defense system became a 'zombie' program." *LA Times*. 24 September 2015. Grazier, Dan. "The JLENS: A Soaring Beacon for Military Reform." *Project on Government Oversight*. 19 November 2015.

8 Cartwright retired in early August of 2011. He joined Raytheon in late January of 2012, per Raytheon's "James E. Cartwright Elected to Raytheon Board of Directors," issued 27 Jan 2012. Schwellenbach, Nick. "Look Out, 4-Star General Coming Through." *Time*. 2 February 2012. By the end of 2014, Cartwright had received $828,000+ in total compensation from Raytheon, per David Willman (*LA Times*, 24 September 2015).

9 "Corporation and Trade Association Donors." *CSIS*. "Missile Defense Project." *CSIS*. Both accessed 14 June 2018.

10 "Total InteGrated Engine Revitalization (TIGER) Program." *Honeywell*. 27 April 2010. Accessed 10 June 2018: <www.youtube.com/watch?v=xG5XOCrAnpI>, (00:50).

11 "The core values of the Army are identical to the core values of both Amazon, Fluor and now Vectrus: integrity, respect, responsibility. The principles and values that are necessary are the same, whether it is delivering fuel to men and women on the battlefield, or delivering material from an Amazon fulfillment center, or running a forward operating base." Quoted in "Executive Spotlight: Interview with Ret. Army Major General Kevin Leonard, SVP of Vectrus" (*Vectrus*, 25 July 2017).

12 "Office of the Inspector General." *U.S. Navy*. Accessed 7 April 2019: <www.secnav.navy.mil/ig/who-we-are/about-us>.

13 Harris, Shane. "The NSA's Cyber-King Goes Corporate." *Foreign Policy*. 29 July 2014. Note: Alexander claims hackers who pilfered industrial secrets from U.S. companies committed the "greatest transfer of wealth in American history." He is wrong. A greater transfer of wealth has been the annual transfer of billions from the U.S. taxpayer (and money raised when Treasury issues debt) to the war industry. Another impressive wealth transfer was the 2017 tax deal, wherein corporations pay even less, and the working class is saddled with an oppressive tax burden. A third great transfer of wealth was when President Obama bailed out Wall Street on the back of the working class in 2009.

14 Sprint sells the Pentagon cellular phone services and fiber telecommunications, among other services. It also reportedly collaborates deeply in NSA domestic and foreign operations. Kappes is also partner in a D.C. private equity firm and a director on the board of the QTech Analytics and Idemia National Security Solutions, which sell intel analyses and software.

15 "General Dynamics Elects James N. Mattis to Board of Directors." *General Dynamics*. 7 August 2013.

16 Asher-Schapiro, Avi and David Sirota. "Donald Trump Pentagon Pick Mattis Made Nearly $1,000,000 On Board of Defense Contractor." *International Business Times*. 2 December 2016.

17 Asher-Schapiro and Sirota (*International Business Times*, 2 December 2016) raise many questions about Mattis, and note that General Dynamics "has spent over $100 million pushing its interests in Washington over the last decade."

18 *Heritage Foundation* pundit and editor of the think tank's 2019 Index of U.S. Military Strength, Dakota Wood, credited Mattis for improving military readiness: "Mattis comes in, during his testimony he says he was 'shocked' at the extent which the military had declined in readiness... To me, that was a big signal," per Aaron Mehta (*Defense News*, 3 October 2018). Heritage draws a big chunk of funding from the U.S. war industry.

19 According to DSCA director Lt. Gen. Charles Hooper, in "How security cooperation advances U.S. interests." *Brookings Institution*. 4 June 2019, (53:55).

20 Reichmann, Kelsey. "General Dynamics re-welcomes Mattis to board of directors." *Defense News*. 8 August 2019.

21 645 instances in FY2016. "Brass Parachutes: Defense Contractors' Capture of Pentagon Officials Through the Revolving Door." *POGO*. 5 November 2018.

22 Unless otherwise indicated, all descriptions in this section were retrieved 11 May 2018 from <www.defense.gov/About/Biographies/Senior-Defense-Officials/>.

23 SRC, formerly known as Syracuse Research Corp., sells such products as electronic warfare and cyber software. Do not confuse this SRC with the Scientific Research Corp. of Atlanta, GA.

24 The official arrived at the Pentagon at the beginning of June 2017. Prior to his arrival at the Pentagon, Kearney & Co. had received 2 recent contracts with the U.S. military: 22 April 2015 and 23 Sept 2016. On 6 July 2017, Kearney & Co. received a Pentagon contract to perform audit and financial services. On 22 Aug 2017, it received more money to help with an upcoming Pentagon audit. On 19 Dec 2017, it received more money for to work on the Pentagon's books. On 22 Feb 2018, it received more money to perform a variety of tasks, including financial management and accounting.

25 Lockheed Martin officially approved of John Rood's Under Secretary nomination in "Lockheed Martin Statement On John Rood's Confirmation As Undersecretary Of Defense For Policy" (4 January 2018). Rood was a VP at Raytheon before LM.

26 General Dynamics sells submarines, surface ships, fire control system for ships, ship maintenance, SATCOM devices, navigation equipment, radios, antennae control systems, Gulfstream aircraft, IT networks & services (including detailed work at U.S. Army Intelligence & Security Command, NSA, and DARPA), public affairs, land vehicles, training devices and simulators, rockets & bombs, and gun turrets, among other weaponry. GD leadership information taken May 2018 from <investorrelations.gd.com/corporate-governance/board-of-directors>.

27 Pearlman, Jonathan. "1 in 5 CEOs are psychopaths, study finds." *The Telegraph*. 13 September 2016.

28 Hewson has met repeatedly with MBS (e.g. Nov 2017, March 2018, April 2018) and MBZ (e.g. 2013 Dubai Air Show, Nov 2015 in Abu Dhabi). On 30 April 2018, at the Global Aerospace Summit in Abu Dhabi, Hewson quoted MBZ flatteringly at the conclusion of her public remarks. Again, she met with MBZ. In the same month, the UN Secretary General noted that Yemen was the world's worst humanitarian crisis. Saudi and Emirati aircraft and ordnance made in the U.S. continued to bombard Yemen. In an earnings call regarding first quarter results, 2018, Hewson remarked, "I had the honor of hosting his Royal Highness, Mohammad Bin Salman the crown prince of Kingdom of Saudi Arabia at our Sunnyvale, California location." She described deals with the Saudis as "something like a $100 billion worth of opportunities." Meanwhile, the Saudi regime was trying female activists in a special court for terrorism cases. Many of the women alleged that their jailors had tortured and sexually assaulted them, according to *BBC News* ("Saudi Arabia puts women's rights activists on trial," 13 March 2019). The *Washington Post* (Reinhard, et al., 21 November 2018) reported on the overall strategy: "Since the start of the war in Yemen, the defense industry—working alongside lobbyists for Saudi Arabia—has successfully beat back congressional efforts, supported by human rights groups, to end or curtail U.S. support for the air war in that conflict."

29 "Yemen: Three years on, U.S. and UK arms supplies to Saudi Arabia-led coalition are devastating civilian lives." *Amnesty International*. 23 March 2018. Amnesty International ("Disappearances and torture in southern Yemen detention facilities must be investigated as war crimes," 12 July 2018) also documented UAE-led torture and systematic disappearances in parts of Yemen under U.S.-Saudi-UAE *de facto* control. Raytheon promotional material best describes the relationship between U.S. war corporations and Gulf regimes: "... When you look at the vision and the values that he set for this country and you look at our core company values, they're very similar," quoted at <www.youtube.com/watch?v=kiXAlMW2PPM> & <www.raytheon.com/uae>. The speaker was referring to Zayed bin Sultan al-Nahyan, the first president of the UAE.

30 U.S. Army Gen. Joseph Votel careful stated that the U.S. Armed Forces did not actively track whether Saudi/UAE aircraft refueled by U.S. tankers killed civilians in ensuing airstrikes or whether U.S.-made bombs were used. However, according to *The New York Times* (Walsh & Schmitt, 25 December 2018), a State Department official who worked with the Saudi-led coalition from 2015 to 2017, said such information was readily available early on in the hostilities. At coalition headquarters in Riyadh, the official said, U.S. liaison officers had access to a database detailing every airstrike, including aircraft, munitions, and target. The data, the official said, could easily be used to pinpoint the role of U.S. aircraft and munitions in a strike. A U.S. military spokesperson stated, "I will not speculate on how the United States could have used or compiled the information the Saudi-led coalition shared for some other function… That is not the mission these advisers were invited to Riyadh to perform."

31 McKernan, Bethan. "Yemen: up to 85,000 young children dead from starvation." *The Guardian*. 21 November 2018.

"Yemen crisis: 85,000 children 'dead from malnutrition.'" *BBC News*. 21 November 2018.

32 Zillman, Claire. "Lockheed Martin CEO Says She'll 'Follow the Government's Lead' in Selling Arms to Saudi Arabia." *Fortune*. 6 November 2018.

33 Turak, Natasha. "Raytheon International CEO on weapons sales to Saudi Arabia: 'We don't make policy.'" *CNBC*. 16 February 2019.

34 "Raytheon CO (RTN) Q3 2018 Earnings Conference Call Transcript." *The Motley Fool*. 25 October 2018.

35 "As a nation we have to uphold our principles. We need to take appropriate action but not have an overreaction," Hawk Carlisle said. "We need to take the long view." Reinhard, Beth, Tom Hamburger, and Emma Brown. "Killing of Khashoggi tests U.S. defense industry as backlash builds on Capitol Hill." *Washington Post*. 21 November 2018.

36 "… that sense of patriotism drew me to the company." She portrayed Lockheed Martin as a "national asset" helping to defend the men and women in uniform and advancing global discovery and knowledge. "WE18 Keynote Presentation: Marillyn Hewson." *Society of Women Engineers*. 19 Oct 2018: <www.youtube.com/watch?time_continue=3237&v=gdQKnPhGCHk>, (58:56). See also Aitoro, Jill. "Lockheed CEO Hewson defends the company's role with DoD: 'We are leading a national asset.'" *Defense News*. 7 March 2018.

37 "WE18 Keynote Presentation: Marillyn Hewson." *Society of Women Engineers*. 19 Oct 2018, (1:11:30).

38 Gurdus, Lizzy. "Female CEOs are scarce, but history shows they can produce huge returns." *CNBC*. 9 March 2019. Hewson's leadership raised Lockheed Martin's stock by 310% through mid-November 2019, per Amanda Macias and Fred Imbert "Lockheed Martin has become a stock market juggernaut under CEO Marillyn Hewson" (*CNBC*, 12 November 2019).

39 "WE18 Day 2 Highlights." *Society of Women Engineers*. 19 October 2018: <www.youtube.com/watch?v=FwmnsfPSRJ4>, available at <alltogether.swe.org/2018/10/video-we18-day-2-highlights>. "WE18 Keynote Presentation: Marillyn Hewson." *Society of Women Engineers*. 19 Oct 2018: <www.youtube.com/watch?time_continue=3237&v=gdQKnPhGCHk>. Among Hewson's accomplishments are forming a women's leadership forum at Lockheed Martin. When asked what traits make her a good leader, she replied, "character and compassion… People trust leaders when they see their values." Regarding the effect of movements for gender equality on business, she said, "Companies should step back and look at, are they living their values?"

40 Honorable mention to Lynn Dugle, CEO of Engility (SAIC acquired Engility in early 2019, and Dugle did not continue on with SAIC), and Pam Wickham, vice president of corporate affairs and communications at Raytheon.

41 Robbins, Carla Anne. "The Spy in General Dynamics' Corner Office." *Fortune*. 11 September 2015.

42 Notable women of war are Andrea Thompson, Under Secretary of State for arms control and international security; Essye Miller, Deputy Chief Information Officer for Cybersecurity at the War Dept.; and a former corporate president and CEO named Lisa Gordon-Hagerty who now heads the National Nuclear Security Administration, the division of the Energy Dept. that builds and refurbishes nuclear weapons. The Deputy Director of the National Geospatial-Intelligence Agency (NGA), the agency focused on mapping earth in multiple wavelengths, is former Intelligence Advanced Research Projects Agency director Stacey Dixon. Kathleen Hicks is senior VP at industry think tank CSIS, and former deputy principal Under Secretary of War for Policy. Anne Marie Slaughter is pro-regime change and pro-responsibility to protect (R2P), an interventionist doctrine that the MIC uses to meddle in others' sovereign affairs. She is currently president of the think tank New America. Samantha Power was a key backer of the U.S. destruction of Libya. Winner of the American Academy in Berlin's Henry Kissinger Prize, Power is a former U.S. Ambassador to the U.N, where she threatened the use of force and bullied smaller nations. Mary Beth Long is a former CIA operations officer (1986-99), former Assistant Secretary of War, former Xe/Blackwater executive, and current owner of a law firm that aids industry's export of weaponry. Avril Haines is former deputy national security advisor and former deputy director of CIA. Haines is great at finessing legalese to help D.C. expand its authority and harm dissenting nations. Michele Flournoy is former Under Secretary of War for Policy, current hawk at Harvard University's Belfer Center, and current advisor to Boston Consulting Group. Recent DARPA chiefs were Regina Dugan and Arati Prabhakar.

43 Cynthia Rapp, deputy director for analysis; Elizabeth Kimber, deputy director for operations; and Dawn Meyerriecks, deputy director for science and technology. Windrem, Robert. "Sisterhood of spies: Women now hold the top positions at the CIA." *NBC News*. 5 January 2019. Additionally, Brittany Bramell is director of public affairs and Sonya Holt is chief diversity & inclusion officer. Journalist Alex Rubinstein (@RealAlexRubi) tweeted on 22 Aug 2018: "Congratulations to Sonya Holt. I'm sure that she'll do an excellent job making sure that when the CIA tries to instigate a coup d'etat against a leftist third world government, agents on the case will be LGBT at a proportional rate to the U.S. population."

44 Mehta, Aaron. "Here's how Ellen Lord grades the Pentagon's most expensive programs." *Defense News*. 1 February 2018.

45 Shane III, Leo. "Air Force secretary: Let's change how we talk about women troops." *Military Times*. 20 March 2018. Wilson has prior experience leading a corporation that helped the War Dept. with its business practices, advising U.S. weapons labs regarding nuclear policy and the industrial base, and serving in the U.S. House of Representatives.

46 Reyes, Jovanni. "'War is the Antithesis of Motherhood:' A Voice From Puerto Rico." *Common Dreams*. 27 September 2014.

47 MSNBC ran a flattering profile of female "defense industry" CEOs. NBC News ran a flattering profile of the "sisterhood of spies" at CIA. See the work of journalist Alexander Rubinstein "The Future is Female (Death Merchants): MSM Celebrates Women in the War Machine" (*MintPress News*, 9 January 2019). *Bloomberg*'s 2019 gender-equality index ranked war corporation Leidos favorably.

48 Unless otherwise indicated, all statements in this section regarding public officials receiving campaign funding were derived from information provided by the Center for Responsive Politics <www.opensecrets.org>, with a focus on the 2016 election cycle. All information is current as of 1 Aug 2018.

49 Anthony N. Cordesman now residing at a war industry think tank, CSIS, once worked for McCain on the SASC and later worked as civilian assistant to the Dep. Secretary of War. He explains McCain's perspective: "He's someone who has lived with underfunding of the military, seen the impact on readiness, seen the strains that impact the force." Cordesman did not mention how the war industry works for sustainment and expansion of the global military footprint. *The New York Times* frames the NDAA as reflecting "Mr. McCain's expansive vision of the role of the United States in world affairs" when talking about "security assistance" measures: $500 million, including weapons, to Ukraine; $100 million for Baltic nations, invoking the fearsome Russians; another $705 million for missile defense programs with Apartheid Israel. Quotes from *The New York Times* ("Senate Passes $700 Billion Pentagon Bill, More Money Than Trump Sought," 18 September 2017).

50 See Lockheed Martin (twitter.com/LockheedMartin; 26 Aug 2018), Raytheon (twitter.com/Raytheon; 27 Aug 2018), Northrop Grumman (twitter.com/northropgrumman; 31 Aug 2018), Boeing (twitter.com/BoeingCEO; 26 Aug 2018). Israeli Prime Minister, Benjamin Netanyahu (twitter.com/israelipm), wrote on 26 Aug 2018: "I am deeply saddened by the passing of John McCain, a great American patriot and a great supporter of Israel. I will always treasure the constant friendship he showed to the people of Israel and to me personally." Former U.S. Sec. of State, Henry Kissinger, also praised McCain, per Bree Burkitt. "Former Secretary of State Henry Kissinger: 'The world will be lonelier without John McCain.'" *USA Today*. 1 September 2018.

51 Fontaine, CNAS president, speaks at "CNAS' Fontaine Remembers McCain" (*Defense & Aerospace Report*, 31 August 2018).

52 Makinson, Larry. "Outsourcing the Pentagon." *Center for Public Integrity*. 29 September 2004. Updated 19 May 2014.

53 Emmons, Alex. "Senate committee votes to raise defense spending for second year in a row to $750 billion." *The Intercept*. 23 May 2019.

54 Kravets, David. "Lawmakers who upheld NSA phone spying received double in defense industry cash." *Wired*. 26 July 2013.

55 "… receiving over three quarters of a million dollars from 2009 through 2011, including $590,000 to his campaign fund and $191,000 to his leadership PAC," according to William Hartung. "Tools of Influence: The Arms Lobby and the Super Committee." *Center for International Policy*. 31 October 2011.

56 War corporations donating to Schiff included Boeing, Harris Corp., Lockheed Martin, Parsons, Raytheon, and Orbital ATK.

57 Wall Street, Harris, General Electric, Carlyle Group, and others have donated to Gillibrand. MIT, Google, Wall Street, Raytheon, and others have donated to Warren. Gillibrand and Warren regularly vote in favor of the NDAA and military appropriations. Warren has an amicable working relationship with the war industry, made clear in *Politico* (Wright and Judson. "Warren takes care of defense business back home." 13 February 2015).

58 All of this revealed in Lambrecht, Bill. "Spy vs. Spy: He's ex-CIA. She was an Air Force intelligence officer. Both want your vote for Congress." *Houston Chronicle*. 2 October 2018.

59 Such hype included but was not limited to NSC 68, the Gaither Report, the bomber gap, the missile gap, Sputnik, Soviet first strike capabilities, Yuri Gagarin orbiting Earth, the "window of vulnerability," SALT opposition, the Committee to Maintain a Prudent Defense Policy, the Committee on Present Danger, and President Reagan's March 1983 claim that Moscow's military might was overwhelming and that D.C. needed to develop (i.e. purchase from industry) an even bigger arsenal. In the War Dept.'s old Office of Systems Analysis there was a Strategic Forces Division. Its director, Ivan Selin, used to say, "Welcome to the world of strategic analysis, where we program weapons that don't

work to meet threats that don't exist." Quoted in Tyson & Lang (*Accessory to War*, p. 485, footnote 51) and Andrew Cockburn ("The New Red Scare." *Harper's*. December 2016, p. 25).

60 Additional Clinton accomplishments benefitting corporate rule included the North American Free Trade Act; the Violent Crime Control & Law Enforcement Act of 1994, which exploded prison populations; the Illegal Immigration Reform & Immigrant Responsibility Act of 1996, forcing many immigrants to the cramped, pliable margins of labor; the 1996 Prison Litigation Reform Act, which violated prisoners' constitutional rights; and the Personal Responsibility & Work Opportunity Act of 1996, which brutalized the destitute and the working poor. Author Thomas Frank and journalist Paul Jay on a 2018 episode of Reality Asserts Itself on *The Real News Network*, <therealnews.com>, got me thinking about many of these. Credit to them.

61 Lisa Stampnitzky's 2013 book *Disciplining Terror: How Experts Invented 'Terrorism'* (Cambridge: Cambridge University Press) analyzes the contemporary understanding of "terrorism" and the emergence of terrorism expertise. Stampnitzky notes that Arab terrorists are often described simultaneously as "evil" and "irrational." She analyzes politicians and punditry who avoid understanding the motivations or justification of terrorists. This "anti-knowledge" can constrain experts.

62 Experts include former Navy helicopter pilots (Rick Nelson at CSIS), Zionist think tank operatives (Toby Dershowitz at the Foundation for Defense of Democracies), and agile climbers within the Silicon Valley/military R&D nexus (Regina Dugan).

63 "Defense: Top Contributors to Federal Candidates, Parties, and Outside Groups." *Center for Responsive Politics*. See also Davies and Benjamin (*Common Dreams*, 7 June 2018), citing "Defense: Lobbying, 2018." *Center for Responsive Politics*. Accessed 14 June 2018: <www.opensecrets.org/industries/lobbying.php?cycle=2018&ind=D>.

64 The war industry divvied out over $129 million on 752 lobbyists in 2016, according to *Politico* (Herb, Jeremy. "Boeing tops defense lobbying." 21 January 2016). In 2018, war corporations spent $127 million on lobbying and paid an additional $29 million in campaign contributions. Mitchell, Ellen. "Defense lobbyists deluged in wake of Trump victory." *Politico*. 11 November 2016. Koshgarian, Lindsay. "For Military Contractors, Tax Day Is Pay Day." *Truthout*. 10 April 2019. Cohen, Alexander. "Defense Contractors Spend Millions to Overturn Limits on Military Spending." *Center for Public Integrity*. 5 August 2015. See also the *Center for Responsive Politics*.

65 Congressman Longley (R-ME), 2 Feb 1995: "You know, jobs are important, not only because of the fact that they give productive employment to our citizens, but they also represent some of the highest paying jobs in the country. But even going beyond that, this is about much more than jobs; it is about making sure that we have a strong national defense and that we are applying the resources that we need to meet the crises that we may be asked to confront." "Congressional Record—House." *H1150*. 2 February 1995: <www.gpo.gov/fdsys/pkg/CREC-1995-02-02/pdf/CREC-1995-02-02-pt1-PgH1149.pdf>, 2120.

66 Some F-35 production locations in the U.S. are Alpharetta, GA; Arlington, TX; Avon, MA; Baltimore, MD; Camden, NJ; Cedar Rapids, IA; Clearfield, UT; East Aurora, NY; Fort Worth, TX; Grand Rapids, MI; Hauppauge, NY; Helena, MT; Inglewood, Garden Grove, Palmdale, San Diego, Torrance, Valencia, City of Industry, El Segundo, Irvine, CA; Marietta, GA; Melbourne, FL; Nashua, NH; N. Amityville, NY; Orlando, FL; Owego, NY; Phoenix, AZ; Plano, TX; Rolling Meadows, IL; Sarasota, FL; St. Charles, MO; Tempe, AZ; Wichita, KS; Windsor Locks, CT; and Williston, VT. Overseas production locations have included Montmorency, Australia; Grenaa, Denmark; Japan; Kjeller and Kongsberg, Norway; British Columbia, Canada; Hoogeveen and Papendrecht, Netherlands; Roma and Torino, Italy; Eskisehir, Turkey; and Cheltenham, Preston, Rochester, and Samlesbury, UK. These countries are customers of the overall U.S. war industry. Denmark, for example, has purchased Boeing missiles, Druck air data test sets, Ellwood National Forge bombs, Engility software, Lockheed

Martin command & control, helicopters & avionics, and navigation devices, and Raytheon missiles, among other products. Foreign suppliers make about half of any given F-35, according to Marcus Weisgerber (*Defense One*, 6 May 2016). Lockheed Martin might have mastered the art of luring and hooking foreign countries, but it is not the only practitioner. Boeing, General Dynamics, Northrop Grumman, Raytheon, and many smaller war corporations do the same thing. Northrop Grumman, for example, produces its E-2D Advanced Hawkeye in Aire-sur-l'Adour, France; Canada (Lunenberg, Novia Scotia; Longueil and Laval, Québec); Latina, Italy; Wimborne, U.K., and other foreign locations. Contracts (4 Aug 2015, 25 Sept 2017, 30 Aug 2018) illustrate worldwide F-35 production. Sometimes this spread causes hiccups. Turkish Aerospace Industries in Ankara had produced some F-35 fuselages. It was suspended from the program after Ankara purchased the Russian-made S-400 air defense system. Poland might take Turkey's place.

67 Baltimore, MD; Bridgeport, WV; Cedar Rapids, IA; Indianapolis, IN; Medford, NY; Moss Point, MS; Newton, ND; Palmdale, Rancho Bernardo, San Diego, Santa Clarita, CA; Red Oak, TX; Salt Lake City, UT; Vandalia, OH; other U.S. locations; Montréal, Canada.

68 Issued 27 June 2018. Locations included Bloomington, MN; Clifton, NJ; East Aurora, Endicott, Greenlawn, NY; Fort Walton Beach, Clearwater, FL; Fort Worth, TX; Hazelwood, MO; Kalamazoo, MI; Mesa, AZ; Ontario, Canada; Santa Ana, El Segundo, Santa Clarita, Torrance, CA; Vandalia, OH; and various locations outside of the contiguous U.S. (OCONUS).

69 Issued 29 June 2018. Locations included Amarillo, Red Oak, Denton, McKinney, Fort Worth, TX; Crestview, FL; East Aurora, Endicott, Rome, NY; East Hartford, CT; Erie, PA; Hazelwood, MO; Irvine, Dublin, Los Angeles, CA; Minden, NE; Park City, UT; Ridley Park, PA; Rockford, IL; Rockmart, GA; Tempe, AZ; undeclared locations, CONUS and OCONUS.

70 Final missile production on Redstone Arsenal in Huntsville, AL. Regular worksites have included Amesbury, Andover, MA; Anaheim, San Diego, San José, San Mateo, CA; Anniston, AL; Clarkston, GA; Dallas, TX; Camden, East Camden, AR; Joplin, MO; Middletown, CT; Middletown, OH; Minneapolis, MN; Orangeburg, NY; Tucson, Phoenix, AZ; Portland, OR; Reisterstown, MD; Tampa, FL; Warrington, PA; Wolverhampton, U.K. Tangential work in Boston, MA; Mesa, AZ; Milwaukie, OR; St. Petersburg, FL.

71 Alamitos, CA; Albuquerque, NM; Anniston, AL; Berryville, AR; Boulder, CO; Burlington, VT; Camden, AR; Chandler, AZ; Clearwater, FL; Dallas, TX; Dublin, GA; East Camden, AR; El Segundo, CA; Farmington, NM; Fort Wayne, IN; Gainesville, VA; Hollister, CA; Hopkinton, MA; Huntsville, AL; Joplin, MO; Kansas City, MO; Lincoln, NE; Mesa, CA; Middleton, PA; Middletown, CT; Minneapolis, MN; Moorpark, CA; Mosheim, TN; Ogden, UT; Pacoima, CA; Rocket Center, WV; San Jose, CA; Santa Ana, CA; Simsbury, CT; South El Monte, CA; Spanish Fork, UT; Tempe, AZ; Torrance, CA; Tucson, AZ; Valencia, CA; Vergennes, VT; Walled Lake, MI; Westminster, CO. Overseas locations include Glenrothes, Scotland, and Midland, Ontario, Canada. This tally includes related technology, particularly Tomahawk launching systems (capsule, tube launch, vertical launch). Not included are JSL Technologies (Oxnard, CA) engineering or Lockheed Martin's Tactical Tomahawk Weapons Control System, built with electronics from Ace Electronics Defense Systems (Aberdeen Proving Ground, MD), Crestwood Technology Group (Yonkers, NY), Gideon Services (Huntsville, AL), RC Electronics (Orange, CA).

72 "Collaborate against the cyber threat: Raytheon CEO speaks on Capitol Hill about strengthening cybersecurity." *Raytheon*. 11 January 2018. "Defense jobs" are "noble jobs," argues Raytheon's CEO (Aitoro, Jill. "Raytheon CEO on Trump meeting: President appears to understand value of UTC-Raytheon tie-up." *Defense News*. 19 June 2019).

73 LPD locations have included Beloit, WI; Brunswick, GA; Columbus, OH; Norfolk, Crozet, VA; Grand Rapids, MI; Pittsburgh, Irvine, King of Prussia, Warminster, York, PA; Mayport, FL;

Milwaukee, WI; Mossville, IL; Muscatine, IA; Pascagoula, MS; Sasebo, Japan; Carson, San Diego, CA; Sumter, SC; Tulsa, OK; Devens, Walpole, MA. This doesn't include propulsion shafts made in New Castle and Bethlehem, PA; MK 46 gun systems made in Anniston, AL, Lima, OH, Scranton, PA, Sterling Heights, MI, Tallahassee, FL; ongoing ship maintenance in Norfolk, VA, San Diego, CA, Bremerton, WA, Everett, WA, Portland, OR, and other locations. Integrated Shipboard Electronic system, a Raytheon product, is produced in many of the aforementioned locations, in addition to Allen, TX; Anaheim, CA; Bohemia, NY; Carlsbad, CA; Fairfax, VA; Providence, RI.

74 See Lockheed Martin's 18 Sept 2018 contract. Such contracts don't even include the locations choking on related goods and services, like Naval Station Mayport, FL, where construction firms are building an LCS training facility. After the building is built, war corporations will sell and install more LCS-related goods and services.

75 Other MMSC locations include Burns Harbor, IN; Crozet, VA; Fridley, MN; Grand Rapids, Iron Mountain, Kingsford, Novi, MI; Louisville, KY; Beloit, Marinette, Milwaukee, WI; Moorestown, NJ; Orlando, FL; Patuxent River, Stevensville, MD; St. Charles, MO; Walpole, MA; and D.C. This doesn't include production of goods that operate on or from MMSC (e.g. Lockheed Martin MH-60R, Lockheed Martin combat management system, Argon ST torpedo decoys, Raytheon and Boeing missiles). Production of MK 41 Vertical Launch System (through which RIM-162 missiles take flight) is sprinkled across congressional districts including Aberdeen, SD; Baltimore, Timonium, MD; Burlington, MA; Clearwater, Orlando, FL; Charlottesville, VA; Minneapolis, MN; Gardena, San José, Ventura, CA; Simpsonville, SC; Sterling Heights, MI; and Tualatin, OR.

76 The Advisory Board will be eyeing labor market data in a bipartisan fashion; increasing privatization of the educational system, including secondary and university levels; and promoting training and educational programs beneficial to the wants of U.S. corporate leadership. Or, as *Industry Week* phrased it on 15 Feb 2019, the "goal is to have varied perspectives on workforce issues facing communities and businesses across the country, while raising awareness of multiple pathways for American workers to obtain family-sustaining careers."

77 Lockheed Martin asserts the "F-35 is built by thousands of men and women in America and around the world. With more than 1,500 suppliers in 46 states and Puerto Rico, the F-35 program supports more than 194,000 direct and indirect jobs in the U.S. alone," per "Lockheed Martin Meets 1,800 Employee Hiring Commitment; Plans to Add 400 More Jobs in Fort Worth." *Lockheed Martin*. 23 July 2018.

78 Harris, Nia, Cassandra Stimpson, Ben Freeman. "Defense contractors are devouring taxpayer dollars and shedding U.S. jobs." *Business Insider*. Posted originally at *TomDispatch.com* on 4 August 2019.

79 "The opening comes 10 months after the project was announced during Maryland Governor Larry Hogan's trade mission to Israel in September 2016," the Elbit press release explains ("Baltimore Cyber Range and Cyberbit Open New Cybersecurity Training and Simulation Center," 3 August 2017). On 21 Sept 2016, Hogan's website <governor.maryland.gov> relayed the words of the Maryland/Israel Development Center (MDIC) executive director: "Maryland and Israel form the backbone of cybersecurity development and defenses in the world." MDIC is comprised of The Associated Jewish Community Federation of Baltimore, Maryland's Department of Commerce, and Apartheid Israel's Ministry of Economy.

80 Gollan, Jennifer. "Defense Contractors Cited for Endangering Workers Continue to Win Big Business." *The Center for Investigative Reporting*. 6 March 2019.

81 Regarding labor rights, workers say Boeing fired them when they tried to bargain collectively, Meg Kinnard reported (*Charlotte Observer*, 22 December 2018). See Sainato, Michael. "'It's because we were union members': Boeing fires workers who organized." *The Guardian*. 3 May 2019. Around

the same time, a machinist union took to the picket lines when a Boeing and Lockheed Martin joint venture proposed changes to the union contract.

82 Garrett-Peltier, Heidi. "Job Opportunity Cost of War." *University of Massachusetts Amherst Political Economy Research Institute*. 25 May 2017.

83 The "military product, whatever its money value, is functionally limited as it cannot be used for ordinary consumption or as a means of production. The jet-powered fighter plane is a technological masterpiece, but you can't eat it, wear it, ride it, live in it, and you can't make anything with it." Melman, Seymour. "Special Interdisciplinary Panel—Barriers to Disarmament." *Towards Preventing Nuclear Omnicide*. St. Louis: First International Conference of the International Philosophers for the Prevention of Nuclear Omnicide, 1 May 1986.

84 Gallagher, Sean. "Boeing downplayed 737 MAX software risks, self-certified much of plane's safety." *Ars Technica*. 18 March 2019.

85 Kindy, Kimberly. "Pork industry will soon have more power over meat inspections." *Washington Post*. 3 April 2019.

86 Contracts issued 12 March 2018, 23 Sept 2014, respectively.

87 One way Saudi Arabia and the UAE tried to counteract criticism was by forming a group called the Joint Incidents Assessment Team in 2015 to investigate civilian deaths. Instead of holding Saudi Arabia/UAE to account, "the body frequently parrots its rhetoric that strikes are unintentional mistakes," according to Kristine Beckerle of Human Rights Watch, per Alex Emmons (*The Intercept*, 20 July 2018). The U.S. State Dept. helped establish the Joint Incidents Assessment Team. "Human rights groups say that its investigations are a sham, and that it rarely finds fault with the coalition's actions. After it examined an airstrike that killed 40 schoolboys in August, [coalition spokesperson] Colonel Malki said that the coalition had struck a 'legitimate target.' … The assessment team also examined the war's deadliest attack at sea—a helicopter strike in March 2017 that killed at least 43 people" on a boat. "The assessment team determined that the coalition had not carried out the attack." Walsh, Declan. "In Saudi Arabia's War in Yemen, No Refuge on Land or Sea." *The New York Times*. 17 December 2018.

88 For example, in autumn 2018 Israeli courts (the Bersheeba District Court, specifically) ruled that the Israeli state is not liable for killing a 15-year-old in Gaza. The Israeli military had shot and killed the child on his own property at close range.

89 Joe Penney, et al. "CIA Drone Mission, Curtailed by Obama, Is Expanded in Africa Under Trump." *The New York Times*. 9 September 2018. CIA reportedly uses General Atomics drones.

90 Williams, Jimmy. "I was a lobbyist for more than 6 years. I quit. My conscience couldn't take it anymore." *Vox*. 5 January 2018. "Unlimited expense accounts, nights out on the town, expensive bottles of wine, elaborate meals with sitting senators and Congress members—that was my life… It was an endless cycle of money trading hands for votes. It's a wonder members of the House and Senate actually have time to legislate when they spend so much of their damn time raising money… Every fundraiser was yet another legal bribe. Every committee hearing I'd look up and think, 'I just bought his vote.' And every time I got a bill passed or, better yet, killed, I'd think to myself, 'That wouldn't have worked if I hadn't bought the outcome.'"

91 Groups have reportedly included ADI; Akin Gump Strauss Hauer & Feld; BGR Group; Brownstein Hyatt Farber & Schreck; Buchanan Ingersoll & Rooney; Burdeshaw Associates; Business Roundtable; The Cohen Group; Denny Miller & Associates; Ernst & Young; Four Star Group; J.A. Green & Co.; McKeon Group; Nuclear Energy Institute; The Podesta Group; The Spectrum Group; U.S. Chamber of Commerce, Van Scoyoc Associates. For the Four Star Group, see Bryan Bender (*Boston Globe*, 26 December 2010). The McKeon Group is led by former chair of the House Armed Services Committee, "Buck" McKeon. More firms are listed on *Lobbydata.com*. Other sources include

Hartung's "Tools of Influence: The Arms Lobby and the Super Committee." *Center for International Policy*. 31 October 2011. The Saudi regime, a big purchaser of U.S. war goods, has hired BGR, BHFS, and others, Ben Freeman reported in *The Nation* ("How Much It Costs to Buy U.S. Foreign Policy," 4 October 2018).

92 Bender, Bryan. "From the Pentagon to the private sector."

93 For example, 22 ex-super committee staffers lobby for the war industry. Eggen, Dan. "Members of debt panel have ties to lobbyists." *Washington Post*. 5 September 2011. Referenced in Hartung, William "Tools of Influence: The Arms Lobby and the Super Committee." *Center for International Policy*. 31 October 2011.

94 "About NDIA." *SOFIC*. Accessed 1 September 2018: <www.sofic.org/about-ndia>. Context at "NDIA announces McConn, Punaro as new heads of board of directors" (*NDIA*, 1 October 2018).

95 "Collaborate against the cyber threat: Raytheon CEO speaks on Capitol Hill about strengthening cybersecurity." *Raytheon*. 11 January 2018: <www.raytheon.com/news/feature/kennedy_aia_speech>.

96 "AUSA Industry Guide." *Association of the United States Army*. Accessed 30 July 2018: <www.ausa.org/industry-guide>.

97 Sordidly, AUSA's lecture series is named after General Lyman Lemnitzer. In 1962, Lemnitzer, Chairman of the Joint Chiefs, signed off on Operation Northwoods, a plan to attack U.S. infrastructure, including passenger jets. According to the now declassified scheme, the attacks would be blamed on the Cuban government and used as a pretext to attack the Caribbean island. AUSA's Lemnitzer lecture series regularly features corporate media and senior Pentagon functionaries.

98 On the NDIA board there's Leidos' Lt. Gen. (ret.) William Bender, Jacobs' Maj. Gen. (ret.) Tim Byers, Dell's Steve Harris, and Sierra Nevada Corporation's Maj. Gen. (ret.) Thomas Andersen. On AIA's board, there's Honeywell's Tom Mahoney, Deloitte's Robin Lineberger, General Dynamics' Phebe Novakovic, and Huntington Ingalls' Mike Petters. AUSA's Council of Trustees features William Brown, CEO of Harris Corp. and Vice Chairperson of AIA; Leanne Caret, chief of Boeing Defense, Space & Security; AM General's Andy Hove; and Frank St. John, executive VP at Lockheed Martin. This is just a sample of populous boards.

99 "How security cooperation advances U.S. interests." *Brookings Institution*. 4 June 2019, (46:50).

100 "Our Mission and Tenets," <www.bens.org/about-bens/our-mission>.

101 BENS' members <www.bens.org/membership/OurMembers> span venture capital, big finance, manufacturing and real estate conglomerates, and war corporations. Hand-in-hand with the U.S. government, they "work to deliver results through varied methods, including round table discussions, red teaming, focused working groups, interviews and research, and regional outreach. Each product will be tailored to meet our government partners needs and timeline." BENS concludes with a humble misdirection: "Credit for achievements goes to our government partners," per "How We Work." *Business Executives for National Security*. Accessed 30 September 2018: <www.bens.org/pages/policy-work/how-we-work>.

102 AOC hosts an annual conference where military flag officers and commanders give speeches. Vice Admiral Charles Richard's speech to the crowd is typical. His first order of business was thanking the conference chair, a Raytheon official ("53rd Annual AOC International Symposium and Convention," 29 November 2016). War corporations sponsor AOC and their events; see <www.crows.org/page/boardofdirectors> and <www.crows.org/mpage/2019Sponsors>. Regarding expanding government spending on signals intelligence in an era of renewed competition with Moscow, AOC organized a forum on Capitol Hill where high-ranking U.S. military officials could promote the need,

so they said, to invest in more SIGINT technology, as reported gently by Sydney Freedberg (*Breaking Defense*, 30 July 2018).

103 "About AIAA," <www.aiaa.org/AboutAIAA/>.

104 "Purpose." *Tidewater Government Industry Council.* Accessed 16 September 2018: <www.tasc-tgic.org/TGIC-Charter>.

105 One Patuxent Partnership presentation (Taylor, Leslie. "Naval Air Warfare Center Aircraft Division." *The Patuxent Partnership.* September 2017, pp. 60-61) boasts of $32.6 billion worth of contracts with private industry flowing through Naval Air Warfare Center Aircraft Division and a $7.5 billion "economic impact to the state of Maryland."

106 Such influence is often phrased as benefitting the people. Notoriously, the head of the War Production Board in 1944 invoked still-understandable worries of the Great Depression when indicating that a permanent war economy could help avoid an economic recession. See Carroll, James. *House of War.* New York: Houghton Mifflin, 2006, p. 546, footnote 91.

107 J.D. Crouch, DPB chair, was CEO of QinetiQ, a U.K.-based corporation that sells counter-IED devices and sensors for drones. Prior to his time with QinetiQ, Crouch was Deputy National Security Advisor in the George W. Bush administration. Other persons and interests include retired Admiral Gary Roughead of the Hoover Institution and the discredited health profiteer Theranos; Frank Miller of The Cohen Group and then the think tank CSIS; Henry Kissinger, a prolific perpetrator of war crimes in southeast Asia and Latin America; Jamie Gorelick, former Fannie Mae executive and D.C. legal guru; former Secretary of State Madeleine Albright, who says that killing 500,000 Iraqi children was "worth it" (*CBS News, 60 Minutes*, 12 May 1996); Michèle Flournoy; and Rudy deLeon, former Under Secretary of War and current senior VP at the think tank Center for American Progress. Full list available at "DOD Announces New Defense Policy Board Members." *U.S. Department of Defense.* 30 November 2017. The new members ascending to DPB in autumn 2017 brought with them a variety of corporate concerns and industry allegiances, including war corporations Rockwell Collins and The Aerospace Corporation; financial firms like The Blackstone Group; and think tanks The Aspen Institute, The Hoover Institution, and The American Enterprise Institute.

108 Ginsberg, Wendy. "Federal Advisory Committees: An Overview." *Congressional Research Service.* 16 April 2009.

109 Censer, Marjorie. "Private-equity firms play major role in defense industry today." *Washington Post.* 2 February 2014.

110 Schroeder, Peter. "Boehner chief lands top job at private equity industry group." *The Hill.* 27 January 2016.

111 "Lockheed Martin Corporation." *Nasdaq.* Accessed 26 February 2019: <www.nasdaq.com/es/symbol/lmt/ownership-summary>.

112 By mid-September 2018, the U.S. Senate had voted to 93-7 to pass the $674 billion official war budget, $717 total. All Senate Democrats voted in favor. Independent Bernie Sanders voted nay. Garamone, Jim. "President Signs Fiscal 2019 Defense Authorization Act at Fort Drum Ceremony." *Defense Media Activity.* 13 August 2018.

113 Public laws 115-232 and -245 authorized and appropriated substantial funding for war corporations to expand the submarine industrial base. Supplementary legal authorities were available via the National Sea-Based Deterrence Fund (10 U.S. Code §2218a). War corporations had pressured Congress by alleging such funding "improves capacity" across industry and "reduces risk" to submarine programs. Funding played out in many ways, prominent among them was when, on 20 May 2019, General Dynamics was allocated nearly half a billion dollars to develop and expand the submarine industrial base, with smaller corporations in subcontracting roles.

114 "NDIA commends passage of defense spending bill in time for new fiscal year." *NDIA.* 28 September 2018: <www.ndia.org/about/media/press-releases/2018/9/28/spending-passes>.

115 Mehta, Aaron. "DOD hands out $7.54 billion in year-end contract bonanza." *Defense News.* 2 October 2018. Pentagon units try to spend the remainder of their coffers during the last week of every fiscal year, and ink long-term contracts for the upcoming fiscal year. The $7.54 billion is a rounded approximation.

116 Stockholm International Peace Research Institute. *SIPRI Yearbook 2016.* Oxford: Oxford University Press, 2016.

117 Damon, Andre. "Democrats back massive Pentagon budget for war and repression." *World Socialist Web Site.* 23 June 2018.

118 Gazis, Olivia. "CIA's top recruiter on how the agency finds—and keeps—its spies." *CBS News.* 11 July 2018.

119 Harris, Shane. "The CIA is returning its central focus to nation-state rivals, director says." *Washington Post.* 24 September 2018. In April 2019, Haspel visited Auburn University in Alabama on a recruitment trip. (A student in the audience berated her: "Tell them who you tortured. You know their names! They're still in Guantánamo Bay!" The student was referring to Haspel's role in the torture of prisoners in Thailand in 2002.) Toward the end of April, CIA joined the social media platform *Instagram*, a continuation of the recruitment drive. Most Instagram users are under 30 years of age. CIA even had a booth at *Awesome Con 2019*, a celebration of graphic novels. As of June 2019, CIA's *Instagram* followed 11 accounts, mostly celebrities who starred in movie or TV that received government support during filming.

120 The *Guardian* (Hopkins, 2 December 2018) reports MI6 director Alex Younger has been trying to change MI6's image and appeal to a broader, more diverse recruiting base. On 3 December, *The Saint*, a student-run newspaper at St. Andrews, quoted Younger: "We are determined to attract people from the widest range of backgrounds to join… This will enable us to bring the widest range of approaches to bear on solving complex problems and so make our missions even more effective."

121 In the latter years of the Clinton administration, Bremer helped lay the legal foundations for the subsequent War on Terror by helming D.C.'s *Report of the National Commission on Terrorism*, which hyped the threat of WMD attacks, demonized Iran and Syria, and recommended designating Afghanistan a sponsor of terrorism, increasing U.S. electronic surveillance capabilities, and expanding CIA's work with "unsavory sources." Text available at <fas.org/irp/threat/commission.html>. In Iraq, Bremer issued Order 39, privatizing Iraqi state assets. According to investigative journalist Max Blumenthal (*The Management of Savagery*. New York: Verso, 2019, p. 111), that order was carried out by a corporation, BearingPoint, which reaped "a $250 million government contract" establishing the legalese required to privatize Iraqi resources.

122 "It's time to advance America's asymmetric advantage by equipping the Air Force." *Defense News.* 26 April 2019.

123 See, *inter alia*, Goodman, Amy. "Access of Evil." *The Nation.* 15 June 2006; Barstow, David. "Behind TV Analysts, Pentagon's Hidden Hand." *The New York Times.* 20 April 2008; "Pentagon suspends retired military analyst program." *Reuters.* 28 April 2008; Greenwald, Glenn. "How the military analyst program controlled news coverage: in the Pentagon's own words." *Salon.* 10 May 2008; "Pentagon's Pundits: A Look at the Defense Department's Propaganda Program." *DemocracyNow.* 22 April 2008; Barstow, David. "Pentagon Finds No Fault in Ties to TV Analysts." *The New York Times.* 24 December 2011; and Nordland, Ngu, and Abed. "How the U.S. Government Misleads the Public on Afghanistan." *The New York Times.* 8 September 2018. Many individuals who were integral to the domestic propaganda program are still in the MIC. Roxie T. Merritt was director of War Dept. press operations at the time. Now she is in charge of corporate communications at the Naval Surface Warfare Center Carderock Division. Larry Di Rita was Secretary of War Donald

Rumsfeld's senior aide. Now Di Rita is on the advisory board at the industry think tank, CNAS. He is also director of The Rumsfeld Foundation and in charge of global marketing & corporate affairs at Bank of America. Victoria Clarke was senior Pentagon spokesperson during the lead up to the 2003 invasion of Iraq. Drawing on this experience and her earlier years as general manager of the PR firm Hill & Knowlton, she went on to work as a commentator for corporate media, work government relations for Comcast, and take charge of corporate affairs for the German software corporation SAP. She's now sitting on the board at The Rumsfeld Foundation.

124 Lutz, Ashley. "These 6 Corporations Control 90% Of The Media in America." *Business Insider*. 14 June 2012. Vinton, Kate. "These 15 Billionaires Own America's News Media Companies." *Forbes*. 1 June 2016. The 1996 Telecommunications Act deregulated the telecom industry and allowed cross-ownership of media. After the 1996 Act passed, a media corporation that specialized in TV info-tainment could purchase local newspapers across the country, as well as invest in internet service providers. Take Sinclair Broadcast Group (Hunt Valley, MD) for example. Sinclair is the largest operator of TV stations in the U.S. Sinclair owns private equity firms and online media assets. (Hunt Valley, incidentally, is home to Textron's drone plant.) Corporate consolidation and cross-ownership wrecked and gobbled up small town newspapers, radio, and TV outlets that once provided two key checks on corporate power (a steady chain of new, hungry journalists and diverse viewpoints refusing to synch with the power centers in U.S. society). In Aug 2019, Gatehouse Media acquired Gannett for $1.4 billion. The resulting corporation now owns at least 1/6 of all daily newspapers in the U.S.

125 Those funding corporate media are able to access the producers and creators of news "by their contribution to reducing the media's costs of acquiring... and producing, news. The large entities that provide this subsidy become 'routine' news sources and have privileged access to the gates. Non-routine sources must struggle for access, and may be ignored by the arbitrary decision of the gatekeepers," Ed Herman and Noam Chomsky explain in *Manufacturing Consent* (New York City: Pantheon, 1988). I also recommend *Inventing Reality: The Politics of News Media*, which the preeminent Michael Parenti published in 1986. Unsurprisingly, Jimmy Dore, an astute comedian and critic of bipartisan corruption in D.C., provides concise analysis of the state of U.S. news organizations: "We used to have journalists investigating corporate criminals in government. And what happened was the criminals got smart, and they just bought the journalists. So now the journalists work for the people they're supposed to be investigating. You know when you watch *Meet the Press*, and you see Chuck Todd throw to a commercial for Boeing—well, nobody's watching that show wanting to buy a jet. [Boeing is] sponsoring NBC News so they *don't* do an investigation." Dore, Jimmy. "Debate Week: Privacy, Surveillance, and Whistleblowers with Jimmy Dore." *RT*. 26 July 2018: <www.youtube.com/watch?v=AdYJDt5QMz8>, (25:30). Other corporations do the same thing. E.g., Monsanto used corporate media when controlling the narrative re: glyphosate in its products (Gillam, Carey. *Whitewash*. Island Press, 2017).

126 Examples include Clear Channel radio banning 158 thought-provoking or nonconforming songs in the wake of 9.11, and MSNBC shedding Phil Donahue's top-rated show because he presented a view that was not sufficiently pro-war.

127 For example, MSNBC has helped rehabilitate war propagandist Bill Kristol as he positions himself as a rational conservative vis-à-vis the Trump administration. See "Watch Fat Joe and 'woke Bill Kristol' cruise New York" (*MSNBC—The Beat with Ari*). Many others who sold us the Iraq War "continue to hold positions of influence" and continue to provide foreign policy advice, according to media watchdog *Media Matters for America* (Hananoki, Eric. "Where Are The Media's Iraq War Boosters 10 Years Later?" 19 March 2013).

128 "New Year 2019: U.S. military apologises for bomb tweet." *BBC News*. 1 January 2019. Lesson *not* learned: DVIDS, a War Dept. media arm you'll encounter momentarily, tweeted on 20 Sept

2019 regarding the plan hatched on social media to storm the Nevada military site known as Area 51: "The last thing #Millennials will see if they attempt the #area51raid today": [a picture of a Northrop Grumman B-2 bomber]. The unit apologized via Twitter the following day.

129 DMA's mission is to "provide a wide variety of information products" to U.S. military members (including contractors and civilians) and "external audiences"; "communicate messages and themes" from senior Pentagon leaders [many of whom come directly from careers in war corporations]; and serve up "visual information products."

"Mission." *Defense Media Activity.* Accessed 8 March 2019: <www.dma.mil/About-DMA/Mission-Vision/>.

130 Published 17 July 2018 and 19 November 2017, respectively.

131 The *AP* elaborates: "What readers are not told: Each of these glowing stories was written by Pentagon staff. Under the free service, stories go out with authors' names but not their titles, and do not mention *Hometown News* anywhere. In 2009, *Hometown News* plans to put out 5,400 press releases, 3,000 television releases and 1,600 radio interviews, among other work—50 percent more than in 2007. The service is just a tiny piece of the Pentagon's rapidly expanding media empire, which is now bigger in size, money and power than many media companies" (Tomlinson, 5 February 2009).

132 "Seth Visits the Pentagon." *Late Night with Seth Meyers.* 14 October 2016: <www.youtube.com/watch?v=Py-jRVMeYk4>.

133 Hollywood removed the antinuclear political message from Gojira ("Godzilla"), effectively neutering the 1954 film for its U.S. release. For more, see Keegan, Rebecca. "The U.S. military's Hollywood connection." *LA Times.* 21 August 2011; Secker and Alford. "Documents expose how Hollywood promotes war on behalf of the Pentagon, CIA, and NSA." *Insurge Intelligence.* 4 July 2017; Tarabay, Jamie. "Hollywood and the Pentagon: A relationship of mutual exploitation." *Al Jazeera.* 29 July 2014; Weisman, Aly. "One Man in the Department of Defense Controls All of Hollywood's Access to the Military." *Business Insider.* 5 March 2014.

134 Jack Shaheen's "Reel Bad Arabs," released in 2006 by *Media Education Foundation* (Northampton, MA), illustrates this clearly. Films denigrating or demonizing Arabs span genres (e.g. comedies, The Dictator; action movies, True Lies).

135 Burgess, Anna. "Female engineers hope to inspire Brockton students with film screening." *The Enterprise.* 14 January 2017.

136 McGrath, Matt. "Final call to save the world from 'climate catastrophe.'" *BBC News.* 8 October 2018; Carrington, Damian. "Earth's sixth mass extinction event under way, scientists warn." *The Guardian.* 10 July 2017; Sutter, John D. "Sixth mass extinction: The era of 'biological annihilation.'" *CNN.* 11 July 2017; "Human health in dire straits if urgent actions are not made to protect the environment, warns landmark UN report." *United Nations.* 13 March 2019; McGrath, Matt. "Nature crisis: 'Shocking' report details threat to species." *BBC News.* 6 May 2019.

137 Carp, Rick. "Who Pays for Think Tanks?" *Fairness & Accuracy In Reporting.* July 2013.

138 The piece is "JDAM: How Boeing's Low-Cost Smart Bomb Revolutionized Strike Warfare" (*Forbes,* 29 August 2018).

139 Former judge advocate Maj. Todd E. Pierce explains: U.S. think tanks fire up the public against a roster of foreign "enemies" in order to justify endless wars, through which weapons manufacturers and other billion-dollar companies profit. Pierce, Todd E. "Inciting Wars the American Way." *AntiWar.com.* 15 August 2016. Rick Carp's "Who Pays for Think Tanks?" (*Fairness & Accuracy In Reporting,* July 2013) itemizes the think tanks taking money from weapon manufacturers. "The companies that most profit from war are using their wealth to shape the discussion in ways that benefit them."

140 Many think tanks, tax-exempt 501(c)3, have affiliated lobbying and PR operations, non-tax-exempt 501(c)4. So, the Heritage Foundation, for example, works with a (c)4 called Heritage Action for America, and the Center for American Progress (CAP) has a (c)4 called the Center for American Progress Action Fund, reported Bruce Bartlett "The Alarming Corruption of the Think Tanks" (*The Fiscal Times*, 14 December 2012). Bartlett is a former policy analyst in the Reagan White House. He explains, think tank output increasingly involves basic, widespread political operations "rather than books and studies." Some might think CAP is aligned with the center-left. Not on matters of war and peace. "Staffers were very clearly instructed to check with the think tank's development team before writing anything that might upset contributors," journalist Ken Silverstein noted in Carp, Rick. "Who Pays for Think Tanks?" *Fairness & Accuracy In Reporting*. July 2013.

141 Post-military, Allen was special presidential envoy to the "Global Coalition to Counter ISIL," leading an effort to purchase, deploy, and use all sorts of weaponry and matériel (which then turned Iraqi cities to rubble). The civilian death count of Operation Inherent Resolve will never be known. The D.C. offensive committed war crimes, though U.S. corporate media downplay these certainties. See Dewan and McGann in "Amnesty International says U.S.-led strikes on Raqqa may amount to war crimes" (*CNN*, 5 June 2018). Bill Van Auken produces a thorough analysis in "Amnesty International report finds U.S. guilty of war crimes in Syria" (*WSWS*, 6 June 2018). Heritage's leadership are bankers, private equity finaglers, and business leaders supportive institutionally of reduced government oversight of extractive and polluting industries. Heritage personnel have pretended the war budget is under attack. By framing the conversation from a defensive posture, Heritage pundits arrogate a moral high ground. They're just trying to save the country's defense. Who could be against that? Illustrative reports are <www.heritage.org/defense/report/maintaining-the-superiority-americas-defense-industrial-base>, <www.heritage.org/defense/report/five-steps-save-americas-defense-industrial-base>. See also <nader.org/2018/03/06/heritages-corporate-lobby-inside-trumps-government-is-not-the-peoples-heritage>. Leadership & staff are current as of 2 Aug 2018. See <csis.org/programs/about-us/leadership-and-staff/board-trustees>; <brookings.edu/about-us/board-of-trustees>; <heritage.org/article/board-trustees>.

142 Tremblay, Rodrigue. "The Five Pillars of the U.S. Military-Industrial Complex." 25 September 2006.

3

Financials and Legalese

To win a war one must go to great lengths to analyze, crack, and understand enemy communications. For the American people, winning means ending the wars and demilitarizing the U.S. economy. Familiarizing oneself with the war industry's language is a crucial first step. War corporations spew forth a hurricane of verbiage and wordplay. Regardless of their capability or effectiveness, goods and services can be marketed by words that pack a punch: descriptors like "agile," "best of breed," and "full-spectrum." Nouns like breadboard, ecosystem, and total package approach. Nouns and adjectives are hyped by turning them into verbs: definitize, operationalize, productionize, ruggedize. Proven execution and "embedded knowledge" are applied to the ho-hum. Interagency is applied to the parochial, kinetic applied to the stagnant. Military officers ape industry's language with alacrity. Everything from statements of commander intent to formal contracts sound more like interns jockeying for intellectual superiority around a water cooler than the grind of a functioning organization. We'll term such jargon by a similarly kineticized label: *pentagonese*. Now that you're introduced to the jargon, you can study the way the War Department conducts business. This business favors industry.

CONTRACT TYPES

Cost-plus and fixed-price are two common contract types.

Cost-plus means the U.S. government assumes the financial burden for a good or service; the war corporations shoulder no risk. The government pays the corporation for all costs incurred. Industry and Pentagon officials tend to claim that cost-plus contracts are awarded mostly for research and development. They argue that this is acceptable because it's very difficult to estimate the total financial resources a corporation needs in order to study, design, test, and evaluate a product. It would be silly, officials claim, for a corporation to enter into a fixed-price contract when developing a new product, because the corporation would have to pay for cost overruns. This is a moot claim, because the Pentagon issues cost-plus contracts for work on all manner of goods and services, not just R&D.[1]

A fixed-price contract ought to function just like it sounds: The corporation receives a fixed amount of money, regardless of how much time it spends or effort it exerts.[2] In practice, there is much variety within fixed-price contracts. A fixed-price contract, which government claims is economical, can be packed with moneymaking incentives and stipulations. Moreover, war corporations often inflate their up-front fees in order to cover any unforeseen costs in a fixed-price contract, ensuring sizeable profit. All war corporations do this, so there is tacit, uniform acceptance of this practice among those in the know in the Pentagon.[3] Cost-plus and fixed-price contracts can both be noncompetitive—that is, awarded without open, free, and fair competition among corporations.

In an indefinite-delivery/indefinite-quantity (IDIQ) contract, a war corporation sells a lot of goods and services within a timeframe set by the Pentagon. These goods and services are usually issued through "task orders" during the timeframe. (The Pentagon sets a minimum quantity, which the war corporation fills. Then, within the timeframe, the Pentagon can place orders beyond the established minimum.) Industry officials assert IDIQ contracts benefit the Pentagon because the U.S. Armed Forces get the products they need (even when the Pentagon cannot initially determine the precise amounts required); IDIQ, officials argue, allows the corporation to be there when the Pentagon needs it. Various arrangements of IDIQ contracts occur,[4] and can contain cost-plus and/or fixed-fee. Military and industry officials assure us that IDIQ contracts help streamline the contracting process. Officials claim that IDIQ contracts are efficient, yet the numbers do not support this. I tallied over $18 billion allocated towards IDIQ contracts during December 2018 alone.[5] Such billions contradict claims of efficiency. Officials also claim IDIQ contracts are mostly used for services that require on-demand ("on-call") work, like random construction projects that might crop up on base. In practice, IDIQ contracts are issued broadly.[6] IDIQ contracts, like all others, favor spending over fiscal responsibility, industry over discipline.

Ultimately, the type of contract is insignificant. Corporate contract negotiators are typically more adept than their War Department counterparts. Moreover, regardless of the contract the War Department issues to a corporation, the underlying profit motive inherent to the entire war industry remains footloose and dominant. The underlying profiteering, to which we draw attention throughout this book, must be addressed if any real change or progress is to be made.

MULTIFARIOUS FUNDING / INCESSANT PURCHASING

Funds used to pay for industry goods and services are raised from U.S. taxpayers or from newly issued government debt. The Pentagon has dozens of funding buckets to use when paying for industry goods and services. These funds, supported by the government's own statutory documentation, allow incessant purchase from industry.

On many occasions, the funds match the type of industry project. For example, the Department of War has used "joint improvised explosive device defeat funds" to purchase technology to disable improvised explosive devices (IED), used "air procurement funds" to acquire avionics for helicopter cockpits, and used "military construction funds" when renovating barracks. The remarkably named "warstopper funds" is more or less used for its intended purpose: to assess risks to the industrial base and/or invest in "critical warfighter capabilities," which can include essential safety items, items with limited shelf life, and items the demand of which might surge in wartime.[7]

However, frequently the funding type does not correspond to the good or service being purchased.

Overseas Contingency Operations (OCO) funds are regularly abused. Originally designed for emergency post-9.11 expenditures, OCO funds now serve as a catch-all to enable the purchase of a wide variety of war goods and services.[8] Corporate media, to the extent that they mention war, parrot the MIC claim that OCO funds are used for "extraordinary costs." OCO funds have become all-purpose monies, a flexible funding source satisfying corporate greed.

Operations & Maintenance (O&M) funds are also used to purchase many different goods and services. Sometimes the War Department uses O&M funds to purchase pertinent—that is, for operations or maintenance functions—goods and services. For example, the War Department has used O&M funds to purchase water distribution and wastewater collection from a utility provider and to purchase BOSS.[9] But O&M are also used when acquiring a variety of goods and services beyond operational, maintenance, or upkeep functions.[10] O&M funds serve one overriding purpose: supporting projects that perpetuate war and military infrastructure (at a time when peaceful, sustainable infrastructure is in the best interest of humans and planet).

Different types of funds engage foreign governments in U.S. industry production to arm and equip allied forces. *Armament cooperation project funds* have the effect of promoting standardization of industry products between the War Department and allied governments, thereby ensuring that purchasing, maintenance and tertiary development of U.S. products is locked in. The War Department uses its allies to share the burden of developing the products. *Building partnership capacity funds* get industry goods and services, including military training, into the hands of allied or allied-for-the-moment militaries. The Pentagon often invokes counter narcotics or counterterrorism when soliciting for and using BPC funds. *Afghan security forces funds* technically fall within the overall BPC program, though Afghan security forces funds have been allocated more frequently in public contracts than general BPC funds. *Counterterrorism partnership funds*, distinct from BPC, are to be used to build the capacity of a foreign military, national police, or border police to conduct what the Pentagon broadly deems "counterterrorism operations." These funds have been used in recent years to purchase surveillance aircraft (19 Sept 2014 for Kenya, Mauritania, and Niger; 28 Sept 2015 for Jordan; 21 Sept 2016 for Cameroon, Chad, and the Philippines) and boats for Naval Special Warfare (2 June 2017). *National Defense Authorization Act Section 2282 funds* have supplemented the Pentagon's authority to build up foreign forces. NDAA Section 2282 funds were used on 9 May 2016 and 21 September 2016, for example—neither contract acquired in free and open competition—when equipping and distributing surveillance aircraft to allied forces in Africa (Chad, Cameroon, and Niger) and Asia (the Philippines). Lastly, under 22 U.S. Code 2795, *special defense acquisition funds* (SDAFs) help purchase goods and services for allied governments and organizations. In recent years, SDAFs have been spent on kits that convert rockets to laser-guided weapons, kits that convert bombs to laser-guided weapons, torpedo parts, bomb fuses, and encrypted communications. SDAFs are supposed to focus on the War on Drugs. It is unclear how torpedo technology aids the War on Drugs. All of the aforementioned funds arm allied forces with goods and services from U.S. industry. Subject to congressional whims, these funding authorities could be shuffled or repealed.

What other types of funding exist? Below is a random selection of funds that the Pentagon has used recently. The most obscure funds come with an explanation.

- aircraft procurement funds
- ammunition procurement funds
- base realignment and closure funds
- consolidated sustainment activity group funds—*focus on maintaining and supplying spare parts*
- cooperative threat reduction funds[11]
- defense health program funds
- defense working capital funds
- family housing operation and maintenance funds
- major range & test facility base funds
- military construction funds
- National Guard and Reserve equipment appropriation funds
- non-U.S. Department of Defense participant funds—*sustain foreign participation in the F-35 program*
- Office of Secretary of Defense funds
- omnibus funds
- other customer funds

- other procurement funds
- Pentagon Reservation maintenance revolving funds
- psychological health / traumatic brain injury funds
- research, development, test and evaluation (RDT&E) funds[12]
- shipbuilding and conversion funds
- space procurement funds
- spectrum relocation special funds
- transportation working capital funds (TWCF)[13]
- weapons activities primary funds[14]
- wounded, Ill, & Injured funds[15]

The Pentagon can access funds from both the past and the future in order to pay for goods and services.[16]

Sometimes funds expire. Sometimes they don't.[17]

Pentagon funding supports industry satisfaction. On 24 July 2014, the War Department used a Miscellaneous Obligation Reimbursement Document (MORD) in support of operations & maintenance funds. A MORD "is a temporary obligating document or, in rare cases, a document in lieu of an actual obligating document. It is used to temporarily record known obligations or reimbursements when the required documents to support the… transactions are not immediately available."[18] Don't have your paperwork in order? No problem. Keep the money flowing by filling out a MORD, and you're good to go!

In a healthy society, the Department of War would not be able to access funds that lie outside its purview. However, since war is profit and we live in a militarized society of pliable laws under the enormous sway of martial authority, the Department of War has access to funds of other departments and agencies. NASA funding, for example, can abet Pentagon procurement.[19] On 6 November 2017, the Pentagon used Department of Homeland Security civil works appropriations funds to build a canine facility in Laurel, Maryland, a municipality home to many industry players. On 29 March 2018, the Pentagon used State Department economic support funds to repair a dam in Iraq. The Pentagon regularly taps into Federal Emergency Management Agency (FEMA) funds. On 29 March 2016, FEMA funds paid a corporation to furnish instructors and subject matter experts[20] and to develop courses at the Naval Postgraduate School in Monterey, California. No reason was given as to how this project has anything to do with FEMA's mission.[21] The Pentagon does not stay in its own funding lane.

The government has a long-standing policy requiring units of all sizes (e.g. squadron, group, wing in the Air Force) to spend their budgets by the end of the fiscal year. If units spend all of their money, they are typically allocated the same amount of money or more in the next budget appropriation. However, if they economize, find savings, or do more with less, they likely get their budget cut in the next appropriation. Going by different nicknames over the years, this policy does not incentivize fiscal responsibility in the U.S. Armed Forces.

WEASLING THE CONTRACTS

Think of the Federal Acquisition Regulation (FAR) as a rulebook that sets out the parameters by which the U.S. government can purchase goods and services. In practice, military and industry can use U.S. legal code and the FAR to keep contracts noncompetitive.

FAR subpart 6.302 codifies when the Pentagon can award a contract without full, open competition. FAR 6.302-1 indicates "full-and-open competition need not be provided for when the contractor is the sole responsible source that is able to satisfy agency requirements." Exemplary is a 30 May 2018 contract with General Dynamics' shipyard, issued noncompetitively in accordance with FAR 6.302-1: The "requirements may be deemed to be available only from the original source in the case of follow-on contracts for the continued provision of highly specialized requirements when it is likely that award to any other source would result in unacceptable delays in fulfilling the agency's requirement."

By far, the most common way to weasel—to issue contracts without full, open competition, that is—is to cite the combination of 10 U.S. Code 2304(c)(1) and FAR 6.302-1. Together, these two say there is "only one responsible source" and "no other supplies or services will satisfy" the requirements set forth by industry and the War Department. Therefore, according to this validation, the good or service must be acquired without competitive bidding. 2304(c)(1) and FAR 6.302-1 are used monthly on dozens of industry products. When contracts are issued without competition, this gives corporate pricing free rein, as there is no assurance that pricing has not been inflated.

Sometimes other excuses supplement U.S.C. 2304 and FAR 6.302-1, altogether hiding important details from the public.[22] There are times when 2304 and FAR 6.302-1 are used in ways recognizable as situations in which "only one responsible source" is genuinely needed and no other supplies or services could get the job done. 2304 and 6.302-1 are applied to all sorts of industry products, which could be supplied by more than one war corporation,[23] but the Pentagon doesn't try earnestly to make that happen. If the Pentagon actually wanted to, it could open up contracts to full and fair competition, which could drive down prices and save money.

Other parts of FAR 6.302 incite noncompetitive contracts.

FAR 6.302-2 allows for the contracting activity to cite "unusual and compelling urgency" to obtain a corporate good or service without competitive bidding.

The urgency and application of FAR 6.302-2 are flexible. In January 2017 a tornado blew through Marine Corps Logistics Base Albany, Georgia. On 27 March 2017, three months after the natural disaster, the War Department issued a noncompetitive contract using 6.302-2 "due to the unusual and compelling nature of the requirement stemming from the tornado damage MCLB Albany experienced."

FAR 6.302-3 is nominally used to maintain or boost industrial or research & development services within the U.S. war industry. Uses of FAR 6.302-3 span the gamut of goods and services, including R&D at Johns Hopkins University and Virginia Tech; geospatial predictive modeling; and costly ships packed with war industry goods.[24]

FAR 6.302-4 can be used to avoid competitive bidding when selling to foreign governments.[25] 10 U.S. Code 2304(c)(4) often supports such noncompetitive contracting processes with foreign governments. Since the cost for same is to be paid by those governments rather than the U.S., why not inflate—and obviate any transparency as to competitive costs?[26] The Department of War echoes and tweaks many Federal Acquisition Regulation stipulations in the Defense Federal Acquisition Regulation Supplement (DFARS). For example, DFARS 206.302-4 describes the rules governing the War Department's international agreements: Citing 10 U.S.C. 2304, "the justifications and approvals described in FAR 6.303 and 6.304 are not required if the head of the contracting activity prepares a document that describes the terms of an agreement or treaty or the written directions, such as a Letter of Offer and Acceptance, that have the effect of requiring the use of other than competitive procedures for the acquisition." It's that simple. Write it out and it be so.

FAR 6.302-5 can be seen as a catchall—a *because we say so* category. It allows for noncompetitive contracting when "a statute expressly authorizes that the acquisition be made from a specified source" or when the contracting activity needs a brand-name commercial item being resold.

The final two gems within this part of the Federal Acquisition Regulation are 6.302-6 and 6.302-7, which provide noncompetitive contracting when contracting officials write the magic words "national security" and "public interest," respectively.[27]

Sometimes multiple Federal Acquisition Regulations are used when justifying a single contract. On 27 September 2018, Syracuse Research Corp., a major not-for-profit research and development corporation, sold lightweight counter-mortar radar (LCMR) systems worth millions of dollars to the Department of War and unnamed foreign governments. When running properly, LCMR can determine the direction of incoming enemy fire and alert U.S. ground forces so they can return fire. The September contract was bid on without open competition. The Department of War justified this decision by invoking FAR 6.302-1 (only one responsible source, and no other supplies/services will satisfy the War Department's requirements), 6.302-4 (international agreement), and 6.302-6 ("national security").

Finally, you can get noncompetitive bidding or opaque contracting processes as long as you have a "unique and innovative concept,"[28] are working on a prototype,[29] or are a small business working on an R&D project of some use to the War Department. Contract types, funding types, and legalese favor industry. With these assets and mighty influence in D.C. (refer back to Chapter Two), corporations are able to rule the contracting process with the War Department.

War corporations use standard, industrywide contracting schemes. The first scheme is to **underestimate** the cost when pitching a product. Expenses accumulate, and the finished product costs way more than initially estimated. Corporations underestimate cost and overestimate performance as a matter of routine. The second scheme involves incorporating regular **upgrades** of software and hardware into the contract. That way, the war corporation remains involved indefinitely. Technicians service, maintain, and upgrade the product, all at great, corporate-determined expense. The third scheme is pushing for **noncompetitive** contracts. When the Pentagon solicits proposals using an open, competitive bidding process, corporations are competing to deliver decent services at the cheapest price. Many major contracts that are awarded through nominally open and free competition are not actually open or free; only a handful of corporations have the technology and the financial clout to place an honest bid. The fourth scheme is piling additional **modifications** onto a supposedly straightforward contract. Years into a contract with a war corporation, a lone Pentagon official might step back and marvel at how the provision of a simple good has metastasized into a ballooning multiyear project that incorporates disparate services and a variety of funding sources. The fifth and final scheme is the sale of **consumables**. Many products produced by war corporations ought to be repaired but are pushed as consumables instead. In other words: use it, discard it, and then buy a new product, instead of using the product and repairing it. In parallel, corporations require many goods sold as reparables to be returned to the corporation within a finite time for scheduled repair, regardless of whether the good actually needs to be repaired at that point. These collective schemes produce contract after contract caring for industry, not necessarily meeting military needs.

INCULPATING SMALL BUSINESS

Federal departments are encouraged to allocate nearly one quarter of their procurement funds to small businesses. The War Department dishes out more money to small businesses than any other government department or agency.[30]

The Department and corporations cite 10 U.S.C. 2304(c)(5), 15 U.S.C. 638, and FAR 6.302-5 in noncompetitive small business contracting. All sides of the MIC are bound symbiotically in the small business game: The Pentagon fast-tracks contracts and militarizes greater portions of the economy, industry gets noncompetitive contracts, and Congress spouts "jobs" rhetoric.

But small businesses are often not small. Small businesses can be quite big, including corporations with over $100 million in War Department deals or corporations with hundreds of employees.[31] Corporations have been known to hold on to Small Business classification even after they became larger than "small." Furthermore, a large corporation can use a smaller subsidiary to enable contracting as a small business, even though the parent company is a behemoth.[32] There are many categories of small businesses.[33]

The War Department and industry have called contracts "competitive" even though the contracts are small business set-asides—not fully open and fair competition. For example, a contract can be "competitively procured using full and open competition, after exclusion of sources in accordance with 10 U.S. Code 2304(b)(2). Set-asides for Small Business Concerns (FAR 6.203)." In other words, it is competitive within noncompetitive environs.

The War Department helps to grow small businesses of war. Large corporations can sign up for the Pentagon's Mentor Protégé Program through which they help small businesses financially and technically meet War Department goals. The small business gains valued guidance and experience, and the large corporation gains a partner for future teamwork and potential merger or acquisition. The Pentagon's Small Business Technology Transfer Program is the same, except it sees small businesses team up with universities, colleges, and research institutes to pursue military goals. The end result is more technology in the War Department's hands, or, in industry terms, "moving research to the marketplace."

Many categories of small business that facilitate noncompetitive bidding seem to exist for altruistic purposes as a means of affording government support—but inescapably their provisioning through the war industry leads to their possible cooptation and to expansion of the war industry's domestic footprint. One such category is the "disabled, veteran-owned small business." This category allows small businesses to get noncompetitive contracts on the merits that the owner of the business is a veteran and disabled. *Veteran* is anyone who has, for one reason or another—mostly economic or nationalist—"served" in uniform. Some veterans now bask in the glory that veteran-worship provides. Other veterans are appalled by war and the militarization of society. *Disabled* can be misleading. I injured my back working out in college. I re-injured it twice more when working out in the military. It was not disabling. It caused me a lot of pain, and then, with stretching and heat, the pain would gradually subside. When I was processing out of the military ("out-processing"), I was encouraged to apply for disability due to this injury. I was informed that it is customary to apply for disability benefits higher than what you think you deserve; it's up to the government bureaucracy to give you what it thinks you deserve. So, for example, if you believe you're only 30% disabled, you're encouraged to apply for higher—say, 60% disabled. Then, the military bureaucracy might give you 30%, 40%, or even more in disability compensation, benefitting you but screwing the taxpayer. I was appalled. "I'm not disabled," I said as the military official encouraged me to take twenty to fifty percent disabled. I did not apply for disability, though many others in the room did, after which they played a competitive game of basketball. I've talked with people who have out-processed different branches of the U.S. Armed Forces, and as far as we can tell the practice is rife across the military. Given the pliable misuse of the *disabled* designation, it is certain that some of the hundreds and hundreds of small businesses, which have received military funding, are abusing their status as "disabled, veteran-owned."

Both the War Department and war corporations boast of helping small businesses. All branches of the U.S. Armed Forces actively court small businesses. Each branch runs an Office of Small Business Programs. Smaller units of organization within the military have similar offices. Space & Naval Warfare Systems Center Pacific, for example, has an Office of Small Business Programs. For a taste of industry courtship of small business, look no further than A, B, C, and D: AAR, Boeing, CACI, and DynCorp. AAR worked with the Salem Baptist Church to fund minority-owned small businesses. Boeing received War Department honors for mentoring small businesses to join the ranks of the war industry. CACI established a Small Business Advocacy Office to achieve the same ends. And the State Department gave DynCorp an award for doing a good job signing up small businesses as subcontractors.[34]

Awarding numerous contracts annually to small businesses further militarizes the economy while shunning competitive bidding, trapping the country in the costly spiral of endless preparation and prosecution of war.

SEDUCING NATIVE AMERICANS

Military force was one of the tools D.C. and colonists used to rid North America of Natives. The military uses Native American tribal names when nicknaming its weaponry.[35] The U.S. Army does obtain permission from tribal authorities. Some of these authorities have thrown in the towel and embraced capitalism. The Pentagon targets Native American communities with recruiters; Native Americans enlist in the U.S. military at very high rates[36] due to a combination of factors—lack of job prospects, mass unemployment, and systemic marginalization of youth. U.S. federal intelligence agencies and corporations have violently, systematically stifled and dismantled Native-led protests against fossil fuel infrastructure being built on Native American land.[37] The war machine continues to harm Natives.

567 federally recognized tribes exist in what is now known as the United States. They follow diverse practices and economic projects. Many tribes have become part of the U.S. war industry. Willing capitalists within Native communities contract with the War Department. One should not shame tribes for acceding to the War Department's might; Native Americans have been brutalized and marginalized for centuries, and now suffer this fully compounded history in addition to living under the capitalist boot. Native corporations sell a variety of goods and services to the War Department, including aircraft and land vehicle maintenance, research and development assistance, contracting support, information technology, medical services, role players for military training, construction, pollution cleanup, supply chain support, and warehousing and distribution.[38]

Native corporations that are Section 8(a)—small businesses—can contract with the U.S. government without limit on the dollar amount of a sole-source contract (noncompetitive bidding). Tribal Governments, Native Hawaiian Organizations, and Alaskan Native Corporations[39] use profits from Section 8(a) contracting with the federal government to care for their respective communities.[40] Tikigaq, Chenega, and Chugach are the Pentagon's go-to Alaskan Native Corporations, while Cherokee is a favorite within the lower 48.

8(a) small businesses are supposed to have a relatively nominal net worth, but that stipulation is not strictly enforced; some 8(a) Native corporations have high net worth. Native corporations contracting with the Pentagon receive good profit margins because of the noncompetitive bidding process and because they can subcontract to other firms on the cheap, as is customary in capitalist circles. The tribes receive funding from the profits generated by selling services to the U.S. Armed Forces but don't have to be the ones actually providing the services, especially in specialized fields. Some 8(a) Native corporations hire a plurality or majority of non-Native employees for a given job. For example, on 25 July 2018, Chenega's offices in Lorton, Virginia, sold English instruction services to the Saudi military. Those who carried out the actual English language training to military forces in Dhahran, Saudi Arabia, were regular contractors looking to make a pretty penny, not specifically Natives, according to someone familiar with the program.

This has been a brief summary of the Native American contribution to the war industry. Why dive into this uncomfortable subject? It not only shines light on some of the Pentagon's operations, but it also shows how all sections of the U.S. population can be coerced or dragged into cooperation with D.C.'s policy of nonstop war, even those who've historically been the victims of such violence. The fact that today some Native tribal structures are part of the MIC is a wake-up call. Oppose war now, or you too will be working for imperial aims sooner or later.

THE (FAILED) AUDIT

The Defense Finance & Accounting Service is the Department of War's primary financial management arm. DFAS' operations show us how little the Pentagon cares for financial responsibility and transparency.

A 2013 *Reuters* investigation concluded that DFAS implements monthly "unsubstantiated change actions"—illegal, inaccurate "plugs"—that forcibly make War's books match Treasury's books:

> Fudging the accounts with false entries is standard operating procedure… Reuters has found that the Pentagon is largely incapable of keeping track of its vast stores of weapons, ammunition and other supplies; thus it continues to spend money on new supplies it doesn't need and on storing others long out of date. It has amassed a backlog of more than half a trillion dollars… [H]ow much of that money paid for actual goods and services delivered isn't known.[41]

DFAS cooks the books. The Pentagon's high-ranking officers and civilian leaders are complicit.[42]

This unconstitutional con has an added bonus: Because the public has no true idea of how much money the Pentagon is wasting, the Pentagon is able to ask Congress every year for more and more money, in brutal contempt of military efficiency and necessity.

Do not expect the Treasury Department to take the War Department to task.[43] (Likewise, do not expect the Labor Department to exert any morality on matters of war and peace.[44])

U.S. Congress passed the Chief Financial Officers Act in 1990. This Act directed all federal departments and agencies to submit to annual audits. The Pentagon has ignored this law year after year. Under Secretary Leon Panetta, a politician with outstanding public relations skills, the War Department agreed to undergo an audit. The audit was designed from the start so the Pentagon could *pretend* to get its great financial con in order.

The audit itself cost a lot. Why so costly? Corporate America saw the audit as yet another opportunity to sell goods and services. Billions had been spent on financial services before the audit even got up and running.[45] Corporate accounting firms then conducted the audit, with some guidance from officialdom, particularly DFAS. Financial firms—primarily the Big Four auditors (Deloitte & Touche, Ernst & Young, KPMG, PwC)—ruled the fiscal landscape from 2015 through fiscal year 2018.

Deloitte & Touche LLP regularly sold reconciliation and financial support services to DFAS.[46] Even just days before the audit was due, Deloitte sold audit services for the Defense Security Cooperation Agency (DSCA) and other War agencies. DSCA helps sell industry products to foreign governments and sponsors U.S. military relationships with foreign militaries. A nod to the incestuous nature of the war industry, Deloitte & Touche has also audited such war corporations as General Dynamics and Vectrus.

Ernst & Young LLP regularly sold to the War Department.[47] Ernst & Young is also a lobbying firm for the U.S. war industry, including titans like AT&T. In general, Ernst & Young lobbies for industries it audits,[48] and bestows awards upon corporations profiting from war.[49] Such gluttonous, fevered conflicts of interest inherent to the Pentagon's audit are vast.

KPMG LLP sold audit and financial management services across the War Department.[50] KPMG also provides audit services to war corporations such as General Dynamics.[51] KPMG officials (e.g. Michael Wood, a KPMG official who became a Raytheon executive) have moved on to war corporations. KPMG is also a major campaign contributor to the Democrats and Republicans. And the profits of war circle round. For what it's worth, the Financial Reporting Council, a U.K. government watchdog, considers KPMG's work to be poor.[52]

PricewaterhouseCoopers, known as PwC, sold audit services across the board—from U.S. War Department units still occupying Japan and South Korea, to the Defense Health Agency, to the Pentagon comptroller.[53] PwC also lobbies for industry.[54] As PwC was auditing the Pentagon, the war industry powerhouse Veritas Capital acquired PwC's U.S. public sector business for an undisclosed price.[55] Congress and the Pentagon didn't even blink. Over the years, Veritas has acquired and dealt war corporations. For example, in the summer before the 9.11 attacks, Veritas purchased pieces of Raytheon and another war corporation (and soon blended the two into a corporation that it turned around and sold to L3[56]). Alion Science & Technology and Vencore are two current Veritas assets that regularly sell goods and services to the War Department.[57] A testament to the military focus of its investments, Veritas recently hired the former chief financial officer of Constellis,[58] which is famous for its armed mercenary activities.

The Big Four auditors—Deloitte & Touche, Ernst & Young, KPMG, PwC—operate out of offices in northeast Virginia and D.C. That is war industry territory.

Sometimes corporations were hired in groups to work on the audit.[59]

A wide variety of corporate interests dove into the audit.[60]

Overall, roughly 1,200 auditors visited over 900 sites at 600 distinct locations, and covered about "$2.7 trillion in assets and $2.6 trillion in liabilities for fiscal year 2018."[61] Those figures give some understanding about the size of the beast, especially when one considers the fact that the auditors skipped most of the Department of War's property. Pentagon comptroller David Norquist, who announced the results of the audit on 14 November 2018, claimed the audit covered all assets (tanks, aircraft, vehicles, ships, computers, bases, depots, etc.) that the Department of War owned. This was misleading. Far fewer than a million pieces of physical military inventory were actually counted. And instead of performing an independent, unbiased accounting, corporate auditors mostly set forth to confirm the Pentagon's existing tallies and appraisals.

This is worth repeating: Auditors didn't review every asset. They didn't even come close. They reviewed what they deemed were "statistically significant samples" in order to present decision-makers with a polished, generalized idea of the Pentagon's possessions. And some of these samples were not statistically significant in the traditional, mathematical sense of the phrase. Most acreage was not covered. Many sites were not visited. Most matériel was not enumerated. Moreover, the audit did not tackle many funding types that pay for wars and corporate goods and services. It mostly tackled broad or generic funding sources, such as working capital funds and the U.S. Air Force general fund.

The Pentagon did not pass its audit.[62] Five units got a clean slate, the equivalent of a passing grade. All the rest failed.[63] Failures included Grant Thornton's audit of Special Operations Command's ledgers.[64] Some Pentagon officials tried to spin the audit by saying that the Pentagon had learned from the proceedings and was already taking steps to address the situation. According to one Pentagon scribe, "Auditors did not find any evidence of fraud, nor did they report any problems for civilian or military pay. And all of the services were able to account for the existence and completeness of all major military equipment."[65] Auditors didn't find any evidence of fraud in a system inherently fraudulent, wasteful, and abusive? Such a conclusion speaks to the collaborative nature of the military-industrial sides of the military-industrial-congressional triangle.

Investigative journalist Dave Lindorff described this miserable situation well: The accounting firms eventually concluded that the War Department's "financial records were riddled with so many bookkeeping deficiencies, irregularities, and errors that a reliable audit was simply impossible."[66] You might say the War Department cheated and still didn't pass. Others might argue it never even tried to pass because its bureaucrats knew there was no accountability coming from the Beltway. (Deputy Secretary of War Patrick Shanahan famously said, "We failed the audit, but we never expected to pass it."[67]) It gets worse.

Shortly after the end of fiscal year 2018, the U.S. government made it legal to cook the books.[68] Around the same time, David Norquist—the man who as the Pentagon's comptroller oversaw the entire audit process—got promoted to Deputy Secretary of War.[69] Norquist is a former partner of Kearney & Co., one of the firms that conducted the audit. After the audit's dust had settled, the Department of War continued purchasing accounting services from big business.[70] All was normal in profit and war.

OFFICES AND ADMINISTRATION

Bureaucratic nooks and crannies provide opportunities for corporate profit. And corporations jostling for elbowroom create more nooks and crannies within which to extract profit. Corporations staff the offices of every large military unit. Systems commands are the primary large bureaucratic divisions in the U.S. Navy. Corporations have had great success assuming dominion across large swaths of systems commands.[71] Unified combatant commands are broad units of control organized based on function (e.g. Special Operations Command, Transportation Command) or geographical jurisdiction (e.g. Africa Command, Southern Command). Corporations work on program management, business processes, planning and analysis, policy recommendations, and acquisition in these commands. Instead of military officers and senior enlisted staff running the show, a corporation is tasked with carrying out basic functions. If high-ranking officials cannot handle paperwork or manage programs, what good are they? That issue does not concern the corporation, which profits from the neoliberal push for privatization and incompetent or apathetic military leadership.

The Pentagon has undergone remarkable corporate growth within its bureaucracy since 2001. Sundry undersecretaries and assistant secretaries residing within the Pentagon, from the Under Secretary of War for Personnel & Readiness to the Under Secretary of War for Policy, exemplify this phenomenon.[72] The case of PE Systems (Fairfax, VA) shows how corporations gobble up minutiae. On 24 November 2015, PE Systems was allocated millions to provide units within the Secretary of the Air Force with expertise, information, and advice, IT tools, training, services, and analyses and evaluations. PE Systems was tasked to focus on many areas that should be taken care of by uniformed troops, including paperwork, looking after workforce numbers, and supervising the acquisition process. Other fields that PE Systems was tasked with, such as "legislative analysis" and "export compliance support," are ripe for graft and conflicts of interest. In a world without corporate greed, the Armed Forces' Secretaries would do their own paperwork.

Understanding how the military and industry operate, exploit and wrangle the legal code, and dance around genuine accountability is crucial to creating an educated population capable of upending the paradigm of endless war. But beware. Manipulating the U.S. legal code is an advantage the MIC will not relinquish willingly.

ENSURING LEGAL IMPUNITY

U.S. law is written for and manipulated by those in authority. Far from constraining war corporations, legal code abets profiteering and military action. And when the law happens to get in the way, the MIC ignores it.[73]

Despite overwhelming evidence that justice does not reach the super-rich and those in authority,[74] war corporations assure us they are scrupulous in following the law. One executive claimed, "Just one or two violations could cause us to be suspended from government contracts. That would destroy our company."[75] Yet the track record of corporations' misdeeds is lengthy. Regular transgressions include overcharging for goods and services and billing the Pentagon for hours not worked. Fines usually amount to a fraction of the overall possible graft. Millions in fines are paid yearly. The fines levied[76] are not prohibitively expensive for multi-billion-dollar corporations. The cases of Lockheed Martin and Raytheon are illustrative. A Lockheed Martin subsidiary, the Sandia Corporation, operated Sandia National Laboratory (SNL) in Albuquerque, New Mexico. SNL develops parts for nuclear weapons. Sandia Corp. settled with the U.S. government (for $4.79 million) over allegations "that it illegally used taxpayer money to lobby for an extension of its management contract," according to the Center for Public Integrity.[77] Sandia Corp. wanted to pay the settlement and legal costs from its direct federal contract revenues. The Justice Department cautioned Sandia against using such revenues to pay for the settlement and legal costs. Shrugging off the Justice Department,[78] the corporation paid its nominal fine using overpriced performance bonuses that it arguably shouldn't have received in the first place. Accused of numerous violations of U.S. export control laws, Raytheon settled with the U.S. government and admitted no wrongdoing.[79] Half of Raytheon's measly $8 million fine was "suspended," i.e. not enforced, on the condition that Raytheon would "use the money for government-approved remedial compliance measures, including increased training and oversight," according to *Reuters*.[80] Industry giants accept a routine slap on the wrist and continue on their way. Paying fines keeps the game going.[81]

Lawyers adept at climbing the D.C. ladder craft the legalese supporting nonstop war. Nathan A. Sales helped draft the USA PATRIOT Act, which took away privacy and civil liberties from the U.S. public. Sales later led the State

Department's Bureau of Counterterrorism. William Wechsler helped craft legalese in the Treasury Department facilitating today's sanctions against anyone who pushes back against the D.C. regime or Israeli hegemony. David Barron and Martin Lederman issued the legal opinion used to justify the murder by corporate missile of Anwar al-Awlaqi, a U.S. citizen and Muslim preacher whom the MIC hyped as an "al-Qaeda leader." Russell Travers, a lawyer with no hands-on counterterrorism experience whatsoever, has guided the National Counterterrorism Center as deputy director. Brian Hook is the career lawyer who currently holds the title U.S. Special Representative for Iran. With no formal training in Iranian history or the Farsi language, he's in charge of crafting the legal justifications that cripple Iran.

Legalese of all shapes and sizes aids military-industry priorities. On the government side, raise the dollar amount where a contract is automatically audited—from $15 million to $250 million—because you're struggling with a backlog.[82] Legal. Shuffle papers and get a few signatures to use the military's special operations forces on a CIA assassination mission.[83] Legal. Characterize a failed ballistic missile test as a "success."[84] Legal. Invoke sovereign immunity in order to dodge lawsuits[85] after industry ordnance poisoned Puerto Rico. Legal. Utilize sundry tactics, techniques, and procedures to enshrine wastefulness and financial fraud.[86] Legal. On the corporate side, transfer sensitive military technology to the despotic House of Saud—technology that can help boost manufacture of advanced ordnance.[87] Legal. Sell products that perform poorly but get plenty of money. Legal. Buy up pristine wilderness, raze the trees, build on the land, pave the rest, sell the whole tract for money. Legal. Rape Colombian girls and women while you get paid a ton to help implement the devastating Plan Colombia. No problem. You're protected under diplomatic immunity.[88] From relatively straightforward contracting trickery to matters of rape and death, the legal system effectively protects and cushions government and industry.

Other actors within or adjacent to the MIC manipulate, massage, and exploit the legal code. If you are a corrupt foreign regime, it is perfectly legal for you to bribe U.S. Congress.[89] The law helps think tanks mask their donors, including war corporations and foreign regimes,[90] tilting Beltway discourse in a more pro-war direction. (Speaking of the Saudi regime and legalese, in July 2018, the Saudi King issued a degree lifting "all military and disciplinary penalties" for Saudi troops and mercenaries fighting in Yemen, in what *The New York Times* called "an apparent amnesty for possible war crimes."[91]) If you are a lobbying firm like The Cohen Group working for the war industry, you too work the legal system to your advantage, often by lobbying War leadership.[92] If you are a public relations official and you write an industry report on a corporation's website, you just cite the Safe Harbor Statement Under the Private Securities Litigation Reform Act of 1995 to cover your behind.[93] If you are a think tank that takes lots of money from the U.S. war industry, you slip a little disclaimer into your publications in order to protect yourself.[94] D.C.'s legalese has fabricated a bizarro world where up is down. Torture is not torture. It's enhanced interrogation. War is not war. It's hostilities. Justice is not served, and peace is nowhere to be seen. Legalese sustains and perpetuates the war on terror—"the vague war on a moving target that has resulted in the ruin of entire countries and the loss of millions of innocent lives since 2001."[95]

Directives, legal opinions, and classified memoranda establish and guide D.C.'s prosecution of nonstop war. The White House Office of Legal Counsel, the Justice Department's Office of Legal Counsel, and CIA's Office of General Counsel are the primary craft breweries of such immoral legal manipulation. An interlocking blend of D.C. officials, war industry personnel, and espionage agencies uses legalese to draw up kill lists for murdering people around the world.[96] Journalists worry they've been put on these kill lists that target accused terrorists using drone strikes.[97] The courts aid and abet, rejecting lawsuits in recent years brought on behalf of Abdulrahman al-Awlaqi and his father Anwar,[98] both of whom were killed by U.S. industry ordnance overseas. CIA legal teams use the law to shield the Agency from legal redress.[99] Lawyers working with the Bush, Obama, and Trump administrations crafted Presidential Policy Guidance governing the use of force and declare entire regions "areas of active hostilities" in order to legitimize the use of weapons of war, particularly General Atomics MQ-9 drones and Boeing/Lockheed Martin missiles, to kill people. The Presidential Policy Guidance permits murder when military forces are unable to capture the suspected enemy—but U.S. military and paramilitary forces make no effort to try to capture suspects. Cleverly, the term "area of active hostilities" has no foundation in domestic or international law. U.S. lawyers just made it up. And when U.S. lawyers don't have the time or inclination to use the "area of active hostilities" excuse, they just issue classified directives[100] or fall back on the 2001 Authorization for Use of Military Force (AUMF), which was for use against al-Qaeda. In 2017, Acting Assistant Secretary of State Charles Faulkner, formerly a Raytheon lobbyist and one-time employee of a firm registered as an agent of the Saudi government, helped the White House broadly cite the 2001 AUMF as a legal authority to engage in war (not formally declared) across the Middle East, including military intervention in Syria.[101] D.C. lawyers are modern-day alchemists, turning countries into battlegrounds.

Intelligence personnel from U.S. government and war corporations hide beneath the "sources and methods" shell. If, for example, you pick fruit with your family in Somalia, Joint Special Operations Command (JSOC) or CIA can kill you from above, just by claiming that you are part of a "terrorist" group called al-Shabaab. If you harvest pine nuts with your friends in Afghanistan, JSOC or CIA can kill you from above, claiming you are part of a "terrorist" group called the Taliban. Government officials will tell journalists, "There are robust procedures in place to avoid civilian casualties." (These robust procedures involve flying aircraft over the scene of the airstrike.) That's all they'll say. Why? U.S. intelligence personnel cowardly hide behind what they claim to be "sources and methods," instead of admitting they have killed innocents: "We do not comment on intelligence, surveillance, or reconnaissance sources and methods." Remember this. Whenever armed U.S. bureaucracies are in a bind, they fall back on "sources and methods."

The war corporations that pressure Capitol Hill and sell the weaponry causing the death and bloodshed are never held accountable.

D.C. uses legalese to sell more weapons. By law, the U.S. government is not allowed to sell weapons to regimes that come to power through coups d'état. So, in 2013 when General Abdel Fattah as-Sisi took control of the Egyptian government in a coup, D.C. simply didn't recognize it as a coup. Problem solved. War industry lawyers have been known to craft the fine print on weapons contracts so that the U.S. government is contractually obligated to sell to recipient nations, regardless of circumstances. In 2018, legal advisers added the word "intentional" to a clause in the existing Conventional Arms Transfer policy,[102] deliberately loosening already slack rules regarding weapon sales. D.C. could block weapon sales if nations that purchase weaponry from the U.S. war industry do not follow the laws of armed conflict. D.C. just ignores this stipulation. No law, writ, or paper obstacle gets in the way. Selling weaponry to the UAE, Apartheid Israel, Saudi Arabia, and other regimes committing war crimes and human rights abuses has been as easy as pie. Similarly, spending billions to "upgrade" U.S. nuclear weapons and deploying such weapons to NATO countries (all signatories of the Nuclear Non-Proliferation Treaty) is a violation of international law. But law doesn't constrain D.C. When all else fails, U.S. academics and think tanks cite the laws of war *jus ad bellum* and *jus in bello* to provide a licit patina—another way for those with the time, money, and inclination to fudge the record in favor of the conqueror.

Perhaps no entity manipulates legalese with greater efficiency and proficiency than the corporatized agency that penetrates and spies on electronic communications: the National Security Agency. Government lawyers write the United States Signals Intelligence Directives (USSID), which provide the legal foundation for NSA's operations. NSA cites Section 702 of the Foreign Intelligence Surveillance Act (FISA) to support invasive espionage against the U.S. public.[103] NSA's Office of General Counsel reinterprets existing rules in order to spy on U.S. phone numbers.[104] NSA invokes the "state secrets privilege" to hide information from the courts.¹⁰⁵ An NSA spokesperson insists that NSA "conducts its foreign signals intelligence mission under the legal authorities established by Congress and is bound by both policy and law to protect U.S. persons' privacy and civil liberties."¹⁰⁶ This legal maneuvering is persistent and formidable. An NSA spokesperson said NSA could "neither confirm nor deny its role in alleged classified intelligence activities."¹⁰⁷ Legalized silence.

Terminology is important. Careful manipulation of legal terms benefits military and civilian intelligence agencies. For example, NSA legal teams have assigned very specific definitions to the following terms: *acquire, citizen, collect, foreign, known, monitor, obtain, person, retrieve, search,* and *target*. When a member of Congress asks questions to the director of NSA during a committee meeting or hearing, the director will utilize precise terminology to respond evasively while the import of his answer seems to comply with civil liberties. This way the director is not lying or committing perjury. *Do you target American communications, sir? No, Senator, NSA does not target American communications.* It's that simple. The director of NSA does not volunteer information that NSA *collects* the communications of U.S. citizens and residents. The director does not volunteer other information that the public should know, particularly how NSA personnel (including corporate contractors) can focus in on a U.S. person's communications based on *reasonable suspicion* instead of the more stringent *probable cause,* or how NSA has a "two-hop" arrangement for surveilling certain persons, citizens, and residents of interest—basically allowing the concordant monitoring of people in two degrees of separation from the person targeted.¹⁰⁸ On the rare occasions that a member of Congress asks a pointed question, a director just lies. In March 2013, Director of National Intelligence James Clapper infamously perjured himself during a congressional committee meeting,¹⁰⁹ but has yet to face any repercussions. Certain individuals of high enough rank within the D.C. regime are, for the time being, immune from prosecution.¹¹⁰

NSA comforts the masses by saying it is not allowed to collect the U.S. public's communications beyond aggregating metadata. The FBI, however, is allowed to do so. But the FBI doesn't have the communications infrastructure to target the masses. So how does the FBI pull it off? NSA monitors U.S. citizens and residents *on behalf of* the FBI. The U.S. government just asserts, on paper, that the FBI is the lead agency, *et voilà,* the might of NSA is directed inward.¹¹¹ NSA public relations assure us: "[O]ne of the biggest misconceptions about NSA is that we are unlawfully listening in on, or reading emails of, U.S. citizens. This is simply not the case."¹¹² Correct. For the most part, NSA's activities are lawful. Immoral, egregious, invasive—and lawful.

The waiver is the consummate legal maneuver. It is the ace up the sleeve and the sword of Attila, all in one.

Say the Pentagon wants to set up a base in the Persian Gulf. The undemocratic regime ruling an Arab country is happy to host U.S. forces, but it wants written assurances that the Pentagon will not use its vast technological superiority to spy on the country. The two parties formally agree, and the War Department establishes its base in the Gulf country. Billions of dollars of industry goods are set up in the country, and billions more flow through the base. Here's the catch: U.S. military-intelligence spies on everyone. How does the Pentagon bypass its formal written agreements with the Gulf country? It just gives itself a waiver, I learned while in uniform. No kidding. In legalese, the Pentagon says it can spy electronically on the Gulf country.

The waiver system also harms the U.S. military. Understanding languages should be essential to the prosecution of global war, yet the *vast majority* of U.S. personnel who work in military-intelligence don't grasp a second language—close to ninety-nine percent according to figures I saw when in uniform. (Most U.S. personnel who work in military-intelligence work in areas such as IT or analysis. Even CIA case officers, the top of civilian intelligence, are often so feeble in foreign languages that they require a Language Officer to accompany them.) The majority of military linguists who studied a Category Four language have no mastery of their language.[113] So what does the military-intelligence bureaucracy do? It issues waivers for these linguists and uses them anyway. It's no wonder that U.S. signals intelligence leads to so many civilian deaths across D.C.'s warzones.

Trying to stop D.C.'s manipulation of the U.S. legal code is like trying to stop professional all-stars from playing basketball by challenging them to a game of basketball. You're playing on their court, by their terms, and are up against their very best. If you use religion or conscience as your guide and engage in direct action against weapons of war, the judge will not allow you to explain your actions fully in court.[114] If you speak to the press about the atrocities abroad that CIA and the War Department carry out in the name of the United States, the D.C. regime will use the Espionage Act of 1917 (which was designed to punish dissidents during World War I) against you.[115] If you publish information damaging to the U.S. oligarchy, including evidence of war crimes and bipartisan corruption, D.C. will use its legal apparatus to get you,[116] while those who ordered and committed the crimes remain free. Journalist Barrett Brown describes the D.C. regime's motivations: "They want an expanded legal toolkit… They understand now that this is a fast-evolving discipline… this sort of unconventional publishing, unconventional journalism, aggressive investigation. [The expanded legal toolkit] is absolutely something they need to have, from their standpoint."[117] D.C.'s legalese will not save you. The U.S. legal code is not there to help you, and it will not protect you in instances where justice and morality are on your side but the U.S. government is not. The 2001 USA PATRIOT Act is the standard bearer.[118]

Remember, war profiteering is legal in the United States. Corporations work with the best lawyers on planet Earth in order to craft and influence the legal system in favor of war and profiteering.

Legalese is the ultimate weapon.

PROPAGANDIZING RECRUITMENT

It is perfectly legal for the war industry to propagandize the U.S. public, convincing them to join and stay in the Armed Forces. The War Department itself does not create such propaganda (e.g. TV ads, social media campaigns, recruitment strategies). The War Department hires Corporate America to do so. This costs a lot.[119] The essence of recruitment and retention is this: corporations receive government money (U.S. tax dollars + money raised from Treasury issuing debt) to persuade and condition the public to venerate or join the military.

The New York City corporation Omnicom Group owns GSD&M (Austin, TX). Many hipsters and liberals work at GSD&M in Austin. It's a strange place. And not the good kind of strange (like "keep Austin weird"). We're talking the bad kind of strange (like "buy into corporate culture and brainwash the masses while sipping a perfectly-poured IPA"). In recent years GSD&M has produced military advertising for national television and social media, online banner ads, and public events.[120] Most of GSD&M's work is for the U.S. Air Force,[121] but other military branches are featured in the ads. Goods and services from war corporations are also found in live-action ads: from Lockheed Martin F-22 jets to Raytheon missiles, from Rockwell Collins headgear to military uniforms produced in Puerto Rican factories, from Boeing bombs to General Atomics drones. It's all there.

Corporations work hard to produce forceful recruitment tools, like thirty-second commercials airing during popular sporting events, attracting a demographic already ripe from years of consumerism, corporate media, and Hollywood bombardment. Consider a commercial released in 2017:[122] Fresh U.S. Air Force basic training graduates march across a field, eyes right. "Every one of us starts out as a wide-eyed recruit, myself included," a strong, reassuring voice tells us as we look at a framed picture of a proud young man. A fighter jet piloted by a wingman banks left, away from our cockpit. A commando parachutes, freefall, from the back of a cargo aircraft, as the voice informs us, "If I could go back, I'd tell that kid, 'Get ready.'" Soldiers and airmen train in urban terrain. A female airman sprints towards a fire truck. In full gear, fire protection troops put out a ferocious blaze. "You're gonna serve alongside some amazing people." Airmen play basketball together near the flight line. They congratulate one another after a long game. In a dark room, a female sergeant assists a male officer, together analyzing information. "They're going to become like family to you." A Northrop

Grumman B-2 bomber cuts through the sky over inhospitable terrain. A pilot in a pressurized suit checks the displays. "And together, you'll see and do things that will help change the world." A proud smile gains traction on the face of a female military training instructor as her trainees march in the haze. "That'll change you." Amid smoke and chaos, a calm airman in combat gear looks up into his partner's eyes. A pilot walks down the flight line, a successful sortie behind him. "One day, you're gonna look up and be a better you." The pristine U.S. flag flaps against blue skies. A pilot wearing a sleek visor speeds along the desert floor. Combat aircraft perform intricate aerial maneuvers. "And this nation will be better for it, too." A 4-star general looks up, framed by brilliant Old Glory in the rafters. Rows of diverse airmen stand before a state-of-the-art aircraft. The general introduces himself. "Come join us." Security personnel patrol the hangar. "Your nation is waiting." AIM HIGH, bold letters instruct us. In thirty seconds, an advertising firm packed alluring imagery, notes of prestige, pokes at your insecurities and the drudgery of daily life, while hinting at possible material wealth, and affirming allusions of belonging.[123]

MullenLowe, based in Boston, Massachusetts, is honest about the extent to which it targets human emotion.[124] The firm has worked with Joint Advertising Market Research & Studies (JAMRS), a program running a database containing detailed information about youth and potential recruits living in the U.S. so the Pentagon can augment recruiting efforts. Fors Marsh Group conducts surveys and market research, leveraging the results to sway the U.S. public toward enlistment.[125] The idea that a community might control its own destiny, let alone its data, is considered heretical within the Pentagon's corporate walls, since the word "freedom" exists only within the confines of advertising, marketing, and military operation—realms that continually relegate most people to consumption, passivity, and spectatorship. This deliberation and confinement takes place in reinforcing and overlapping contexts of economic and social inequality, in which surveillance capital (largely Silicon Valley firms, operating in coordination with the Pentagon—a circular support group of sorts) collects your data in order to know almost everything about you.[126]

The remaining corporate division of labor among the military branches is clear.[127] One firm, DDB Chicago Inc. (Chicago, IL), boasts, "Our ideas are big and powerful enough to create consumer enthusiasm about the brand and ultimately build our clients' business."[128] Yes. That's why you were hired. Altogether these corporations sustain war by enticing youth to enlist.[129] Most recruits don't become cannon fodder, but they do become vessels for corporate goods and services.

Multiple corporations often work together on a single contract. On 23 February 2017, for example, the U.S. Navy contracted five firms: three war corporations (Alion, Booz Allen Hamilton, and CSRA, which is now part of General

Dynamics), in addition to the PR firm kglobal and the media production firm, Media Fusion. These five got to work on such fields as communication, information, environment management and training; communication integration and strategy; community outreach, media relations, public affairs, professional and community development; public information materials development and production; and visual information systems and imagery marketing.[130] On 3 August 2018, the Navy gave another five corporations duties loaded with conflicts of interest, such as assessing & supervising manpower levels; managing financial programs; forecasting & assessing performance; leading strategic assessments & plans; and evaluating & managing policies and programs pertaining to personnel, training, and education. In other words, profit-driven corporations help determine the direction, strategy, and outward appearance of an entity the ultimate concern of which is preparing for and prosecuting (profitable) war. Notably, each corporation in the second set of five has sold goods and services in other sectors of war.

Corporate interests go anywhere, covering most angles.[131]

Recruiting requires substantial physical infrastructure: construction at recruiting depots in Illinois, South Carolina, and California; bullet-resisting paneling for recruiting stations on the mainland and overseas colonies; and furniture for recruiting offices, for example.[132] Construction on Guard and Reserve units in recent years has spanned the country.[133] This is part of the overall process (military recruitment run by industry) that ensures enough bodies are available to fill out MIC objectives. Corporations building this Guard and Reserve infrastructure are located across the country, from Massachusetts to California. In addition to recruiting men and women to put on the military uniform, Corporate America is in charge of refining methods of selection and training: Aptima Inc. (Arlington, VA) measures trainee performance for the Army and Navy, while KBRWyle (Houston, TX) tries to improve selection, training, and retention of enlisted airmen. General Electric researches technologies to track biological processes (genetic, metabolomic) that influence cognitive, physical, and behavioral qualities, with the aim of improving the troops' performance during training through deployment.[134] Across the board, Corporate America is in charge, providing no incentive to arrest or conclude the wars.

This brief summary reflects just what has been made available publicly in daily contract announcements. It does not reflect off-the-books or covert propaganda campaigns against the global public. Investigative journalism has brought a few propaganda operations to light. Psychological operations (PSYOPS) is a propaganda subdiscipline. In recent years, parts of the War Department had PSYOPS units intern at CNN and NPR,[135] paid professional sports teams to display traditionally patriotic ceremonies,[136] and targeted U.S. officials to sway their opinions on matters of war and peace.[137] These operations could not have occurred without the tangential, infrastructural, or direct support of war corporations. In Iraq alone, the U.S. military and a corporation wrote news articles and placed them in Iraqi media as the objective accounts of journalists, and British firms received hundreds of millions of dollars to produce dark content.[138] The important takeaway is this: Corporations run much of today's war propaganda. Activities include manipulating media (print, online, and TV), bolstering the credibility of local allies, and working to spread narratives that dissuade armed resistance. Corporations are often allowed to grade their own performance, relying heavily on volume, not effectiveness. Billions of U.S. dollars have been sacrificed in recent years. The Pentagon has dramatically increased its spending on influencing public opinion.[139]

"This is nothing new," you say. "Capitalists spread advertisements in order to get more people to buy their product. Nothing new." Dig deeper. Industrial capitalism, avaricious as it is, requires modern advertising in order to sustain its needs;[140] military recruitment and advertising are a direct response to the needs of the MIC. Capitalist propaganda in the form of advertisements metastasizes. Remember the boards around a professional ice hockey rink in the 1980s? Clean. Now look at them. Packed with corporate logos and slogans. War corporations (e.g. Boeing, Leidos, Red River) even grace the boards at Washington Capitals' home games. Remember when a corporation didn't sponsor every pause, intermission, break, goal camera, and television segment? Remember when professional sports teams didn't sell advertising space on players' jerseys (e.g. Chevy on Manchester United)? Remember when your go-to video-sharing website didn't cram an advertisement (sometimes two) at the beginning and end of every clip? Remember when a TV show didn't have corporate logos and advertisements squirming in the corners? Remember when corporations (selling cars, insurance, soft drinks, beer, etc.) didn't exploit the U.S. Armed Forces in order to sell a product? Remember when billboards didn't climb the sides of buildings? By design, the trend grows. Now take a moment to stand up and stretch, sponsored by your friendly neighborhood war corporation. War corporations colonize every possible space with advertisements and product placement.

The War Department relies on a strong stable of corporations to advertise, propagandize, explain, recruit, and retain. Given the corporatization of the Pentagon and its subsidiary organizations and agencies, U.S. corporations are now performing multiple roles: (1) promoting themselves as corporations; (2) pursuing the Pentagon's designs inside the United States and in warzones abroad; (3) informing the public about curated perspective through a variety of media; and (4) ensuring that plenty of people continue to enlist in the U.S. Armed Forces to become vessels for corporate goods and services. These lines blur and fade over time until the corporatized Pentagon exists simply to exist, in the process destroying country after country, no end in sight. All abetted by U.S. law.

ENDNOTES

1 One need only examine the first 5 duty days of Dec 2018 to see the diversity of cost-plus projects on which corporations work. These established projects do not reach the threshold of risk that would justify cost-plus contracts, yet they receive cost-plus funding. They include maintenance of submarines and surface ships; fighter jet parts and engineering; ship weapon systems; parts for the Aegis weapon system; simulation for Army and Marine training; and nuclear propulsion for navy boats. Some contracts issued the first week of Dec 2018, such as academic institutions demonstrating small satellite engineering and DARPA missile studies, are indeed R&D deals reaching the acceptable level of risk for cost-plus funding.

2 A spokesperson for the Defense Contract Audit Agency says large firm-fixed price contracts are most prone to "excess profits" wherein corporations are jacking up prices, reported Tony Capaccio (*Bloomberg*, 14 September 2019).

3 It is even common to see a contract or contract modification issued as firm-fixed-price *and* cost-plus-fixed-fee, negating some potential savings while allowing government officials to pass tales of thrift up the chain of command.

4 Arrangements include but are not limited to single award, IDIQ contract; IDIQ cost-plus-fixed-fee contract; IDIQ cost-plus-fixed-fee, multiple-award contract; IDIQ contract with firm-fixed-price, cost-plus-fixed-fee, and cost provisions; IDIQ contract with firm-fixed-price, time-and-materials, cost-plus-fixed-fee, and cost reimbursable line items; multiple award IDIQ contract (MAIDIQ); single-award IDIQ, firm-fixed–price, and cost reimbursable contract.

5 The 67 transactions logged during Dec 2018 pertaining to IDIQ contracts totaled over $18,379,900,000. This is a conservative estimate. Transactions covered fruit, clothing, petrol-based lubricants, targeting pods for aircraft, GPS satellite sustainment, privatized real estate services, special operation helicopter upgrades, signals intelligence training, and Silicon Valley R&D. Some of these goods and services were sales to foreign governments.

6 In my analysis spanning 2014-18, IDIQ contracts were issued for diverse projects: BOSS in the U.S. and in Singapore; IT communications support; Defense Security Service administrative & business support; document destruction & menial labor; hardware & software development; environmental services at U.S. bases in Europe; financial management; hand-held radios; oversight of military exchange students; mobile stations that integrate different streaming video & data; R&D on thermal power; satellite hosting services; ship maintenance; aircraft radar; supply chain management & equipment services; support of an anti-ballistic missile system; transducers; and worldwide work on counter-WMD activities.

7 Warstopper funds were only used for fuel and medical supplies in the 2.5 years I sampled. I included aviation fuel and transportation of fuel. Medical supplies included pharmaceuticals and medical equipment. Relevant contracts issued 4 May 2015, 11 June 2015, 2 Sept 2015, 17 Dec 2015, 1 July 2016, 12 Dec 2016, 26 June 2017, 31 Aug 2017, 22 Sept 2017, 28 Sept 2017, 29 Sept 2017, 3 Nov 2017, 17 Jan 2018. I saw no clear evidence in these contracts of studying risks to the industrial base.

8 On 7 February 2017, the *Congressional Research Service* ("Overseas Contingency Operations Funding: Background and Status") explained that procedural limits on discretionary spending in congressional budget resolutions do not apply to OCO funds. Definitions of what constitutes OCO shift and are flexible, so the Pentagon is able to spend OCO funds on anything, ranging from big corporate undertakings, like Northrop Grumman airborne countermeasures (29 June 2017) and aircraft that relay communications (22 May 2017), to smaller services, like dental care (28 Sept 2017) and audiovisual equipment (29 Sept 2017). Other uses of OCO funding in recent years include nursing (1 May & 14 June 2018), moving cargo in Iraq (1 Aug 2017), and KBR prepositioning matériel (5 April 2018).

9 Relevant contracts issued 6 June 2018 and 17 May 2018.

10 O&M were allocated during 2018 to the following corporate goods and services: IT software for the Defense Health Agency (1 June), IT and cyber support (26 June), financial assistance for the Dept.'s chief financial officer (25 May), ship repair (10 May), ship engine repair (23 May), aircraft helping the Navy practice engaging enemy planes (17 May), basically running the National Space Defense Center at Schriever AFB in Colorado Springs (28 June), production and upkeep of ballistic missiles (16 May) that threaten life on Earth, upgrading aircraft countermeasures (8 June), educational services for kids of Dept. personnel (29 June), satellite communications infrastructure (17 May). Hundreds of other allocations of O&M funding occurred.

11 Per 50 U.S.C. 48, cooperative threat reduction funds are supposed to be used for counter-proliferation, particularly in the former Soviet Union and China. The interpretation of what constitutes "threat reduction" is strictly military and adversarial. These funds are explicitly not to be used for peacekeeping, elimination of conventional weaponry, or conversion of war industry to peaceful industry.

12 Some funds—like O&M and RDT&E funds—can be "defense-wide": many contracting activities across the four branches of the Armed Forces can tap into the funds to pay for industry products. For example, construction contracts issued on 13 Sept 2018 used defense-wide military construction funds for construction (Naval Special Warfare facilities in Coronado, CA, and building a small arms testing & evaluation center at Joint Expeditionary Base Little Creek-Fort Story, VA). Some RDT&E funds are specified further as hailing from certain offices. For example, on 17 Dec 2018, ongoing development of a Raytheon glide bomb, capable of striking a target from great distances, was paid for using RDT&E (Strategic Capabilities Office) funds.

13 Funds are often bundled together in order to pay for a specific good or service. An example of this is from 30 Sept 2016, when the following funds were used to pay for transportation services: Groups Operational Passenger System TWCF operations; operations and maintenance; TWCF capital; TWCF information technology operations; and RDT&E.

14 Issued 24 April 2018, for building a National Nuclear Security Administration Complex in Albuquerque, NM. The project broke ground that July. U.S. senators and representatives attended the ceremony. NNSA chief Lisa Gordon-Hagerty said the Complex would "modernize" Cold War-era infrastructure.

15 From summer 2014 to summer 2018, WII funds were allocated only on medical-related projects. I have seen no indication that these funds were misallocated during this timeframe.

16 On 10 Dec 2018 the Army bought modulating valves from Honeywell using working capital funds that date to the year 2023. On 1 March 2019 the Defense Logistics Agency allocated O&M funds that date to the year 2069 for electricity at Keesler AFB, MS. This is not time travel. It's just the War Dept. banking on having access to future funding. Similarly, a contracting activity in the War Dept. can use old funding. This was seen on 15 March 2019 when the U.S. Army Corps of Engineers used military construction funds from 2016 to pay for construction in Kuwait that is to take place during 2019-21.

17 The Financial Management Regulation known as DOD 70000.14-R, lays out how to use expired funds for "antecedent liabilities or liabilities that arise under the terms of the original contract." It helps if the original contract cited FAR 52.216-16, which allows the price revision at a later date, as long as the cumulative final contract price does not exceed the contract ceiling price. Got that?

18 "The MORD should be reversed when the actual document becomes available," per "Air Force Materiel Command Instruction 20-102," <static.e-publishing.af.mil/production/1/afmc/publication/afmci20-102/afmci20-102.pdf>.

Financials and Legalese 119

19 The Pentagon regularly uses the National Aeronautics & Space Administration (NASA) "Solutions Enterprise Wide Procurement" website to acquire industry goods and services. Examples from 2017 include 18 Sept, 29 Sept, 25 Oct, and 11 Dec. Goods and services acquired included servers, Oracle licensing, and laptops that use Microsoft Windows.

20 Industry provision of subject matter experts (SME) is profitable and problematic: There is no commonly accepted standard within the U.S. war industry for awarding the title *subject matter expert* to personnel. For example, I've come across an Air Force technical sergeant who is a subject matter expert on an area of the world he's never set foot in, an area whose population speaks a dialect he does not understand. Expertise, as found in so-called subject matter experts, can include rookie naïveté, cultural illiteracy, and self-assured ignorance. Subject matter experts can be in any field. Popular fields where SME frolic are maintenance, IT, and transportation. SME are often administrative in nature (e.g. SME for a financial management system or for the Office of the Under Secretary of War for Policy to help set up an oversight body). Sometimes SME are relatively harmless (e.g. aiding Military Sealift Command logistics or U.S. Army Corps of Engineers energy projects). SME can be more aggressive: SME for cyberspace operations and network systems; military training; support of Special Operations Command; communications and network infrastructure, including within overseas bases and warzones; missile systems in the UAE; and testing how to shoot down ballistic missiles. Whether indirectly or directly belligerent, corporate SME lack uniform, concrete standards of quality. Relevant SME contracts issued 23 Sept 2014, 2015 (31 July, 8 Sept, 18 Sept, 29 Sept, 13 Oct), 2016 (8 March, 22 March, 29 March, 28 June, 29 June, 9 Aug, 15 Aug, 25 Aug), 2017 (28 Feb, 15 March, 27 April, 5 May, 18 Sept, 29 Sept, 1 Nov), 2018 (26 April, 2 July, 17 July, 14 Sept, 21 Sept).

21 The FEMA funds were allocated under the Stafford Act, a federal law whose stated intent is to help people recover from natural disasters. FEMA's mission statement, per <fema.gov>, is "Helping people before, during, and after disasters."

22 For example, on 24 June 2016 Boeing's subsidiary, Insitu, was allocated millions in O&M funds to provide drone services to Special Operations Command. "Justification and approval (J&A) number 16-842 was signed on March 16, 2016. The redacted J&A will be posted to Federal Business Opportunities in accordance with FAR 6.305." Gratuitous redactions cloud democracy, one might say. J&A is the primary document the Pentagon uses when excusing noncompetitive contracts. It helps to have someone in authority sign off on your noncompetitive bidding while citing opaque J&A. A research & analyses contract on 21 March 2016, for example, was not procured with fair and open bidding. The Office of Naval Research cited J&A numbers 14-15, "approved by Assistant Secretary of the Navy (Research Development & Acquisition) on Aug. 26, 2015," under request for proposal. That Assistant Secretary of the Navy was Sean Stackley, a man who has touched all three sides of the MIC: A former Navy officer who worked his way up through the Senate Armed Services Committee, Stackley worked as an Assistant Secretary of the Navy before joining L3 as a senior vice president.

23 Examples of relevant industry products—just from August 2018—that could be supplied by more than one corporation include air conditioners for certain landing craft; display units, electric components, and windows for military vehicles; engine parts; heat exchangers for aircraft; night vision technology; processors used on transport aircraft; parts for and repair of tiltrotor aircraft; binocular displays; research & data collection on ways to measure student performance for the Naval Surface Warfare Center; rocket propelled grenade netting kits for armored vehicles; software for Marine Corps System Command; spare parts for Boeing F/A-18 and P-8A aircraft; and helicopter yoke assemblies and rotary wing blades.

24 Costly ships include littoral combat ships and Arleigh Burke-class destroyers. Relevant contracts: 15 Feb 2013, 26 Aug 2013, 14 June 2016, 18 Sept 2018, 27 Sept 2018.

25 6.302-4 invokes the terms of an international agreement or treaty between the U.S. and an allied government or invokes the "written directions of a foreign government reimbursing the agency" for the good or service. Examples of 6.302-4 being used to avoid competitive bidding on international deals include maintenance and repair of Australia's Lockheed Martin MH-60R helicopters (12 Dec 2012, 15 Sept 2016); maintenance and repair of Iraqi ships (24 April 2017); maintenance on Kuwait's Boeing F/A-18 aircraft (30 May 2017) and instructing Kuwait how to operate KC-130J aircraft and simulators (19 March 2014); and Raytheon's Seasparrow missile (developed with nine NATO nations, including the Netherlands and Germany) used on Navy ships (24 Aug 2018). FAR 5.202 (a)(3) can have a similar effect. A 20 May 2016 contract wherein Northrop Grumman helped arm the Saudi regime was not competitively procured, citing FAR 5.202 (a)(3), used when foreign government is going to reimburse the U.S. contracting agency for the cost of the product *or* an international agreement / treaty between D.C. and a foreign government "has the effect of requiring that the acquisition shall be from specified sources." In other words, if you're dealing with a foreign government, and you feel like it, feel free to make it a noncompetitive contract.

26 An example of 10 U.S.C. 2304(c)(4) is a 29 June 2018 contract, which disclosed that Northrop Grumman was working on parts of the Lockheed Martin Trident II submarine-launched ballistic missile. The contract modification was justified, in part, using (c)(4) and citing an international agreement: the 1963 Polaris Sales Agreement between the U.K. and U.S. London and D.C. had amended this agreement in the 1980s in order to justify sales of the Trident II missile to London. BAE Systems makes the U.K. submarines (the Vanguard class from the 1990s and the upcoming Dreadnought class) that hold the Trident II. As of spring 2016, an upgrade to the Trident in the U.K. was expected to cost £205 billion, according to the anti-war coalition Stop the War (Kate Hudson, 12 May 2016).

27 Written out in its entirety: -6) Full and open competition need not be provided for when the disclosure of the agency's needs would compromise the national security unless the agency is permitted to limit the number of sources from which it solicits bids or proposals. -7) Full and open competition need not be provided for when the agency head determines that it is not in the public interest in the particular acquisition concerned.

28 In accordance with FAR 6.302-1(a) (2)(i)(A) and DFARS 206.302-1. A corporation is exempt from full & open competition when the "source has demonstrated a unique and innovative concept."

29 10 U.S. Code §2371b is used to justify noncompetitive contracts when developing a prototype.

30 In 1982 U.S. Congress passed the Small Business Innovation Development Act. The Pentagon has cited U.S. Public Law 106-554, which the 106th Congress enacted in the year 2000 reauthorizing and revamping the 1982 Act. The Small Business Innovation Research (SBIR) program arose as a result of the 1982 Act. Under SBIR, the federal government issues grants and loans to small businesses.

31 See Larry Makinson's reporting ("Outsourcing the Pentagon." *Center for Public Integrity*. 29 September 2004). Makinson sampled FY1998-2003.

32 Giant war corporations have claimed their smaller divisions or subsidiaries are stand-alone small businesses. For example, on 14 June 2018, numerous small businesses were awarded their share of an ultimately $7.5 billion contract to supply the Defense Information Systems Agency with systems engineering and technology. Among the corporations awarded were BAE Systems, Booz Allen Hamilton, Leidos, Northrop Grumman, and Parsons. These are not small businesses.

33 You've got small business, woman-owned small business, small disadvantaged business, disadvantaged woman-owned small business, and disadvantaged woman-owned small business in a historically underutilized business zone. Likewise, you've got veteran-owned small business,

disadvantaged veteran-owned small business, service-disabled veteran-owned small business, and service-disabled veteran-owned woman-owned small business operating in a historically underutilized business zone.

34 "Aerospace CEO Creates $500,000 Venture Capital Fund for Minority Small Businesses." *AAR*. 21 November 2013. "Boeing Recognized for Successful Small Business Mentorship." *Boeing*. 16 March 2015. "CACI Small Business Advocacy Office." *CACI*. Accessed 20 March 2019. "DynCorp International Wins Department of State Prime Contractor Subcontract Award." *DynCorp International*. Last updated 9 April 2013.

35 War products included Boeing Apache helicopter; Boeing Chinook helicopter; Boeing-Sikorsky Comanche helicopter (which cost around $7 billion in R&D before being cancelled); Lockheed Martin (Sikorsky) Black Hawk helicopter; MD Helicopter Cayuse (and its Ute variant) helicopter; Raytheon Tomahawk cruise missile; Sikorsky Choctaw helicopter; Textron (Beechcraft) Huron surveillance airplane; Textron (Bell) Iroquois "Huey" helicopter; and Textron (Bell) Kiowa helicopter. One ought to consider all the military unit patches featuring problematic or even racist imagery.

36 Sebastian Junger's *Tribe* explains, "American Indians, proportionally, provide more soldiers to America's wars than any other demographic in the country" (p. 118). See also "American Indian and Alaska Native Servicemembers and Veterans." *Department of Veterans Affairs*. September 2012: <www.va.gov/TRIBALGOVERNMENT/docs/AIAN_Report_FINAL_v2_7.pdf>.

37 Brown, Alleen, Will Parrish, and Alice Speri. "Leaked documents reveal counterterrorism tactics used at standing rock to 'defeat pipeline insurgencies.'" *The Intercept*. 27 November 2017. "Mercenary firm providing security at DAPL Protest did covert ops for Blackwater." *Telesur*. 31 October 2016. "TigerSwan Security, Linked to Blackwater, Now Coordinates Intel for Dakota Access." *DemocracyNow*. 21 November 2016.

38 Relevant Native contracts: 2014 (29 Aug, 26 Sept), 2015 (1 April, 14 May, 24 June, 22 July, 25 Sept, 28 Oct), 2016 (29 Jan, 10 Feb, 30 June, 19 Aug, 6 Sept, 7 Oct, 1 Dec, 22 Dec), 2017 (10 Feb, 15 May, 7 Sept, 27 Sept, 28 Sept, 29 Sept, 3 Oct), 2018 (20 Feb, 6 April, 17 April, 1 May, 5 June, 2 July).

39 Tribal leaders signed the Alaska Native Claims Settlement Act of 1971. The Alaskan Native people as a whole did not vote on the Act or the previsions contained within. D.C. conceded titles to millions of acres of land, some monetary compensation, and acknowledgement of Alaskan Natives' aboriginal ancestry. Native leaders agreed not to pursue reparations and/or any unresolved territorial claims. The Act created corporations to manage Alaskan Native operations, effectively shoehorning Alaskan Native wellbeing into the corporate realm while binding Native prosperity to D.C.'s needs.

40 Some differences: Tribal Governments can provide governmental services (e.g. public works, some law enforcement, some healthcare and education allotment) to the respective community, but ANCs must instead divvy out contracting profits to ANC stakeholders (typically via supplementary income, land stewardship, academic scholarships, and donations to local non-profits). In any case, Natives' prosperity is bound to D.C.'s contracting largess.

41 Paltrow, Scot J. "The Pentagon's doctored ledgers conceal epic waste." *Reuters*. 18 November 2013. Plugs are illegal per the Antideficiency Act. "Former military service officials say record-keeping at the operational level throughout the services is rife with made-up numbers to cover lost or missing information."

42 Dave Lindorff ("Exclusive: The Pentagon's Massive Accounting Fraud Exposed." *The Nation*. 27 November 2018) noted that though the Pentagon inspector general knew and acknowledged DFAS was falsifying financial statements on a grand scale, the inspector general did not push for punishment of DFAS personnel. This could only happen with the top tier of military leadership approving tacitly or

formally of the financial fraud and the IG's neglect. Scot Paltrow (*Reuters*, 18 November 2013) came to a similar conclusion: "The secretary of defense's office and the heads of the military and DFAS have for years knowingly signed off on false entries..." It is my experience that high-ranking officers and civilians—under the assumption that their vast coteries and support staff have covered all the bases—perfunctorily sign off on items that cross their desks.

43 The War Dept. "is continuing to take steps to strengthen its financial reporting. ... We're supportive of those efforts and will continue to work with DOD as they make additional progress," a Treasury spokesperson said, quoted *Reuters* (Paltrow, 18 November 2013). Treasury also aids MIC and Zionist maneuvers by sanctioning and separating from their funds people who chart their own strong, independent foreign policy (e.g. Iran) or defy Zionist rule of the eastern Mediterranean (Hezbollah).

44 The U.S. Department of Labor has aided, for example, Lockheed Martin's exploitation and propagandization of the working classes, approving the war corporation's National Standards of Apprenticeship, thereby "establishing a common framework for the company to develop and expand registered apprenticeship programs across its U.S. facilities." "U.S. Department Of Labor Approves Lockheed Martin National Standards Of Apprenticeship." *Lockheed Martin*. 13 November 2018. The Department of Labor has also granted Raytheon's operations at White Sands Missile Range, NM, the highest level of achievement in employee health and safety (the pollution and toxins that come from missile production and testing were not factored in Labor's assessment). "U.S. Department of Labor's OSHA recognizes Raytheon Mission Capability and Verification Center for safety and health achievement." *U.S. Department of Labor*. Release No. OSHA-09-1110-DAL. 2 December 2009.

45 Before the audit kicked off, the Pentagon "spent tens of billions of dollars to upgrade to new, more efficient technology in order to become audit-ready. But many of these new systems have failed, either unable to perform all the jobs they were meant to do or scrapped altogether—only adding to the waste they were meant to stop," according to *Reuters* (Paltrow, 18 November 2013). No matter which way you turned, industry was there. When think tanks and industry analysts circulated news that the audit would fail because the War Department was using a snarl of mismatched, disparate, and outdated accounting systems, the war industry said, *Great! We have a solution for that*. And the war industry went on to market more business management systems and personnel.

46 Deloitte & Touche is a U.K. firm, but the offices handling the Pentagon are based in Virginia. Relevant contracts: 29 Sept 2016, 15 Sept 2017, 17 April 2018, 25 May 2018, 27 Sept 2018. The 17 April 2018 contract was worth $800 million.

47 2017 and 2018 were big years for the firm. It made millions auditing the Army, Navy, and Air Force, and Defense Logistics Agency. Relevant contracts: 2017 (11 July, 7 Sept, 25 Oct, 27 Dec, 28 Dec), 21 Sept 2018. Audit work on U.S. Army and the Pentagon's Office of Inspector General were issued, for example, 4 Nov 2015, 2016 (27 Jan, 23 Dec, 13 May, 23 Dec).

48 Aubin, Dena, et al. "Exclusive: Ernst & Young tightropes between audit, advocacy." *Reuters*. 9 March 2012.

49 Ernst & Young gave its 2012 "Entrepreneur of the Year" award to AAR's chairman of the board, David Storch. In a particularly crude example, Ernst & Young bestowed a "corporate social responsibility" award upon Green Beans Coffee (the corporation that employs third-country nationals when selling expensive coffee and pastries to U.S. troops and mercenaries on military bases in the Persian Gulf, Djibouti, Afghanistan, and Iraq). Green Beans Coffee is owned by Elevate Gourmet Brands (San Rafael, CA) as of this writing. Since Sept 2001, Green Beans Coffee's "growth rate has exceeded an astonishing 1,400 percent," *National Public Radio* reported (Raz, Guy. "U.S. Contractors in Iraq Rely on Third-World Labor." 10 October 2007).

50 The beginning of FY2015 was a strong quarter for KPMG sales to the War Dept. They sold audit services on 29 Oct, 31 Oct, 1 Dec, 4 Dec 2014. Other contracts issued 18 Nov 2015, 27 Jan 2016, 15 Dec 2016, 22 Aug 2017, 29 Dec 2017, 9 Feb 2018.

51 "Management's Report on Internal Control Over Financial Reporting." *General Dynamics Annual Report 2017*, p. 81.

52 "KPMG's audit work unacceptable, says watchdog." *BBC News*. 18 June 2018.

53 Relevant contracts: 12 May 2016, 26 May 2017, 29 March 2018, 16 May 2018, 28 July 2015, 31 July 2015, 18 Dec 2015.

54 "PwC collected $1.8 million from 11 lobbying clients in 2011. Most of them were trade associations and industry coalitions." Aubin, Dena, et al. "Exclusive: Ernst & Young tightropes between audit, advocacy." *Reuters*. 9 March 2012.

55 Wilkers, Ross. "Veritas closes deal for PwC U.S. public sector arm." *Washington Technology*. 1 May 2018. Veritas already had a stable of war corporations (assets under management), including Peraton (from Harris' IT division) and DXC Technology.

56 "L-3 To Buy Vertex for $650 Million." *Bloomberg*. 23 October 2003.

57 Alion has sold unmanned underwater vehicle technology, business support, engineering, R&D, and C4ISR support services. Vencore has sold IT products, many different cyber programs, data collection services, R&D of defenses against distributed denial of service attacks, and machine-learning R&D on the energy-grid. Vencore works regularly for DARPA and AFRL.

58 The CFO, Deborah Ricci, had also worked for A-T Solutions (now owned by PAE) and Centerra. Around the same time, Tim Reardon became the new Constellis CEO. He had been a high-ranking official at Lockheed Martin and then a president at Leidos.

59 4 corporations sold "audit finding remediation support" on 22 Aug 2017: RMA Associates led Ernst & Young, Kearney & Co., and KPMG. Later, Deloitte and KPMG sold—up to $980 million on 21 Dec 2017—financial improvement and audit readiness.

60 Such war corporations as Accenture and Booz Allen Hamilton sold to the Navy. Kforce Government Solutions sold to the Defense Threat Reduction Agency, an agency in charge of monitoring and countering chemical, biological, radiological, nuclear, and high explosive weaponry. (In addition to financial services, KGS has sold a variety of products to the U.S. government in recent years, including hospital equipment, C4ISR engineering support, and medical training devices.) Seneca Solutions, a Native small business, sold financial & accounting services. Cotton & Co., Kearney & Co., and Grant Thornton helped audit the War Dept. Small tech firms sold business activity monitoring services and cost assessment. All of these corporations contracted through their offices in northeast Virginia. Relevant contracts: 9 Sept 2014, 3 Dec 2014, 30 March 2015, 30 April 2015, 20 April 2015, 29 Feb 2016, 29 April 2016, 23 Sept 2016, 26 Sept 2016, 6 Feb 2017, 30 May 2017, 6 July 2017, 22 Aug 2017, 15 Dec 2017, 19 Dec 2017, 8 May 2018, 16 Aug 2018, 21 Aug 2018, 17 Sept 2018, 18 Oct 2018.

61 Vergun, David. "The Biggest Audit in Human History ... Really?" *U.S. Department of Defense*. 16 November 2018.

62 Cancian, Mark. "The DOD Audit: No Pot Of Gold At The End Of That Rainbow." *Forbes*. 19 November 2018.

63 The few that received a passing grade, an "unmodified opinion" in pentagonese, were the Defense Contract Audit Agency; the Defense Finance & Accounting Services, Working Capital Funds; the Defense Health Agency, Contract Resource Management; the Military Retirement Fund; and the U.S. Army Corps of Engineers, Civil Works.

64 Grant Thornton couldn't issue an audit opinion because "USSOCOM management was unable to provide sufficient appropriate audit evidence to conclude that the financial statements taken as a

whole are free of material misstatements." Full criticism available at "FY 2018 USSOCOM Financial Statement Reporting Package." *U.S. Special Operations Command.* 30 Sept 2018: <www.socom.mil/Documents/FY2018_USSOCOM_Financial_Statement_Reporting_Package_UNCLASSIFIED.pdf>, p. 47.

65 Vergun, David. "The Biggest Audit in Human History ... Really?" *U.S. Department of Defense.*

66 Lindorff, Dave. "Exclusive: The Pentagon's Massive Accounting Fraud Exposed."

67 Lindorff, Dave. "Exclusive: The Pentagon's Massive Accounting Fraud Exposed."

68 Journalist Matt Taibbi (*Rolling Stone*, 16 January 2019) explains how the Federal Accounting Standards Advisory Board (FASAB) legalized classified war and military intelligence spending: "The new guidance, 'SFFAS 56—CLASSIFIED ACTIVITIES' permits government agencies to 'modify' public financial statements and move expenditures from one line item to another. It also expressly allows federal agencies to refrain from telling taxpayers if and when public financial statements have been altered." Dave Lindorff contextualizes the new guideline in *The Nation* on 27 November 2018.

69 Mehta, Aaron. "Pentagon comptroller to serve as acting deputy defense secretary." *Defense News.* 2 January 2019.

70 Issued 6 Nov 2018, 30 Nov 2018, 13 Dec 2018, 19 Dec 2018, 30 Dec 2018, 21 Dec 2018, 29 Jan 2018. Corporations included CACI, KPMG, Kearney & Co., Ernst & Young, and Diligent Consulting (San Antonio, TX). The pentagonese in the latter's contract is stunning: Diligent Consulting will work to "better align capabilities with user needs by realigning the fielding strategy to match the needs of individual units through the use of agile methods, and incorporate two financial processes necessary to be compliant with Financial Improvement and Audit Readiness and the Federal Information System Controls Audit Manual."

71 Consider a few corporations in Naval Air Systems Command: StraCon Services Group (Fort Worth, TX) leads strategic planning and evaluation of administrative systems and military activities for Program Executive Offices, Total Logistics (Manassas, VA) helps manage Industrial & Logistics Management Planning / Sustainment Department, and Integri (Tampa, FL) has supported the corporate business office.

72 Examples include but certainly are not limited to Concurrent Technologies Corp. (Johnstown, PA) running and managing portions of the Under Secretary of War for Personnel & Readiness; Strategic Analysis Inc. (Arlington, VA) guiding research and engineering objectives within sundry offices under the Assistant Secretaries of War; and E3 Federal Solutions (McLean, VA) covering over three dozen "separate offices headed by senior level individuals" within the Office of the Under Secretary of War for Policy. E3 has also sold analytical and administrative services for the Office of the Under Secretary of War for Acquisition, Technology, and Logistics. Pertinent contracts: 19 July 2018, 26 July 2018, 13 Sept 2018, 26 March 2018, 6 Feb 2018, 25 April 2018, 23 May 2018, 11 Aug 2016, 21 July 2017, 19 July 2018, 5 Sept 2017. On 30 April 2019, the Institute for Defense Analysis (Alexandria, VA) was contracted to support the Office of the Secretary of War Joint Staff, combatant commands, and agencies. Support included research, analyses, technical evaluation, and test & evaluation involving "comprehensive evaluation of national security issues, including systems and technologies at all stages of development, deployment, and use." Such contracts are common occurrences. Corporations have also overrun Washington Headquarters Services, the Pentagon's primary stand-alone unit focused on administrative activities.

73 Examples of ignored laws include the Kellogg-Briand Pact of 27 August 1928, an international agreement which barred armed conflict as a way of settling disputes, and the War Powers Act of 1973, which stipulates that U.S. troops can only be deployed into combat when U.S. Congress

declares war. U.S. Congress has willingly ignored its obligation under the War Powers Act during ever-expanding post-9.11 global war.

74 White-collar criminologist Bill Black has noted that today's widespread corporate criminality stems from (1) egregious executive compensation packages, (2) limited liability companies permitting great flexibility and corporate authority, and (3) a lack of willingness in D.C. to prosecute white-collar crime. White-collar criminal behavior is not punished with any consistency, substance, or sting. Not one Wall Street official went to jail for crashing the global economy in 2008-9. The only person who went to jail was Bernie Madoff, because he stole from the super-wealthy. Wall Street firms received windfalls in 2009, per "Wall Street Doled $20B in Bonuses in 2009" [*CBS News*, 23 February 2010]. Journalist Matt Taibbi has noted that the sub-prime mortgage plot was an effort to pull the remaining savings out of the U.S. working class. The most war corporations will ever see are fines and lenient, soft penalties levied. War criminality and profiteering are not touched.

75 Gorman, Siobhan. "Little-known contractor has close ties with staff of NSA." *Baltimore Sun*. 29 January 2006. The executive was talking about hiring individuals who recently worked in government.

76 E.g. penalties & fines: "Key Trends in POGO's Revamped Contractor Misconduct Database." *Project on Government Oversight*. 12 November 2015; Fang, Lee. "Contractors that defraud the government the most also spent the most on lobbying." *The Intercept*. 13 November 2015; Hartung, William "Tools of Influence: The Arms Lobby and the Super Committee." *Center for International Policy*. 31 October 2011; Esterbrook, John. "Halliburton To Pay Pentagon $6.3M." *CBS News*. 23 January 2004; Mehta, Aaron. "Department of Justice forces $30M from Northrop for fraudulent costs." *Defense News*. 3 November 2018; "Defense Contractor Agrees to Pay $4.63 Million to Settle Overcharging Allegations." *U.S. Department of Justice*. 28 September 2015; Vine, David. "Contractors Raked in $385 Billion on Overseas Bases." *Mother Jones*. 14 May 2013.

77 Malone, Patrick. "Lockheed Martin Nuclear Subsidiary Fined for Paying Lobbyists with Federal Funds." *Center for Public Integrity*. 24 August 2015: <time.com/4007950/nuclear-weapon-sandia-lockheed/>.

78 "The amount represents 8 percent of the bonus payments Sandia Corporation received while the lobbying effort was under way, according to federal contract records," the *Center for Public Integrity* reports (Malone, 24 August 2015).

79 Shalal-Esa, Andrea. "Raytheon to pay fine for U.S. export control violations." *Reuters*. 30 April 2013.

80 Raytheon PR officials said the corporation would continue to work with the U.S. State Department "to achieve its goal of full compliance and industry-leading practices." Some of Raytheon's violations were related to mishandling or improper oversight of classified material. *Reuters* concludes: "Last year, United Technologies Corp, another large U.S. exporter, agreed to pay $75 million in fines for export violations, including the sale of software later used by China to develop its first modern military attack helicopter." Shalal-Esa, Andrea. "Raytheon to pay fine for U.S. export control violations." 30 April 2013.

81 But, one might argue, the very act of fining war corporations is proof that the U.S. government is in charge and taking action. Right? No. At the end of the day, the U.S. war industry gets what it wants: war. With the deck stacked in its favor, the war industry writes some legislation pertaining to "defense" and "national security." Lobbyists, armed with drafts of legislation written by corporate legal teams, meet with congressional aides and hash out the finer points of whatever bill is in question. The larger legal code is ultimately crafted or approved by the very politicians the war industry owns. The executives running war corporations are happy to keep paying relatively nominal fines as long as the racket of war continues.

82 The Defense Contract Audit Agency "raised to $250 million from $15 million the threshold value at which a contract is automatically audited." DCAA justified this by saying it's now mostly concentrating on the bigger contracts where serious money can be recouped. "Still, hundreds of thousands of contracts that would eventually have been audited now won't be," reported Scot J. Paltrow (*Reuters*, 18 November 2013).

83 D.C. wanted to conduct combat operations inside Pakistan. Pakistani President Pervez Musharraf opposed this. CIA proposed a legal solution: "In order to get special-operations troops inside Pakistan, they would simply be turned over to the CIA and operate under Title 50 covert-action authority. Special-operations troops would be 'sheep-dipped'—the SEALs would become spies." Special operations forces were then legally able to operate in Pakistan, and D.C. wouldn't have to tell Musharraf. The same legal trick was used in the raid on OBL's compound in Abbottabad. Mazzetti, Mark. *The Way of the Knife* (New York: Penguin Press, 2013, pp. 133, 287).

84 Willman, David. "A flawed missile defense system generates $2 billion in bonuses for Boeing." *LA Times*. 2 September 2016. In another instance, MDA apparently altered very the criteria needed to pass a missile test. An MDA spokesperson prevaricated: "In recent contract terms, the words 'hit-to-kill' have been changed to support the more detailed documented objectives of each respective flight test. For intercept flight tests conducted under the current design and sustainment contract, a successful intercept remains a key performance objective." An MDA spokesperson defended paying Boeing billions for the shoddy Ground-based Midcourse Defense system: Boeing had "earned" such payment "based on the criteria specified in the contract." And MDA was merely complying "with all appropriate acquisition regulations." A Boeing spokesperson said the corporation "has met contractual requirements and a variety of incentives across a wide range of program objectives."

85 Natasha Bannan, associate counsel at LatinoJustice PRLDEF, notes that the U.S. military often operates under the notion of sovereign immunity, a legal doctrine that protects the U.S. federal government from lawsuits or other legal challenges. "This was why a district court and then the U.S. Court of Appeals for the First Circuit dismissed Sanchez et al. v. United States, a case filed against the U.S. in 2007 by more than 7,000 Vieques residents. The Supreme Court declined to hear the case in 2013," reported Valeria Pelet ("Puerto Rico's Invisible Health Crisis." *The Atlantic*. 3 September 2016).

86 Courtesy of journalists Matt Taibbi (*Rolling Stone*, 16 January 2019) and Dave Lindorff (*The Nation*, 27 November 2018), we know that the U.S. government has made it legal to cook the books. This legalization just enshrined what U.S. intelligence agencies and the Pentagon have been doing for decades: manipulating financial ledgers in order to obtain funding for classified projects, some of which are the work of Lockheed Martin's Skunk Works or Boeing's Phantom Works. CIA, for its part, has had no obligation to be honest about its finances. It relies on 50 U.S. Code § 3510: "The sums made available to the Agency may be expended without regard to the provisions of law and regulations relating to the expenditure of Government funds; and for objects of a confidential, extraordinary, or emergency nature, such expenditures to be accounted for solely on the certificate of the Director and every such certificate shall be deemed a sufficient voucher for the amount therein certified." Additionally, CIA generally reserves the right to determine whether its own activities are criminal or not and whether to report them.

87 When transferring sensitive military technology to the Saudi regime to boost weapon production, a Raytheon spokesperson leaned on legalese: "Industrial participation by local partners has been an element of international sales of military equipment for decades... These activities and related technologies are governed by the Arms Export Control Act, controlled by the International Traffic in Arms Regulations, and conform to all licensing rules and restrictions of the United States government." Quoted in LaForgia and Bogdanich (*The New York Times*, 7 June 2019).

88 *The Nation* explains: "Under a series of treaties dating back to 1962, members of the U.S. military stationed in Colombia are immune from prosecution. That immunity has since been extended to private security firms, which have been implicated in a series of crimes in Colombia related to drug-running, money laundering and rape." Grandin, Greg. "U.S. Soldiers and Contractors Sexually Abused at Least 54 Children in Colombia Between 2003 and 2007." *The Nation*. 7 April 2015. Status of Forces Agreements, negotiated by D.C.'s lawyers, protect U.S. troops and mercenaries around the world.

89 "While it's true that foreign nationals and foreign governments are prohibited from making contributions to political campaigns, there's a simple work-around for that, one the Saudis obviously made use of big time. Any foreign power hoping to line the pockets of American politicians just has to hire a local lobbyist to do it for them." Freeman, Ben. "How Much It Costs to Buy U.S. Foreign Policy." *The Nation*. 4 October 2018.

90 Federal law does not mandate public disclosure of think tank benefactors. Donations above $5,000 are reported to the IRS. One must comb tax documents to figure out what corporations and governments are spending on think tanks. See Rick Carp ("Who Pays for Think Tanks?" *Fairness & Accuracy In Reporting*. July 2013).

91 Walsh and Schmitt. "Arms Sales to Saudis Leave American Fingerprints on Yemen's Carnage." *The New York Times*. 25 December 2018. Pre-amnesty is a theme among the brutal. Acting President of Bolivia, Jeanine Áñez, pre-exonerated the federal police forces (through a decree, DS-4078) after she came to power in a D.C.-backed coup in autumn 2019.

92 Hilzenrath, David. "From Public Life to Private Business: Former Pentagon Chief Cohen's Firm Serves Defense Contractors." *Washington Post*. 28 May 2006.

93 A typical Safe Harbor disclaimer: "Except for historical information contained herein, the matters set forth in this news release are forward-looking statements. Statements that are predictive in nature, that depend upon or refer to events or conditions or that include words such as 'expects,' 'anticipates,' 'intends,' 'plans,' 'believes,' 'estimates,' 'will,' 'could' and similar expressions are forward-looking statements. The forward-looking statements set forth above involve a number of risks and uncertainties that could cause actual results to differ materially from any such statement, including the risks and uncertainties discussed in the company's Safe Harbor Compliance Statement for Forward-Looking Statements included in the company's recent filings, including Forms 10-K and 10-Q, with the Securities and Exchange Commission. The forward-looking statements speak only as of the date made, and the company undertakes no obligation to update these forward-looking statements."

94 A typical think tank disclaimer: "This report is written and published in accordance with [think tank name] policy on intellectual independence. The author is solely responsible for its analysis and recommendations. The [think tank] and its donors do not determine, nor do they necessarily endorse or advocate for, any of this report's conclusions."

95 Quote by Cindy Sheehan, "SJR 54 will not end the war in Yemen (Statement from March on the Pentagon)" (*PopularResistance.org*, 5 December 2018).

96 Cobain, Ian. "Obama's secret kill list—the disposition matrix." *The Guardian*. 14 July 2013. Becker, Jo and Scott Shane. "Secret 'Kill List' Proves a Test of Obama's Principles and Will." *The New York Times*. 29 May 2012. Saletan, William. "Beyond the Kill List." *Slate*. 30 May 2012. Broze, Derrick. "Obama Administration Forced to Release Drone Kill List 'Playbook.'" *MintPress News*. 11 August 2016.

97 Gerstein, Josh. "Judge green-lights 'kill list' lawsuit." *Politico*. 13 June 2018.

98 The judge rejecting the Al-Awlaqi suit wrote that the people alleged to have exercised this legal authority "are alleged to have followed a known procedure that occurred in Washington or its environs." See Josh Gerstein (*Politico*, 13 June 2018).

99 "A lawyer representing the CIA refused to acknowledge that the CIA had anything to do with drones, even under cross-examination from skeptical judges who questioned him about public statements by former CIA director Leon Panetta," journalist Mark Mazzetti explains (*The Way of the Knife*, p. 313).

100 Both Secretary of War and Combatant Commander have signed off on such directives. War Secretary Donald Rumsfeld issued a classified directive in 2004 expanding the reach of U.S. special operations forces to capture, kill, and spy in over a dozen countries (e.g. Pakistan, Philippines, Somalia, Syria). David Petraeus, CENTCOM commander (Oct 2008–June 2010), signed a directive expanding U.S. military activity in the greater Middle East. These activities "prepare the environment," allowing military units and mercenaries to "develop clandestine operational infrastructure that can be tasked to locate, identify, isolate, disrupt/destroy" bad guy networks and individual leaders of "terrorist groups" (Mazzetti, *The Way of the Knife*. pp. 128-9, 206-7). Both Rumsfeld and Petraeus have had intricate ties to Wall Street and Corporate America. Petraeus is now a partner at the New York investment firm KKR.

101 A letter Faulkner sent to U.S. Senators "argued that military action in Syria is 'consistent with the inherent right of individual and collective self-defense.'" Fang and Emmons. "State Department team led by former Raytheon lobbyist pushed Mike Pompeo to support Yemen war because of arms sales." *The Intercept*. 21 September 2018.

102 Alex Emmons of *The Intercept* (20 July 2018) explains: "While the previous policy prohibited arms transfers to countries that perpetrate 'attacks directed against civilian objects or civilians,'" the new policy "bars such transfers to countries that commit 'attacks intentionally directed against civilian objects or civilians.'"

103 FISA Section 702 allows NSA to surveil without a warrant U.S. persons who communicate with people overseas. Toomey and Peracha. "The NSA Is Using Secrecy to Avoid a Courtroom Reckoning on Its Global Surveillance Dragnet." *ACLU National Security Project*. 29 June 2018. Note: There is no adversarial legal process in FISA courts.

104 NSA has changed its legal interpretation of inconvenient laws. Online phone call services allow users "to dodge long-distance calling fees and to take their number with them anywhere around the world." In NSA's view, such online calling "might allow targets to acquire phone numbers with U.S. area codes and thus become off-limits to the agency, which is not supposed to conduct domestic spying," *The Intercept* explains. NSA once interpreted USSID 18 "as barring the targeting of U.S. numbers, and built safeguards into various online systems, causing U.S. numbers to be 'minimized upon presentation'" and restricted from a process in which NSA maps people's networks and associations. "NSA developed techniques 'for identifying the foreign status' of phone numbers," and NSA's Office of General Counsel "ruled that U.S. phone numbers affiliated with online calling services" could be deemed as foreign and surveilled "if the number was 'identified on foreign links' and was associated with an online calling service such as Vonage." Margot Williams, et al. *The Intercept*. 15 August 2018.

105 Toomey and Peracha. "The NSA Is Using Secrecy to Avoid a Courtroom Reckoning on Its Global Surveillance Dragnet."

106 Gallagher and Moltke. "The Wiretap Rooms: NSA's Hidden Spy Hubs in 8 U.S. Cities." *The Intercept*. 25 June 2018.

107 Gallagher and Moltke. "The Wiretap Rooms: NSA's Hidden Spy Hubs in 8 U.S. Cities."

108 In order to easily surveil anyone in contact with the target, NSA lawyers craft legalese, classifying major telecom corporations as a "person," thereby opening up NSA surveillance over any

and all Joes and Janes. NSA can say, for example, *alright, we're targeting Bob*. And one of Bob's contacts—under the two-hop rule and the associated NSA legalese—is the telecom provider that Bob uses. Hence, NSA can monitor any communication going through the telecom in order to surveil the population and any of Bob's associates. NSA whistleblower William Binney explained this in detail on the 1 April 2019 episode of *Empire Files* ("NSA Whistleblower: Government Collecting Everything You Do," <www.youtube.com/watch?v=SjHs-E2e2V4>) and "NSA Whistleblower Tells How NSA Tracks You" (*The Jimmy Dore Show*, 14 December 2017).

109 Clapper should face "charges for an admittedly false statement to Congress in March 2013, when he responded, 'No, sir' and 'not wittingly' to a question about whether the National Security Agency was collecting 'any type of data at all' on millions of Americans." Nelson, Steven. "Lock Him Up? Lawmakers Renew Calls for James Clapper Perjury Charges." *U.S. News & World Report*. 17 November 2016. For more information, see <www.hasjamesclapperbeenindictedyet.com>.

110 Clapper is an industry man. He led the National Geospatial-Intelligence Agency (NGA), which works to map the earth for military purposes, during the early war on terror. NGA corporatization accelerated under Clapper's leadership. Clapper retired from the Air Force in 2006 as a Lieutenant General. He immediately went to work for war corporations. The great investigative journalist, Tim Shorrock, reported in *The Nation* on 8 Sept 2016 that one of these jobs was director of intelligence programs for SRA International (which sells such goods and services as intelligence collection technology, IT services, and biomedical research). Clapper soon returned to government as Under Secretary of War for Intelligence and then ascended to Director of National Intelligence. After leaving government in 2017 Clapper wrote a book, joined a think tank that receives much funding from the U.S. war industry, and joined CNN as a national security analyst.

111 For a recent instance of FBI utilizing NSA databases, see Aaronson, Trevor. "A declassified court ruling shows how the FBI abused NSA mass surveillance data." *The Intercept*. 10 October 2019. Ongoing analysis at <icontherecord.tumblr.com>.

112 "U.S. agency denies data center to monitor citizens' emails." *Reuters*. 15 April 2013.

113 Category 4 languages (e.g. Arabic, Mandarin, Pashto) are the hardest for an English speaker to learn. A 3/3 on the Interagency Language Roundtable scale indicates professional working proficiency in reading & listening. A 4/4 indicates full professional proficiency (i.e. rarely taken for a native speaker but can respond appropriately even in unfamiliar situations; makes rare and minor errors of grammar and pronunciation). 3/3 is rare among Cat 4 military linguists. 4/4 is exceptionally rare. DLI aims to get students around 2/2, according to pressure group AUSA <ausa.org/articles/dlis-language-guidelines>.

114 James Carroll (*House of War*. New York: Houghton Mifflin, 2006, pp. 418-9) details peaceful action well: Acting on their morals and the message of Jesus, Philip Berrigan and five others snuck aboard USS *The Sullivans* in February 1997, damaged some of its weaponry, and poured blood. They also "damaged the casement for the nuclear-capable cruise missiles," Carroll noted. The U.S. has a deep tradition of religious pacifism, anti-war activism, and active Christian resistance to nuclear weaponry. The judge did not let them fully argue the religious or moral necessity of their actions. In July 2012, religiously motivated humans broke in to the Y-12 nuclear complex in Tennessee. Again, a judge did not allow the defendants to argue the moral or religious necessity of their actions in court. In April 2018, seven Catholic activists broke in to Naval Submarine Base Kings Bay, Georgia, and protested peacefully. In court in October 2019, the judge would not permit the seven to cite the Religious Freedom Restoration Act as part of their defense. For more information, go to <kingsbayplowshares7.org>. Similarly, those charged under the Espionage Act of 1917 (e.g. Edward Snowden, Julian Assange) are not allowed to argue a moral defense to the jury in the court of law, while the state is allowed to use classified evidence and witnesses against the defendant.

115 "[W]ith this indictment, [Assange] has become the target for a case that could open the door to criminalizing activities that are crucial to American investigative journalists who write about national security matters," *The New York Times*' Charlie Savage wrote ("Assange Indicted Under Espionage Act, Raising First Amendment Issues," 23 May 2019).

116 D.C. used a classified grand jury to go after Julian Assange. When Assange was dragged out of the Ecuadorian Embassy in London, the legal proceedings against him were unsealed. And where were the proceedings to take place? In the *heart* of the war industry: the eastern district of Virginia, where war corporations are *the* watershed.

117 "The war on Wikileaks, Assange and other outlets exposing the inner workings of power." *On Contact with Chris Hedges*. 4 August 2018: <www.youtube.com/watch?v=4EVPBwrj3RI>.

118 Do not confuse the USA PATRIOT Act (Uniting and Strengthening America by Providing Appropriate Tools Required to Intercept and Obstruct Terrorism) with a Raytheon missile system (Phased Array Tracking Radar to Intercept On Target). The USA PATRIOT Act allowed the U.S. government to get away with otherwise unjust and anti-democratic behavior, namely shredding the 4th Amendment and entrenching the surveillance state. The USA PATRIOT Act is not an anomaly. It is part of a broader legal tyranny designed to sustain war and suppress dissent.

119 Nationwide, in 2007, the Pentagon spent about $12,000 on advertising and other recruitment efforts per enlistee, according to Bill Carr, Deputy Under Secretary of War for Military Personnel Policy, as cited by the *AP* (30 September 2007). The War Dept. spent $2 billion spent on advertising during fiscal years 1998-2003. Makinson, Larry. "Outsourcing the Pentagon." *Center for Public Integrity*. 29 September 2004. Updated 19 May 2014.

120 Relevant contracts issued 28 Sept 2016, 30 Sept 2016, 24 July 2017, 27 July 2017, 18 Sept 2017, 12 March 2018, 4 April 2018, 18 July 2018, 2 Oct 2018. USAF contracts point to GSD&M selling "full-service advertising" with "all necessary management, supervision, labor, material, and equipment" required to "plan, create, design, produce, place, evaluate, and measure the effectiveness of advertising & special events" across national, regional, and local markets.

121 The 12 March 2018 contract with GSD&M cost $741 million for 9.5 years of advertising and event marketing.

122 "U.S. Air Force: Letter :30 Commercial." *U.S. Air Force Recruiting*. 13 June 2017: <www.youtube.com/watch?v=OAINshm-vHg>.

123 Peddling "great power competition" during his time in uniform, Gen. David Goldfein (featured in the ad) pushed to expand the Air Force by 74 squadrons. He also advocated increasing the network connectedness of Air Force units, pleasing industry.

124 The firm states, "U.S. Department of Defense tasked MullenLowe with creating a campaign specifically for young adults who have a passion they want to turn into a profession. Our platform—'You have a calling. We have an answer.'—speaks directly to those youth who know what they want out of life. It presents the U.S. Military as a transformative option, offering the most direct path to a fulfilled future. These spots exceeded expectations…" See "Calling/Answer." *MullenLowe U.S.* Accessed 8 March 2019: <us.mullenlowe.com/work/jamrs-calling-answer/?t=0>. The firm boasts, "With many long arms, each able to deliver a powerful blow, several hearts that beat in unison and one sharp mind that shares a bold vision, MullenLowe is really unlike any other agency out there… MullenLowe U.S.'s culture is entirely about limitless possibilities and a relentless belief in a future that is bigger than the past," per <https://us.mullenlowe.com/about/>.

125 Relevant contracts 22 Nov 2016, 6 Dec 2017. FMG's work sometimes involves tapping into Defense Human Resources Activity (DHRA) and JAMRS, exploiting databases for what can only be described as propaganda purposes. The missions of DHRA and JAMRS are broad, flexible, and

overlapping. FMG has a vice president of "military personnel analytics," per <www.forsmarshgroup.com/about/leadership/katherine-ely/>, accessed 1 May 2019.

126 I applied Stuart Ewen's words (*Captains of Consciousness*, pp. 211-3) to the war industry. His wisdom was: "to assert the idea that a community might control its own destiny was 'communistic'"; and freedom is "the version of freedom that continually relegates people to consumption, passivity, and spectatorship." The note about economic and social inequality was derived from the pioneering work of Prof. Shoshana Zuboff (*The Age of Surveillance Capitalism*. New York: PublicAffairs, 2019).

127 Recruitment and retention sales flow along the following tracks: Blaine Warren Advertising (Las Vegas, NV) to Air Force Reserve Command; Laughlin, Marinaccio & Owens (Arlington, VA) to Air National Guard; Jacob's Eye (Atlanta, GA) and Lempugh Inc. (Laurel, MD) to Army National Guard; Buchanan & Edwards (Arlington, VA) and Wunderman Thompson (Atlanta, GA) to the U.S. Marine Corps; and Young & Rubicam (New York, NY) to the Navy. Y&R recently worked on a new motto for the Navy, surveying veterans, enlisted sailors, and "influencers" during testing. It focused on ages 17-21. The campaign debuted at the end of 2017. See Seck, Hope. "'Forged By the Sea': New Service Slogan to Debut at Army-Navy Game." *Military.com*. 5 December 2017. Viewsport (Penfield, NY) has produced promotional gear for Marine recruiters. Industries for the Blind (Milwaukee, WI) customized Air Force promotional items. WPP plc (London) owns Wunderman Thompson and Y&R.

128 Available at <www.ddb.com/offices/north-america/usa/ddb-chicago/>.

129 Relevant contracts issued 6 April 2017, 21 Feb 2018, 20 May 2016, 6 April 2015, 6 Nov 2015, 28 Aug 2017, 25 Sept 2017, 3 Oct 2018, 1 June 2018, 14 June 2017, 10 June 2016. B&E designs, develops, manages Marine Corps Recruiting Information Support System (MCRISS) offline capability for recruiters. MCRISS tries to "digitize the entire enlistment and officer accessions processes." It is billed as a time saver that leads to "automating data entries" and "electronically scheduling applicants" for steps throughout the recruitment process. Accessed 8 March 2019: <www.candp.marines.mil/Programs/Focus-Area-1-People/Marine-Corps-Recruiting-Information-Support-System-MCRISS>. A 10-year deal to DBB Chicago worth $4 billion was issued 20 Nov 2018. McCann World Group (New York, NY) had previously run Army Marketing & Advertising Program.

130 Issued 23 Feb 2017. This is nothing new for Booz Allen Hamilton, which is regularly contracted to work on media relations with the public.

131 The IT firm MicroTech has helped run the Pentagon's Public Affairs Information Resource Management Office. General Dynamics has produced public affairs equipment and "visual information systems support." CACI, the corporation that sells IT and intel services across the War Dept., also works marketing and advertising for the National Guard. Issued 18 July 2016, 11 May 2017, 18 May 2016, 16 Feb 2018. Note the unquenchable nature of a 16 Feb 2018 contract for "strength maintenance program resource development and delivery of Army National Guard specific messaging for appropriate calls-to-action across key markets to generate leads required to achieve Army National Guard end strength."

132 Contracts: 2016 (10 June, 22 Nov), 11 Sept 2017, 2018 (30, 31 July; 7, 25, 27 Sept; 3 Oct), 2019 (31 Jan, 12 Feb, 10 July).

133 Construction on Guard & Reserve units has stretched from South Burlington, VT, to Kingsley AB in southern OR. Issued 24 Oct 2016, 2017 (28 Apr, 7 July, 24 Aug, 1 Sept, 7 Sept, 20 Sept, 21 Sept, 25 Sept, 27 Sept, 28 Sept) 2018 (11 & 24 Sept).

134 Issued 2018 (8 June, 13 July, 22 Aug). GE issued 25 Sept 2019. Full description at <darpa.mil/program/measuring-biological-aptitude>. The Institute for Human & Machine Cognition (Pensacola, FL) works on similar efforts.

135 "The placements at CNN were reported in the European press in February of this year and the program was terminated," *National Public Radio* ("Army Media Intern Flap," 10 April 2000) reports.

136 The War Dept. paid professional U.S. sports teams to engage in traditionally patriotic ceremonies, like singing hymns ("God Bless America"), spreading massive U.S. flags across the field, and recognizing troops as "heroes." The independent news organization *TruthDig* cites ESPN's Stephen A. Smith for context: "Until 2009, no NFL [National Football League] player stood for the national anthem because players actually stayed in the locker room as the anthem played... The players were moved to the field during the national anthem because it was seen as a marketing strategy to make the athletes look more patriotic." The War Dept. spent roughly $12.1 million during 2011-15 on these ceremonies, all "part of military-recruitment budget line items." See Peralta, Eyder. "Pentagon Paid Sports Teams Millions for 'Paid Patriotism' Events." *NPR.* 5 November 2015; and Niles, Emma. "How the Pentagon Paid for NFL Displays of Patriotism." *TruthDig.* 26 September 2017.

137 Hastings, Michael. "Another Runaway General: Army Deploys Psy-Ops on U.S. Senators." *Rolling Stone.* 24 February 2011.

138 Mazzetti and Daragahi. "U.S. Military Covertly Pays to Run Stories in Iraqi Press." *LA Times.* 30 November 2005; Cloud, David S. "Quick Rise for Purveyors of Propaganda in Iraq." *The New York Times.* 15 February 2006. The *Bureau of Investigative Journalism* (Black, et al. "Lord Bell ran $540m covert PR ops in Iraq for Pentagon." *The Sunday Times.* 2 October 2016) reported that the Pentagon paid a U.K. firm, Bell Pottinger, roughly $540 million USD (during 2007-11) to produce al-Qaeda-like videos (to see who watched them) and write fake news made to look like the work of Arab media. The firm worked out of Camp Victory, Baghdad, as part of U.S. task force. Gen. David Petraeus reportedly approved many of the videos personally.

139 Tomlinson, Chris. "Pentagon ups public relations spending." *AP.* 5 February 2009. Total Pentagon media expenditures were cited at $4.7 billion/year. Funding amounts included $1.6 billion for recruitment & advertising, $547 million for public affairs, and $489 million for PSYOPS (the fastest-growing part of War Dept. media). Costs cited in the *AP* report didn't include classified budgets or off-the-books operations. By 2013, annual Pentagon PR had increased to approx. $626 million. The War Dept. used roughly 63% of the U.S. government's overall PR spending and 40% of overall federal PR staff during 2006-15. See "Public Relations Spending: Reported Data on Related Federal Activities." *Government Accountability Office.* 30 September 2016: <www.gao.gov/assets/690/680183.pdf>.

140 Ewen, Stuart. *Captains of Consciousness.* p. 31.

4

The Tricks of the Trade

COOPERATION

Intra-industry cooperation demonstrates how the unifying profit motive of war corporations ultimately trumps competition among them. While corporations unite to wield influence and legalese for profitable advantage, they also cooperate by working together on the same military contract. For example, Constellis' Academi division (formerly known as Blackwater), Boeing, PAE, and Textron have worked together on a single worldwide drone contract. AECOM, Jacobs, and other engineering firms have worked together on a worldwide construction contract.[1] Elsewhere and ominously, industry giants have come together as a "single extended entity" to develop and manage standards for open computer architecture "via pre-planned product improvement initiatives."[2] One contract alone can facilitate industry cooperation.

War corporations also cooperate through providing goods and services for one another's products. For example, Textron's Bell brand makes a popular attack helicopter, the AH-1Z. General Electric makes the aircraft's engines. General Dynamics makes the rockets. Lockheed Martin makes the targeting system. Northrop Grumman makes the mission computers. Raytheon makes the missiles. Aircraft are platforms for a variety of corporate goods and services.

Joint ventures are another way war corporations cooperate. A joint venture (JV) is a partnership between corporations allowing them to share expertise and/or pool resources. Prominent JVs in the U.S. war industry include:

- United Launch Services (a.k.a. United Launch Alliance): Lockheed Martin and Boeing selling satellite launch services
- Javelin: Raytheon and Lockheed Martin selling portable anti-tank missiles
- Longbow: Northrop Grumman and Lockheed Martin selling fire control radar and missiles (to be used on Boeing's AH-64 attack helicopter)

Boeing and General Motors team up as HRL Laboratories, researching everything from microelectronics to large sensors. General Dynamics and Raytheon form Range Generation Next, or RGNext, to operate sites where war corporations launch vehicles into space for the government. Joint ventures keep U.S. military facilities up and running around the world.³ Governments allied to the U.S. war industry get into the mix. Boeing and the Swedish corporation Saab develop a training jet, the T-X. Rockwell Collins and the U.K.'s BAE Systems operate Data Link Solutions, which makes communications equipment.

Working on the same contract, producing goods and services for one another's platforms, and joint ventures are some ways in which war corporations cooperate. They're all in the racket of war together.

MEMES

In order to keep the military budget elevated, sustain industry, and confine D.C. to a violent foreign policy, the public must be fed a constant stream of fear-inducing pretexts. Such pretexts, which must be carefully crafted and promoted, effectively serve as advertising to sell the public on the need for war-related production. The U.S. war industry, its think tanks, its politicians, and its media affiliates hyped the Soviet menace during the Cold War while simultaneously the U.S. war industry sold weaponry to all manner of allies, including despots and dictatorships. Today, after pumping the War on Terror for trillions in military spending, the war industry is returning to targeting Russia and China through "great power competition."

Facing off against Russia and China is more comfortable territory for war corporations insofar as, in the calculus of industry boardrooms, the big-ticket items inherent to competition with another major industrial nation are where the real money can be made. A war on terror was lucrative for a decade or two, and it will continue, but the enemies in such a war are not sufficient in composition and operations to justify excessive spending on cyber, submarines, satellites, ballistic missiles, nuclear weaponry, and aircraft carriers.

So now we return again to great power competition, the new Cold War—but containment is out the window this time around. Energy expert Professor Michael Klare explains, the U.S. view of great power competition demands that it

> retain military and technological superiority over Russia and China (and all other potential challengers) for as far into the future as we can see. In this vision, America sits alone at the top of the global hierarchy; there can be no partnership among the major powers.[4]

Moreover, competition against Moscow and Beijing continues the militarization of U.S. society, channeling anger (which might otherwise manifest itself as class awareness and/or physical protest against D.C.'s corruption) into outrage against a stereotypical enemy that resides overseas—just as the War on Terror did.

The U.S. war industry tells us that Russia and China are the great powers competing against the United States. Ellen Lord, the former Textron executive who is now the Pentagon official in charge of acquiring goods and services from the war industry, promotes fear of a narrowing capabilities gap between the U.S. military and the militaries of Russia and China. Arguing that D.C.'s technological superiority "has been diminishing over the past few years, because we have not embraced new technologies" in sufficient pace "to develop applications and field systems," Lord says that the Department of War needs "a whole new level of capability, so you will see an energized focus on hypersonics... You will see an enormous amount of effort on artificial intelligence and utilizing that. You will see hardened electronics being looked at. Command and communications to make sure that we are truly interoperable... A lot of cybersecurity focus as well... A lot more focus on space."[5] That's a heck of a shopping list. And it overlaps with the list of Mark Esper, former Raytheon vice president and current Army Secretary.[6] In this, the war industry is the greatest volleyball player ever: setting up the fear, then spiking it into monetary rewards. All military production-related options are on the table; none for the pursuit of peace, deconfliction, and conversion to civilian, peaceful industry.

The war industry has a variety of new, costly goods and services in mind for great power competition: artificial intelligence, autonomous weapons, drones in the sky and underwater, hypersonic propulsion, Navy ships (such as littoral combat ship and Zumwalt-class destroyers), nuclear weaponry, signals intelligence hardware and software, Silicon Valley tech, and other weapons. A U.S. Army colonel unwitting echoed more of industry's wish list of products: "exquisite situational awareness," i.e. integration of satellite maps, on-the-ground sensors, and other costly gizmos (understanding of local culture and historical grievances not included); "organic capability" across more than ninety countries, i.e. more hard facilities and infrastructure, and the legal authorities backing up the deployment of forces and industry products; "hyper-enabled operators," grunts loaded with all the gear they could handle, supported with costly information technology and satellite infrastructure; and assured communications, i.e. dominating the electromagnetic spectrum.[7] Transitioning special operations forces—whose training, equipment, and weaponry comprise a growing sector of industry—to great power competition,[8] war corporations have even pushed ground robots.[9] Great power competition is marvelous from a corporate perspective, because it directly targets multiple enemies, in this case Russia and China, while actively turning all aspects of life (economy and trade, energy and resources, science and technology, internet and communications) into battlefields and then selling goods and services to dominate those battlefields.

The War Department eagerly adjusts to more expensive war. In early October 2018, the Pentagon issued its regular assessment of the U.S. war industry base. The report made clear that the U.S. war industry and the Pentagon are shifting to great power competition.[10] The industrial base, the report makes clear, includes everything: public and private academia, research and development organizations, Corporate America. Everything. The report bemoans the decades of "erosion of American manufacturing," but ignores how corporate leaders caused this erosion by pushing manufacturing jobs overseas where labor is relatively cheaper. Of course, the report frames this erosion as a threat, one that could "undermine the ability of U.S. manufacturers to meet national security requirements." The report doesn't mention (perhaps its scribes are unaware) that corporate authority is the one that largely determines what national security requirements are. Though the report talks about labor, it doesn't mention any working-class perspective.[11] A former Boeing executive named Pat Shanahan delivered the report in his capacity as Deputy Secretary of War. By January 2019, Shanahan was acting Secretary of War and pushing China as the main enemy.[12] (Shanahan is alleged to have helped out Boeing from his new position,[13] though an internal review cleared his name. Former U.S. Ambassador to the United Nations Nikki Haley was soon nominated to Boeing's board of directors.[14]) The Pentagon's 2020 budget looks to be taking "significant steps" toward a "focus on great power conflicts," the industry-friendly bulletin *Breaking Defense* noted.[15]

Think tanks across the board hyped great power competition throughout 2018.[16] A senior research fellow at Heritage reminds us that the biggest change to the operating environment is a positive one: that U.S. allies have in the last year truly "awakened to the fact that everybody is back in big power competition."[17] Federal allies are onboard, too. The director of CIA (the organization whose essential purpose is the protection and promotion of capitalism) asserts, "We are sharpening our focus on nation-state rivals."[18]

Great power competition is already playing out in profitable ways. The Center for Strategic & Budgetary Assessments (CSBA) think tank issued a study stating that great power competition obligates the U.S. Air Force to dramatically expand its number of aircraft squadrons. CSBA also found severe shortfalls in a variety of weapon categories, including aircraft (bombers, tankers, fighters, drones) and space assets.[19] CSBA is funded by the war industry and appendages of the U.S. Department of War.[20] It was established in the 1980s as an alternative to the Congressional Budget Office, which is less influenced by corporations. CSBA, on the other hand, reliably produces reports favorable to industry's bottom line. U.S. Air Force civilian leaders, who recently worked in industry, are responding auspiciously. Industry goods and services had already encircled the bogeymen (Russia and China) prior to the launch of great power competition.

The great power competition pretext has given the Pentagon an excuse to deploy more corporatized troops, mercenaries, and goods and services right up to Russia's borders,[21] while Pentagon leadership has stylized such a permanent war footing as conducive to peace.[22] More frequent deployments and the conducting of war games with a greater intensity of corporate products ensue. The deployment of U.S. and North Atlantic Treaty Organization (NATO) troops to Russia's borders entails provision of AM General and General Dynamics vehicles, Boeing jets, Harris radios, Raytheon radar, Lockheed Martin/Raytheon anti-tank missiles, and AeroVironment drones. The U.S. Air Force regularly sends bombers to bases in Europe—Boeing B-52s and Northrop Grumman B-2s in spring and summer, 2019, for example. The U.S. Navy stood up a new Fleet and sent it to Russia's coastal waters.[23] Mainstream media organizations do their part by uncritically portraying Moscow as racing for global dominance while underplaying the Pentagon's colossal overseas reach.[24] In fiscal year 2020, the U.S. Air Force will spend $278 million to position more equipment "throughout Europe and $241 million on construction efforts to support expeditionary basing."[25] Meanwhile, weapon sales to China's neighbors are flourishing,[26] and the U.S. Armed Forces are conducting regular unilateral exercises near China and drills with Southeast Asian militaries. A variety of products are involved in such efforts, including Lockheed Martin cargo aircraft and jets, Boeing ordnance, General Dynamics submarines, Raytheon electro-optical/infrared sensors, and littoral combat ships packed with industry products. Some U.S. exercises have focused on seizing territory and setting up airstrips, a process known as Expeditionary Advance Base Operations (EABO). War corporations held an EABO "industry day" in 2018 in concert with the Armed Forces to present and promote relevant industry goods and services.

Industry's activity requires physical infrastructure. With an eye on Moscow, such infrastructure is expanding across Europe, including in the Czech Republic, Germany, Iceland, Poland, and Romania.[27] The U.S. Army Corps of Engineers in Wiesbaden, Germany, administers many construction projects. U.S. corporations profit from upgrading U.S. military bases under the European Reassurance Initiative. A construction firm from Colorado Springs, Colorado, building infrastructure at Mihail Kogalniceanu Air Base, Romania, is a good example of this.[28] The War Department is also upgrading military infrastructure in the Far East,[29] in Beijing's face. Meanwhile, Beijing's construction is framed as a threat. "I mean, this is insane. Look at all that crazy construction," remarked a U.S. Navy officer as she observed Chinese military construction projects in the South China Sea.[30] Though a useful bogeyman, Chinese military construction in the South China Sea does not hold a candle to what U.S. construction firms have built up overseas.

High-ranking military officials are on board with great power competition, prioritizing careers and corporate largess. Some officials justify their participation in this pretext by claiming that all branches of the U.S. Armed Forces are "depleted" after decades of fighting. Basically, so their argument goes, recent wars have left the troops with degraded equipment, substandard weaponry, and not enough supplies. (Keep in mind, these officials do not propose to end the needless wars. They propose to spend more resources on these wars and preparation for new great power wars.) Ergo, Pentagon officials justify the pursuit of great power competition (and sky-high military budgets and nonstop purchasing of costly goods and services) by claiming the U.S. military is "under-resourced."[31] Great power competition is now fully entrenched in the Pentagon. The 2018 National Defense Strategy, developed in 2017, emphasized, "inter-state strategic competition, not terrorism, is now the primary concern in U.S. national security."[32] Etching the National Defense Strategy into stone, Chairman of the Joint Chiefs of Staff Joseph Dunford officially declared that great power competition was here to stay, demanding a shift in Pentagon funding priorities and weapons development.[33] Dunford was speaking at a forum sponsored by war corporations Boeing, CAE, and United Technologies, and NATO, among other powerful groups, including energy firms and IT corporations.[34] The National Defense Industrial Association later presented General Dunford with its most prestigious award.[35] Dunford soon retired and joined the board of Lockheed Martin.

The great power competition dogma's near-term implications for the state of the nation are scary: further starvation of the diplomatic corps, diminishing its talent and effectiveness; increased militarization of an already militarized U.S. economy and public life; and greater likelihood of wars big and small. Great power competition also has major implications for humanity, other animals, and Earth itself: more pollution (notably toxic particulates, carbon emissions, and radiological contamination) in an era of climate catastrophe and mass extinction;[36] nuclear weapons on a hair trigger; and relentless corporatization of the Pentagon, the world's mightiest organization. The pretext known as great power competition is off to a great start, financially, bureaucratically, and industrially.

THREAT FABRICATION

When war is your business, peace is your enemy. The MIC incessantly fabricates threats. Threats—both specific and vague—sustain the racket.

The world is filled with all kinds of threats, including advanced persistent threats, affiliates, black identity extremists, dark networks, destabilizing regimes, great powers, guerrillas, hackers, insurgents, malicious actors, non-compliant governments, non-state actors, a non-state hostile intelligence service, people who don't accept state violence or intimidation, rogue states, special interest aliens, terrorists, unaccompanied immigrant children, and unprivileged enemy belligerents. Some of these threats are real. Some are not. All are hyped. All serve a common purpose: sustain and increase industry profit while glazing the public with layers of fear.

Military officials, industry officials, and congresspeople are indistinguishable in their hype of armed threats. The Pentagon says, an increased budget allows effective "adapt[ation] to an array of changing global threats."[37] A war corporation chimes in: "To address evolving threats with more confidence and greater efficiency, customers need 'next-generation' systems that connect across domains."[38] The late U.S. Senator John McCain notes that provisions in a bill will help address "a growing array of threats."[39] Each side of the military-industrial-congressional triangle plays from the same sheet of music.

The U.S. Armed Forces bureaucracy has fully internalized the "threat"-filled world, to a large degree swallowing its own propaganda and that of the war industry. Accordingly, various organizations operating within the War Department have christened themselves in opposition to open-ended threats: the Defense Threat Reduction Agency is concerned with nuclear proliferation; the Defense Insider Threat Management & Analysis Center shares information across the Department vis-à-vis potential insider threats; and the Airborne Threat Simulation Organization within Naval Air Systems Command imitates enemy electronic warfare devices and radar systems for training. And all require industry products.

The war industry is so creatively dominant in its relationship with the Pentagon that its own unproven corporate claims about threats and product performance have appeared in public contracts. Booz Allen Hamilton sells the U.S. Armed Forces "reliable and secure" IT operations for "anywhere in the world," so the Department of War regurgitates the corporation's unproven claims about "threats" when stating that Booz Allen Hamilton "enables rapid aggregation, fusion, and dissemination of operational information, intelligence, and technology to respond to emerging threats."[40] The corporate website advertising a Lockheed Martin fire control system positioned on the nose of a Textron attack helicopter boasts that such a system will "provide pilots with enhanced capabilities… significantly enhancing platform survivability and lethality." Although the system has been accused of being involved in civilian deaths in the Middle East and received mixed feedback regarding user friendliness, the Department of War's contracting site echoes corporate claims, alleging the system "provides the capability to identify and laser-designate targets at maximum weapon range, significantly enhancing platform survivability and lethality." Contracts for expensive Multi-Mission Surface Combatant ships claim the product is "a lethal and highly maneuverable surface combatant capable of littoral and open-ocean operation," though testing and trials have indicated that the ship can be error prone and is hardly as agile as advertised.[41] It is unacceptable that Pentagon contracting officials uncritically regurgitate the claims of war corporations.

War corporations get away with having their "threats" and fearmongering echoed in War Department contracts for several reasons: (1) Anyone who speaks up about the problem risks their career. (2) Many U.S. military officers are unable or unwilling to distinguish between the production bias of a war corporation and the actual needs of a professional uniformed military. These U.S. military officers don't see war corporations as pursuing a self-interested agenda; rather, they see a total force effort in which military and industry work together to fight the enemy. (3) The tight nature of coordination and cooperation within the MIC leads to an overlap and imbrication of actors, roles, and duties. (4) There is a lack of moral courage in the War Department.

Many will undoubtedly argue that the U.S. war industry is merely responding to a threat that has arisen, after the Pentagon has turned to industry to help confront it. This is incorrect for several reasons. The war industry—through means of influence noted in Chapter Two—is able to continually promote war and bellicose policies prior to any possible foreign military aggression or any other pretext to be exploited. In other words, the cart comes before the horse (or the missile system comes before the conflict). Goods and services of the U.S. war industry are created and marketed prior to the missions in which industry and Pentagon officials then praise said goods and services. Look at the Mine Resistant Ambush Protected vehicle, or MRAP (say it: em-rap). Oshkosh Defense and Navistar Defense are primary manufacturers of MRAP vehicles. SAIC has worked on logistics programs for MRAP vehicles.[42] Kongsberg Defence & Aerospace of Norway makes the Common Remotely Operated Weapon Station (CROWS), a joystick-operated weapon system often mounted on MRAP. The list goes on. Corporations selling MRAP and associated products bend Congress prior to hostilities abroad.[43] Applauding the MRAP for its role supporting recent Western military operations inside Syrian territory or Libyan territory—not to mention Hometown, USA, where police departments from California to South Carolina have acquired such vehicles from the Pentagon—ignores the fact that MRAP had been in development and production long before initiation of hostilities in those areas.[44]

Threats can sell any good or service imaginable. Cruising around in a military vehicle? Raytheon's Active Protection System can "engage threats fired from any angle or elevation, providing all weather, full 360-degree hemispherical vehicle and crew protection with each countermeasure."[45] On a ship? "Every day ships across the world are facing a variety of evolving threats," says a program director at Lockheed Martin. The corporation's electronic warfare system "will help create a coordinated attack against these threats, to keep our warfighters safe by controlling the electromagnetic spectrum and disrupting adversaries."[46] Trying to hide? Concealment systems are "important, particularly now, because the threat on the battlefield has increased."[47] Just going about your day in the U.S. ("the Homeland")? Raytheon's "partnership with the U.S. Air Force ensures air, missile and space threats are identified and understood for NORAD action."[48]

War corporations put the word "threat" into product names to sell more units. "Threat" goods and services include advanced and tactical threat displays, advanced threat warning sensors, airborne threat simulators, counter-threat technologies, cyber infrastructure threat assessments, real-time cyber threat detection, global threats operations and logistics support, joint threat emitter, opposing force threat simulation, next-generation threat systems, threat analysis services, threat management services, threat radar emitter simulations, threat adaptive countermeasure dispensing systems, threat warning technology, and the unmanned threat emitter.[49] The unfortunately named Isis Defense (Alexandria, VA) has worked on a research project for DARPA called the "Threat Intelligence Platform."

The word "threat" dazzles corporate names.[50]

Providing "threat warning" alone is a lucrative gig.[51]

Industry frames development of any major weapon system as a response to the activities of a dreadful enemy. Pentagon officials including Secretary of the Navy Richard V. Spencer—a former Wall Street executive and long-time member of the Defense Business Board, the group that basically advises the Pentagon on how to best help the war industry and vice versa—even promote the Arctic as a threat.[52] At the Sea Air Space Forum of 2019 (sponsored by CACI, Lockheed Martin, Northrop Grumman, and shipbuilder Huntington Ingalls, among others) war officials cited great power competitors as expanding military power into the Arctic. They ignored the real threat: the U.S. Armed Forces' rampant carbon-based military activity contributes to anthropogenic climate change, which melts Arctic ice, which opens up northern sea lanes, into which the Pentagon projects its polluting arsenal, which puts more carbon in the atmosphere.

Whole military units—themselves requiring industry goods and services—have been created in this profitable climate of fear. The National Space Defense Center, which is effectively run by Harris Corp. as of this writing, "was created out of increasing fear that America's enemies would make satellites a wartime target,"[53] a fear hyped by the U.S. war industry and its think tank and media affiliates. Other units created in this climate include the Defense Threat Reduction Agency, the Defense Insider Threat Management & Analysis Center within the Defense Security Service, and the Missile Defense Agency (est. 2002, blaming Moscow). And why does the University of Maryland's Center for Advanced Study of Language exist? September 11, 2001.[54] The U.S. Armed Forces' bureaucracy operates in opposition to the "threat"-filled world, which was largely created by the U.S. war industry.

War corporations have landed many contracts in recent years to work on combatting "insider threats"—people who might intentionally or unintentionally disclose information or tell the public details about military excesses or abuses. Many corporations sell goods and services addressing insider threats.[55] Relatedly, the Department of War is now purchasing goods and services to continuously monitor the eligibility of cleared personnel to maintain a security clearance.[56] Raytheon offers products to counter "the threat within." Leidos sells "insider threat solutions." A Lockheed Martin vice president assures us, insider threats "pose one of the highest risks to an organization."[57] So, buy Lockheed Martin Insider Threat Identification.

It should be clear by now that threats don't just appear. They get hyped. The Secretary of War reminds us, "Threats today in the world know no boundaries," and "Threats today in the world are not indigenous to countries or borders or regions."[58] In other words, this isn't your grandfather's threat. This is abundant, different, modern, new—the methods more dangerous and sophisticated, the ensuing fear more overwhelming. "Our enemies' ability to transition is outpacing us," claims the acquisitions chief of Special Operations Command.[59] En garde! The threat is always "changing in its diversity."[60] It's never-ending, by design. So, naturally, "it's going to take a different approach" from the U.S. war industry. Hint, hint: costly. The current official in charge of U.S. military acquisition (a former Textron honcho herself) and the chiefs of the premier industry pressure groups (such as NDIA and AIA) insist more must be done to help the industrial base.[61] The war industry wins no matter whom they hype—"rogue nations" such as Iran and North Korea, "great power competition" with China and Russia. Hype the threat, pitch your product. Threats everywhere!

Likely threats are numbered, but the range of conceivable threats, imaginable threats, things that just might happen if you brainstormed the possibilities, are innumerable. You, the U.S. government or an allied regime, need a solution (a good or a service) for each threat. War corporations market their goods and services as "solutions." An industry executive explains, engaging "with senior members of government" is just "providing solutions to our customers," providing "integrated solutions to meet our customers' needs," and even "figuring out how we can solve our customers' problems using a dispassionate system approach."[62] This is problem solving, not selling products. The "solutions" trick works well when selling to the Pentagon. Booz Allen Hamilton offers digital solutions, CACI offers information solutions, Leidos offers innovative solutions, and Raytheon offers cyber solutions.[63] Industry "solutions" show up in Pentagon contracts as well.[64] Capitalists mimic one another, inserting "solutions" into the very names of their corporations⁶⁵ or divisions within their corporations.⁶⁶ U.S. military bureaucracy has taken the cue, using the term "solutions" for various offices and divisions, including the Solutions Delivery Division of the Defense Health Agency's Health IT Directorate and the Special Communications Mission Solutions Division of the Naval Air Warfare Center Aircraft Division. Through the harmful, anti-democratic activities covered in Chapter Two, the war industry creates the miserable conditions for which it then offers "solutions," of course without ever taking responsibility for the dismal state of affairs (i.e. nonstop war) that it helped create. "Providing solutions" sounds prettier and more generous than "making money selling death and destruction." Corporations big and small perform this trickery.⁶⁷

RUSES

Great powers and threats galore line up against the United States. Providing solutions to these problems requires a palatable presentation, so the U.S. War Department (and willing collaborators) conceals the government's imperialism, weapon sales, and war-first foreign policy by means of ruses. Ruses are banana peels that corporations throw onto the military-industrial-congressional circuit to neutralize potential criticism and garner fanfare.

Robert Gates, Secretary of War from 2006 to 2011, promoted a bloated war budget by claiming it was the "best we could do to protect our men and women in uniform, to give them the tools they need to deter our enemies, and to win our wars today and tomorrow."⁶⁸ Testifying before Congress, Gates' successor, Leon Panetta, claimed that the development of military and intelligence capabilities had "provided the key tools that we need" for battlefield success.⁶⁹ Panetta's successor, Chuck Hagel, averred, the money saved when limiting pay-raises and increasing retirees' medical co-pays "will go toward ensuring that our troops have the training and the tools they need to accomplish their missions."⁷⁰ Hagel's successor, Ash Carter, initiated reforms to the military promotion process and strengthened ties to Silicon Valley "to ensure our services have the tools they need to always ensure we're promoting, retaining, and bringing in the best possible officers to lead our all-volunteer force."⁷¹ President Donald J. Trump sang a similar, though garbled, tune: "To keep Americans safe, we must provide the men and women of the U.S. military with the tools they need to prevent war and, if they must they have to fight and they only have to win."⁷²

MIC elites use this ruse for diverse objectives, belligerent and profitable alike. When awarding Boeing a massive contract to produce aircraft that refuel other aircraft midflight, Secretary of the Air Force Michael Donley was "confident that when our young pilots, boom operators and maintainers receive this aircraft, they will have the tools they need to be successful at what we ask them to do."[73] In his position as Deputy Secretary of War, former Boeing executive Pat Shanahan pushed the need to work with industry in order to address cyber necessities: "We must keep pace with the threat, get our warfighters the tools they need, and stay closely coordinated."[74] Keep your eyes and ears peeled for a similar phrase that industry executives use all the time: "We've listened to the warfighter." In this way, war industry spokespeople position themselves as compassionate relatives rather than the profiteers that they are.

The "tools they need" has been applied to all manner of issues, including military recruitment and retention;[75] the militarization of Puerto Rico;[76] and even educating youth in the official history of the United States.[77] U.S. military officers utilize "the tools they need" to justify ongoing occupation of foreign lands. Speaking from the comfort of an air-conditioned conference room and claiming that U.S. military forces were still needed in Iraq, the commander of Task Force Lion asserted in 2018, "We are at a critical juncture right now where if we don't continue our work and support for the [Iraqi Security Forces], if we don't continue our work to professionalize them as a military, to give them the tools they need and set the conditions for security and stability in this country then we risk a return to the conditions like they were in 2014."[78] Regarding the training of U.S. National Guard troops for deployment to Kosovo, the U.S. European Command liaison officer for nonlethal weapons affirmed, "When you are doing pre-deployment training, you go that extra mile to ensure they have the tools they need to accomplish their mission."[79] When discussing the arming of Ukrainian soldiers and mercenaries, U.S. Air Force General Paul Selva stated, "This will be a policy choice on whether or not we're going to give the Ukrainian government the tools they need to defend themselves against what we believe to be a Russian-supported insurgency movement in the Donbass."[80] War goods and services are not weapons of death, in this view. They're solutions or tools, which the Pentagon's master gladly sells.

While government officials typically cite "tools they need," war corporations invoke "our troops." Navistar Defense, a major corporation producing military vehicles, introduces us to this ruse. Navistar asserts that it "builds the world's best military vehicles because we care most for the people who drive them… No matter where our vehicles serve, our troops will never ride alone."[81] Other vehicle manufacturers play the same ruse.[82] Vectrus—motto: "True to Your Mission"—sells base operations support services, IT expertise, and supervision of pre-positioned matériel. The history is rich. Halliburton's slogan was "Proud to Serve Our Troops"[83] while the corporation profited in the invasion and occupation of Iraq. A Raytheon slogan in 2012 was "Customer Success Is Our Mission" while the corporation increased the amount it pays stockholders for the eighth consecutive year.[84] A regular Lockheed Martin motto is "We Never Forget Who We're Working For." War industry personnel, from salespeople to chief executives, refer to "our men and women in uniform" in their spiels, even though the U.S. war industry sells weapons of war to governments around the world.

Industry spouts effective hogwash. Corporate executives and political operatives usually invoke the safety of the troops to sell weaponry or expand operations.[85] But sometimes D.C. elites invoke the safety of the troops in order to protect themselves. For example, when Secretary of State Mike Pompeo revoked the entry visa of Fatou Bensouda, the Chief Prosecutor of the International Criminal Court (ICC) in March 2019 who had requested ICC judges to make an investigation into alleged war crimes in Afghanistan by, among others, U.S. troops, Pompeo said he was doing so to protect U.S. troops in Afghanistan from ICC prosecution. But the ICC doesn't target low-level troops. It focuses on politicians and high-ranking officers who order war crimes. Pompeo was using the troops' wellbeing to cover the hindquarters of the D.C. regime.

Exploitation of the purported interests of the troops is often flagrant. Even non-martial corporations are on the record exploiting the troops,[86] but war corporations take it to another level. Northrop Grumman markets products under the headline, "Protecting SOCOM's Most Important Asset—Its People. The Value of PROTECTING OUR GREATEST ASSET"[87] (emphasis theirs). SAP NS2, a corporation that sells expertise and technology to military-intelligence, flashes imagery of a soldier saluting sharply in front of the U.S. flag when pitching services that help "solve mission owner challenges, and produce meaningful intelligence for decision makers."[88] A product made by Data Link Solutions "saves lives."[89] Another corporation, Peraton, claims to "protect and promote freedom around the world."[90] These corporations flagrantly position themselves as benevolent or altruistic. If war corporations truly cared about the troops, they wouldn't lobby and push for policies that end up killing/maiming the troops.

Leanne Caret is CEO of Boeing Defense, Space & Security. She also sits on the board of the United Service Organizations. The USO entertains the troops, providing moments of amusement for the soldiers, sailors, airmen, and Marines stationed around the world. Boeing is a major sponsor of the USO. Thus, Boeing finances congressional campaigns and lobbies for war while working through the USO to soothe the troops whose deployments underpin the very profits that allow Boeing executives to live in luxury.[91]

Another example: Leanne Caret's boss, the head of Boeing Corporation, was Dennis Muilenburg. He grieved publicly after the corporation's relentless drive for profit maximization led to two crashes of 737 MAX civilian aircraft in 2018 and 2019. "Frankly, these last few weeks have been the most heart-wrenching of my career," Muilenburg told a crowd at the George W. Bush Presidential

Center in Dallas, Texas.[92] (Boeing made billions from George W. Bush's launch of global war in 2001 and from the invasion and occupation of Iraq in 2003.) To my knowledge, however, Muilenburg has never grieved publicly for the victims of Boeing's ordnance or aircraft. Nor, to my knowledge, has he ever grieved publicly for the men and women of the U.S. Armed Forces who died overseas in elective wars. He made $23 million in 2018 and, after being unable to get the Max aircraft flying again, walked away from Boeing with $62.2 million in compensation.

BUILT-IN OBSOLESCENCE

Now that great power competition has arrived, and threats are everywhere, war corporations are happily engaged in selling solutions and tools for "our troops." There's just one catch: Corporations in all industries deliberately design products to function as expected for a specific duration, after which they pitch upgrades, additional goods and services, or an entirely new product. This is called planned obsolescence. Planned obsolescence is everywhere in the civilian world. The charger for your old smartphone is not compatible with the new smartphone that you purchased from the same corporation. Your laptop is not designed to be upgradable with more memory. Printer cartridges don't work in other printers made by the same company.

The U.S. war industry is no different. It too plans obsolescence into products to get the customer to purchase goods and services again and again. "Of course we do it," said one midlevel engineer I spoke with who worked for one of the major war corporations doing substantial business with Naval Sea Systems Command. The war industry has so thoroughly imbued its products with planned obsolescence that it has opened yet another business opportunity: obsolescence monitoring. You're in luck! the war corporation pitches. We provide obsolescence monitoring—for a price.[93]

Historically, missiles were one of the first products for which the industry introduced planned obsolescence, blaming the shelf life of certain missile components in order to regularly or prematurely take them back to perform upgrades. Industry charges for obsolescence on a variety of different missiles and "missile defense."[94]

Industry sells new aircraft. Bell-Boeing debuted the V-22 tiltrotor aircraft roughly four years into the 2003 occupation of Iraq. The V-22 takes off like a helicopter, rotates its engines during flight to a horizontal position, and flies long distances as a conventional fixed-wing prop plane. The aircraft's development was fraught with engineering challenges, and several people died in its testing and early introduction. Safety remains a worry within certain military circles, though the industry downplays these concerns. The Pentagon has certified the

V-22 as operational, and the aircraft now flies regularly, yet Bell-Boeing still sells engineering to address V-22 obsolescence. This is a new aircraft—if it's already having obsolescence problems to such an extent, then one might wonder whether obsolescence upgrades serve as a means of addressing design flaws in the original or whether obsolescence was planned from day one.[95] Bell-Boeing did not reply to my inquiries.

The U.S. Navy purchases and operates a large Northrop Grumman drone, the MQ-4C, to be used in conjunction with Boeing's P-8A aircraft to surveil large swaths of ocean. The MQ-4C took its maiden flight in the spring of 2013. Yet, by 17 February 2016, Northrop Grumman had sold services to address obsolescence on MQ-4C production. Roughly a year and a half later, on 1 August 2017, Northrop Grumman sold the U.S. Navy more efforts aimed at solving "near-term emerging obsolescence issues" on the MQ-4C. This pattern points to planned obsolescence. On 18 July 2018, Northrop Grumman sold the Pentagon upgrades of MQ-4C software to "integrated function capability (IFC) 4.0." While not explicitly pertaining to obsolescence, the deal on 18 July demonstrates how industry markets and sells upgrades to the Pentagon, no different from how an electronics firm suggests you upgrade your smartphone or a computer software giant suggests you upgrade your computer operating system. Northrop Grumman did not reply to my inquiries.

A state-of-the-art product, the aforementioned Boeing P-8A aircraft was introduced into the U.S. Navy fleet toward the end of 2013. Remarkably, Boeing sold obsolescence work, including obsolescence monitoring, to the U.S. Navy less than two years later.[96] After another five months Boeing sold $2.47 billion worth of P-8A aircraft to the U.S. Navy and Australia—with obsolescence monitoring included in the deal.[97] In 2017, Boeing sold more obsolescence work on four separate occasions.[98] This evidence points to obsolescence as part of corporate business plans. Boeing sold more obsolescence monitoring on P-8A aircraft as I was editing this paragraph.[99] Boeing declined to comment.

Similar patterns occur in ships. The brand-new littoral combat ships (LCS) are marketed as "stealthy" and able to operate close to shore. With standards straight out of a Michael Bay blockbuster, the LCS variants are named *Freedom* and *Independence*. Lockheed Martin led the design and construction process for the *Freedom*, General Dynamics for the *Independence*. Like most modern, pricey weapons platforms, LCS have underperformed in early tests and trials. The ships are over budget and have been prone to major failures. These facts don't matter, as LCS manufacturers—Austal, General Dynamics, and Lockheed Martin, primarily—continue to receive deal after deal. LCS contracts flourished in 2017, for example,[100] though the Pentagon is expected to purchase fewer LCS than initially scheduled. On 8 August 2018, General Dynamics was allocated $33.5 million to work on LCS. This work included "engineering, planning, ship configuration, material and logistics support to maintain and modernize" the LCS variants. Impressive: General Dynamics got funding to "modernize" a ship that was *just* released into the fleet. Throwing salt in fiscal wounds, the war industry keeps on producing the LCS, and the U.S. Navy keeps on purchasing them at great cost.

The same pattern appears again and again in the war industry's design, development, and marketing of goods and services, drumming home the notion that the Pentagon can only compete on the battlefield by purchasing the latest goods and services (whatever we, industry, define as the state-of-the-art or smart choice). A corporation will bill the Pentagon for obsolescence monitoring during the life of the product. There is no authority within the U.S. Armed Forces pushing back firmly against the obsolescence business model. War officials position goods and services as tools the troops need, while corporations invoke the best interests of "our troops" (all while planning obsolescence to sell products).

EUPHEMISMS

A euphemism is a kinder, gentler term used in place of a direct, often more accurate one. The MIC loves euphemisms. PR gurus know the English language very well. Recall George Orwell's 1946 essay *Politics and the English Language*: "In our time, political speech and writing are largely the defence of the indefensible... Thus political language has to consist largely of euphemism, question-begging and sheer cloudy vagueness."[101] With the care of a sommelier, MIC propagandists select the perfect euphemisms to mask their activities and present death and destruction in comfortable terms. The public's use of these euphemisms aids and abets endless war. The list below will help readers begin to recognize euphemisms, expose their use, and get going on a path toward peace. By decoding and debunking the MIC's lingo we can demilitarize language and take a necessary step toward truth in all matters concerning war.

Euphemism is intricately linked to exploitation and crafting of the legal code and underpins nonstop war. Senator Hiram Johnson warned in 1917, "The first casualty when war comes is truth." We—people living inside the U.S. war industry and people overseas living under industry's ordnance and aircraft—deserve a language that accurately depicts the MIC. Getting rid of euphemisms, pursuing an honest language, is one step toward achieving a system that benefits people and planet. In doing so, we shed the harmful assumption the Department of War is here to protect us. Truth shows that the Department of War responds to the U.S. war industry's priorities, imposes an injurious global order, fights brown and black people,[102] bombs recalcitrant states' populations, supports Apartheid Israel, sells to despotic regimes, and loathes democracy.[103]

Euphemism	Reality
acquire the full range of counterspace capabilities	develop weaponry to blow up other countries' satellites
additional contract requirement	exorbitant public treasure spent on mediocre weapons platform
administrative detention	solitary confinement
advisor	CIA officers / special operations personnel
anticipatory self-defense	Bush Doctrine of pre-emptive strike, regardless of validity of threat
arms trade	selling weapons of death
armed combatant	civilian or resistance fighter, armed or unarmed
"at the request of the [allied govt.], the United States is conducting unarmed reconnaissance flights accompanied by armed escorts who have the right to return fire if fired upon"	"we bomb civilians" to assure the survival of client governments
outpost, facility, station, forward operating location, defense staging post, contingency operating site	base
building partner capacity	selling arms and training to foreign military forces
collateral damage	civilian deaths
communistically inclined	progressive, independent, promoting domestic interests over U.S. government's
counterinsurgency	military occupation, quelling popular resistance for client governments
counterterrorism pursuit teams	hit squads funded by CIA and armed and trained by U.S. war corporations
courageous restraint	resisting the urge to shoot civilians
data collection	mass surveillance
defensive actions of the free world	protection and advancing of U.S. hegemony
degrade	we can't defeat [group X], so we won't use 'defeat'
designated defense marksman	sniper
detainee	prisoner
developing nations	exploited peoples
disinformation website	(accredited Russian) or alternative news site
dual-use target	bombable civilian infrastructure

Euphemism	Reality
economy-of-force initiative	using different resources and more tax dollars in creative ways to sustain U.S. military interventionism
eco-terrorist	land protector
enduring camp	U.S.-only enclave
"enhance security in the region"	"sell devastating weaponry to despotic regimes"
enhanced interrogation	abuse, torture
entry operation conducted under the auspices of a competent authority	black bag job / illegal breaking & entering
erroneous deprivation of life	murder via corporate missile, launched from corporate drone
executive action	political murder (usually on U.S. soil)
expedition targeting force	JSOC raid team, death squad
extraordinary rendition	kidnapping
federal solutions	war profiteering
fiscal consolidation	austerity
foreign investment	corporate takeover of land and resources; privatization of the commons
forward defense	aggressive offense
forward deployed	in someone else's territory
freedom, American values	neoliberalism; opening of markets to U.S. corporate plunder
free fire zone	area where you kill anything that moves
free trade	governments captured by corporate interests allow corporations to do business across borders regardless of the cost to the environment or the workers
general	warlord
habitability set	tent
highly reliable informant	microphone or eavesdropping device
identity management solutions	massive databases containing biometrics of people
information from a confidential informant	dirt, illegally obtained
information warfare, strategic communications	misinformation, disinformation, propaganda, lies, false flags

Euphemism	Reality
insurgents, militants	resistance, freedom fighters
intervention	military attack
intimidation	violent political suppression
joint priority effects list	capture / kill list (mostly kill)
legacy aircraft	old aircraft, obsolete in many ways but still profitable to sell
lethal defensive aid	weaponry used by mercenaries to destabilize regions or topple governments
logistics civil augmentation program (LOGCAP)	War Dept. outsourcing its logistics responsibilities within its flailing empire by throwing money at corporations
manage dollars wisely	Impose austerity; gut social programs, environmental protections, the State Department budget
message force multipliers	retired military personnel who propagandize via corporate media
military information support operations	PSYOPS
military operations	ambushes, acts of war
modernization	updating nuclear weapons; more arms spending
national interest	oligarchical interest (Wall Street profits)
national security	actions that keep war profiteers plump and the people fearful
naval cordon	blockade—an act of war
negative treatment	cold-blooded assassination
online persona management service	sock puppets to spread D.C.'s propaganda
operational mishaps	e.g. murder of Gazans who protest during Great March of Return
operational pause; indications of a "desperate enemy"	setback; route
outsourcing	suppressing labor
protective reaction	pretending radar activity looks provocative so you can bomb infrastructure and other targets
rebels	armed jihadists
refocus of client procurement	war industry lobbying

Euphemism	Reality
regime	a government resisting U.S. hegemony
reinventing government	privatizing everything under the sun
residual training force	continuing military occupation
retrograde operation, redeployment, reposturing	withdrawal
reverse geometry	entering Palestinian homes through their walls, rather than their doors
sanctions	blockade causing high civilian suffering to induce popular uprisings
self-radicalize	via alternative information sources discover and reject U.S. gov criminality
security initiative	monitoring and attacking
sensitive investigative techniques	break-ins
settlement	Israeli colony on Palestinian land
shock & awe	blitzkrieg, 21st century version
sleep management	depriving prisoners of sleep, a form of torture
special expeditionary targeting force	a (200+ SOF/intel) deployment to Iraq, December 2015
strongman	U.S.-allied dictator
support free trade	support corporate rule
surrogates	see: *message force multipliers*
targeted killings	extrajudicial assassination
targeted preventive acts	assassination
tender age shelter	prison for babies
theater	warzone
threat finance	the budget of any group that opposes D.C.'s dictates
tribe	faction
unsubstantiated change actions	cooking the books
un-vouchered funds	off-the-books cash bribes
village stability operations	night raids

ENDNOTES

1 The contract for drones, maintenance, and tech support, worth a potential $1.73 billion, was issued on 8 June 2017. "Global contingency construction" issued 29 March 2019.

2 Corporations were Boeing, General Atomics, Harris, Lockheed Martin, Northrop Grumman, Raytheon, United Technologies, and the U.K.'s BAE Systems. Issued 27 Dec 2018 and 2 Jan 2019. The open architecture contract stressed that the following "business goals" would guide corporate cooperation: accommodating different cybersecurity parameters; adaptability, flexibility, and expandability; enabling independent development and deployment of system elements; making sure the technology can be updated regularly; simplifying integration; and supporting a variety of missions and domains. Reducing "technical risk and overall cost of ownership of weapon system programs" was also a business goal.

3 Notable JVs are National Defense Energy & Environmental Alliance (E2A), which is Concurrent Technologies Corporation and Battelle together selling environmental, energy, and safety expertise in order to keep War Dept. ranges and installations running smoothly; AC First, which is AECOM and CACI selling logistics, maintenance, and supply services for use at U.S. military bases overseas, particularly in Afghanistan; DZSP 21, which is Parsons and others running BOSS on Guam; and BREMCOR, which is Burns & Roe and EMCOR selling BOSS, including services at Naval Station Guantánamo Bay, Cuba.

4 Klare, Michael T. "Why 'Overmatch' Is Overkill." *The Nation*. 20 December 2018. The Pentagon's National Security Strategy (which was crafted in part by employees of war corporations, I might add), released towards the end of 2017, said as much, Klare points out.

5 Lord, Ellen. "DOD's Lord on 'Falling Fast,' Fast-Tracking Foreign Military Sales Authorities, Reorganizing AT&L." *Defense & Aerospace Report*. 29 May 2018. Lord had stated in her 7 Dec 2017 testimony to the Senate Armed Services Committee, "The current pace at which we develop advanced capability is being eclipsed by those nations that pose the greatest threat to our security, seriously eroding our measure of overmatch." 2 of the 3 other Pentagon officials testifying that day had extensive experience as high-ranking officials in the war industry. All hyped threats from great powers. Testimony accessed 27 June 2019 at <www.armed-services.senate.gov/hearings/17-12-07-department-of-defense-acquisition-reform-efforts>.

6 Esper's list: new command & control, long-range artillery, attack aircraft, reconnaissance aircraft, missiles, and helicopters. Weisgerber, Marcus. "Army Secretary Reveals Weapons Wishlist for War with China & Russia." *Defense One*. 16 April 2019.

7 "USSOCOM's Reim on Great-Power Competition, Communications Challenges, Acquisition Lessons Learned." *Defense & Aerospace Report*. 26 May 2018: <www.youtube.com/watch?v=W0qMgJhRUYQ>, (4:00).

8 Larter, David. "After years fighting terrorism, the SEALs turn their eyes toward fighting big wars." *Defense News*. 17 January 2019.

9 Gregg, Aaron. "Defense mergers and acquisitions poised to keep pace in 2019." *Washington Post*. 12 January 2019.

10 The report is titled *Assessing and Strengthening the Manufacturing and Defense Industrial Base and Supply Chain Resiliency of the United States*. According to a Pentagon press release (#NR-285-18, 5 October 2018), the "report provides recommendations to address immediate risks identified in the manufacturing and defense industrial base and initiates follow-on efforts to create a strategy for building this base for next-generation technologies. This comprehensive and government-wide effort demonstrates that manufacturing and the defense industrial base are vital to not only our Nation's economic security, but also to our national security."

11 Andre Damon explains a perspective of the working class: The vision in the document manifests the war machine's strategy of integrating diverse elements of national power (diplomacy, economics, financial power, information, intelligence agencies, law enforcement, the War Department). The tech sector, which comprises many war corporations, receives political protection while implementing censorship of independent media on their platforms—media that often shine an honest light on D.C. The alliance between powerful corporations and the D.C. regime rends the Bill of Rights asunder. "The central target of such measures will be the forcible suppression of the class struggle in the name of promoting 'national security,'" Damon asserts in "Pentagon report points to U.S. preparations for total war" (*World Socialist Web Site*, 11 October 2018).

12 "In one of his first meetings of the day, Shanahan told civilian leaders of the U.S. military to focus on 'China, China, China,' even as America fights militants in Syria and Afghanistan, a U.S. defense official said." Stewart, Phil and Idrees Ali. "For Shanahan, a very public debut in Trump's cabinet." *Reuters*. 2 January 2019.

13 Johnson and Brown. "New Pentagon chief under scrutiny over perceived Boeing bias." *Politico*. 9 January 2019.

14 Haley defended Apartheid Israel at every turn. See Falk, Pamela. "Nikki Haley's U.N. mission: Sticking up for Israel" (*CBS News*, 16 Feb 2017) and "Nikki Haley defends Israel after Gaza violence, walks out of meeting" (*CBS News*, 16 May 2018) for mainstream coverage of Haley's ardent Zionism. Boeing shareholders approved Haley's nomination at the end of April 2019.

15 Cancian, Mark. "2020 Budget: One Half Step Towards A Great Power Strategy." *Breaking Defense*. 25 March 2019.

Jen Judson (*Defense News*, 17 June 2019) suggests the new Army Futures Command, which got up and running in summer 2019, was "aimed at accelerating modernization and staying ahead of" Russia and China. In June 2019, the War Dept. created a new position: Deputy Assistant Secretary of Defense for China.

16 For example, CNAS and the *Washington Post* held a conference at the Washington Hilton Hotel on 21 June 2018 about "Strategic Competition—Maintaining the Edge," while Heritage sounded the alarm about U.S. military weakness in its 2019 "Index of U.S. Military Strength" vis-à-vis purchases abetting prosecution of great power competition. CSIS on 12 Feb 2018 addressed great power competition in Central Asia on its "Chinapower Podcast." See also Brimley and Hendrix, et al. "Building the Future Force: Guaranteeing American Leadership in a Contested Environment" (*CNAS*, 29 March 2018). CNAS' Elbridge Colby testified before SASC in January 2019 and hyped great power competition. Colby was the perfect person to testify, because he was a key figure in drafting the Pentagon's National Defense Strategy, which hyped Moscow and Beijing as threats.

17 Mehta, Aaron. "The U.S. may not be able to fight two big wars at once." *Defense News*. 3 October 2018.

18 Harris, Shane. "The CIA is returning its central focus to nation-state rivals, director says." *Washington Post*. 24 September 2018. There is certainly an institutional impetus to return to facing off against Moscow: CIA needs Russia's foreign intelligence service, SVR, and SVR needs CIA. Neither could justify their authority or budget without the rival. CIA has extensive AI / machine learning programs for great power competition: CIA's privacy and civil liberties officer stated, "We at the Agency have over 100 AI initiatives that we're working on, and that's going to continue to be the case," per "A conversation with the CIA's privacy and civil liberties officer Ben Huebner." *Brookings Institution*. 3 June 2019: <www.youtube.com/watch?v=B9PB2Mh192w>, (1:00:10).

19 Insinna, Valerie. "What aircraft does the U.S. Air Force need to beat China and Russia? This new study has an answer." *Defense News*. 20 March 2019.

20 "Contributors." *Center for Strategic & Budgetary Assessment.* Accessed 17 April 2019: <csbaonline.org/about/contributors>.

21 In testimony to U.S. Congress in 2018, the head of U.S. European Command referred to Russia as "malign" no less than 5 times in 2018. In 2019, he stepped up his game, calling Russia "malign" 6 times. In 2019, the general bemoaned, "Moscow seeks to assert its influence over nations along its periphery, undermine NATO solidarity, and fracture the rules-based international order." "Rules-based international order" means D.C. makes the rules and economically and militarily bullies other nations into abiding. The general advocated for more [war industry] weaponry to be shipped to D.C.-backed militants operating in eastern Ukraine. At the time of the general's testimony, the Pentagon had already shipped command & control technology, vehicles, radars, arms, and other industry goods to Ukraine—transportation, maintenance, and supply via the U.S. war industry. "Statement of General Curtis M. Scaparrotti Commander United States European Command." *House Committee on Armed Services.* 28 March 2017. "Statement of General Curtis M. Scaparrotti, United States Army Commander United States European Command." *United States Senate Committee on Armed Services.* 8 March 2019. Raytheon's new customers purchasing its PATRIOT missile defense system—roughly $18 billion in deals—had been all European "and were responding to what they perceive as Russian aggression in the region," says Jen Judson (*Defense News*, 13 August 2019).

22 "I think, from a U.S. military perspective, it is incumbent upon us to continue to develop those capabilities that give our allies and partners the confidence that we can meet the commitments that we have, and also ensure that Russia and China understand that we do have the capability to respond if deterrence fails... That conventional relative capability that we have had over the past couple of decades is actually a fundamental element of peace." "Statement of General Curtis M. Scaparrotti Commander United States European Command."

23 McLeary, Paul. "New 2nd Fleet To Confront Russia From Day One." *Breaking Defense.* 3 May 2019. The Second Fleet was sent off the coast of Kaliningrad in the Baltic Sea.

24 Adam Johnson of *Fair & Accuracy in Reporting* (FAIR) wrote accurately and critically in "To Ramp Up Fear of Russia in Africa, NYT Downplays Massive U.S. Military Presence on Continent" (4 April 2019).

25 Insinna, Valerie. "Denied hot meals and indoor toilets, U.S. airmen prepare for the fog of war." *Defense News.* 28 August 2019.

26 Sales to Taiwan alone are staggering. "U.S. approval of $300 million military sale to Taiwan draws China's ire." *Reuters.* 24 September 2018. "Taipei Economic and Cultural Representative Office in the United States (TECRO)—F-16C/D Block 70 Aircraft and Related Equipment and Support." *Defense Security Cooperation Agency.* Transmittal No 19-50. 20 August 2019.

27 Some relevant contracts issued 5 July 2018, 6 July 2018, 28 Aug 2018, 6 Nov 2018, 20 Dec 2018. For more information about U.S. posture in Iceland and Germany, see "Iceland's Sigurjónsson on U.S. Return to Iceland, Climate Change Impact, China" (*Defense & Aerospace Report*, 15 June 2019) and "U.S. Ramstein Base Key in Drone Attacks" (*Der Spiegel,* 22 April 2015).

28 The European Reassurance Initiative (ERI) kicked off in June 2014 after heavy industry lobbying to do something to "respond" to Moscow's annexation of Crimea. To my knowledge no war industry lobbyists ever mentioned any causative factors such as NATO's expansion up to Russia's borders or the 2014 U.S.-backed coup in Kiev. The U.S. war industry got all it wanted in ERI: increased deployments of U.S. troops and mercenaries, increased sales to European countries, more pre-positioned goods from industry, more infrastructure that will necessitate keeping U.S. forces (and war industry goods) in Europe, and increased combined exercises. "Fact Sheet: European Reassurance Initiative and Other U.S. Efforts in Support of NATO Allies and Partners." *The White House—Office of the Press Secretary.* 3 June 2014. ERI budget is now around $5 billion annually. Pellerin, Cheryl.

"2018 Budget Request for European Reassurance Initiative Grows to $4.7 Billion." *Defense Media Activity*. 1 June 2017.

29 Projects include construction at military facilities in Sembawang, Singapore; Gyeongsangbuk-do, South Korea; and Yamaguchi, Nagasaki, Kanagawa, and Okinawa, Japan.

30 Beech, Hannah. "China's Sea Control Is a Done Deal, 'Short of War With the U.S.'" *The New York Times*. 20 September 2018.

31 Talk of the U.S. military being under-resourced and under-funded was everywhere in 2018. Peruse, for example, testimony of war industry operatives and Pentagon officials in front of congressional Armed Services Committees. A good example is the April 2018 testimony of the Under Secretary of War for Research & Engineering at the House Armed Services Committee (Griffin, Mike. "Promoting DOD's Culture of Innovation." *HASC, Second Session, 116th Congress*. 17 April 2018). Elsewhere, the Chairman of the Joint Chiefs of Staff stressed that the Pentagon was in a poor financial state—the dominant military advantage the U.S. military once enjoy had "eroded," and required "sustained predictable, adequate levels of funding" to remedy. Garamone, Jim. "Great Power Strategy Affects DOD Priorities, Allocations, Dunford Says." 17 November 2018.

32 "Summary of the 2018 National Defense Strategy of the United States of America." Accessed 2 January 2019: <dod.defense.gov/Portals/1/Documents/pubs/2018-National-Defense-Strategy-Summary.pdf>.

33 Garamone, Jim. "Great Power Strategy Affects DOD Priorities, Allocations, Dunford Says." *U.S. Department of Defense*.

34 "Partners & Sponsors." *Halifax International Security Forum*. Accessed 23 November 2018: <https://halifaxtheforum.org/partners-sponsors/partners-sponsors/>.

"Members of the Halifax Canada Club." *Halifax International Security Forum*. Accessed 23 November 2018: <https://halifaxtheforum.org/partners-sponsors/halifax-canada-club/>.

35 "Dunford is NDIA's pick for its highest honor, the Eisenhower award." *NDIA*. 25 March 2019. In his acceptance speech, Dunford spread fear of Russian and Chinese technological advancements. See Jim Garamone's "Dunford Accepts Eisenhower Award, Calls for Industry, DOD Cooperation" (*DOD News*, 12 May 2019).

36 For more information on the sixth extinction in which humans are currently living and at least partially culpable for, consult Carrington, Damian. "Earth's sixth mass extinction event under way, scientists warn." *The Guardian*. 10 July 2017; Drake, Nadia. "Will Humans Survive the Sixth Great Extinction?" *National Geographic*. 23 June 2015; Sutter, John D. "Sixth mass extinction: The era of 'biological annihilation.'" *CNN*. 11 July 2017. Also pertinent are Ferreira, Becky. "Arctic Warming Will Cost At Least $24 Trillion More Than We Thought, Study Finds." *Vice News*. 23 April 2019; Watts, Jonathan. "Military buildup in Arctic as melting ice reopens northern borders." *The Guardian*. 24 January 2019; Watts, Jonathan. "We have 12 years to limit climate change catastrophe, warns UN." *The Guardian*. 8 October 2018; "Human health in dire straits if urgent actions are not made to protect the environment, warns landmark UN report." *United Nations*. 13 March 2019; McGrath, Matt. "Nature crisis: 'Shocking' report details threat to species." *BBC News*. 6 May 2019; Smedley, Tim. "Deadly air in our cities: the invisible killer." *The Guardian*. 17 March 2019. For more on the effect of plastics on the natural world, consult "Millions of Tons! Scientists Tally Up Plastic Pollution in Oceans." *NBC News*. 12 February 2015; "Ocean plastic could triple in a decade." *BBC News*. 21 March 2018; "Plastic pollution reaching record levels in once pristine Arctic." *BBC News*. 8 Feb 2018; "Plastic pollution: Scientists' plea on threat to ocean giants." *BBC News*. 5 February 2018; "Remote island has 'world's worst plastic rubbish density.'" *BBC News*. 16 May 2017; "Study Finds Plastic Waste and Toxics in Remote Parts of Antarctica." *DemocracyNow*. 7 June 2018; "Whale that died off Thailand had eaten 80 plastic bags." *BBC News*. 2 June 2018; Briggs, Helen. "Plastic patch in Pacific

Ocean growing rapidly, study shows." *BBC News.* 22 March 2018; Gill, Victoria. "Marine plastic: Hundreds of fragments in dead seabirds." *BBC News.* 23 June 2018; Shukman, David. "Giant plastic 'berg blocks Indonesian river." *BBC News.* 19 April 2018.

37 Pope, Charles. "Air Force's fiscal 2020 budget focuses on modernization, readiness, confronting global threats." *Secretary of the Air Force Public Affairs.* 12 March 2019.

38 "Lockheed Martin advances system that links capabilities across domains to create a unified battlespace picture." *Lockheed Martin.* 17 July 2018. The quote is from a Lockheed Martin vice president in charge of C4ISR & Unmanned Aerial Systems.

39 Mason, Jeff. "Trump signs defense policy bill with watered-down China measures." *Reuters.* 13 August 2018.

40 Booz Allen Hamilton literature at "Managed Threat Services Provides Worldwide Protection," <www.boozallen.com/c/insight/publication/managed-threat-service-provides-worldwide-protection.html>; "Meet Brad—Senior Vice President," <www.boozallen.com/s/bio/leadership/brad-medairy.html>. Contract issued 13 Feb 2017.

41 Contracts issued 10 July 2015, 17 March 2017, 29 March 2017, 27 Sept 2017, 30 March 2018, 19 Nov 2018, 27 Sept 2018. Relevant Lockheed Martin Target Sight Systems contracts include 22 Dec 2016; 28 Sept 2017; 31 Aug, 30 Nov 2018.

42 The Pentagon's Inspector General (report #D-2011-081, 11 July 2011) found War Dept. officials administering the SAIC contract very poorly. This included allowing SAIC to take charge of inherently governmental functions (e.g. disciplining War Dept. employees). The IG also found SAIC ignobly laying the groundwork for the next MRAP contract, which (surprise!) SAIC ended up getting. Finally, "the contracting officer awarded a contract type which provides no incentive to the contractor for cost control or labor efficiency and significantly increased risk to DOD."

43 One part of this is the millions that Oshkosh Corporation (parent company of Oshkosh Defense) and Navistar, together, have allocated in recent years to lobbying D.C. and congressional campaigns. MacAndrews & Forbes (owner of AM General) is another major campaign contributor. Figures available at the Center for Responsive Politics, <www.opensecrets.org>.

44 "What about Iraq?" industry voices inquire. The standard industry narrative claims that the MRAP was created as a response to the fatalities that U.S. military forces were suffering in Iraq as a result of improvised explosive devices that insurgents were planting. Inaccurate. Since at least the 1970s, the U.S. war industry had been prototyping and manufacturing light and heavy armored vehicles designed to resist landmines. (Iraqis who were fighting the U.S. troops in Iraq, especially during 2003-11, were often called "insurgents." Most U.S. corporate media and think tanks didn't attempt to understand their grievances or even figure out why people would fight a foreign army occupying their country.)

45 "Active Protection System (APS)." *Raytheon.* Accessed 2 September 2018: <www.raytheon.com/capabilities/products/aps>.

46 "Lockheed Martin's latest electronic warfare system for helicopters to safeguard U.S. Navy against anti-ship missile threats." *Lockheed Martin.* 12 January 2017. Accessed 31 August 2018: <news.lockheedmartin.com/2017-01-12-Lockheed-Martin-s-Latest-Electronic-Warfare-System-for-Helicopters-to-Safeguard-U-S-Navy-Against-Anti-Ship-Missile-Threats>.

47 "SOFIC 2018 Day 2—Special Operations Force Industry Exhibition Tampa United States." *DefenseWebTV.* 28 May 2018: <www.youtube.com/watch?v=mDQUP4Cz0h0>, (6:55).

48 NORAD is the North American Aerospace Defense Command. See "NORAD Operations and Sustainment." *Raytheon.* Accessed 2 September 2018: <www.raytheon.com/capabilities/products/nissc>.

49   Prominent examples of "threat" in product naming include the Lockheed Martin Advanced Radar Threat System, the Northrop Grumman Advanced Threat Warning Missile Warning Sensor, and the Logos Technologies Persistent Threat Detection System. Persistent Threat Detection Systems are blimps. Lockheed Martin also works on PTDS. A Lockheed Martin executive describes it as having "saved countless lives through its capability to identify threats, track insurgents, and enhance overall readiness for the men and women in theater... We're honored by this award and the role we play supporting our troops." ("Threats" *and* "our troops!") See "Lockheed Martin Persistent Threat Detection System team wins aviation week award." *Lockheed Martin.* 12 November 2015. Some relevant contracts: 29 July 2016, 21 Aug 2014, 18 Nov 2015, 1 Feb 2016, 5 May 2016, 2 Sept 2016, 18 Nov 2016, 28 April 2017, 8 Sept 2017, 15 Sept 2017, 27 Sept 2017, 5 June 2018, 29 June 2018.

50   Among them: ChemImage Bio Threat LLC (Pittsburgh, PA), Global Threat Reduction LLC (Reston, VA), Global Threat Response Group (Cape Canaveral, FL), Threat Management Group LLC (Ladson, SC), and Threat Tec LLC (Hampton, VA).

51   Raytheon's Common Sensor Payload for General Atomics MQ-1C drone provides threat warning. Raytheon's multi-spectral targeting system for Northrop Grumman's MQ-4C drone provides threat warning. Shipboard electronic warfare products from General Dynamics and Lockheed Martin also provide threat warning. FLIR (North Billerica, MA) electro-optical/infrared sensors for patrol boats provide threat warning. R&D from Leidos advances Air Force threat warning systems. And Northrop Grumman aircraft countermeasure systems provide threat warning. At least, that's what contract announcements say, repeating industry marketing. Contracts referenced: 2014 (18 Aug; 22, 25 Sept), 25 June 2015, 2016 (23, 30 Sept 2016), 2017 (25 April; 15, 25, 28 Sept 2017), 2018 (15 Feb; 13 April; 3, 4, 31 May; 27 Aug).

52   Jonathan Watts ("Military buildup in Arctic as melting ice reopens northern borders." *The Guardian.* 24 January 2019) quotes U.S. Secretary of the Navy Spencer: "Everyone's up there but us... The threat is back on. This is an area ... we need to focus on." See also Rempfer, Kyle. "NORTHCOM: Arctic now America's 'first line of defense.'" *Defense News.* 6 May 2019.

53   "National Space Defense Center begins 24-hour operations." *Associated Press.* 19 February 2018.

54   "Why does CASL exist?" Accessed 5 August 2018: <www.casl.umd.edu/about>.

55   For example, Cloud Lake Technology (Herndon, VA) sold management and analytic support (2 Oct 2017) to the Insider Threat Group within Defense Intelligence Agency (DIA). ITG "identifies anomalous behavior indicative of an insider threat and works with other DIA elements to mitigate the threat." Because the corporation is categorized as a small business and is an Alaskan Native Corporation, the contract was not procured in a competitive manner. The Design Knowledge Co. (Fairborn, OH) sold its R&D expertise (5 June 2018) to monitor and make sure Air Force cyber assets and microelectronics infrastructures are free from insider threats. ForcePoint (Herndon, VA) has monitored the activity of cleared personnel on classified networks, Novetta (McLean, VA) has helped get the System of Systems up and running within Defense Security Service's Defense Insider Threat Management & Analysis Center, and Potomac River Group (Ashburn, VA) has helped administer polygraph exams for Naval Criminal Investigative Service insider threat efforts. Issued 17 Aug 2018, 19 Sept 2016, 20 Aug 2015.

56   The Continuous Evaluation Program went into effect 27 July 2018. "Since the start of this new policy, 1.1 million clearances have been enrolled and over 38,000 cases have been flagged." A major component of the program is monitoring the financial status, including credit reports, of cleared personnel. Fink and Barrett. "Major financial changes could affect your security clearance." *U.S. Army.* 19 September 2018.

57 Insider threat documentation available at <www.raytheon.com/cyber/news/feature/threat-within>, "Insider Threat." *Leidos.* Accessed 22 July 2019: <www.leidos.com/competencies/cyber/insider-threat>; and "Lockheed Martin Commercial Cyber announces insider threat detection solution with interest." *Lockheed Martin.* 13 June 2016. Raytheon's SureView product "captures human behaviors such as policy violations, compliance incidents or malicious acts at the endpoint that serve as warning signs leading up to a breach." SureView technicians have "pioneered an active strategy to protect critical data by monitoring technical observables, including not only data's location and movement, but also the actions (including precursor actions) of users who access, alter and transport that data." See "SureView" (*Raytheon*, 2014).

58 "Joint Press Briefing by Secretary Hagel and Minister Pinzon in Colombia." *U.S. Department of Defense.* 10 October 2014.

59 Erwin, Sandra I. "Secretive SOCOM opens up to private sector." *National Defense.* 25 January 2016.

60 The threat is also "changing in just the sheer number of them that are out there," and attaining a high overall quality, a Northrop Grumman executive tells us. He describes the threat quality as "better lethality, better countermeasures, more ability to impact a battle space." "Northrop Grumman's Todorov on $9.2B Orbital ATK Acquisition, Missile-Defense Space, Evolving Threats." *Defense & Aerospace Report.* 6 August 2018: <www.youtube.com/watch?v=gnADkxrX5tI>.

61 Mehta, Aaron. "White House warns of 'domestic extinction' of suppliers in industrial base report—and DOD is ready to help with cash." *Defense News.* 4 October 2018.

62 "Raytheon's Harris on Global Product Demand, International Sales, Partnerships." *Defense & Aerospace Report.* 2 August 2018: <www.youtube.com/watch?v=phCJaKWZ-pE>, (1:10), (2:52), (11:40).

63 For more information, consult <www.boozallen.com/expertise/digital-solutions.html>, <https://investor.caci.com/file/Index?KeyFile=396549116>, <www.leidos.com/company/our-business>, and <www.raytheon.com/cyber/solutions>.

64 For example, on 7 Aug 2018, Textron (AAI) sold an "ISR solution," which entailed the corporation's drones flying over Afghanistan. On 24 Aug 2018, Infoscitex (Littleton, MA) sold its R&D expertise, comprising "software solutions."

65 Some corporate names that fall into this category (sample: summer 2018 contracts) include American Technology Solutions International, AOC Program Solutions, Applied Training Solutions, C4 Planning Solutions, Credence Management Solutions, DLT Solutions, E3 Federal Solutions, Engineering & Software System Solutions, Entrust Government Solutions, Envision Innovative Solutions, Epsilon Systems Solutions, Innovative Scientific Solutions, Middle Bay Solutions II LLC, Modern Technology Solutions, National Aerospace Solutions, Pioneering Decisive Solutions, Primus Solutions, Sawdey Solutions Services, Space Ground System Solutions, Spectrum Federal Solutions, and Synectic Solutions.

66 Corporate divisions include but are not limited to Bowhead Operations & Maintenance Solutions, CACI National Security Solutions, CACI Six3 Intelligence Solutions, Chenega Applied Solutions, Chugach Federal Solutions, Fluor Federal Solutions, KBRwyle Technology Solutions, Kratos Technology & Training Solutions, PAE National Security Solutions, Rockwell Collins Simulation & Training Solutions, and Textron Geospatial Solutions. The telecoms also do this when selling to government: AT&T Government Solutions and Motorola Solutions, based in Vienna, VA, and Linthicum Heights, MD, respectively.

67 Lockheed Martin is providing the Navy "with the solutions they need to maintain freedom of the seas and deter aggression" <www.lockheedmartin.com/en-us/capabilities/maritime-systems.html>. Boeing pitches cyber tools as "provid[ing] a comprehensive suite of interactive solutions"

<www.boeing.com/defense/cybersecurity-information-management>. Northrop Grumman boasts that it provides "innovative systems, products and solutions to government and commercial customers worldwide" <www.northropgrumman.com/AboutUs/Welcome/default.aspx>. General Atomics, a major drone manufacturer, "provides best value field support solutions" for its fleet of drones <www.ga-si.com/aero-services>. "By establishing a close partnership with users and providing engineering support from the rear," Palantir "delivers a solution for defense customers that is constantly improving, constantly incorporating user feedback, and constantly adapting to meet future needs and solve new problem" <www.palantir.com/solutions/defense/>. L3 (maker of fuses, surveillance devices, training systems, and SATCOM antennae) says, "diverse needs require trusted solutions" <www.l3aviationproducts.com/solutions/>. CACI markets itself: "Information Deployed. Solutions Advanced. Missions Accomplished" <www.caci.com/about.shtml>. "By combining a passion for science with precision engineering, [United Technologies] is creating smart, sustainable solutions the world needs" <www.utc.com/news/news-center/pages/united-technologies-reports-second-quarter-2018-results-raises-2018-outlook.aspx>.

68 "Secretary of Defense Speech—Economic Club of Chicago." *U.S. Department of Defense*. 16 July 2009.

69 "Secretary of Defense Testimony—House Armed Services Committee." *U.S. Department of Defense*. 13 October 2011.

70 Simeone, Nick. "Hagel: Proposed Defense Budget Tailored to Meet Future Threats." *American Forces Press Service*. 18 June 2014.

71 "Remarks on 'The Next Two Links to the Force of the Future.'" *U.S. Department of Defense*. 9 June 2016.

72 "Trump calls for 'one of the largest defense spending increases in history.'" *Fox 5*. 2 March 2017.

73 Garamone, Jim. "Boeing Wins Aerial Tanker Contract." *American Forces Press Service*. 24 February 2011. The first contract, for four aircraft, cost $3.5 billion. The whole program would produce over 170 aircraft. Donley was a D.C. insider, former think tanker, and veteran political operative. Boeing's KC-46 program has been plagued with problems. As of December 2019, problems included malfunctioning camera systems airmen use to direct the refueling boom, debris in aircraft compartments, and malfunctioning cargo locking systems.

74 Shanahan, Patrick. "October Message to the DoD Team." *U.S. Department of Defense*. 2 November 2018.

75 "Remarks on 'The Next Two Links to the Force of the Future.'" *U.S. Department of Defense*. 9 June 2016. "Let me start with what we're doing on the military side, to ensure our services have the tools they need to always ensure we're promoting, retaining, and bringing in the best possible officers to lead our all-volunteer force," Secretary of War Ash Carter began.

76 In June 2012, the Army broke ground on a new Reserve Center in San Juan, part of a wider revamp of infrastructure in Puerto Rico. The senior Army reserve officer in the Caribbean claimed, "With this ceremony we continue taking the critical steps to ensure our troops have the resources and facilities needed to conduct administrative activities, plan operations and train personnel." Cuebas, Maj. Carlos. "Army Reserve investing big in Puerto Rico." *United States Army*. 1 June 2012.

77 "We must prepare our children and grandchildren with the tools they need to be informed, engaged citizens who care about individual liberty and democracy... We must teach them history. We must insist they understand the government they are blessed to live under," said Laura W. Bush, wife and whitewasher of one of the great war criminals in modern U.S. history.

"Texan of the Year 2018: Laura W. Bush." *Dallas Morning News Editorial*. 30 December 2018.

78 "Department of Defense Press Briefing by Colonel Folsom via teleconference from Al Asad Airbase in Iraq." *U.S. Department of Defense*. 20 March 2018. Col. Seth W.B. Folsom led Task Force Lion, which operated under Operation Inherent Resolve. Navy Captain Jeff Davis, director of Pentagon press operations, spoke about the Iraqi military: "We will stand by them... and we have given them the tools they need to succeed in this [fight against jihadists]." Quoted in Cronk, Terri Moon. "Iraqi Troops Advanced Toward Mosul as ISIL Tries to Hide Movements." *DMA*. 18 October 2016.

79 DeFilippis, Sgt. Rocco. "Marine Forces Europe instructors sharpen incoming Kosovo Forces soldier's [sic] non-lethal weapon skills." *Marine Forces Europe*. 9 February 2009. The troops were deploying to be a part of the U.S.-backed, NATO-led Kosovo Force, which is still going strong as of this writing.

80 Garamone, Jim. "Selva Addresses Global Challenges, Readiness in Capitol Hill Hearing." *DMA*. 18 July 2017. The Pentagon refers to this escalation of the conflict as supplying "lethal defensive aid." The U.S. Defense Security Cooperation Agency has assigned a retired senior Pentagon official to advise the Ukraine Defense Ministry in the pursuit of great power competition, Lt. Gen. Charles Hooper explains in "How security cooperation advances U.S. interests" (*Brookings Institution*, 4 June 2019).

81 "Defense." *NAVISTAR*. Accessed 15 July 2018: <www.navistar.com/navistar/globalportfolio/products/defense>.

This assertion rings hollow, especially when Navistar sells its MaxxPro vehicle to Pakistan. FMS to Pakistan issued 19 Dec 2014, for example.

82 Lenco Armored Vehicles' slogan is "Protecting Our Nation's Defenders." Oshkosh Defense's slogan right now is "Your Mission. Our Honor." Geoff Howe, of Howe & Howe Technologies, says he created a popular tracked vehicle "to save the lives of those fighting for ours—plain and simple." Howe & Howe Technologies designed and sold land vehicles. Geoff Howe was talking specifically about the Ripsaw, <www.howeandhowe.com/defense.html>. Textron now owns Howe & Howe.

83 Esterbrook, John. "Halliburton To Pay Pentagon $6.3M." *CBS News*. 23 January 2004.

84 "Raytheon Company increases dividend by 16 percent its eighth consecutive annual increase." *Raytheon*. 21 March 2012: <raytheon.mediaroom.com/index.php?s=43&item=2062>. Other Raytheon notables from early 2012 include producing its 1,000[th] "Paveway" guidance kit for bombs; celebrating Pi Day; collaborating with the Smithsonian museum; putting retired Gen. James Cartwright on the board of directors; selling Stinger missiles to Taiwan (5 Jan); selling aircraft sensor systems and software to Malaysia (10 Feb); selling satellite communication terminals to Canada's Navy (14 Feb); selling aircraft radar to Qatar (1 March); selling missiles to Singapore (1 March) and Saudi Arabia (1 and 30 March); and upgrading vehicle computers in the Los Angeles County Sheriff's Department, and inaugurating the Public Safety Regional Technology Center in Downey.

85 When pitching "concealment systems," a representative from TYR Tactical states, "In terms of concealment and protection of our troops and sustainability on the battlefield, we think it's critical, so that's why we're bringing it to market now." William Lynn, former U.S. Deputy Secretary of War and current head of the Italian corporation Leonardo DRS, affirms, the goal "is to do equally well going forward... to make similarly targeted investments that will ensure that our fighting forces retain that technological advantage." When celebrating new corporate infrastructure stateside, a vice president at Harris Corp. avers, "This facility demonstrates Harris' commitment and long-term dedication to our customers in the Tampa region and support to our military around the globe." "We feel strongly that the defense, intelligence and national security communities deserve access to the best technology in the world and we are committed to supporting their critical missions of protecting our citizens and defending our country," an Amazon spokesperson declares. The premier pressure group, NDIA, claims, "Budget instability hurts the defense industrial base's ability to supply warfighters with the

equipment they need to defend our homeland." TYR Tactical rep quoted at (7:08) in "SOFIC 2018 Day 2—Special Operations Force Industry Exhibition Tampa United States" (*DefenseWebTV*, 28 May 2018: <www.youtube.com/watch?v=mDQUP4Cz0h0>). Lynn quoted in "Leonardo DRS' Lynn on CNAS' 'Building the Future Force' Report, DOD Technology Investment" (*Defense & Aerospace Report*, 10 April 2018: <www.youtube.com/watch?v=t_zX4Avr35Y>). Harris VP quoted in "Harris Corporation Opens New Office in Tampa, Florida" (*Harris Corp*, 2 May 2011). Amazon quoted in Levi Pulkkinen "From books to bullets: inside Amazon's push to 'defend' America" (*The Guardian*, 31 January 2019). NDIA quoted in "NDIA commends passage of defense spending bill in time for new fiscal year" (*NDIA*, 28 September 2018).

86 For example, Budweiser is "proud to serve those who serve." Fritos honors "our nation's heroes" by teaming with Carry the Load, a non-profit "dedicated to providing active, meaningful ways to honor and celebrate the sacrifices made by our nations heroes," as made clear at <www.carrytheload.org>. USAA makes billions in annual profits selling insurance and banking services to the troops and military veterans.

87 "Capabilities." *Northrop Grumman*. Accessed 25 July 2018: <www.northropgrumman.com/Capabilities/C4ISR/specialops/Pages/default.aspx>.

88 "SAP NS2—Turn Thinking Into Everything." *SAP NS2*. 25 April 2018: <www.youtube.com/watch?v=WR2oIAP-y0g>, (00:18).

89 "MIDS JTRS terminal." *Data Link Solutions*. 2017: <https://datalinksolutions.net/pdf/MIDS-JTRS-data-sheet.pdf>.

Data Link Solutions makes the same claim about its Multifunctional Information Distribution System Low Volume Terminal (MIDS LVT) in <www3.rockwellcollins.com/dls/MIDS%20LVT%201%20Data%20Sheet%200209.pdf>.

90 "About Us." *Peraton*. Accessed 13 December 2018: <www.peraton.com>. And Robertson Fuel Systems has used the slogan "Extending the Reach of Freedom."

91 Caret earns millions each year from selling weapons of war to the War Dept. and governments worldwide. Mcintosh, Andrew. "Boeing reveals pay for top five highest paid executives in 2018." *Puget Sound Business Journal*. 15 March 2019.

92 DiFurio, Dom. "Boeing CEO Dennis Muilenburg says the last few weeks were the 'most heart-wrenching' of his career." *Dallas Morning News*. 11 April 2019.

93 Recent contracts involving obsolescence management or obsolescence monitoring include 30 March, 10 Aug, 28 Aug, 15 Dec, 21 Dec 2017; 25 June, 7 Aug, 5 Sept, 26 Sept, 17 Dec, 20 Dec 2018.

94 On 10 May 2017, Raytheon sold obsolescence components and other services for medium-range air-to-air missiles. On 7 March 2018, Raytheon sold testing and obsolescence work on anti-tank missiles. On 22 Dec 2016, Raytheon and Lockheed Martin (in the JV known as Javelin) sold efforts to resolve obsolescence issues. On 7 July 2017, Javelin JV sold anti-tank missiles, command launch units, and obsolescence work. On 31 March 2016, Raytheon sold "electronic equipment unit modification kits and obsolescence mitigation" on the radar used in Lockheed Martin's Terminal High Altitude Area Defense (THAAD). On 28 Aug 2017, Raytheon was tasked with manufacturing SM-3 missiles, which are marketed as being able to destroy short- and intermediate-range ballistic missiles. And, yes, the contract included "obsolescence monitoring," among other efforts. On 3 July 2018, Raytheon sold more obsolescence work on SM-3 missiles.

95 On 29 Sept 2016, Bell-Boeing Joint Project Office sold engineering efforts for the design and development of the Mission Computer Obsolescence Initiative Operation test program set for V-22. On 6 June 2017, Bell-Boeing JPO sold design and development of Midwing Avionics Obsolescence Vibration Structural Life & Engine Diagnostic operational test program set.

96 Issued 27 Aug 2015.

97 Issued 28 Jan 2016.

98 On 15 Feb 2017, Boeing was tasked with R&D, integration, and testing efforts on P-8A aircraft. This task order included obsolescence mitigation. On 24 Feb 2017, Boeing sold $41.3 million worth of P-8A systems and software engineering sustainment association with obsolescence, improvements, and enhancements. On 30 March 2017, Boeing sold $2.19 billion worth of P-8A aircraft to the U.S. and unspecified FMS customers. The deal covered "segregable efforts consisting of unknown obsolescence, class I change assessment, obsolescence monitoring, and integrated baseline/program management reviews." On 21 Dec 2017, Boeing sold over $1.2 billion worth of P-8A aircraft to the War Dept. and the U.K. This again included "segregable efforts consisting of unknown obsolescence."

99 Issued 25 Jan 2019.

100 Austal USA (Mobile, AL) was allocated up to $1,217,292,787 in 2017: $36,608,865 on 20 March for LCS core class services and special studies; $584,200,000 (max.) on 23 June to build an LCS; $12,283,922 on 6 Sept for engineering & management for advance planning and design on LCS-12 post shakedown availability; and $584,200,000 (max.) on 6 Oct to build an LCS. (Austal did not answer multiple inquiries asking whether the 23 June and 6 Oct announcements of $584.2 million were part of the same contract or separate contracts.) General Dynamics took in around $50,892,000: $7,973,506 on 20/24 April for LCS sustainment; $24,481,878 on 17 Aug for LCS planning yard services (engineering, ship configuration, material & logistics support); $9,214,089 on 28/29 Sept for LCS maintenance/support; and $9,222,928 on 27 Oct for LCS planning yard services. On 14 July, Lockheed Martin was allocated $8,617,000 for LCS services, and on 6 Oct it got up to $584.2 million to build an LCS. This accounting doesn't include corporations selling goods & services for LCS (e.g. Arête Associates Coastal Battlefield Reconnaissance & Analysis systems that go on Northrop Grumman MQ-8 drones, which launch from LCS; General Dynamics gun weapon systems; Lockheed Martin services for LCS sales to foreign governments; Northrop Grumman LCS gun mission modules; Raytheon maintenance on a sonar mine detecting set towed behind LCS; Raytheon Mine Neutralization Systems deployed from a Lockheed Martin helicopter launched from LCS; and Trivec-Avant antennae).

101 Available at <www.orwell.ru/library/essays/politics/english/e_polit>.

102 For example, just as cops protect largely white property, police the color line, deprive minorities of freedom in their own communities, and target black & brown people (e.g. shooting Stephan Clark in the back on his grandmother's property, supported by helicopters in the air) so does the U.S. military-industry police D.C.'s periphery (shooting Ahmed in his own country, supported by drones and helicopters in the air). Just as greater Los Angeles is monitored and policed by the largest municipal helicopter force in the world, so too were Baghdadis monitored and policed by the largest collection of helicopters (and other air assets) in the world, by my count, during 2007.

103 Genuine worldwide democracy would reduce the war industry's customer base, since unpropagandized citizens of countries in the Persian Gulf, for example, would kick out their despotic oppressors and reject U.S. weaponry. Likewise, genuine democracy in the U.S. would reject permanent corporate war and embrace a system that cares for the working class.

5

Foreign Military Sales

RATIONALIZATIONS

Through foreign military sales (FMS), the U.S. government procures and transfers industry goods and services to allied governments and international organizations. The most belligerent regimes on Earth are frequent customers, including London, Riyadh, Abu Dhabi, and Tel Aviv. The Leahy Law, which is intended to prevent U.S. military assistance from reaching militaries that have committed serious human rights violations, is not enforced when it comes to FMS.

FMS exists to profit the U.S. war industry. Publicly, U.S. military officers repeat the industry assertion that FMS reduces the cost of military systems to the U.S. Armed Forces. Privately, U.S. military officers support FMS because foreign militaries dependent on U.S. equipment, knowhow, training, parts, and software are more likely to listen to the Pentagon on military matters, the direction to take in regional conflicts, and international policy—and indeed, be effectively locked long term into the U.S. orbit. The director of the Defense Security Cooperation Agency (DSCA)—the agency in charge of administering FMS and military education exchange programs—touches upon these core reasons, explaining, DSCA programs are

> a foundation for human relationships. The strength of our programs is that we don't leave our partners behind at the point of sale. We are with them for the long run. When we use the same equipment, we speak the same language, use the same doctrine, and attend the same schools. We break bread together. This is the foundation of the long-term relationships between our leaders, our warriors, and our respected military professionals...[1]

Let me clarify. In actuality, this purported foundation for human relationships primarily serves as a conduit to guarantee future sales from U.S. war corporations to foreign governments. When the DSCA director says programs "don't leave their partners behind at the point of sale," the subtext is that corporations work hard to sell upgrades, maintenance, equipment, technical support, logistics, and other goods and services for as long as possible; DSCA's job is to facilitate these initial and follow-on sales. "We are with them for the long run." Common terminology, doctrine, and formal military education unite U.S. military-industry and foreign militaries.

FMS is framed as altruistically helping a country defend itself. The DSCA director says FMS is just the U.S. government providing "capability to address common challenges," helping allies' "ability to defend themselves," and "building partner capacity."[2] Defensive justifications play out in a variety of locations. Raytheon is building a sizeable radar system for the Qatari regime. According to the country director for Bahrain and Qatar (a position within the U.S. Secretary of the Air Force for International Affairs), the Raytheon radar "will better protect Qatar's people, culture and infrastructure against current and future medium- and long-range ballistic missile threats."[3] When selling the F-35 fighter jet to Japan, Lockheed Martin's CEO says, "The security alliance between Japan and the United States has been a cornerstone of peace and prosperity in the Asia-Pacific region for generations."[4] DSCA claims a potential sale of United Technologies engines, General Electric rotary cannons, Lockheed Martin jets, and other weapons to Slovakia would help "improve the security of a NATO partner that is an important force for ensuring peace and stability in Europe."[5] Stability, peace, defense—worldwide, wherever U.S. weaponry goes. "Solutions."[6] On any given day, DSCA is managing "14,000 open foreign military sales cases with 185 countries," the director explains.[7]

THE MQ-4C TRITON

Northrop Grumman's MQ-4C "Triton" is a large, expensive, unarmed drone that operates at high altitudes. Northrop Grumman spreads work on the MQ-4C across the U.S.[8] In June 2018, the Australian Prime Minister disclosed that the Australian military would purchase six of these drones. (Australia uses the General Atomics MQ-9 as its armed drone.) Corporations from Nevada to Pennsylvania view the MQ-4C as a platform for their products.[9] The total cost of these drones must take into account new infrastructure needed. *Reuters* calculates this as roughly $6.9 billion AUD to be paid by Australian taxpayers.[10]

These Northrop Grumman drones are designed to operate with Boeing P-8A maritime patrol aircraft. Boeing regularly sells additional P-8A-related goods and services.[11] Australia has already purchased a few of these aircraft and is in line to purchase more. War corporations view the P-8A as a platform for a range of their products.[12] In order to achieve initial operational capability, Australia must have in place the requisite infrastructure, including new facilities, logistics, management, supplies, support, and training areas. Corporations, including many from the U.S., sell this.[13]

Enter the Kiwis. In July 2018, Australia's neighbor, New Zealand, inked a deal to purchase four P-8A aircraft at a price of $2.2 billion (NZ$2.34 billion). Neighbors bound by industry's chains operate together. The deal was marketed as a "Pacific reset," "promoting regional stability," and countering "the rise of China"—part of the terminological cluster surrounding the new great power competition pretext. The hundredth P-8A aircraft was produced in October 2018. Australia, India, Norway, and the U.K. operate the aircraft. South Korea might purchase it. Boeing is looking to increase international sales.[14]

Corporations consider a country like Australia to be a wealthy shopper. FMS to Australia has spanned radios, targeting systems, missile launchers, and more. More means everything from aircraft countermeasures and avionics to kits that turn artillery shells into "smart" weapons. Boom goes the explosive (and the wire transfer).

Industry often crafts FMS contracts with stipulations requiring the purchase of a variety of goods and services in the future, including computer program development, data, documentation, equipment, engineering, engineering change proposals, incidental materials, in-country support, logistics, maintenance, mission support, parts, performance-based logistics, program management, refresh, spares, staging, sustainment, technical manuals, and training.

FMS to Australia from the beginning of July 2014 through the end of the 2015 calendar year amounted to 110 distinct transactions worth approximately $2,219,764,000, I tallied. FMS to just one country can be a bonanza for the U.S. war industry. You have to ask: is this "building partner capacity"—or tribute from a vassal state?

A SINGLE MONTH'S SALES

You've witnessed how one sale of one product easily snowballs into many additional, tangential, or complementary purchases from the U.S. war industry. And you've gaped at how much one government among many can purchase from the U.S. war industry. But what happens in just one month? A mere month of FMS—June 2018, selected at random—is detailed below. One month teaches us about the priorities of authority, conflict zones, unnamed customers, contract bundling, and Europe's war industry.

Textron sold T-6 aircraft to Argentina. The T-6 is a single-engine prop plane often used to train pilots. There was an uptick in FMS to Argentina after President Mauricio Macri took power at the end of 2015. Macri spends millions on foreign weapons[15] while enforcing austerity measures against the Argentinian people.[16]

In 2018, Macri's government took out the largest ever loan from the International Monetary Fund, $57 billion, requiring cuts in social spending. Governments that purchase weaponry from U.S. industry often claim there isn't enough money for domestic social programs, as if the left hand doesn't know what the right hand is doing.

The U.S. war industry profits from high tensions: Japan v. China, South v. North Korea, and Taiwan v. China. Without tensions, military provocations, and ongoing war (in the case of Korea, as the July 1953 armistice ended hostilities, not the state of war), the U.S. war industry would lose billions in annual sales. Industry goods and services sold in June 2018 to allies in East Asia covered frequency converters, mission computers, early warning aircraft, tiltrotor aircraft, ship networking systems, and the Aegis missile defense system.[17] Increasingly, sales to Pacific nations are being painted as necessary under great power competition.

The military and industry can avoid disclosing the recipient of U.S. weaponry by classifying an FMS transaction or by simply not stating the recipient's name in the contract announcement. Unnamed FMS announced during the month in question, June 2018, included Boeing goods and services for its jets; Harris Corp. electronic warfare equipment production; and Lockheed Martin Autonomic Logistics Information System software and installations. ALIS is the error-ridden, IT-heavy maintenance "mission support" product for Lockheed Martin's costly F-35 fighter jet. (ALIS is such a poor product that U.S. Air Force pilots and students have stopped using it, *Defense News* has reported.[18]) Unnamed FMS has increased in recent years in public contracts. Reasons could include a desire to hide sales to non-state actors, as well as recipient countries wishing to conceal their business ties to the U.S. war industry for domestic political purposes.

Governments are often bundled together in FMS, as sales in June 2018 demonstrate.[19] Bundling customers guarantees reliable, regular, uniform, worldwide bulk sales, and, the war corporations emphasize, economies of scale.

Europe has a war industry of its own. London has BAE Systems, Paris has Thales and Safran, Rome has Leonardo DRS, Brussels has Fabrique National (owned by the Herstal Group), and Stockholm has Saab—to name a few. But European governments also purchase from the U.S. war industry. In June 2018, DynCorp sold aircraft maintenance to Croatia, Lockheed Martin sold missile services for Romania's arsenal, a U.S.-German team sold equipment for naval surface-to-air missiles to Germany, and Raytheon sold communication security units for NATO allies. Oh, and SAIC sold torpedo components to Turkey. It was an average month.

FMS customers within greater Middle East are the big prizes. All Gulf Cooperation Council (GCC) countries—Bahrain, Kuwait, Oman, Qatar, Saudi Arabia, and the UAE—host U.S. military forces and bases. Oman keeps the lowest profile of all. No GCC country is democratic. The Pentagon and U.S. war corporations like it this way; if the people of the Gulf had their say, the War Department likely wouldn't be allowed in. Absolutist Gulf regimes purchased billions from the U.S. war industry in June 2018.[20]

Even as the civilians of Afghanistan and Pakistan suffered under D.C.'s longest war, their governments purchased from the U.S. war industry: MD Helicopter maintenance for Afghanistan, and L3 upgrades on Lockheed Martin F-16 training devices for Pakistan in June 2018. MD Helicopter's June 20th sale included engineering support, failure reporting, maintenance support, management, repair, spares procurement, support system readiness, and total asset visibility. My, how many categories! U.S. war corporations don't just provide maintenance. They craft additional, profitable categories of service.

Lebanon pops up once or twice a year in FMS. Boeing's Insitu unit sold unarmed ScanEagle drones—wingspan about three meters—to Lebanon in June 2018. Medico Industries sold 120mm explosives, practice charges, and fuse parts to Lebanon. Lockheed Martin sold logistics and technical assistance to Iraq regarding ground equipment, spares, repairs, and training on cargo aircraft. Iraqi government officials can't keep the power on,[21] but somehow find enough money to purchase weaponry regularly from U.S. industry. Neither D.C. nor Baghdad has demonstrated genuine, sustained concern for the people.

The FMS contracts listed in the above eight paragraphs were issued in June 2018. That month was relatively mild: by my count, U.S. industry sold $5,408,112,575 of FMS goods and services. The industry leitmotifs you saw crop up in June 2018 included governments bundled together in one contract, regional tensions being good for business, governments purchasing weaponry while neglecting their citizens, and the Middle East being a great market. Only concerted education and action, inducing, among other results, a forced withdrawal of U.S. military and industry from the region, will change this miserable status quo.

ZIONISM, AN INDUSTRY PERSPECTIVE

Zionism is the ideology that justifies the occupation and colonization of Palestine, and the maintenance and expansion of the occupation, using various forms of violence. Zionists had weighed colonizing other locations, but much of the ideological rationale demands locating in historic Palestine. Zionists established Israel in Palestine in May 1948, ethnically cleansing hundreds of thousands of Arabs from the land. U.S. President Harry S. Truman immediately recognized Israel's independence. (Formal, *de jure* recognition from D.C. was finalized in January 1949.) Many of Truman's top military and diplomatic advisors were astonished at his decision. General George C. Marshall was vehemently opposed to recognizing the nascent Israel.

Heartbreak defines the ensuing U.S.-Israel relationship. A small faction within the War Department reportedly colluded to cover up Israel's 8 June 1967 attack on the USS *Liberty*.[22] By the October 1973 war, the Pentagon's leadership had committed fully to arming the Israeli military: In Operation Nickel Grass, the Pentagon and the U.S. war industry worked together to restock Israel's arsenal. Since the 1980s, Israel War Ministers and their coteries have been routinely flying to D.C., where they're feted like kings. In 1999, the Israeli Ministry of War and U.S. Department of War established the Defense Policy Advisory Group through which both countries review "global and regional security challenges and set priorities" for the "partnership over the coming year."[23] The War Department across Republican and Democratic administrations has worked hand-in-hand with Israel to attack Iran and Hezbollah,[24] a social welfare provider in Lebanon capable of deterring Israeli aggression.

A notable major resupply of Israel's massive arsenal came in the last week of July 2014. Israel was engaged in murdering 2,200 civilians in Gaza, so when Israeli officials asked for access to U.S. war matériel, including high explosives, that had been prepositioned within the apartheid state, the Pentagon complied immediately. Israel didn't miss a beat in its onslaught against Palestinians, including multiple attacks against schools belonging to the United Nations Relief and Works Agency in Gaza's Jabaliya refugee camp. Today, every new U.S. Secretary of War affirms that the U.S.-Israel relationship has never been stronger. The 501(c)3 Zionist think tank known as Jewish Institute for National Security Affairs (JINSA) has been indispensable in cultivating political support among active and retired U.S. military officers.

The U.S. war industry typically sells to Israel through U.S. Army Contracting Command's Europe District. This makes sense, since many of the Zionists that colonized Palestine hailed from European countries, Israel plays basketball in the European league, and Israel competes in the Eurovision song competition. These facts align well with what the Israeli founding father, David Ben Gurion, said—to paraphrase: Israel is part of the Middle East in geography only, and never intended to be a part of the region.

The U.S. war industry leadership loves Apartheid Israel. Foreign military financing is money, usually loans or grants, which D.C. sends to other governments so they can buy from U.S. industry. Each year, D.C. gives roughly $3.8 billion to Israel. (The number can increase with congressional supplements.) Israel is supposed to use all of the money to purchase U.S. weaponry, according to the most recent agreement signed with D.C. in September 2016. In addition to the billions of dollars routed through Israel to the U.S. war industry, U.S. corporate leaders love Israel because of teamwork: Both groups lobby Capitol Hill together. It is hard for Capitol Hill to say no when two of the most powerful lobbies are advocating for military conflicts. The final major reason the U.S. war industry loves Israel is because the occupation of Palestine and Zionist aggression against neighboring countries ensures ongoing conflict, providing the U.S. war industry with a valuable slice of its portfolio: an outsourced proving ground to test, evaluate, and improve weaponry. U.S. war corporations do not care about innocents dying. Palestinian lives, Syrian lives, Lebanese lives, Egyptian lives, and Arab life in general—the U.S. war industry couldn't care less. When war is profit, death ensures a healthy bottom line. The aggressive military posture inherent in Zionism is a commercial asset.

Human rights groups pinpoint Boeing, Caterpillar, General Electric, Lockheed Martin, Motorola, Northrop Grumman, and Raytheon as contributing to Israel's systematic abuse of Palestinians. Products include Boeing missiles and attack helicopters; Lockheed Martin fighter jets, cargo aircraft, and mobile rocket launchers; and Raytheon PATRIOT missile systems and air-to-air missiles.[25] But they are not the only U.S. war corporations that sell to the Zionist regime. Israel's recent purchases span the gamut: FLIR Systems weapon sights, Nammo Talley light assault weapons, National Test Pilot School (Mojave, CA) training, and ViaSat communications systems.[26] U.S. corporations help keep the Israeli military mobile.[27] Sales, you see, go beyond such typical offenders as Boeing and Raytheon, and attest to the deep relationship between the U.S. war industry and Israel. Israeli officials across government and industry are quick to note the benefits that Israel brings to the U.S. war industry's table: Israel was the first country to use Lockheed Martin's F-35 jet in combat;[28] Israel has used Raytheon's PATRIOT missile system against drones;[29] and, in general, Israel has killed Arabs quite effectively with a variety of aircraft and weaponry purchased from U.S. corporations. The U.S. State Department turns a blind eye.[30] Israel regularly claims self-defense when using U.S. and Israeli weaponry to kill Arabs.

The Egyptian regime must be mentioned within the context of U.S. support for the Zionist regime. D.C. supports the Egyptian regime for two main reasons: U.S. industry says so, and the Zionist lobby says so. U.S. industry wants to sell weapons, and the Zionist lobby wants D.C. to continue giving Egypt diplomatic support and the $1.4 billion annuity in foreign military financing—an amount large enough to keep the Egyptian military compliant and locked in. The U.S. war industry reequipped a pacified Egyptian military after the October War, 1973, en route to the 1978 Camp David Accords and the 1979 Egypt-Israel peace treaty. And it hasn't stopped arming Egypt ever since.[31] In recent years, the Egyptian dictator, General Abdel Fattah as-Sisi, jailed thousands, executed dissidents, tortured opponents, and disappeared citizens. D.C. likes as-Sisi because he enforces the peace with Apartheid Israel, purchases weaponry from U.S. corporations, and opens up Egypt to foreign corporations.

Many Israeli war corporations have set up shop inside the U.S. The Israeli corporation Elbit Systems has a strong presence in Fort Worth, Texas. The Pentagon purchases aircraft technology, communications systems, surveillance products, and other goods from Elbit. Elta North America, a subsidiary of Israeli Aerospace Industries, is headquartered in Annapolis Junction, Maryland, just west of Fort Meade (home to NSA). Elta sells radar, communications, and surveillance products. Israeli technology has been purchased and deployed to the U.S.-Mexico border. The presence of Israeli war corporations inside the U.S., including in Silicon Valley, profits Apartheid Israel and encourages combined U.S.-Israeli military proficiency and ferocity.[32]

The U.S. and Israeli war industries collaborate.[33] One of the most productive alliances between the two is Rockwell Collins and Elbit Systems, together known as Vision Systems International. VSI produces a helmet display system that pilots wear to see the battlefield and track humans and vehicles. Work takes place across the U.S. (including Merrimack, NH, down to Atlanta, GA, west to Wilsonville, OR) and Israel. VSI sells to at least thirteen foreign militaries, by my count, including Australia, Belgium, Canada, Chile, Finland, Iraq, Pakistan, Portugal, Switzerland, and Thailand. In April 2019, the U.S. industry pressure group NDIA signed an agreement with the Manufacturers Association of Israel, bringing the latter into the former's International Division.[34] CEOs of U.S. war corporations travel to Israel regularly. U.S. war corporations have offices there to benefit from collaboration and the foreign military financing that flows through the apartheid state.[35]

U.S. construction firms aid and abet the occupation of Palestine. Israel is not the only country that uses U.S. construction firms, but it is by far the most egregious. Contracts are often noncompetitive. U.S. construction firms that have worked regularly for Israel include AECOM, Conti, and KBR. (Nibor, also popular with Israel, is a U.S.-Israeli firm.) Notable construction projects include an Israeli military recruitment center and ammunition storage facilities, issued 8 July 2014 and 5 April 2019 respectively. Most projects involving U.S. construction firms in the apartheid state lack details. Such secrecy is how D.C. operates in general: Deny the public the necessary information to make decisions regarding the fate of the nation—information which if disclosed would cause outrage regarding the MIC's posture. Conti Federal of Edison, NJ, has been Israel's favorite U.S. construction firm.[36] On 31 July 2015, Conti received a contract to build a photovoltaic power plant at an Israeli military base. The Israeli military bombed Gaza's electrical infrastructure in their 2008-9 assault and again on 29 July 2014. Electricity for Zionist colonists, good. Electricity for Palestinians, bad.

Heavy Israeli espionage and lobbying ensure the D.C. regime does not stray from unconditional support of Israel. Israel has worked hard to establish espionage cells, lobbies, and think tanks within the Beltway. That much is fairly well known. (While Israeli law equates NGO receipt of foreign funding with disloyalty, the U.S. fails to regard Zionist lobbies operating in D.C. as disloyal to the U.S. and require their registration under the U.S. Foreign Agents Registration Act.) New members of U.S. Congress submit to AIPAC in exchange for political backing and helpful funding. Some U.S. Senators take this allegiance to the extreme. Mossad case officers (*katsa*, in the singular) and personnel from Israeli military intelligence are dug into the Baltimore-D.C. corridor like ticks. Sometimes brazen, sometimes difficult to uncover, Israeli recruitment of U.S. officials spans military, politics, industry, and intelligence. Israel's operations are conducted with an eye on long-term development. Israel has unfiltered signals intelligence on U.S. persons,[37] thanks to NSA's leadership. This intel can easily be used to support Israeli operations in the U.S. (And when the Israelis dislike an intel sharing agreement, they work hard to get one that is better—for them.[38]) Israel takes full advantage of FMS.[39]

Israel cares about Israel. Full stop. Look at the track record. A decent chunk of what Israeli spy Jonathan Pollard stole from U.S. intelligence agencies went to the Soviet Union. Israel reportedly traded the information to Moscow in exchange for supporting Zionist immigration to Israel.[40] Israel lobbied hard and secured Pollard's released in 2015. Israel stole nuclear triggers and uranium from the United States.[41] "Intelligence" the Israelis give to the U.S. is usually politicized—designed to steer U.S. foreign policy in a direction favorable to Mossad's long-term strategic goals.[42] And Israel always gets more than it gives: *Want this? How about giving us access to those satellites of yours?* The U.S. government says, "Okay."

Terrorism is politically-motivated violence. It occurs when a state, a group, or an individual uses violence against ordinary people with the aim of coercing them, intimidating them, or instilling fear in them. Zionist terrorism was instrumental in bringing about the creation of Israel, ethnically cleansing Palestine and murdering British officials.[43] Even the *Associated Press* couldn't turn a blind eye to Zionist terrorism. Reporting in 2016 on the contents of declassified British documents in the U.K. National Archives, which included hundreds of creative Zionist plots against the British, the *AP* revealed Zionist forces' attempted assassination of Evelyn Barker, commander of British forces in Palestine during the British Mandate.[44] "Railways, bridges, government facilities and officers clubs were all targeted."[45] Assassinating a U.S. Ambassador was also not out of the question.[46]

For decades now, U.S. and Israeli goods and services have helped Israel violate Palestinian human rights. In the West Bank, Israel monitors and raids Palestinian communities regularly, killing Palestinians and subjecting them to indefinite detention, interrogation, and torture. Israeli military courts boast a near 100% conviction rate against Palestinians from the West Bank. But what about Gaza? The Israelis dismantled their colonies in Gaza in 2005, a strategic maneuver designed to double down on colonization of the West Bank.[47] The Israeli military regularly massacres Gazans (e.g. winter 2008-9, November 2012, summer 2014, and ongoing bombing and sniping). In its day-to-day oppression of Palestinians, Israel has developed a wide variety of invasive espionage technology. A sizeable portion of the Israeli war industry is now focused on population control and counterinsurgency technologies: surveillance equipment, drones, border sensors, "homeland security" products, and oppressive know-how.[48] Brutal regimes use Israeli technology.[49] Israeli sales to the likes of Saudi Arabia and the UAE bring many benefits: increased normalization between Arab regimes and Apartheid Israel; lots of money; and an alliance of the worst human rights abusers against a common enemy, Iran.

Israel is more than just an apartheid state that purchases heavily from U.S. industry. It is a location of warfare production, testing, terror, and collaboration.

A TALE OF TWO REGIMES: D.C. AND THE HOUSE OF SAUD

The U.S. war industry's relationship with the House of Saud encapsulates D.C.'s approach to foreign policy: corporate and immoral. U.S. weaponry is the backbone of the Saudi military, including its National Guard, which leads the way in quashing the Saudi citizenry whenever deprived groups rise up in demand of basic human rights (notably the Shi'a in early winter of 1979 in al-Hasa', and in 2011-2 in al-Hufuf, al-Awamiya, and other towns). DynCorp, Northrop Grumman, Rockwell Collins, and other U.S. war corporations have been instrumental in training and sustaining the Saudi National Guard.

Saudi Arabia purchases a lot of weaponry from U.S. industry. *The New York Times* cited the Stockholm International Peace Research Institute regarding U.S. products going to the Saudi regime during 2010-17: thirty Boeing F-15 aircraft, 84 combat helicopters, 110 air-to-surface missiles, and roughly 20,000 guided bombs.[50] The D.C. regime did not object when in 2015 the Saudi regime turned U.S. weaponry on Yemen, murdering innocents.[51]

News of Yemen's destruction was hard to ignore. The Pentagon implemented stricter safeguards in summer 2017, including expanding a no-strike list to more than 33,000 targets, which the U.S. Secretary of State, a former oil tycoon, then used to gain elites' support "for the sale of more than $510 million in precision-guided munitions to the kingdom."[52] The Saudis simply disregarded these "safeguards." As did their arms suppliers. The Saudi coalition reportedly killed at least 370 children in Yemen during 2017. On 9 August 2018, the coalition attacked a school bus carrying Yemeni children. A Mark 82 bomb was one type of ordnance used to attack the school bus. General Dynamics (Garland, TX) has been a main producer of the Mark 82, which it has sold to the three main aggressors in Yemen: D.C., Riyadh, and Abu Dhabi. Other buyers have included Canada, France, Iraq, Oman, Taiwan, and Turkey. Seven transactions involving Mark 82 sales have netted General Dynamics nearly a billion dollars ($970,580,786) in recent years. *CNN* reported that Lockheed Martin had manufactured the particular Mark 82 dropped on the school bus on 9 August 2018. It is quite possible that General Dynamics manufactured the bomb, while Lockheed Martin manufactured the bomb's guidance kit. The Saudi-led coalition later investigated themselves regarding the school bus attack. The head of the investigation insisted the strike had hit a "legitimate" military target, according to the *BBC*. As of mid-September 2018, *Save the Children* reported that 5.2 million Yemeni children faced famine. *The New York Times* reported 18,000 coalition airstrikes struck Yemen from 2015 to autumn 2018. By the end of 2018, coalition airstrikes had killed at least 4,600 civilians, a low estimate from *The New York Times*. Bombing runs continue from King Khalid Air Base and other Saudi bases where U.S. war corporations sustain activities. The death toll rises. On the fourth anniversary of the start of aggression against Yemen, the Saudi coalition bombed a hospital.[53]

The U.S. military provided aerial refueling to the Saudi coalition until the end of 2018. The U.S. military still provides "intelligence" to the Saudi coalition. Yemenis suffer from raging famine, disease outbreaks, and crippled infrastructure. Civilians are hit (school field trips, funeral processions, weddings, markets, etc.) and humanitarian aid is prevented from entering. In autumn 2018, the head of the State Department's legislative affairs team (a former Raytheon lobbyist) certified that Saudi Arabia and the UAE were taking steps to reduce civilian deaths in Yemen.[54] The overall death toll in Yemen passed 100,000 in autumn 2019, according to Armed Conflict Location & Event Data.[55]

Lockheed Martin's business is one of the major links between the D.C. and Saudi regimes. The corporation's sales to the Saudi regime center around seven products.[56] Joe Rank recently finished up a career in the U.S. Army that spanned three decades. His final job in Army uniform was helping guide Middle East policy for the U.S. Secretary of War. Now he is in charge of Lockheed Martin's business with Saudi Arabia.

Vision 2030 is the Saudi regime's campaign to diversify its economy. U.S. public relations and consulting firms, corporations, and media outlets play a large role. As it stands, the Saudi regime is highly dependent upon the fossil fuel corporation, Saudi Aramco.[57] On the ground, Vision 2030 provides suave cover for the House of Saud to shore up power during a time of instability. In parallel to Vision 2030, U.S. war corporations have been expanding facilities in Saudi Arabia. Subsidiaries like *Boeing Saudi Arabia, General Dynamics Arabia*, and *Raytheon Saudi Arabia* are growing. Gentle terminology—"indigenous development," "strengthening partnerships," "being a meaningful part of the Kingdom," "diversification"—cushions such expansion. Raytheon's executive in charge of international sales adds a teaspoon of honey: Indigenous development is about giving partners an opportunity to make investments in their capability, with Raytheon as the "trusted advisor" and the "go-to resource."[58] Other U.S. war corporations are involved in the Vision 2030 effort. For example, Kratos sells planning, technical & instructional services, and logistics for the naval portion.[59]

Saudi corporations move to operate in greater concert with U.S. weaponry. Established in 1988, Advanced Electronics Co. works with major war corporations like United Technologies and Lockheed Martin. It has netted worthwhile contracts for work complementing U.S. goods and services. Other Saudi corporations like Al-Raha Group for Technical Services (RGTS) and Al-Salam Aircraft Company (AAC) work with U.S. war corporations and provide integral support to the U.S.-manufactured Saudi arsenal. U.S. war corporations often have large financial stakes in these Saudi corporations. These Saudi corporations are working to bring the professionalization and standardization of U.S. war corporations to Saudi Arabia—such "Saudization" helps the House of Saud play extra innings (crushing internal dissent while prolonging Saudi participation in the MIC).

At the same time, Saudi lobbyists go to extreme lengths to purchase support and stay in favor within D.C. The public relations and lobbying firm Qorvis/MSLGroup has long been a Saudi regime favorite. Firms cultivate MIC officials, promote pseudo-scholarship, network with think tanks, sponsor corporate media campaigns, and entice the pro-war political class in D.C. Sometimes the lobbying and public relations firms on Saudi payroll also work for U.S. war corporations (from which the Saudis purchase war goods and services). Firms working for the Saudi regime even reportedly purchased rooms at D.C. hotels for U.S. military veterans, who were then sent to Capitol Hill to lobby for the Saudi regime.[60]

The congressional side of the military-industrial-congressional triangle has done its job. One faction of Congress resorted to procedural ploy in the U.S. House of Representatives—attaching a one-line rule change to a resolution about wolves[61] in order to avoid a vote about the U.S.-backed, Saudi-led war against Yemen. The matter eventually came up for a vote. Neither a Senate vote in December 2018 nor one in March 2019 banned the U.S. military or mercenaries from operating in the Arabian Peninsula, though both votes were praised as "ending U.S. military support for Saudis in Yemen." Political operatives from the U.S. war industry crafted language—including a deliberately vague part about "associated forces"—and watered down the text in these bills, creating loopholes to facilitate ongoing military operations. Neither vote touched ongoing sales from U.S. war corporations to the Saudi regime. Neither vote touched U.S. drone operations in the skies over Yemen. The bills explicitly allowed U.S. troops to operate in "hostilities" in Yemen against what commanders or officials deem to be al-Qaeda. D.C.'s forces only need to claim that al-Qaeda has a presence in a given region, and then the Pentagon and/or intelligence agencies are free to operate and kill in and around that area. Notably, both the December and March votes took care of Zionist priorities.[62] Both votes can be understood as political rebukes to the Trump White House, not to the destruction of Yemen. The congressional side of the MIC will not harm the pillars of the D.C.-Saudi relationship. The MIC wants to keep a friendly, compliant Saudi regime in power for as long as possible. It's good for business.

SELLING TO COUNTRIES WITHIN CENTRAL COMMAND

The Pentagon has divided the world into geographical areas of responsibility so it can better manage the imperium. U.S. Central Command (CENTCOM) is the geographic combatant command in charge of the greater Middle East. CENTCOM stretches from Kazakhstan in the north, Afghanistan and Pakistan in the east, westward across the Arabian Peninsula, ending in Egypt. U.S. Africa Command (AFRICOM) is in charge of the African continent, minus Egypt. An added bonus of these administrative divisions is greater ease in partnering with anti-democratic regimes and selling them U.S. industry products. In less than one year—from May 2015 through March 2016—U.S. war corporations sold over $30 billion of goods and services to anti-democratic Gulf allies.[63]

Selling weaponry takes a little work. Navy Vice Admiral Barry McCullough retired as Commander of U.S. Fleet Cyber Command and then got a job with Lockheed Martin. In no time he was vice president of business strategy. In March 2018, Vago Muradian of the *Defense & Aerospace Report* joked that Barry was "ready to become a Saudi citizen" because Barry was "spending so much time over there" in Saudi Arabia.[64] Hard work pays off. In May 2018, Barry was promoted to vice president of strategy & business development in Lockheed Martin's Rotary and Mission Systems division.[65] FMS represents a sizable chunk of Lockheed Martin's overall sales,[66] and countries within CENTCOM are the corporation's favorite customers. Goods and services Lockheed Martin sold to governments in CENTCOM during 2016-17 involved missiles, cargo aircraft, helicopters, and aircraft sensors.[67] And that's just one corporation. Ask yourself "Why sow conflict in the Middle East?" as you familiarize yourself with foreign military sales.

Weapons sales to CENTCOM regimes are broad, as Raytheon's 2016-17 transactions demonstrate. Sales were missile-heavy (air-to-air, rocket motors for air-to-air, HAWK, anti-tank, surface-to-air), but spanned the region (from thermal weapon sites for Pakistan to running Qatar's air & missile defense operations center). Given its long sales history to regimes like Bahrain, Saudi Arabia, and the UAE, Raytheon stands firmly on the side of profit, and firmly against democracy. Or, as the corporation puts it: "With more than 50 years in the Middle East, Raytheon's steadfast commitment and uninterrupted presence in the region is a testament to the tremendous value we place on being there for our customers."[68] And where war corporations go, construction and logistics follow.[69]

SELLING TO THE U.S. FOR OPERATIONS WITHIN CENTRAL COMMAND

The end of World War II saw the British Empire fading fast. The U.S. Empire was *the* superpower. The U.S. War Department already had thousands of military installations worldwide in 1945, including many in the Middle East. The 1945 Quincy Pact between U.S. President Franklin D. Roosevelt and King Abdul Aziz al-Saud sealed the deal: D.C. would entrench regional bases and protect the House of Saud, while the latter would keep the oil flowing and give preferential treatment to U.S. corporate interests. The Saudi regime would later agree to use the dollar in international oil trading. The U.S. War Department refined its Middle East basing over the years. The 1980 Carter Doctrine accelerated this process.

Units of the U.S. Armed Forces now deploy regularly to Middle Eastern countries—countries where it fights (e.g. Afghanistan, Iraq) and countries where it launches aircraft, conducts information gathering, stores matériel, and stations troops (e.g. Bahrain, Kuwait, Qatar, Saudi Arabia, Jordan, and the UAE). You know by now that the U.S. war industry makes a lot of money selling goods and services to Middle East governments. But you might not be familiar with how the U.S. war industry sells goods and services to the U.S. War Department for U.S. military units that are *deployed or stationed within* Middle East countries. Gulf countries house some of the War Department's biggest and most active overseas installations. U.S. military units use war industry goods and services on deployment (and are often outnumbered in their deployment location by mercenaries, a.k.a. contractors).

Before a unit can deploy to the Middle East, it needs to be trained. All branches of the U.S. Armed Forces are heavily dependent on corporations to train.

The Marines are arguably the least corporatized when it comes to training, yet they too suffer. At great expense, corporations provide role players for semi-realism; run "immersive training range support"; train Marines on corporate counter-IED curricula; teach how to best command a military convoy and respond to an ambush; help run and synchronize command and control training; practically run the Marines' Training & Education Command at Quantico, Virginia; develop Marine training plans and doctrine; provide physical instruction and lectures; help run Marine Corps Installations Command HQ; run the Multi-Mission Parachute Course; provide distance education for Training Command; manage security and support training at installations; and work on injury prevention. For Pete's sake, what's left for the Marines? Training requires substantial physical infrastructure. Recent construction on military training facilities spans east coast to west.[70] Once built, training facilities require the Pentagon to purchase more and more goods and services (e.g. instructors, simulators, dummy and live ordnance, maintenance, technical expertise) in order to process more troops to fill out the billets prosecuting nonstop war.

Just getting to a single warzone can be incredibly costly.[71] U.S. Transportation Command (TRANSCOM) is the military unit in charge of global transportation. TRANSCOM and the Pentagon have corporatized most international movement of personnel and cargo. Troops often fly to and from U.S. bases in Europe and Asia on massive aircraft (e.g. DC-10) run by companies, not by the military. Cargo aircraft like the Boeing C-17 and the Lockheed Martin C-5, some of the greatest single burners of fossil fuel in the U.S. arsenal, fly in cargo and some troops. Corporations such as American Airlines, FedEx, and UPS[72]—without which the war machine would grind to a halt—handle a lot of the cargo load. Such corporations are members of the Civil Reserve Air Fleet (CRAF) program. CRAF was established in 1950 as part of the Defense Production Act, leading D.C.'s war mobilization sending goods and services to the fight in Korea (where D.C.'s forces committed war crimes[73]). The Defense Production Act has been in effect ever since. It's yet another way that politicians encourage corporations to get aboard the war train. Contracted air services (CAS), a distinct category of service, involves corporations flying all sorts of aircraft within the U.S. and abroad in support of training and aerial refueling.

Certain aircraft corporations, such as AAR Airlift Group (Palm Bay, FL), Berry Aviation (San Marcos, TX), and Phoenix Air Group (Cartersville, GA), spend a fair amount of time in D.C.'s warzones. AAR's helicopters operate in U.S. Indo-Pacific Command and U.S. Central Command, particularly the U.S. Fifth Fleet, based out of the kingdom of Bahrain, where the unelected regime has violently repressed and tortured its citizens who are protesting for democratic rights.[74] AAR has been very active in Afghanistan, providing aircraft, personnel, and maintenance to transport passengers, cargo, and human remains in, around, and out of the country. Notably, AAR's board of directors is stacked with bankers, Wall Street pros, and war industry executives, including those with great experience moving troops and matériel around the Middle East, such as former commander of U.S. Transportation Command retired General Duncan McNabb and former Chairman of the Joint Chiefs of Staff retired General Peter Pace. Columbia Helicopters (Aurora, OR) provides services similar to AAR. Berry Aviation moves passengers, casualties, and cargo throughout the Middle East and North Africa, often supporting special operations. Phoenix Air Group has provided air transportation across Europe and Africa.

U.S. corporations are in charge of a lot of seaborne transportation. In general, seaborne transportation involves moving cargo and fuel to and from military installations worldwide. Cargo destinations include such outposts as Diego Garcia in the Indian Ocean and Naval Station Guantánamo Bay on the eastern end of Cuba, and installations in the Middle East, the Korean peninsula, and on the U.S. coastline. Seafaring corporations transport and deliver war matériel, troops, and mercenaries (though the latter two take air travel, too); manage and repair transportation equipment; repair the Navy's lighterage system, which helps get matériel, food, and industry products ashore; and operate tugboats and blocking vessels that help cargo ships maneuver. Other corporations operate and maintain Expeditionary Transfer Dock ships, getting equipment and supplies to and from ships, troops, and mercenaries around the world. Yet other corporations charter ships positioning war matériel *at sea*. Seaborne transportation is in corporate hands.

Foreign maritime companies have sold to the War Department.[75]

Many corporations sell software helping TRANSCOM keep track of assets, personnel, and industry products it has deployed around the world.

The Middle East—where despotic regimes, U.S. military infrastructure, and fierce fossil fuel corporations often overlap—is the arena for which U.S. industry designs land vehicles. Perhaps the single most productive manufacturing hub for U.S. military vehicles is greater Detroit, particularly Sterling Heights and Warren. U.S. military contracts involving vehicles are issued regularly through Army Contracting Command's Warren office. Civilian automobile manufacturers like Chevy may have closed up shop in parts of Motor City, but the war industry remains. The major U.S. war corporations that manufacture land vehicles are AM General, General Dynamics, Navistar Defense, and Oshkosh Defense. Respectively, they operate out of South Bend, Indiana; Sterling Heights, Michigan; Lisle, Illinois; and Oshkosh, Wisconsin. AM General makes the famed High Mobility Multipurpose Wheeled Vehicle commonly known as the "Hummer," and sells widely, including to two countries that D.C. destabilized:

Iraq and Afghanistan. General Dynamics makes an eight-wheeled fighting vehicle known as Stryker, a mine resistant ambush protected (MRAP) vehicle, and the M1 Abrams tank. It has sold vehicles to Australia, Egypt, Iraq, and Gulf regimes in recent years. Navistar's best-selling line of vehicles is the MaxxPro MRAP, which has been sold to Afghanistan, Iraq, Pakistan, and the UAE. Oshkosh makes a variety of heavy and light vehicles, including MRAP. Oshkosh's recent customers stretch from Cameroon to Somalia to Oman. Again: corporations don't just sell vehicles. Following the greed inherent to all corporate entities, they sell upgrades, enhancements, components, repairs, maintenance, recapitalization, life cycle support, displays, tech support, containers, parts, and storage to the U.S. War Department and allied governments.[76] Solutions galore![77] Over a hundred U.S. companies have sold goods and services (not including fuel) for military land vehicles in recent years.

You dismount a corporate ride and stroll around a U.S. military installation—say, Camp Arifjan in Kuwait. You run into a variety of corporations carrying out different governmental tasks. Mission 1st Group manages network and communications infrastructure. Your peer stateside receives you on his new audiovisual equipment, maybe purchased from Wildflower International. Perhaps he works for Serco, Inc., which manages programs, runs intelligence logistics and air operations centers, and plans operations for CENTCOM. Your stomach growls, so you end the call and exit the building, which was built by CH2M Hill (now Jacobs). You pass a group of AECOM personnel rigging up infrastructure to support U.S. Navy surveillance operations. CGI Federal maintains nearby software. On your way to the chow hall, which is run by Vectrus, you pass a warehouse in which AECOM personnel using General Dynamics software sort and track matériel. Leidos expertise helps account for munitions. You glance to your right at the distant gate, where SAIC personnel are arranging the latest entry control systems. Triple Canopy personnel guard the gate. Vectrus personnel are fueling the military police vehicles. Members of the 595th Transportation Brigade are driving cargo (unloaded at the ports by Cargo Transport System) onto the base. New construction is taking place across the installation. KBR runs morale, welfare, and recreation, including the gym you hit every morning. The chow hall isn't open yet, so you duck into a safety briefing, featuring materials from Kaiyuh Services.

U.S. firms have been hard at work constructing a variety of military facilities around the Middle East. At a U.S. military installation in Azraq, Jordan, they're building roads and routing utilities to the flight line. In Bahrain, they're replacing a pier in the southeast of the capital city, al-Manama. Some structure is always being built or renovated at the major U.S. air base in Qatar, named al-'Udeid. The Department of War hired construction firms to build a medical administration building and a squadron operations facility at al-'Udeid, in autumn 2015 and 2019, respectively, though most construction activity on base is not announced publicly. From central Jordan to the Persian Gulf, U.S. construction firms build the infrastructure through which U.S. war corporations then route profit. Firms sell services to the U.S. Army Corps of Engineers Transatlantic Middle East District (USACE TAM).[78] USACE TAM works on helping allies with construction needs,[79] benefiting the local, undemocratic ruling regimes, oil corporations, and U.S. industry. And who is monitoring the U.S. Army Corps of Engineers? Corporate America: On 4 September 2018, The Solution Foundry (Woodstock, GA) was contracted for environmental management system consulting services, training, planning requirements, budgeting, and implementation, operation, and management review for the U.S. Army Corps of Engineers.

War matériel and weaponry made by U.S. industry sit at strategic locations around the world. These matériel and weaponry are known as prepositioned stock. Big business is made from servicing Army Prepositioned Stock (arranging, cataloguing, logistics, maintenance, supply, transportation, guarding). APS is divided numerically by region, with APS 2 covering Europe, APS 3 based in South Carolina, APS 4 focusing on South Korea and Japan, and APS 5 for Southwest Asia. Camp as-Sayliyah in Qatar holds APS and features prominently in provocative U.S. military exercises, such as Eagle Resolve. Camps Doha and 'Arifjan in Kuwait hold APS and are major staging points for U.S. military forces en route to occupying Afghanistan and Iraq. Many corporations service APS.[80] Locating products overseas is part and parcel of industry's profit-making arrangement.

OUTPOSTS, DEATH, AND AIRWARS

CIA had Somali warlords on its payroll shortly after the 9.11 attacks. By 2006 the bond had evolved into a broader, formal arrangement wherein the warlords functioned as a coalition known as the Alliance for the Restoration of Peace & Counter-Terrorism. Operating out of Nairobi, CIA funneled weaponry and funding to the coalition. A zealous White House and many at CIA saw the coalition as a way to face off against the Islamic Courts Union (ICU), which brought strict *sharia* law and a degree of order to the country. Al-Shabaab were a faction operating under the ICU. Al-Shabaab were quite distinct from al-Qaeda, but they accommodated one another to a degree. Many Somalis saw the ICU as an option through which to rid the country of the CIA-backed coalition of corrupt gangsters. The ICU soon drove the coalition from Mogadishu. Al-Shabaab fighters gained more authority within the ICU. D.C. then backed an Ethiopian invasion of Somalia. Ethiopia invaded to dislodge the Islamists over the border. D.C. supported the invasion in part because it provided cover for U.S. special operations missions into Somalia. Somalis understandably loathed the Ethiopian military occupation, which committed such war crimes as gang rape and indiscriminate targeting of civilians. Al-Shabaab's ranks grew in size.[81] Some Islamists were kicked out of Mogadishu. Many returned. It's ongoing.

U.S. Africa Command (AFRICOM) got up and running during the Ethiopia-Somalia conflict, though U.S. military operations out of Camp Lemonnier in Djibouti predate AFRICOM's activation. AFRICOM enjoys plenty of funding. Nick Turse, the preeminent U.S. journalist covering AFRICOM, gives us a lesson: U.S. military installations of impressive size and scope span Africa, including an outpost in Mali, a drone base in Niger, and NSA facilities in Ethiopia. U.S. special operations on the continent are extensive and broad; U.S. allies, like Cameroon military forces, torture enemies; and the U.S. drone program now covers the skies over countries as vast as Libya and Somalia.[82] AFRICOM churns through billions each year in budget and war industry goods and services. But that doesn't satisfy.

Funding for operations is very opaque. Franklin "Chuck" Spinney, a former War Department employee who tried in the 1980s to draw attention to the Department's fraud and waste, explains pertinent accounting tricks: the Department "routinely over-estimated inflation rates for weapons systems… When actual inflation turned out to be lower than the estimates, they did not return the excess funds to the Treasury, as required by law, but slipped them into something called a 'Merged Surplus Account.' In that way, the Pentagon was able to build up a slush fund of almost $50 billion," which is roughly $120 billion in 2018 dollars. Spinney believes the Pentagon is using tricks like this to fund classified operations,[83] like special operations activity in Africa. Other funds, like overseas contingency operations funds discussed in Chapter Three, are available for use.

U.S. law provides additional funding for special operations on the continent. 10 U.S. Code Section 127e is used to aid such operations. Section 127e funds U.S. special operations forces' effective control of foreign military units ("surrogate forces"), guiding these units to assume the burden of fighting D.C.'s list of enemies. In the industry-led shift to "great power competition," Section 127e is exceptionally helpful because in exploiting foreign troops it frees up more U.S. special operations forces to operate around the borders of China and Russia. According to *Politico*, Section 127e funding has quadrupled to $100 million. The quadruple increase in Section 127e funding took place "in part thanks to the glowing testimony generals and admirals have given to Congress. Congress has reauthorized the temporary [funding] authority every year until last year, when lawmakers made it permanent."[84]

Military leaders sitting in the Pentagon support Section 127e and a high operations tempo across Africa and the Middle East. And why shouldn't they? There is no downside for high-ranking officers who support nonstop war. They'll retire soon with full benefits, and likely go work for a war corporation. They know, at least intuitively, that D.C. doesn't hold high-ranking military officers accountable. U.S. generals and admirals regularly describe SOCOM and AFRICOM operations with the following misrepresentations: *fraction of the cost of other commands*, *low-cost*, *progress*, *removing senior terrorists from the battlefield*, *small footprint*, and *successful*. Put these phrases on a bingo card and then listen to a U.S. 3- or 4-star officer testify about AFRICOM. You'll have bingo before your Irish coffee is cold.

A *Reuters* news article about the death of a U.S. soldier in Somalia unintentionally highlights an important piece of the profitable AFRICOM puzzle. The soldier had been on a mission to clear al-Shabaab from areas under al-Shabaab control, and establish a permanent combat outpost, according to AFRICOM.[85] Let's take these objectives one at a time. First of all, the U.S. military trying to clear al-Shabaab from urban areas and villages in Somalia is like a lifeguard trying to clear chlorine from the community pool using a teabag: flawed mission, deficient knowhow, and unsuitable means. Secondly, "clear, hold, and build" has been thoroughly debunked; it was a fantasy in Vietnam, it was a fantasy in General Petraeus' Iraq, and it's still a fantasy in Somalia.

Look at the establishment of a combat outpost from industry eyes. What construction conglomerates would build the perimeter and permanent structures within? What goods and services would the outpost consume? What weaponry might it need? What transportation firms would ferry troops and mercenaries in and out? Could Somalia ever purchase significant quantities of product from the U.S. war industry? No matter: U.S. military forces and corporate personnel have already helped build outposts across Somalia.[86] AFRICOM's director of operations told *The New York Times* that al-Shabaab dislikes these outposts and attacks them.[87] Refusing to concede that al-Shabaab can be viewed as "a local resistance movement against foreign intervention,"[88] the U.S. military launches airstrikes.

CIA is operating drones in Africa's sky.[89] In 2017, the White House aided the overall air war (drone strikes + helicopter strikes + fixed-wing aircraft strikes) by declaring large portions of Somalia an "area of active hostilities"[90]—legalese that relaxes rules of engagement and allows the U.S. government greater leeway in conducting operations. Even prior to that 2017 declaration, U.S. aircraft could kill over a hundred people at a time.[91] Understandably, U.S. bombing of Somalia causes the local people to get angry.[92] In 2019, the White House rescinded an Obama-era rule that had required the head of CIA to publish annual tallies of how many people die in its drone strikes,[93] while continuing Obama policies regarding drone strikes and global war.[94]

Profit is the common denominator of U.S. military and paramilitary operations in Somalia. Airstrikes are composed entirely of industry products—aircraft, bombs, missiles, maintenance, avionics, satellite guidance, training for pilots and maintainers, etc. Profitable ground activities include U.S. troops training the Somali National Army using all sorts of industry goods and services, corporate helicopter services aiding U.S. Naval Special Warfare, U.S. mercenaries reportedly working for Bancroft Global Development training Somali commandos, and AECOM construction at Camp Baledogle.[95] Meanwhile, civilians die.[96] Though airstrikes have no overall effect against the local militants' presence or capabilities,[97] the Pentagon and CIA have been launching more and more strikes on Somalia lately.[98] The air strategy does not change. It does not change because the only "success" that is unmistakable is the success of profiteers.

Once the corporatized U.S. Armed Forces are allowed in a space, the self-fellating operation—or self-flagellating operation, depending on your view of the war industry—takes on a circular, relentless life of its own. For example, U.S. forces in Somalia employ corporate matériel in coordination with private mercenaries. This involves, in part, corporatized intelligence operations, including but not limited to invasive ground and airborne signals intelligence (SIGINT) hardware and software. Taking their cue from SIGINT, U.S. special operations forces go on house raids. After U.S. and Somali forces raid a building, they collect cellphones, thumb drives, documents, pictures, even laptops from the scene. Corporatized shops within U.S. government and U.S. corporate facilities (in Maryland or Virginia, typically) then get to work arranging information from the material gathered, generating more "leads" that U.S. forces use as justification to attack other Somalis, by ground or by air. And the cycle repeats itself, spinning off new, identical series. (Afghans, too, loathe house raids,[99] as would anyone on the receiving end of one. Industry mercenaries are deeply involved in the parallel running of CIA's *counterterrorism pursuit teams*, a.k.a. death squads.[100]) Any given series becomes supercharged whenever locals take the initiative to attack the outpost of a foreign military. Despite all signs to the contrary, the U.S. military leadership indicates progress is being made in the country.[101]

U.S. troops are not playing a support role in Africa; they're in the lead. They're in the lead in conventional military operations. They're in the lead in special operations. And they're in the lead in Section 127e special operations. Officials from the U.S. government and the U.S. war industry regularly frame operations on the continent as supporting local forces: The locals are "in the lead." This is a familiar lie.[102] U.S. Armed Forces and mercenaries engage in combat across Africa. They target homes, compounds, trade routes, villages, civilian vehicle convoys, and celebratory events, like graduations and weddings. Their enemy is "suspected terrorists." (They lump in the "suspected terrorist" group anyone who picks up arms against the foreign military, in this case against Western troops.) Classification, well-funded public relations, and compartmentalization keep programs away from the critical eyes and ears of global citizenry. Corporate media ask softball questions. Violence skyrockets.[103]

U.S. military and mercenary deployments often coincide with FMS.[104]

After establishing U.S. Africa Command (for which the war industry lobbied), the U.S. military showed up in Niger and Nigeria[105] to fight "extremists" and "terrorists" (who posed no threat, existential or otherwise, to the United States). Foreign military sales followed. A notable sale was the 28 November 2018 deal involving A-29 aircraft to the government of Nigeria.[106] Niger is rich in uranium—the French first discovered uranium deposits in 1958 in a region called Agadez[107]—and the French corporation Orano controls most of the uranium extraction business there. U.S. war corporations recently built an expensive drone base in Agadez.[108] The French-led Operation Barkhane pursues a variety of groups across G-5 Sahel countries (Burkina Faso, Chad, Mali, Mauritania, Niger). The Sahel is a geographic band south of the Sahara Desert, the governments within which U.S. industry has been cultivating for weapon sales, marketing such sales as "solutions" to armed violence. Western militaries portray Operation Barkhane as aiming to "stop a region on Europe's doorstep [from] becoming a launchpad for attacks at home,"[109] a well-worn excuse that has been used to extend military occupations of Afghanistan, Iraq, and Palestine. Operation Barkhane is based in N'Djamena, Chad, but many French General Atomics MQ-9 drone operations are run out of Naimey, Niger. U.S. MQ-9 drones also roam the skies over Niger— same drone brand, different droned country. "But these drones are unarmed," you protest. "They're just for monitoring the situation." The first U.S. and French MQ-9 drones deployed to Niger were unarmed. Now they're armed.[110] The French and U.S. intervene against many different groups with distinct grievances, rooted in a variety of problems, including lack of economic opportunity, climate crises, globalization, inequality, governance, neocolonialism, religion, secessionist movements, and the European conquest of Africa (1880–1914). The West uses military force—often indiscriminate and bumbling—against these groups while Western corporations go after the natural resources, including minerals. The French war industry profits. The U.S. war industry profits. Western media and legislatures frame armed violence and/or resistance to Western military-corporate presence as "terror" attacks and "terrorist" activity.

The Pentagon has put forth no coherent strategy for U.S. military operations in Africa, and top members of U.S. Congress have been ignorant of such operations.[111] The war industry, on the other hand, has a strategy: lobby, cajole, bribe, and push for more funding, wider deployments, and more weapon acquisitions. The Pentagon and Congress accede. Neither the effectiveness nor the need for U.S. operations in AFRICOM is weighed. (By any objective measure that doesn't have to do with profit, AFRICOM has been a disaster: Since its full inception in

2007, AFRICOM has witnessed money squandered, U.S. lives lost, dead civilians, and people taking up arms against a foreign army. No war has been "won." That is the definition of failure.) Some military officers in the Pentagon confuse a transient aim (e.g. "degrade" the "terrorists") with strategy. Others, typically those who have profited professionally from post-9.11 global war or those looking to profit financially from an imminent position in industry, pay neither strategy nor a peaceful endgame any attention. The drive and momentum of the war industry guides U.S. military operations. As it stands, U.S. Armed Forces using corporate weaponry and products roam Africa with little oversight—exactly the type of situation for which the U.S. war industry worked so hard.

GOTTA GET THAT CASH

The Executive Branch functions as an international arms dealer. Presidents from both D.C. factions participate: Carter, Reagan, Bush Sr., Clinton, Bush Jr., Obama, Trump—all. Recipients over the years have included the Shah of Iran, Gulf Arab monarchies, European governments, military dictatorships in South America, Apartheid Israel, "contras" in Central America, and jihadis in 1980s' Afghanistan. With panache, President Barack H. Obama sold to Saudi Arabia, Qatar, and other Gulf regimes. Obama's hard work putting a palatable shine on weapons of death didn't last long. President Donald J. Trump's braggadocio dulled the shine, though the policy remained. The White House in 2018 was blunt about its intentions, promising to "advocate strongly on behalf of United States companies."[112] The State Department said it would energize a "whole-of-government effort to expedite transfers that support" D.C.'s "essential foreign policy and national security objectives."[113] The State Department later erroneously claimed that this added "thousands of jobs to the U.S. economy" and sustained "many thousands more."[114] The U.S. government, captured by corporate interest, couches these steps as "reform," "modernization of the arms transfer process," and "removing outdated regulations." War goods and services advocacy is a bipartisan affair.

Senior war leaders are candid about their roles as arms merchants. As Deputy Secretary of War, former Boeing executive Patrick Shanahan affirmed, "To strengthen our relationships, Secretary [of War] Mattis, our combatant commanders, and other senior leaders have traveled extensively, demonstrating our commitment to allies and partners." FMS "grew 62% over three years and exercises grew 17%, enhancing interoperability."[115] Secretary of the Air Force (former industry executive) Deborah Lee James noted, "We're in the business of killing terrorists, and business is good."[116] Mid-ranking officers get the picture, having internalized the lessons of upper leadership: An Army colonel named Jim

Brashear in an obscure office conceded that part of his job is to help the war industry: "All of our business is foreign military sales."[117]

Coordination is emphasized within DSCA's corporate-first environment. One of the first actions Lieutenant General Charles Hooper took upon becoming director of DSCA, he says, was instructing security cooperation officers to work even closer with industry. (DSCA itself is increasingly corporatized. Corporations are in charge of security cooperation programs within DSCA, including management, budgeting, evaluation, and institution building.) Under Secretary of War (former Textron executive) Ellen Lord convenes monthly meetings with State and War personnel in which she prioritizes FMS paperwork by region, and works "with everyone in the room to highlight any issues so that we can simultaneously, quickly work through the issues."[118]

Pressure from the U.S. war industry is one of the reasons why the U.S.-Pakistan relationship of two-faced cordiality slugs on. Selling weapons to Pakistan is big business.[119] And Pakistan is a relatively minor customer of the U.S. war industry. U.S. Congress appropriated roughly $3.6 billion in foreign military financing to Pakistan from 2001 through mid-2015, according to the Congressional Research Service,[120] as cited favorably by the Lexington Institute, a think tank.[121]

When bragging about selling weapons internationally, a Raytheon executive provides us context:

> It really is about focus. Of putting to bear the right resources with the right capability and authority to partner with our allied nations—with the U.S. government's allied nations—and provide meaningful bespoke capability to them. When we've done that and look at a country as a market with multiple customers, we've now seen the opportunity to deliver more capability even in those nations where we've been there for some long time.[122]

Weapon sales drive policy.

THE KEY TO MILITARY POLICY

Without looking at military adventurism through the lens of the war corporation, analysts are bound to produce error-filled studies. For example, after three U.S. troops died from a roadside bomb in Afghanistan in November 2018, *The New York Times* cited the Taliban's territorial expansion, al-Qaeda's presence, relatively low U.S. troop levels (using mostly air power and Afghan military and police forces), and insider attacks as the reasons that U.S. troops still fight and die there.[123] The war industry did not feature in the *Times*' calculus. The *Times* article appeared online on a Tuesday. That Wednesday, U.S. airstrikes killed at least thirty civilians.[124]

Academics also can miss industry's role. Rami Khouri, a brilliant academic whom I respect greatly, contends, "Military force is almost never going to achieve your political aims. The Americans learned this in Vietnam. They're learning it in Afghanistan. They're learning it in Syria… So Obama supporting the Saudis/Emiratis in Yemen is a sign really of incoherence on the part of the United States."[125] Far from incoherence, the behavior is quite rational. A portfolio of conflicts, disparate and seemingly futile, is *precisely* the aim. Permanent warfare—producing untold mountains of profit for war corporations—is the goal.

Similarly, some journalists believe the U.S. war industry is pushing for the war between South and North Korea to turn hot again. But war corporations do not always want all-out war. Rather, U.S. war executives want to maintain the profitable status quo on the Korean peninsula: An endless cold war, engendering ongoing sales to the South Korean government *and* to the U.S. government (maintaining the massive U.S. military presence south of the 38th parallel—28,500 troops as of autumn 2019—imagine the goods and services cash gusher, there).

U.S. policy doesn't have to make sense beyond the logic of profit. Look at Syria. As of late 2018, U.S. military forces were

- fighting the "Islamic State" (IS), which was fighting President Bashar al-Assad;
- allied with many Kurdish groups, which had alliances with President al-Assad;
- selling weaponry to Turkey, which considers most Kurdish groups to be terrorists;
- providing air support for al-Qaeda-linked groups like al-Nusra and Ahrar ash-Sham, which were fighting President al-Assad;[126]
- based in eastern Syria as a bulwark against the ebb and flow of Iranian forces, which were allied with President al-Assad against the jihadists;
- and allied with Israel, which aided Sunni jihadists (e.g. giving medical aid to them in the Golan Heights) and bombed Lebanese Shi'a fighters and Syrian troops.

Israel has worked hard to Balkanize Syria, so Syria would no longer be a strong Arab nation. This aligns with the war industry's Syria policy, which is to arm divergent factions inside the country; let the conflict boil, and then sell to a U.S.-allied regime if it crops up down the road.

The nature of these allies is irrelevant. In Yemen, the Saudi-UAE-U.S. coalition has paid al-Qaeda to do its bidding,[127] overlapping with the UAE's work buying and transferring U.S. weaponry to jihadists, including al-Qaeda-linked groups,[128] and the UAE hiring of U.S. mercenaries (working for U.S.-based Spear Operations Group) to carry out political assassinations.[129] UAE also hired U.S. desk mercenaries to target the Emirati regime's foes, including political dissidents seeking democracy and human rights groups.[130] Meanwhile, the U.S. military helped the UAE interrogate (read: torture) prisoners in Yemen,[131] rescued UAE troops in Yemen,[132] and trained members of the Saudi-led coalition to fight in Yemen,[133] all while telling Congress that there was no "evidence of detainee abuse by U.S. allies in Yemen."[134]

The war industry pursues a portfolio of conflicts just as any powerful industry views the global marketplace, parses demographics, shapes consumer tastes, and pursues profit maximization at all costs. The portfolio approach took off after the attacks of 11 September 2001, which shed any remaining constraints on the war industry. Observe the breakdown of the war industry's portfolio of conflicts, as appraised during summer 2018:

- Afghanistan—old faithful
- Colombia—the mountainous test bed
- Iraq—the consummation
- Iran—the future
- Korea—the long-term callous
- Libya—the down-low
- Mexico—the collaboration
- Palestine—the outsourced proving ground
- The Philippines—the simmer
- Somalia—the big easy
- Syria—the jumble
- The Sahel—the stadium
- Ukraine—the cold brew
- Yemen—the jamboree

Each conflict has advantages and disadvantages, unique terrain and unique obstacles. Testing, evaluating, using, repairing, and maintaining weaponry varies across population centers. Products monitor, control, or destroy populations. The weaponry selected is not the point here. The point is: from the eyes of the corporate boardroom, conflict must endure.[135] Peace is not profitable. A strong portfolio of conflicts, which vary in intensity and scope, is what industry has accrued.

By design, the military-industrial-congressional triangle is completely insulated from the reactions of the U.S. public, and particularly from those aware of the class struggle and the profitable nature of war. The tiny sliver within the MIC that still possesses a shred of empathy is co-opted and coerced over time to judge the wars in terms of numbers (dollars spent, weapons purchased, bases active, troops deployed) instead of clear soldierly goals and the true national security interests of the American people.

Global capitalism demands infinite growth. War corporations' portfolio approach demands endless, dispersed armed conflicts of varying intensity but short of a world war—though the threat of that is immensely rewarding. Robust FMS is integral to the racket of war. Weapon sales drive government policy. Most of the time, U.S. flag officers who worked on FMS then doff the uniform and go profit from their knowledge: "The last seven generals and admirals who worked as Department of Defense gatekeepers for international arms sales are now helping military contractors sell weapons and defense technology overseas," the *Boston Globe* has reported.[136] Across the board—from millionaire CEOs to members of U.S. Congress who accept corporate influence, to think tanks that advocate for weapon sales and alliances with brutal regimes, to foreign elites who ink deals with U.S. corporations—profit is the tie that binds.

ENDNOTES

1 Hooper, Charles. "Foreign Military Sales (FMS) Video." *Defense Security Cooperation Agency*. 20 March 2018. Accessed 18 July 2018: <www.youtube.com/watch?v=hlAghDl_fJ0&feature=youtu.be>, (1:22).

2 Hooper, Charles. "Foreign Military Sales (FMS) Video." *Defense Security Cooperation Agency*.

3 Newell, Benjamin. "Hanscom awards $1 billion for Qatar's new radar." *66th Air Base Group Public Affairs*. 15 March 2017.

4 Stump, Dominique. "Lockheed Unveils Initial F-35A for Japan Air Self Defense Force; Marillyn Hewson Comments." *ExecutiveBiz*. 26 September 2016.

5 "Slovakia—F-16 Block 70/72 V Configuration Aircraft." *Defense Security Cooperation Agency News Release*. Transmittal No. 18-10. 4 April 2018: <www.dsca.mil/sites/default/files/mas/slovakia_18-10_0.pdf>.

6 FMS as solutions: Harris sold "tactical communications solutions" to governments in the Middle East, North Africa, and elsewhere. Raytheon sold glide bombs—"a very cost effective solution"—to the Turkish government. The CEO of L3 boasted about the corporation having "affordable, state-of-the-art solutions" when setting up units to focus exclusively on international sales. See "Harris Corporation Awarded $20 Million in Orders to Provide Tactical Radios to Middle East and North African Nations." *Harris Corp*. 15 April 2016. "Harris Corporation Awarded $1.7 Billion Foreign Military Sales IDIQ Contract for Tactical Communication Solutions." *Harris Corp*. 23 June 2016. "Raytheon Makes First International Joint Standoff Weapon Sale to Turkey." *Raytheon*. 6 April 2006. "L3 Establishes International Boards to Drive Growth in Key Markets." *L3*. 4 January 2018.

7 "How security cooperation advances U.S. interests." *Brookings Institution.* 4 June 2019. DSCA director Lt. Gen. Charles Hooper notes that DSCA processes 50% of FMS cases within 52 days or less.

8 Baltimore, MD; Bridgeport, WV; Cedar Rapids, IA; Indianapolis, IN; Medford, NY; Moss Point, MS; Newton, ND; Red Oak, TX; Salt Lake City, UT; Vandalia, OH; Palmdale, Rancho Bernardo, San Diego, Santa Clarita, CA; and other locations, disclosed and undisclosed. The multi-function active sensor (MFAS) on the MQ-4C scans the water below. MFAS is produced in Andover, MA; Annapolis, Baltimore, Hampstead, Linthicum, MD; Exeter, NH; San Diego, CA; Stafford Springs, CT, and elsewhere.

9 L3 makes a system for line-of-sight and satellite communications. Curtiss Wright (Newtown, PA) sells airborne instrumentation hardware. Druck LLC (Billerica, MA) sells engineering change kits to upgrade the drone's air data sets. Raytheon sells the targeting system sensor turret. Rolls-Royce's North American branch makes the engine. Sierra Nevada Corp. sells "electronic support measures" that ride on the underbelly. L3 and others manufacture the Automatic Identification System, which helps the MQ-4C track, locate, and identify ships. Other corporations provide training curricula and instruction for uniformed personnel and mercenaries who operate and service the MQ-4C. Other equipment includes datalinks and ground control stations, to name a few.

10 "Australia to buy six U.S. Triton drones for $5.1 billion." *Reuters.* 25 June 2018. "The total cost for the six drones, including facilities upgrades and support, will be A$6.9 billion, a person familiar with the transaction said," *Reuters* reported.

11 Boeing regularly comes out with more updates and change proposals for the P-8A. For example, Boeing received millions on 24 Aug 2018 to update the repair manual. Exactly one month later, on 24 Sept, as the fiscal year was winding down, Boeing received millions to incorporate engineering changes into eighteen P-8A aircraft in the U.S. Navy's arsenal.

12 Corporate goods and services for Boeing P-8A aircraft include Aviall Services engine components, Avox Systems oxygen systems, Pole/Zero Acquisition antennae, Honeywell auxiliary power units, Raytheon radar, and Telephonics identification friend or foe (IFF) interrogators. Spirit AeroSystems assembles the fuselage in Kansas. CFM International, a JV between GE and the French corporation Safran, produces the engines. AAR services the airframe and modifies the engines. Then there is Boeing and Raytheon ordnance that the aircraft can use. Progeny Systems Corp. services the Raytheon torpedo used. Boeing makes equipment that allows the P-8A to launch Raytheon torpedoes from high altitude. Northrop Grumman makes countermeasures for the Boeing P-8A to jam incoming missiles.

13 4 May 2015: Boeing to provide training (systems, courseware, materials) in support of Australia P-8A in Edinburgh. 11 Dec 2015: Boeing to supply P-8A more training systems and services to Australia. 28 April 2017: Northrop Grumman ALQ-213 electronic warfare management system and antenna and related services for Australia's P-8A. Aircrew training takes place at NAS Jacksonville, FL, USA. 9 April 2018: Boeing to upgrade P-8A maintenance device training systems in Edinburgh. 30 April 2018: Boeing to support Australia's P-8A aircrew and maintenance training devices in Edinburgh. 12 Sept 2018: Boeing to upgrade the P-8A training system. The contract tells us, these upgrades "are required for training devised to be ready for initial training to meet future mission capabilities." Boeing confirmed to me that this phrasing was correct. The P-8A only recently entered military service, yet Boeing is already selling the U.S. Navy and Australia upgrades to the training system.

14 "New Zealand to buy Boeing P-8 aircraft in $2.2 billion deal to boost monitoring of Pacific." *Reuters.* 9 July 2018. Boeing's deputy program manager: "We have many active (sales) campaigns... We think we'll sell another 100." Quoted by Dominic Gates (*Seattle Times*, 2 May 2018).

15 U.S. corporations selling to Argentina during Macri's tenure included Textron, Honeywell, L3. Relevant contracts: 25 April 2017, 7 Dec 2017, 29 Jan 2018. Macri also opened up Argentina to greater foreign corporate rule, including lithium mining.

16 Partington, Richard. "Argentina launches fresh austerity measures to stem peso crisis." *The Guardian*. 3 September 2018.

"Police and protestors clash as worker strike paralyzes Argentina." *Reuters*. 6 April 2017.

17 In June 2018, Aviation Ground Equipment Corp. sold static frequency converters for various aircraft for Japan. Boeing sold upgrades on Japan's mission computers. Northrop Grumman sold Japan one E-2D aircraft ($153.2 million). (Bigger pay dirt came in Nov 2018 when Northrop Grumman inked a deal, worth over $489 million, to sell Japan the RQ-4 Global Hawk drone. The deal was announced on 19 Nov, but awarded on 20 Nov. The U.S. military presence in Japan had been previously operating its own Northrop Grumman RQ-4 drones, some jointly with the Japanese.) In June 2018, Bell & Boeing sold Japan four V-22 aircraft. Bell & Boeing also sold modifications and engineering on Japan's existing V-22. Boeing sold Australia, Japan, and South Korea engineering services on ship networks that coordinate navigation, propulsion, and helm signals. Communications & Power Industries sold Australia, Japan, and South Korea traveling wave tubes (installed in the fire control system on board Aegis-equipped ships). Lockheed Martin sold Aegis development, operation, and maintenance to Australia, Japan, South Korea.

18 Insinna, Valerie. "Key piece of F-35 logistics system unusable by U.S. Air Force students, instructor pilots." *Defense News*. 8 March 2019. LM regularly receives substantial ALIS funding: 2018 contracts (24 May, 25 June, 29 June, 17 Aug, 20 Dec).

19 In June 2018, General Dynamics sold various rockets, warheads, and components to Afghanistan, Qatar, Saudi Arabia, Jordan, Kenya, and Nigeria. Intuitive Research & Technology Corp sold technical support services for cruise missile defense systems to Egypt, Finland, India, Indonesia, and Qatar. Kaman sold fuses to Netherlands, Qatar, Iraq, Saudi Arabia, Egypt, Nigeria, Indonesia, UAE, Taiwan, and South Korea. Kilgore Flares sold flares to Kuwait, Romania, and Pakistan. Raytheon sold software development and "system integrity services" on Boeing jets to Australia, Canada, Kuwait, and Switzerland.

20 In June 2018, Boeing sold Kuwait system configuration sets ($179 million) for F/A-18 software. Boeing sold Kuwait F/A-18 aircraft ($1.5 billion). Harris Corp. sold Kuwait map computers ($2.3 million) for Textron helicopters and Boeing fighter jets, along with aircraft housings. Integral Aerospace sold fuel tanks for Kuwait's Boeing tactical aircraft ($11.2 million). Lockheed Martin sold Bahrain F-16 aircraft ($1.12 billion). Lockheed Martin sold Modernized Target Acquisition Designation Sight/Pilot Night Vision Sensor, M-TADS/PNVS, to the UAE. M-TADS/PNVS (sold at $288.3 million) is used on attack helicopters. Raytheon sold Qatar Air & Missile Defense Operation Center support for $49.4 million.

21 Protestors' grievances (summer '18, autumn '19) included inadequate utilities and government corruption. Saeed Kamali Dehghan. "Protests spread through cities in Iraq's oil-rich Shia south" (*The Guardian*, 18 July 2018); "Iraq anti-government protests lead to deadly clashes" (*BBC News*, 2 October 2019); "Internet access cut across much of Iraq" (*Middle East Monitor*, 2 October 2019); "Protests in Iraq turn deadly and spread nationwide" (*France24*, 3 October 2019).

22 Joan Mellen's *Blood in the Water* (Amherst, NY: Prometheus, 2018, pp. 214, 241-288, 323-349) is the definitive study of the USS *Liberty*. The *Liberty* was a special reconnaissance ship in international waters. A false flag attack against a U.S. warship could provide the pretext for D.C. to intervene militarily against the Egyptians in the Six Day War. U.S. President Lyndon B. Johnson quickly recalled the U.S. rescue party headed to the *Liberty*. Attacks against U.S. assets are a regular occurrence. Israeli intelligence agencies had prior knowledge of and perhaps (given Israel's command

of the car-bomb scene in Lebanon in the 1980s) were involved in bombing the U.S. Embassy in April 1983 and bombing the U.S. Marine Barracks at Beirut's airport in October 1983. The U.S. Embassy in Beirut had been the epicenter of CIA's familiarization with and outreach to Palestinian factions (most notably the operations of CIA case officer Robert Ames). Mossad had been furious with this familiarization. Former Mossad officer Victor Ostrovsky (*By Way of Deception*. New York: St. Martin's Press, 1990, written with Claire Hoy) discusses Israeli prior knowledge of the attack. Ronen Bergman (*Rise and Kill First*. New York: Random House, 2018, pp. 240-5, *passim*) lays out how Israeli intelligence agencies dominated the car bomb scene in Lebanon in the 1980s. Mossad's old motto was *By deception, wage war*, alternatively translated as *For by stratagem, you wage war*. Journalist Whitney Webb ("Newly Released FBI Docs Shed Light on Apparent Mossad Foreknowledge of 9/11 Attacks." *MintPress News*. 17 May 2019) discusses Israeli intelligence's possible prior knowledge of 9.11.

23 "U.S.-Israel Defense Policy Advisory Group." *U.S. Department of Defense*. Release No. NR-173-19. 30 June 2019.

24 For cyberattacks against Iran, see Sanger's "Obama Order Sped Up Wave of Cyberattacks Against Iran" (*The New York Times*, 1 June 2012) and Nakashima and Miller's "U.S., Israel developed Flame computer virus to slow Iranian nuclear efforts, officials say" (*Washington Post*, 19 June 2012). For military operations in Iranian territory, see Hersh's "Our Men In Iran?" (*New Yorker*, 5 April 2012) & Naylor's *Relentless Strike* (New York, St. Martin's Press, 2015). Jeff Stein of *Newsweek* reported on 31 Jan 2015 that CIA and Mossad had worked together to murder a man Stein hyperbolically called a "terrorist kingpin." Careerists (e.g. Gen. Michael Hayden) are crucial to Tel Aviv's effective maneuvering within the MIC.

25 Relevant contracts issued 2014 (15 Aug; 9, 20, 28, Oct; 21 Nov; 2, 11, 19 Dec), 2015 (13 Feb; 30 June; 14 July; 27 Aug; 25, 30 Sept; 3, 30 Nov; 21, 29 Dec), 2016 (15 & 29 Jan; 11 Feb; 7 & 11 March; 15 April; 19 May; 21 Sept), and on and on.

26 Relevant contracts issued 2014 (24 Sept, 10 Dec), 2015 (2 March, 20 March, 26 March, 28 May), 2016 (16 Feb, 26 Feb, 20 Sept), 23 Aug 2018. Intuitive Research & Technology (Huntsville, AL) assists in developing Israeli missile systems.

27 Diesel Engineering (Englewood Cliffs, NJ) works on the engine and transmission for Israel's Achzarit heavy armored personnel carrier. Goodyear (Akron, OH) sells tires. BP North America (Chicago, IL), Petromax (Bay City, TX), and Valero (San Antonio, TX) sell fuel. Issued, for example, 12 Sept 2014, 29 April 2015, 14 Sept 2015, 30 Sept 2015, 29 Feb 2016.

28 Rosie Perper (*Business Insider*, 25 May 2018). Israel flies the F-35, which they call "*Adir*," out of Nevatim AB in northern Negev (*an-Naqab*, in Arabic). The Zionist terrorist group known as *Haganah* used the area before Israel's '48 establishment to develop and deploy its nascent air assets. Haganah units were later absorbed into the Israeli military. Lockheed Martin has an office in the Negev. LM's CEO Hewson attended the office's opening. Hewson visits Israel regularly. In summer 2019, she spoke at an IDC Herzliya (northern Tel Aviv) conference and touted the F-35's ability to target Hezbollah's rockets.

29 "Israel fires missile at drone that entered from Syria." *Associated Press*. 11 July 2018.

30 Kane, Alex. "Inside Sources Say the State Department Refuses To Trace Whether Israel Is Using U.S. Military Aid Illegally." *In These Times*. 13 December 2018.

31 Recent sales to the Egyptian regime have involved a United Technologies pod that is bolted onto the bottom of Egypt's F-16 aircraft for imagery; building facilities at Cairo West Air Base; tanks and vehicles; cartridges that release weaponry from aircraft; countermeasure flares; fuses; mission planning software; maintenance on vehicles; mobile surveillance sensor security systems; motors for air-to-air missiles; Raytheon missiles and radar systems; small boats; maintenance and engineering

on fighter jets; and Lockheed Martin targeting devices for use on Boeing helicopters. U.S. industry sales to Egypt during January 2018 through September 2018 (fiscal year end) illustrate a fair cross-section of products. Jan-Sept 2018 sales (11, 17 Jan; 12, 16 Mar; 10 May; 1, 29 June; 20 July; 29 Aug; 13, 24, 26, Sept) to Egypt involved small drones; antennae for electronic countermeasures; aircraft maintenance; GPS and navigation engineering & maintenance; technical support on missile defense systems; fuses and engineering; advisory & assistance; missiles, spares, and engineering; and ejection seat parts.

32 Elbit also owns M7 Aerospace (San Antonio, TX) and Kollsman (Merrimack, NH), and recently purchased Harris' night vision line prior to Harris' merger with L3. Elta built a see-through prototype Mexico-U.S. border wall, per "Israeli Firm Chosen to Build Prototype of U.S. Border Wall With Mexico" (*Jewish Telegraphic Agency*, 13 September 2017). Technology from Elbit patrols the U.S. border, including the Tohono O'odham nation, which spans U.S. and Mexico sides of the Sonoran Desert.

33 Elbit Systems produces composite materials for Northrop Grumman's production of F-35 fuselages. Northrop Grumman works with IAI on radar satellite technology. Textron works with Israel's MDT Armor Corp. to produce vehicles. Honeywell and IAI develop GPS anti-jamming technology. Boeing has invested in Israeli startups, like Assembrix, and works with IAI on missile systems. Raytheon has collaborated with Rafael to produce missile interceptors, the technology of which Raytheon then uses to produce more goods for European customers—or, in industry lingo, providing "our customers alternatives that meet their specific demands." (See "Raytheon's Harris on Global Product Demand, International Sales, Partnerships." *Defense & Aerospace Report*. 2 August 2018, 12:15.) Portions of other U.S. work—from an experimental Boeing vertical takeoff & landing plane (issued 26 Aug 14) to Raytheon mortars (issued 8 Dec 15)—take place inside Israeli territory.

34 "Israel signs on as 17th member of NDIA's International Division." *National Defense Industrial Association*. 1 April 2019. Reps from war corporations were present for the signing. The keynote speaker was Brennan Grignon, director of policy and industry outreach for the U.S. Under Secretary of War for Acquisition & Sustainment. Grignon came to that position from the U.S. financial sector and the consulting firm LMI (Tysons Corner, VA). David Zolet is in charge of LMI. His roots are with the IT/cyber corporation known as DXC Technology, IBM, and Northrop Grumman. Avowed American Zionists also invest in the U.S. war industry. Prominent examples include Ron Perelman's MacAndrews & Forbes owning AM General, and Stephen Feinberg's Cerberus Capital owning DynCorp and other war corporations.

35 Lockheed Martin invested "over $1 billion on reciprocal procurement deals with Apartheid Israel between 2010 and 2017." Boeing has a reciprocal purchase agreement with Apartheid Israel wherein Boeing "will invest and partner with Israeli companies on certain contracts." See Perper, Rosie. "Lockheed Martin, maker of the F-35 stealth fighter jet, is opening a preschool in Jerusalem." *Business Insider*. 25 May 2018. Azulai, Yuval. "Lockheed Martin spends over $1b in Israel." *Globes*. 12 February 2017. Boeing will allocate at least 35% of contract value (on contracts over $1 million) to Israeli war industry. Boeing CEO Leanne Caret stated: "This agreement ensures that the relationship and partnership [between Boeing and Israel] will continue to grow and prosper in the coming decades." Forrester, Anna. "Boeing Signs Deal for Investment, Partnership With Israeli Companies; Leanne Caret Quoted." *Executive Mosaic*. 28 November 2018.

36 For example, Conti has built aircraft shelters and underground bunkers; led environmental work; constructed a drone facility; upgraded the defenses of military sites; upgraded fuel stations; and worked on sites 13414 and 13558. Contracts: 25 July 2018, 2016 (18 Oct, 15 Sept, 23 June), 2015 (18 June, 1 May), 2014 (21 Nov, 18 Dec), 26 Feb 2013. Conti is charge of building a "secret underground complex," as *Business Insider* (Robert Johnson, 7 March 2013) puts it, for the U.S. in Israel.

37 Greenwald, Glenn, Laura Poitras, and Ewen MacAskill. "NSA shares raw intelligence including Americans' data with Israel." *The Guardian*. 11 September 2013.

38 NSA's own rules didn't allow NSA to share certain info (particularly geolocation data) with Israeli military-intelligence, so the Israelis went all the way to the Office of the Director of National Intelligence to obtain an exemption. The director granted it, reported *The Intercept* (Hussain Murtaza, 29 May 2019). Tel Aviv and D.C. now have a new intel sharing arrangement, quite favorable to Israel, I note.

39 For example, say a U.S. corporation in Greenville, TX, produces an encrypted communications device for military aircraft. The corporation sells this product to Israel. Israeli military professionals work hard to know everything about its technology. Israel military-intelligence is outstanding at obtaining U.S. weapons (legally and illegally), breaking the protections, and studying the components and features, using the process to boost Israel's own military knowhow, which already is top-notch.

40 See Sy Hersh's *Reporter* (New York: Knopf, 2018, pp. 293-294).

41 Grant Smith of the *Institute for Research: Middle Eastern Policy* is one of the more dogged researchers regarding these cases and Israeli espionage in the U.S. in general.

42 Recent examples in the public realm of Israeli intelligence steering the U.S. foreign policy apparatus include the 2002 presentation of "evidence" to the U.S. War Dept. regarding Iraqi President Saddam Hussein's [fabricated] ties to al-Qaeda, Zionist think tanks in D.C. repeating narratives built in Tel Aviv, Israeli PM Benjamin Netanyahu's May 2018 presentation of "Iran's secret nuclear files," and "evidence" of Iran's "malign activity" given to U.S. military officials to get D.C. to co-sign Israeli airstrikes against Iraqi Shi'a militias inside Iraqi territory during summer-autumn 2019. Manipulation of U.S. intelligence can be read in Netanyahu's infamous words, spoken in 2001: "I know what America is. America is a thing you can move very easily, move it in the right direction." For additional information on Zionist operations, see *The CIA Insider's Guide to the Iran Crisis*, by John Kiriakou and Gareth Porter (New York: Skyhorse, 2020).

43 Early Zionist terrorism, as chronicled in Ronen Bergman's *Rise and Kill First*, includes assassinating British officials (4-6), a Bedouin policeman (8), and an Arab police officer (9); "personal terror operations" against British officials (17-20), including, but not limited to, bombing a British embassy and the King David Hotel in 1946 (19), and mailing letter bombs to "every senior British cabinet member in London" (20); posing as British officials when beating Arabs to death (24), using truck bombs to kill and maim (25), and murdering a United Nations envoy (28). Post-1948, state-sponsored Zionist terrorism includes attacking Western targets—including the U.S. and U.K.— and blaming it on non-Zionist parties (34-35); bombing civilians, including the use of car bombs (41, 238, 242, 379, 407); shooting missiles at innocents (396); attacking whole villages / cleansing population centers (44, 131); systematic arson (357); bombing and murdering scientists (67, 75, 349, 507, 608); raiding civilian homes (132, *passim*); torture (305, 413, 417); forced displacement (418-419); development of weapons of mass destruction (454); religious extremism (314-315, 348); extra-judicial murder, including women and children (133-134, 212, 231, 294, 396, 504, 507, 520-521, 532, 537, 549, *passim*); forced disappearance (294, 324); luring civilians to pick up arms, only to murder them as soon as they do (538-539); murdering police officials in a foreign nation (171); murdering foreign nationals—British, German, Lebanese, Iranian (224, 232, 294); destroying an apartment complex (168-173) and other buildings (256, 257); killing a pool attendant (183), a gardener (321), a preacher (378); kidnapping / abduction (199); and murdering prisoners (201, 228, 232), among other crimes. Unfortunately, Bergman refuses to understand Palestinian resistance as arising against Zionist colonization. He portrays the Zionist aggressors not as terrorists but as victims responding to the angry Arab. Nonetheless, his book is a carefully curated chronicle of Israeli state terror, although

he would euphemize most of the state's activities as "interception," "assassination," "interdiction," or "accidental damage." The ethnic cleansing of Palestine is described well in Ilan Pappe's *The Ethnic Cleansing of Palestine* (Oxford, U.K.: Oneworld, 2006).

44 "Barker was particularly controversial because of his incendiary comments after [Zionist] militants bombed Jerusalem's King David Hotel... The King David Hotel blast killed more than 90 people and infuriated Barker, whose offices were in the hotel." Katz, Gregory. "UK opens secret files about 'Jewish terrorists' in 1940s." *Associated Press.* 27 September 2016.

45 Katz, Gregory. "UK opens secret files about 'Jewish terrorists' in 1940s."

46 A terrorist organization that Israel created, funded, and armed tried to assassinate U.S. Ambassador John Gunther Dean on 28 August 1980 in a Beirut suburb. Dean was a critic of Israeli aggression and was working towards peace in southern Lebanon. Ronen Bergman's book, *Rise & Kill First*, contains some background information about the terrorist organization, known as the Front for the Liberation of Lebanon from Foreigners, but Bergman omitted the attack on the U.S. Ambassador from his book. Independent media outlets provide greater context: "New book sheds light on Israel's attempted assassination of U.S. ambassador" (*Middle East Monitor*, 24 August 2018); Weiss, Philip. "New book gives credence to U.S. ambassador's claim that Israel tried to assassinate him in 1980" (*Mondoweiss*, 22 August 2018).

47 Look at the numbers. The *AP's* Josef Federman ("Israeli settlements have grown during the Obama years," 16 September 2016) reports that construction of colonies—he uses the euphemism "settlements"—in the West Bank increased during the Bush and Obama administrations. Colony construction during Obama's tenure "matched and even exceeded" construction that took place under the Bush administration. Hanan Ashrawi, a senior Palestinian official, commented on U.S. complicity: "They did nothing to stop it. On the contrary, they looked the other way." As of summer 2018, over 600,000 colonists occupy Palestinian land in the West Bank and East Jerusalem, per "Settlements." *The Israeli Information Center for Human Rights in the Occupied Territories.* Accessed 15 August 2018: <www.btselem.org/topic/settlements>.

48 Shir Hever is an astute analyst of the Israeli war industry. He wrote *The Privatization of Israeli Security* (London: Pluto Press, 2017). His 8 Aug 2018 conversation with *The Real News Network* ("Israel is turning from a security state to a private security state") is worth watching in its entirety. Hever elaborates in a later interview (17 Oct 2018) with the network: Israeli war/intel corporations use the perceived prestige of Israeli military units for promotion and marketing. Private individuals are one of their main customer bases. The technology is often developed in and/or with Israeli government intel agencies. The bigger picture, Hever stresses, is that these Israeli war/intel corporations are outstanding with SIGINT, likely at the expense of their human intelligence capabilities. For information on Black Cube, a Tel Aviv-based firm implicated in scandals in the U.S. and Europe, see Bayer, Lili. "Israeli intelligence firm targeted NGOs during Hungary's election campaign." *Politico.* 7 July 2018. Israeli software created by veterans of military intelligence Unit 8200 have targeted people from all walks of life, including human rights groups. "Amnesty: We Were Targeted With Israeli NSO Cyberweapons." *Haaretz.* 1 August 2018.

49 "Report: Saudi Arabia Used Israeli Cyberweapons to Target Dissident in Canada." *Haaretz.* 2 October 2018. In 2018, Israel reportedly sold Saudi Arabia $250 million in espionage technology, said the *Jerusalem Post* and the UAE news service *Al-Khaleej*, as reported by journalist Randi Nord of *MintPress News* (31 October 2018). Edward Snowden told the *Jerusalem Post* (6 November 2018) that the Saudi regime used Israeli technology to target Jamal Khashoggi, a man the House of Saud murdered. Saudi Arabia later purchased $300M worth of Israeli tech, reported 20 June 2019 by *Middle East Monitor*. Historically, Israel has sold to such brutal regimes as Apartheid South Africa, Iran

during the reign of the Shah, and dictatorships in Latin America during the Dirty Wars of the 1970s and 1980s. India under Narendra Modi is a major purchaser of Israeli war goods and services.

50 See William Maclean "Saudi Arabia outpaces India to become top defense importer: IHS" (*Reuters*, 8 March 2015); Jeffrey Stern "From Arizona to Yemen: The Journey of an American Bomb" (*The New York Times*, 11 December 2018); Alex Kane "Here's Exactly Who's Profiting from the War on Yemen" (*In These Times*, 20 May 2019); William Hartung "'Little Sparta': The United States-United Arab Emirates Alliance and The War in Yemen" (*Center for International Policy*, 7 February 2019). Kane writes, "Since the war [in Yemen] began in March 2015, General Dynamics' stock price has risen from about $135 to $169 per share, Raytheon's from about $108 to $180, and Boeing's from about $150 to $360." Booz Allen Hamilton sustained the Saudi armor corp., which consists of a lot of heavy artillery and tanks. Issued 8 Sept 2014, 6 Dec 2017.

51 A full report is available at Ruhan Nagra and Brynne O'Neal. "Day of Judgment: The Role of the U.S. and Europe in Civilian Death, Destruction, and Trauma in Yemen." *James L. Cavallaro, Ed., Mwatana for Human Rights, University Network for Human Rights & Pax for Peace*. 6 March 2019. The report makes clear that Paveway bombs are one of the biggest killers of Yemeni victims. A lot of contract activity surrounds Paveway bombs in recent years, I note: Raytheon sold Paveway to the Saudi regime on 21 Nov 2014. Similar FMS was issued 28 July 2017, 9 Aug 2018. Paveway sold to U.S. Air Force and perhaps others unnamed on 9 May 2016. Further GBU-49 ("Enhanced Paveway II") deals were issued 22 Nov 2017, 24 May 2018. Archer Technologies International (Shawnee, OK), a Native corporation, sold repair services and supplies for Paveway bombs to the U.S. Navy on 29 Nov 2018. Meanwhile, Northrop Grumman sold training devices and navigation equipment to the Saudis. Issued 29 Sept 2016, 1 Nov 2017, 20 May 2016. Aircraft and boats killed civilians at sea: *The New York Times* (Declan Walsh, 17 December 2018) concedes, "Although American military support for the Saudi-led coalition is not as extensive in the sea as in the air, there is tight cooperation in many areas." The U.S. Navy shares information with the Saudi Navy and "has bombed Houthi radar stations." The Saudis use U.S. helicopters, and Saudi "officers have been trained by a Virginia-based contractor." A spokesperson for the U.S. Fifth Fleet said the U.S. military had no knowledge of the attacks on fishing vessels. "Last year the United States sold 10 maritime helicopters to Saudi Arabia in a $1.9 billion deal," and "Booz Allen Hamilton, earned tens of millions of dollars training the Saudi Navy over the past decade. A spokesman for the company said its last contract ended in July 2017." A retired U.S. Army officer, Stephen Toumajan, commands the UAE military helicopter fleet, *The Times* reported.

52 Walsh and Schmitt. "Arms Sales to Saudis Leave American Fingerprints on Yemen's Carnage." *The New York Times*. 25 December 2018.

53 McKernan, Bethan. "Airstrike on remote Yemen hospital kills at least seven." *The Guardian*. 27 March 2019; "Thousands Attend Funeral of 40 Yemeni Children Killed in Saudi Airstrike" *DemocracyNow*. 14 August 2018; "Report: U.S.-Backed, Saudi-Led Coalition Responsible for Half of All Child Deaths in Yemen in 2017." *DemocracyNow*. 27 June 2018; Nima Elbagir, et al. "Bomb that killed 40 children in Yemen was supplied by the U.S." *CNN*. 17 August 2018; "Yemen Conflict: Saudi-led coalition admits mistakes in deadly bus strike." *BBC News*. 1 September 2018; "Yemen conflict: A million more children face famine, NGO warns." *BBC News*. 18 September 2018; Walsh, Declan. "This is the front line of Saudi Arabia's invisible war." *The New York Times*. 20 October 2018; Walsh and Schmitt. "Arms Sales to Saudis Leave American Fingerprints on Yemen's Carnage." *The New York Times*. 25 December 2018; Davies and Benjamin. "In Yemen and Beyond, U.S. Arms Manufacturers Are Abetting Crimes Against Humanity." *Antiwar.com*. 27 September 2018; Wintour, Patrick. "U.S.-made bomb killed civilians in Yemen residential building, says Amnesty." *The Guardian*. 22 September 2017; "Yemen: Three years on, U.S. and UK arms supplies to Saudi

Arabia-led coalition are devastating civilian lives." *Amnesty International.* 23 March 2018; Summers, Hannah. "Scale of Yemen famine was 'initially underestimated' by aid agencies." *The Guardian.* 16 October 2018. Relevant GD Mark 82 contracts issued 14 Aug 2014, 9 July 2015, 2016 (26 Feb, 28 July, 30 Aug), 2017 (14 Sept, 21 Dec).

54 Fang, Lee and Alex Emmons. "State Department team led by former Raytheon lobbyist pushed Mike Pompeo to support Yemen war because of arms sales." *The Intercept.* 21 September 2018.

55 "Press Release: Over 100,000 Reported Killed in Yemen War." *ACLED.* 31 October 2019: <www.acleddata.com/2019/10/31/press-release-over-100000-reported-killed-in-yemen-war/>.

56 These 7 products are the Multi-Mission Surface Combatant, a ship marketed as being able to operate close to shore as well as the open-ocean; THAAD, marketed as being able to intercept ballistic missiles; the UH-60 helicopter, which the regime has used to stay in power; PATRIOT Advanced Capability-3 (PAC-3) missiles; satellite communications; C-130J cargo aircraft; and a targeting and fire control system for helicopters. It sells other products to the regime, but the aforementioned 7 bring home the most bacon. Lockheed Martin sells upgrades and tangential services on these 7 products.

57 Saudi Aramco took in a net income of $111.1 billion USD in 2018. *Bloomberg* tells us the "kingdom's dependence on the company to finance social and military spending, as well as the lavish lifestyles of hundreds of princes, places a heavy burden on Aramco's cash flow." Aramco pays 50% of its profit "on income tax, plus a sliding royalty scale that starts at 20 percent of the company's revenue and rises to as much as 50 percent with the price of oil." The House of Saud exerts major influence on Aramco "through regulating the level of production, taxation and dividends." Blas, Javier, Matthew Martin, and Archana Narayanan. "Aramco Unveils Financial Secrets of World's Most Profitable Firm." *Bloomberg.* 31 March 2019.

58 "Raytheon's Harris on Global Product Demand, International Sales, Partnerships." *Defense & Aerospace Report.* 2 August 2018: <www.youtube.com/watch?v=phCJaKWZ-pE>, *passim.* Retired Vice Admiral Andy Winn (a Lockheed Martin VP) explains an underlying, lucrative impetus: "We pay particular attention to the life cycle costs… So, many times when we offer systems we offer the full package." Quoted in "Lockheed Martin's Winns on Regional Market Prospects for MMSC, F-35." *Defense & Aerospace Report.* 23 March 2018: <www.youtube.com/watch?v=ZpQW0nbRVO0>.

59 Issued 7 Aug 2017, 12 July 2018.

60 Fahrenthold, David and Jonathan O'Connell. "Saudi-funded lobbyist paid for 500 rooms at Trump's hotel after 2016 election." *Washington Post.* 5 December 2018. For Saudi operations in D.C., see Lee Fang in *The Intercept* ("Inside Saudi Arabia's Campaign to Charm American Policymakers and Journalists," 1 December 2015) and Ben Freeman in *The Nation* ("How Much It Costs to Buy U.S. Foreign Policy," 4 October 2018). After the Saudi regime had a *Washington Post* columnist murdered, the newspaper noted the "defense industry has long had a guiding hand on American foreign policy, facilitated by a parade of former military and government officials moving between corporate jobs and key State Department and Defense Department posts. U.S. defense companies have spent between $125 million and $130 million annually on lobbying in recent years, plus tens of millions more on contributions to federal candidates, according to the nonpartisan Center for Responsive Politics." Reinhard, Hamburger, and Brown. "Killing of Khashoggi tests U.S. defense industry as backlash builds on Capitol Hill." 21 November 2018.

61 Borger, Julian. "Republicans block Yemen war vote by sneaking rule change on wildlife bill." *The Guardian.* 14 November 2018.

62 "Another amendment made it explicit that the resolution did not affect joint military operations with Israel, which convinced some wavering Republicans that it would not have unforeseen consequences for other alliances."

Borger, Julian. "Senate Votes to end U.S. military support for Saudis in Yemen." *The Guardian*. 13 December 2018.

63 Dillow, Clay. "U.S. Sold $33 Billion in Weapons to Gulf Countries Last Year." *Fortune*. 28 March 2016.

64 "Lockheed Martin's Winns on Regional Market Prospects for MMSC, F-35." *Defense & Aerospace Report*. 23 March 2018: <www.youtube.com/watch?v=ZpQW0nbRVO0>, (2:47).

65 Liang, John. "Lockheed names new rotary and mission systems VP." *Inside Defense*. 9 May 2018.

Major war corporations have a person in charge of each Gulf country ("customer"). For example, Lockheed Martin's man in charge of the UAE has been Vice Admiral (ret.) Robert Howard. Howard has worked with the *ABC News* team, too.

66 28% of the corporation's $53.8 billion 2018 net sales were from international customers, according to Lockheed Martin's 2018 Annual Report (p. 3). 30% of the corporation's $51.0 billion 2017 net sales were from international customers, according to Lockheed Martin's 2017 Annual Report (p. 3).

67 The bulk of these sales involved C-130 cargo aircraft spares & work to Saudi Arabia; F-16 engineering & technical services to Bahrain, Egypt, Iraq, Jordan, Oman, Pakistan, and Turkey; Hellfire missiles to Jordan, Lebanon, and the UAE; firing range infrastructure to Saudi Arabia; PATRIOT goods & services to Kuwait, Qatar, Saudi Arabia, and UAE; sustainment of targeting pods & navigation equipment to Egypt, Jordan, Kuwait, Oman, Pakistan, and Turkey; UH-60 helicopters and/or related goods & services to Jordan and Saudi Arabia; and THAAD goods & services to a variety of customers. Additionally, Raytheon sold radar work & spares for THAAD to the UAE. Relevant contracts: 2016 (26 July, 1 Aug, 25 Aug), 2017 (31 Jan, 28 March, 15 May, 18 May, 1 June, 2 June, 28 June, 30 June, 14 July, 28 Aug, 28 Sept, 31 Oct, 27 Nov, 21 Dec). Corporate products flowing through War Dept. offices are part of FMS pertaining to UH-60 helicopters for CENTCOM nations: The Utility Helicopter Project Office works with governments on coordinating sustainment and upgrades for the Lockheed Martin UH-60. Project office work included CAS Inc. (29 Sept 2016), Iron Mountain Solutions (15 Nov 2017), and Quantitech (16 May 2017). Corporate work in project offices is commonplace. These offices regularly engage in FMS to Gulf regimes. Relevant contracts: 2016 (26 Feb, 19 May, 5 Dec, 16 Dec), 2017 (28 Feb, 13 Oct). SAIC also sold MH-60 systems support/sustainment to the Saudis.

68 "Collaborating in the Middle East." *Raytheon*. Accessed 15 April 2019: <www.raytheon.com/ourcompany/global/middle_east>.

69 Relevant sales, 2016-7, include general architect-engineer services, issued 5 May 2017 to Bahrain, Kuwait, Oman, Qatar, Saudi Arabia, UAE; architect-engineer services, issued 1 June 2017 to Bahrain, Kuwait, Oman, Qatar, Saudi Arabia, UAE; and construction, issued 16 Dec 2016 to Kuwait.

70 Relevant contracts issued 20 April 2017, 28 April 2017, 25 May 2017, 7 June 2017, 16 June 2017, 20 June 2017, 13 July 2017, 19 Sept 2017, 27 Sept 2017, 3 Oct 2017, 8 March 2018, 8 June 2018, 23 Aug 2018, 24 Aug 2018, 29 Aug 2018, 11 Sept 2018, 21 Sept 2018, 28 Sept 2018, 1 Oct 2018, 12 Oct 2018, 8 Feb 2019, 14 March 2019, 8 April 2019. Stateside training locations where Advancia Technologies provides role players include NC (Bogue Field, Camp Lejeune), VA (Fort A.P. Hill, Fort Story, Marine Corps Base Quantico), CA (Bridgeport, Camp Pendleton, Twentynine Palms, Fort Hunter Liggett), Yuma, AZ; and across HI. Corporate remit running TECOM included such areas as education & planning, policy, training, and developing the corporatized military "product." Combat Convoy Simulator virtual training takes place in Camp Pendleton, Twentynine Palms, Camp Lejeune, Kaneohe Bay (HI), and Okinawa. Services to USMC Installations Command HQ included managing programs, supporting IT, helping run operations, and "government and external affairs support." Counter-IED training is at Camp Lejeune, Twentynine Palms, Camp Pendleton. Recent

construction on Armed Forces training facilities includes new barracks at Camp Parks, CA; training facility additions at JB McGuire-Dix-Lakehurst, NJ; renovations to cadet barracks at West Point; new facilities at Joint Readiness Training Center, Fort Polk, LA; infantry platoon battle course range at Fort Hood, TX; training support center at Fort Indiantown Gap, PA; mission training complex at Fort Hood; operation training facility at MCAS Miramar, CA; F-35 training detachment at Eielson AFB, AK; and a support facility, Fort Sill, OK.

71 Paying Pakistan to use Pakistani airspace to move matériel, troops, and goods and services into Afghanistan has easily cost the U.S. government $100 million/month compared to certain ground routes, per Steve Coll (*Directorate S*. New York: Penguin Press, 2018, p. 626). This amount does not include monies that go to war corporations transporting cargo or the cost of U.S. military cargo aircraft (parts, maintenance, fuel, etc.) flying to and from Afghanistan via Pakistani airspace.

72 Much of the Pentagon's international airlift services is contracted out to the following corporations: ABX Air, Air Transportation International (Wilmington, OH), Alaska Airlines (Seattle, WA), Allegiant Air (Las Vegas, NV), American Airlines (Fort Worth, TX), Atlas Air (Purchase, NY), Delta (Atlanta, GA), Bighorn Airways (Sheridan, WY), FedEx (Memphis, TN), Hawaiian Air (Honolulu, HI), JetBlue (Long Island City, NY), Kalitta Air (Leesburg, VA, and Ypsilanti, MI), Lynden Air Cargo (Anchorage, AK), Liberty Global Logistics (Lake Success, NY), Miami Air International (Miami, FL), MN Airlines (Mendota Heights, MN), National Air Cargo Group (Orlando, FL), Northern Air Cargo (Anchorage, AK and Greensboro, NC), Omni Air International (Tulsa, OK), Polar Air Cargo Worldwide (Purchase, NY), Sierra Pacific Airlines (Tucson, AZ), Sky Lease I (Greensboro, NC), Southern Air (Norwalk, CT), Southwest (Dallas, TX), Tatonduk Outfitters (Fairbanks, AK), United Air (Houston, TX), United Air (Elk Grove Village, IL), UPS (Louisville, KY), U.S. Airways (Phoenix, AZ), USA Jet Airlines (Belleville, MI), Western Global Airlines (Estero, FL). Notice that different offices of the same corporation receive contracts. Transportation contracts typically feature multiple corporations and are often expensive (e.g. $357 million issued 18 Nov 2015, $284.9 million issued 22 March 2019). Even design, maintenance, and support of the aircraft that transport the U.S. President have been handed over to corporations. DynCorp was in charge of such maintenance on behalf of the 89th Airlift Wing as of 2018. Boeing is manufacturing the next presidential airplane, Lockheed Martin the next presidential helicopter.

73 Harden, Blaine. "The U.S. war crime North Korea won't forget." *Washington Post*. 24 March 2015; "Prof. Bruce Cummings: U.S. Bombing in Korea More Destructive Than Damage to Germany, Japan in WWII." *DemocracyNow*. 12 June 2018; Shorrock, Tim. "Can the United States Own Up to Its War Crimes During the Korean War?" *The Nation*. 30 March 2015.

74 For more on Bahraini human rights, see *Amnesty International* <www.amnesty.org/en/countries/middle-east-and-north-africa/bahrain/report-bahrain/> and *Human Rights Watch* <www.hrw.org/world-report/2017/country-chapters/bahrain>. See also El Yaakoubi, Aziz and Ali Abdelaty. "Bahrain executes three, including Shi'ite activists." *Reuters*. 27 July 2019.

75 The Australian firm Austal has chartered U.S.-flagged passenger/cargo vessels. Maersk (Denmark) prepositions matériel at sea and charters tankers. Maersk also operates ships packed with high-powered radar that track missile launches, and operates ships that use industry surveillance products to conduct underwater reconnaissance. U.S. corporations also provide these services. The surveillance ships usually operate under Military Sealift Command's Special Missions Program.

76 Relevant contracts: 2016 (6, 29 Jan; 23, 25 Feb; 21, 31 March; 19 May; 24 June; 29 July; 21-23, 27-28 Sept; 1, 2, 28 Nov), 2017 (16, 28 Feb; 28, 30 March; 27 April; 18 May; 21 Sept), 2018 (16 March; 14, 24 Sept).

77 AM General markets goods and services as "global vehicle solutions." General Dynamics' positions upgrades to its Stryker as "solutions." Oshkosh markets goods and services as "solutions"

that "directly respond to the needs of those who serve." See <www.amgeneral.com/news-events/news/am-general-displays-modified-and-diversified-mobility-solutions-highlighting-innovative-partnerships-at-ausa-2017/>; <oshkoshdefense.com/engineering-solutions/>; and "04 Gen Dynamics Stryker Upgrades AUSA 2018." *Breaking Defense.* 9 October 2018: <www.youtube.com/watch?v=NvTsuVHtfoU>. Navistar markets its MRAP as "the perfect solution for extreme theaters like Afghanistan" because of maneuverability, tight turn radius and increased payload," per <www.navistardefense.com/NavistarDefense/vehicles/maxxpromrap/maxxpro_dash_dxm>.

78 Issued 14 March 2018, 12 June 2019.

79 "Middle East District—I Am TAM." *USACE.* Accessed 1 December 2018: <tam.usace.army.mil>. Projects over the years run by USACE TAM and its predecessor organizations include work in Afghanistan (highway system), Bahrain (Sheik Issa AB; Naval Support Activity Bahrain), Iraq, pre-1979 Iran, Jordan (King Abdullah II Special Operations Training Center), Kuwait, Pakistan, Libya, Saudi Arabia (King Khalid military city, King Abdul Aziz Military Academy), and Turkey.

80 AECOM and Defense Support Services (Arlington, TX) in Europe, with a focus on U.S. military activities in Mannheim and Dulmen, Germany; Honeywell and KBR in South Carolina and South Korea, with a focus on military bases in Daegu; and Vectrus and AECOM in Kuwait and Qatar. Other corporations play more precise roles. CACI, for example, has arranged expeditionary medical matériel within APS, while General Dynamics has maintained vehicles within APS. CGI Federal's Stanley Associates has administered APS overseas in Afghanistan, Europe, the Gulf, South Korea, and stateside (IL, SC, VA).

81 This summary was largely taken from Mark Mazzetti's *The Way of the Knife,* pp. 139-143, 147-151.

82 See, *inter alia,* "Commandos Sans Frontières: The Global Growth of U.S. Special Operations Forces." *TomDispatch.* 17 July 2018; "Pentagon stands by Cameroon—despite forensic analysis showing soldiers executed women and children." *The Intercept.* 27 September 2018; "Secret U.S. Military Documents Reveal a Constellation of American Military Bases Across Africa." *The Nation.* 27 April 2017; "The stealth expansion of a secret U.S. drone base in Africa." *The Intercept.* 21 October 2015; "A Wider World of War." *TomDispatch.* 14 December 2017; "Secret War: the U.S. has conducted 550 drone strikes in Libya since 2011—more than Somalia, Yemen, or Pakistan" (with Henrik Moltke and Alice Speri). *The Intercept.* 20 June 2018.

83 Lindorff, Dave. "Exclusive: The Pentagon's Massive Accounting Fraud Exposed." *The Nation.* 27 November 2018.

84 Morgan, Wesley. "Behind the secret U.S. war in Africa." 2 July 2018.

85 "U.S. soldier killed in Somalia firefight identified." *Reuters.* 10 June 2018.

86 Savage, Charlie and Eric Schmitt. "U.S. Airstrikes Kill Hundreds in Somalia as Shadowy Conflict Ramps Up." *The New York Times.* 10 March 2019.

87 Al-Shabaab view these outposts "as an irritant, and masses to go after it," the director of operations stated. Savage, Charlie and Eric Schmitt. "U.S. Airstrikes Kill Hundreds in Somalia as Shadowy Conflict Ramps Up."

88 Savell, Stephanie. "When is America going to end its shadow war in Somalia?" *The Guardian.* 5 September 2019. Savell argued persuasively, "Today, U.S. military policy in Somalia ignores al-Shabaab's deep ties to the Somali government, business interests, Somali national security forces, the African Union Mission in Somalia (Amisom) and regional entities… America's counterterrorism strategy has not lessened the impact of al-Shabaab activities." A scholar of anthropology and militarism, Savell was writing based on a 5 September 2019 report written by Catherine Besteman of Colby College, issued by the *Watson Institute for International and Public Affairs at Brown University.*

89 The Executive Branch allows CIA to conduct drone strikes in the region, per to *Wall Street Journal* (Nissenbaum, Dion. "U.S. Forces Get More Freedom to Strike Militants in Somalia." 30 March 2017). These drones are likely General Atomics MQ-9.

90 Savage, Charlie and Eric Schmitt. "Trump Eases Combat Rules in Somalia Intended to Protect Civilians."

91 Uncritical reporting available in Cooper, Helene. "U.S. Strikes in Somalia Kill 150 Shabab Fighters." *The New York Times.* 7 March 2016.

92 Journalist Jamal Osman ("A Trump decree is killing innocent civilians in Somalia." *Al Jazeera English*. 14 January 2018) explains: Indiscriminate killings of civilians "gives legitimacy to the militant group as a resistance movement, especially within communities living under its rule. Every innocent person killed by the U.S. is a gain for al-Shabab. Victims' family members and fellow clansmen will seek retaliation. To them, revenge is an act of justice. Most of the victims of U.S. military operations in Somalia are farmers and nomads who have no animosity towards the American people."

93 "Trump revokes Obama rule on reporting drone strike deaths." *BBC News.* 7 March 2019.

94 The Obama White House conflated Somali militants & gangs with al-Qaeda and used Executive legal prowess, including the 2001 Authorization for Use of Military Force to actively help AFRICOM conduct military operations in Somalia. Obama had issued an Executive Order during his tenure that asked CIA to provide numbers regarding people killed in its drone strikes. CIA begrudgingly conceded and published very low numbers that made its drone program look like a precise and accurate killing machine. The important part, Prof. Daniel Brunstetter of UC-Irvine reminds us, is that the Obama Executive Order institutionalized the policy of extrajudicial drone strikes outside of a "hot battlefield." See Brunstetter's full analysis on a 21 March 2019 episode of *The Real News Network*: "Trump's Secrecy Insulates U.S. Public from CIA Drone War."

95 Training seen in Harwood, Tech. Sgt. Joseph. "101st Airborne Division platoon provides secure training area for historic Somali National Army training." *DVIDS.* 24 May 2017. Approximately 500 U.S. troops in Somalia train Somali troops around the country, according to *The New York Times* (Savage and Schmitt, 10 March 2019). See corporate services in Turse and Naylor "Revealed: The U.S. military's 36 code-named operations in Africa" (*Yahoo News*, 17 April 2019) and Rempfer, Kyle. "Secret U.S. Base in Somalia is getting some 'emergency runway repairs.'" *Air Force Times*. 4 October 2018. AECOM issued 24 Sept 2018.

96 "A surge in American airstrikes over the last four months of 2018 pushed the annual death toll of suspected Shabab fighters in Somalia to the third record high in three years," *The New York Times* reported ("U.S. Airstrikes Kill Hundreds in Somalia as Shadowy Conflict Ramps Up," 10 March 2019). 2019's pace was on track to eclipse the 2018 tally. Investigative journalist Amanda Sperber spent weeks in Somalia, interviewing men and women and investigating the Pentagon's air war: Her investigation "tracked down evidence that AFRICOM's claim of zero civilian casualties is almost certainly incorrect. And it found that the United States lacks a clear definition of 'terrorist,' with neither AFRICOM, the Pentagon, nor the National Security Council willing to clarify the policies that underpin these strikes." And "nearly every Somali" she spoke with "was certain that people with no connection to Al Shabab were being killed in the air strikes" ("Inside the Secretive U.S. Air Campaign In Somalia." *The Nation*. 7 February 2019). On 20 March 2019, Amnesty International ("The Hidden U.S. War In Somalia: Civilian Casualties from Air Strikes in Lower Shabelle") added further evidence of civilians killed in U.S. airstrikes. There were at least 46 U.S. airstrikes in Somalia during Jan-July 2019, according to John Vandiver (*Stars & Stripes*, 26 July 2019).

97 Burke, Jason. "U.S. airstrikes fail to weaken al-Shabaab's grip on Somalia." *The Guardian.* 11 November 2018.

98 Airstrikes continued. On 17 Dec 2018, for example, the *BBC* ("Al-Shabab in Somalia: Air strikes kill 62 militants, U.S. says") reported, the "U.S. military says it has killed 62 fighters from the Islamist group al-Shabab in six air strikes in Somalia. Four air strikes on Saturday killed 32 militants and a further two on Sunday killed 28, it said in a statement." These were the deadliest strikes in Somalia since Nov 2017 "when the U.S. said it had killed 100 militants..." BBC reported at least 40 strikes "carried out in Somalia so far this year, compared with 35 recorded in 2017... No civilians were killed in the latest air strikes, which were carried out in co-ordination with the Somali government, *the U.S. military said*" (my emphasis). Writing in *The Nation*, Journalist Amanda Sperber (7 Feb 2019) cited figures confirmed by the Pentagon: U.S. airstrikes have tripled since January 2017.

99 In *The Nation*, Jeremy Scahill ("Killing Reconciliation," 27 October 2010) reports on how night raids reduce the possibility of peace in Afghanistan, not to mention damaging (whatever is left of) U.S. standing in the region.

100 Mashal, Mujib. "C.I.A.'s Afghan Forces Leave a Trail of Abuse and Anger." *The New York Times*. 31 December 2018. Astri Suhrke and Antonio De Lauri. "The CIA's 'Army': A Threat to Human Rights and an Obstacle to Peace to Afghanistan." *Watson Institute for International and Public Affairs at Brown University*. 21 August 2019. "CIA-backed Afghan troops 'committed war crimes': report." *BBC News*. 31 October 2019.

101 Garland, Chad. "AFRICOM commander sees recent signs of progress in Somalia." *Stars & Stripes*. 12 June 2019. "In Somalia, AFRICOM leaders say they have seen important progress over the past couple years," as *Stars & Stripes* put it on 26 July 2019 (Vandiver, "AFRICOM's new boss to face threats in Somalia and beyond"). "These gains in Somalia are extremely fragile, but they are gains nonetheless," said Gen. Thomas Waldhauser, who was retiring after helming AFRICOM.

102 Such a lie reminds observers of other D.C. maneuvering: (1) Peace talks with the Taliban were "Afghan-owned and Afghan-led," according to *The New York Times* (Nordland and Abed, 7 September 2018). (2) Combined U.S.-Iraqi military operations during the Bush and Obama administrations were presented as "Iraqi-led." (3) Combined U.S.-Afghan military operations were presented as "Afghan-led." Afghan and Iraqi forces were never regularly in the lead.

103 Turse, Nick. "Violence has spiked in Africa since the military founded AFRICOM, Pentagon study finds." *The Intercept*. 29 July 2019.

104 Countries on the receiving end of U.S. military and mercenary operations—including but not limited to Cameroon, Libya, Mauritania, Niger, Somalia—are recipients of U.S. arms sales and transfers, formal and discrete. FMS to Cameroon, a former European colony sitting on the Bight of Biafra, exemplifies the steady, under-the-radar approach that some of these sales take. Sales to Cameroon in recent years include Mack Defense and Oshkoskh Defense vehicles and small drones from Boeing (Bingen, WA). Textron, North American Surveillance Systems, and L3 collaborate to sell prop planes and onboard reconnaissance packages. Issued 2015 (25, 29 Sept), 2016 (9 May; 21, 23 Sept). This FMS is also troubling because of recent human rights abuses committed by the Cameroonian military. Consider a massacre in spring 2015, as detailed by Nick Turse in *The Intercept* ("Pentagon stands by Cameroon—despite forensic analysis showing soldiers executed women and children," 27 September 2018). On 18 Feb 2016, 5 corporations sold weapons parts and accessories to Afghanistan, Pakistan, Jordan, Iraq, Somalia, Niger, Burkina Faso, Djibouti, Chad, Congo. The U.S. military has been operating in the Congo for years. In spring 2019, *The New York Times* cited questionable evidence—a book, a banner, and an Israeli think tank—to announce that ISIS had arrived in the Congo (Rukmini Callimachi. "ISIS, After Laying Groundwork, Gains Toehold in Congo." 20 April 2019). For more overlap between FMS and U.S. deployments, consider the 21 Dec 2018 contract to PAE for surveillance systems operating in Benin, Congo, Djibouti, Kenya, Nigeria, São Tomé & Príncipe, Togo, and Tunisia. U.S. military operations in these nations include but are not limited to

Odyssey Resolve, Observant Compass, Paladin Hunter, Kodiak Hunter, Jupiter Nimbus, and Jupiter Shield. For a fuller list of operations, see Nick Turse and Sean D. Naylor (*Yahoo News*, 17 April 2019).

105 Pro-war media like the *Army Times* (Rempfer and Meyers, 12 December 2018) use pentagonese, excusing U.S. military operations: "The U.S. military provides training and security assistance to the Nigerien Armed Forces, including support for intelligence, surveillance and reconnaissance to facilitate their efforts to target violent extremist organizations in the region. This training includes advising and assisting the Nigeriens to increase their organic ability to bring stability and security to their country." The *Army Times* is owned by Sightline Media Group, which is owned by the Beverly Hills private equity firm Regent, L.P. Side note: Business terms like "organic ability" are a telltale sign of the corporatization of military operations. The think tank CSIS indicated that "the number of radical Islamist-linked attacks in the Sahel has doubled each year since 2016," France's state-owned *France 24* reports ("West African leaders pledge $1 billion to tackle terrorism," 15 September 2019).

106 Naturally, this included costly spares, support equipment, contractor logistics support, mission planning systems, training devices, mission debrief systems, and service. Sierra Nevada Corp. has also sold A-29 aircraft to Lebanon and Afghanistan.

107 Klare, Michael. *The Race for What's Left.* New York: Picador, 2012, p. 135.

108 Penney, Joe, Eric Schmitt, Rukmini Callimachi, and Christoph Koettl. "CIA Drone Mission, Curtailed by Obama, Is Expanded in Africa Under Trump." *The New York Times*. 9 September 2018.

109 Quoted is the wording of Van Der Perre, Christophe and Benoit Tessier in *Reuters* ("French troops in Mali anti-jihadist campaign mired in mud and mistrust," 12 August 2019). Boeing C-17 cargo planes resupply French forces.

110 Petesch, Carley. "U.S. confirms drones in Niger have striking capabilities." *AP*. 30 July 2018. "France turns to armed drones in fight against Sahel militants." *Reuters*. 5 September 2017. France has purchased U.S.-made GBU-12 Paveway II ordnance for its MQ-9. For small business activity on GBU, see 29 Nov 2018 contracts. *Jane's Defence Weekly* ("French Air Force introduces new UAV pilot training scheme," 23 May 2019) reports that the French Air Force aims to expand its fleet of MQ-9 drones to 24 by the year 2030. When bestowing France's *Légion d'honneur* upon the vice chairman of the U.S. Joint Chiefs of Staff, France's Ambassador to the U.S. thanked the vice chairman for his "efforts in the enhancement of information sharing and the help you provided for access to munitions needed for the fight in the Sahel," Jim Garamone quoted ("France Honors Vice Chairman for Fostering Cooperation Between U.S., French Militaries," 18 July 2019).

111 Haltiwanger, John. "How many troops does the U.S. have in Africa? Top senators didn't know military was in Niger." *Newsweek*. 23 October 2017.

112 "National Security Presidential Memorandum Regarding U.S. Conventional Arms Transfer Policy." *The White House—Presidential Memoranda*. 19 April 2018.

113 "Implementation of the Conventional Arms Transfer (CAT) Policy." *U.S. Department of State*. 16 July 2018. For sound analysis of this policy, see Emmons, Alex. "How a one-word loophole will make it easier for the U.S. to sell weapons to governments that kill civilians." *The Intercept*. 20 July 2018.

114 "U.S. Arms Transfers Rise 13 Percent in 2018, Highlighting Administration's Success Strengthening Security Partners While Growing American Jobs." *U.S. State Department Office of the Spokesperson*. 8 November 2018.

115 View Shanahan's Sept 2018 message at <www.defense.gov/Our-Story/Meet-the-Team/Deputy-Secretary-of-Defense>.

116 Dillow, Clay. "The U.S. Is Running Low on Hellfire Missiles." *Fortune*. 10 December 2015.

117 Bledsoe, Sofia. "Non-Standard Rotary Wing team has new leader." *The Redstone Rocket.* 29 July 2015. "[Brashear] said an unspecified facet of the mission is that the office strives to use its mission to help strengthen the American aviation industry."

118 "How security cooperation advances U.S. interests." *Brookings Institution.* 4 June 2019, (45:35). Hooper makes clear that FMS is a policy tool. When a country has purchased, DOD and industry bureaucrats can arrange all of the relevant paperwork (cost & analysis, pricing sheets, DCMA docs), and, according to Lord, "leverage that to quickly go and sell to another country." See "DOD's Lord on 'Falling Fast,' Fast-Tracking Foreign Military Sales Authorities, Reorganizing AT&L." *Defense & Aerospace Report.* 29 May 2018: <www.youtube.com/watch?v=mfyE7W7CrfM>. Illustrative DSCA corporatization issued 30 Sept 2019.

119 Recent sales include but are not limited to infrared flares (7 June 2016, 29 June 2018); hardware & data for small drones (29 Sept 2015); acquisition support (21 June 2016); carbines (20 April 2017); work in an Army project office (30 Nov 2015, 1 Dec 2015) that facilitates helicopter-related FMS worldwide; communication devices for aircraft (16 June 2015); miniguns and parts (18 Aug 2015); kits upgrading test sets used on aircraft (28 Feb 2018); engineering & software (28 May 2015); rockets (29 May, 25 June 2015) often launched from attack aircraft; gun turrets for attack helicopters (7 Dec 2017); auxiliary power units and ground carts for cargo aircraft (29 Jan 2018); missile approach warning systems (21 Dec 2016); engineering, technical services, training (8 Dec 2014, 28 Aug 2017); air-to-surface missiles & equipment (15 Sept, 23 Sept, 7 Dec 2015; 16 Nov 2016); systems that help laser-guided weapons find a target (15 Jan 2016, 22 Dec 2016); targeting pods and navigation equipment, engineering, and support (1 June 2017); training devices for teaching maintenance personnel (29 Sept 2017); logistics on various products, including cruise missile systems and mission planning systems (17 June 2016); aircrew training device upgrades (8 June 2018); vehicles and support (19 Dec 2014, 16 Feb 2017); engineering on computer-guided 20mm rotary cannon for ships (31 Dec 2015); weapon sights, spares, training (5 April 2016); radios and support (28 May 2015); and Textron helicopter support (17 Aug 2015), auxiliary fuel kits for helicopters (25 Aug 2015, 4 April 2016), and aircraft & sustainment packages (20 April 2016). Many contracts to Pakistan exemplify corporate cooperation: Northrop Grumman logistic support on Textron surveillance aircraft (27 Sept 2016); Northrop Grumman mission computers and equipment for Textron attack helicopters (9 Sept 2016); and Rockwell Collins avionics for Lockheed Martin cargo aircraft (15 Jan 2016).

120 "Major U.S. Arms Sales and Grants to Pakistan Since 2001." *Congressional Research Service.* 4 May 2015.

121 Gouré, Daniel. "Foreign Military Sales Remain An Important Tool Of U.S. National Security." *Lexington Institute.* 26 February 2016.

122 "Raytheon's Harris on Global Product Demand, International Sales, Partnerships." *Defense & Aerospace Report.* 2 August 2018: <www.youtube.com/watch?v=phCJaKWZ-pE>, (6:22-6:50), *passim.* "My charge since I've been in this job is basically to change the game with respect to the growth of our international business. I'm happy to say that this past year, 32% of our revenue was international… And we also were able to successfully achieve a 14th consecutive year of international growth."

123 *The New York Times* ("3 U.S. Soldiers Died in Afghanistan: Why This Fight Drags On," 27 November 2018) ignored Afghanistan's mineral resources, potential for oil pipelines, geostrategic location vis-à-vis China, and opium productivity, let alone the main reason U.S. troops fight and die in Afghanistan: war = profit. Moreover, *The Times* portrayed the dead—3 Army Special Forces soldiers—as saviors, having been sent to Ghazni City, Afghanistan, "to save that city from falling to the Taliban." *The Times* then implied that D.C.'s troops have "rejoined the fray" fighting in Afghanistan, though they never actually left the country, despite 2014's formal end to combat operations. Regarding

troop levels, *The Times* did not mention "contractors" or private mercenaries paid by D.C. One of the pioneers of the modern use of mercenaries, Erik Prince, is investing in mineral resources in the region. "Blackwater founder launches fund to invest in car battery metals: FT." *Reuters*. 1 January 2019. Minerals like gallium—used in weapons of war, particularly radar systems—are said to be in abundance across Afghanistan and portions of U.S. Africa Command. Elsewhere, the War Dept. and war industry are preparing the mineral base. On 6 June 2019, the Pentagon paid millions for research & development of a dedicated U.S.-based production source of gallium nitride. On 29 August 2019, Northrop Grumman continued work on gallium nitride efforts for mobile radar. Another Northrop Grumman gallium nitride-related purchase occurred on 19 November 2019.

124 "Thirty Afghan civilians killed in U.S. air strike, officials say." *Reuters*. 28 November 2018.

125 "Can Trump, Israel, and Gulf Allies Get Putin to Turn On Iran?" *The Real News Network*. 14 July 2018, (16:23).

126 In Syria, the U.S. government is helping jihadists, many of them openly allied with al-Qaeda. Eqbal Ahmad and David Barsamian (*Terrorism: Theirs and Ours*. New York City: Seven Stories Press, 2001) makes clear this phenomenon (D.C.'s use of jihadists as a tool of foreign policy). For a thorough history, see Max Blumenthal (*The Management of Savagery*. New York: Verso, 2019). See also "Weapons of the Islamic State" (*Conflict Armament Research*. 2017: <www.conflictarm.com/publications>,) which documents how D.C. and Riyadh violated international law by funneling weaponry to militant and terrorist groups operating within Syria.

127 "Yemen: U.S. allies don't defeat al-Qaida but pay it to go away." *Associated Press*. 6 August 2018.

128 Mackintosh, Eliza. "UAE 'recklessly' supplying Yemeni militias with foreign arms, Amnesty reports." *CNN*. 5 February 2019.

129 Roston, Aram. "A Middle East Monarchy Hired American Ex-Soldiers To Kill Its Political Enemies. This Could Be The Future Of War." *BuzzFeed News*. 16 October 2018. The Saudi regime also reportedly inquired about using private corporations to assassinate its enemies, in this case Iranian officials. See Mazzetti, Bergman, and Kirkpatrick. "Saudis Close to Crown Prince Discussed Killing Other Enemies a Year Before Khashoggi's Death." *The New York Times*. 11 November 2018.

130 Bing, Christopher and Joel Schectman. "UAE Used Cyber Super-Weapon to Spy on iPhones of Foes." *Reuters*. 30 January 2019. Bing and Schectman. "Inside the UAE's Secret Hacking Team of American Mercenaries: Ex-NSA operatives reveal how they helped spy on targets for the Arab monarchy—dissidents, rival leaders and journalists." *Reuters*. 30 January 2019. UAE deemed its political opponents in Yemen "terrorists" in order to reduce them to viable military targets.

131 Michael, Maggie. "In Yemen's secret prisons, UAE tortures and U.S. interrogates." *Associated Press*. 22 June 2017.

132 Trevithick, Joseph. "A USAF C-17 Flew A Secretive Mission Into Yemen To Rescue Wounded Emirati Troops In 2017." *The Drive / The War Zone*. 13 December 2018.

133 Turse, Nick. "Despite denials, documents reveal U.S. training UAE forces for combat in Yemen." *Yahoo News*. 16 January 2019.

134 Emmons, Alex. "See no evil: Pentagon issues blanked denial that it knows anything about detainee abuse in Yemen." *The Intercept*. 7 January 2019.

135 You might disagree with my specific characterization of a conflict zone (perhaps you believe certain parts of Libya have become more high-speed than the low intensity conflict I have generalized). That's fair. But my characterization of the overall lens through which the U.S. war industry leaders view the world has been demonstrated.

136 Bender, Bryan. "From the Pentagon to the private sector." 26 December 2010. This phenomenon continued after 2010.

6

The Academy

Institutions of higher education provide the intellectual foundations of society. They teach students, preserve history, develop new theories, make discoveries, and expand our understanding of the world around us. Colleges and universities are supposed to be open environments where students can grow, play, and learn. Unfortunately, the war industry is embedded in U.S. academia. The Department of War pays colleges and universities to enhance military and intelligence technological capabilities. American academia's support for the War Department is too vast to catalogue, so the focus here is primarily on illustrative patterns and the greatest academic offenders, among them, MIT and Johns Hopkins.[1] Along the way we learn about languages, various forms of militarized research, and how the war industry is preparing for the future.

BEANTOWN AND BEYOND

We lead off with Boston area institutions. Boston College helps the Air Force Research Lab develop military technology. The University of Massachusetts-Lowell helps the U.S. Army develop nanotechnology.[2] Tufts University works with the U.S. Army to improve soldiers' cognitive and physical performance on the battlefield.[3] Complementing this activity, industry executives sit on the Boards of New England universities.[4]

The Massachusetts Institute of Technology (MIT) is a twenty-minute bike ride south-southeast of Tufts. Professors Ruth Perry and Yarden Katz explain MIT's history: When Perry first arrived at MIT, the Pentagon largely subsidized the university's budget. Many faculty and students "objected to the way this funding by the war machine changed research priorities and slanted educational objectives." This pushback caused MIT to diversify its funding. Corporate America stepped in, effectively corrupting the academic process even further.[5] MIT now gets money from the Pentagon *and* war corporations—a harder arrangement for conscientious students, faculty, and staff to stop.

Partnering with corporations, Perry and Katz explain, results in "an association whose precise terms are hidden, but whose public aspect is neutral, professional, and sanitized. MIT's partnerships are generally negotiated confidentially, without input from the greater campus community. These partnerships have become more normalized over time, and more explicit..." For example, IBM sponsoring a research lab at MIT gives IBM access to students, university resources, and faculty. "Yet such alliances are presented as if there's no tension between the corporate agenda and MIT's professed educational and research mission."[6]

Corporate ties to MIT are antithetical to an educational mission, but the money and prestige entice university administrators. Examples abound. The university organizes *MIT Seminars,* forums wherein MIC elites working on behalf of militant aims, departments, or organizations, study, network, and exchange ideas.[7] MIT administrators named the university's College of Computing after Stephen A. Schwarzman, the CEO of Blackstone Group (the largest private equity firm in the U.S.), which invests heavily in the war industry (and allocated millions to crush an affordable housing ballot measure in California[8]). Schwarzman had personally donated $350 million to MIT.[9] The university's Provost defended the College's naming, the *Boston Globe* reported.[10] The Schwarzman College of Computing soon teamed up with the U.S. Air Force to launch an artificial intelligence accelerator.[11]

MIT has deep, opaque history with the centers of D.C. power. Some of the shadiest characters in D.C.'s history have operated at MIT and the MIT Media Lab.[12] Today, MIT's Media Lab is stronger than ever. U.S. war corporations and martial organizations sponsor the Lab,[13] which aims to create "disruptive technologies that happen at the edges, pioneering such areas as wearable computing, tangible interfaces, and affective computing."[14] No wonder military and industry are interested in such technologies. The applications to warfare are almost endless. MIT has its hands in many war pots. Though nominally independent from MIT, Charles Stark Draper Laboratory ("Draper," from here on out) draws heavily from the MIT faculty, staff, and student body. Draper develops technology for the military's Global Positioning Systems operations at Los Angeles Air Force Base and tweaks guidance systems for the Trident II (D5) submarine-launched ballistic missile, a nuclear weapon. The Trident II costs the U.S. and U.K. taxpayer billions. The Department of War has roughly 220 of these missiles deployed at any given time, according to the U.S. State Department's Bureau of Arms Control, Verification, and Compliance. Draper and Lockheed Martin spread work on the Trident II across dozens of locations.[15]

Draper and MIT personnel venture beyond campus. Draper helps the Naval Undersea Warfare Center in Newport, Rhode Island, develop underwater drones.[16] MIT personnel work at the university's Lincoln Lab, which is located at the eastern end of Hanscom Air Force Base, a one-hour bike ride northwest of Cambridge.

Hanscom is one of the hottest nodes for technology development within the war industry. MIT has juggled many projects at Lincoln Lab, one of which was voice matching and analysis technology used by the National Security Agency.[17] Back on the university's campus in Cambridge, researchers develop software that monitors computer systems in order to distinguish between harmless users and Advanced Persistent Threats (APT).[18] MIT receives millions annually in exchange for supporting the Pentagon's research priorities. MIT is a war corporation.

The nation's most reputable academic institution, Harvard University, is a stone's throw from MIT. Harvard faculty have long prioritized war. Harvard's James D. Watson, a Nobel Prize winning academic who helped discover the double helix DNA structure, served on a classified Pentagon advisory panel for chemical and biological weaponry.[19] James B. Conant, a man who served on many War Department boards, commissions, and committees, was Harvard's president (1933-53). Harvard academics invented Napalm during World War II. They haven't looked back since.

Harvard is a full partner with military and industry. Though it works on goods and services for the Pentagon, Harvard University does not appear in the Pentagon's daily contract listings. This is likely due to strict nondisclosure agreements signed between the two parties and due to careful parsing of funding allocations, keeping tranches below the $7 million level at which public disclosure is required. Nonetheless, Harvard's broad public relations apparatus has touted substantial projects with the Defense Advanced Research Projects Agency.[20]

Harvard hosts many military programs, including the Pentagon's Leadership Decision Making Program at the John F. Kennedy School of Government. Having gobbled up the blue pills (war funding and D.C. edicts), Harvard's senior administrators offer many "national security" courses as well as a National Security Fellows Program. The National Security Fellows Program "is a closed-enrollment, ten-month postgraduate research fellowship for U.S. military officers who are eligible for senior development education and equivalent civilian officials from the broader Intelligence Community. *Selection for this program is handled internally by the respective military services and federal government agencies*" (emphasis mine).[21] The Saudi regime has endowed many professorships at Harvard. Money talks.

Harvard considers where you stand on matters of war and peace. The war industry, the War Department, CIA, and other corporatized U.S. intelligence agencies recruit heavily at Harvard. (Like most youth, Harvard students are susceptible to CIA's highly polished prestige and allure.) Harvard revoked the fellowship of whistleblower Chelsea Manning.[22] The D.C. regime later jailed Manning for refusing to again testify regarding *WikiLeaks*.[23] The Harvard administrator who informed Manning of the snub, Doug Elmendorf, did not reply when I asked him about Manning's imprisonment. Less than a year after rebuffing Manning, Harvard honored Hillary Clinton with the Radcliffe Medal for her "transformative impact on society."[24] As Senator and Secretary of State, Clinton regularly advocated for the use of military force and was a primary driver behind the 2011 destruction of Libya. Harvard's behavior reflects the way the D.C. regime operates: jail whistleblowers, extol war criminals.

Harvard's Belfer Center for Science and International Affairs is ground zero for MIC elites. Ash Carter (former Secretary of War) is now in charge of the Belfer Center. Others finding a home at Harvard include Belfer's director of global communications and strategy, Josh Burek, who used to head marketing and communications at a think tank, the American Enterprise Institute; Eric Rosenbach, a loyal Ash Carter aide and leader of the "Defending Digital Democracy" project at Harvard; and Michael Sulmeyer, the former head of cyber policy at the Pentagon and current leader of the Cyber Security Project at Belfer. The steering group of the Cyber Security Project features current Harvard fellows: James Cartwright (industry think tanker, member of Raytheon's board, retired 4-star general), David Petraeus (former general, former CIA director, and he-who-gave-highly-classified-material-to-his-mistress), James N. Miller (industry think tanker, former senior Pentagon official and House Armed Services Committee senior staffer), and James A. Winnefeld (current member of Raytheon's board and former Vice Chairman of the Joint Chiefs of Staff, where his dominion covered "investment, personnel, intelligence, and strategy, policy, and operations"[25]). Principled courage is hard to find. The Center's namesake, Bob Belfer, who made his fortune in fossil fuel and private equity, is a strong member of the war industry pressure group known as Business Executives for National Security and the Zionist pressure group known deceptively as the American Jewish Committee. Rounding out our brief dive into Harvard's war elite is Michael Blake Greenwald, a man who at the U.S. Treasury Department helped freeze the monies of anyone who opposed D.C. dictates or wars and/or Israeli regional hegemony. He joined Belfer in 2018. Speaking on behalf of the Center, Ash Carter said, "We are honored to have him join our community of researchers committed to a more secure, peaceful world."[26] Members of the Center push great power competition[27]—good men to have on your war team.

All Ivy League universities are complicit in the expansion of military technology and research that builds a more effective warfighter. For example, Brown and Columbia have worked on DARPA's Neural Engineering System Design program, which aims to turn brain signals into machine readable data and readable data into chemical and electrical signals. Yale has worked with DARPA on restoring vision in the blind. Princeton has worked on developing hardware for design and verification of open-sourced integrated circuits. Cornell chemists have attempted to design two-dimensional polymers. DARPA has sponsored conferences about machine learning at Dartmouth. The University of Pennsylvania has worked on artificial intelligence and computational linguistics to understand diverse languages. Do these universities believe their contributions to the military will be confined to the realms of altruism and benevolence?

Universities across the country are scrambling to get War Department money. The University of Arizona (UA) is one example. "Developing new, synergistic strategies for partnerships that help drive innovation are central to the UA strategic plan," says the vice president of UA's *Tech Launch Arizona*. Tech Launch Arizona is the university's overall plan to become "a recognized national resource" for "commercializing UA-created knowledge." Commercializing exactly what knowledge? Might the fact that Arizona has the "fifth largest aerospace and defense economy in the nation" be a factor? Luke Air Force Base is near Phoenix. Raytheon has a massive missile factory in Tucson. Boeing has a helicopter factory in Mesa, east of Phoenix. Davis-Monthan Air Force Base is in southeast Tucson. The Army's Fort Huachuca is farther southeast of Tucson. Accordingly, UA recently established the Defense & Security Research Institute (DSRI). This institute is "expected to make the University an even more attractive partner" to the war industry. The university's leadership pushes hard in favor of militarizing university academics and luring military-industry funding. DSRI's partners include the Air Force Research Lab, the Army Research Lab, the Navy Research Lab, the Department of Homeland Security, and DARPA. A former Deputy Assistant Secretary of War leads DSRI. Second in command at DSRI is a former Raytheon official who "works to support faculty across all colleges" and help them "engage with external defense and intelligence communities." The Institute hopes to double university "research expenditures from $600 million to $1.2 billion by 2023." Money and corporate authority are at home there.[28]

DARPA is a magnet for academics with wobbly morals and a love of money. DARPA contracts were integral in the creation of computer science departments in universities across the country, and tied universities closely, "through funding and personnel," to the War Department.[29] DARPA money feeds engineering and physics departments, too. A two-hour bus ride northeast of DSRI, Arizona State University is working with DARPA on cyber warfare.[30] The University of Southern California helps DARPA speed up circuit design and production,[31] and helps the Air Force Research Lab (AFRL) develop three-dimensional imaging of integrated circuits and design a search program to sift through data and extract important information. The University of Delaware helps DARPA develop composite materials and reconfigurable technologies to improve and even simplify the war industry's manufacturing processes. Six universities (Minnesota, UCLA, Notre Dame, Michigan, Illinois, and UC-Berkeley) work on DARPA's

Focus Center Research Program Semiconductor Technology Advanced Research Network (STARnet). This program aims to keep the U.S. war industry leagues ahead of Moscow and Beijing in the fields of microelectronics and integrated circuits. Others, too, examine the itty-bitty. For DARPA, MIT tries to synthetically manufacture high-value molecules,[32] and the University of Wisconsin at Madison studies neural networks and learning patterns of mice and pigs. The knowledge gained will eventually be used to produce a deadlier warfighter.[33] Through funding and bestowing fellowships and Young Faculty awards, DARPA works to bring pre-tenure academics into the fold of war research academia.

Without modern medical advancements and just-in-time logistics, the U.S. death toll from D.C.'s post-9.11 global wars might just pass the U.S. death toll from D.C.'s war against Southeast Asia (1955-75). The Pentagon and academia collaborate to advance medical research that mollifies our perceptions of the physical and mental effects of war while propitiating the poor and marginalized communities that fight and are maimed in war. Contributing to such medical innovation, Case Western Reserve University in Cleveland, Ohio, works with DARPA to restore feeling and motor function to surgically reattached limbs. Johns Hopkins University Applied Physics Lab works to create prosthetic arms that the human brain can control. The University of Pittsburgh helps improve trauma and emergency services to save U.S. infantry. DARPA works overtime with academia in order to address traumatic brain injury,[34] which is one of the great cripplers of U.S. troops. Many universities work in the medical field for the War Department. The University of Minnesota crafts modular manikins for medical research. At the University of Central Florida (Orlando), Army medical units from Fort Detrick work on psychotherapies for treating post-traumatic stress. The University of Alabama at Birmingham supports clinical research of blood infusion therapies. (Lockheed Martin's CEO has given the University of Alabama a lot of money, helping the university achieve record fundraising in FY2018.[35]) Georgia Tech provides IT security to Army Medical Command. A healthy fighting force is a deployable, operational fighting force. By mollifying our perceptions of the effects of war and propitiating the poor and marginalized communities that are harmed in war, the Pentagon and academia effectively postpone the period of political and educational reconciliation necessary to end the wars.

STANFORD UNIVERSITY

Two of the biggest players in militarized academia are MIT on the east coast and Stanford University on the west coast. Stanford and the surrounding area comprise the west coast core of U.S. microprocessor and computer research and development. Though Stanford has a deep relationship with the military and industry, the university's name is hardly mentioned in the Pentagon's daily contract announcements. In this sense, Stanford University is a subtler operator than its peers in academia.

The Stanford Research Institute (SRI) of Menlo Park, California, is another story. Founded by Stanford immediately after World War II, SRI became an independent organization in the 1970s. Headquartered in Silicon Valley, SRI is now known as SRI International. Like Draper Lab, SRI International is nominally independent from its respective university. Both Draper and SRI International vacuum up academic talent and prioritize the development of war technology.

SRI International has a long history of work within the war machine. SRI was a major ARPA contractor, the early name of DARPA. Its work spanned counterinsurgency technology and early internet development. SRI helped ARPA refine and implement chemical warfare in Vietnam.[36] In recent years, SRI International has become a practical west coast extension of DARPA. The head of SRI International, William Jeffrey, is a former high-ranking DARPA official. SRI International's military contracts teach us about the MIC's goals and its domestic and foreign posture.

When U.S. grunts were perishing daily as a result of improvised explosive devices (IED) in Iraq and Afghanistan, the U.S. war industry jumped in and pitched technology to recognize, avoid, and neutralize the devices. Industry produced a reconnaissance aircraft packed with sensors designed to discern the distinctive characteristics of the ground below to see if any IEDs have been planted. SRI International works on this program, known as Desert Owl.[37] Desert Owl is a good example of the corporatization of war: Textron and L3 have owned and operated the platform. Leidos works on a complementary program known as Night Eagle in Princeton, New Jersey, where SRI International has offices and recruits talent. Corporate work honing Desert Owl and improving its sensors advances U.S. military occupation of lands from the Mediterranean Sea to the Hindu Kush.

The actions of SRI International unveil the overall hypocrisy of the war machine. SRI International and Northrop Grumman have worked on microcircuit technology and a DARPA program known as Supply Chain Hardware Integrity for Electronics Defense (SHIELD), which tries to come up with a way to authenticate components anywhere in the war industry's supply chains to assure that parts are not counterfeit.[38] At the same time, U.S. and Israeli intelligence agencies slip faulty parts into the supply chain of Iran's space program.[39]

SRI International has worked on DARPA's World Modelers Program. By inputting historical data, news figures, and multiple online sources, the World Modelers Program aims to furnish the U.S. military with qualitative and quantitative analyses and forecasts of complex global and regional issues.[40] The Pentagon could apply this technology, for example, to analyze the effects of engineering austerity measures in Athens, food shortages in Caracas, or the expansion of petroleum infrastructure in the Niger delta. If successful, the World Modelers Program will enable Pentagon bureaucrats, and, ultimately, their betters in Corporate America, to scrutinize the implementation of and reaction to capitalist policies in a thorough, user-friendly manner. Corporate America benefits in another way: If the World Modelers Program is effective, the Pentagon might forego long-term development of good human analysts,[41] making the government even more reliant on corporate gizmos.

You've heard of the Internet of Things—extensive integration and overlap of devices (e.g. laptop, tablet, household appliances, vehicle, medical devices, smartphone, wearable technology) connected to the internet. Well, SRI International is developing the Internet of Battlefield Things.[42] This contract points to a never-ending feature of the war industry: war corporations push for a more interconnected, IT-driven military; the Pentagon accedes; war corporations say, "But your systems are unprotected!"; and the Pentagon solicits more corporate devices and personnel to shore up the Pentagon's increasingly interconnected, "vulnerable" systems. The only winners here are the war corporations.

COMPUTING, COLONIZATION, AND LANGUAGE CAPACITY

The Department of War operates five High Performance Computing Centers. Industry giants and academic institutions support this. Hewlett Packard (HP) and its subsidiary Cray maintain and modernize high performance computers. SAIC, a corporation with deep ties to NSA, upgrades the computing capabilities. The High Performance Computing Centers are located at the Army Research Lab at Aberdeen Proving Ground on the Maryland coast; the Engineer Research & Development Center in Vicksburg, Mississippi; the John C. Stennis Space Center in southwest Mississippi; Wright-Patterson Air Force Base, Ohio; and a research lab in Hawai'i.

A brief history of Hawai'i illustrates the crushing nature of U.S. militarism. The U.S. Department of War invaded the islands of Hawai'i in the late nineteenth century. It overthrew the Native's constitutional monarchy and colonized the islands.[43] The U.S. military establishment "arrived en masse" after the 7 December 1941 attack on Pearl Harbor.[44] Outsiders ("haole") wrapped up a major phase of the colonization of Hawai'i in the 1950s. After admitting Hawai'i into the union on 21 August 1959, D.C. turned the Hawaiian island of Kaho'olawe into a firing and bombing range. (Kaho'olawe is still polluted and rife with unexploded ordnance, though, after popular protest, the War Department no longer uses it for bombing and live fire. The War Department did spend $400 million on a somewhat ineffective cleanup effort there.) Like all areas of intense military-industry activity, the island chain suffers from pollution. Native Hawaiians continue to protest militarization on their land.

What does military-industrial infrastructure on Hawaiʻi tell us about the state of the nation? During the 2020 run for Presidency of the United States, Rep. Tulsi Gabbard (D-HI) spoke out against "regime-change wars"—U.S. military interventions in such sovereign nations as Iraq, Syria, and Libya. Let's assume for a moment that Gabbard is genuinely a peace candidate, despite a few blots on her record spouting MIC pabulum (e.g. *troops fight for freedom,* and *military deployments serve the country*) and voting for bloated military budgets. What are Gabbard and her supporters up against? U.S. military installations and land comprise roughly 25% of Hawaiʻi—a larger percentage of territory than the Pentagon has in any other state.[45] Major military facilities include Camp H.M. Smith, Marine Corps Base Hawaiʻi, and Joint Base Pearl Harbor-Hickam on Oʻahu; the Pacific Missile Range Facility on Kauai; the Pōhakuloa Training Area on the island of Hawaiʻi; and the High Performance Computing Center located at the Maui Research & Technology Park.[46] Substantial military-intelligence facilities pockmark the colony, including NSA's cryptologic center on the island of Oʻahu. The military's presence in Hawaiʻi is expanding: Military construction is ongoing at all of the aforementioned sites. Notable projects include a communications facility at Marine Corps Base Hawaiʻi, an electrical distribution facility at the Pacific Missile Range Facility, telecommunications infrastructure at Pōhakuloa Training Area, and warehouses at Joint Base Pearl Harbor-Hickam. Industry is also entrenched in Gabbard's home state. War corporations pulsating in the Aloha State have included AECOM contractors, Boeing cargo aircraft, CACI signals intelligence software, DynCorp technicians, ECS information technology, Fluor supervisors, General Dynamics submarines, Huntington Ingalls aircraft carriers, and InDyne launch control. Expansive military-industry infrastructure forestalls any chance of peace.

In order to conquer, expand, and subdue, an empire must grasp the languages spoken within its existing and anticipated imperium. Columbia University helps the Air Force Research Lab (AFRL) develop machines that perform automatic speech recognition and language translation. The ultimate aim is to integrate these technologies into compact, user-friendly systems, which the U.S. Armed Forces can use to better control local populations. The University of Pennsylvania helps AFRL sift through multiple streams of media in real-time in order to reconcile conflicting pieces of information, making it easier to wage agile, comprehensive warfare. Draper tries to extract specific portions of language from cluttered media. The University of Pennsylvania supports a program that aims to develop a way to translate rare or "low-resource" languages (good for whenever the War Department is looking to co-opt, coerce, or harm a new country). The University of Southern California helps the War Department research quantum computing, speech recognition, and machine translation. On a parallel track, Johns Hopkins University helps AFRL develop software that translates and interprets any language into English.

Why is the War Department turning to academia and industry to fulfill its language needs?

The answer is twofold.

Firstly, the War Department's linguists are not up to the task.

The Defense Language Institute (DLI) in Monterey, California, is the War Department's premier foreign language training facility. The examination the Department uses to gauge language proficiency is the Defense Language Proficiency Test (DLPT). When I arrived at DLI, students were passing the fourth version of the Arabic DLPT, the DLPT 4, with flying colors. But military-intelligence units were not happy because the students passing the DLPT 4 didn't know Arabic well. The DLPT 4 was not accurately assessing students' knowledge, allowing subpar linguists to matriculate. So, the military brass in the Pentagon commissioned an expensive study and paid a third party handsomely to come up with the next version of the proficiency test, the DLPT 5. The DLPT 5 was a challenging upgrade that tested a student's language skills. Passing rates dropped overnight. Only students who really knew the Arabic language passed. Military-intelligence units were finally getting competent Arabic linguists. But the high rate of failure was not good news to the military brass. *Now we don't have enough linguists going into military-intelligence units! What do we do?!* The bureaucracy was panicking. Did they revamp the training procedures? No. Did they recycle or wash out more of the slackers? No. Did they raise the scores required on the DLAB (the language aptitude test given to aspiring linguists)? No. Instead, the War Department ordered the Arabic DLPT 5 test results to be scaled. So now, once again, most students were passing and graduating, including the sub-par students. Lazy, undedicated students were graduating and going on to positions within U.S. military-intelligence. The Pentagon was back where it started: shitty Arabic linguists. Tales like this serve as important context for why the War Department is turning to academia and the war industry in general to devise language translation and interpretation tools.

Hardworking teachers in the public-school system are forced to emphasize standardized testing and deemphasize creativity, curiosity, and innovative study skills. Largely abandoned by Capitol Hill, the public-school system does not raise many people who are intellectually curious, let alone many who value studying. The War Department relies on the lower and middle classes in the U.S. to carry out the nonstop wars abroad. These enlisted ranks are the ones who, by the numbers, receive most foreign language training. These men and women, graduates of the neglected public-school system, do not learn Category Four languages satisfactorily. (Category Four languages, including Mandarin and Arabic, are the hardest for a native English speaker to learn.) Additionally, instructors at DLI are working with batches of students that have grown up in an age of technological plushness. Enlisted troops are used to finding answers quickly on search engines and relying on smartphones and apps to solve problems. Many refrain from the hard work of sitting down, hashing out an issue over conversation, or dedicating months to achieving intellectual understanding. This ties into a larger facet of U.S. Empire: the mercenaries and enlisted men and women comprising the linguist core of military-intelligence (not to mention the grunts fighting D.C.'s wars) typically do not have the will to understand the cultures of the people they are fighting or snooping on in Asia and Africa, cultures deemed implicitly inferior to American exceptionalism. The result is an intelligence backbone largely clueless about any motivations (e.g. historical, cultural, religious, nationalist, socio-economic, anti-imperial) circulating among the enemy-of-the-day. The officials supervising this activity are too busy (getting rich off war, climbing the career ladder, and rotating between government and industry) to change the system. Battling for "hearts and minds" notwithstanding, if we see those we fight as inferior and simply to be defeated, why should we care what they think?

The second reason the War Department is turning to the academy and industry to fulfill its language needs is that, with installations and operations stretching around the globe, the Department, including NSA, is simply overwhelmed with spoken and written communications. The War Department is eavesdropping on and interfering in[47] so many countries that it's difficult to keep pace with the flood of information coming in.

This is really the paradox confronting the NSA et al.'s extensive information retrieval system. The war industry knows that the War Department is overwhelmed and unable make effective use of all that data it has collected. It is, of course, ready to step up to the plate.

Selling language instruction and skills to the U.S. War Department and allied militaries is big business. Corporations sell their services to keep the Defense Language Institute up and running in Monterey, D.C., and Lackland Air Force Base, Texas. Corporate personnel who passably speak or mumble a foreign language "enhance realism" in military training across the country. Construction companies build language training facilities, like a multi-million-dollar facility for special operations forces in Fort Carson, Colorado. U.S. corporations sell English language instruction to foreign militaries, especially militaries of the Gulf Cooperation Council. Providing interpreters, translators, and linguists for warzones and "intelligence" matters is another profitable slice. (After their military enlistments are up, linguists move like ants on a trail into war corporations, where they do the same desk job for thrice the pay. NSA is a major customer, purchasing corporate linguists, desk mercenaries, of varied motivations and skills.) No single War Department entity enforces contracting or strict supervision of these disparate language programs.

Where there's language, there's industry. MIT professors with ties to the war industry established Bolt, Beranek, and Newman (BBN) shortly after World War II, a time when the titans of capital were working hard to solidify and entrench the MIC. BBN worked with parts of the War Department, including NSA, to develop and upgrade early versions of the internet.[48] Raytheon purchased BBN in autumn 2009. Raytheon BBN works on the hardest war projects, including targeted electronic warfare attack, dispersed computing capabilities for forces deployed in areas of limited connectivity, and drone technology. Raytheon BBN also tackles the same language R&D projects on which the University of Southern California and Columbia University have worked: cross-language information retrieval, machine translation, and automatic speech recognition.

Well at least the Pentagon, not the profit-motivated U.S. war industry, is in charge of administering portions of the U.S. government's language assets, you say. Unfortunately, this is not the case. Booz Allen Hamilton administers the National Language Service Corps (NLSC), an organization established post-9.11 to gather people with language skills that the U.S. government can use during extended emergencies. NLSC resides bureaucratically under the National Security Education Program, the governing organization that develops language initiatives for U.S. espionage purposes, including encouraging partnerships with allied militaries.[49] In an administrative capacity, Booz Allen Hamilton helps recruit U.S. citizens to join NLSC, collects and retains their information, provides this "information to government organizations that are NLSC partners or are interested in becoming partners," and helps activate and certify members while "ensuring compliance with privacy act regulations."[50] War corporations benefit from and are in charge of government language capabilities.

JOHNS HOPKINS, THE STAR

Maryland colleges and universities provide stomping grounds of the War Department and the war industry. For example, the Naval Air Warfare Center Aircraft Division has ties to the University of Maryland, the Southern Maryland Higher Education Center, the College of Southern Maryland, and Morgan State University.[51] One university stands out in Maryland: Johns Hopkins University, an icon of the war industry. Johns Hopkins University's Applied Physics Laboratory, or JHU APL, is close to D.C.—geographically and financially—and it has no qualms accepting War Department funding. The lab is located in Laurel, Maryland, equidistant between Baltimore and D.C. The Baltimore-D.C. corridor is home to many war corporations and government facilities. Many senior fellows at JHU APL are prominent MIC individuals.[52] JHU APL is comparable to Harvard's Belfer Center in the sense that it hosts a familial chamber where MIC elites dwell before rotating back into government or industry.

Other academic institutions are repositories of U.S. war elite. The Texas A&M board of regents is a longtime proponent of bellicose foreign policy and state violence, judging by its appointments. Robert Gates spent roughly twenty-seven years at CIA, including a stint as director. Gates went on to become dean of Texas A&M's George H.W. Bush School of Government & Public Service. (George H.W. Bush was director of CIA, briefly, and an implementer of state terror—that is, the deliberate use of state violence as foreign policy tool intended to coerce, kill, or intimidate—throughout his time in government.) Gates was then appointed President of Texas A&M. After a stint as Secretary of War (2006-11), Gates returned to private life and soon became the Chancellor of the College of William & Mary in Williamsburg, Virginia. Former CIA counterintelligence chief James Olson is a professor at the Bush School of Government & Public Service. Retired General Mark Welsh, former Chief of Staff of the U.S. Air Force and proponent of the most expensive weapons platform in the history of warfare,[53] is the current dean of the Bush School. Many within the university's student body join the U.S. Armed Forces.[54] Retired Air Force General T. Michael Moseley sits on the board of directors of the university's Former Students' Association. The University of Texas isn't much better. Among other War duties, the University of Texas helps the U.S. Navy engineer acoustics, navigation, command & control, and weapons systems. The University of Texas at San Antonio is a major hub for research about military cyber technologies. William McRaven, a retired admiral and career officer in Naval Special Warfare, was chancellor of the entire University of Texas system during 2015-18. Political operator Karl Rove is on the University of Texas Chancellor's Council Executive Committee. Former Secretary of the Air Force Heather Wilson became president of the University of Texas at El Paso.[55] The war elite find shelter and an opportunity to influence in academia from Texas to Maryland and beyond.

What do scientists and engineers at Johns Hopkins University Applied Research Lab do?

Johns Hopkins gets millions from the War Department for the following work:

> assessments and alternatives of offensive capabilities within the domains of air, land, sea, space & cyberspace, missions & warfare areas that asymmetrically mitigate threat effectiveness, impose cost, and/or create ambiguity in adversary decision-making.[56]

What does it mean to advise the U.S. Department of War in *asymmetrically mitigating threat effectiveness, imposing cost, and creating ambiguity in adversary decision-making*? It means that Johns Hopkins is helping the Department develop technologies that put the official enemies of the D.C. regime at a disadvantage. This disadvantage can occur across different battlefields, both declared and undeclared, as the contract phrasing implies.

The official enemies list of the D.C. regime is quite lengthy. It ranges from sub-state and non-state groups like the FARC [*Fuerzas Armadas Revolucionarias de Colombia*] and the Afghan Taliban, to state and social welfare providers like Hezbollah in Lebanon, to great powers like Moscow and Beijing. It is safe to presume that Johns Hopkins is helping to develop technology to harm such official enemies. Surely Johns Hopkins students hail from Afghanistan, Colombia, the People's Republic of China, Lebanon, or Russia. (I sought confirmation. No response.) Johns Hopkins' mission statement says it aims to "bring the benefits of discovery to the world" —contrary to its activities helping the War Department harm or prepare to harm the nations and peoples of the world.

JHU APL also conducts experiments and studies to boost U.S. Special Operations Command's scientific and military knowledge. MIC elites have abused U.S. Special Operations Command, sending SEALs, Army Special Forces, Air Force pararescue, Marine Raiders, and others across the globe on all sorts of imperial errands. Such heavy-duty troops have committed numerous atrocities in Iraq, Afghanistan, and elsewhere. This is a tragedy, a tragedy supported by JHU APL.

In line with demonization of Moscow and Beijing, JHU APL is hard at work researching and developing weapons of war and advanced military technology. JHU APL is a leader in research about hypersonics, air vehicles and missiles that fly over five times the speed of sound. JHU APL also designs tactical devices that perform three-dimensional laser scanning; helps the Air Force engineer nuclear weapons and develop nuclear planning and strategy; and helps the Defense Intelligence Agency engineer and test new sensors. Industry is pushing these technologies, a slice of JHU APL research, via great power competition.[57]

Johns Hopkins University is working on a program called Machine Translation for English Retrieval in Any Language, or MATERIAL. MATERIAL got its start in the Pentagon's Intelligence Advanced Research Projects Agency. The Pentagon established the Intelligence Advanced Research Projects Agency in 2006, as if DARPA and the numerous other military research labs were not enough. Johns Hopkins' work on MATERIAL involves honing machine learning and software to better translate writing and interpret speech. Since MATERIAL has direct applications to signals intelligence, you can bet the program will be used against allied governments as well as official enemies. Understanding the world's languages expands warzones and improves the ability of signals intelligence organizations, like NSA, to monitor people around the world.

Johns Hopkins fashions itself a cosmopolitan academic institution dedicated to human progress and the advancement of the global good. But its intricate ties to the War Department show the university's true colors: caring more about government funding than the fate of mankind or the nobility of academia. It is no different than MIT, Harvard, or Georgia Tech in this regard. Georgia Tech, a regular recipient of War Department funding, focuses on everything from espionage to missile technology.[58]

In 2019, students at Johns Hopkins launched an occupation of the campus administration building in protest of the university's contracts with the Department of Homeland Security's Immigrations & Customs Enforcement. They were also protesting the university's plans for an armed campus police force and dissenting in favor of union rights. With no sense of irony, JHU administrators called in the Baltimore Police Department, an organization with a horrid track record of corruption and brutality, in order to evict protestors.

HIGHER EDUCATION

Aside from paying academia directly, the War Department sets up events that cultivate an academic interest in working for the war industry. One popular initiative is Hacking for Defense (H4D)[59] in which university students are given complex problems to brainstorm and tackle. Many universities have teamed up with H4D.[60]

H4D tangibly abets D.C.'s aggression, the website explains:

> The Hacking for Defense program combines rapid problem sourcing processes developed in Afghanistan with innovative Silicon Valley business models... Corporate Sponsors support and mentor students during this process and develop close bonds with their teams.[61]

Help corporations and the Pentagon in exchange for kudos, job prospects, and a potentially cushier lifestyle for you and yours. But—buyer beware. What goes around could surely come right back around.

The war industry wins in other ways via H4D. It gets to spot talent, cultivate favorable press, and expand its pool of eligible thinkers, programmers, engineers, and scientists. The founder of the war corporation Arête (Northridge, CA) is currently the managing director of H4D's superordinate National Security Technology Accelerator program (MD5). MD5 aims to develop "human capital," a.k.a. people with the technical skills the war industry wants, or people developing products the war industry could use. Arête has sold the Pentagon a variety of goods and services in recent years.[62] And just when MD5 couldn't get any more corporate, the Pentagon paid millions on 25 September 2018 to Eccalon (Hanover, MD) to help administer the Office of Manufacturing & Industrial Base Policy within MD5. MD5, like the military as a whole, is run for corporations by corporations.

While academia creates military goods and services as part of the war industry, the War Department is hard at work educating personnel *within* the Department itself. The Department has its own institutions of higher learning, which include Air University, Army Command & General Staff College, Army War College, Defense Acquisition University, Marine Corps University, National Defense University, Naval War College, and Naval Postgraduate School.[63] These institutions sequester the soldier, sailor, airman, or Marine from possible exposure to countervailing views, leading to a degree of indoctrination that hampers their clear understanding of what the U.S. war project is. Civilian universities like Salve Regina of Newport, Rhode Island, supplement these efforts by educating many rising officers in international relations and political science.

Civilian colleges and universities educate U.S. troops overseas. The University of Maryland provides graduate programs for U.S. troops deployed to Africa and Southwest Asia. This includes educating U.S. troops who are stationed in the Sinai. Central Texas College provides technical and vocational programs to deployed U.S. troops. (The U.S. military and the Israelis are key players in the Sinai, along with the military of Egyptian dictator Abdel Fattah as-Sisi.[64] The Egyptian military's brutality in the Sinai is now coming to light in Western media.[65]) Neither the University of Maryland nor Central Texas College responded to my inquiries asking if they research where the Pentagon deploys troops before they sign such educational deals.

Organizations that seem peaceful on the surface can actually abet the War Department. The National Academy of Sciences in D.C. assembles a board that will advise the U.S. Army on scientific and technical topics to give the military a distinct war-fighting advantage. The National Academy of Sciences has also established a post-doctoral research position in alliance with the Air Force Research Lab. This program cultivates the next generation of pro-war scientists (whose research will ultimately contribute to the military's ability to kill and destroy). By accepting War Department funding, the National Academy of Sciences puts itself at odds with the International Council for Science (ICSU), of which it is a member. The ICSU prioritizes the ethnical responsibility of scientists.[66] The U.S. War Department, on the other hand, demonizes and attacks certain groups of people. I called the accounts department of the ICSU in 2018. They were unaware of any financial transactions between the National Academy of Sciences and the Pentagon. The ICSU staffers with whom I spoke declined to comment further on the matter, and I was told that senior ICSU officials who might have been able to speak authoritatively about the National Academy of Sciences were traveling abroad at the time of contact. I followed up with no success. The National Academy of Sciences' work with the U.S. military is part of a wider pattern wherein professional groups and associations aid the War Department, only to regret it later. The American Psychological Association (APA) aided CIA and the War Department in approving torture and inhumane treatment. Other medical professionals have helped torture of prisoners in U.S. custody worldwide.[67]

A policy of permanent warfare entails the coopting of apolitical scientific endeavors by creative means.

LABS AND CENTERS

The U.S. government runs many research labs pursuing military and intelligence R&D.[68]

U.S. academics work at these labs. For example, the Air Force Research Lab attracts a wide variety of academic minds. The University of Dayton Research Institute is a short drive from Wright-Patterson Air Force Base. In recent years it has worked on improving materials and designs of military aircraft, advancing engine combustion, researching reusable hypersonic vehicles, analyzing thermal technologies, and developing small drones. Utah State University develops sensors to help AFRL identify and track hazards in space. Utah State also works on navigation and boosts AFRL's capacity to process imagery and analyze data. Some of this work overlaps with Utah State's commitment to the Missile Defense Agency. The University of New Mexico works on developing semiconductors and electronic components for AFRL, while New Mexico State University (NMSU) teams up with the Army Research Lab to assess vulnerabilities and lethality of industry products. NMSU is a thirty-minute drive to White Sands, where the U.S. government tests propulsion, aerospace materials, and explosives. (TRAX International, Las Vegas, runs mission support at White Sands. A joint venture called Southwest Range Services runs test operations.) The academic-corporate presence at military labs is typically much larger than the military presence.

Funding research centers is another effective way to monopolize academia. Research Triangle Park is one of the biggest research facilities in the U.S. The Park's campus draws academic talent from nearby institutions, such as Duke, the University of North Carolina, and NC State University. Industry projects involving Research Triangle Park and paid for by the War Department have focused a lot in recent years on developing technology for crushing insurgencies and rebellions of all sizes. This technology includes digital low light imaging; capabilities to "decisively establish the identity of adversaries and effectively link that identity to other information"; counteracting "asymmetrical threats"; detecting explosives at checkpoints; finding improvised explosive devices based on telltale and subtle signatures; human identification from a variety of distances; maximizing infantry performance using drones and secure communications; radar for special operations; "red team" operations run out of the Pentagon; three-dimensional laser mapping; and DARPA counterinsurgency projects, the nature of which is undisclosed. Funding research centers outsources the development of counterinsurgency technologies.

University-Affiliated Research Centers (UARCs) are War Department research units that operate with and are often embedded in a university. JHU APL is one. UARCs respond to the Pentagon's research priorities, as seen in the University of Alaska Fairbanks Geophysical Institute teaming with the War Department to run a UARC focused on detection of nuclear proliferation. Third parties regularly get involved, like Stevens Institute of Technology (Hoboken, NJ) selling R&D services to assist the Systems Engineering Research Center, a UARC affiliated with the University of Southern California. Federally Funded Research & Development Centers (FFRDC) are public-private partnerships. They research mostly war-related topics for the Departments of War and Energy, the latter of which administers nuclear weapons research. FFRDC pose as "independent, not-for-profit" organizations, explicitly without "commercial conflicts of interest"[69]—but they largely cater to the MIC. MITRE is a good example of an FFRDC. MIT established MITRE as a non-profit in part to avoid scrutiny of a dismal, failing radar program, according to a former employee.[70] MITRE has evolved into a not-for-profit engineering and technology corporation. Its board of directors is packed with war titans.[71] MITRE currently runs a few FFRDC, including the War Department's National Security Engineering Center, the DHS Homeland Security Systems Engineering & Development Institute (est. 2009), and a cybersecurity FFRDC (est. 2014) within the Commerce Department.[72] The Aerospace Corporation runs the FFRDC at the Space & Missile Systems Center, Los Angeles Air Force Base, the center of space militarization. The Aerospace Corporation even has its own educational endowment fund and scholarship programs.[73]

MILITARIZING EDUCATION

Education in the United States exists within narrow confines. People educated in elementary and secondary schools are not given the opportunity to learn about the horrific nature and devastating effects of the U.S. war industry. They are not taught about how the interests of elites (the Pentagon's leadership, industry executives, the Wall Street managerial class, and Congress) clash head-on with the interests of ordinary Americans. An uneducated population will not mobilize against its oppressors—or if it does, its analysis is faulty and easily deflected. This atmosphere of ignorance greatly benefits the MIC. By attracting students into science, technology, engineering, and math (STEM) careers, the war industry and the War Department prepare and safeguard their profitable future.

The saga of NSA wooing children introduces us to militarized educational initiatives. The chief of external recruiting and hiring at NSA says that the agency succeeds by "recruiting directly to middle school and high school kids, planting the seeds of a desire to serve upon graduation," according to the *Army News Service*.[74] It is no accident that in Howard County, Maryland—one of six counties that Fort Meade (NSA's home) encompasses or encroaches upon—residents enjoy superb schools.[75] The *Washington Post* reports, the "schools, indeed, are among the best, and some are adopting a curriculum this fall that will teach students as young as 10 what kind of lifestyle it takes to get a security clearance and what kind of behavior would disqualify them."[76] NSA's role in education illustrates a circle of corporate entanglement: War corporations take over most of NSA's workload, and the agency woos youth, sucking them into the military-industry pipeline and providing the agency with a future workforce, all while perverting the very meaning of education and erudition.

The Pentagon throws money and resources at elementary and secondary school education within the United States. The National Defense Education Program is the primary vehicle through which the War Department militarizes education, funding STEM programs and offering scholarships.[77] Even seemingly random units within the War Department push STEM campaigns. For example, Naval Surface Warfare Center Dahlgren Division sponsors STEM events at museums, and Naval Air Warfare Center Aircraft Division hosts STEM students for "National Week at the Labs."[78] The War Department promotes STEM in order to foster a technologically literate workforce and future generations of enlisted troops who are smart enough to operate the war industry's products.

Every major war corporation promotes STEM. Boeing is committed "to developing the future workforce." Lockheed Martin identifies STEM education as a "critical focus." Raytheon calls it a "key strategic business concern." Northrop Grumman calls it "critical for our business and for U.S. competitiveness, so we've embraced programs that we think will help build a diverse employee pipeline." CACI supports STEM education "both nationally and locally." Harris Corp. helps "foster the next generation of space innovators."[79] The industry pressure group NDIA has STEM initiatives in its many chapters to "compete as an innovative country."[80] Indeed, many different industry pressure groups promote STEM.[81] Industry promotion of STEM lays the groundwork for future design, engineering, and production capacity.

STEM efforts are comprehensive. Grants and scholarships for educators who teach STEM in K-12 proliferate. Unique programs include Raytheon sponsoring an MIT summer camp where youth learn STEM and design drones, and giving millions of dollars to help the Boys & Girls Clubs of America establish Centers of Innovation, spanning such industry hotspots as Huntsville in Alabama and Aberdeen Proving Ground in Maryland; and Lockheed Martin funding the largest STEM event in the States,[82] and partnering with the Ministry of Education in Apartheid Israel to educate children, including kids as young as five.[83] Get 'em early, while their guard is down, and you own them for life.

Locations are selected carefully. For example, Lockheed Martin has given a $2 million STEM grant to Orange County, Florida,[84] a major war industry node.[85] By giving Orange County money for STEM education, the war corporation is aiming to cultivate future employees in an area rife with corporate interests and production facilities. The goal is to put programs in place to inspire students already well located to pursue technical careers with Lockheed Martin, the corporation's executive vice president for Mission Systems & Training makes clear.[86] This is the same Mission Systems & Training, mind you, that has produced deadly weaponry like MH-60 helicopters and boondoggles like the Aegis combat system.

Major war corporations allocate resources to strengthen female interest in science and technology. Northrop Grumman sponsored a panel—"The Science of Confidence: How Women and Girls can Master the Tech Revolution"—on 8 April 2017 in Baltimore, Maryland. The CEO of Sierra Nevada Corp. (a company that sells logistics for strike packages for AC-130 gunships, which have killed civilians, including women) has sponsored the Ozmen Center for Entrepreneurship and the Center's Women's Entrepreneurship Symposium at the University of Nevada-Reno. *Women in Defense,* affiliated with NDIA, funds STEM. Lockheed Martin's *Girls, Inc.* targets ages 9-12.

STEM endeavors are consistent with corporations' leveraging of empathy and progressive ideals to promote profitable war. Lockheed Martin's use of Langston Hughes' poem, *A Dream Deferred*, when promoting STEM education among female students[87] is particularly nauseating. Langston Hughes was a groundbreaking African American poet acutely aware of the lack of racial justice in the United States. It is tragic to see a corporation, whose weaponry regularly kills black and brown people worldwide, exploit Hughes' poetry.

But then, war corporations are adept at exploiting whatever way the wind blows. Consider the case of Dr. Martin Luther King Jr., a man steadfast in his commitment to nonviolence and his rejection of war. Dr. King famously asserted, "Our only hope today lies in our ability to recapture the revolutionary spirit and go out into a sometimes hostile world declaring eternal hostility to poverty, racism, and militarism."[88] AAR named one of its job fairs the *MLK Day of Service Job*

Fair. The press release stated, "On a history-making day—and a day off for many Americans—AAR will honor Dr. Martin Luther King's legacy with an economic opportunity: access to 70 open positions at its aircraft repair station near the airport."[89] AAR, a corporation that specializes in transporting U.S. troops and cargo around warzones, also has robust STEM operations. In 2019, war corporations honored the memory of Dr. King and Black History Month. Lockheed Martin even re-tweeted the War Department (@DeptofDefense), which had brazenly quoted MLK: "The time is always right to do what is right."

War corporations have no problem exploiting anyone's memory in their pursuit of profit. The war industry regularly remembers the 9.11 attacks.[90] War corporations issued press releases or commentary on Memorial Day, 2019, paying tribute to those "who sacrificed for our freedom" (Raytheon's tweet, General Dynamics' tweet) and "those who've made the ultimate sacrifice in the name of freedom" (Lockheed Martin's tweet). This is an average, mild day in industry communications.[91]

STEM enablement and promotion is part of corporations' overall insistence that they're doing good deeds. The philanthropy of war corporations is mostly dispensed in academic scholarships and charitable giving. Raytheon's 2017 corporate responsibility report—war corporations assure us they are leaders in "corporate responsibility," an oxymoron—emphasizes sustainability, environmentalism, renewable energy, support for veterans and military families, support for small businesses, promotion of STEM, and LGBTQ rights. An interesting note occurred on page 70 of 82 of the report: "In 2017, our GLBTA employee resource group promoted awareness and support by circulating an ally wall for Raytheon leaders and employees to sign. This was an important opportunity to express our shared values by supporting a vulnerable GLBTA community that faces unfavorable policy changes in some states where we operate." I assume Raytheon was referring to U.S. states. There was no mention of the Saudi regime, a major Raytheon customer, which beheads men and women for offenses like witchcraft and homosexuality. General Dynamics' corporate sustainability report of the same year was equally remarkable. There, General Dynamics made clear that its "ethos" is its "distinguishing moral nature." Its "ethos is rooted in four values: Transparency. Trust. Alignment. Honesty." The war corporation goes on to affirm its support of human rights, small businesses, ethical leadership, business ethics, environmental responsibility, diversity, and youth education.[92] These corporate responsibility reports seek to whitewash the crimes, carnage, and death that sustain their business model.

Early recruitment into STEM is also a marketing opportunity. Corporations just lean on the advertising skills they have perfected over decades of capitalist exploitation. Corporate advertisers have mastered the art of targeting youth, getting them to consume more and more goods and services at younger and younger ages. Youth are now the most powerful demographic among consumers. Correcting the acceptance of the war industry, or pro-war ideologies, or military culture, ingrained since childhood, is difficult to reverse. Industry's work is effective and devastating—like when a nine-year-old boy drew a futuristic bomber aircraft for the Deputy Secretary of War,[93] or when a PhD student fondly recalled Raytheon's impact on her life.[94] All U.S. war corporations of significant weight have educational and/or STEM initiatives in the works. From a boardroom perspective, such machinations are a smart investment. From a community, environmental, or loving perspective, such machinations are disastrous and go far to explain the general bellicosity of the American public.

Major foreign procurers of U.S. war industry goods and services contribute to the degradation of U.S. academia. According to the *Project on Government Oversight,* Gulf countries like Bahrain, Kuwait, Qatar, Saudi Arabia, and the UAE have invested billions in U.S. colleges and universities in recent years. MIT, Harvard, and others feted the Saudi regime's leading despot, Mohammed bin Salman, on his first official U.S. tour. Other U.S. universities with strong ties to the Saudi regime include the University of New Haven and Yale University. NATO, a major purchaser of products from the U.S. war industry, received a student delegation from Emmanuel College of Boston at a firing range in the Mediterranean. When "universities decide to sell themselves to the highest bidder, they become deaf to the interests of their students and the wider societies in which they operate," Grif Peterson and Yarden Katz teach us. "Subservience to war criminals and corporate overlords tends to follow,"[95] hence the *Lockheed Martin Leadership Institute* at the University of Miami.

The sequence of corruption and neglect of the common good is sickening. The U.S. government spends most of its discretionary spending on war, weapons of war, and preparing for war. It then claims there is no money for programs that take care of people: the social safety net, infrastructure, education, or universal healthcare. Government imposes austerity measures on the masses and privatization of public schools. Schools are strapped for cash, so war corporations—the very war corporations benefiting from this dreadful status quo—step in and fund the science and math programs!

BRAIN DRAIN

"Brain drain" happens when industry herds intelligent people toward purposes of war, like when a graduate of engineering school goes to work for a war corporation instead of a municipality. Humanity loses the efforts of skilled human beings which might otherwise benefit the common good. Brain drain is a great tragedy, and the war industry's biggest success. In Boston, the U.S. Air Force alone funds ninety different research projects, according to the Air Force Secretary.[96] That's just the publicly declared actions of *one* branch of the military in *one* city. Likewise, the Space and Naval Warfare Systems Center Pacific in San Diego, California, employs thousands, cornering numerous ideas ("intellectual property") in the process.[97] The "largest number of mathematicians in the world" works for NSA.[98] Lockheed Martin alone employs nearly 50,000 scientists and engineers.[99] Imagine the possibilities if these minds were working on problems and projects for the betterment of humanity and the planet, instead of devising more ingenious ways to surveil or murder.

The war industry and the Pentagon have established many more programs to exploit U.S. academia. Covering a fraction of publicly available contracts, this chapter has demonstrated the problems associated with academia's role in the war industry. Many contracts between U.S. academia and the Pentagon are not even disclosed; the public will never know the true extent of the collaboration. Universities have transformed themselves into war corporations because it's financially and professionally profitable. But there is an added bonus for the Pentagon: Dominating academia with war funding crowds out those who wish to use academia for non-military scholarship. Effective science is based on free, open discussion. Pentagon funding and stipulations (compartmentalization, shoehorned focus, classification, near-term deadlines, stovepiped fields) oppose free, open discussion. Science at the service of war-related innovation is suffocated at best, stagnant and deviant at worst. Breakthroughs require the open, secure inquiry and inquisitive self-determination of an unrestrained academia. Major breakthroughs do not happen regularly when academics are tied to military-industry funding priorities, schedules, and narrow mental confines. The military and industry shun and condemn the polymath, the free thinker, and the uninhibited tinkerer, instead embracing and funding the careerist, the complicit academic, the rigid functionary, the greedy corporatist, and the aspiring bureaucrat. These people may possess strong minds, but theirs are minds that will never be directed toward the kind of scientific breakthroughs society needs. The corruption of colleges and universities inhibits genuine academic growth. The fields of science and mathematics, integral to the war industry, are particularly corrupted.

Universities are swiftly becoming corporations in outlook, soul, and deed—full members of the war industry.

ENDNOTES

1 As always, unless otherwise stated all information has been derived from contracts at <www.defense.gov/News/Contracts/>, before summer 2018; during summer 2018–spring 2019 at <https://dod.defense.gov/News/Contracts/>; and after spring 2019 at <www.defense.gov/Newsroom/Contracts>.

2 The initiative goes by the servile backronym *Harnessing Emerging Research Opportunities to Empower Soldiers* (HEROES). More information available at UMASS-Lowell's Center for Advanced Materials (CAM): <www.uml.edu/Research/CAM/default.aspx>.

3 One of their big initiatives is the Center for Applied Brain & Cognitive Sciences (CABCS). Benson, Jane. "Natick and Tufts to hold grand opening for Center for Applied Brain and Cognitive Sciences." *Natick Soldier Research, Development, and Engineering Center (NSRDEC)*. 18 October 2016.

4 Mark Russell, a Raytheon VP, is on the Worcester Polytechnic Institute board. Gary Labovich, Booz Allen Hamilton executive VP, is on Clark University's board. Liz Cahill Lempres, senior partner emeritus at McKinsey & Co., is on the Dartmouth board of trustees. (McKinsey & Co. regularly sells consulting services and strategic analyses to the War Dept.). Scott Donnelly, Textron CEO, is on the Bryant University board of trustees. Bob Lupone, Textron general counsel, is involved in Brown University fundraising and alumni relations. Executives from investment banks and private equity typically have a greater presence than executives from war corporations on New England university boards.

5 Corporate funding turned out to have "less tolerance for educational purposes" and less interested in "'basic' research." Corporate priorities were "focused more narrowly on their own special business interests," and "results were expected more quickly." Perry, Ruth and Yarden Katz. "Is This Any Way to Run a University?" *MIT Faculty Newsletter*. Vol. XXX, No. 5, May/June 2018. Perry works at MIT and Katz works at Harvard.

6 Perry, Ruth and Yarden Katz. "Is This Any Way to Run a University?"

7 See more at <semxxi.mit.edu/about>.

8 "Housing Is A Human Right Exposes Billionaire Landlord Stephen Schwarzman." *Housing is a Human Right*. 14 June 2019: <www.housinghumanright.org>. "Celebrating war criminals at MIT's 'ethical' College of Computing." *The Tech.com*. 14 February 2019. In calling on the MIT administration to reconsider its *modus operandi*, academics at MIT report: Schwarzman, "who has a net personal worth of over $12 billion, invested $350 million in the initiative." The man has also hosted Saudi despot Mohammed bin Salman. "For the MIT administration, as for Schwarzman, money trumps concerns for human rights and economic justice… Underlying the whole of this is MIT's growing quest for private sponsorship, military contracts, and the wrong kind of prestige. Rather than promoting thoughtful discussion about the direction of the university, the administration stages Davos-like spectacles, of which the Schwarzman College celebrations are a prime example."

9 Schwarzman then donated £150 million ($188.17 million) to the U.K.'s Oxford University, which will use the money for a new institute to study artificial intelligence, philosophy, and ethics.

10 McDonald, Danny. "MIT's invitation to Henry Kissinger is controversial." *Boston Globe*. 18 February 2019. The *Globe* quoted a spokeswoman for Schwarzman: Addressing the "pressing challenges of our times" "should transcend politics." "Steve is proud to support an institution that is making a major commitment to be at the epicenter of the technology's evolution by allowing the free and open discussion of its development and impact." The *Globe* quoted Yarden Katz, who emphasized the need to establish a democratic procedure for "the broader university community to be able to vote on partnerships."

11 Crichton, Danny. "MIT and U.S. Air Force team up to launch AI accelerator." *Tech Crunch*. 20 May 2019.

12 John Negroponte, the first ever U.S. Director of National Intelligence (2005-7), helped lead D.C.'s dirty wars against the people of Latin America during the 1980s. Yasha Levine (*Surveillance Valley*, p. 130) explains that John's younger brother, Nick, worked on military programs at MIT and for the predecessor to today's Defense Advanced Research Projects Agency. He also ran his own government-funded research outfit at MIT called the Machine Architecture Group (MAG). In 1985, Nick folded MAG into the MIT Media Lab, "a hub that connected business, military contracting, and university research." There, he pursued corporate funding even more aggressively. Levine also points out that MIT's Center for International Studies has received CIA funding (p. 65).

13 War corporations include MacAndrews & Forbes and Northrop Grumman. Organizations that sponsor MIT's Media Lab and are also affiliated with the U.S. War Dept. include Aramco, Cisco, Dell, Deloitte LP, IBM, Intel, Motorola, and Thales, among others. Research contracts and special funds come from Charles Stark Draper Laboratory, Lincoln Laboratory, the U.S. Army, and the U.S.-Israel Binational Science Foundation. Full list available at <www.media.mit.edu/files/sponsors.pdf>.

14 "The MIT Media Lab at a Glance." *MIT Media Lab*. Spring 2018: <dam-prod.media.mit.edu/x/2018/05/07/at-a-glance.pdf>.

15 Draper's Trident II work is spread out across MN, FL, and MA. Lockheed Martin divvies out work to Sunnyvale, Rialto, & Palo Alto, CA; Denver & Colorado Springs, CO; Cape Canaveral & Merritt Island, FL; Kings Bay & St. Mary's, GA; Silverdale & Poulsbo, WA; Magna, UT; Gainesville & Manassas, VA; Elkton & Baltimore, MD; Atlanta, GA; Cincinnati, OH, and **over 80 other** U.S. towns and cities. Overseas locations include Aldermaston, England; Coulport, Scotland; Borgo San Dalmazzo, Italy.

16 The Woods Hole Oceanographic Institute also helps develop unmanned undersea vehicles.

17 Williams, Margot, Talya Cooper, Henrik Moltke, Micah Lee. "328 NSA Documents Reveal 'Vast Network' of Iranian Agents, Details of a Key Intelligence Coup, and a Fervor for Voice Matching Technology." *The Intercept*. 15 August 2018.

18 A tranche of NSA hacking tools leaked online in 2017 revealed "a collection of scripts and scanning tools the NSA uses to detect other nation-state hackers on the machines it infects." These scripts and tools show that NSA has tracked "at least 45 different nation-state operations" deemed Advanced Persistent Threats. An NSA team, Territorial Dispute, had created these scripts and tools. Territorial Dispute's mission was "to detect and counter sophisticated nation-state attackers more quickly, when they first began to emerge online... But their mission evolved to also provide situational awareness for NSA hackers to help them know when other nation-state actors are in machines they're trying to hack, according to *The Intercept* (Kim Zetter, 6 March 2018). The MIT APT contract was issued 29 June 2015.

19 Hersh, Seymour. *Reporter*. New York: Alfred A. Knopf, 2018, p. 65.

20 Mowatt, Twig. "Harvard's Wyss Institute receives $2.6M from DARPA to develop suit." *Harvard Gazette*. 19 July 2012. Kusek, Kristen. "Wyss Institute wins DARPA grant to further develop its Soft Exosuit." *Harvard Gazette*. 11 September 2014.

21 "National Security Fellows." *Educational Programs*. Accessed 2 October 2018: <www.hks.harvard.edu/educational-programs/executive-education/national-security-fellows>.

22 For coverage of the incident, see the work of journalists Katharine Q. Seelye ("With Chelsea Manning Invitation, Harvard Got a Discussion It Didn't Want." *The New York Times*. 15 September 2017) and Ed Pilkington ("Chelsea Manning hung up phone on Harvard dean who delivered fellowship snub." *The Guardian*. 15 September 2017).

23 Manning was jailed on 8 March 2019 for being in "contempt of court." Remember: the MIC regularly exploits legalese to advance a pro-war agenda. Jamiles Lartey writing in *The Guardian* on 24 March 2019 notes, "Extended periods of solitary confinement 'amount to torture,' according to the United Nations special rapporteur Juan Méndez, who has argued that 'solitary confinement should be banned by states as a punishment or extortion technique.' Manning's supporters said: 'Chelsea is a principled person, and she has made clear that while this kind of treatment will harm her, and will almost certainly leave lasting scars, it will never make her change her mind about cooperating with the grand jury.'"

24 Walsh, Colleen. "Hillary Clinton receives Radcliffe Medal." *Harvard Gazette*. 25 May 2018. Many Democratic operatives call Harvard home. Cass Sunstein, current Harvard professor, worked for the Obama administration by monitoring government regulatory agencies and spiking pending improvements in workers' health or muscular environmental protection.

25 Cited on <www.belfercenter.org/person/james-winnefeld-jr>.

26 Wilke, Sharon. "Greenwald joins Kennedy Schools as Belfer Center fellow." *The Harvard Gazette*. 13 July 2018.

27 A good example of this is the duo of Ambassador/Lt. Gen. (ret.) Doug Lute and Former NATO Ambassador Nick Burns, both living the cushy life at the Belfer Center. Lute is a Senior Fellow and Burns is a professor. Lute and Burns are unapologetic in their support for D.C.'s militarism vis-à-vis NATO. Lute pushes great power competition ("Putin's Russia" and "the increase in competition with China," in Lute's phrasing) in order to strengthen NATO. Burns provides the bluster: As the "core of the alliance," the U.S. is "the strongest country. We always have been since 1949—we always will be... It's in the self-interest of the United States to have our troops in Europe. That's how you defend the United States, from Europe; we're a continent closer to the conflicts we sometimes have to be in." Burns' lies are bold and aggressive: NATO member countries are "all countries that believe in what we believe: democracy, human rights, the rule of law... The Russians have no allies in the world." This interview with Lute and Burns was conducted at CNAS. "Harvard's Lute, Burns on New NATO Report, Challenges, Alliance's Importance." *Defense & Aerospace Report*. 15 March 2019: <www.youtube.com/watch?v=AW6mq8s8uoI>.

28 Esham, Gary. "The University of Arizona and Motorola Enter Agreement to Streamline Research and Innovation." *Tech Launch Arizona*. 27 January 2015. "What We Do." *Tech Launch Arizona*. Accessed 30 June 2018: <techlaunch.arizona.edu/tla/about-ott>. "UA Launches Defense & Security Research Institute." 10 March 2014. "Our Partners." *DSRI*. Accessed 6 August 2018: <dsri.arizona.edu/our-partners>."DSRI Leadership." Accessed 6 August 2018: <dsri.arizona.edu/dsri-leadership>. The Arizona Commerce Authority <www.azcommerce.com/industries/aerospace-defense> explains what attracts military and industry to Arizona. "Raytheon will continue to rely on the University of Arizona for engineering grads and other talent the company needs, said [Missile Systems President Taylor] Lawrence," reported the *Arizona Daily Star* (David Wichner, et al., 18 November 2016). Capitalist malfeasance runs deep. The UA Center for the Philosophy of Freedom is funded by oligarch oil money (the Koch Brothers' in particular) and promotes corporate ideologies like neoliberalism. Similarly, the Center corrupts academia by trying to sponsor local high school courses and imbue them in corporate ideologies. See "High School Dual Enrollment: Ethics, Economy, and Entrepreneurship" at <freedomcenter.arizona.edu/eee>. Also see Natalie McGill's segment on Episode 234 of *Redacted Tonight*, <www.youtube.com/watch?v=WbnOz9fGQCI>, for hilarious and edifying journalism about academic corruption. For a language skills partnership with a local air force base, see "D-M strengthens ties with Tucson community," <www.dm.af.mil/Media/Art/igphoto/2001345825>.

29 Levine, Yasha. *Surveillance Valley*, p. 51.

30 Issued 11 April 2018. The DARPA research project is called Harnessing Autonomy for Countering Cyberadversary Systems. Georgia Tech also works on HACCS. Issued 30 April 2018.

31 Some of the work on CRAFT, Circuit Realization At Faster Timescales, took place at USC's Information Sciences Institute. The head of USC's ISI at the time of this writing is Prem Natarajan, former director of Raytheon's BBN Technologies.

32 DARPA's Living Foundries program aims to produce critical, high-value molecules using biomanufacturing. DARPA and industry partners have already developed the basic physical technologies and tools (re: design, automation, modular devices, genetic editing). MIT and others are working on the scaling and expansion (using genome editing and machine learning) of these biomanufacturing systems. "As a proof of concept, DARPA aims to produce 1,000 molecules and material precursors spanning a wide range of defense-relevant applications including industrial chemicals, pharmaceuticals, coatings, and adhesives that can be customized to continuously evolving" specifications and requests from the War Dept. Wegrzyn, Renee. "Living Foundries." *Defense Advanced Research Projects Agency*: <www.darpa.mil/program/living-foundries>.

33 "Computer Science Study Group (CSSG)." *Defense Advanced Research Projects Agency*. Accessed 13 December 2018: <www.darpa.mil/program/computer-science-study-group>.

34 DARPA's TBI projects include "Targeted Electrical Stimulation of the Brain Shows Promise as a Memory Aid" (<www.darpa.mil/news-events/2015-09-11a>) and "Restoring Active Memory (RAM)" (<www.darpa.mil/program/restoring-active-memory>). Corporate entities work separately on TBI efforts for the War Department. Three examples among many are Abbott (Princeton, NJ) conducting lab research (issued 28 April 2017); Neural Analytics (Los Angeles, CA) developing a device to monitor physiology (issued 26 Sept 2017); and General Dynamics (Fairfax, VA) IT support of Veteran Affairs medical centers (issued 25 March 2019). Pertinent keep-the-troops alive fields include Kforce supplying traumatic amputation task trainers (30 Jan 2019) and R.B. Allen Co. procuring communications systems for casualty control (12 March 2019).

35 Hewson gave the largest single financial donation in the school's history ($15 million, July 2018) to benefit the Culverhouse College of Business. The college will construct a new building named after Hewson. In 2017, Hewson gave $5 million for the Marillyn Hewson Faculty Fellows Program in Data Analytics & Cyber Security, "a high-tech data analytics and cyber security lab, and an endowed undergraduate scholarship and graduate assistantship," per "University of Alabama sets new fundraising record" (*Birmingham Business Journal*, 22 October 2018). #culverhouse100. In 2019, Hewson made an appearance in a University of Alabama recruiting video titled "Where Legends Are Made."

36 Yasha Levine (*Surveillance Valley*, pp. 112, 50, 247).

37 Work on Desert Owl sensors has taken place in CA, CO, MI, OH, and VA, as well as in overseas warzones. Issued 15 Sept 2014. Other military-industry entities have worked on Desert Owl, including redundant capacities within the U.S. Army Corps of Engineers' well-funded Engineer Research & Development Center in Vicksburg, MS; corporations in the greater Huntsville, AL, area; and the Air Force Research Lab at Wright-Patterson AFB, east-northeast of Dayton, OH.

38 Northrop Grumman's work took place at its facilities in Linthicum, MD, as well as sites in CA, GA, MD, NM, TX, VA. SRI International's work took place at the same CA site (Santa Clara), and also at Menlo Park and San Diego, CA, and Portland, OR. Nimbis Services (Oro Valley, AZ) has worked for AFRL to design & implement a program to verify the life cycle of microelectronics and manage risks to the supply chain. Relevant contracts: 13 Jan, 14 Jan 2015; 13 Feb 2019.

39 Sanger, David E. and William J. Broad "U.S. Revives Secret Program to Sabotage Iranian Missiles and Rockets." 13 February 2019. Other hypocrisy involves the U.S. government and corporations claiming that foreign hackers aim to remotely wreck U.S. energy infrastructure

(Johnson, Tim. "Preparing the battlefield: Hackers implant digital grenades in industrial networks." *McClatchy.* 27 June 2018), while the U.S. government and corporations attack Russia's power grid (Sanger and Perlroth. "U.S. Escalates Online Attacks on Russia's Power Grid." *The New York Times.* 15 June 2019). The U.S. government is also suspected of being behind a March 2019 cyber-attack on Venezuela's electrical grid.

40 Cohen, Paul R. "World Modelers." *DARPA Information Innovation Office.* Accessed 26 June 2018: <www.darpa.mil/attachments/WorldModelers%20v2.pdf >.

41 Humble career analysts could be seen as public servants whose minds are the modelers—as opposed to those who rotate in and out of government, recycling stale observations into new jargon and creative phraseology and boosting résumés.

42 "SRI International Leading Security Research for U.S. Army Research Lab Initiative to Develop and Secure the Internet of Battlefield Things (IoBT)." *SRI International Newsroom.* 21 February 2018. IoBT aims to "connect soldiers with smart technology in armor, radios, weapons, and other objects, to give troops 'extra sensory' perception, offer situational understanding, endow fighters with prediction powers, provide better risk assessment, and develop shared intuitions." Corrupted disciplines include cognitive science, cryptography, cyber-physical computing, information theory, machine learning, networking, and cybersecurity. Partners include Carnegie Mellon University, University of Illinois, University of Massachusetts, and some of the California clique (UC-Berkeley, UCLA, USC).

43 *Cultural Survival Quarterly* magazine (Trask and Haunani-Kay. "The Struggle of Hawaiian Sovereignty—Introduction," vol. 24, no. 1, March 2000) explains the situation: "Our language was banned in 1896, resulting in several generations of Hawaiians, including myself, whose only language is English. Our lands and waters have been taken for military bases, resorts, urbanization and plantation agriculture. Under foreign control, we have been overrun by settlers: missionaries and capitalists, adventurers and, of course, hordes of tourists… [T]ourism has appropriated and cheapened our dance, music, language, and people, particularly our women… In the meantime, shiploads and planeloads of American military forces continue to pass through Hawai'i on their way to imperialist wars in Asia and elsewhere… Now, caught in a political system where we have no separate legal status—unlike other Native peoples controlled by the United States—we are by every measure the most oppressed people living in our ancestral homeland."

44 "The newly arrived men, their wallets bulging, turned the tourist drag of Hotel Street into a gold mine. Eight parlors supplied some four hundred to five hundred tattoos a day ('Remember Pearl Harbor' was a favorite). The overcrowded brothels, doling out services in three-minute increments, cleared $10 million a year…" Martial law in the islands, characterized by summary rulings and harsh punishments, lasted 3 years, "which was two and a half years longer than Japan posed any plausible threat to the islands" (Immerwahr, *How To Hide an Empire*, pp. 173, 177). Trask and Haunani-Kay indicate that throughout WWII Hawai'i was under martial law for 7 years, "during which time hundreds of thousands of acres of land were confiscated, civil rights were held in abeyance, and a general atmosphere of military intimidation reigned."

45 Percentages are made clear in the Pentagon's FY2018 Base Structure Report, available at <www.acq.osd.mil>. Annual military construction on the islands consistently reaches into the hundreds of millions of dollars. Brum, Aiko and USACE. "MILCON: Rebuilding U.S. Army Hawaii." *U.S. Army.* 18 March 2008. "Hawaii Approved for $400 Million in Military Construction." *Hawaii Reporter.* 24 May 2013.

46 Overlooking Mā'alaea Bay on the west coast of the island of Maui, MRTP is home to many corporations. Pacific Defense Solutions works at MRTP to develop electro-optical systems. (Integrity Applications Incorporated recently purchased PDS. IAI then rebranded as Centauri.) Boeing, too, has

a presence at MRTP. Generous incentives, such as low taxes, help attract these corporations. Such industry towns as Huntsville, AL, and Tucson, AZ, lure war corporations with similar incentives.

47 Regarding "eavesdropping on," see: Greenwald, Glenn. "The crux of the NSA story in one phrase: 'collect it all.'" *The Guardian*. 15 July 2013. Regarding "interfering in," see: Costs of War Project's "Current United States Counterterror War Locations" and Savell, Stephanie and 5W Infographics. "Where We Fight," <watson.brown.edu/costsofwar/papers>.

48 Levine, Yasha. *Surveillance Valley*, pp. 92, 94.

49 "I believe that languages and foreign, you know, just the skills of understanding other cultures is actually pretty much the bedrock of what we need, the foundation of the Department of Defense. Having a rich population of people who are diverse, understand, have been exposed to language and education and the cultures, that's what's gonna help us be a stronger nation," said Maj. Gen. (ret.) Clifford Stanley, Under Secretary of War for Personnel & Readiness (2010-11), discussing NSEP in "Boren Alumni and Federal Employment Video—Celebrating 20 Years of NSEP." *Boren Awards*. 12 September 2011: <www.youtube.com/watch?v=mE3bI4Z6OiI>, (1:36-1:56).

50 Issued 14 March 2018. The announcement makes clear, "There is no known congressional interest pertaining to this acquisition."

51 Taylor, Leslie. "Naval Air Warfare Center Aircraft Division." *The Patuxent Partnership*. September 2017, pp. 62-63. NAWCAD works with the University of Maryland on drone testing, for example.

52 Senior fellows at JHU APL should be familiar to the reader: Robert Work, former Deputy Secretary of War and former CEO of war industry think tank, CNAS; John Allen, former commander of the U.S. war in Afghanistan and former presidential envoy to counter the latest enemy-of-the-day, the "Islamic State"; and Richard Danzig, a member of the Defense Policy Board, a RAND corporation trustee, a director of an investment firm, a director at CNAS, and former Secretary of the Navy under President Clinton. Avril Haines massaged the legal code within the Office of White House Counsel so the Obama administration could expand warzones and target foreign populations with freer rein. She was rewarded with rapid promotions to deputy director of CIA and then Deputy National Security Advisor. At JHU APL Haines is accompanied by former deputy director of Central Intelligence John E. McLaughlin and retired Admiral Sam Locklear, former head of U.S. Pacific Command.

53 Gen. Welsh supports the F-35 in "Virtually Undetectable," <www.f35.com/about/capabilities/stealth>.

54 Secretary of State Mike Pompeo told the student body in 2019, "I understand that this institution has sent more of its graduates into the military than any university, other than our military academies. It's because you all are tough. You're committed and you want to serve. Aggies have a long history in the military, but you also have a long history, serving America's diplomatic mission at the State Department, and I'd love that to continue." The full quote is available in Mekena Rodriguez (*KWTX 10*, 16 April).

55 In her time as Secretary, Wilson helped make the case for expanding the U.S. Air Force by 74 squadrons "as part of the Pentagon's overall shift to focus on great power competition," Stephen Losey reported in *Air Force Times* (8 March 2019). Wilson used to work on the National Security Council and then as a Congressperson from New Mexico (1998-2009).

56 Contracts for this work have been issued at regular intervals [15 March 2017, 22 Sept 2017, 7 Feb 2018, 9 July 2018, 26 Sept 2018, 9 Jan 2019, 14 Feb 2019] over the last two years. These contracts have totaled $72,799,000.

57 JHU's work on nuclear weapons can be seen as part of an upgrade of the U.S. nuclear arsenal. The total value of the overall upgrade may very well top $1.7 trillion USD. Johns Hopkins has a "strategic partnership" with the Air Force Nuclear Weapons Center at Kirtland AFB, NM. A relevant

contract was issued 17 July 2017. War corporations flock to the Air Force Nuclear Weapons Center at Kirtland and at Hill AFB, UT, constantly selling maintenance, upgrades, and "modernization" to the War Department. For the Air Force Nuclear Weapons Center, Johns Hopkins conducts R&D, assesses the capability of nuclear weaponry, and, frankly, improves the Pentagon's ability to conduct a nuclear first strike. As the expert Daniel Ellsberg pointed out in his 2017 book *The Doomsday Machine*, the mere existence of nuclear weapons is a threat to all life on Earth. See also Sneiderman, Phil. "Google's ATAP and Johns Hopkins University Team Up in Tech Development Pact." *JHU Office of Communications*. 7 August 2014. "APL Leaders Appointed to Defense Task Force on the Future of U.S. Military Superiority." *JHU APL*. 4 March 2019.

58 Georgia Tech's main pro-war unit is its Applied Research Corporation, Atlanta, GA. Georgia Tech (GT) helps develop drones, radar, cyber warfare software, ballistic missile sensors, SIGINT electronics, equipment mimicking enemy missile systems, rocket engines, aircraft countermeasures, and communications infrastructure. GT has also curated special access programs. GT helps the National Ground Intelligence Center analyze the hardware of foreign militaries. Some of GT's strongest partnerships are with DARPA and Redstone Arsenal.

59 Not to be confused with *Hack the Pentagon*, a program crowdsourced to Silicon Valley firms, individuals, and corporations across the U.S. to find bugs and security flaws in War Dept. assets and websites.

60 Of course pseudo- and semi-academic institutions within the War Dept.—like the Defense Acquisition University—are involved in H4D, in addition to perennial war players like Stanford, JHU, and the University of Southern California. H4D also reaches out to non-traditional partners like the University of Southern Mississippi and the University of West Florida.

61 "Pairing Students With Corporate Mentors and Technical Advisors," <www.h4di.org/about.html>.

62 Arête has worked with the Navy to develop sensors for ships to detect hazards in the water. Arête has worked with the Office of Naval Research to develop ways to link to underwater mines while operating in enemy or unfriendly waters. The corporation's Tucson branch has helped engineer reconnaissance technology to be used on Northrop Grumman drones launched off ships to neutralize mines. Relevant contracts: 29 Sept 2016, 2017 (17 Feb, 22 June, 26 Sept, 20 Nov).

63 New colleges are cropping up all the time. In 2015 Maxwell AFB began establishing its first Cyber College, and the Pentagon will soon inaugurate a Defense Security Cooperation University to liaise with and train people from across the War Dept. whose jobs involve military-to-military cooperation and FMS. DSCA director Lt. Gen. Charles Hooper reportedly first pitched the DSCU idea to industry during AUSA's 2017 conference.

64 CENTCOM locations openly specified in the relevant contracts (31 Jan 2017) include Afghanistan, Bahrain, Egyptian Sinai, Jordan, Kuwait, Qatar, Saudi Arabia, and UAE. The only AFRICOM country specified in the contract was Djibouti, even though U.S. military forces are deployed in many African nations—around 46 distinct sites according to journalist Nick Turse (*The Nation*, 27 April 2017). David Kirkpatrick explained Sinai operations in "Secret Alliance: Israel Carries Out Airstrikes in Egypt, With Cairo's O.K." (*The New York Times*, 3 February 2018). Relatedly, 2,100 U.S. combat aircraft overflew Egypt in 2016, per "How security cooperation advances U.S. interests" (*Brookings Institution*, 4 June 2019).

65 "Egypt's Sinai: 'War crimes' being committed, says Human Rights Watch." *BBC News*. 28 May 2019.

66 ICSU "promotes the Universality of Science on the basis that science is a common human endeavor that transcends national boundaries and is to be shared by all people," as stated at <icsu.org/what-we-do/freedoms-and-responsibilities-of-scientists>.

67 See Kelly, Erin. "Report: Top psychologists bolstered CIA, Pentagon torture" (*USA Today*, 10 July 2015) and "Doctors aided U.S. torture at military prisons, report says" (*BBC News*, 4 November 2013).

68 The Army Research Lab and the Intelligence Advanced Research Projects Activity are located in Maryland. DARPA and the Office of Naval Research are in Arlington, Virginia. The Air Force Research Lab is run out of Wright-Patterson Air Force Base, northeast of Dayton, Ohio, with branches in New Mexico and upstate New York. The U.S. Army Corps of Engineers' Engineer Research & Development Center is in Vicksburg, Mississippi. Then there are such organizations within the Pentagon as the Secretary of the Air Force's Concepts, Development, and Management Office. No officer, person, or program coordinates research among these entities with the aim of eliminating waste, though it's only a matter of time before a corporation realizes this and pitches a service to ostensibly fill that gap.

69 "FFRDC Whiteboard Explainer Video." *MITRE Corp.* 19 October 2015. Accessed 25 December 2018: <www.youtube.com/watch?v=AQqJlxI8-9g>.

70 The former employee, Lester Earnest, was interviewed by journalist Paul Jay in "Cold War Radar System a Trillion Dollar Fraud—Lester Earnest on RAI (1/4)" (*The Real News Network*, 24 December 2018).

71 The Chairman, Donald Kerr, is former director of the National Reconnaissance Office and former principal deputy director of national intelligence. Kerr is current director of war corporations, including Areté Associates. He is a former director at SAIC. The MIRE Vice Chairman, Mike Rogers, is former chair of the House Permanent Select Committee on Intelligence. He is on the board of (former NSA Director) Keith Alexander's corporation, IronNet Cybersecurity. He is a distinguished fellow at the think tank Hudson Institute. Other directors at MITRE include a director emeritus at McKinsey & Co., a Navy admiral, an Air Force general, and chairmen of industry pressure groups like AFCEA.

72 "We Operate FFRDCs." *MITRE*. Accessed 25 December 2018: <www.mitre.org/centers/we-operate-ffrdcs>.

73 "Shooting for the Stars: STEM Scholarship Superheroes." *The Aerospace Corp.* Accessed 17 February 2019.

74 Vergun, David. "Leaders offer solutions to cyber personnel challenges." *Army News Service*. 3 August 2018. Targeting poor kids ("youth in lower socioeconomic areas") who might have cyber aptitude and interest but who "lack the information" is also an NSA priority, *ANS* reports. CIA also woos children. See <www.cia.gov/kids-page/k-5th-grade>. It is worth noting that NSA's subservient U.K. partner, Government Communications Headquarters (GCHQ), achieves similar goals by planning Cyber Schools Hubs, which aim to "send staff into local schools to 'encourage a diverse range of students into taking up computer science,' in effect grooming the next generation of cyber-competent spies." Kennard, Matt. "Business is booming for the U.K.'s spy tech industry." *The Intercept*. 11 May 2018.

75 The executive of Howard County stated of the county's residents, "They demand good schools and a high quality of life."
Priest and Arkin. "Top Secret America: The secrets next door." *Washington Post*. 21 July 2010. These schools function well, in part, because locals (in relatively high-paying jobs as desk mercenaries for the war corporations that do most of NSA's work) fund the schools well. The vast majority of NSA's work is done by war corporations (see Chapter Seven).

76 Priest and Arkin. "Top Secret America: The secrets next door."

77 "Research, Development, Test & Evaluation Budget Item Justification." *Office of the Secretary of Defense*. February 2015. See also "Smart Scholarship Program." *U.S. Department of*

Defense. Accessed 14 March 2019: <smartscholarshipprod.service-now.com/smart>. Corporations can also cover early childhood development *within* the War Dept. For example, Dynamic Systems Technology (Fairfax, VA) is contracted to "promote and sustain the quality of life and resilience of Army National Guard children and youth by providing secure, timely, flexible, high-quality support services and age-appropriate development programs." Issued 10 Sept 2018.

78 "NSWCDD Biomedical Engineer Teams Up with High School STEM Champion to Mentor Students—'Fun Twist on Math.'" *NSWC Dahlgren Division Corporate Communications*. 24 May 2018. "NAWCAD National Week at the Labs 2017." *Naval Air Warfare Center Aircraft Division (NAWCAD)*. 17 March 2017: <www.youtube.com/watch?v=giR436BdN14>. Students and teachers ate it up. The Navy's warfare centers offer Educational Partnership Agreements so educational institutions can collaborate with the War Department and the Department can encourage STEM among local and regional youth.

79 "Boeing, National Science Foundation announce partnership, $21 million investment in workforce development and diversity in STEM." *Boeing*. 24 Sept 2018: <https://boeing.mediaroom.com/2018-09-24-Boeing-National-Science-Foundation-announce-partnership-21-million-investment-in-workforce-development-and-diversity-in-STEM>. "Impacting Education." *Lockheed Martin*. Accessed 3 Oct 2018: <www.lockheedmartin.com/en-us/who-we-are/communities/stem-education.html>. "Education—Corporate Responsibility." *Raytheon*. Accessed 4 Aug 2018: <www.raytheon.com/responsibility/stem/>. "Education—Corporate Responsibility." *Northrop Grumman*. Accessed 28 Aug 2018: <www.northropgrumman.com/CorporateResponsibility/CorporateCitizenship/Education/Pages/default.aspx>. "CACI Cares." *CACI*. Accessed 21 Nov 2019: <www.caci.com/CaciCares/education.shtml>. "Harris Corporation Provides Grants to Support STEM Training." *Harris Corp*. 23 Aug 2018: <www.harris.com/press-releases/2018/08/harris-corporation-provides-grants-to-support-stem-training>.

80 "About STEM." *NDIA*. Accessed 28 March 2019: <www.ndia-mich.org/initiatives/stem>.

81 AIA has worked with the state of Arizona at United Technologies facilities in Phoenix to address anticipated STEM workforce issues. AUSA has brought students from Alabama colleges and universities to Redstone Arsenal to promote STEM and learn about careers in the war industry. November 2018 was AOC's 4th annual STEM Outreach Program. The Patuxent Partnership held a Science & Engineering Special Awards Reception for middle and high schools in Saint Mary's County, and it has field office managers in charge of STEM outreach. Some, like AFCEA, even have their own 501(c)(3) educational foundations to get youngsters on board with the militarized economy. AFCEA is honest: "Our programs exist to ensure tomorrow's work force has the necessary technical skills to be competitive in the fast-paced, ever-changing global security arena," per "Why We Do It." *AFCEA*. Accessed 30 September 2018: <www.afcea.org/site/?q=Educational-Foundation>. Pluribus, former employer of alleged leaker Reality Winner, has teamed up with the Fort Belvoir chapter of AFCEA to fund scholarships in STEM "technical fields and those supportive of our national security," per "May 2016: Pluribus Partners with AFCEA Belvoir to Raise STEM Scholarship Funds." *Pluribus International*. (The private equity-backed LLC known as Metis Solutions purchased Pluribus in summer 2019.)

82 LM STEM details—including the programs *Code Quest, FIRST Robotics, Generation Beyond, Great Minds in STEM, K-12 STEM Match, STEM on Wheels, Project Lead the Way*—available at <www.lockheedmartin.com/en-us/who-we-are/communities/stem-education.html>. The $24 million was allocated in 2016.

83 "Weapons manufacturer to offer primary education to Israel kids in Jerusalem" (*Middle East Monitor*, 31 May 2018). Perper, Rosie. "Lockheed Martin, maker of the F-35 stealth fighter jet, is opening a preschool in Jerusalem" (*Business Insider*, 25 May 2018). No distance is too far. Raytheon's

deputy of Space Systems met with school kids in the UAE, encouraging them to go into science and math careers. LM has teamed with the Japan Assoc. of Rocketry to cultivate female STEM interest.

84 Roth, Lauren. "Lockheed Martin grant will grow STEM offerings in Orange schools." *Orlando Sentinel*. 5 February 2015.

85 Orlando is the dominant metropolis in Orange Country. Lockheed Martin's work in Orlando has included attack helicopter logistics, night vision, and sensors; targeting pods; anti-submarine warfare products; B-52 bomber instrumentation; aircrew trainers; DARPA projects; cyber testing; data links; digital data recorders; clunky electronic hardware units used for repairing Navy aircraft; fighter jet parts; missiles; IT services; missile launchers; navigation & targeting prototypes capable of homing against a mobile weapon platform without reliable GPS; and logistics for the Saudi regime's National Guard. Governments recently benefiting from FMS through LM's Orlando branch include Egypt, India, Indonesia, Iraq, Jordan, Kuwait, Pakistan, Qatar, Romania, Saudi Arabia, Thailand, Tunisia, and the U.K.

86 Roth, Lauren. "Lockheed Martin grant will grow STEM offerings in Orange schools." *Orlando Sentinel*. 5 February 2015.

87 "Realizing a Dream with Lockheed Martin." *Lockheed Martin*. <www.lockheedmartinjobs.com/women-in-stem>.

88 King also said in his "Beyond Vietnam" speech, "When machines and computers, profit motives and property rights, are considered more important than people, the giant triplets of racism, extreme materialism, and militarism are incapable of being conquered." This speech took place on 4 April 1967, exactly a year before he was assassinated.

89 "AAR to Honor Dr. King's Legacy with Access to Career Opportunities." *AAR—Doing it Right*. 17 January 2013.

90 A few examples of many include CACI CEO Ken Asbury's "Special Announcement" (September 2014), Raytheon's "Remembering 9/11: Fifteen Years Later, Raytheon Honors Those Lost" (8 September 2016), and Northrop Grumman's "Northrop Grumman Volunteers Choose Community Service on Anniversary of 9/11 Attacks" (12 September 2011). Northrop Grumman helped refurbish the Tomorrow's Aeronautical Museum in Compton, Los Angeles, as part of the corporation's drive to attract youth into the overlapping war and aerospace industries. Corporate PR officials framed the volunteerism as helping disadvantaged youth. For its part, SAIC "Teams Up with the Washington Nationals to Sponsor the Patriotic Series" (4 April 2017). See "SAIC Sponsors Washington Nationals Patriotic Series for Fifth Consecutive Year" (*SAIC*, 11 April 2018) and "Nationals Patriotic Series & Military Branch Days return for 2018" (*MLB*, 10 April 2018). Corporate officials appreciate the military, of course; industry profits when the Pentagon purchases goods and services and the troops implement nonstop war.

91 Black Engineer of the Year Awards (BEYA) is run by a corporate conglomerate known as the Career Communications Group, whose events are consistently sponsored by war corporations, branches and units within the War Dept., and intelligence agencies. The 2019 BEYA STEM Conference was co-hosted by Lockheed Martin; the Lockheed Martin CEO invoked African American sacrifice: "Aaron was thrilled that this role involved engineering work on the F-35 advanced fighter program. These days, Aaron is enjoying making his impact on the F-35 training systems team… His example serves as an inspiration—and a call to action." Deen, Lango. "Lockheed Martin CEO to speak at BEYA Conference." *BlackEngineer.com*. 10 January 2019. CEOs from Boeing, LM, Northrop Grumman, and Raytheon spoke at the 2018 BEYA Stars & Stripes Awards.

92 "Engineering a Safer World: 2017 Corporate Responsibility Custom Report." *Raytheon*. "Corporate Sustainability Report." *General Dynamics*. 2018. Accessed 7 March 2019.

93 Banusiewicz, John. "Fiscal Crisis Requires Responsible Approach, Lynn Says." *American Forces Press Service*. 19 June 2011.

94 Courtney Roberts, finishing up her PhD at UNC-Chapel Hill, recalls thankfully how a Raytheon mentor impacted her: "I wouldn't be where I am today if it wasn't for FIRST and the support of Raytheon." FIRST, *For Inspiration & Recognition of Science and Technology*, is a Raytheon-supported STEM initiative. "Real Encounters With STEM Learning." *Raytheon*. 31 January 2018. Accessed 16 July 2018.

95 Dennett, Lydia. "Universities on the Foreign Payroll." *Truthout*. 5 March 2019. Peterson and Katz. "Elite universities are selling themselves—and look who's buying." *The Guardian*. 30 March 2018. Public relations, a friendly-faced form of propaganda, runs wild: (1) When called out on accepting money from and wooing the Saudi regime, Harvard's assistant VP of communications stated, "As a global research university, Harvard has a broad and robust scholarly engagement in the Middle East, including in the Kingdom of Saudi Arabia, and has benefited immensely from the intellectual contributions of Saudi-based individuals over the years... We are following recent events with concern and are assessing potential implications for existing programs." 2) When questioned about collaborating with the Saudi regime, a spokesperson for the University of New Haven wrote, "The goal, then as now, was to help modernize and professionalize criminal justice activities in Saudi Arabia through this educational partnership... We have been pleased with the academic professionalism of our partners, and we look forward to continuing the relationship." See "Saudi Ties to U.S. Universities Under Question Amid Ongoing Crisis over Khashoggi Murder" (*DemocracyNow*, 26 October 2018) and "Does Saudi Forensic Doctor Who Allegedly Dismembered Khashoggi Have Ties to Univ. of New Haven?" (*DemocracyNow*, 26 October 2018). "Delegation of Emmanuel College of Boston Visits NAMFI." *NATO Missile Firing Installation*. Accessed 16 July 2018: <www.namfi.gr/delegation-of-emmanuel-college-of-boston-visits-namfi/>. As of July 2018, the website of Emmanuel College—its motto, "God With Us"—boasts of ethical decision-making among its students and graduates. The universities receiving the most money from Gulf regimes (e.g. Georgetown, Harvard, Johns Hopkins, MIT, University of Southern California) tend to be the ones most intimately tied to the MIC.

96 Lisinski, Chris. "Air Force chief: Future bright at Hanscom." *Lowell Sun*. Last updated 6 April 2018.

97 Space and Naval Warfare Systems Center Pacific (SSC Pacific) has substantial brainpower, swimming among the ocean of brilliance circling the MIC drain. SSC Pacific employs "more than 4,700 scientists, researchers, engineers, technicians, technical specialists and more, who hold 194 Ph.D./J.D. degrees, and 1,356 master's degrees." The lab "is ranked as a top generator of patents and license agreements (155 patent disclosures, 100 patent applications filed, and 50 patents issued in fiscal year 2017)." See <www.public.navy.mil/spawar/Pacific/Pages/About-SSC-Pac.aspx>. Speaking of San Diego, Northrop Grumman partners with the University of California system to present "The Dynamic Leader" forum series. If you attended in 2017 you got to hear Northrop Grumman leaders, the Distinguished Executive Guest Speakers!

98 Priest and Arkin. "Top Secret America: The secrets next door." *Washington Post*. 21 July 2010. I stress that the dungeons of NSA on the Fort Meade campus are packed with even more scientists and engineers—whose collective mental prowess could be used to better humankind.

99 "WE18 Keynote Presentation: Marillyn Hewson." *Society of Women Engineers*. 19 Oct 2018: <www.youtube.com/watch?time_continue=3237&v=gdQKnPhGCHk>.

7

Information Technology

INFORMATION TAKEOVER

Networking equipment, servers, hardware, and software that process, relay, and distribute data are known as information technology (IT). Information technology is one of the most lucrative sectors of the U.S. war industry. By my count, IT-related contracts are more common than those in any other sector (e.g. aircraft, land vehicles, nuclear weaponry). In the glut of the last twenty years, the U.S. government has funneled money to high-tech hardware, software, and major IT acquisitions (arguably at the expense of refining the caliber of in-house uniformed military personnel or prioritizing pound-for-pound human intelligence). In such an environment, which the war industry fostered, corporations are allowed to market and sell endless IT services to fill military or intelligence deficiencies, whether simply perceived or authentic. Worth mentioning off the bat, some of the major U.S. corporations selling IT-related goods and services to the War Department include Booz Allen Hamilton, CACI, Dell, General Dynamics, Harris, HP, Oracle, SAIC, and Vectrus.

Waste is the defining characteristic of the war industry's IT sector. And no single organization consumes more IT goods and services than the National Security Agency. The job of NSA (along with its Fort Meade partner, Central Security Service) is to aggregate money and resources to find ways into, around, and through electronic devices, to eavesdrop on those devices, and to ensure devices used by U.S. forces are cryptographically protected. War corporations, primarily SAIC, pitched a program known as Trailblazer to NSA shortly after 11 September 2001. Trailblazer was designed to help NSA track electronic communications. War corporations pitched it as "modernization," a "much needed" upgrade to NSA's lagging capabilities. Trailblazer cost billions of dollars.[1] While some former officials placed the figure at around $1.2 billion,[2] NSA whistleblower William Binney clarifies its actual cost:

> See, the Trailblazer program actually produced nothing. It was a total failure by 2005. And it wasted over four billion dollars. It was

continued as a funding mechanism for some time, for about another three or four billion [dollars].[3]

Trailblazer was a failure in many respects, but not for corporations.

Trailblazer. It is an appropriate name for a program that blazed a corrupt trail, lined with U.S. tax dollars and government-issued debt. The corruption was vast: former director of NSA Bobby Ray Inman and other former NSA honchos worked for SAIC at the time of Trailblazer, and the NSA official initially in charge of Trailblazer (William Black) used to work for SAIC as an assistant vice president. Pertinent war corporations followed the classic contracting schemes of underestimating the cost, overhyping what a product can allegedly do, and adding additional contract modifications and upgrades.

Thomas Drake, a courageous individual who complained about Trailblazer to the Pentagon's Inspector General, was pursued and punished.[4] The Inspector General's full report was classified, thereby avoiding public discussion, debate, and scrutiny. (It's a regular Department of War practice to classify damaging information, preventing the public from understanding and acting against entrenched, costly militarism.) None of the corporations that worked on Trailblazer received any notable punishment. In fact, they all continued on their merry way, selling goods and services to NSA. The CEOs and high-ranking officials received bonuses like any other year. No harm (to war industry bosses), no foul.

Trailblazer is not an anomaly. It is a salient example of the U.S. war industry's standard operating procedures.

There are ostensible, token measures within U.S. government through which employees can report instances of fraud, waste, or abuse. But these measures don't make a dent, because the War Department as a whole is fraudulent, wasteful, abusive—and huge. No measure or internal mechanism can address it. Corporate executives know—intuitively or consciously—that the War Department is a slush fund for corporate greed. They also know they run the show.

War corporations choke the landscape around Fort Meade. These corporations specialize in IT, cyber, and signals intelligence products and personnel, which they pitch to NSA with unrivaled zeal. NSA has increasingly come to rely on war corporations to carry out its activities. The war corporations running NSA monopolize most of the agency's budget, which hovers around $11-12 billion annually, fluctuating according to supplementary funding.[5] Near NSA looms National Business Park (NBP), perhaps the most ostentatious display of corporate greed in the Baltimore-D.C. corridor. NBP is home to offices of war corporations eying the NSA budget spigot. Dana Priest and William Arkin of the *Washington Post*: "More than 250 companies—13 percent of all the firms in *Top Secret America*—have a presence in the Fort Meade cluster. Some have multiple offices, such as Northrop Grumman, which has 19, and SAIC, which has 11. In all, there are 681 locations in the Fort Meade cluster where businesses conduct top-secret work."[6]

NSA's implicit mission (and that of NSA's superior, the Under Secretary of War for Intelligence) is to "collect it all." This mission generates too much information, flooding the system and overwhelming the analysts, linguists, and technicians on the receiving end in Fort Meade, Fort Gordon, Lackland Air Force Base, Hawai'i Cryptologic Center, and facilities around the world. The "collect it all" approach is ineffective—it doesn't even stop the handful of people who rarely attempt to attack U.S. civilians.[7] "Collect it all" is nonetheless promoted for two main reasons: (1) The flood of information allows the war industry to develop, market, and sell very expensive information technology, including but not limited to software and hardware that aggregate or merge information, allegedly simplifying the big picture. (2) Collecting it all requires, more broadly, the expansion of the surveillance state—additional technology, contractors, maintenance and repair, upgrades, facilities. The corporations that have captured the War Department know a good thing when they have it. They'll never willingly surrender this self-licking ice cream cone.

The vast expansion of IT contracting within the War Department over the past two decades is akin to a professional hockey league quadrupling in size during the off-season. What happens to the caliber of play? What arenas will the new teams play in? How does the league schedule and juggle all of the new games? Imperfect analogy aside, the War Department is in a situation right now where the U.S. war industry, in cooperation with major software giants like Microsoft, has overwhelmed the system and is now functionally in charge of that system. The War Department has so thoroughly outsourced all major networks and IT functions that it is now like the rest of U.S. society—entirely dependent on corporate greed to accomplish the most basic tasks in everyday life.

The total dollar amount the Pentagon spends on IT is difficult to ascertain in part because many contracts featuring IT are part of wider orders of goods and services from the war industry, which can lead to underestimates in IT spending figures. So, for example, a contract that contains the provision of IT in conjunction with command, control, communications, computers, intelligence, surveillance, reconnaissance (C4ISR) operations out of San Diego would likely be billed to the Pentagon through Space & Naval Warfare Center Pacific using sundry funds (e.g. Navy research, development, test, and evaluation funds; Navy other procurement funds; and/or Navy operations and maintenance funds) and not necessarily counted in overall government IT expenditures, even though it includes integrated IT support and works with NSA and the Defense Intelligence Agency, among other corporatized units.[8] (C4ISR is the use of all sorts of sensors, IT, computers, and communications systems to develop a picture of what's happening for military leaders.)

Government figures, nonetheless, illustrate the vast scope of IT spending. Total War Department spending on IT reportedly hit $42.52 billion during FY2018,[9] while spending on IT within U.S. intelligence agencies hit $8 billion in 2013, according to documents leaked by Edward Snowden, as cited in *The Atlantic*.[10] These figures give the reader a good starting point regarding IT spending within the War Department.

INTEL

"Intelligence" is the most hackneyed word in the MIC. Drop the hype about shadows, cloaks, and daggers. Intelligence is nothing more than information. Plain and simple. Sometimes information is accurate, sometimes inaccurate. Demystifying this language helps us deflate and debunk some of the allure that keeps the wars going.

Intelligence is corporatized.[11] Most intelligence positions within the "intelligence community" are simply people sitting at desks. Desk mercenaries make up the bulk of the workload in both military and civilian intelligence agencies within U.S. government. These mercenaries span the young analyst at the Office of the Director of National Intelligence to the longtime signals intelligence contractor, mother of two. The major corporations that keep NSA up and running include Accenture, Booz Allen Hamilton, CACI, General Dynamics, Harris, Leidos, L3, ManTech, PAE, and SAIC.

The Defense Intelligence Agency (DIA) is a tale of corporatization and waste. DIA was created in 1961 to consolidate separate, parochial intelligence fiefdoms within the War Department. The Secretary of War, Robert McNamara, aimed to establish an agency that had "a commitment to gathering and evaluating information based on a higher loyalty than to any one service."[12] DIA today gathers information on the leaders and militaries of foreign nations, guerilla organizations, and citizens of foreign countries. DIA's work often overlaps with other intelligence agencies. For example, it runs case officers, which traditionally has been CIA's domain. (Case officers recruit foreign spies and manage their activities.) And DIA's analysts are largely superfluous, along with multitudes in the other sixteen U.S. intelligence agencies.

DIA is increasingly corporate, from the ground up, from day one, from training through operations. Parra Consulting Group (Gaithersburg, MD) screens and processes DIA candidates. ADC Ltd. NM (Albuquerque, NM) conducts background investigations for DIA's Personnel Security Division. Corporatization of background investigations and personnel vetting is not unique to DIA. Deloitte, a corporation intimately involved in the Pentagon's audit, has been running the Personnel Vetting Transformation Office under direction of the Under Secretary of War for Intelligence. In this capacity, Deloitte has played an integral role in the transfer of background investigations of federal government employees from the Office of Personnel Management (OPM) to the War Department.[13] The bigger picture profits corporations: The War Department is purchasing a new online system potential employees use to fill out their initial forms and is purchasing IT systems designed to *continually* vet cleared personnel. Sensitive data—one's credit information, significant financial transactions, social media, encounters with law enforcement—can be poured into the latter systems. War corporations pitch these systems as freeing up personnel to focus on the backlog of employees awaiting clearances.

Corners of DIA have been corporatized: training, including DIA's Joint Counterintelligence Training Academy in Quantico, Virginia; pre-deployment training; and DIA's Insider Threat Group, basically snooping on employee behavior, trying to catch the next Snowden, Manning, or worse. Speaking of Edward Snowden, his former employer, Booz Allen Hamilton, produces and disseminates intelligence within DIA's Directorate of Analysis. Other corporatized corners include physical security, determining who can enter and leave DIA facilities; training personnel on security practices in DIA facilities; information technology at DIA's Defense Logistics Operations Center; R&D; human resources; and information classification. Corporatization of DIA's operations includes monitoring disease and running the Missile & Space Intelligence Center (MSIC).[14] Located on Redstone Arsenal in Huntsville, Alabama, DIA's MSIC is a curious corporate case: A portion of the information gathered at MSIC about the capabilities of foreign governments' missile systems finds its way, per the Center's inherent mission and design, back into the hands of U.S. corporations (that develop platforms and missile systems that will be sold to the U.S. government). In this narrow sense, MSIC is a unit run for war corporations by war corporations, potentially increasing the capabilities of corporate goods while definitely increasing corporate profit.

Working on a top-secret special access program? The Department of War, its intelligence agencies, and other agencies outside the Pentagon's purview run thousands.[15] Think a foreign intelligence service is sniffing too close? Prescient Edge (McLean, VA) and Grand Ground Enterprise (D.C.) run a lot of counterintelligence for DIA.[16] DIA employees better hope these corporations have their act together and are putting the public good ahead of profit. Regrettably, this corporatization of compartmentalized espionage activity has occurred across the federal government. For example, Georgia Tech is working on improving the information systems underpinning special access programs.[17]

Some corporations play a larger role within DIA than others. Engility specializes in research and development.[18] Its goods and services are diverse.[19] Engility sells audio and video forensics services to DIA's National Media Exploitation Center (NMEC), which, in part, works on making sense of some of the physical "intelligence" gathered in U.S. warzones. "Intelligence," in this sense, can be gathered in house raids, discussed in Chapter Five. Countries targeted by the MIC loathe house raids. SAIC acquired Engility in early 2019. NMEC is fertile ground for corporate growth.[20]

Rapid construction on intelligence projects, particularly the corporatized world of military-intelligence, is ongoing. Investigative journalists Dana Priest and William Arkin inform us, in the greater D.C. area "33 building complexes for top-secret intelligence work" were built from September 2001 through summer 2010. "Together they occupy the equivalent of almost three Pentagons or 22 U.S. Capitol buildings - about 17 million square feet of space."[21] These facilities then add to the ceaseless harvest of information about sundry populations worldwide. CIA expanded (increasing the Agency's office space by one-third) and the National Geospatial-Intelligence Agency, or NGA, expanded (a new $1.8 billion headquarters in Springfield, Virginia, "the fourth-largest federal building in the area"[22]). NSA's presence in Maryland is huge, as its buildings' footprints take up well over a square kilometer, not including a new data center in Bluffdale, Utah, south of Salt Lake City. Construction on intel facilities proceeds steadily across the United States.[23] Some construction firms work on multiple intel sites.

Corporate America learns by doing. It knows that attaching "cyber" to a proposal, initiative, or project is a good way to obtain funding.[24]

A Sensitive Compartmented Information Facility, or SCIF (say it: *skiff*), is an enclosed space designed to keep eavesdroppers out. Persons with authorized clearance and access congregate in a SCIF, discussing and handling classified information. The War Department has hired construction corporations to build SCIFs from the east coast to the west: Fort Belvoir, Washington Navy Yard, and Naval Air Station Oceana, Virginia; Department of War facilities in Fairfield, Pennsylvania; Naval Air Station Jacksonville, Florida; Vandenberg Air Force Base and Naval Base Ventura County, California. The dirty south gets new SCIFs, too: Goodfellow Air Force Base, Texas, and Naval Air Station New Orleans, Louisiana. Overseas, SCIFs crop up with equal vigor, notably at Camp Humphreys in South Korea and at the penal colony aboard Naval Station Guantánamo Bay, Cuba.[25] (Most people imprisoned at Guantánamo are not terrorists and are already cleared for release.[26])

Just as corporations have worked tirelessly to cultivate a consumer culture across the United States, so too have war corporations worked tirelessly to cultivate a consumer culture for war-related goods and services within the high ranks of the U.S. Armed Forces. Consume and build to increase your status.

I witnessed a flood of construction projects while I was in the military. An actual flood. The leadership of one Wing was very proud of a new building, the core of which was basically one big SCIF. From the Wing commander on down, Air Force leaders patted themselves on the back day after day during construction. They held a ceremony to inaugurate the facility. Water flooded the building a few days after its grand opening. The SCIF might have been impermeable when it came to eavesdropping, but a little rain found its way in, no problem.

The Pentagon's intelligence leadership will not rein in or reverse the corporatization of intelligence. Military-intelligence leaders come from Corporate America.[27]

Many problems arise from the corporatization of intelligence: reduced public oversight of an already opaque realm, decreased transparency, congressional ignorance, and increased incentivizing of ongoing espionage activities, cold wars, and military operations for the sake of profit. Another disturbing problem arises from such corporatization: greater permeability. Cash payments are one of the tried-and-true ways that foreign intelligence organizations recruit employees of a rival or allied government. Given that profit is the number one motivator of corporate activity, foreign intelligence organizations have an easier time recruiting within a corporatized intelligence establishment than recruiting within a tight network of non-corporate, traditional patriots.

Secrecy is key. Classification to prevent public knowledge happens all the time. You saw how classification of the Pentagon's Inspector General report of Trailblazer prevented the public from learning about wasted billions and government corruption. When reporters requested copies of unclassified documents that detailed a potentially permeable alloy used to seal nuclear waste inside Yucca Mountain, the Departments of Energy and War reportedly convinced a federal judge to go along with the claim that such documents were now classified.[28] When U.S. Congress during the Reagan administration criticized the cost of anti-ballistic missile systems (for political points, not because they were against the Cold War), the Pentagon just classified the systems' cost, preventing public knowledge. The war industry is especially adept at the manipulation of secrecy. High-ranking U.S. war industry officials have clearances and are privy to all types of classified material. Industry, as you know, is in the driver's seat, fabricating threats, corrupting Congress, *and* classifying and declassifying information. MIC elites are taking more and more information away from the people.[29] Secrecy is profit's chainmail. Currently, when it comes to oversight, the U.S. Congress doesn't ask for much from the U.S. military and intelligence. The average congressperson is clueless on matters of war, espionage, and peace. The average congressperson on armed services or intelligence committees is more aware, but their views are carefully circumscribed by the information that the agencies selectively divvy out.

Secrecy harms the country. The public can't make decisions about the fate of the country or the world when they're denied the relevant information. Secrecy effectively gelds the democratic process.

MANAGING DATA OVERLOAD

We came across Space & Naval Warfare Systems Center Pacific (SSC Pacific) earlier. Situated in picturesque San Diego, California, SSC Pacific throws dollars at contracts that blend IT, space technology, command & control systems, and intelligence, surveillance, reconnaissance (ISR).[30] Hyperbole aside, it's a hell of a hullabaloo.

A typical deal between the war industry and SSC Pacific is as follows: A corporation based in San Diego is contracted to provide SSC Pacific with technical expertise. In industry jargon, the corporation has been contracted to provide integration, design & testing, deployment, and life cycle support for electronic and computer systems. SSC Pacific says it spends roughly $1.2 billion per year,[31] and nearly all of that goes to contracts involving at least some component of IT.

Consolidated Afloat Network Enterprise Services (CANES) was one of SSC Pacific's programs. CANES scrapped older IT networks and merged them into a new single network to be used on boats and some shore facilities. Industry has promised that the new network will be more efficient than existing networks. Many corporations have been involved in CANES. Costs rose, corporations appealed Pentagon choices, and goods and services piled on. Several contracts were awarded without true competition. Work on CANES was spread across the U.S., from Virginia to California. CANES cost billions of dollars.

Producing technology that merges data is a deep leitmotif in the war industry.

War corporations have already succeeded in selling the U.S. Department of War more goods and services than the military knows what to do with. Now, war corporations are selling technology that is marketed as helping the military merge and make sense of all the data it is drowning in. Leaning on historical precedent,[32] war corporations are marketing technology that merges data involving a wide range of Department activity. For example, Raytheon has worked on a product marketed as improving troops' understanding of the battlefield by extracting and distributing from sensors information "such that the superset of this data is available" to all participating units.[33] SRI International sells TerraSight, marketed as being able to take information from a variety of distributed sensors and present the information in a single, understandable common operating picture. FD Software Enterprise has sold its work on the Network-Centric Early Warning

System, which is marketed as integrating the data from people using different mobile devices in different areas.[34] Technology that merges data includes DARPA's extensive work. For example, the corporation Isis Defense (hell of a name!) of Alexandria, Virginia, has sold its expertise to DARPA for work on the Threat Intelligence Platform, using high-performance computing and storage to blend and analyze DARPA's big data research information.[35]

The next step is industry's push (citing great power competition) to develop Multi Domain Command & Control—corporate products aiming to develop a worldwide system that shares and blends data and information from any and all sources, eventually offering predictive analysis. Another goal, as Air Force General David Goldfein presented at industry's 2019 Air Space & Cyber symposium, is to connect everything—aircraft, satellites, ships, artillery batteries, and other weapon systems—into a single network, tentatively known as Advanced Battle Management System (ABMS), which shares data, with machine learning aiding decision-making.[36] Industry would design and sell the network and associated components and, through the provision of mercenaries ("contractors"), play an active role in running ABMS.

Everything is fair game in the data blending push, including buildings[37] and logistics.[38] All such goods and services are sold to the U.S. government for the same purpose: merging the glut of data and information (a problem caused originally by the goods and services of the U.S. war industry) into a semi-decent picture, presentation, or set of data. A corporate executive unintentionally touched upon the underlying weakness of it all: "The more we become connected, the more we are vulnerable."[39] Yup.

CLOUDY WITH A CHANCE OF FLEECING

IT corporations sell their computing power and storage to a customer who then accesses these services over the internet. That is called "the cloud." To clarify: the cloud is a corporate computing service. In fiscal year 2017, the War Department spent roughly $2.3 billion on cloud computing.[40] The Department has 3.4 million users and 4 million personal devices,[41] and climbing. Corporations eye these numbers lasciviously. Such giants as Microsoft and Amazon, allies of the Pentagon for years, have succeeded in marketing the cloud as the latest and greatest military advantage. The cloud is presented as (1) employing "emerging technology" to "meet the warfighter needs," while increasing "speed and agility in developing and procuring technology" and (2) giving the troops "a tactical edge on the battlefield" and enhancing technological development in a "cost-recovery way." In other words, a "solution."[42] The War Department is fully on board.

Amazon

In the summer of 2014, Amazon Web Services (AWS) began providing CIA with cloud computing. The deal was worth $600 million. The U.S. government framed its decision to pick AWS as being about security and keeping pace with industry and commerce.[43] This AWS contract overlapped with other work Amazon was doing for intelligence agencies. For example, an Amazon subsidiary was building a data center in northeast Virginia, just west of the traditional Virginian den of war corporations.[44]

Government and Amazon tout many benefits of AWS cloud computing. The AWS cloud would allow users from intelligence agencies to easily work together and share information. It would maximize automation and provide users with a straightforward, standardized interface. It would allow desk workers within U.S. intelligence to order different services (analytics, computing, storage) with ease. CIA's layers of managerial staff favor the cloud, asserting that its scalable features allow CIA to save money.

Political researcher Evan Blake suggests another benefit to Amazon's intelligence dealings: stanching leaks. Recent leaks by people of conscience working for the U.S. government scare and anger the elites within the military-industrial-congressional triangle. MIC elites don't want their crimes and political corruption exposed. Using encryption and features developed by AWS and augmented by NSA Central Security Service, intelligence agencies are able to centralize and monitor data storage on the privatized cloud. Security personnel use such features—including automatic notification when someone shifts large amounts of data—to monitor government intelligence users, Blake notes.[45] Amazon is lined up on the side of secrecy and, I note, is complicit in any government violence carried out directly or indirectly with the aid of AWS.

Other U.S. intelligence organizations do not sit idly by. Though government and industry market cloud computing as a way to share services responsibly, reality dictates that all agencies clamber for their own clouds of varying scopes and capacities. Other intelligence organizations like DIA, NRO, and NGA have their own bureaucratic and territorial incentive to go along with the corporate push toward cloud computing. They mask their cloud march as ensuring that all organizational components and individual projects are cared for, and that all personnel and operations are able to thrive.

A year into the deal with Amazon, CIA was reportedly "happy" with the move to the cloud, despite some bugs.[46] Amazon spends a small fortune on lobbying,[47] and has "more federal authorizations to maintain government data across agencies than any other" tech firm.[48] Other corporations are allied with Amazon. For example, Applied Research Associates (Albuquerque, NM) helps develop cloud-based software within a classified AWS cloud service region.[49] In 2018, thirteen percent of Amazon's profit came from its cloud services.⁵⁰ Its customers, aside from government, included such war corporations as General Electric, which makes aircraft engines. A new cloud deal called Commercial Cloud Enterprise (C2E) for CIA and other agencies is in the works.⁵¹

A group of Amazon staff asked Amazon CEO Jeff Bezos to cease sales of Amazon's facial recognition technology to police departments and the U.S. government, and to stop selling cloud services to Palantir,⁵² a big data analytics firm with ties to political operatives and intelligence agencies alike. Bezos dragged his feet and changed the subject.

Amazon's support of federal intelligence agencies takes place against the backdrop of exploited Amazon warehouse workers. These workers are subject to intense workplace monitoring, many don't make ends meet, and they work without robust collective bargaining. After taking a lot of heat for being the world's richest man while many of his employees did not make a living wage, Bezos approved a wage increase for certain low-wage workers in the United States and United Kingdom.⁵³ Jay Carney, Amazon's chief propagandist, spun it well: "We will be working to gain Congressional support for an increase in the federal minimum wage. The current rate of $7.25 was set nearly a decade ago."⁵⁴ Jay Carney's name sounds familiar because he was U.S. President Barack Obama's press secretary. Moving from government to Silicon Valley is a fairly common move these days.⁵⁵ Tellingly, a new Amazon headquarters will open in Crystal City, Virginia, less than a mile from the Pentagon. Bezos frames Amazon's support for the Pentagon as a matter of traditional patriotism.⁵⁶ In September 2019, Bezos initiated plans for eliminating medical benefits for Amazon Whole Foods' part-time workers.

Joint Enterprise Defense Infrastructure (JEDI) is a big prize. Through JEDI, one or more corporations of the Pentagon's choosing would receive up to $10 billion to migrate a good chunk of the U.S. military's IT infrastructure to the cloud and maintain that cloud infrastructure. Amazon hired a man with War Department experience (he worked on the JEDI contract during his tenure at the Department⁵⁷) to the chagrin of tech rivals. Amazon was seen as the frontrunner for the JEDI contract, but the Pentagon selected Microsoft in October 2019. Amazon has appealed the selection.

Meanwhile, tech giants such as Amazon, Google, and Microsoft are efficiently and tenaciously aiding Big Oil in the search for and extraction of fossil fuels.⁵⁸ The overlapping corporate interests are stark: In this era of climate catastrophe, military and industry dominate a pro-oil Silicon Valley while the War Department simultaneously burns through record amounts of fossil fuel,⁵⁹ *in addition to* running operations that assist Big Oil (like the 2003 invasion of Iraq and the 2019+ covert assault on Venezuela)! Tellingly, the U.S. government spends comparable amounts on fossil fuel subsidies and the military.[60] The war machine runs on fossil fuels, and Corporate America goes where the money is.

There was a time when NSA's own in-house employees took care of maintaining the bulk of the agency's infrastructure. But, true to form, government bureaucrats willingly acceded to corporate seduction; Groundbreaker got off the ground in 2001 with the aim of outsourcing NSA's physical IT work. Its first contract, worth billions, went to a corporate consortium led by what is now part of General Dynamics' IT division.[61] NSA's IT infrastructure is now almost entirely corporate. And, with the agency's current collect-it-all, cover-it-all approach, the agency would collapse without corporate personnel ("contractors"). NSA hopped to the cloud in the blink of a cursor. By June 2018, NSA had moved most of its mission data into a cloud computing environment known as the Intelligence Community GovCloud (IC GovCloud), which was marketed as allowing intelligence agencies to connect the dots in a big data environment.[62] The stated aim was to get much of NSA's data—disparate, dispersed, and in different formats—into a single pool where it may be visualized, fused, rearranged, and manipulated at will. Automation and the use of various algorithms are said to speed up and/or enhance the pace of NSA personnel (military and corporate).

And none of this could happen without Microsoft.

Microsoft

Microsoft's strong support for NSA goes back decades.[63] Microsoft aids an impressive range of military-intelligence operations, in fact.[64]

Auspicious clouds were approaching.

In spring 2018, Microsoft agreed to provide intelligence agencies with cloud computing,[65] then snagged the aforementioned JEDI contract in 2019.

The Department of War has paid Microsoft billions of dollars. Microsoft sells "Premier Support Services" to units across the U.S. Armed Forces, from Marine Corps Systems Command in Quantico, Virginia, to SSC Pacific in San Diego, California. Microsoft also experiments setting up commercial data & voice networks (for mobile and remote users working in or with the Department), focusing particularly on opaque units at Hurlburt Field in Florida, Maxwell Air Force Base in Alabama, and Cannon Air Force Base in New Mexico. And, daily, Microsoft personnel arrive at Department facilities across the country to fix software and support operations. This includes "access to Microsoft source code when applicable to support DOD's mission." Microsoft engages its significant resources to help the Department become a more powerful, comprehensive fighting force.[66]

Third parties also sell Microsoft products to the Department of War.[67]

CANES, one of many products designed to merge technology and data, rounds out the incestuous haze: Insight (Tempe, AZ) sells Microsoft goods and services to the War Department providing support for CANES, and Northrop Grumman has marketed CANES as being able to give sailors access to the cloud.[68] The Assistant Secretary of the Navy for Research, Development, and Acquisition (ASN RDA) signed off on the legalese that justified a non-competitive procurement to Insight: "This award is supported by a brand name limited source justification…"[69] Many contracts dealing with Microsoft products are not competitive.[70] The ASN RDA at the time was Sean Stackley. He soon left government to become a vice president at the war corporation L3.[71] Ka-ching!

In addition to serving as the software backbone of the War Department, Microsoft sells its goods and services to mainstream war corporations.[72]

At least fifty Microsoft employees have (belatedly) called for the corporation to stop working with the Pentagon on one particular contract,[73] missing the fact that Microsoft is *the foremost* supporter of U.S. war overall. U.S. military computers mostly run on Microsoft Windows. From the most sleep-inducing PowerPoint to the most crippling cyber operation—Microsoft is integral.

Google

Though not as crucial to the military as Microsoft, Google is coming on strong. Google's former CEO, current Alphabet advisor Eric Schmidt, leads the Pentagon's Defense Innovation Board, an advisory panel packed with corporate executives and pro-war academics who help the Secretary of War bring Silicon Valley into military activities and vice versa. Google also signs research agreements with colleges and universities, which can be used to enhance the business of war.[74] It gets worse. Google's business model demands behavioral data of immense volume and breadth. Surveillance capitalists analyze your experiences with algorithms and high-powered processors, and turn both data and experiences into information to sell.[75] And U.S. intelligence agencies are in bed with this Silicon Valley surveillance giant: Google sells "versions of its consumer data mining and analysis technology to police departments, city governments, and just about every major U.S. intelligence and military agency," reports journalist and author Yasha Levine. Google has "supplied mapping technology used by the U.S. Army in Iraq, hosted data" for CIA, indexed the NSA's "vast intelligence databases, built military robots," and even "colaunched a spy satellite with the Pentagon…"[76] In 2015, the War Department took it up a notch, establishing the Defense Innovation Unit in Mountain View, California, with the goal of leveraging a broad range of new Silicon Valley technology for, of course, surveillance and war.

Recently, Google applied its machine learning technology to help the War Department identify objects seen from drones.[77] After employee backlash went public, Google executives made clear they were toning down that deal with the Pentagon. (Some executives tried to spin Google's work with the Pentagon as helping to save lives.[78]) Google executives didn't cancel the contract, mind you. They just let it expire in about a year. That gave the Pentagon plenty of room to utilize and benefit from the technology. (Peter Thiel's Palantir Technologies has since taken over Google's role in this drone project.) ECS Federal, one of Google's subcontractors on the drone software project,[79] has not stopped working with the War Department: ECS sells management of military programs and businesses; IT networks used by U.S. and allied militaries to collaborate; data mining and algorithm research; administrative and financial assistance; and strategic planning. Prior to inking the deal with the Pentagon, Google executives had met with high-ranking officials: Patrick Shanahan (a former Boeing official, and second-in-command in the Pentagon at the time) told executives that he wanted "a built-in AI capability" in weapons platforms.[80] War's wish was Google's command. As of this writing, Google was already drafting what it called "ethical guidelines,"[81] which I expect will be used to help PR officials temper future public backlash regarding military contracts. Google still supports war and intel agencies in ways known and undisclosed.

D.C. is at home in Silicon Valley. A group of insiders from the bellicose Obama administration, for example, help liaise between Silicon Valley and the Pentagon via WestExec Advisors, a consultancy that got its start as a strategic partner of Google's in-house think tank (aiming to bring together the Pentagon, intelligence agencies, cybersecurity experts, and Silicon Valley's best and brightest).[82] Nomenklatura include Blinken, former Deputy Secretary of State; Cohen, former CIA deputy director; Flournoy, former Under Secretary of War for Policy; Monaco, a lawyer and former Executive Branch counterterrorism advisor who is on the board of Accenture, a war corporation; and Shapiro, former U.S. Ambassador to Apartheid Israel. Robert Work, former Deputy Secretary of War, got Google's machine learning drone program up and running while in the Pentagon. Now he's with WestExec. WestExec functionaries overlap a lot with the Democratic cadre in the policy group / think tank known as National Security Action.

The closed, self-serving circle of war corporations, academia, despotic regimes, and war profiteers is tightening: Cloud contracts are becoming a regular presence in daily Pentagon expenditures; as war corporations increasingly adopt Silicon Valley approaches to creating profit;[83] as the War Department operates a fast lane, called the Defense Digital Service, which helps employees at Silicon Valley tech companies rotate briefly into the War Department; as academic institutions like Georgia Tech develop and sell cloud technology to the War Department; as the Saudi regime, a major purchaser of goods and services from the U.S. war industry, provides the *single largest source of funding* for U.S.-based tech companies.[84] This circle could tighten until it pops, or until outside pressure makes it pop.

The detrimental consequences of these profitable intersections are clear. (1) D.C.'s love for neoliberal economic policies blends smoothly with Silicon Valley's ideological preferences. Silicon Valley has been at the forefront pushing neoliberal economic policies, which includes reliance on "flexible or contingent employment" (non-core work going to subcontractors, temporary workers being juggled by third party agencies) as most production is sent overseas. These forms of exploitation help Silicon Valley executives become some of the richest people in the world.[85] (2) The blurring of for-profit surveillance capitalism with the goals of the surveillance state (itself thoroughly motivated by profit) puts capitalist motivation on steroids. (3) The smooth interface inherent to Silicon Valley technologies, particularly cloud storage, allows intelligence agencies and government departments to share information easily, facilitating increased monitoring of the U.S. public under the guise of "national security" and "protecting the Homeland." Flimsy legal protections, already diluted from decades of war, lay shredded and burned.

A TASTE OF C4ISR AND CACI

Much of the U.S. war industry benefits from an information technology subset fancily named command, control, communications, computers, intelligence, surveillance, and reconnaissance (C4ISR). In the simplest terms, C4ISR encompasses all the IT and technical wizardry through which commanders wield information across the battlefield. C4ISR is a catchall term. It is often applied to drones and piloted aircraft, but it also applies to ships or any weapon of war that requires a lot of IT inputs and technical integration to produce an overall surveillance picture. War corporations hype up the need for the Pentagon and its allies to purchase and expand C4ISR capabilities. Studying C4ISR teaches us lessons about the industry's posture and activities, profitable avenues, and nefarious undertakings.

Many corporations sell C4ISR products. Vendors often reside in the Baltimore-D.C. corridor. They sell hard to military-intelligence, particularly units affiliated with NSA, the National Geospatial-Intelligence Agency, and the Air Force. Goods and services can be marketed as improving the sensors on airborne platforms—drones, helicopters, and fixed-wing planes—and satellites on a quest to identify and track targets among the chaff of buildings, businesses, families, and florae on the ground. Corporate employees work on complex, nitty-gritty problems, like how to best combine information gathered from different sensors and different units. Some work develops new "exploit" capabilities for C4ISR. Exploitation in this context involves identifying the target, tracking it, registering the target across U.S. and allied IT systems, and fusing information gained from U.S. operations in a given region into an understanding of the situation on the ground. Sometimes work involves refining algorithms to perform with greater speed and smoothness. With great challenge comes great profit. Recent C4ISR sales focus on making processes more autonomous and anticipating and avoiding problems that might arise in or around hostile territory.

A hefty challenge, indeed. But that is the point. Industry stokes whims, illusions, and dreams of fantastic technological capabilities. Industry promises the moon, and ends up flooding the War Department with product after product, causing more problems for which industry offers solutions. Many products are unable to communicate with each other, for example. An individual unit will complain up the chain of command. The complaints eventually reach some high-ranking brass in the Pentagon. The brass might issue requests to the corporations involved. These then pitch an upgrade or an entirely new product to take care of the particular communication problem. And the U.S. government pays more money. Malleable phrases like "homeland defense" and "established industry practices" and "sustainment activities" varnish this process, inevitably making their way into Pentagon contracts.

Now is a good time to discuss CACI, a formidable corporation based in Chantilly, Virginia. CACI sells a lot of goods and services, particularly IT products and cleared personnel. Its operational depth within the War Department is impressive. A tour of some undertakings reveals worrying activities and astonishing growth of organizations of War.

CACI has recruited heavily for the military, crafting advertising for the National Guard and developing marketing techniques for the Department of War.[86] CACI activities include advertising on social media platforms, "media buying," directing promotional events, and creating and deploying targeted job postings. Benevolent wording cushions such activities.[87] The implications are grotesque: A corporation lobbies Capitol Hill and makes a lot of money selling goods and services for nonstop wars, the cogs and cannon fodder of which the corporation helps recruit through marketing and advertising efforts.

People across the Middle East and Africa use improvised explosive devices to resist military occupation of their respective countries. Guerillas who plant IEDs "employ improvised-threat weapons for strategic effect," in military jargon. CACI technology has provided "a key component" to enable the War Department "to counter improvised threats with tactical responsiveness" and "through anticipatory, rapid acquisition" in support of efforts "to prepare for, and adapt to, battlefield surprise in support of counter-terrorism, counter-insurgency, and other related mission areas." CACI has made a lot of money selling goods and services to the Joint Improvised-Threat Defeat Organization (JIDO), an organization that didn't even exist before 2006. JIDO grew from a task force to an agency to an organization in a few years. Now it's consuming corporate counter-IED products at a rapid pace.

Many organizations have sprung up over the past two decades of war. The Defense Forensics & Biometrics Agency (DFBA) is one. Predecessor units—the Biometrics Management Office became a task force, which became a field operating agency—evolved into DFBA. DFBA oversees and coordinates forensic and biometric capabilities. (Sales of biometrics products to the government have increased in recent years. For example, General Technical Systems makes Gatekeeper On The Move – Biometrics, or GOTM-B. Used by special operations forces in touch with NSA, GTS' GOTM-B is an "innovative, non-contact, on the move, multimodal biometric" device that can ingest identifying finger, face, and iris features. Corporations euphemize sales as "solutions in identity management.") DFBA's work—collecting and analyzing fingerprints, retinal patterns, facial images, palm prints, and other biometrically identifying features—is not limited to battlefields overseas. Its expertise is deployed to U.S. borders. DFBA coordinates with DHS and FBI, operating a database with data from over "16 million encounters," according to the official website.[88] "Every day, immigration and border authorities use DOD biometric information to intercept persons with nefarious histories attempting to enter the U.S.," Army Public Affairs explains.[89] Silicon Valley corporations (e.g. Amazon, Microsoft, and Palantir) sell a variety of products to DHS Immigration & Customs Enforcement (ICE),[90] assisting directly and indirectly in attaining a staggering number of humans in detention.[91]

The investigative journalists Dana Priest and William Arkin contextualize post-9.11 growth.

> With the quick infusion of money, military and intelligence agencies multiplied. Twenty-four organizations were created by the end of 2001, including the Office of Homeland Security and the Foreign Terrorist Asset Tracking Task Force. In 2002, 37 more were created to track weapons of mass destruction, collect threat tips and coordinate the new focus on counterterrorism. That was followed the next year by 36 new organizations; and 26 after that; and 31 more; and 32 more; and 20 or more each in 2007, 2008 and 2009.[92]

To the war industry, an increase in the number and size of organizations equals more avenues through which to route goods and services.

Industry profits from repeated incarnations of long-term pet projects, redundancy, and proliferation of technology.

CACI acquired a corporation, Six3, in 2013. Now, the division of CACI known as Six3 Intelligence Solutions works on some of the toughest projects. CACI Six3 has been working on developing a program that "combines human and unmanned assets, ubiquitous communications and information, and advanced capabilities in all domains" to maximize "performance in increasingly complex environments." Dating back through projects like the Future Combat Systems and the Brigade Combat Team Modernization, industry has been pushing the Department of the Army to purchase massive "modernization" programs for the soldier. Marketing officials consistently paint these systems as begetting flexible, networked squads moving fluidly on the battlefield. These modernization programs cost billions, far more than initially estimated. They consisted of components largely awarded without truly free and open competition; and featured regular upgrades and contract modifications. Developing incessant, interconnected technology for U.S. infantry is resurging in today's products marketed as addressing great power competition. The jury is still out on CACI Six3's performance-maximizing program.

Redundancy favors the bottom line. CACI Six3 has helped run the Counter Insurgency Targeting Program in the U.S. Army National Ground Intelligence Center, or NGIC, in Charlottesville, Virginia, in coordination with the U.S. military occupation of Afghanistan. Part of U.S. Army Intelligence & Security Command, NGIC works on some tasks duplicating what other entities (e.g. Defense Intelligence Agency at Joint Base Anacostia-Bolling and in Reston, Virginia; the National Air & Space Intelligence Center at Wright-Patterson Air Force Base, Ohio) are already doing. Meanwhile, Corporate America regularly cites employee redundancy as an excuse to fire their workers. Money saved pads executives' pockets. I repeat: Military and industry entrench redundancy to expand domains and make money, respectively, while Corporate America cites worker redundancy to fire people.

CACI technology aids special mission aircraft.[93] Do not be pulled into the allure of "special missions." In most configurations, these aircraft possess the technology to monitor electronic communications, even track a human based on identifying electronic traits. These aircraft are not cool or beneficial. They are a way that corporations profit—profit through monitoring. Corporations have honed the design and operation of such aircraft, like the C-12, and the technology onboard during the past twenty years in Afghanistan, Iraq, the Horn of Africa, Latin America, and elsewhere. CACI's work on special mission aircraft is an expected outgrowth of its traditional IT and SIGINT focus. Corporations demand a constant search for new applications for technology. Testing spans Navy, SOCOM, and corporate facilities, primarily on the U.S. east coast. (Armed bureaucracies with a domestic mandate and National Guard units receive comparable technology, raising questions about personal privacy and the relative effectiveness of the Posse Comitatus Act.[94]) Industry executives know that software and C4ISR products are extremely profitable, so they're marketing, pitching, and pushing these goods and services with zeal.

CYBER

The war industry works to attract bright minds into cyber careers. The executive director of cyber at ManTech incentivizes recruits with financial inducements. "However, service to country still trumps salary for the most part," he says, thereby underscoring the notion that ManTech and its desk mercenaries' primary motivation is patriotism.[95] An executive at Booz Allen Hamilton cites tenacity and diversity as desired traits in a cyber recruit.[96] Cyber "is a core element of our growth strategy," a prominent Raytheon official reports.[97] A Northrop Grumman official tells us, "We don't make any move in terms of our development of a system, in terms of development of missile defenses, without thinking about cyber and how it impacts the equation."[98] Understood.

Any war industry appendage worth its weight in transistors has been hyping "cyber" as the next big thing. "Cyber," a broad category, involves products related to the internet and information technology and the protection of these products. Industry develops, markets, and sells "cyber" goods and services to increase profit margins. All levels of organization within the Department of War must acquire a cyber capability or risk succumbing to the "threat." Cyber threats resonate powerfully with us all because our lives are immersed in the internet age. Industry taps into feelings of dread, regularly citing a variety of dangerous groups that can use cyber as offensive weaponry: great powers, terrorists, and rogue states—even for-profit criminals. Targets of bad guys using cyber weaponry include the electricity grid, the internet backbone, oil refineries, and public transportation, according to *McClatchy*.[99] Any place could be targeted. But in reality, D.C. is always the first to use devastating new weapons against others. It was the first to use nuclear weapons (Little Boy and Fat Man; victim Japan) and cyber weapons (Operation Olympic Games/Stuxnet; victim Iran). The rest of the world, except for the Israelis, is fairly self-restrained.

People across the MIC benefit from the hype of cyber threats. These individuals tend to fall into a few main categories: the industry executive who spent his formative years working at NSA or other military-intelligence units; the managing director of a "security advisory corporation" who once worked as a high-ranking official in the Department of Homeland Security or the Pentagon, perhaps occupying one of the many assistant secretary or deputy positions that have proliferated in recent years; a sitting civilian intelligence czar (e.g. Director of National Intelligence) whose organization, career, and reputation was made through seeking out threats and then defending against them and who is ogling a lucrative position within the war industry; the mid-level consultant working at one of many brand-new cybersecurity firms; and the expert whose think tank receives the lion's share of its funding from war corporations.

An important part of hyping cyber is declaring existing weaponry to be inadequately protected. Fortunately, the war industry is there to sell updates, secure your arsenal, and train your personnel on the newest technology. War corporations know exactly what they're doing. *Defense & Aerospace Report* editor Vago Muradian, a man who knows more about industry than most executives, recalls a conversation with Ken Kresa, the former Northrop Grumman CEO: "Northrop was one of the companies way before cyber became cool. [It] had them on its advertising campaigns. I remember talking to Ken Kresa about that. That it's like, 'Wow,' you know. He's like, 'It's something that we're really good at and we think it's going to be the future.'"[100] Turns out, Northrop Grumman was right. That future arrived (due to industry pressure, as seen in Chapter Two, not necessarily due to "organic" threats).

Beware! The CEO of Raytheon warns, "Cybersecurity is becoming more and more of an important issue… It's a matter of national security and the safety of our infrastructure and our warfighters."[101] Expanding that market, a Booz Allen Hamilton executive says every organization has been or will be hacked.[102] Cyber threatens you.[103] *Flight Global* paraphrases a Raytheon vice president: "As aircraft become increasingly networked and rely more heavily on software, they have become vulnerable to cyberattacks."[104] Deputy Secretary of War Pat Shanahan (former Boeing senior vice president) pushed the need to work with industry in order to foist cyber.[105] Industry leadership, across the board, hyped cyber in 2018.[106] The Pentagon and the D.C. regime are happy to go along for the ride, eager to militarize the world's global electronic infrastructures[107] in an attempt to retain waning hegemony. Industry convenes panels, corporate media host industry representatives, academic institutions like Vanderbilt and Georgia Tech suit up, think tanks publish studies, and Congress funds the whole sector of the racket. Profit rolls in.[108]

Corporate personnel work hard so legislation reflects industry priorities. On a macro scale, legislation promotes war as an ingrained part of D.C. foreign and domestic policy. On a micro scale, operatives (liaisons, corrupted congresspeople, lobbyists, aides, advisors, et al.) place language in bills that benefit industry. A vice president at Raytheon concedes, "If you look at the 2016 National Defense Authorization Act, there is a mandate for all weapons systems to have a vulnerability assessment"[109]—operatives crafted the language. The war industry works the usual legislative angles (lobbying, campaign finance, and hands-on drafting of legislation), as producing and marketing increasingly interconnected weaponry requires more software, which must then be protected from cyberattacks.

Pretexts such as great power competition ripple throughout the IT industry. Beijing possesses more than double the number of major supercomputers D.C. has. And, as *The New York Times* reports, Beijing is looking to introduce at least three exascale supercomputers in 2020.[110] Exascale computing makes a quintillion calculations per second. That's the number one followed by eighteen zeros. The U.S. Department of War views this development as a threat. U.S. industry views it as an opportunity. You can't compete with a great power like China unless you have the right computing muscle, so the war industry taps on the shoulder the Department of Energy, a longtime ally of the Department of War on matters of computing and nuclear weaponry. DOE is now developing a $500 million machine called *Aurora* to reach exascale status. War industry regulars, like Cray and Intel, are in charge of designing Aurora. Much of the work on Aurora takes place at Argonne National Lab in Illinois. Argonne, which got its start working on the atomic bomb in the Manhattan Project, now works on nuclear propulsion for the U.S. Navy. Jacobs, a construction and engineering firm that sells frequently to the Pentagon, helps run the lab in partnership with the University of Chicago. More exascale computing systems are headed to other national labs (Lawrence Livermore, which is run by industry giants like AECOM and Bechtel; and Oak Ridge, which is run by industry giants like Battelle). A perceived threat begets profits.

I conclude this cyber section with a note about the War Department's hypocrisy. Keep this in mind whenever military and industry shriek about "cyber" weaknesses: Exploiting vulnerabilities is a key advantage of U.S. military-intelligence. NSA utilizes cyber vulnerabilities that it finds in commercial software. These vulnerabilities are known as *zero day exploits*. NSA reportedly uses these exploits as part of its daily operations. NSA could easily help fix these vulnerabilities, enhancing humanity's collective cybersecurity overnight. It doesn't, because NSA would lose a tool and because war corporations that run NSA would lose revenue. The status quo is more profitable.

DMT AND SPECIAL RELATIONSHIPS

Intimately tied to U.S. military and intelligence activities are corporations that sell DMT (data links, microelectronics, or telecommunications) and other valuable rudiments.

Military ships or aircraft need to communicate. They do so with data links. In pentagonese, such communications equipment provides "secure, high capacity, jam resistant, digital data and voice communications capability" and broadband. The main U.S.-based sellers of this technology are ViaSat (Carlsbad, CA) and a joint venture between Rockwell Collins and the U.K's BAE Systems known as Data Link Solutions (Cedar Rapids, IA). The customer base is huge. It spans Apartheid Israel, Austria, Chile, Finland, Jordan, Japan, Kuwait, Malaysia, Morocco, Oman, Pakistan, Qatar, South Korea, the Saudi regime, Singapore, Sweden, Switzerland, Taiwan, Thailand, the UAE, Australia, Canada, New Zealand, UK, and NATO.

The joint venture known as Data Link Solutions plunges us into the London-D.C. Special Relationship. London typically follows D.C.'s dictates on matters of war and peace. The U.S. and U.K. militaries have a long history of operating and training together, even sharing military bases. The U.S. military operating out of the British colony of Diego Garcia in the Indian Ocean and RAF Lakenheath in Suffolk England, are good examples of this. In addition to defense pacts and banking ties between the U.K. and U.S., war industry underpinnings have a great foundational impact on the Special Relationship.

U.K. corporations sell to the U.S. government. Rolls-Royce and BAE Systems are the U.K.'s most lucrative war corporations. Rolls-Royce sells mostly aircraft engines and maintenance, while BAE Systems' sales are very diverse.[111]

U.S. war corporations sell a variety of goods and services to London, including aircraft and missiles.[112] MAG Aerospace (Newport News, VA) manages the U.K.'s drone operation centers at RAF Waddington, just south of Lincoln, England, and Creech Air Force Base, Nevada, USA.[113] One of London's major purchases from the U.S. war industry in recent years has been the Lockheed Martin F-35 Joint Strike Fighter, the most expensive weapon in history. In a functioning democracy, the British public would weigh the fact that the F-35 is a costly, underperforming aircraft, and London would decline the purchase. Nuclear weapons like the submarine-launched ballistic missile known as Trident II fortify the London-D.C. relationship. The Trident II is a Lockheed Martin product, but many other war corporations (including BAE Systems) work on the missile (see Chapter Nine). Trident II missiles that London purchases are kept at Naval Base Clyde in western Scotland, where protests regularly take place. London purchased the Trident II against the wishes of many of its citizens,[114] who know there is only so much quid to go around, and the more the government spends on nuclear weapons the less the government spends on healthcare, housing, and education. While BAE Systems is involved heavily in the design/manufacture of U.S. nuclear weapons, Lockheed Martin is part of the conglomerate that runs the British Atomic Weapons Establishment. Financial transactions go both ways across the pond.

NSA entrenches the Special Relationship. The U.K.'s primary signals intelligence organization is Government Communications Headquarters (GCHQ). One of NSA's most effective outposts is in the town of Cheltenham in the U.K. Another is at Menwith Hill, which is located near Harrogate, about an hour-and-a-half bike ride north of Leeds. A third is at the Air Force Station known as Croughton in Northamptonshire. GCHQ effectively functions as a branch of NSA. And NSA, as you've seen, is captured by war corporations. You've encountered them before: Accenture, Booz Allen Hamilton, CACI, General Dynamics, Harris, Leidos, L3, ManTech, PAE, and SAIC. If NSA is captured by U.S. war corporations, and GCHQ functions as a branch of NSA, then, according to the transitive property, GCHQ is captured by U.S. war corporations. The corporatized NSA-GCHQ bond raises many questions regarding democracy, or lack thereof, within the United Kingdom and the United States, and indeed the possibility of other tangential uses of the information thus secured.

The Defense Microelectronics Activity (DMEA) is a repository of knowledge about the miniature electronic components and semiconductors known as *microelectronics*. DMEA oversees development and prototyping of new technology. It has engineers and highly tailored equipment on hand to produce microelectronics. Corporate America is integral to War Department efforts to direct and control the microelectronics base. Corporations also smoothly sell goods and services to DMEA via ATSP, the Advanced Technology Support Program, which aims to "rapidly augment the DMEA mission and capabilities to respond to the warfighter needs." Under the guise of "quick access," "lower procurement time," and "rapid acquisition," corporations tap ATSP for billions. ATSP also caters to small businesses, a profitable hustle.[115] DMEA can be described as a corporate lodestar.

DMEA is distinct from the Defense Information Systems Agency (DISA). Headquartered at Fort Meade, DISA is one of the main military organizations that administers delivery of corporate IT across the Armed Forces. An exemplary contract of corporate services within DISA is the $7.5 billion systems engineering and technology deal, issued 14 June 2018, which LinQuest—a regular presence within the space sector of the war industry—shared with other giants (e.g. Booz Allen Hamilton, IBM, Leidos, Northrop Grumman). Both DISA and DMEA are under immense pressure from MIC elites to find ways to increase U.S. processor capacity. Many contracts have been issued to address this.

Wars cannot launch or function without cables and wires. Millions of miles of cables run within U.S. military infrastructure, including domestic bases, aircraft, and deployed locations. Corporations sell fiber optics, fiber optic repair sets, high temperature superconducting cables, dark fiber, and various assemblages (including synthetic ropes and fabric assemblies). Corporations sell military activities involving ocean cable systems (e.g. shipboard loading systems and undersea cabling). Corporate America supplies the nervous system coordinating the actions sustaining nonstop war.

Giant telecommunication corporations such as AT&T, Verizon, Sprint, and Motorola abet the War Department and other armed bureaucracies. Notable sales include networks, communications, and support of troop training.[116] Telecom cooperation with NSA is documented well.[117] Telecoms accede to Foreign Intelligence Surveillance Court orders to hand over the private communication records of U.S. citizens and residents. Established under the guise of preventing undue intrusion into privacy, the Foreign Intelligence Surveillance Court is actually a rubber stamp, with only twelve requests declined out of thousands approved in a period covering three decades.[118] Telecoms routinely cough up metadata. Metadata tells personnel at corporatized intelligence agencies about the source, route, recipient, time, duration of call, and phone number (and, for email, addresses and header). An enormous amount can be learned through metadata. Industry is involved in every step of this process.[119] Metadata also serves as a reference so governments and corporate actors can later refer back to the actual content of electronic communications that have been stored in NSA data centers, which run on corporate IT.

What do data links, microelectronics, telecommunications, and information technology all have in common? Aside from their pervasive place in our lives and their dominant role in the prosecution of war, these goods and services require minerals—from bauxite, cobalt, copper, iron, lithium, nickel, tin, and titanium, to the rarer lanthanum, niobium, rhodium, samarium, tantalum—whose extraction regularly exploits local populations, inflicting a caustic environmental toll and catalyzing domestic resistance requiring further suppression. The war industry would not exist without extractive industries: No fossil fuels for its vehicles, planes, and naval fleets. No erbium for laser repeaters in fiber-optic cables. No indium coating cockpit avionics, gallium integrating missile and IT circuits, or vanadium strengthening aircraft bodies. Nowhere does the War Department take into account the pollution and environmental costs associated with the extraction process of the minerals (rare earths included) that constitute weaponry. Such a lack of accountability aligns flawlessly with the rest of the Department's unaccountable pollution, death, and destruction, and the war industry's role in stoking it all.

ENDNOTES

1 Sieff, Martin. "NSA's New Boss Puts Faith In Hi Tech Fixes." *United Press International*. 18 August 2005.

2 Gorman, Siobhan. "Little-known contractor has close ties with staff of NSA." *Baltimore Sun*. 29 January 2006.

3 "NSA Whistleblower Tells How NSA Tracks You, with Bill Binney." *The Jimmy Dore Show*. 14 December 2017. Accessed 27 June 2018: <www.youtube.com/watch?v=PoeJeWfoSpQ>, (12:10).

4 For more information on Trailblazer and whistleblowers, see Nakashima, Ellen. "Former NSA executive Thomas A. Drake may pay high price for media leak." *Washington Post*. 14 July 2010. Most charges against Drake were eventually dropped after expensive, extensive legal processes.

5 I put the total U.S. intel budget—the two budget portions are the national intelligence program and the military intelligence program—at roughly $80B/year. Around 2/3 of that goes to corporations for provision of IT, cleared personnel, and products.

6 Priest and Arkin. "Top Secret America: The secrets next door." *Washington Post*. 21 July 2010.

7 Note: People living in the United States are far more likely to perish in a lightning strike than in a terrorist attack. These figures and more are documented by the community awareness organization known as *War on Irrational Fear*, <waronirrationalfear.com/facts>.

8 Another example: 3 corporations including Carahsoft Technology share up to $100 million to provide software and IT maintenance. The contract is purchased through Army Contracting Command's Rock Island Arsenal using operations and maintenance funds or "other procurement" funds. Therefore, on paper it might get excluded from the War Department's accounting of intelligence IT contracts, even though its work overlaps considerably with intel-IT undertakings.

9 $42.52B spent on IT in the War Dept. is 44.4% of federal IT spending. "Information Technology." *Office of Management & Budget*. Accessed 22 July 2018: <www.whitehouse.gov/sites/whitehouse.gov/files/omb/budget/fy2018/ap_16_it.pdf>. Shawn McCarthy cites roughly $30B FY2016 DOD spending on IT in "The State of DOD IT Spending—In Three Charts" (*IDC Community*, 29 July 2015). Prof. Paul Strassmann estimates spending on the aggregate of DOD computers, software, and IT at more than $50B annually. Strassmann, Paul A. "The Efficiency of Defense Department Information Technology Spending." *Signal Media*. May 2012.

10 Konkel, Frank. "The Details about the CIA's Deal With Amazon." *The Atlantic*. 17 July 2014.

11 The seminal book on the privatization of intelligence is Tim Shorrock's *Spies for Hire* (New York: Simon & Schuster, 2008).

12 Carroll, James. *House of War*. New York: Houghton Mifflin, 2006, p. 257.

13 Relevant contracts: 29 Aug 2017, 13 & 28 Sept 2018. iWorks (Reston, VA) provides personnel to the Defense Vetting Directorate within the War Dept.'s Defense Security Service. Issued 12 March 2019. As of 1 Oct 2019, employees of OPM's background investigation agency were realigned (not physically moved) to the War Dept. Industry reigns. Charles Phalen Jr., acting director of the Dept.'s new Defense Counterintelligence & Security Agency in charge of background investigations, came from Northrop Grumman. Joseph Kernan, Under Secretary of War for Intelligence, came from industry (including SAP NS2).

14 Relevant contracts: 20 Sept 2012, 2017 (2 Oct, 15 Sept, 8 Sept, 29 Sept), 2018 (30 Mar, 22 Aug, 13 Sept, 6 Dec), 25 Sept 2019. Major intel contract—16 corporations—with DIA issued 5 Aug 2019. Nisga'a Tek (Herndon, VA) monitors and tracks worldwide disease, viral outbreaks, and nations' healthcare capabilities for DIA. Parsons is one of the main corporations running DIA's MSIC at Redstone. COLSA provides high performance scientific computing to MSIC. Rounding out some

of DIA's activities is an amalgam of war corporations and telecom giants—including AT&T, Harris, Lockheed Martin, and Northrop Grumman, as well as NSA regulars like Booz Allen Hamilton and KeyW—that conduct research, development, test & engineering services for DIA's Directorate for Science & Technology. Issued 2018 (8 May, 25 June, 14 Sept), 28 Sept 2016. The latter contract announcement stresses, MSIC "responds to the technical intelligence requirements" of the War Department's "planners and decision makers."

15 Investigative journalists Priest and Arkin (*Washington Post*, 19 July 2010) explain: The "Pentagon's list of code names for them runs 300 pages." Other U.S. intelligence has "hundreds more of its own, and those hundreds have thousands of sub-programs with their own limits on the number of people authorized to know anything about them."

16 Issued 24 and 27 Sept 2018. Prescient Edge and Grand Ground "procure services to identify and neutralize threats to DIA personnel, information and missions."

17 Issued 26 Sept 2018, 2 Jan 2018. G-Tech's work is within the Office of the Secretary of War.

18 Engility operates out of Chantilly, VA, and Andover, MA. It has financial dealings and operations with Qatar, Saudi Arabia, Australia, Japan, and other industry allies. Relevant Engility contracts: 2016 (12 Jan, 10 Feb, 18 Feb, 7 Apr, 29 July, 21 Nov, 28 Nov, 20 Dec), 2017 (7 Feb; 30 Mar; 7, 10 Apr; 31 July; 8, 12, 21 Sept; 23 Oct), 2018 (30 Mar, 6 July, 14 Aug, 26 Sept, 28 Sept).

19 Some of the services Engility has sold to the War Dept. include advisory & assistance to the Defense Threat Reduction Agency, which fancies itself as a unit promulgating nuclear safety and security; research with AFRL on understanding radiation (ultraviolet, visible, infrared) devices; upgrades on electronic warfare systems for aircraft; and developing communication tools for U.S. Central Command. Other goods & services include software development and engineering; engineering & design, including work on aircraft launch & recover equipment; engineering for Defense Technical Information Center's (DTIC, pronounced: *dee-tick*) Information Analysis Center; and R&D helping to guide munitions on target. A sizeable component of Engility's sales goes to the Space & Missile Systems Center at Los Angeles Air Force Base, one of the primary conduits through which corporate technology militarizes space.

20 Such corporations as MultiLingual Solutions and Leidos translate material for NMEC. Vexterra Group has analyzed and processed media and worked on digital forensics within NMEC. Global Professional Solutions has worked on a lot within NMEC at the new DIA campus in Bethesda, Maryland: financial services, managing programs and facilities, logistics, and aiding high-ranking executives. It has also helped determine when/how/why to disclose information to allied governments, including sanitizing, reclassifying, and releasing information. Relevant contracts: 28 July 2018; 2 Oct 2017; 20, 28, 29 Sept 2017.

21 Priest and Arkin. "Top Secret America: A hidden world, growing beyond control." *Washington Post*. 19 July 2010.

22 Priest and Arkin. "Top Secret America: A hidden world, growing beyond control."

23 Recent intel facility construction has taken place at U.S. Army Intelligence and Security Command on Fort Belvoir; National Air & Space Intelligence Center on Wright-Patterson Air Force Base, Ohio; the Baltimore-D.C. corridor; the Intelligence Community Campus in Bethesda, Maryland; and in St. Louis, Missouri (where NGA got a whole new campus). Recent construction at Fort Gordon, Georgia, reportedly home to NSA facilities focused on the Middle East, proceeds apace: Relevant contracts 29 Aug 2016, 14 Sept 2018, 5 Sept 2018, 25 Sept 2016, 12 Sept 2018.

24 Issued 12 Feb 2018, 23 Aug 2018, 23 Aug 2016, 13 June 2016, 30 March 2017, 15 Aug 2018. NASIC keeps updated files on the weapon systems that foreign militaries possess. NGA works on detailed mapping and imagery of Earth. NGA uses war industry software and satellites (run by the National Reconnaissance Office and the U.S. Air Force) to create this imagery. War corporations

selling "intelligence" services cluster like barnacles in the Baltimore-D.C. corridor. The Intelligence Community Campus – Bethesda (ICC-B) is where NGA used to have its headquarters. NGA's new headquarters is a massive $1.7 billion facility at Fort Belvoir in Springfield, VA. DIA is now one of the main players at ICC-B, though the Campus is designed to house representatives of all 17 U.S. intelligence agencies. "Multiple intel sites" e.g.: HDR Architecture building facilities for NGA in St. Louis, MO, and NSA in Fort Gordon, GA (issued 29 Sept 2015, 23 Oct 2017). Recent construction projects for cyber facilities include but are not limited to an academic building for Cyber Security Studies at the U.S. Naval Academy, Spellman Hall Army Cyber Institute Building 2101 at the U.S. Military Academy, and a new cyber facility for the Maryland Air National Guard.

25 Issued 29 Sept 2015, 2016 (30 March, 15 June, 23 Aug, 27 Sept), 2017 (25 Jan, 29 June, 3 Oct), 2018 (20 April, 28 Dec), 23 May 2019. Goodfellow is home to some Air Force intel training, including IMINT and SIGINT classes. The NAS New Orleans SCIF is part of a Joint Reserve Intelligence Center being built. The Fairfield, PA, contract did not specify the facilities. Raven Rock Mountain Complex is a possibility. A contract for SCIF construction in 5 European countries was issued 27 Sept 2019.

26 "Closing Guantanamo." *Human Rights First*. 10 October 2018: <www.humanrightsfirst.org/resource/closing-guantanamo>.

27 The current deputy director of DIA, who assumed the role in October 2018, whetted her talents at General Dynamics. The Principal Deputy Under Secretary of War for Intelligence previously worked as policy director for the House Armed Services Committee. Before that, she worked for a war corporation, SRA International, which sells IT services, tracking using RFID technology, research on "autonomy for human-machine teaming," and Distributed Common Ground System (DCGS) operations and maintenance, among other goods & services. DCGS are typically user-unfriendly systems through which troops and mercenaries gather and share information from drones and other platforms. The Principal Deputy Under Secretary of War for Intelligence had also worked for The Aerospace Corporation, which operates the only federally funded research & development center focusing on space. Her boss, the Under Secretary of War for Intelligence, worked as a senior VP at SAP National Security Services, which sells the U.S. government IT and cyber security goods and services. The acting Director of National Intelligence (as of 16 Aug 2019) came from Booz Allen Hamilton vice presidency.

28 D'Agata, John. *About a Mountain*. New York: W. W. Norton & Co., 2010, p. 56.

29 Three examples suffice. The Obama administration utilized the Espionage Act of 1917 to prosecute and silence whistleblowers and truth-tellers. In March 2014, the Director of National Intelligence, James Clapper, prohibited U.S. intelligence community personnel (including those working for war corporations) from leaking information to the press, stifling one of the pillars of journalism. In spring 2019, MIC elites achieved a long-term goal, removing the anti-secrecy pioneer Julian Assange from the Ecuadorian embassy. These acts send a strong message: Do not resist our secrecy.

30 ISR is basically using satellites, drones, and sensors to know what the enemy is up to. This definition is modified from Tyson & Lang (*Accessory to War*, p. 157) who said ISR is "knowing what the enemy is up to."

31 In FY2016, for example SSC Pacific spent roughly $1,230,348,000. Pritchard, Sharon. "SSC Pacific FY17 Contract States." *SSC Pacific*. 17 October 2017: <www.public.navy.mil/spawar/Pacific/Documents/SSC-Pacific-FY17-Contract-Stats.pdf>, p. 2.

32 Selling technology that merges data has historical precedent. Lester Earnest worked on System 438-L, a computerized intelligence system used by Strategic Air Command HQ, during the Cold War. "The goal was not to improve anything, it was to computerize it," Lester recalls. See

"Military-Industrial-Congressional Frauds—Lester Earnest on RAI (2/4)." *The Real News Network.* 26 December 2018.

33 According to Raytheon contract announcement, the Cooperative Engagement Capability improves "overall situational awareness" and enables "longer range, cooperative, multiple, or layered engagement strategies." CEC focuses on air and missile defense. ULTRA Electronics (Austin, TX) sells & sustains the Air Defense Systems Integrator, which blends info from a variety of data links, sensors, and radar systems and puts the resulting mixture on a somewhat intelligible display.

34 I.e., NEWS should standardize communications among War Dept. employees and federal and state officials operating on dissimilar devices (e.g. cell phones, tablets, PDAs) across a disaster zone or a region of the U.S. NEWS is marketed as providing such a good common operational picture that it might even help detect the onset of a major disaster. Issued 8 Aug 2018.

35 Relevant contracts for the paragraph issued 2018 (15 June, 21 Sept, 15 Nov), 31 May 2017. DARPA contract: 6 March 2015.

36 Erwin, Sandra. "Air Force paints a digital future where data from satellites play central role." *Space News.* 30 September 2019. Pope, Charles. "Goldfein details Air Force's move toward a 'fully networked,' multi-domain future." *Secretary of the Air Force Public Affairs.* 17 September 2019. The Air Space & Cyber symposium is presented by the Air Force Association, an industry pressure group that accepts sponsorship and funding from war corporations. Sponsorship levels around the 2019 event included *3-star partner* ($50,000-$99,000), *4-star partner* ($100,000-$199,999), and *5-star partner* ($200,000 or more). Gen. Goldfein cited Russia and China when justifying the shift to ABMS.

37 Quanterion Solutions (Utica, NY) runs the Homeland Defense & Security Information Analysis Center in Fort Belvoir, providing the Defense Technical Information Center "centralized operation" of War Dept. databases, systems, and networks for acquisition, storage, and dissemination of scientific and technical information with an eye on R&D and engineering. Issued 12 Sept 2018. This is in addition to the existence of fusion centers, physical structures in cities across the U.S. and abroad within which federal and state officials use industry goods and services to gather, share, and merge information ("intelligence") about foreigners, U.S. citizens and residents, and recent immigrants.

38 Journalist Scot Paltrow (*Reuters*, 18 November 2013) reports: The Air Force's Expeditionary Combat Support System was supposed to replace older systems and become a single system tracking acquisition, maintenance, supplies, and transportation. It cost roughly $1.03 billion. Development lasted 2005-12. Computer Sciences Corp, now part of DXC Technology, was the main corporation in charge. Defense Integrated Military Human Resources System (2003-10) was a pay & personnel system. It cost over $1 billion. The Air Force's Defense Enterprise Accounting & Management System (estimated total cost $1.77 billion) was for basic accounting. It cost $466 million as of autumn 2013. Accenture was a major contractor.

39 "Raytheon's Harris on Global Product Demand, International Sales, Partnerships." *Defense & Aerospace Report.* 2 August 2018: <www.youtube.com/watch?v=phCJaKWZ-pE>, (3:02).

40 Rossino, Alexander. "FY2017 Cloud Contracting Trends at the Department of Defense." *Deltek.* 14 March 2018.

41 Nix, Naomi and Ben Brody. "Microsoft Wins Lucrative Cloud Deal With Intelligence Community." *Bloomberg.* 16 May 2018.

42 For solution marketing, see "IBM Cloud solutions." *IBM.* Accessed 17 April 2019: <www.ibm.com/cloud/solutions>, "Cloud Solutions." *Cisco.* Accessed 17 April 2019: <www.cisco.com/c/en/us/solutions/cloud/overview.html>, and "AWS Solutions." *Amazon.* Accessed 17 April 2019: <https://aws.amazon.com/solutions/?ncl=h_ls>, among others.

43 Konkel, Frank. "The Details about the CIA's Deal With Amazon." *The Atlantic.* 17 July 2014. The deal was inked in 2013.

44 Smolaks, Max. "Amazon to build data center on a classified U.S. intelligence campus." *Data Center Dynamics.* 13 November 2015. Judge, Peter. "Impact assessment reveals new U.S. intelligence data center." *Data Center Dynamics.* 20 July 2018. The Amazon subsidiary is *Vadata*. The work involves Warrenton Training Center, a signals intelligence complex with multiple sites in Fauquier County. Vadata got millions in tax exemptions for working on the project. The construction demolished pristine forest. State and federal regulators, including those in the U.S. Fish & Wildlife Service, approved the construction. The traditional Virginian den encompasses the northeast Virginia towns of Fairfax, Herndon, McLean, Falls Church, Vienna, Arlington, Tysons Corner, and others. Amazon has substantial property in Herndon.

45 Blake, Evan. "Amazon & the CIA: A Match Made in Hell." *WSWS.* 13 July 2017.

46 Darrow, Barb. "Intelligence community loves its new Amazon cloud." *Fortune.* 29 June 2015.

47 Korosec, Kirsten. "Here's What Amazon Spent on Lobbying Washington Last Year." *Fortune.* 5 April 2018. "Amazon lobbied more government agencies than any other tech company," per Brody, Soper, and Jacobs. "Amazon Severs Ties With Top Lobbying Firms in Washington" (*Bloomberg*, 30 March 2018).

48 Levin, Sam. "Tech firms make millions from Trump's anti-immigrant agenda, report finds." *The Guardian.* 23 October 2018.

49 Issued 19 Dec 2018.

50 Weinberger, Sharon. "Meet America's newest military giant: Amazon." *MIT Technology Review.* 8 October 2019.

51 C2E looks to "expand and enhance" the 2013 Amazon-CIA cloud arrangement. C2E should be awarded around 2021.

Konkel, Frank. "CIA Considering Cloud Contract Worth 'Tens of Billions.'" 9 April 2019.

52 Bright, Peter. "Amazon staff to Bezos: Stop selling tech to law enforcement, Palantir." *Ars Technica.* 22 June 2018. Pulkkinen, Levi. "From books to bullets: inside Amazon's push to 'defend' America." *The Guardian.* 31 January 2019. Suppe, Ryan. "Amazon's facial recognition tool misidentified 28 members of Congress in ACLU test." *USA Today.* 26 July 2018. Dearden, Lizzie. "Facial recognition wrongly identifies public as potential criminals 96% of time, figures reveal." *The Independent.* 7 May 2019.

53 "Amazon raises wages for lower-paid workers." *BBC News.* 2 October 2018.

54 "Amazon raises wages for lower-paid workers." *BBC News.*

55 The director of the National Counterterrorism Center (a man who previously was NSA general counsel) moved from government to Uber in the summer of 2018. Matt Olsen's official title at Uber is Chief Trust and Security Officer. Between his days at NSA and Uber, Olsen had worked at IronNet Cybersecurity (the firm set up by former Director of NSA Keith Alexander).

56 "This is a great country and it does need to be defended... If big tech companies are going to turn their back on U.S. Department of Defense, this country is going to be in trouble," Bezos says. Quoted in Pulkkinen, Levi. "From books to bullets: inside Amazon's push to 'defend' America." *The Guardian.* 31 January 2019. In December 2019, Bezos spoke at the Reagan National Defense Forum: It is "on the senior leadership team to say, 'I understand these are emotional issues, that's OK. We don't have to agree on everything. But this is how we are going to do it. We are going to support the Department of Defense. This country is important.'" Quoted in Mehta (*Defense News*, 8 December 2019).

57 The War Department employee, Deap Ubhi, worked at Amazon, then the War Department, and then returned to Amazon. See Chris Isidore ("Pentagon probes whether Amazon improperly hired defense department employee." *CNN Business.* 25 January 2019), and Alex Emmons ("Amazon

offered job to Pentagon official involved with $10 billion contract it sought." *The Intercept.* 3 June 2019). Other conflicts of interest plagued the JEDI bidding process, as Paul McLeary reported in *Breaking Defense* ("New Evidence of Conflict of Interest in JEDI Contract," 19 February 2019).

58 Merchant, Brian. "How Google, Microsoft, and Big Tech Are Automating the Climate Crisis." *Gizmodo.* 21 February 2019. Tech giants provide a variety of services, including automation, big data assistance, and machine learning. A former BP executive is leading Google's new fossil fuel division.

59 Crawford, Neta C. "Pentagon Fuel Use, Climate Change, and the Costs of War." *Watson Institute for International and Public Affairs.* 12 June 2019.

60 Dickinson, Tim. "Study: U.S. Fossil Fuel Subsidies Exceed Pentagon Spending." *Rolling Stone.* 8 May 2019. Military spending exceeds fossil fuel subsidies, I note, if one factors in nuclear weapons funding (stashed in the Dept. of Energy) and overseas contingency operations funding.

61 General Dynamics finished its acquisition of CSRA in the spring of 2018.

62 Konkel, Frank. "NSA 'Systematically Moving' All Its Data to The Cloud." *NextGov.* 21 June 2018.

63 Greenwald, Glenn, Ewen MacAskill, et al. "Microsoft handed the NSA access to encrypted messages." *The Guardian.* 12 July 2013. Goodin, Dan. "NSA backdoor detected on >55,000 Windows boxes can now be remotely removed." *Ars Technica.* 25 April 2017. Zetter, Kim. "How a crypto 'backdoor' pitted the tech world against the NSA." *Wired.* 24 September 2013. Microsoft's VP of Trustworthy Computing Group says, "If I put a backdoor in our product, our market capitalization goes from $260 billion to zero overnight. I can't even sell it. It's nuts! Economic suicide! So, no backdoors." Thomson, Iain. "Microsoft: NSA snooping? Code backdoors? Our hands are clean!" *The Register.* 25 February 2014.

64 Major organizations and locations heavily reliant on Microsoft include Maxwell AFB, a hub of cyber operations; Lackland AFB, TX; Fort Meade, MD; Fort Gordon, GA; JB Langley-Eustis, VA; Ramstein AB, Germany; Peterson AFB, CO; JB Pearl Harbor-Hickam, HI, and elsewhere on Oʻahu; McConnell AFB, KS (home to the 184th Intelligence Wing); and Fort Huachuca, AZ.

65 Nix, Naomi and Ben Brody. "Microsoft Wins Lucrative Cloud Deal With Intelligence Community." *Bloomberg.* 16 May 2018.

66 Relevant Microsoft contracts: 2014 (24 Sept, 25 Sept, 3 Dec), 2015 (9 June, 28 Aug), 2016 (22 April, 1 Dec, 20 Dec, 30 Dec), 25 Sept 2017, 2018 (28 June, 26 Sept), 11 Jan 2019.

67 Third parties include InfoReliance Corporation (Fairfax, VA) Microsoft Consulting Services; Regan Technologies (Wallingford, CT) Microsoft IT software & support; En Pointe Gov (Gardena, CA) and SHI International (Somerset, NJ) Microsoft software assurance & maintenance; Minburn Technology Group (Great Falls, VA) expertise using Microsoft products for acquisition/contracting at SOCOM.

68 "CANES: An Open Systems C4I Networks Design." *Northrop Grumman.* Accessed 23 June 2018. Additionally, on 4 May 2018, Insight sold Microsoft software licenses, software assurance, and cloud offerings to the Department of the Navy as a whole.

69 Insight delivery order issued 22 June 2017 in accordance with FAR 8.405-6(b). Work expected to continue through 31 May 2018. Approved by ASN RDA on 25 March 2015.

70 Among them 11 July 2014, 9 June 2015, 20 Dec 2016, and 30 Dec 2016.

71 Aitoro, Jill. "Former Navy official Sean Stackley joins L3 Technologies." *Defense News.* 8 January 2018. Stackley said of his new job, "It's a whole new world." The CEO of L3 had called Stackley to woo him. The CEO "has worked with Stackley on government projects on and off for about a decade."

72 For example, Northrop Grumman works on radar programs that have run Microsoft Windows. Northrop Grumman's test stand for ballistic missiles uses Windows. Lockheed Martin programs within the Space & Missile Systems Center use Windows to help plan missions and run SATCOM systems. L3 uses Windows when updating Mission Training Center hardware & software for Lockheed Martin F-16 aircraft. Raytheon uses Windows to run the DHS National Cybersecurity Protection System.

73 Microsoft agreed in Nov 2018 to sell headsets, called *HoloLens*. The deal ($479M) specified that Microsoft would help "increase lethality by enhancing the ability to detect, decide and engage before the enemy," according to the *BBC*. Microsoft employees voiced their disagreement in a letter, which read in part: "Microsoft must stop in its activities to empower the U.S. Army's ability to cause harm and violence." A Microsoft spokesperson condescended: "We always appreciate feedback from employees and have many avenues for employee voices to be heard." Lee, Dave. "Microsoft staff: Do not use HoloLens for war." *BBC News*. 22 February 2019.

74 Research agreements between academia and Silicon Valley develop technology that can benefit the nexus of industry and military-intelligence. (A Multi-University Research Agreement, MURA, delineates the rules and guidelines for collaboration between universities and Google. Facebook has a program just like MURA. It is called Sponsored Academic Research Agreement, SARA.)

75 Prof. Shoshana Zuboff educates us: Google does not offer any free services. You are Google's source of free, raw material. Many tech platforms comb through your experiences and turn them into data. Your happiness or wellbeing is irrelevant. Prof. Zuboff explains this in her book (*The Age of Surveillance Capitalism*. New York: PublicAffairs, 2019) and on the 1 March 2019 episode of *DemocracyNow*.

76 Levine, Yasha. *Surveillance Valley,* pp. 176-8, *passim*. A "full-fledged military contractor," Levine reports, Google has worked hand-in-hand with corporations like SAIC and Lockheed Martin.

77 Amadeo, Ron. "Google helps Pentagon analyze military drone footage—employees 'outraged.'" *Ars Technica*. 6 March 2018.

78 "Google to scrub U.S. military deal protested by employees—source." *Reuters*. 1 June 2018.

79 Shane, Scott and Daisuke Wakabayashi. "'The Business of War': Google Employees Protest Work for the Pentagon." *The New York Times*. 4 April 2018.

80 "Google to scrub U.S. military deal protested by employees—source." *Reuters*.

81 "Google to scrub U.S. military deal protested by employees—source." *Reuters*.

82 Fang, Lee. "Former Obama officials help Silicon Valley pitch the Pentagon for lucrative defense contracts." *The Intercept*. 22 July 2018.

83 For example, L3 uses "innovation sprints," an intense brainstorming technique pioneered by Silicon Valley firms. In 2017, L3 used these sprints four times. "In 2018, they did 65 sprints and are on pace to do even more this year," per Marcus Weisgerber ("How L3 Technologies Is Culture-Shifting Its Way into the Industry's Top Tier." *Defense One*. 16 June 2019).

84 Brown, Eliot and Greg Bensinger. "Saudi Money Flows Into Silicon Valley—and With It Qualms." *Wall Street Journal*. Updated 18 October 2018. For Google's operations with the Egyptian regime, see Ryan, Vic. "Google is deepening its involvement with Egypt's repressive government." *The Intercept*. 18 August 2019.

85 Greater detail is presented in Richard Walker's *Pictures of a Gone City* (Oakland: PM Press, 2018). In an interview ("On Contact: Silicon Valley and The New Capitalism." *RT America*. 3 November 2018), Walker starts off by impersonating a Silicon Valley PR specialist: "Well, look, our average worker makes $250,000 a year." Walker continues, critiquing the system: "But that's because they don't include in their statistics all the work that they put out to low-wage firms," which do "the

food service, the cleaning, security, transport, and so-on." The final, lowest tier, is global labor, mostly those making Silicon Valley's products in China, because "capitalism never weans itself off of cheap labor. It's always in there."

86   CACI marketing has been issued repeatedly, in particular 14 April 2015, 18 May 2016, 16 Feb 2018. See also Ross Wilkers "CACI keeps $60M Army National Guard media support contract." *Washington Technology*. 20 February 2018.

87   CACI helps "each state and local region tailor national recruitment strategies to local needs, with an emphasis on state-based messaging and media placements. In turn, state recruiters sharpen their ability to recruit in local markets, maximize the impact of their media budgets, and reduce time spent on media procurement activities," per "CACI Awarded $60 Million IDIQ Contract to Provide Advertising and Media Support for Amy National Guard" (*CACI*, 19 February 2018).

88   "About FAQs." *DBFA*. Accessed 4 September 2018: <www.dfba.mil/about/faqs.html>.

89   McLaughlin, Matt. "Defense Forensics and Biometrics Agency uncases colors for the first time." *Army Public Affairs*. 28 July 2014.

90   Tools help surveil, track, detain, monitor, and deport humans targeted for deportation, according to a coalition of immigrant rights groups: "Who's Behind ICE? The Tech and Data Companies Fueling Deportations." *National Immigration Project, Immigrant Defense Project, and Mijente*. October 2018. Available at <mijente.net>. Microsoft has aided ICE, though Microsoft's CEO has said that the corporation was not selling machine learning-based technology to ICE—*only* services for communications, document management, and similar office tasks that help an organization run. See "Microsoft Employees Up in Arms Over Cloud Contract with ICE" (*Gizmodo*, 18 June 2018). Peter Bright (*Ars Technica*, 22 June 2018) reports, "But in a blog post announcing its work with ICE," a Microsoft rep "expressed the desire to sell machine learning services to the agency."

91   44,631 humans was the average daily population in ICE custody as of 20 Oct 2018, according to Ackerman (*The Daily Beast*, 11 November 2018).

92   Priest and Arkin. "Top Secret America: A hidden world, growing beyond control." *Washington Post*. 19 July 2010. Another example, NCTS Hampton Roads, has grown physically and bureaucratically in recent years from a detachment to a command, per Lori Blann (*Defense Visual Information Distribution Service*, 20 July 2016).

93   For CACI airborne SIGINT careers, see <careers.caci.com/sema_pilot_program>.

94   For reported concerns about domestic use, see Jeremy Scahill "Were U.S. Special Forces Involved in the Arrest of Faisal Shahzad?" (*The Nation*, 4 May 2010); and Aldhous and Seife "Spies in the Sky" (*Buzzfeed*, 6 April 2016).

95   Vergun, David. "Leaders offer solutions to cyber personnel challenges." *Army News Service*. 3 August 2018.

96   Vergun, David. "Leaders offer solutions to cyber personnel challenges."

97   "Raytheon's Harris on Global Product Demand, International Sales, Partnerships." *Defense & Aerospace Report*. 2 August 2018: <www.youtube.com/watch?v=phCJaKWZ-pE>, (2:55).

98   "Northrop Grumman's Todorov on $9.2B Orbital ATK Acquisition, Missile-Defense Space, Evolving Threats." *Defense & Aerospace Report*. 6 August 2018: <www.youtube.com/watch?v=gnADkxrX5tI>, (14:00).

99   Johnson, Tim. "Preparing the battlefield: Hackers implant digital grenades in industrial networks." 27 June 2018.

100   "Northrop Grumman's Todorov on $9.2B Orbital ATK Acquisition, Missile-Defense Space, Evolving Threats." *Defense & Aerospace Report*. 6 August 2018: <www.youtube.com/watch?v=gnADkxrX5tI>, (12:59).

101 "Collaborate against the cyber threat: Raytheon CEO speaks on Capitol Hill about strengthening cybersecurity." *Raytheon.* 11 January 2018. The Raytheon CEO was in D.C. for AIA's National Aerospace Week, a forceful pressure / PR effort. He spoke inside the U.S. Capitol building. Sen. Mark Warner (whose biggest '16 campaign contributions came from Big Tobacco, private equity, investment banks, and war powerhouses like Carlyle, Harris, and Huntington Ingalls) and Sen. Jerry Moran (whose biggest '16 campaign contributions came from a major military construction firm, Burns & McDonnell, coincidentally) were co-chairs of the Aerospace Caucus. They hosted the event. The Pentagon's Dep. Chief Information Officer for Cybersecurity spoke and schmoozed with the industry reps present. On 14 May 2019, the Raytheon CEO teamed up with the governors of Arkansas and Louisiana to hype cyber threats at the state level. Their piece ran on *FoxNews* and *The Hill* websites.

102 Vergun, David. "Leaders offer solutions to cyber personnel challenges." *Army News Service.* 3 August 2018.

103 "Critical national infrastructure, commercial aircraft and personal health and financial data each face cyber threats," Raytheon tells us. "And in the consumer sector, the IP addresses of devices like phones, household appliances, thermostats and cars have become threat points, or vectors, that bad actors can use to shut down our homes, invade our privacy, or crawl deeper into the network to reach critical infrastructure or networks," per <www.raytheon.com/responsibility/cyber>.

104 Reim, Garrett. "FARNBOROUGH: Raytheon to advise Jordan on aircraft cybersecurity." *Flight Global.* 17 July 2018.

105 "We are working hand-in-hand with industry—from traditional defense to banking, energy, and technologies companies—to protect critical data, technology, and infrastructure. Our military superiority and security—in cyber as in other areas—depends on their strength and security. Together, we are raising the bar on cybersecurity and enhancing our coordination through DOD-Industry partnerships such as the Enduring Security Framework and the Defense Industrial Base Cybersecurity Program. The days of analyzing this problem are over. We are taking action..." Shanahan, Patrick. "October Message to the DoD Team." *U.S. Department of Defense.* 2 November 2018.

106 In early 2019, I looked at the 2018 statements of executives at the biggest war corporations. The leadership within Lockheed Martin, Boeing, Raytheon, Northrop Grumman, General Dynamics, L3, Booz Allen Hamilton, Honeywell, Textron, CACI, ManTech, Leidos, SAIC, and Harris Corp. all hyped cyber in 2018.

107 Phrasing borrowed from Stephen Graham (*Cities Under Siege.* London: Verso, 2011, p. 272).

108 One example is the Air Force Research Lab. Cyber contracts purchased for the lab increased greatly in frequency and amount in recent years after war corporations started earnestly hyping cyber.

109 Reim, Garrett. "FARNBOROUGH: Raytheon to advise Jordan on aircraft cybersecurity." *Flight Global.* 17 July 2018.

110 Clark, Don. "Racing Against China, U.S. Reveals Details of $500 Million Supercomputer." 18 March 2019.

111 Rolls-Royce Holdings sells aircraft engines to the U.S. War Department. (General Electric, Honeywell, and United Technologies are the major U.S. engine sellers.) Rolls-Royce engines propel U.S. Navy landing craft, Lockheed Martin cargo planes and aerial refuelers, the V-22 tilt-rotor aircraft, Northrop Grumman early warning aircraft, and Northrop Grumman drones. Rolls-Royce also regularly gets money from the War Department to research the next generation of aircraft engine technology. BAE Systems is one of the U.K.'s most powerful corporations. Its headquarters is a stone's throw from Whitehall, the center of the British government. BAE's most productive facilities are located in the United States. (Most productive in terms of matériel output and combined revenue.) BAE Systems

has sold many goods and services to the Pentagon: ship maintenance, battle management software, machine learning, signals intelligence, conversion of rockets into more accurate weapons, decoys that lure incoming missiles away from aircraft, systems that jam enemy radar, technology that detects buried explosives, "intelligence" products for the U.S. occupation forces in Afghanistan, machine guns, missile launching systems, land vehicles, and artillery. BAE has also run ammunition plants (Holston in Tennessee and Radford in Virginia). Newer corporations also bind London and D.C.: The U.K. once had the Defence Evaluation & Research Agency. DERA was the British military's primary research & development wing. It was comparable to the U.S. Defense Advanced Research Projects Agency. In 2001, most of DERA's work was privatized and turned into a corporation, QinetiQ. In autumn 2004, QinetiQ (pronounced: *kinetic*) acquired a Waltham, Massachusetts, company named Foster Miller, which sells robots that help analyze and diffuse explosives. QinetiQ now sells a lot to the U.S. War Department, including robotics, controllers for drones, and mission planning software. QinetiQ's journey shows how neoliberal economic policies, like the privatization of government functions, help expand the war industry.

112 Recent sales from U.S. industry to the U.K. include Boeing aircraft, Boeing and Raytheon missiles, General Dynamics communications systems, General Dynamics missile tubes for submarines, Telephonics identification friend or foe devices, ViaSat data links, anti-tank missile systems, Lockheed Martin cargo aircraft, and General Atomics drones.

113 Issued 21 March 2019. MAG Aerospace has grown leaps and bounds since its establishment in 2010. The corporation's website puts it best: "In 10 years, MAG has become the leading independent provider of manned/unmanned full-spectrum outsourced ISR services, with 1,000+ employees operating 200+ platforms over 100,000 flight hours annually *on 6 continents...* MAG serves its customers' ISR needs anywhere in the world under extreme and austere operating conditions ranging *from the jungles of South America to the mountains of Afghanistan to the coasts of the world's oceans*" (emphasis mine).

114 Townsend, Mark. "Trident rally is Britain's biggest anti-nuclear march in a generation." *The Guardian*. 27 February 2016.

115 ATSP's aims stated in "Defense Microelectronics Activity (DMEA) Advanced Technology Support Program IV (ATSP4) Technical Requirements and Objectives" (*DMEA*, 18 March 2014, p. 3). ATSP4 is the fourth iteration of the program. A 31 March 2016 contract announcement explains: DMEA ATSP4 aims to "resolve problems with obsolete, unreliable, unmaintainable, underperforming, or incapable electronics hardware and software through development of advanced technology insertions and applications to meet" War Dept. requirements "for a quick reaction capability." A lot of money is up for grabs; the first 3 iterations of ATSP offered combined aggregate ceilings of roughly $7.4 billion, per p. 5 of the initial citation in this endnote. The 31 March 2016 ATSP4 contract catering to bigger war industry players, like General Dynamics and Honeywell, was capped at $7.2 billion. One small business slice of ATSP4, issued 12 Jan 2018, was capped at $800 million. DMEA (p. 20) states, "Subcontracting to small business will be encouraged, monitored, and will influence performance rating."

116 **AT&T** abets the occupation of Afghanistan and other foreign lands by facilitating the training of U.S. grunts at Fort Polk and in the Sierra Nevada Mountains. Facilitation involves constructing and servicing telecom and radio infrastructure through which troops train to shoot, move, and communicate. AT&T has also sold cyber support at Maxwell AFB's Gunter Annex; DISA network support, domestic and worldwide; maintenance of classified communication networks at Los Angeles AFB; UHF/line-of-sight communications; wireless technology. Relevant contracts: 2015 (24, 29 April; 15 May; 21 Dec), 2016 (1, 20 April; 31 Aug), 2017 (31 March, 15 Sept, 30 Oct), 2018 (2, 23 April; 10 July; 14, 26 Sept; 18 Oct). See also "AT&T Government Solutions, Inc." *Federal Supply*

Service General Services Administration. Contract No. GS-23F-0174S. Contract Period 05-05-2006 through 05-04-2016. AT&T helps sustain the Defense Intelligence Agency's Directorate for Science & Technology (issued 14 Sept 2018), working alongside Booz Allen Hamilton, Harris, Leidos, Lockheed Martin, Northrop Grumman, and others on "research, development, technical, and engineering services." AT&T owns CNN, which, as covered in Chapter Two, pushes pro-war propaganda (and is home to "national security analyst" former Director of National Intelligence James Clapper). **Verizon** sells telecom services and devices across the War Department, including voice and data to the Naval Computer & Telecommunications Area Master Station Atlantic (NCTAMS LANT), which looks after some of the U.S. Navy's computer and communications systems. Pertinent Verizon sales issued 21 Dec 2015, 2017 (12 April, 14 Sept, 30 Oct). One NCTAMS LANT subordinate unit is Naval Computer & Telecommunications Station (NCTS) Hampton Roads, VA, which is the third largest DISA Node worldwide, according to Lori Blann "Parish Assumes Command Over Newly Established Naval Computer and Telecommunications Station" (*DVIDS,* 20 July 2016). Verizon is "strategic partner" of the industry pressure group, Armed Force Communications & Electronics Association (AFCEA), per <www.afcea.org/site/StrategicPartners>. Telecoms have cozy relationships with industry pressure groups (e.g. AIA, NDIA, AUSA). On a lighter side of this coin, an AT&T Corporate Historian was featured on a panel during AUSA's annual meeting in 2018. On a darker side, Motorola has sponsored AUSA's wounded warrior golf outing. **Sprint** operates and maintains fiber infrastructure across the European continent for the Pentagon. Sprint's work in Europe is expansive and steady, with a lot of effort aiding the Pentagon's own global telecom service, Defense Information System Network (DISN). Stateside, Sprint has supported military activity on the small and large scale, providing mobile service for the Army at Fort Knox, KY, and developing high-speed wireless service for military use. **Motorola**'s bread and butter involves furnishing the U.S. military with land mobile radio systems, which are advanced walkie-talkies. Motorola also modernizes radio subsystems for the U.S. Army and the National Guard. Motorola's work takes place worldwide, including expanding infrastructure in Japan and on the Korean peninsula. Smaller telecoms sell to the War Department. For example, Oceus Networks plans out and sustains the Mobile Cellular Network for SOCOM. Blending multiple circles of the MIC's destructive actions, we see General Dynamics on the last day of FY2018 getting millions of dollars to upgrade the telecom network across U.S. military infrastructure in Hawaiʻi, abetting further militarization of the colony. Relevant contracts: 2014 (1 Oct; 14, 18 Dec), 2015 (27 Apr, 23 & 30 June, 23 Dec), 2016 (27 June, 30 Aug; 21, 27 & 29 Sept; 20 Oct), 2017 (17 March; 9 June; 6 July; 25, 28 Sept; 30 Oct; 15 Nov), 2018 (13 April; 24 May; 18, 28 June; 31 July).

    117 Gallagher and Moltke. "The Wiretap Rooms: The NSA's Hidden Spy Hubs in Eight U.S. Cities." *The Intercept.* 25 June 2018; Zetter, Kim. "What we know about the NSA and AT&T's spying pact." *Wired.* 17 August 2015; Julia Angwin, et al. "AT&T Helped U.S. Spy on Internet on a Vast Scale." *The New York Times.* 15 August 2015; Gallagher, Ryan. "NSA Collecting Phone Records for Millions of U.S. Verizon Customers." *Slate.* 6 June 2013; Bowcott, Owen. "Intelligence services 'creating vast databases' of intercepted emails." *The Guardian.* 18 July 2014; Froomkin, Dan. "NSA backs down on major surveillance program that captured Americans' communications without a warrant." *The Intercept.* 28 April 2017; Konkel, Frank. "AT&T Won Secret $3.3 Billion NSA Contract Despite More Expensive Bid." *NextGov.* 21 March 2018; Greenwald, Glenn. "NSA collecting phone records of millions of Verizon customers daily." *The Guardian.* 6 June 2013. "An opinion from the secret Foreign Intelligence Surveillance Court, which was declassified in September [2013], said no company that has received an order to turn over bulk phone records has challenged the directive," the *AP* reported ("Verizon plans transparency report on phone record requests, working with NSA," updated 3 November 2015).

118 "Since 1979 through to 2015, the last round of reporting figures, the [FISA] court has approved 38,365 warrants but only rejected a dozen. That's a rejection rate of 0.031 percent," reported Zack Whittaker in "Here's how many U.S. surveillance requests were rejected in 2015" (*ZDNet*, 30 April 2016). FISC approved 1788 of 1789 U.S. government special surveillance requests during 2012, according to Glenn Derene "Why the NSA Wants All That Verizon Metadata" (*Popular Mechanics*, 6 June 2013). 2013-18 saw comparable approval rates, with a slight uptick in rejections in 2015, 2017. See *Electronic Privacy Information Center* <epic.org/privacy/surveillance/fisa/fisc>.

119 One such process: Develop analytical tools. Use large data sets to map out relationships among people. Target certain communications (based on geographical location, name, call time, etc.). Parse the data. Build a picture, spokes from anchors. Refine technological capabilities, understanding social networks to greater degrees of accuracy.

8

"Our" Hemisphere

SOUTHCOM

U.S.-based capitalists and their extractive industries (oil, logging, palm, coffee, biofuels, fruit, minerals) operating in Latin America have stolen land, destroyed subsistence farming, displaced millions, turned locals into laborers, and killed indigenous peoples and land protectors. D.C.-backed oligarchs in the region have used U.S.-trained military and paramilitary forces to protect this extraction. Local elites in Latin American countries back D.C. for their own reasons, often economic. Overt and covert activity suppresses progressive movements that resist this exploitation.

D.C.'s war on drugs runs parallel to and overlaps this capitalist exploitation. Successive administrations—Reagan, Bush Sr., Clinton, Bush Jr., Obama, Trump—all drew the bulk of their senior-level cliques from Wall Street, neoliberal institutions, and the war industry, and all consistently opted for militarized foreign policy choices.[1] D.C. implements the war on drugs in such a way as to control the hemisphere, including the U.S. population.[2] The U.S. war industry is a full partner in the war on drugs because supplying military goods and services to the U.S. and allied governments is a profitable venture.[3] In exchange for money, U.S. war corporations provide weaponry and carry out public relations campaigns, narcotics interdiction, satellite surveillance, airborne reconnaissance, signals intelligence, privatized policing, crop eradication, and other activities throughout Latin America. As of 2010, the militarized drug war had cost the U.S. over $1 trillion,[4] a low estimate that didn't factor in pertinent Pentagon activities.

Headquartered in Miami, Florida, Southern Command (SOUTHCOM) is the Pentagon's organization (unified combatant command, in official lingo) in charge of South America, Central America, and parts of the Caribbean. The head of SOUTHCOM, Admiral Kurt Tidd, introduces us to how industry profits through SOUTHCOM. In testimony to the Senate Armed Services Committee consisting of two parts fearmongering and one part asking for more weaponry, Admiral Tidd referred to SOUTHCOM as "an economy of force Combatant Command."[5] For perspective, SOUTHCOM operated with an annual budget around $190 million,[6] significantly more than U.S. European Command (EUCOM) received.

Tidd's initial round of carping is worth reading.

> Yet the combined impacts of defense spending caps, nine years of continuing resolutions, and insufficient spending in the diplomacy and development arenas make it increasingly difficult to sustain this regional network. Because our global security responsibilities outpace the resources available to meet them, we have had to make a series of tough choices, resulting in compounding second and third order effects. The net result is the perception among our friends—and the palpable anticipation among our competitors—that we no longer stand by our commitments, that we are relinquishing our strategic position, and that we don't take the challenges in this region seriously.[7]

With no actual, demonstrable threat coming from Latin America, Tidd scrounged up every possible scary situation and presented them to U.S. Congress as if the sky was about to fall. Threats he cited included migration, non-state actors, unmet development goals, violent crime, and political corruption. One of Tidd's favorite phrases, and a vogue phrase within the war industry at the time, was "threat networks," a frightful, all-encompassing term that evokes Hollywood-style menaces lurking around every corner. Tidd included arms dealers, drug traffickers, human traffickers, terrorist supporters, and money launderers within this "threat network" category. (Military contracts pursue the same nebulous amalgam of baddies that Tidd cited.[8]) Tidd did not mention Western banks laundering drug money[9] or the Pentagon laundering tax dollars.[10] Or that U.S. domination and exploitation was likely a causal factor in much of what he labeled as threats.

The "threats" Tidd cited had been hyped at think tanks long before Tidd testified.[11] Think tanks sow, testimony waters, and industry harvests the flowering weapon sales.

Tidd's bouquet of bad guys would not suffice. Tidd rolled out Islam, the most reliable of talking points that scares the zippers off of congressional purses. "Global threat of violent extremism has gained a small foothold within Latin America's growing Muslim populations," Tidd asserted.[12]

Let us pause and consider terrorism rationally.

The likelihood of being a victim of a terrorist attack in the U.S. is astonishingly small. Having compiled robust studies and reports about terrorism, the community awareness organization known as *War on Irrational Fear* provides facts. The organization emphasizes, "Americans are eight times more likely to die from a lightning strike than a terrorist attack."[13] The likelihood of being a victim of a terrorist attack by an immigrant is miniscule, almost nothing.[14] With this calm perspective, we can see how absurd Tidd's hyperbole is. Yet hyperbole sustains war.

SOUTHCOM's official mission is to work "to build regional and interagency partnerships to ensure the continued stability in the Western Hemisphere and the forward defense of the U.S. homeland." Such a loaded mission statement requires candid dissection.

- *Partnerships* actually means "relationships through which D.C., armed with industry's arsenal, protects and promotes neoliberal economic projects in Latin American countries and local elites who, while taking a slice of the profitable pie, sign off on U.S. capitalists' pillage of natural resources and privatize state assets."
- *Continued stability* means "the political and economic conditions in which U.S. capital can thrive and exploit the population."
- *Forward defense* means deploying SOUTHCOM (in conjunction with units from the Department of Homeland Security, the Drug Enforcement Agency, and CIA) in order to make sure no troublemakers, typically of the Left variety, are successful in achieving self-determination or charting an independent foreign policy.[15] Aggressive "forward defense" means people die. In May 2012, for example, the U.S. Drug Enforcement Agency killed four civilians (including a schoolboy and two pregnant women) in northeast Honduras, and then lied about the incident.[16] The DEA fired from a modified Textron (Bell) Huey gunship.[17]

D.C. has a long history of enforcing corporate control over the natural world in the Western Hemisphere. U.S. military and/or espionage interference (clandestine, covert, and open) in Latin American affairs is lengthy.[18] Human Rights is featured prominently on SOUTHCOM's website, though military and industry do not care about human rights. Rather, Human Rights serves as a diplomatic and propaganda tool used to accost "great power" rivals like Moscow and Beijing or countries that do not conform to D.C. policy. SOUTHCOM develops ties with military officers across Latin America, cultivates the next generation of dictators, provides neoliberal regimes with military and financial support, and conducts foreign internal defense. Foreign internal defense involves the U.S. military building up the military, paramilitary, or national police forces of another country, which historically act as the front-line in suppression of democratic movements. The U.S. Army's Seventh Special Forces Group traditionally carries out foreign internal defense in Latin America. The armed wings of U.S. capital have interfered in each and every nation in Latin America.

War corporations are particularly adept at exploiting SOUTHCOM's three "lines of effort:" *countering threats*, *building our team*, and *strengthening partnerships*.

- *Countering threats* involves conducting operations, deploying troops throughout Latin America, and dominating the Caribbean while hunting for narcotics traffickers.
- *Building our team* is best described by SOUTHCOM: "Knowledge matters: we must have a trained, educated, and highly competent work force." And who does most of the recruiting, military training, and educating? War corporations. Candid history about the U.S. role in Latin America is not given to U.S. troops during this training and educating.
- *Strengthening partnerships* used to be called "building partner capacity," but that was too obviously pro-industry. *Strengthening partnerships* involves training militaries and supplying them with products from the U.S. war industry. A lot of training is run through industry goods and services (e.g. "private contractors," a.k.a. mercenaries; simulators; hardware and software; ordnance) and formal study at the Western Hemisphere Institute for Security Cooperation, the rebranded School of the Americas.

SOUTHCOM's lines of effort are better viewed as threads of profit.

Other ways to strengthen partnerships in SOUTHCOM include Public-Private Cooperation, the State Partnership Program in Latin America and the Caribbean (SPP), and the Caribbean Basin Security Initiative (CBSI) Technical Assistance Field Team (TAFT).

- Public-Private Cooperation initiatives align U.S. academic institutions, corporations, and non-governmental organizations into the War Department's priorities for hemispheric control.
- SPP pairs U.S. National Guard troops from various states, Puerto Rico, and the District of Columbia with military forces from Latin American nations. Past pairings include Arkansas with Guatemala, Connecticut with Uruguay, and Kentucky with Ecuador. The South Carolina National Guard has hosted units from the Colombian Army and trained them on goods and services from the war industry. Responses were positive from an industry perspective. Colombian Brigadier General Cesar Parra affirmed, "The Colombian military is going through a transformation

and wants to become more interoperable with U.S. forces."[19] In addition to exposing foreign militaries to U.S. industry products, pairings are designed to bring Latin American militaries under U.S. cultural and military influence and build goodwill to be leveraged at a later point in time. (Other goodwill to be cashed in at a later date includes USAID projects, U.S. Army Corps of Engineers construction, and medical training programs.)
- CBSI TAFT perform essentially the same function as SPP, except CBSI TAFT focus on maintaining small ships and watercraft belonging to Latin American navies and coast guards. Standardization is repeatedly stressed among participating navies. Standardization encourages all militaries to use the same boats and riverine craft, providing industry more opportunity to sell wares into the future. The U.S. pioneered this technique with the North Atlantic Treaty Organization, through which mandatory standardization led to member countries purchasing billions and billions of dollars of products from the U.S. war industry over the years. Such standardization operates within the overarching priorities of corporate-induced globalization. Globalization is the vast project by which Western-based capital forces open markets abroad, demands free flow of capital (not humans), uses cheap labor around the world, and exploits natural resources on or beneath other people's land. Globalization homogenizes formerly diverse cultures via the imposition of monolithic, corporate goods and services, and their cultural baggage.

BRAZIL

U.S. Secretaries of War serve as weapons dealers when they travel.[20] For example, in the spring of 2012, Secretary of War Leon Panetta toured Latin America. This was business as usual.[21] Brazil is a future prize in industry eyes. War corporations paved the way for Panetta's arrival. At least seven of them toured Brazil prior to Pentagon officials' April 2012 visit.[22] Panetta confirms, "This offer is about much more than providing Brazil with the best fighter available... With the [Boeing F/A-18E/F] Super Hornet, Brazil's defense and aviation industries would be able to transform their partnerships with U.S. companies, and they would have the best opportunity to plug into worldwide markets."[23] The Defense Security Cooperation Agency (DSCA), which administers the U.S. foreign military sales program, had long ago notified U.S. Congress of the pending sale of new fighter jets to Brazil.[24] Boeing was salivating.[25] Other corporations named in the DSCA notification to Congress included General Electric, Lockheed Martin, Northrop Grumman, and Raytheon. Once in Brazil, Panetta built upon the U.S.-Brazil

Defense Cooperation Agreement (DCA). The DCA is almost entirely about benefitting U.S. industry.[26] Panetta affirmed, the best way to deal with "common challenges" is "to work together, not apart." He stopped in Brazil "because this is an important place to start that kind of relationship."[27] According to the *American Forces Press Service,* the meeting with Brazil's military establishment was designed to follow up on the DCA, including a focus on cyber security technology, logistics, and technology transfer.[28] Panetta resorted to a tired war industry talking point: "provide jobs and opportunities for [Brazil's] people as we provide jobs and opportunities for ours."[29]

Alas, it wasn't meant to be, for the time being. In a twist of irony, word of NSA's activities tanked the whole weapons deal. The sale was all set up, but then Edward Snowden's leaks hit the press and the world found out about mass NSA surveillance of Brazilian citizens, politicians, and petroleum corporations.[30] Brazil's political establishment recoiled. Brasília gave D.C. and Boeing's headquarters a firm "no" regarding the Super Hornet, selecting the Swedish Saab Gripen instead.[31] These events show how investigative journalism can impact the war industry. The U.S. war industry nodded and planned for another day. It wasn't all tears and condolence flowers back in boardrooms of U.S. war corporations. Industry still sold Brazil plenty of weaponry and matériel;[32] industry plays the long game. Boeing soon inked a joint venture with a Brazilian aerospace corporation.[33] Brazil then joined the State Partnership Program, teaming up with the New York National Guard.[34] Things were looking up for the U.S. war industry in Brazil.

Other Secretaries of War (e.g. Chuck Hagel, Ash Carter) followed behind Panetta and had more success. Aside from visiting individual countries, Secretaries of War attend the Conference of the Defense Ministers of the Americas, a grand venue for pitching weaponry and entrenching hegemony. The Conference was created in 1995 as part of an MIC push—during the relatively lean years between the Cold War and the War on Terror—to increase weapon sales to Latin American nations. At the Conference, U.S. Secretaries of War look to sign agreements with Latin American ministries of defense. Agreements typically focus on expanding military cooperation and deepening research on terms favorable to U.S. industry. All who purchase from the U.S. war industry are reliable partners to some degree, but Honduras holds a particular space in the industry's cold heart.

HONDURAS

Pentagon officials view the nation of Honduras as a base of operations. The U.S. war industry views U.S. military installations in Honduras as avenues through which to route goods and services. A lot of the cocaine that the United

States consumes travels through Honduras.[35] The War Department and war industry assert that U.S. military activities help counter this flow. Construction corporations have built up many military installations, old and new, in Honduras in recent years. SOUTHCOM's Joint Task Force-Bravo operates out of Soto Cano Air Base, a two-and-a-half-hour walk, south-southeast of the town of Comayagua. Soto Cano AB is home to a Forensic Exploitation & Analysis Center wherein industry goods, including biometric devices and document analysis software, try to make sense of traces left behind by men and women who are suspected to have participated in some level of the narcotics trade. The U.S. food service provider Sysco has fed the troops at Soto Cano. An Aviation Regiment belonging to Joint Task Force-Bravo focuses on the Gracias a Dios department, specifically Puerto Lempira. This is in the country's east. And U.S. Navy and Marine assets flow in and out of Catarasca in the east and the island of Guanaja. Other U.S. military and intelligence outposts in the country include Forward Operating Base (FOB) El Aguacate, FOB Mocorón, and FOB Puerto Castilla. Meanwhile, D.C.-backed militants reportedly kill peasants and support the Honduras élite.[36]

COLOMBIA

U.S. military and industry also have a large presence in Colombia. Colombian elites and the U.S. war machine exist on the same side of the neoliberal coin. U.S. war corporations sell Colombia a variety of weaponry, including Boeing attack helicopters, Colt carbines, General Dynamics rockets, armored vehicles, and parts and accessories for a variety of goods. The relationship between the U.S. war industry and the Colombian government is intimate.[37] For its cooperation, Colombia receives foreign military financing, typically two-dozen million dollars every year, serving as an indirect transfer to the U.S. war industry. The pattern goes like this: the recipient country spends U.S. military aid to buy goods and services from U.S. war corporations. Then SOUTHCOM chips in with support (training, information sharing, and logistics support) that complements the sale.

The MIC packages sales to Colombia as "solidarity with Colombia" and its campaign against the *Fuerzas Armadas Revolucionarias de Colombia,* known as the FARC. "We will continue to provide training, equipment and assistance that Colombia has requested in order to defeat this common enemy" is a refrain coming from U.S. Congress, the Pentagon, and war corporations. It's a clever gambit: impose a war upon Colombia (through the United States' insatiable demand for narcotics, Capitol Hill's profit-over-people policy response, and the Pentagon's military expansion) and then require that Colombia purchases goods and services from the U.S. war industry in order to address this war.

The FARC signed a definitive ceasefire in 2016, after which the Colombian state and right-wing paramilitaries murdered hundreds of Colombian community leaders and former FARC fighters.[38] U.S. weapon sales to Colombia didn't stop after the FARC signed the ceasefire. Post-peace treaty, the U.S. war industry and the Pentagon increased their branding of the Colombian government as an "exporter of security" in the region.[39] An "exporter of security" can be leveraged for financial gain and regional domination. SOUTHCOM Commander Admiral Tidd in autumn 2018 painted a positive picture of Colombia—a Colombia, in his estimation, far from the "terrorists" and armed revolution of the 1980s.[40] In spring 2018, Colombia and NATO agreed to work together on "cyber security, maritime security, and terrorism and its links to organized crime," among other areas.[41] Colombia is now a full NATO partner. The Colombian government will purchase more weaponry from the U.S. war industry to further standardize (lock in) its arsenal with that of NATO member countries.

U.S. war corporations in Colombia have benefited from the corporatization of the U.S. military by running missions in coordination with U.S. military and intelligence forces against the FARC and other groups; detecting and eradicating Colombian crops, including coca;[42] and advising U.S. government officials implementing Plan Colombia and its successor Peace Colombia. (With the support of Colombian elites, these Plans leveraged U.S. diplomatic and military might to entrench and expand U.S. corporate power in Latin America.) The U.S. war industry tests and deploys many advanced reconnaissance and surveillance aircraft and sensors in Colombia, operated by uniformed U.S. troops as well as mercenaries getting paid hefty stipends by war corporations. Perhaps the most infamous example of corporatized airborne reconnaissance is Northrop Grumman operations. In 2003, mercenaries working for a Northrop Grumman subsidiary were flying an airborne counter-narcotics mission in the skies over Colombia when their plane crashed. The crew had repeatedly expressed worries that their aircraft was not up to the rigors of reconnaissance missions over mountainous terrain. After the crash, Northrop Grumman folded the subsidiary and created new corporations, moves that had the effect of avoiding paying compensation and avoiding legal liabilities for the deaths.[43] The surviving mercenaries were held by the FARC for over five years. SOUTHCOM and the U.S. Joint Personnel Recovery Agency worked to locate the mercenaries in FARC custody. In summer 2008, Colombian military personnel posed as humanitarian workers in order to rescue the captives. U.S. military personnel were in the loop during the operation. SOUTHCOM Commander Admiral James Stavridis later presented the mercenaries with the Defense of Freedom Medal after they had returned to the U.S. (via Boeing C-17 aircraft) and had recuperated. The incident didn't deter corporatized U.S. reconnaissance operations, which continue to this day. Airtec Inc. (California, MD), for example, has helped run reconnaissance operations out of Bogotá using corporate aircraft, including the Bombardier Dash 8 and possibly the Falcon 10.[44]

U.S. military bases dot Colombian territory. Some are nominally run by the Colombian military, but all parties know who is boss. U.S. Secretary of War Hagel explained in 2014: "And as we all know, right here on this base [is] where so much of Colombia's defense capabilities are built, and Colombia's defense cooperation with other nations across Central and South America evolve and strengthen… I also had an opportunity to meet with U.S. troops here, serving in Colombia: Special Forces troops and aviation specialists who have worked closely with their Colombian counterparts."[45] (The Pentagon concedes that all Colombian military leaders have received some U.S. military training.[46]) Hagel was talking about Tolemaida Air Base, which is located southwest of Bogotá. Tolemaida has been packed with U.S. war industry goods and services, including carbines, mercenaries, helicopters, and personnel helping to run mobile air surveillance systems.[47] Forces from U.S. Special Operations Command and other U.S. military commands run in and out of bases like Tolemaida, armed with the latest gear.[48] U.S. equipment shows up at combined training exercises in the Western Hemisphere and beyond. It is showcased carefully to allied militaries. These militaries often purchase such gear after seeing it in action. Prior to, during, and after combined exercises, executives and officials from U.S. war corporations get in touch with allied ministries of war to lay the groundwork for future purchases.

Colombia's National Training Center in Tolemaida is one place where war industry goods are always on display, and featured in annual special operations training exercises. The U.S. Department of War and U.S. war industry cooperate to establish such training centers. As the grunts shoot, move, and communicate, high-ranking U.S. officials promote U.S. war products and explore ways to further imbricate allied militaries with the U.S. (i.e. "enhance military cooperation"). The war industry is ever present at these competitions at training centers.[49]

High-ranking leaders (civilian and military) from the U.S. War Department visit U.S. warzones like Colombia. They tour Potemkin villages—wherever Pentagon VIPs go, subordinates and bootlickers polish the panorama and pretend the current approach is working well—and reiterate what has already been decided. Language, like "progress," sustains military actions. The war industry goes unmentioned. Even though the products of war corporations are often the most visible aspects of SOUTHCOM's operations, the corporations that produce them are regularly omitted from the command's literature, speeches, and official briefings. This contrasts with a reality in which the U.S. war industry markets its products throughout Latin America and to SOUTHCOM, an enthusiastic participant which monitors, reports on, and engages drug traffickers, migrants, activists, left-wing organizers, peasants, and diverse civilians. And U.S. Congress goes along for the ride, happy to accept war money in their campaign coffers and war lobbyists in their offices. Keep this in mind next time a U.S. congressperson takes a tour of a U.S. base, whether in Asia, Africa, or Latin America.

This militarized approach to the drug war—featuring all of the aforementioned war industry goods and services—doesn't reduce coca production. Cocaine production in Colombia during 2017 hit record levels.[50]

Meanwhile, U.S. military and corporate actions in Colombia inflict devastating costs. On a broad level, unconditional, forceful martial actions against social issues in the Western Hemisphere have unleashed ferocious levels of violence upon the people of Colombia—tearing families apart, assassinating trade unionists, poisoning cropland, displacing millions of Colombian citizens, and destroying their communities. Locals despise the presence of gringos and U.S. sponsorship of the Colombian military. (General Martin Dempsey fraudulently alleged the Colombian people have become fond of the Colombian Armed Forces' presence.[51]) U.S. personnel (uniformed troops and mercenaries) allegedly sexually abused and raped Colombian minors.[52] D.C. argues that the Status of Forces Agreement (SOFA) signed between Colombia and the U.S. provides immunity to U.S. Armed Forces and mercenaries so such personnel cannot be prosecuted in Colombian courts; all matters should be resolved in U.S. courts or not at all. The War Department's bureaucratic obstructionism in Colombia vis-à-vis sexual abuse is not an aberration.[53]

In spring 2018, the Colombian president Juan Manuel Santos presented the *Orden de San Carlos* to SOUTHCOM, recognizing "distinguished service to the nation, especially in the area of international relations"[54]—drawing on a thirty-year relationship between MIC and Colombian élites, SOUTHCOM commander Kurt Tidd later called Colombia "a modern, thriving, capable partner"[55]—bringing to full circle Colombia's role in this sector of the racket.

MEXICO

The U.S. government plies Latin American governments with loans, grants, and giveaways, much of which comes back to the U.S. war industry in the form of weapon purchases. In 2017, for example, Mexico received $5 million.[56] The Mexican Army and Navy purchase a lot from the U.S. war industry.[57] Civilians suffer. Violence in Mexico is through the roof. (Mexico is technically part of NORTHCOM, not SOUTHCOM, though SOUTHCOM units often operate in/ around the country in coordination with such NORTHCOM units as Theater Special Operations Command – North.) In 2017, the nation's homicide tally hit a record high, with 28,702 victims—men, women, and children. *The New York Times* indicated that the homicide rate was even higher in the first half of 2018.[58]

Different groups battling for control of drug trafficking routes and markets cause most of this violence. The firearms usually come from the United States. 130 Mexican politicians and candidates were killed from autumn 2017 through early summer 2018, according to *Deutsche Welle*, perhaps an undercount.[59] Mexico remains one of the most dangerous countries in the world for journalists. There are civilian victims inside the U.S. as well: the taxpayers who subsidize the drug war, the black and brown people who are disproportionately policed and prosecuted, and the families who are terrorized when their homes are raided by armed bureaucracies. To say nothing of the suffering of those who succumbed to the allure of drugs targeting their communities.

SPECIAL MARKETING OPS

Task forces abet corporate profits. A task force is a temporary arrangement of military units and corporate personnel under a single military commander to perform a specific assignment (e.g. kill insurgents or guerillas, interdict narcotics). U.S. military task forces regularly cycle through Latin America. In June 2018, SOUTHCOM deployed a task force comprised of Marines and sailors loaded with industry products and traveling on industry ships. It stopped in Belize, El Salvador, Guatemala, Honduras, and Colombia. Belize received roughly $35,826,000 in aid from the U.S. government during 2012-17.[60] Belize, which purchases firearms from Colt (West Hartford, CT), is where U.S. war corporations send technicians running technical and analytical support "to include conduct and analysis of structured operational and integrated test and evaluation" of U.S. Navy systems.[61] El Salvador hosts the U.S. Navy's Cooperative Security Location (CSL) Comalapa. There are more U.S. mercenaries at CSL Comalapa than U.S. uniformed military personnel among the non-flying staff.[62] U.S. task forces in Latin America have included Joint Task Force-Vulcano, Joint Task Force-Bravo, and Joint Interagency Task Force-South. A task force is a show of might from a military perspective and a product magnet from a corporate perspective.

Military exercises create demand for corporate goods and services. The Pentagon brass and U.S. government agencies promote exercises because exercises extend their reach and influence. Military exercises are showcases, displaying the seductive weaponry that your nation could have for the right price. From an industry perspective, all exercises are an opportunity to present goods and services. In advance of an exercise, officials and representatives from the U.S. war industry can be dispatched to the countries participating. These reps familiarize key military brass and senior ministry officials in the participating nations with the goods and services that will be on display. War corporations maintain close contact with Pentagon personnel in case any dates are changed.

SOUTHCOM exercises have included CRUZEX, PANAMAZ, Tradewinds, UNITAS, and Fused Response. Billed as the "largest bilateral exercise of its kind in the Western hemisphere," Fused Response has involved training in the field, command post instruction, communications work, senior-level staff planning, and reconnaissance drills. It is designed to enhance nations' ability to "work together in any circumstance." Exercises are an effective tool to make sure foreign units under the War Department's command are able to use the weaponry and matériel of U.S. war corporations. Exercises are training for operations.

Operations entail short- and long-term, coordinated military activity. Operations require extensive planning across the U.S. War Department, U.S. federal agencies, U.S. war corporations, and the militaries of allied capitalist governments. SOUTHCOM runs Operation Martillo. *Martillo* is Spanish for "hammer." The Operation's main aim is to track and pursue humans on both sides of the Central American isthmus.[63] Operation Martillo openly involves DHS and the Defense Intelligence Agency.[64] The War Department retains the right to VBSS (Visit, Board, Search, and Seize) any private property traveling in SOUTHCOM's area of responsibility. Sometimes Operation Martillo provides tips to regional partners—like the U.S.-supplied navies of El Salvador and Guatemala or the U.S.-supplied air force of Colombia—who then pursue the "bad guys." They capture or kill the bad guys using weaponry from U.S. war corporations. Profitable operations never end because the war on drugs never ends. And vice versa.

War corporations profit extensively from SOUTHCOM's task forces, exercises, and operations. A wide range of products (e.g. craft, training, intelligence) is sold to the War Department for SOUTHCOM use.[65] Of course, corporations follow up these sales with additional sales of everything from parts and maintenance to field service representatives, training, and logistics. Such sales are relatively small; many purchases (for example, most signals intelligence technology monitoring the people of Venezuela and Colombia) used in the drug war are cloaked in secrecy, further separating the public from understanding the true costs of war.

Some people think it's a chicken-or-egg scenario. They argue that it's difficult to tell which came first—the war industry or the need to go after bad guys in the hemisphere. But it's not even a situation where there's a problem, and then the war industry comes up with a solution for the problem. It's just the opposite: The war industry inflates an issue, avoids addressing the root causes, manufactures weaponry, and markets the weaponry, which the Pentagon purchases for use in military operations. This process is comparable to the process Corporate America uses to get you, a consumer, to purchase a product that you don't need. The only difference is that the war industry has more incisive forms of marketing.

THE PUERTO RICAN COLONY

By now you know how war corporations operate. You know that human lives mean nothing. You know that Wall Street and the MIC prioritize the almighty dollar. The way Capitol Hill deals with Puerto Rico is exemplary. Puerto Ricans are U.S. citizens, but their citizenship can be revoked because it is statutory, not granted by the Constitution. The political representation of Puerto Rico in U.S. Congress cannot vote. Puerto Ricans are not allowed to vote for the U.S. President. They are treated as second-class citizens on paper and in real life.

The D.C. regime has a long history of exploiting Puerto Rico. The armies of D.C. captured the island of Puerto Rico in the Spanish-American War. In July 1898, U.S. troops invaded Puerto Rico and imposed a military government. The December 1898 Treaty between D.C. and Madrid was negotiated in Paris. While D.C. purchased the Philippines from Spain for $20 million, D.C. got Puerto Rico and Guam for free. D.C.'s policies and wars have continuously devastated Puerto Rico's people.[66] For decades the Occupation banned the teaching of Spanish in schools. Though traditionally answerable to the Governor of Puerto Rico, the Puerto Rico National Guard is still subject to D.C.'s edicts and the Pentagon's whims. The War Department built up military infrastructure on the island during and after World War II, continuing throughout the 2000s.[67] Puerto Ricans are regularly ordered to deploy in support of D.C.'s wars, including operations in U.S. Africa Command and U.S. Central Command. The Pentagon also uses the Puerto Rico National Guard as a key part of its SOUTHCOM operations. Major General (ret.) Felix Santoni, the lead civilian assistant in Puerto Rico for the Secretary of the Army, claimed that the U.S. Army Reserve has a long tradition helping Puerto Rico. He made these claims in an Army recruitment video (before the video offered up to $20,000 dollars for joining the U.S. Army Reserves).[68]

Puerto Rico has a long history of resisting D.C.'s machinations. In the 1960s, the Young Lords, men and women of Puerto Rican heritage in New York City, educated the public and raised awareness about D.C.'s abuse of Puerto Rico. Different armed groups have attacked U.S. military infrastructure (recruiting stations, uniformed military personnel, mercenaries, and draft stations) in Puerto Rico. The most famous of these groups is the *Macheteros*, to whom a January 1981 attack against military planes on Muniz Air National Guard base is often ascribed. It is no accident that the perpetrators targeted products of the U.S. war industry.[69] Puerto Ricans peacefully oppose D.C. recruiting their youth for military purposes.[70] *Madres Contra la Guerra,* a Puerto Rican anti-war group, has protested, educated the public, fundraised for veterans, and helped veterans find medical care.[71]

The MIC has treated Vieques, an island to the east of the main island, with exceptional brutality. During 1940-41, the U.S. Navy kicked Vieques residents out of their homes. Some locals were dispossessed and then abandoned in fields of sugar cane. Compensation ranged from zero to a couple of hundred U.S. dollars. Many people didn't want to move, but they were forcefully relocated. Roughly two-thirds of Vieques was taken. Vieques, a community whose economic livelihood centered around fishing, was further devastated when the U.S. Navy banned commercial fishing in the newly designated military waters. Navy patrols regularly harassed local fishermen who disobeyed the War Department. The U.S. military used the island of Vieques as a bombing and training range for decades. All sorts of industry munitions have landed on Vieques, including Boeing, General Dynamics, and Raytheon products. Heavy metals and toxic compounds like arsenic, cadmium, cyanide, lead, and depleted uranium poisoned the flora and fauna, and leached into the water table.

Vieques residents came together, mobilized, and successfully resisted the abuse of their land. The U.S. military no longer uses Vieques as a practice range, but the area is now very polluted.[72] The War Department tasked corporations to lead the environmental remediation of Vieques.[73] According to locals, cleanup on the island has included open-air detonation of unexploded ordnance and burning vegetation, potentially exacerbating the pollution.[74]

Nonetheless, the U.S. military and industry continue to lean on Puerto Rico. Though the formal U.S. military presence in Vieques was said to have ceased by early 2004, war corporations have stuck around. Raytheon, for example, works on Navy surveillance equipment in Vieques, specifically the Relocatable Over-the-Horizon Radar (ROTHR) system.[75] The Raytheon site in Vieques, with some work in Juana Diaz, violates the spirit of the U.S. military withdrawal. ROTHR was originally designed to notify the Navy about incoming missiles and ships. After the Cold War ended in the early 1990s, industry marketed ROTHR anew, pitching it as a counter-narcotics surveillance device. The Pentagon bought the pitch hook, line, and sinker. The new counter-narcotics mission required war corporations to adjust the ROTHR system, costing even more money.

The military and congressional sides of the MIC work together to militarize Puerto Rico by publicizing "jobs" and "investment." The Department of War claims its Army Reserve invested "over 140 million U.S. dollars" in Puerto Rico in 2011,[76] a figure that local functionaries use to justify the pernicious military presence. Later, the Pentagon moved this figure higher, placing the Army Reserve's investment in Puerto Rico at roughly $285 million U.S. dollars per year.[77] Congress' NDAA of 2012 granted the Pentagon greater authority to call up and use Army Reserve forces, like those in Puerto Rico, for flexible "emergencies" inside the U.S. (the "Homeland") and overseas for "theater security missions."[78] In 2012, the Pentagon again expanded its Reserve presence in Puerto Rico.[79] In 2016, D.C.'s fiscal control board (*never* elected by the public) began governing

Puerto Rico, imposing austerity measures on the masses in order to repay wealthy mainland creditors. (D.C.'s imposition of neoliberal economic policies exacerbates unemployment, further ripening Puerto Ricans for military exploitation.) This isn't the first time mainland capitalists have interfered in the Puerto Rican economy. Beginning in the 1940s *Operación Manos a la Obra* began converting the island's economy from agriculture to tourism and manufacturing.

Capitalists in D.C. and on Wall Street have privatized much of Puerto Rico's economy, including the healthcare sector, over the past two decades. Slowly but surely, a profit-over-people model enveloped most public services in Puerto Rico, contributing to a lack of preparedness in responding to major crises. In autumn 2017, Hurricane Maria struck. One of the most powerful tropical cyclones ever recorded, Maria tore apart Puerto Rico's electrical and transportation infrastructure. The hurricane made a terrible situation (food insecurity, poor health care, resource-starved public transit) even worse.[80]

D.C. did not give Puerto Rico the help it needed to recover from the hurricane. Rather, D.C. treated the island like a colony.

In previous disaster responses D.C. sent the troops. Ansel Herz writing in *The Nation* pointed to the 2010 earthquake in Haiti: The arrival of U.S. military personnel clogged airports, commandeered infrastructure, and brought with it its own overwhelming demands (e.g. feeding, housing, and cleaning for all the U.S. troops).[81] In most locations, the War Department is quick to use its vast military capabilities to provide disaster relief, because it is easy for the War Department and U.S. intelligence agencies to later leverage that goodwill for geostrategic aims and espionage efforts. While D.C.'s responses to the 2010 Haiti earthquake, 2005's Hurricane Katrina in the Gulf Coast, and 2019's Cyclone Idai in southeast Africa were more militarized, the response to Hurricane Maria was far subtler, more privatized. D.C. sent the Federal Emergency Management Agency (FEMA), a few uniformed military personnel, and a lot of corporate power to Puerto Rico. Puerto Rican medical workers did their best in very difficult circumstances. Understaffed and underequipped as a result of years of privatization, they were unable to access patients in a timely manner, leading to many deaths. D.C. could have employed a robust, well-funded, interagency effort. Instead, it took advantage of the disaster to double down on its neoliberal economic policies of privatization and corporate welfare.[82]

The War Department played a central role in this profiteering.

The War Department paid three corporations—The Louis Berger Group, Fluor, and PowerSecure—to restore electrical power in Puerto Rico. The Louis Berger Group was allocated one payment: $860 million.[83] Fluor received three allocations totaling over $1.3 billion for construction services to help restore electricity. (Fluor is a long-time Pentagon favorite. It has renovated U.S. Embassies, operated military installations, and built maintenance facilities for bomber aircraft.) In years immediately prior to Hurricane Maria, the Pentagon had issued PowerSecure only one contract. By early May 2018, PowerSecure had received its ninth allocation for repairing Puerto Rico's electrical grid. This brought the total amount of funds allocated to PowerSecure since Hurricane Maria to $517,375,000.

Yet much of the island still teetered on the brink of darkness[84] due to the shoddy work and corruption inherent to the capitalist model.[85]

In the beginning of April 2018—by which point PowerSecure had been allocated over $367 million, and Fluor and the Lewis Berger Group combined had been allocated over $2 billion—the island suffered a serious blackout, reportedly because a contractor accidentally drove an excavator into a critical electrical facility.[86] Reduced government oversight is an intended consequence of neoliberal economic policies.

All of these Pentagon contracts raise critical questions. Why were corporations like the Louis Berger Group, which had a record of defrauding the U.S. taxpayer,[87] awarded contracts to assist a people in need on an island long treated as a colony? Why was the War Department, which for decades contaminated parts of Puerto Rico using ordnance, the go-to department through which electricity was being provided to U.S. citizens? The answer is tragic: The D.C. regime has so thoroughly neglected and depleted the non-militarized portions of the U.S. government that it's no longer capable, let alone willing, of summoning aid to its citizens without turning to the War Department and the incorrigible war industry. The U.S. government possesses no robust, homegrown, non-military capacity to care for its citizens during and after a natural disaster. The people cannot rely on the D.C. regime to care for them. Genuine care is not profitable. If D.C. truly wanted to help Puerto Rico recover, it could cancel Puerto Rico's debt.[88] But the D.C. regime and Wall Street remain primarily concerned with abetting the war industry while grabbing Puerto Rico's land, pillaging resources, and imposing austerity measures.[89] Over 4,600 U.S. citizens died in Puerto Rico as a result of Hurricane Maria.[90] In the summer of 2019, U.S. Congress passed a disaster relief bill, allocating roughly $1.4 billion for Puerto Rico. For perspective, the unelected fiscal control board that runs Puerto Rico has a $1.5 billion, five-year budget. Echoing the Pentagon's modus operandi,[91] about two-thirds of the fiscal control board's budget goes to consultants and corporate advisers.[92]

War industry players, collaborators, and associates—academia, Big Finance, and Big Fossil Fuel—interact to abet Puerto Rico's destruction. The Baupost Group is one of a handful of hedge funds that holds Puerto Rico's debt. Baupost also invests in war corporations and fossil fuel infrastructure. (Seth Klarman is the billionaire Zionist in charge of the Baupost Group, based in Boston. He is a major donor to federal election campaigns.) The Massachusetts Institute of Technology, an academic institution in the war industry, has deep financial ties to the Baupost Group.[93] Contemporaneously, the U.S. fossil fuel industry and federal government have maneuvered to push liquefied natural gas onto the Puerto Rican population, further burdening Puerto Ricans and the planet with heavy-duty fossil fuel infrastructure and exacerbating the climate crisis.[94] Big Finance, Big Fossil Fuel, and academia support the war industry and altogether harm Puerto Rico.

Political repression against assertive Puerto Ricans continues. In autumn 2005, the FBI shot dead Filiberto Ojeda Rios, an elderly Puerto Rican independence activist wanted in connection with a robbery that took place decades ago at a Wells Fargo depot.[95] "We went to arrest him but when the gunfire started we had to defend ourselves," said the FBI official in charge of the colony.[96] (This is an old trick. Federal agents claimed self-defense after murdering four Honduran civilians in May 2012.[97] U.S. mercenaries in Iraq claimed self-defense when shooting civilians. Across the U.S., police officers who kill black youth regularly claim self-defense. Customs & Border Protection trains its officers to reach for their sidearms and vocalize that they feel threatened in order to freeze a detainee.) The FBI had deemed Ojeda Rios a terrorist, effectively dehumanizing him long before the shooting began. The FBI detained a pro-independence activist named Orlando González-Claudio while he was driving in his car on 20 April 2016, reported Puerto Rican journalist Carmelo Ruiz. DNA samples were taken from González-Claudio.[98] The FBI took DNA samples from other pro-independence activists during that same week in April. Carmelo Ruiz reports, "Many *independentistas* suspect that these U.S. government moves also have the purpose of intimidating and undermining popular struggles against neoliberal austerity measures that the government is imposing in response to the wishes of bondholders who want to collect on the island's ballooning $72 billion public debt."[99] On May Day 2019, hundreds of U.S. citizens marched in San Juan's financial district against D.C.'s fiscal control board. Puerto Rico pushes back, an example to all.

In addition to suffering political persecution, Puerto Rico is used as a sweatshop of sorts. Stateside, the War Department utilizes the Thirteenth Amendment to the U.S. Constitution, which permits slavery as punishment for a crime. Therein, prison labor provides the War Department with cheap products, ranging from body armor to clothing.[100] (The prison system in the United States is an annual $182 billion drain on taxpayers, with much of that money going toward corporate greed. Nationally, roughly six percent of corrections spending goes toward education, even though educating prisoners is very cost effective.[101]) Abroad, the Department of War has purchased clothing from unscrupulous and inhumane contractors.[102] Deals for clothing, uniforms, and footwear produced at factories in Puerto Rico appear regularly in the Pentagon's contract announcements.[103]

Contracts for clothing and gear manufactured in Puerto Rico continued to be issued after Hurricane Maria struck. The Pentagon made sure the companies making its uniforms were up and running. The rest of Puerto Rico didn't receive such concern.

Pentaq Manufacturing (Sabana Grande), M&M Manufacturing (Lajas), Puerto Rico Apparel Manufacturing (Mayagüez), or PRAMA, and Propper International (Mayagüez) are some of the leading manufacturers of U.S. military uniforms, from physical fitness uniforms to parkas. Pentaq, M&M, PRAMA, and Propper have made uniforms for Afghanistan's military and national police. (In mid-2017, the Special Inspector General for Afghanistan Reconstruction called out the Pentagon for spending $28 million on "forest" pattern uniforms for the Afghan National Army; 97.9% of Afghanistan is not wooded.[104]) Sitnasuak, an Alaskan Native Corporation, owns API LLC. As you've seen, Native Corporations are often granted a preferable bidding process. Though its parent company is headquartered in Alaska, API LLC is based in Puerto Rico, capitalizing on the pliable labor force. API LLC has produced military apparel, load carrying equipment, and duffel bags. Sitnasuak also owns Aurora Industries of Camuy, Puerto Rico. In recent years Aurora has produced military uniforms, apparel, and duffel bags. Many other manufacturers of clothing and small equipment dot the colony.[105] Some have headquarters or other manufacturing locations within the mainland. Some operate entirely in the colony. One example is illustrative: In 1998, two Israelis were charged with defrauding the Pentagon.[106] Their headquarters were in Brooklyn, New York. Their textile plant was in Puerto Rico.

Contracts with work taking place in Puerto Rico must be seen as part of the neoliberal economic policies D.C. has used when dealing with Latin America in general: Under the rules of the game, capital can move freely across borders, because it benefits the structures of authority (in Wall Street, war corporations, and the Pentagon). Undesirable humans and excess population are not allowed, under these same rules, to move freely across borders.

Formal MIC jurisdiction grows. By the end of 2018, the Pentagon had solidified its bureaucratic control over Army Reserve units in Puerto Rico, forming them into a new Army Reserve Caribbean Geographical Command.[107] In January 2019, the Pentagon used this new Command to deploy Puerto Ricans in the Army Reserve to Afghanistan.[108] On 27 September 2019, the Army issued a contract to build a new Reserve training building on Fort Buchanan in San Juan, and an Atlanta firm took over a decent portion of maintenance, repair, and administrative services for the 81st Reserve Division in Puerto Rico. But don't worry, Puerto Rico. The Pentagon named a boat after you.[109]

GUANTÁNAMO: OCCUPIED TERRITORY

Established in 1903, Naval Station Guantánamo Bay (NSGB) is one of the War Department's longest-running overseas facilities. *Guantánamo* means "land between the rivers" in Taíno, an indigenous language spoken in the Caribbean.[110] The naval station expanded institutionally, financially, and geographically as a detention camp for immigrants in the early 1990s.[111] CIA and the War Department used it as a prison after the 9.11 attacks. Most Muslim men imprisoned aboard NSGB had not been captured by U.S. forces.[112] Even under D.C.'s brutal legal posture, only 9 out of 779 Muslim men kidnapped and brought to Guantánamo were charged with any criminal activity.[113]

On the campaign trail, Barack Obama swore he would close the prison at Guantánamo Bay. (Let's assume he was genuine about this campaign pledge.) He never got it done. The conventional wisdom states that President Obama failed because of domestic politics, bipartisan obstructionism, and the intricate legal process surrounding the transfer of prisoners. Those factors certainly played a major role. Another factor is the MIC. Corporations pitched a variety of upgrades to NSGB. Eager to maintain the overseas garrison, the Pentagon poured millions of dollars into renovating and improving the naval station.[114] This soon settled into a fluid, well-paced contracting sequence. Infrastructure upgrades came quickly.

On 13 April 2016, Leidos was put in charge of providing interpreters, translators, stenographers, and court reporters to assist case preparations within the Office of Military Commissions in Virginia and Guantánamo. Let's be clear: A corporation that pressures (using lobbying and campaign financing) Capitol Hill in favor of war then sells services to aid D.C.'s prosecution of those who got rolled up in D.C.'s wars. Leidos also happens to sell plenty of goods and services to corporatized intelligence agencies monitoring global communications. Industry officials could easily portray construction as "jobs." Lest this be viewed positively, it should be emphasized: A dollar spent on clean energy, education, healthcare, or infrastructure creates more jobs than a dollar spent on military matters.[115] From aircraft maintenance and IT to physical education and construction, the message is clear: military operations at Guantánamo go full steam, and no transient president has the political muscle or the institutional capability of stopping it.

Base operation support services (BOSS) keep a military installation up and running, and usually involve a combination of the custodial arts, grounds maintenance, facility upkeep, emergency services, pest control, and minor vehicle service. Corporations that have sold BOSS for Guantánamo include IAP, Centerra, G4S, and a joint venture between Burns & Roe and EMCOR known as BREMCOR. Roughly one-third of people living at the naval station are guest workers from countries like Jamaica and the Philippines[116] who carry out the BOSS tasks. Sysco has kept U.S. personnel fed well aboard the naval station.

Construction and infrastructure projects for Naval Station Guantánamo Bay continued after Obama left office: laying fiber optic cable linking U.S. government facilities in Guantánamo Bay and Puerto Rico; supplying medical equipment and software; renovating the Tierra Kay housing area in which U.S. troops reside; building new schools (pre-K through high school); upgrading the Villamar substation; renovating an aviation hangar; building a new solid waste facility, and building a new fire station.

Construction projects are a useful indicator of policies the MIC would like to see implemented. On 22 February 2018, RQ Construction was contracted to build a Mass Migration Complex at Naval Station Guantánamo Bay.[117] The contract included *ten* potential options—options are extensions to an initial contract—for more construction on the site. A SOUTHCOM spokesperson claimed, "There are no detention facilities involved in this project,"[118] yet the very nature of the project (building sprawling concrete pads, establishing sites for tents, and installing a mass public address system) says otherwise. Such infrastructure could be converted overnight to a fortified detention facility. Who will be housed there? Anyone military and industry are able to deem a "threat"—like *Special Interest Aliens*, a new category of threat concocted by unelected bureaucrats. A Special Interest Alien is a foreign national from a country with potential or established terrorist links. On 20 April 2018, the War Department allocated more money to expand the Legal Complex at NSGB. More facilities to process enemies foretells ongoing, undiscerning, worldwide military operations. Legal proceedings aboard NSGB cost millions of dollars annually. The corporatized military presence at Guantánamo is going nowhere. Like every other outpost, Naval Station Guantánamo Bay is a mecca for war corporations. Except at Guantánamo they've had longer to dig in.

ENDEMIC TUNNEL VISION

The MIC's wars mirror one another. U.S. military and industry train military and police forces across Latin America and the Middle East. MIC elites frame their War on Drugs and War on Terror as a "responsibility" that the U.S. has to the rest of the world. The MIC always frames corruption in the Middle East and Latin America as a major obstacle to success (ignoring the corruption inherent to the MIC operations there). The MIC supports tackling the supply side (pursuing narcotics traffickers and whack-a-mole-ing "terrorist leaders"), while never addressing the U.S. demand for narcotics or capitalists' demand for the fruits of war. U.S. military installations in Central America are patterned after U.S. bases in Iraq and Afghanistan, and U.S. military compounds in northern Mexico are modeled after U.S. "fusion intelligence centers" in Afghanistan.[119] Even U.S. personnel cross over from the War on Terror to the War on Drugs.[120] MIC officials cite the porous Colombia-Venezuela border as a prime shipping point for cocaine and "terror" activities. Similarly, the porous Afghanistan-Pakistan border is often cited as teeming with terrorist activity and narcotics. MIC officials conveniently view borders, not policy, as the problem. Both the War on Drugs and the War on Terror involve hyping amorphous, unsubstantiated threats. Drugs and terror are blended together until, now, *narco-terrorists* are the main threat in the Hemisphere.

And with borders comes profit.

The war industry's military power—as projected through the U.S. Armed Forces—increases emigration; men, women, and children flee their treasured homes in order to get away from D.C.'s wars. Those fleeing don't want to leave. They're forced to leave.[121] Then military and industry use potential immigration of these refugees into the U.S. as a fear-inducing reason to spend even more money on wars abroad and surveillance technology, IT, "intelligence" software, contractors, and militarized borders at home. MIC elites crafting and imposing the policy of war become so wealthy that they can move, fly, and generally avoid any face-to-face, hard consequences of their policies. They're protected—for the time being—by members of the very working class (including cops, mercenaries, FBI, DHS, and other enforcers) that D.C. has neglected by forsaking programs of social uplift in favor of endless, for-profit war.

U.S. military flag officers are a party to this destruction and militarization, home and abroad.

Since the end of the Cold War, every single officer who has commanded SOUTHCOM—from George Joulwan at General Dynamics to John Kelly at Beacon Global and Caliburn International (owned by DC Capital Partners)—has moved from military to industry.

At the beginning of this chapter, we were introduced to Admiral Kurt Tidd, the latest commanding general of U.S. Southern Command, by citing how he spread fear and hyped various "threats" to the U.S. emanating from the south. Well, now the Admiral helps us close the chapter:

> What these groups are really engaged in is an assault on the rule of law, and everything it stands for. This assault comes in many forms... We see it in the corruption of institutions and government officials. And we see it in the slowly expanding spaces of lawlessness, alternative order, and criminal control... The cumulative effects of these groups eats (*sic*) away at core democratic values.[122]

No, Admiral Tidd was not describing how the MIC harms U.S. democracy. He was hyping threats to justify SOUTHCOM's existence, just as the war industry hypes threats to justify weapon procurement and exorbitant military budgets. Lest you worry that the great power competition meme does not apply in the Western Hemisphere, SOUTHCOM commanders have fearmongered Russia and China prominently to Congress.[123]

Tunnel vision is the name of the game. Regarding an "anti-American regime" in South America, Tidd states, "... the political, economic, and humanitarian crisis in Venezuela worsens by the day. Its citizens (especially the most vulnerable) are suffering. The health care system has nearly collapsed. Child malnutrition rates are past the crisis threshold and infant mortality rates have risen sharply. Some reports suggest that 93% of Venezuelans claim they cannot afford the food they need."

So the MIC focuses on that, but not on genuine threats to the public: The political, economic, and humanitarian crisis in the United States worsens by the day. Its citizens (especially the most vulnerable) are suffering. Though it has the highest GDP in the world, neither political faction advocates for free healthcare for the citizens. The present healthcare system benefits the pharmaceutical and insurance industries. Roughly 85% of Americans lack essential vitamins.[124] Infant mortality rates have risen sharply.[125] Most U.S. workers live paycheck to paycheck.[126] In no state can a person earning minimum wage afford a 2-bedroom apartment.[127] The wealth gap is astonishing.[128] Some reports suggest that half of people in the United States are poor or low income.[129] Poverty is rampant.[130]

Real threats to national security—endemic poverty, systemic pillaging of the Treasury by a rapacious industry, and D.C.'s corruption—were not on Tidd's radar.

The only people who ultimately benefit from the militarized drug war are perfidious flag officers, the D.C. regime, executives in war corporations, and a few Latin American elites. The colony of Puerto Rico is nothing more than fertile recruiting ground and a sweatshop in the eyes of military and industry. Naval Station Guantánamo Bay is a profitable outpost of many. The war industry hypes threats, which the War Department eagerly hops aboard in order to sustain hegemony in the hemisphere. Weapon sales to Latin American governments ice a rich cake. Analysis undertook in this chapter—breaking down how the war industry profits via a command's lines of effort, locations, task forces, exercises, and operations—can be done with any of the bigger combatant commands. SOUTHCOM is a good example precisely because it's a smaller command. The other, bigger commands possess more corporate products, more ties to war corporations, and other forms of violence. Industry has a field day with U.S. combatant commands.

The Puerto Rican independence leader Pedro Albizu Campos once noted, "We live in the era of the scientific savage, where all the wisdom of science, mathematics and physics are used for the purposes of assassination."[131] His words were accurate then and now.

ENDNOTES

1 No, Obama was not a significant aberration to this trend. See Alexander, Michelle. "Obama's Drug War." *The Nation*. 9 December 2010; Corones, Mike. "Tracking Obama's deportation numbers." *Reuters*. 25 February 2015; and Harrington, Rebecca. "Obama deported 3 million immigrants during his presidency—here's how Trump's new immigration order compares." *Business Insider*. 22 February 2017. The Obama administration did, however, allow states to legalize cannabis and helped pass the Fair Sentencing Act, an improvement on existing laws.

2 See Douglas Valentine's *The CIA As Organized Crime* (Atlanta, GA: Clarity Press, 2017, pp. 175-223) for thorough analysis of CIA's role in the war on drugs.

3 In industry parlance, a war corporation merely offers and expedites unique military platforms, personnel, systems and capabilities that support federal agencies and foreign security forces involved in counter-narcotics missions.

4 "After 40 years, $1 trillion, U.S. War on Drugs has failed to meet any of its goals." *Associated Press*. 13 May 2010. The *AP* found that the U.S. "repeatedly increased budgets for programs that did little to stop the flow of drugs… 'Current policy is not having an effect of reducing drug use, but it's costing the public a fortune,' says Harvard economist Jeffrey Miron."

5 "Posture Statement of Admiral Kurt W. Tidd, Commander, United States Southern Command." *115th Congress—Senate Armed Services Committee*. 15 February 2018. Later in his tenure as Commander of SOUTHCOM, Tidd began frowning upon the phrase *economy of force*: "I like to think of us an elite welterweight punching above our weight class and able to go after problems as they present themselves." Garamone, Jim. "Central, South American Nations Demonstrate Power of Democracy." *U.S. Department of Defense*. 21 November 2018.

6 "Operation & Maintenance Overview Fiscal Year 2016 Budget Estimates." *Office of the Under Secretary of Defense (Comptroller) / Chief Financial Officer*. February 2015, p. 104.

7 "Posture Statement of Admiral Kurt W. Tidd, Commander, United States Southern Command." *115th Congress—Senate Armed Services Committee*. 15 February 2018.

8 For example, on 10 Feb 2016, eight corporations sold "training support services, equipment, material, instruction, and products to improve U.S. and partner nation agencies' capability and expertise to detect, deter, disrupt, and degrade national security threats posed by illegal drugs, trafficking, piracy, transnational organized crime, threat finance networks, and any potential nexus among these activities."

9 Western banks have laundered money for drug cartels. See Farrell, Greg. "HSBC Sued Over Drug Cartel Murders After Laundering Probe." *Bloomberg*. 9 February 2016. Protess and Silver-Greenberg. "HSBC to Pay $1.92 Billion to Settle Charges of Money Laundering." *The New York Times*. 10 December 2012. Taibbi, Matt. "Outrageous HSBC Settlement Proves the Drug War Is a Joke." *Rolling Stone*. 13 December 2012. Smith, Michael. "Banks Financing Mexico Drug Gangs Admitted in Wells Fargo Deal." *Bloomberg*. 29 June 2010. Fitzpatrick, Dan. "Bank Accounts Figure in Drug Probe." *Wall Street Journal*. 9 July 2012.

10 "Among the laundering tactics the Pentagon uses: So-called 'one-year money'—funds that Congress intends to be spent in a single fiscal year—gets shifted into a pool of five-year money. This maneuver exploits the fact that federal law does not require the return of unspent 'five-year money'

during that five-year allocation period," per Dave Lindorff "Exclusive: The Pentagon's Massive Accounting Fraud Exposed." *The Nation.* 27 November 2018.

11 The fear sown prior to Tidd's testimony was notable. Think tanks polished SOUTHCOM's activities with a pseudo-intellectual sheen, confining the narrative inside the Beltway to emphasize the utility of military options as often the best way to pursue "U.S. interests" in the Western Hemisphere. Relevant reports and studies include CSIS' "Alternative Governance in the Northern Triangle and Implications for U.S. Foreign Policy," issued 18 Sept 2015; CSIS' "Why Venezuela Should be a U.S. Foreign Policy Priority," issued 17 Aug 2017; CNAS' "Security Through Partnership: Fighting Transnational Cartels in the Western Hemisphere," issued 21 March 2011; Heritage Foundation's "Top Priorities for U.S. Policy Toward Latin America and the Caribbean in 2016," issued 29 Jan 2016; Brookings' "Rethinking Latin America's Development Strategy," issued 19 April 2010; and Brookings' "State Capacity in Latin America," issued 20 April 2010, among many others. The promotion of military solutions to social problems is a key feature of think tanks. While this brief collection is not a quantitative study of all think tank publications over time, a cursory qualitative analysis indicates no publications from war industry think tanks foreswearing military approaches to the drug war or the hemisphere in general.

12 "Posture Statement of Admiral Kurt W. Tidd, Commander, United States Southern Command."

The war industry screeds, laid months and years in advance, that support Tidd's contention are too many to count. A few examples are illustrative: Asher, David and Scott Modell. "U.S. Must Push Back against Threat Posed by Iran's Global Revolutionary Network Say Authors of CNAS Report." *Center for a New American Security.* 6 September 2013; "Violence and Terrorism in Latin America in a Global Context: An Overview." *Hudson Institute.* 24 August 2017; Quintana, Ana and Charlotte Florance. "Regions of Enduring Interest: Latin America, the Caribbean, and Africa." *2015 Index of U.S. Military Strength.* D.C.: The Heritage Foundation, 2015; Benjamin, Daniel. "Is Iran about to unleash a wave of terrorism against the United States?" *Brookings Institution.* 13 August 2015; Kopp, Jason. "As Islamic extremism grows in Latin America, some want Trump to take action." *Fox News.* 31 March 2017; and Ottolenghi, Emanuele. "Hezbollah in Latin America is a threat the U.S. cannot ignore." *Foundation for the Defense of Democracies.* 11 June 2017. Note the overlap among war industry think tanks and pro-Zionist operatives regarding Hezbollah.

13 Available at <waronirrationalfear.com/facts>. "Six Americans have died per year at the hands, guns, and bombs of Islamic terrorists (foreign and domestic)," *Business Insider* reported ("How likely are foreign terrorists to kill Americans? The odds may surprise you," 31 January 2017).

14 Beauchamp, Zack. "You're more likely to be killed by your own clothes than by an immigrant terrorist." *Vox.* 26 June 2017. The "chance of being murdered in an attack committed by an illegal immigrant is an astronomical 1 in 10.9 *billion* per year," the *CATO Institute* concedes (Alex Nowrasteh. "Terrorism and Immigration: A Risk Analysis." 13 September 2016).

15 Professor Stephen Graham in *Cities Under Siege* (London: Verso, 2011, p. 134) explains *forward defense*: "Homeland security is thus increasingly seen as an 'away game.'"

16 Those murdered were Candelaria Trapp Nelson, a mother of six; Juana Jackson Ambrosia, a mother of two; Hasked Brooks Wood; and Emerson Martínez, a father of one. Nelson and Ambrosia were pregnant at the time of their murders. Glaser, John. "U.S. DEA Agents Kill up to Six Civilians in Honduras." *Antiwar.com.* 16 May 2012. Buncombe, Andrew. "Video shows U.S. commando-style operation that killed four Honduran civilians after five-year cover-up by Washington." *The Independent.* 24 October 2017. Lakhani, Nina. "U.S. admits DEA lied about Honduras 'massacre' that killed four villagers." *The Guardian.* 25 May 2017. Professor Dana Frank (*The Long Honduran Night.* Chicago: Haymarket Books, 2018) explains on Chris Hedges' show *On Contact* (*RT America,* 8

December 2018) that the Honduran military and private mercenaries on behalf of foreign corporations (sweatshop owners, plantation owners, etc.) kill Honduran citizens who protest the status quo. Frank explains that President Barack Obama and Secretary of State Hillary Clinton backed the 2009 coup against Honduran President Manuel Zelaya through creative diplomatic wording and an eventual increase in funding to the Honduran regime. I add intelligence support to that list. Leon Panetta was only a few months into his job as director of CIA at the time of the coup. It is unclear how much the Directorate of Operations (a.k.a. the "National Clandestine Service") and its chief Jose Rodriguez clued Panetta in during the run-up to the coup. The Honduran military stormed Zelaya's home in the early hours of the morning and put him on a plane to Costa Rica. Zelaya wasn't a leftist, but he did favor some relatively progressive measures (backing some labor rights, halting some privatization, putting a survey measure about constitutional convention on the ballot) that angered D.C. economic interests and Honduran elites. These elites doubled down, post-coup, on their program of assassinating labor organizers and campesinos, boosting their paramilitary forces, increasing mining concessions to giant Western corporations, removing subsistence agriculture in favor of palm oil, sowing commodity goods, pushing for privatizing public education, and increasing the use and abuse of local labor in maquiladoras / "export processing zones."

17 The *New Yorker*'s Mattathias Schwartz ("A Mission Gone Wrong," 29 December 2013) indicates the helicopter was a Huey.

18 Interventions include Bolivia 1964; Brazil 1961; Chile 1973; Costa Rica; Dominican Republic 1963; Ecuador 1960; El Salvador 1980; Grenada 1983; Guatemala 1954; Guyana 1953; Haiti 1959, 1987, 1994-1995, 2004; Honduras and Nicaragua in the 1980s; Honduras 2009; México and Colombia 1980s-present, most intensely; Panamá 1900s, 1989; Perú 1965; Uruguay 1969; Venezuela 2002, 2018-present. This is an abbreviated list. Earlier incarnations of SOUTHCOM controlled the Panamá Railroad by force, providing logistics and transportation to a variety of illicit actions like the 1954 coup in Guatemala. One of the better books on U.S. actions in Guatemala in the 1950s is *Bitter Fruit* (New York: Doubleday & Co., 1983), written by Stephen Kinzer and Stephen Schlesinger. Panamá's creation dates back to D.C.'s desire for land to facilitate the transportation requirements of empire. Historian Daniel Immerwahr explains, U.S. Navy Captain Alfred Thayer Mahan "suggested opening a canal through the Central American isthmus... and [Teddy] Roosevelt agreed. He tried to buy territory from Colombia, without luck. He tried threatening and got no further." So Roosevelt "threw his support behind rebels, who declared Panama's independence from Colombia" (*How To Hide an Empire*, p. 280).

19 Baker, Chelsea. "South Carolina Guard, Colombian army hold artillery exchange." *U.S. Department of Defense*. 20 November 2017.

20 Industry officials often use the phrase "technology transfers" instead of "arms sales." Pentagon officials follow suit, mentioning "technology transfers" as one of the "common interests" uniting Latin America and USA.

21 Panetta confirmed on his stop in Colombia that the U.S. "is prepared to facilitate the sale of 10 helicopters," five Lockheed Martin UH-60 helicopters and five others, "to help Colombia's governmental efforts against the FARC." Pellerin, Cheryl. "Panetta Promises Continued Support to Colombia." *American Forces Press Service*. 22 April 2012.

22 "Boeing, Super Hornet Suppliers Tour Brazilian Companies." *Boeing Media Room*. 13 April 2012.

23 Garamone, Jim. "Panetta Calls for Closer Military Relations With Brazil." *American Forces Press Service*. 25 April 2012.

24 "Brazil – F/A-18E/F Super Hornet Aircraft." Transmittal No. 09-35. *Defense Security Cooperation Agency*. 6 August 2009.

25 "Boeing, U.S. Navy Deliver Proposal to Equip Brazil's Air Force With Super Hornets." *Boeing Media Room.* 3 February 2009.

26 "U.S.-Brazil Defense Cooperation Agreement." *Office of the Spokesman of the U.S. Department of State.* 12 April 2012.

The State Department's summary of its text stressed the need to (1) cooperate in "the fields of research and development, logistics support, technology security, and the acquisition of defense products and services"; (2) exchange information "on topics such as operational experiences, defense technology, and international peacekeeping operations"; (3) promote combined training and military exercises, in addition to exchanging military students and instructors and conducting port calls; (4) collaborate "relating to military systems and equipment"; (5) and, quite openly, promote "commercial initiatives related to defense matters."

27 Pellerin, Cheryl. "Panetta: U.S., Brazil Partnership 'Is the Future.'" *American Forces Press Service.* 26 April 2012.

28 Pellerin, Cheryl. "U.S., Brazil Launch New Defense Cooperation Dialogue." *American Forces Press Service.* 24 April 2012.

29 Pellerin, Cheryl. "U.S., Brazil Launch New Defense Cooperation Dialogue."

30 Borger, Julian. "Brazilian president: U.S. surveillance a 'breach of international law.'" *The Guardian.* 24 September 2013.

31 McLaughlin, Tim. "Snub of Boeing-made fighter rattles Missouri manufacturers." *Reuters.* 21 December 2013.

32 Boeing's St. Louis branch later sold missiles to Brazil on multiple occasions, including parts and spares. One of BAE Systems' North America branches (York, PA) has upgraded Brazil's armored personnel carriers, sold Brazil amphibious assault vehicles, and repaired the country's howitzers. CAE sold flight-training devices. CAS Inc. (Huntsville, AL), Iron Mountain Solutions (Madison, AL), and Quantitech (Huntsville, AL) have helped bring Brazil into the U.S. Army's Utility Helicopter project office, which works heavily with the Lockheed Martin UH-60 helicopter. Engility (Chantilly, VA) sold acquisition management software, engaging Brazilian reps vis-à-vis Naval Air Warfare Center locations. Dillion Aero (Scottsdale, AZ) sold mini-gun parts, training included. Druck LLC (Billerica, MA) sold upgrades for air data test sets. General Dynamics' presence in Sorocaba, Brazil, west of São Paulo, does a strong business. As does L3's office in Rio de Janeiro. L3 sold sonar and other goods. Separately, L3's old Vertex Aerospace branch in Madison, MS, provided maintenance, logistics, upgrades, and repairs to the U.S. Air Force C-12 aircraft in Brazil. SAIC has helped maintain Brazil's fleet of Lockheed Martin MH-60 helicopters. Lockheed Martin has also helped manage the supply chain for tires on Brazilian aircraft. Raytheon sold torpedoes and thermal imaging sensors. The list goes on.

33 Boyle, Alan. "Boeing and Brazil's Embraer set terms for commercial (and defense) joint venture." *Geek Wire.* 17 December 2018.

34 The Commander of SOUTHCOM noted, "The State Partnership Program is an opportunity to accelerate the transformation of our security relationship with Brazil…" Brazilian Navy Rear Admiral Guilherme da Silva Costa stated, "There has been a long-standing partnership between the armed forces from both our countries exchanging experiences and knowledge, training together, fighting together… With the State Partnership Program, by the exchange of experiences, both sides will be able to enlarge capacities, so as to better serve our countries, better serve our people." Goldenberg, Col. Richard. "Signing ceremony formalizes New York and Brazil partnership." *New York National Guard.* 15 March 2019.

35 "In 2012, 80% of cocaine destined for the United States passed through the region, doubling its share from 2009," the 8-14 issue of *The Economist* reported (p. 35). "Much of it arrived on the

Mosquito Coast of Honduras going up the northern coast and through San Pedro Sula, which became the world's most violent city."

36 Lakhani, Nina. "Honduras and the dirty war fuelled by the west's drive for clean energy." *The Guardian*. 7 January 2014.

37 In autumn 2013, for example, a Colombian military delegation met with officials from Textron and the U.S. government in Louisiana to discuss FMS. The country program manager for the SOUTHCOM directorate within U.S. Army Security Assistance Command (USASAC) explains the benefits: "The in-progress review provided the customer an in-depth overview of the case and provided an opportunity for the customer and vendor to better define the requirements... One of the most important aspects of a face-to-face meeting is building relationships with the partner nation... This allows the customer to interact with the personnel who are developing their case and also helps to provide assurance that if they have any questions or concerns, they have a team of subject matter experts standing by to assist in meeting their mission requirements..." Quoted in Stevenson, Paul J. "Colombians review Foreign Military Sales case" (*USASAC*, 26 November 2013). Lt. Gen. (ret.) William Phillips explains this process more broadly: "Don't be afraid to talk to industry. Pull industry in. Do that early, up front. Make sure they have a chance to look at your requirements and then give you feedback on those requirements... Bring 'em in one-on-one. Have discussions with them." Lt. Gen. Phillips once led U.S. Army acquisition of industry goods. He's now a Boeing vice president. He was quoted in "Boeing's Phillips on Army Programs, Chinook Cut, Futures Command, Program Management Advice" (*Defense & Aerospace Report*, 15 April 2019).

38 *The New York Times* (Nicholas Casey, 17 May 2019) explains: The government's promise to help rural areas with infrastructure, education, and utilities was a major reason the rebels stood down. The govt. never came through with this promise. Since the peace deal was signed, at least 500 activists and community leaders have been killed, and more than 210,000 people displaced from their homes amid the continuing violence. That undercuts a core selling point of the deal: that it would bring safety and stability." Many militants have taken up arms again. See also "Colombia: Missing Farc leader Iván Márquez re-appears on video" (*BBC News*, 13 January 2019) and "Colombia murders: Anger as indigenous leaders are buried" (*BBC News*, 14 August 2019). The ceasefire was supposed to provide space and opportunity for the state to better share resources and authority. Instead, the state seized the ceasefire to inflict violence (sometimes with SOUTHCOM's knowledge).

39 Garamone, Jim. "Central, South American Nations Demonstrate Power of Democracy." *U.S. Department of Defense*. 21 November 2018. This phrase came into fashion when War Secretary (and former DCI) Robert Gates used it to describe Colombia in spring 2010. Secretary Panetta used the phrase in his April 2012 tour of Latin America, Secretary Hagel said the same in Oct 2014, and Secretary Carter said the same in 2016.

40 "The Colombian military benefitted from" SOUTHCOM's "internal controls and training," a Pentagon scribe said, describing Tidd's view. Accomplished, trained, increasingly well-rounded, the Colombian military is "working in Central America to help these militaries to deal with internal security challenges, and at the same time incorporating this fundamental respect for human rights." Tidd goes on to credit SOUTHCOM as having played a key role in this apparent transformation. "We have worked side by side with them for decades, and now our Colombian partners are shoulder to shoulder with us, very capable and mature in their leadership... They are able to play important security roles helping other countries develop their own capabilities. It really has become what folks hoped for and dreamed about years ago." Garamone, Jim. "Central, South American Nations Demonstrate Power of Democracy."

41 "Relations with Colombia." *North Atlantic Treaty Organization*. Accessed 31 May 2018: <www.nato.int/cps/ic/natohq/topics_143936.htm>. U.S. war corporations even find a way to benefit

when Colombia purchases aircraft from rival country's war industry. The A-29 Super Tucano, made by a Brazilian corporation, is supported by technology from Sierra Nevada Corporation (Mary Esther, FL).

42 Private war corporations like DynCorp have dumped carcinogenic glyphosate from airplanes in Latin American nations. DynCorp threw enormous legal and financial resources to deflect criminal charges. See "Ecuador Farmers Sue U.S. Defense Contractor DynCorp over Toxic Fumigation" (*Telesur*, 3 April 2017). Chevron, which polluted the Ecuadorian Amazon, has followed the same playbook, throwing legal might and financial resources at those who resist, Clifford Krauss ("Big Victory for Chevron Over Claims in Ecuador." *The New York Times*. 4 March 2014) makes clear. For a thorough analysis of Chevron's legal actions against some indigenous peoples in Ecuador, consult "Chevron Arbitration Ruling Against Ecuador 'Completely Off Base'" (*The Real News Network*, 17 September 2018).

43 "'It's been sheer hell,' said Ralph Ponticelli, the father of one of the pilots killed. 'We are just not satisfied.' ... Family members, former pilots and a high-ranking official who worked with contractors for years in Colombia contend that the contract switch was aimed at shielding Northrop Grumman from liability." Forero, Juan. "Private U.S. Operatives on Risky Missions in Colombia." *The New York Times*. 14 February 2004.

44 Corporations running counter-narcotics operations in the skies over Colombia can bill the U.S. War Dept. for flight hours, maintenance, operations, and development, testing & evaluation of aircraft ground systems. Relevant contracts include 28 Aug 2014, 29 Sept 2014, 26 June 2015, 27 Sept 2018—all awarded without open, free, and fair competition.

45 "Joint Press Briefing by Secretary Hagel and Minister Pinzon in Colombia." *U.S. Department of Defense*. 10 October 2014. For more information, see Cronk, Terri Moon. "Hagel Touts Colombia's Role in Helping World Meet Threats." *Defense Media Activity*. 11 October 2014.

46 Garamone, Jim. "Dempsey: Colombia Has Strategy to Take Down Terror Group." *American Forces Press Service*. 29 March 2012.

47 As illustrated in contracts issued 31 Aug 2015, 19 Oct 2016, 2 Oct 2017. Surveillance systems are from Telecommunication Support Systems (Melbourne, FL).

48 U.S. Special Operations Forces are armed with the latest gear from the U.S. war industry, constantly upgraded and marketed anew. Among the equipment that SOCOM contracted in 2016 were Armtec airborne countermeasures, Battelle vehicles, Berry Aviation transportation, Boeing drones, Broadbay Group aviation support, CACI geospatial analysis software, Camgian Microsystems radar, Dillon Aero mini-guns, FLIR Surveillance sensors, IGOV Technologies voice communications, L3 rangefinders and night vision devices, Nammo Talley light anti-armor weapon, Wing Inflatables watercraft, and dozens of other products, big and small. Among the equipment that SOCOM contracted in 2017 were Boeing drones, L3 SATCOM devices, Mustang Survival maritime assault suits, Optics 1 laser range fingers, Raytheon radar, Raytheon tracking software, Rockwell Collins cockpit avionics, SNC counter-IED systems, Textron drones, Trelliswar Technologies radio systems, ViaSat communication gear, and Vigor Works watercraft. Not all of this gear has been seen in Tolemaida.

49 See, *inter alia*, Donna Miles. "Commando competition promotes special ops skills, collaboration." *American Forces Press Service*. 10 June 2012. In 2009, U.S. military and industry teamed up to establish the King Abdullah II Special Operations Training Center (KASOTC), which is located just north of the Jordanian capital of Amman. *The New York Times* reports, "The base was built by a U.S. construction firm on land donated by the king and paid for by a Defense Department program that provides weapons and infrastructure to friendly foreign governments" (Eells, "Sleep-Away Camp for Postmodern Cowboys," 19 July 2013). Like Colombia's National Training Center, KASOTC is a playground for U.S. Special Operations Command, allied and familiar special operations units, and

U.S. mercenaries. Teams compete in tests of marksmanship, endurance, and tactical prowess. From Boeing helicopters to Colt carbines to General Electric engines, U.S. corporate goods and services cover KASOTC. U.S. corporations even sponsor events there, and are allowed to market goods and services to U.S. and allied special operations forces. Corporations typically run training at these sites: ViaGlobal Group (Annapolis, MD) and GovSource (Reston, VA) have run training at KASOTC, and GovSource has coached Iraqi special operations recruits there.

50 "Colombia cocaine production acreage at 'record level.'" *BBC News*. 20 September 2018.

51 Garamone, Jim. "Dempsey: Colombia Has Strategy to Take Down Terror Group." *American Forces Press Service*. 29 March 2012.

52 Wyss, Jim. "Investigations, questions swirl around reports of U.S. military sexual abuse." *Miami Herald*. 7 May 2015. "Colombia to investigate alleged child abuse by U.S. military." *Agence France-Presse*. 6 May 2015.

53 The Pentagon's obstructionism in Colombia parallels the instructions given to U.S. troops in Afghanistan to ignore sexual abuse committed by their Afghan allies. For more on this sexual abuse, see *The New York Times'* Joseph Goldstein ("U.S. Soldiers Told to Ignore Sexual Abuse of Boys by Afghan Allies," 20 September 2015).

54 "Colombian president visits, thanks SOUTHCOM for its support." *U.S. Southern Command*. Release No. 18-003. 25 April 2018.

55 Garamone, Jim. "Southern Command Chief Says South American Allies 'Got Game.'" *U.S. Department of Defense*. 7 June 2018. Colombian President and former War Minister Juan Manuel Santos (a man who studied at the University of Kansas, the London School of Economics, Harvard's School of Government) had recently visited Brussels and toured NATO headquarters in order "to further the nation's position as the first Latin American nation to become a global partner of the alliance."

56 "Foreign Military Financing" (*Security Assistance Monitor*, accessed 16 June 2018).

57 Corporate goods and services sold in recent years to the Mexican military include helicopter and maintenance, GPS navigation systems, auxiliary power units, flight simulators, acquisition support, programmatic support on helicopter projects, IT systems and data/voice networks, cargo aircraft, ejection seat parts, miniguns, land vehicles, integrated warfare systems.

58 Semple, Kirk. "In Mexico, a Truck Full of Corpses Takes a Mystery Road Trip." 18 September 2018.

59 Anarte, Enrique. "Mexico: Election campaign tainted by political violence." 30 June 2018. A 12-month period, roughly August 2017 through August 2018, saw 175 Mexican politicians killed, as reported by the independent news organization *DemocracyNow*: "Mexico: Mayor Assassinated House After Taking Office." 4 January 2019.

60 "Security Aid Pivot Table—Programs: Belize." *Security Assistance Monitor*. Accessed 19 June 2018.

61 Issued 5 Feb 2016.

62 The War Department and DHS personnel fly many war industry products out of CSL Comalapa, including Lockheed Martin C-130, Northrop Grumman E-2, and Boeing P-8A, which replaced the Lockheed Martin P-3 Orion. Details of staffing and war industry products are quoted in "History—Cooperative Security Location Comalapa, El Salvador." *U.S. Navy*. Accessed 15 June 2018. The presence of the P-8A is stated in Wasik, Mallory. "P-8A Poseidon comes to 4th Fleet." *U.S. 4th Fleet Public Affairs*. 29 June 2016. AECOM employees maintain U.S. aircraft at Comalapa. War Dept. operations based out of Comalapa increased steadily after Ecuadorian President Rafael Correa closed the U.S. Air Base in Manta in summer 2009. Ecuador under President Lenín Moreno

reestablished cooperation with the U.S. War Dept. and deepened ties with other U.S. governmental agencies.

63 In industry lingo, operations like Martillo use "persistent surveillance to force traffickers to move their shipping routes into international waters," denying "transnational criminal organizations the ability to move narcotics, precursor chemicals for explosives, bulk cash and weapons along Central American shipping routes."

64 Behind the scenes it involves CIA and tips from NSA, the latter often working in conjunction with U.S. Air Force satellites and reconnaissance aircraft built by the likes of Lockheed Martin or Boeing.

65 The U.S. Navy operates Boeing P-8A out of Central America. The U.S. Air Force operates reconnaissance aircraft (made by Lockheed Martin or Boeing, often featuring L3 technology) throughout Latin America. Airtec (California, MD) supports airborne surveillance out of Bogotá using corporation-owned, corporation-operated Bombardier Dash 8 aircraft. Telecommunication Support Services (Melbourne, FL) provides technical support to SOUTHCOM's Mobile Air Surveillance System. This is run through assets in Colombia and a satellite communications facility in Key West, FL. Harris Corp. (Rochester, NY) provides tactical radios and training in support of counter-narcotics activities. AOC Intel (Chantilly, VA), CULMEN International (Alexandria, VA), METIS Solutions of Arlington, VA—a corporation, like many, backed by private equity investors—and ITA International (Yorktown, VA) support the Air Force's Counter Narco-Terrorism Program office (CNTPO), including its technology development. Hornbeck Offshore Operators (Covington, LA) charters ships for SOUTHCOM. [Charter of HOS Mystique supporting SOUTHCOM and Military Sealift Command was issued 7 Sept 2018 "to provide proof of concept for a single vessel to meet various training, exercise, experimentation, and operational mission support requirements." HOS Mystique was piddling around the western edge of Key West as of 15 Oct 2018.] Hornbeck is owned by private equity and investment firms like D.C. Capital Advisors and Cyrus Capital Partners. The Rockhill Group (Molino, FL) trains and instructs U.S. aircrew at Hurlburt Field and Cannon AFB. Brunswick Commercial & Government Products (Edgewater, FL) sells Boston Whaler boats, parts, and maintenance to interdict drug smugglers on the open water. Metal Shark (Jeanerette, LA) sells near coastal patrol vessels with sensors to SOUTHCOM and allied nations (e.g. Dominican Republic, El Salvador, Honduras). Support Systems Associates (Melbourne, FL) upgrades avionics in RC-26 aircraft, which roam the skies.

66 "In 1917 U.S. citizenship was imposed on all Puerto Ricans. Those who refused citizenship were automatically ostracized," explains Sonia Santiago, a Puerto Rican anti-war leader. "That same year the U.S. entered the First World War and was in desperate need of a large army... Not coincidentally, that same year, 27,786 Puerto Rican men were recruited to fight..." Roughly 90% of the members of the National Guard and Army Reserves in Puerto Rico have been deployed to Afghanistan or Iraq. "Of those, there are about 1,650 maimed [soldiers]." Santiago is quoted in Reyes, Jovanni. "'War is the Antithesis of Motherhood:' A Voice From Puerto Rico." *Common Dreams*. 27 September 2014. Various estimates place the number of Puerto Ricans who enlisted in World War II around 60,000.

67 "In Puerto Rico," historian Daniel Immerwahr notes, "workers moved from faltering sugar plantations to jobs building and operating military bases. By 1950, the federal government had spent $1.2 billion there" (*How To Hide an Empire*, p. 173). "The war had brought military investment in Puerto Rico, but it had also brought soldiers, censorship, the threat of martial law, shipping shortages, and frequent unrest" (p. 243). Notable recent projects include renovating family housing at U.S. Naval Station Roosevelt Roads and reinforcing U.S. military infrastructure in Aguadilla. Relevant contracts

issued 25 Nov 1998, 22 July 2009 (awarded 17 July 2009). Aguadilla is home to the 141st Aircraft Control Squadron, among other U.S. Air Force units.

68 "Army Reserve Giving Back to Puerto Rico (Spanish Version)." *U.S. Army Recruiting*. 8 August 2014: <www.youtube.com/watch?v=iTvZ7GGmYPo>.

69 "People call them terrorists... But terrorists want to terrify a society. These groups have not directed themselves to terrifying the people, but to striking blows against the armed forces of the United States," said Juan Antonio Corretjer in *The New York Times* (Thomas, Jo. "Armed Puerto Rican Groups Focus Attacks on Military." 16 January 1981). Other attacks against sites and personnel supporting the D.C. regime have included: Oct 1979, bomb at federal buildings; Dec 1979, attack on a bus transporting D.C. military personnel west of San Juan; March 1980, shooting officer trainees in San Juan; and July 1980, bombing federal navigation facilities.

70 "Puerto Rico Anti-Military Recruiting Campaign Ignites Independent Movement." *Associated Press*. 30 September 2007.

71 Reyes, Jovanni. "'War is the Antithesis of Motherhood:' A Voice from Puerto Rico." *Common Dreams*. 27 September 2014.

72 Valeria Palet ("Puerto Rico's Invisible Health Crisis." *The Atlantic*. 3 September 2016) reports: "Thousands of residents have alleged that the military's activities caused illnesses. With a population around 9,000, Vieques is home to some of the highest sickness rates in the Caribbean." U.S. Navy denies links between military activity and Vieques' illnesses. See also "Punishing Vieques: Puerto Rico Struggles With Contamination 10 Years After Activists Expel U.S. Navy" (*DemocracyNow*, 2 May 2013). Dr. Spencer Sullivan, medical coordinator for medical research on Vieques, referenced the work of Dr. Carmen Ortiz Roque whose testing of hair samples of Vieques residents revealed toxic levels of heavy metals in their bodies. Sullivan, Spencer. "Helping the helpless in Vieques." *Orlando Sentinel*. 18 January 2018.

73 Relevant contracts issued 23 March 2017, 31 March 2016, 31 July 2014, 14 March 2013, 30 Nov 2017, 13 Aug 2015. Industry giants like CH2M have worked the Superfund sites at the former Vieques Naval Training Range and Naval Ammunition Support Detachment. Conducting "community relations" is part of CH2M's 31 March 2016 deal. On 21 Dec 2015, CH2M Hill was contracted with two other corporations for a possible half-billion-dollar effort for environmental services, location unspecified. The engineering colossus Jacobs acquired CH2M near the end of 2017. USA Environmental (Oldsmar, FL) has also cleaned up Vieques in what the corporation and the Pentagon deem "munitions response action." Industry pollutes, industry cleans up. Region 2 of the Environmental Protection Agency, which includes Puerto Rico, shows up often in War Dept. environmental contracts. For example: 8 Jan 2015 for toxic, hazardous, and radioactive waste remediation; 10 Feb 2016 for environmental remediation; 14 March 2017 to remediate radiological contaminants; 28 April 2017 for environmental remediation services; 2 Feb 2018 for environmental remediation.

74 Pelet, Valeria. "Puerto Rico's Invisible Health Crisis."

75 Relevant Raytheon contracts issued 31 July 2015, 24 Aug 2015, 25 Sept 2017. Related ROTHR facilities are in Virginia (in Chesapeake and Kent) and Texas (in and around Corpus Christi in Freer, Pounce, and Premont). The colony is used for other services, like fuel from San Juan's Airport Aviation Services. Meanwhile, one year of "global business support" in Puerto Rico raked in roughly $65 million for Corporate [mainland] America. (On 24 Aug 2011, corporations received $730 million for 3 years of "global business support." The work on PR amounted to roughly 26.78% of the total contract.) Business support included administrative support and IT; financial management; handling war matériel; helping to operate some military facilities; information & arts; instruction & training; and providing some healthcare services (not doctors and nurses).

76 Cuebas, Maj. Carlos. "Army Reserve investing big in Puerto Rico." *United States Army*. 1 June 2012.

77 Cuebas, Lt. Col. Carlos. "Caribbean Geographical Command is a reality." *U.S. Army 1st Mission Support Command*. 11 December 2018.

78 Cuebas, Maj. Carlos. "Army Reserve investing big in Puerto Rico."

79 In June 2012, the U.S. Army Reserve started building a new Army Reserve Center in the Puerto Nuevo neighborhood of San Juan. This was "part of a larger modernization of the Army Reserve infrastructure across the island." The War Dept. built other costly reserve centers in nearby Fort Buchanan and on the west of the island. Prior to that, new Army Reserve Centers had been opened in the island's east and south (e.g. Ceiba and Juana Díaz). See Cuebas, Major Carlos. "Army Reserve investing big in Puerto Rico" (*United States Army*, 1 June 2012). On 8 May 2017, the Pentagon allocated millions to build entrance barriers at a gas station in Puerto Rico—another example in the ongoing, often ridiculous militarization of the island. A construction firm based out of Ponce is currently building an Army Reserve training facility in Aguadilla.

80 "These three problems will dramatically complicate Puerto Rico's recovery," Lauren Lluveras explains in "Puerto Rico's Bankruptcy Will Make Hurricane Recovery Brutal—Here's Why" (*Truthout*, 30 September 2017). Take food insecurity. Puerto Rico imports more than 85% of its food. Before World War II, Puerto Rico had a sound agricultural base. But industrialization and neoliberal economic policies (not to mention imposition of ponderous multinational agribusiness) gutted Puerto Rico's self-sufficiency. Austerity measures also wrecked medical infrastructure. Hospitals and health care facilities suffered budget cuts. Hospitals went bankrupt, clinics closed, and some doctors left for more comfortable jobs on the mainland. And D.C. capped Medicaid reimbursements.

81 Herz, Ansel. "Wikileaks Haiti: The Earthquake Cables." *The Nation*. 15 June 2011.

82 Aronoff, Kate. "Citigroup drove Puerto Rico into debt. Now it will profit from privatization on the island." *The Intercept*. 21 February 2018.

83 Issued 22 Nov 2017.

84 Weissenstein, Michael. "Puerto Rico grid 'teetering' despite $3.8 billion repair job." *Chicago Tribune*. 30 May 2018.

85 For an explanation of this process, read Richard Wolff "Political Corruption and Capitalism." *Truthout*. 2 February 2014.

86 "Puerto Rico hit by first island-wide blackout since Hurricane Maria." *BBC News*. 18 April 2018.

87 Zambito, Thomas. "Ex-CEO gets home confinement, fined $4.5 million for padding bills on work overseas." *New Jersey Advance Media*. 8 May 2015.

88 Mark Weisbrot ("If You Want Puerto Rico To Recover, Cancel Its Debt." *Common Dreams*. 2 October 2017) also advocates repealing the Jones Act, a federal statute from 1920 concerning maritime commerce from U.S.-to-U.S. ports. There is evidence that the Jones Act in practice harms the Puerto Rican economy.

89 For more details about austerity and resource grabs, consult Noami Klein's *The Battle for Paradise* (Chicago: Haymarket Books, 2018); and "Puerto Rico Anti-Austerity Protests Continue, Defying Police Violence" (*DemocracyNow*, 3 May 2018).

90 "Hurricane Maria 'killed 4,600 in Puerto Rico.'" *BBC News*. 29 May 2018.

91 Whitlock, Craig and Bob Woodward. "Pentagon buries evidence of $125 billion in bureaucratic waste." *Washington Post*. 5 December 2016.

92 Mark Weisbrot, co-director of the *Center for Economic & Policy Research*, explains this well in "Puerto Rico to Receive New Disaster Relief, but Colonial Status Prevents Economic Recovery." *The Real News Network*. 7 June 2019.

93 Perry and Katz. "Is This Any Way to Run a University?" MIT Faculty Newsletter. Vol. XXX, No. 5, May/June 2018.

94 "Toxic Coal Ash Afflicts Puerto Rico and the Dominican Republic." *The Real News Network*. 1 April 2019. "Puerto Rico Faces a Flood of Fracked Gas in Wake of Hurricane Maria." *The Real News Network*. 28 March 2019.

95 The robbery took place in September 1983. Fast forward to 2018: Even within D.C.'s leniency and the lightest regulation imaginable, Wells Fargo has been fined multiple times for alleged criminality. Well Fargo's record includes forcing goods on customers and opening up millions of fraudulent accounts without customer consent. Like criminologist Bill Black says, "The best way to rob a bank is to own one."

96 "Puerto Rican Nationalist Killed in FBI Shootout." *Associated Press*. 24 September 2005.

97 Lakhani, Nina. "U.S. admits DEA lied about Honduras 'massacre' that killed four villagers." *The Guardian*. 25 May 2017.

98 "Afterwards he was released and taken back to his car. The agents would not tell him what were they investigating, and he was not charged with anything." Ruiz, Carmelo. "The New Wave of Repression in Puerto Rico." *Counterpunch*. 6 May 2016.

99 Ruiz, Carmelo. "The New Wave of Repression in Puerto Rico."

100 These jobs could be going to high-paying union workers or, at least, to prisoners being paid a living wage. Writing in *AlterNet*, Mike Elk ("Defense Contractors Using Prison Labor to Build High-Tech Weapons Systems," 28 April 2011) reports on prisoners building missile parts: These workers earn a starting wage of 23 cents/hour and make $1.15/hour, maximum. Nearly 1 in 100 adults are in jail in the U.S. and are exempt from minimum wage laws, creating a sizable captive workforce, Elk reports. In 2013, federal inmates "stitched more than $100 million worth of military uniforms," per Ian Urbina (*The New York Times*, 22 December 2013). For more reporting on the Pentagon and prison labor, see Samee Ali, Safia. "Federal Prison-Owned 'Factories With Fences' Facing Increased Scrutiny." *NBC News*. 4 September 2016; Kelley, Michael B. "More jobs lost as the government decides to have military uniforms made by convicts." *Business Insider*. 7 September 2012; Jordan, Bryant. "Industry Upset Over Prison Defense Contracts." *Military.com*. 19 October 2012; Jane Fox, Emily. "Factory owners: Federal prisoners stealing our business." *CNN Money*. 14 August 2012; and Flounders, Sara. "The Pentagon & slave labor in U.S. prisons." *Workers World*. 6 June 2011.

101 "Every dollar that is spent on prison education... saves 4.5 dollars spent on other costs associated with imprisonment," according to Professor Drew Leder of Loyola University, as detailed in Eddie Conway's reporting for *The Real News Network* ("Prison Programs That Work," 30 December 2018).

102 Urbina, Ian. "U.S. Flouts Its Own Advice in Procuring Overseas Clothing." *The New York Times*. 22 December 2013.

Torture, inhuman working conditions, abuse, unpaid overtime, barefoot and underage workers, lack or absence of safety precautions, and theft of workers' pay has occurred regularly at factories producing goods in Asia that the U.S. military stocks and sells, often at exchanges on base. These exchanges, stores run by the War Department, "do big business, selling more than $1 billion a year in apparel alone. Exempt from the Berry Amendment, the exchanges get more than 90 percent of their clothes from factories outside the United States, according to industry estimates," the *Times* reports. The Berry Amendment obligates the War Dept. to favor U.S. companies when purchasing products (especially textiles, food, and metal).

103 Many PR manufacturing facilities (Sabana Grande, Cabo Rojo, and Lajas) are located in the southwest. Mayagüez is on the west coast. Camuy and Arecibo are along the northwest coast. I have

never seen deals involving factories in Southeast Asia in the Pentagon's daily contract listings, most likely because U.S. corporations subcontract the work to Asian sweatshops.

104 "Pentagon 'wasted $28m' on Afghan camouflaged uniforms." *BBC News*. 21 June 2017.

105 These manufacturers include Altama Footwear (Atlanta, GA), Atlantic Diving Supply (Virginia Beach, VA), Bluewater Defense (Corozal and San Lorenzo), Bronze Star Apparel Group (San Juan), Eagle Industries Unlimited (Fenton, MO), Kandor Manufacturing (Arecibo), Rocky Shoes & Boots (Nelsonville, OH), Short Bark Industries (Vonore, TN), The Original Footwear Co. (Arecibo), Tullahoma Industries (Cabo Rojo), and Wellco Enterprises (Morristown, NJ).

106 They allegedly used poor-quality fabric when making uniforms for the U.S. military. In order to pass tests, they showed inspectors pre-selected samples of quality uniforms, while most of the uniforms shipped were substandard. The Pentagon estimated it lost at least $10 million on the deal, as reported by Joseph Fried in "4 Men Charged With Selling Faulty Uniforms to Pentagon" (*The New York Times*, 7 October 1998).

107 Cuebas, Lt. Col. Carlos. "Caribbean Geographical Command is a reality." *U.S. Army 1st Mission Support Command*. 11 December 2018.

108 "There are approximately 500 Army Reserve-Puerto Rico Soldiers deployed around the world, in countries such as Cuba, Poland, Honduras, Guatemala, Afghanistan, and Texas. Since 2001, the Army Reserve in Puerto Rico has deployed a hundred percent of its units, in support of the needs of the Nation." Quoted in "Caribbean Geographic Command starts off the year with a deployment to Afghanistan" (*United States Army*, 1 January 2019).

109 "Navy to Christen Expeditionary Fast Transport Puerto Rico." *U.S. Department of Defense*. 8 November 2018.

110 Murphy, Jessica Bram. "On life and the pursuit of death in Guantánamo Bay." *The College Hill Independent*. 15 March 2019.

111 Pitzer, Andrea. *One Long Night: A Global History of Concentration Camps*. New York: Little Brown, and Company, 2017.

112 Ackerman, Spencer. "Only three of 116 Guantánamo detainees were captured by U.S. forces." *The Guardian*. 25 August 2015. Most had been captured by various government or warlord factions in Afghanistan and Pakistan. For more on CIA, see Johnson and Mazzetti. "A Window into C.I.A.'s Embrace of Secret Jails" (*The New York Times*, 12 August 2009) and "CIA turned Guantánamo Bay inmates into double agents, ex-officials claim" (*Associated Press*, 26 November 2013).

113 Murphy, Jessica Bram. "On life and the pursuit of death in Guantánamo Bay."

114 NSGB contracts issued in the lead-up to Obama's inauguration include 30 April 2008 construction; several deals issued 17 July 2008; and 29 Sept 2008 design/build Building 1661. Hardliners in the Pentagon's E-ring were eager for NSGB upgrades. Salient construction projects at NSGB during the Obama administration included refurbishing Beacon Tower; designing and building a major medical complex; replacing residential units; refurbishing the Taurman Avenue electrical substation; repairing HVAC systems and roofs; and building fuel storage tanks. Other corporate work at the naval station included but was not limited to increasing capacity to maintain and refuel military aircraft; replacing a pier and a truckload facility; revamping a seawater treatment plant; building a chow hall; and upgrading IT operations.

115 As explained earlier, military construction does provide some jobs, but the jobs are temporary. Worse yet, the entire process—building more infrastructure for the War Dept. and war industry—only extends and exacerbates the militarization of U.S. society and its collective dependency on corporatized military solutions to domestic and international problems. Congressional representatives and communities in California, Florida, North Carolina, Ohio, Pennsylvania, Texas, and Virginia were targeted with the jobs ruse vis-à-vis construction at NSGB. A dollar spent on clean

energy, education, healthcare, or infrastructure creates more jobs than a dollar spent on military matters, as clarified by Heidi Garrett-Peltier "Job Opportunity Cost of War" (*The Watson Institute for International and Public Affairs at Brown University,* 24 May 2017).

116 Rosenberg, Carol. "A Look Inside the Secretive World of Guantánamo Bay." *The New York Times.* 18 July 2019.

117 RQ Construction is no stranger to work at NSGB. The corporation had previously repaired Wharf Bravo and repaved blacktop surfaces around the installation. Stateside, RQ Construction is one of the War Department's favorite building contractors. Its projects have included building a Marine battalion complex at Camp Lejeune, building a battalion facility for special operations units at Joint Base Lewis-McChord in Washington state, and building SEAL facilities in and around San Diego. (Most of the work on SEAL facilities takes place in Coronado, CA, at the "Naval Special Warfare Coastal Campus," long-time SEAL/UDT stomping grounds with a new, lame, corporate-ish name.)

118 Rosenberg, Carol. "Attorney General, Director of National Intelligence tour Guantánamo Bay." *Miami Herald.* 7 July 2017.

119 See Thom Shanker "Lessons of Iraq Help U.S. Fight a Drug War in Honduras" (*The New York Times,* 5 May 2012); and Ginger Thompson "U.S. Widens Role in Battle Against Mexican Drug Cartels" (*The New York Times,* 6 August 2011).

120 The Commander in charge of U.S. military operations in Central America was once in charge of U.S. military operations in Baghdad, per Thom Shanker (*The New York Times,* 5 May 2012). According to Gen. Martin Dempsey, the War Department is sending military personnel with experience in Iraq and Afghanistan to Colombia, because "the challenges they face are not unlike the challenges we've faced in Iraq and Afghanistan." See Garamone, Jim. "Dempsey: Colombia Has Strategy to Take Down Terror Group." *American Forces Press Service.* 29 March 2012.

121 Consider some examples: D.C. supported brutal right-wing paramilitary death squads and military regimes throughout Latin America during the 1970s and 1980s. Families fled north. In the 1990s, D.C. enacted the North American Free Trade Act (NAFTA), which completely wrecked the Mexican economy and the life of the Mexican working class in favor of Wall Street and U.S.-based multinational corporations. Families fled north. Today, humans flee into Europe from Afghanistan, Iraq, Libya, Syria, Yemen, and many other countries that D.C. has destabilized or destroyed, economically and/or militarily. Worldwide, the number of humans fleeing armed conflict is the highest since World War II, as reported by *The New York Times,* citing United Nations' statistics (Cumming-Bruce, Nick. "Number of People Fleeing Conflict Is Highest Since World War II, U.N. Says," 19 June 2019).

122 "Posture Statement of Admiral Kurt W. Tidd, Commander, United States Southern Command." *115th Congress – Senate Armed Services Committee.* 15 February 2018.

123 "Posture Statement of General John F. Kelly, United States Marine Corp, Commander, United States Southern Command." *114th Congress – Senate Armed Services Committee.* 12 March 2015. "Posture Statement of Admiral Kurt W. Tidd, Commander, United States Southern Command." *115th Congress – Senate Armed Services Committee.* 15 February 2018. "Posture Statement of Admiral Craig S. Faller, Commander, United States Southern Command." *116th Congress – Senate Armed Services Committee.* 7 February 2019.

124 Bush, Barbara and Hugh Welsh. "Hidden hunger: America's growing malnutrition epidemic." *The Guardian.* 10 February 2015. "United States of America (The)—Global Database on Child Growth and Malnutrition." *World Health Organization.*

125 "United States of America statistics summary (2002–present)." *World Health Organization.* Accessed 17 June 2018.

126 Picchi, Aimee. "Vast number of Americans live paycheck to paycheck." *CBS News.* 24 August 2017.

"Vulnerability in the Face of Economic Uncertainty." *Prosperity Now*. January 2019.

127 Andone, Dakin and Jessica Campisi. "There's not a single U.S. state where a minimum wage worker can afford a 2-bedroom rental, a report says." *CNN*. 15 June 2018. "How Much do you Need to Earn to Afford a Modest Apartment in Your State?" *National Low Income Housing Coalition*. Accessed 18 June 2018: <https://nlihc.org/oor>.

128 Mishel, Lawrence and Julia Wolfe. "CEO compensation has grown 940% since 1978." *Economic Policy Institute*. 14 August 2019. Available at <www.epi.org/publication/ceo-compensation-2018/>. Fry, Richard and Rakesh Kochhar. "America's wealth gap between middle-income and upper-income families is widest on record." *Pew Research Center*. 17 December 2014. Fu, Lisa. "The Wealth Gap in the U.S. Is Worse Than In Russia or Iran." *Fortune*. 1 August 2017. Thompson, Brian. "The Racial Wealth Gap: Addressing America's Most Pressing Epidemic." *Forbes*. 18 February 2018. Professor Soshana Zuboff (*The Age of Surveillance Capitalism*) notes that amid this devastating inequality, the U.S. populace also faces social inequality like never before: private surveillance capital knows almost everything about you.

129 "Census data: Half of U.S. poor or low income." *CBS News*. 15 December 2011.

130 Alston, Philip. "Extreme poverty in America: read the UN special monitor's report." *The Guardian*. 15 December 2017. Jarvie, Jenny. "UN's poverty and human rights special rapporteur finds U.S. policies reward wealthy, punish poor." *LA Times*. 2 June 2018.

131 Quoted in Immerwahr's *How To Hide an Empire*, p. 259.

9

The Nuclear Arsenal

OGDEN

On Saturday, November 3, 2018, the mayor of a Utah town lay dead on the ground in Afghanistan. An Afghan had opened fire on D.C.'s occupation forces. The mayor hailed from North Ogden and was in Afghanistan with fellow members of the Utah National Guard. The significance of greater Ogden went unnoticed in all press accounts. Ogden is centered just north of Hill Air Force Base. The base is home to the Air Force Sustainment Center and the Air Force Nuclear Weapons Center. One of the largest mainland bases in terms of acreage and population, Hill gives rise to many corporate goods and services. Construction firms in and around Ogden get paid for infrastructure upgrades and expansion at Hill and throughout the U.S. As mayor of North Ogden, the deceased wasn't just another vessel on deployment (his fourth), a vessel through which the most powerful assemblage of corporate interests in world history routes goods and services. He also represented the industry node of Ogden.

The Afghan attacker, reportedly a commando trainee, likely did not know the mayor's full background. To the attacker, the mayor was just one of hundreds of thousands of foreign troops who had rotated through Afghanistan in recent years. Insider attacks like this one that killed the mayor are a steady feature of D.C.'s occupation of Afghanistan, an indicator of the profound antipathy the domestic population has toward the foreign forces. Yet D.C. persists.

The mayor's death is tragic. What is more tragic is that D.C. continues to use and abuse the U.S. citizenry in pursuit of its own ends. Drowning in propaganda (a great deal of which emanates from corporations, think tanks, and PR firms working for the Pentagon), American men and women actually believe they're "serving" the United States when they enlist in the Armed Forces and are deployed around the world, some tasked to occupy a country thousands of miles from the continental United States. On 30 June 2019, yet another Ogden native died in Afghanistan.[1]

BEYOND RECKLESS

What happens when a nuclear weapon detonates? Steel melts, lakes boil, and cities blow away. Radioactive fallout soon poisons the surrounding area—far beyond the blast radius. But the worst is yet to come. A great power competitor has launched retaliatory strikes. Enter nuclear winter. The ash and dust resulting from multiple strikes cloud the atmosphere, preventing photosynthesis. The byproducts of the nuclear reaction wreak havoc on Earth's fragile ozone later. Humanity peters out worldwide.

Human possession of nuclear weaponry is beyond reckless. Did you know the U.S. government set off nuclear weapons *in Earth's atmosphere* during the late fifties and early sixties? (Moscow responded with a string of their own atmospheric tests in autumn 1961 and autumn 1962.) Did you know the U.S. government set off 900 nuclear weapons at the Nevada Test Site between 1951 and 1992? Cancer rates increased dramatically across the Midwest United States. The full effects on humanity and the natural world will never be known. One social media user (YouTube handle: Privacy Lover) accurately captures the horrible idiocy of this situation: The U.S. government detonated nearly 1,000 nuclear bombs *on its own soil* "to protect themselves against someone dropping a nuclear bomb on them?" Elsewhere, U.S. military and industry have regularly polluted the United States with radiation and nuclear waste.[2] This pollution will continue to kill, long into the future.

Humans live life on the brink, but mostly can't fathom it. Though many people are familiar with how close the Cuban Missile Crisis brought us to nuclear war in autumn 1962, there have been many more close calls. In spring 1967, a solar flare and coronal mass ejection messed with some equipment belonging to the North American Aerospace Defense Command. Many high-ranking U.S. military personnel interpreted this as the Soviet Union jamming U.S. radar prior to a nuclear attack. U.S. military personnel advocated for launching a nuclear attack on the Warsaw Pact. Cooler heads prevailed, barely. In autumn 1983, NATO conducted its annual multinational Able Archer exercise. Moscow interpreted the exercise, especially the radio silence and military maneuvers, as preparation for nuclear war. Moscow readied to attack. Fortunately, the exercise soon ended, and humanity lucked out. In January 1995, Norwegian scientists launched a rocket to study the Northern Lights. Russian early warning systems thought the rocket could have been a submarine-launched ballistic missile. The Russian military went on full alert. The decision—launch a strike or not—was on the shoulders of a single human, an alcoholic, Russian President Boris Yeltsin. These are just a handful of examples. And they're taken only from the incidents we know about. Many other mishaps, near misses, and close calls are still classified. Investigative journalist and author Eric Schlosser notes that between 1950 and 1968 "at least

1,200 nuclear weapons had been involved in 'significant' incidents and accidents."³ Recklessness. After U.S. military-industry's poor security practices came to light, the Pentagon classified the extent of its nuclear incompetence.⁴ Here again, secrecy prevents the public from being informed on matters of war.

The opaque nature of Corporate America (working in the secretive nuclear sector) makes understanding the total financial cost of nuclear weapons a difficult task. At a minimum, the U.S. government has spent trillions of dollars since the 1940s on nuclear weapons.⁵ Government neglect abets both the expense and the irresponsibility. The Department of Energy's National Nuclear Security Administration is the federal organization in charge of applying atomic science to military goals. It has corporatized the national weapons labs in charge of nuclear design and testing.⁶ And it does not monitor subcontractors with any scrupulousness. So, in a corporatized environment where profit is a priority, a corporate practice of subcontracting to another war corporation and avoiding a lot of fiscal or regulatory oversight leads to instances of inadequate design and assembling of nuclear components, and abundant opportunity for fraud and waste.

The international campaign known as *Move the Nuclear Weapons Money* cites sixteen major U.S. war corporations involved in producing nuclear weapons and their delivery systems. Running all manner of nuclear weapon production, Boeing, General Dynamics, Honeywell, Lockheed Martin, Northrop Grumman, and Raytheon gain the most from the nuclear weapon sector of the war racket.⁷ Other major beneficiaries are Huntington Ingalls and Jacobs, according to the peace movement *PAX*, as cited by *The Intercept*.⁸

Construction firms and war corporations benefit from regular upgrades to the nuclear infrastructure.⁹ By the time this book hits shelves, the Department of War will have cut the ribbon on its new $1.3 billion nuclear command center at Offutt Air Force Base, Nebraska. Industry played this one well: It cost roughly $600 million/year to keep the old nuclear facilities at Offutt up and running, so Pentagon officials gave the green light to build a new facility, which ended up costing even more and was riddled with major structural flaws.¹⁰ New facilities, once all the kinks are worked out, will have new communications in order to direct the nuclear triad and, terrifyingly, make it easier to conduct nuclear war. Many new facilities are being built to support nuclear activities.¹¹

The war industry's nuclear weapons are spread out in a triad: land-based intercontinental ballistic missiles (ICBM), submarine-launched ballistic missiles (SLBM), and bombs and missiles released from aircraft. The Third Reich's V-2 rockets, upon which the U.S. military's rocket program was based, were the first ICBMs that humans created. Hundreds of Boeing "Minuteman III" ICBMs are spread across bases, from Nebraska to North Dakota, Montana to Wyoming. Maintenance, control, and targeting of these missiles and training of missile personnel take place at multiple sites across the U.S., particularly in Nebraska, Colorado, Utah, and California. A few hundred Lockheed Martin Trident II submarine-launched ballistic missiles roam the seas aboard General Dynamics and Huntington Ingalls submarines and sit at Navy ports often run by corporations. The Trident II is a Lockheed Martin product, but many other corporations work on the missile.[12] The third part of the triad, air-launched nuclear ordnance, is loaded onto aircraft, like Boeing B-1, Northrop Grumman B-2, and Boeing B-52 bombers. These bombers operate out of bases from North Dakota to Louisiana. Corporations are constantly selling maintenance and upgrades for all three legs of the triad.

Nuclear weapons drain human resources in many ways, not just through devastating violence. There's brain drain, which we discussed at the end of Chapter Six. There's also a lot of time and effort that goes into designing, constructing and maintaining the nuclear complex that could be spent elsewhere. Like many who work in the war industry, people working at national labs (including coders, mathematicians, and physicists) explain away their participation in such a wasteful and ghoulish endeavor thusly: they're just technical experts; the military is the one that makes the decisions.[13] But consider this: The national labs could be used fulltime to study plate tectonics, brain injuries, climate catastrophe, photosynthesis, global plastic pollution, cancer, figuring out the most sustainable human population size, monitoring the sun for coronal mass ejections, and other complex problems facing humans and other animals. The possibilities are endless.

MDA

War corporations long loathed the restrictions that the 1972 Anti-Ballistic Missile (ABM) Treaty had imposed on their potential sales. Boardrooms and corporate strategists saw the ABM Treaty as blocking a very lucrative field: the design, production, and sale of missiles and technology marketed as being able to intercept and shoot down incoming ICBMs.

The Strategic Defense Initiative was the industry-led push during the Reagan administration to channel government money into a harebrained system to defend against ballistic missiles. Never operationally effective, the SDI system easily chewed through $30 billion during its first decade in existence. This system was rebranded variously as National Missile Defense and Ballistic Missile Defense under the George H. W. Bush and William J. Clinton presidencies. Corporate groundwork laid during the Reagan, Bush, and Clinton administrations consisted of long-term lobbying, strategic allocation of campaign finance, cultivating ideologues who revolve in and out of government, and building narratives through think tank publications and companions in corporate media. Part of the full-court corporate press for getting rid of the ABM Treaty was hyping the "ballistic missile threat" from Russia, North Korea, Iran, and China. The U.S. needed an organization dedicated to confronting such a threat, so the story went. Industry caught its big break when the war-friendly George W. Bush administration took office. The Bush administration, a hotbed of corporate greed, withdrew from the ABM Treaty in the spring of 2002. The Pentagon heeded industry counsel and immediately established the Missile Defense Agency, rolling all previous ABM technology and efforts into this agency designed to nurture, promote, and deploy such systems. MDA's initial budget was around $10 billion (in 2017 dollars).

Products routed through the MDA ballistic missile defense program are marketed as intercepting ballistic missiles at different layers of their trajectory. The Lockheed Martin Aegis system uses Raytheon missiles to hit ballistic missiles as they ascend. Aegis, on ships and ashore, integrates a wide variety of corporate operations.[14] A contract announcement from 31 August 2016 conveys this best: Aegis sites "incorporate highly integrated, classified, real-time networks that connect numerous contractor and U.S. government facilities required to build, integrate, test, and deliver computer code baselines." Smaller corporations get in on Aegis.[15] Threats sustain it all.[16] Corporations are also working on drones to track and potentially disable enemy ballistic missiles shortly after launch.[17] Raytheon PATRIOT missile batteries (that "create new, high-tech jobs"[18]) target shorter-range ballistic missiles, and Lockheed Martin Terminal High Altitude Area Defense, or THAAD (supporting over 18,000 jobs in forty states, Lockheed Martin says[19]), aims to hit an incoming missile during its final phase of flight.

The middle layer in the MDA ballistic missile defense program is ground-based midcourse defense (GMD). It aims to use kinetic energy (e.g. a Raytheon projectile and Aerojet Rocketdyne motor) to knock out the missile between ascent and descent. Many big corporations profit from GMD; two stand head and shoulders above others. Northrop Grumman is in charge of a lot of the computer stuff, fire controls, and flight test boosters. Boeing is the prime contractor in charge of overall GMD development, integration, testing, operations, and sustainment. The CEO of Northrop Grumman styles the team as a smooth blend of "experience" with "heritage." Boeing public relations paint Boeing as caring for a dear customer, MDA.[20] Corporate America leaves no corner un-corporatized. LSINC Corp. (Huntsville, AL) runs human resources at MDA.[21] Major war corporations work together on GMD pieces through cooperation and subcontracting.

Corporations also maintain and sustain radar systems that work with satellites to warn of inbound ballistic missiles.[22]

The Missile Defense Agency and the war industry test the interception of ballistic missiles regularly—at least ten publicly-acknowledged tests from the time D.C. dissolved the ABM Treaty in 2002 through March 2019. Intercepting an incoming ICBM with ground-based interceptors is like hitting a bullet with a bullet. Actually, it's harder; an incoming ICBM travels much faster than any pistol's bullet. So, what is the Missile Defense Agency to do?

All tests involving ground-based interceptors are rigged. In real life, if a country launched a ballistic missile towards the United States, the Missile Defense Agency would have to figure out the location of the launch and the exact trajectory of the missile, then launch the correct interceptor missile(s) at the right time and place. In tests, MDA has had such information (launch location, time of launch, etc.) ahead of time and has operated against a single missile; no test has been close to real-world circumstance.[23]

After a lull in testing, MDA took a new approach to increase its ability to declare success: launching multiple projectiles at one incoming missile.[24] MDA declared its March 2019 test a success,[25] despite glaring issues strongly suggesting a cover-up.[26]

Whenever MDA finally hits a target during a test, industry think tanks cheer wildly.[27]

Testing shows us industry's comprehensive monopoly over U.S. nuclear/space infrastructure. The typical stateside test of GMD is centered around Vandenberg Air Force Base, the coastal California enclave. Uniformed military personnel are in the loop, but numerically inferior to corporate personnel during tests. Vandenberg is home to a wide variety of corporate interests.[28] In ground-based interceptor tests, war corporations operating within MDA launch a mock ICBM from the Kwajalein Atoll, a U.S. colony and part of the Marshall Islands in the Pacific Ocean. The war industry runs the Kwajalein launch site,[29] which is named after Ronald Reagan. (The U.S. Department of War has conducted nuclear tests on atolls in the Marshall Islands and throughout the Pacific, leaving behind poisonous, radioactive debris.[30] For example, the U.S. exploded twenty-three nuclear bombs in the Bikini Atoll—east of Enewetok Atoll, north/northwest of Kwajalein Atoll—during 1946-58.[31]) Corporations within MDA launch the interceptor missile from Vandenberg. Even in these rigged tests, GMD has failed about half the time. No matter. For tests that took place from 2002 to 2015, the Pentagon forked over "more than $21 billion total for managing the system" including $2 billion in performance bonuses to Boeing according to the *LA Times*.[32] Vandenberg and Kwajalein are major industry avenues.

Some locations are almost entirely corporate. Wake Island is a U.S. colony located about 4,000 kilometers west of Hawai'i as the crow flies. The War Department refers to Wake Island as a "strategic possession," though Wake Island could be more accurately described as a business possession. Ninety-six of the 100 personnel based at Wake Island are corporate mercenaries. Corporate America is constructing and upgrading facilities on the island. MDA conducts tests on the island. Over 400 military aircraft, including Boeing and Lockheed Martin products, pass through Wake Island each year.[33] Environmental remediation at Wake Island is ongoing. The Naval Facilities Engineering Command (NAVFAC) Pacific is often in charge of cleanup of the lands and waterways in and around the majestic Pacific. NAVFAC hands off this work to Corporate America.[34]

Waste is normal. By autumn 2016, the GMD portion of the anti-ballistic missile program had cost over $40 billion, according to the *LA Times* (Willman, 2 Sept 2016). On 22 May 2017, the Pentagon allocated $1.088 billion to redesign the failing "exoatomospheric kill vehicle" of the GMD interceptor. This "redesigned kill vehicle" was developed by an industry team of Boeing, Lockheed Martin, and Raytheon. The team worked on the redesign for a little over two years; the Pentagon cancelled the redesign on 14 August 2019 because of "technical design problems." A corporate apotheosis named Mike Griffin (in charge of Pentagon research) explained on 3 September 2019 that the Pentagon was not asking for its $1.088 billion back because the money had gone to "the acquisition of knowledge, which will inform our future."[35] None of this well-defined waste stopped the Pentagon from then going ahead with the design and development of *another*, newer, "next-generation" interceptor for the GMD. The request for proposals was handed out to corporate reps at an industry day on 29 August 2019.[36]

Bipartisan support for "great power competition" allows industry expansion. The George W. Bush administration laid the groundwork for ground-based interceptors in Europe. The Barack H. Obama administration came through, approving the European Phased Adaptive Approach (EPAA), an industry-driven initiative that has promoted two lies: Iranian "threats" and "cost-effective" technology. The realities—that Iran doesn't pose a missile threat to Europe or the U.S. and that the industry technology was quite costly—don't matter to D.C. The EPAA is currently in full swing: warships with Lockheed Martin's Aegis technology operate out of Naval Station Rota, Spain; Lockheed Martin THAAD (with Raytheon radar) and Raytheon PATRIOT systems (with Lockheed Martin missiles) operate in Turkey; an Aegis site in Deveselu, Romania, is up and running; and corporations are building another Aegis site in Poland, where U.S. military infrastructure has expanded under Obama and Trump. Missile defense is bipartisan in its hype and waste.

Great power competition lights the way. The Deveselu location deserves scrutiny. Deveselu is one location of many where the U.S. war industry, through the Missile Defense Agency, deploys missile technology that menaces both target and host nations. The site is designed to operate against Russian missiles, but corporate officials and think tanks insist it is to counter the always-hyped Iranian threat.[37] Even the most casual observer can recognize this as a ruse, since Iranian missile engineers lack capacity, funding and intent to develop anything close to a functioning long-range intercontinental ballistic missile program;[38] Iran's missile program is regional, defensive, and tightly focused. Moscow appropriately views D.C.'s envelopment of Romania as an aggressive move. The missile "defense" equipment in Deveselu can be modified overnight for offensive capability.

In late spring, 2016, U.S. Deputy Secretary of War Bob Work inaugurated the missile installation in Deveselu. Prior to his term as Deputy Secretary of War, Work was head of one of the war industry's favorite think tanks, the Center for a New American Security. CNAS' major financial donors during 2016-17 represented a cross section of industry actors: major banks such as Bank of America and JPMorgan Chase; giant war corporations such as Raytheon and General Dynamics; war corporations that have grown in leaps and bounds in recent years such as CACI and Harris Corp.; foreign governments that purchase from the war industry such as the United Arab Emirates; foreign corporations such as BAE Systems (U.K.) and Leonardo DRS (Italy) that function as extensions of the U.S. war industry; and industry pressure groups such as NDIA.[39]

Lockheed Martin set up its Aegis product at the site in Deveselu. The product uses Lockheed Martin radar, Raytheon missiles, and Lockheed Martin launchers. KBR built many of the facilities on the 269-acre site. Soon, the whole gang showed up: CGI Federal matériel management software, Jacobs logistics, Parsons contractors, General Dynamics (CSRA) IT services, Vectrus (Exelis) IT infrastructure support, and IAP base operations support services. D.C. sold weapons to the Romanian government while the Deveselu Aegis site was getting up and running.[40] The metastasizing implantation at Deveselu reminds us how industry is pushing us all closer to war. The establishment of the Deveselu site is a provocation, a massive middle finger: threatening the Russian public with attack, putting U.S. tax dollars into unnecessary products, and increasing Treasury debt issuance.

The anti-ballistic missile portion of the nuclear sector of the war racket is lucrative for many reasons. First, it requires the ongoing development of newer and ever newer technology. This is a limitless sinkhole: MDA funds pouring into war corporations. Second, per corporate modus operandi, for each generation of technology sold, tangential programs and technical support (e.g. transportation, ongoing maintenance, fiber optics, communication devices, associated satellite deployment and usage, radars, sensors, command & control facilities, R&D) will also be sold. Third, there is no accountability, as evinced by MDA's track record.

Corporations are thrilled. Northrop Grumman, for example, is "really excited" about "the missile defense space." The corporation has tentacles in the entire missile defense/offense process: launch preparation, acquiring a missile, tracking the missile, intercepting the incoming missile, and using software and personnel to assess whether it hit its target, in addition to nuclear missile work, like the launcher subsystems it produces for Trident II ballistic missiles. A Northrop

Grumman official couches this as being "more responsive to our customer set."[41] We end on that note.

THE MODERNIZATION SCAM

Industry pushed hard during the Bush and Obama administrations for a massive overhaul of the U.S. nuclear weapons complex. War corporations, their lobbyists, and PR firms pitched this to Capitol Hill as "rebuilding" a "crumbling" nuclear weapon infrastructure. When this was met with brief hesitation by some members of the Obama administration, the war industry assured them that a refurbished nuclear arsenal would lead to new arms control treaties that would ultimately *reduce* the number of deployed nuclear warheads. The Obama administration actually bought it,[42] and gave a green light to "modernization." Less surprisingly, Congressional proponents of nuclear modernization receive money from the war industry.[43]

This $1.74 trillion effort is currently underway and is expected to last for years.[44] Corporations know that once "modernization" is underway it is difficult to stop. Costs will go through the roof. Facilities, bombs, warheads, command & control systems, weapons lab management, tactical aircraft, bomber aircraft, ballistic missiles (submarine-launched and land-based), and submarines are coming down the pike. Each weapon of war comes with more mandatory purchases—such goodies as hardware, software, launchers, bomb racks, guidance equipment, satellite technology, training, maintenance, and facility modifications. Simultaneously, industry cooks up new related fields of profit (e.g. anti-area denial technology, low-yield nuclear weapons, hypersonic missiles) within the nuclear sector, and markets those fields as delivering a "flexible" and "tailored" "solution," keeping the industrial gas pedal to the floor.

The New York Times justified modernization with a spoonful of great power competition: "With Russia on the warpath, China pressing its own territorial claims and Pakistan expanding its arsenal, the overall chances for Mr. Obama's legacy of disarmament look increasingly dim, analysts say."[45] All corporate media have to do is blame Russian President Vladimir Putin. They do not provide context, like mentioning that the *mere increase* in the U.S. war budget from 2018 to 2019 was more than the *entire* Russian war budget,[46] or that Russia's economy, as measured by GDP, is smaller than Italy's. Smaller than California's, too.

This "modernization" of the U.S. nuclear arsenal was well underway by the time the 2018 Nuclear Posture Review came out. The NPR was issued from the Office of the Secretary of War, but employees of war corporations had significant input in its preparation and crafting. The Review warned of "aging components" and insufficient integration into the War Department's existing nuclear command

& control infrastructure, especially in the face of "growing twenty-first century threats,"[47] like Moscow and Beijing. The War Department's fiscal year 2019 budget shifted the expansion of nuclear arsenal into high gear, providing funds to actively develop different types of low-yield nuclear warheads and banning any reduction in the number of ICBMs. The chiefs of corporatized U.S. intelligence agencies (e.g. CIA, DIA, NSA) and the Director of National Intelligence appeared before Congress to hype "worldwide threats."[48]

Meanwhile: Danger. On 25 July 2018, Boeing received millions of dollars to work on Flight Termination Receiver 2.0 for the Air Force Nuclear Weapons Center at Hill Air Force Base, Utah. Because this Receiver can "self-destruct" a U.S. nuclear missile *after launch*, it increases the likelihood that U.S. military officers or the Executive Branch will launch a nuclear weapon toward a human population overseas. This is how war corporations jeopardize us all—contract by contract.

Under industry pressure and with its own parochial bureaucratic interests in mind, the U.S. Air Force is now developing a costly[49] hydrogen bomb known as the B61-12. The B61-12 will replace other versions (among them, the -3, -4, -7, and -11). Industry presents this as a cost savings method. There are no government savings, however; the hundreds of B61-12 bombs to be manufactured, in addition to associated costs (maintenance, spare and consumable parts, ongoing R&D, travel, field service reps, and other billable categories) outweigh potential savings. Corporate interests align behind the B61-12. Lockheed Martin is a main contractor. Boeing is selling a GPS-guided tail kit for the bomb based on knowhow developed for its Joint Direct Attack Munition (one of the corporation's most popular and deadly products in the post-9.11 binge). The B61-12 will likely be carried on Northrop Grumman B-2 and B-21 bombers, and Boeing and Lockheed Martin fighter jets. Corporatized national weapons labs help design the B61-12. The B61-12—costly in part because it will probably feature a variable "dial-a-yield" capability (50-350 kilotons, roughly 3-23 times what blew apart the civilian population of Hiroshima)—will be deployed to NATO bases in Europe against the will of the European public and in violation of the Nuclear Non-Proliferation Treaty. Most "military leaders believe that short-range 'tactical' nuclear weapons based in Europe have virtually no utility," according to a former White House National Security Council director for defense policy and arms control.[50] True. Which is why the war industry and its D.C. goons are trying (and succeeding!) in pumping up the meme of great power competition to override any sense of restraining norms. They need an enemy in order to justify their nuclear revamp. Journalist Joseph Trevithick, who usually fawns over war industry wares, described the B61-12 as having "proven to be time-consuming and very costly."[51]

Testing of the B61-12 is ongoing, with plans to deploy it by the early 2020s. If history is any indication, costs will only go up.[52]

The war industry develops new weaponry, too, under the guise of modernization: a new cruise missile (the "Long Range Standoff missile," for example, which can carry nuclear warheads) to be used on Northrop Grumman and Boeing bombers; a new fuse that increases threefold the destructive power of nuclear weapons, making Russia's civilian and military forces more vulnerable to a U.S. first strike;[53] the new Northrop Grumman B-21 bomber, featuring such goodies as United Technologies avionics and engines; new nuclear warheads marketed as interoperable across the triad; new General Dynamics Columbia class submarines, featuring the upgraded Trident II; new ICBMs;[54] and new "low yield" nuclear warhead, the W76-2, which debuted aboard the U.S. submarine fleet in 2019. Ultimately, spiffy new technology just makes nuclear weaponry easier to use.

Modernization is theft.

But modernization was not enough. International treaty protections that hinder profit had to be scotched.

The Intermediate-Range Nuclear Forces (INF) Treaty barred deployment of land-based cruise missiles and ballistic missiles with the ability to hit targets between 500 and 5,500 kilometers away. War corporations loathed the INF Treaty, as there is much money to be made in the development, sale, deployment, maintenance, and upgrade of short- and intermediate-range land-based missiles and missile launchers. Through the end of the Obama administration and into the first years of the Trump administration, war corporations lobbied hard against it behind closed doors. Yes-men, military careerists, and ideologues in government were eager to comply. But in order to withdraw from the INF Treaty, D.C. needed to find an excuse. Enter Russian President Vladimir Putin, the most effectively demonized man by U.S. corporate media. Industry think tanks, pundits, and politicians blamed Russia (its SSC-8 missile in particular) to justify reneging on the INF Treaty. Industry media affiliates followed tightly scripted coverage:

- Do not mention the fact that NATO has expanded into former Warsaw Pact countries, right up to Russia's borders.
- Do not mention the war industry's missile batteries in Eastern Europe.
- Do not mention major NATO construction projects in Central and Eastern Europe.[55]
- Do not mention D.C.'s $1.74 trillion-dollar upgrade to U.S. nuclear weaponry.
- Do not mention the context in which the INF Treaty had been signed.[56]

Blaming Russia, D.C. withdrew from the INF treaty in August 2019.[57] D.C.'s withdrawal from the INF Treaty was the natural result of the corporate capture of U.S. government and a continuation of D.C.'s 2002 withdrawal from the ABM Treaty. Once free from the ABM Treaty, the U.S. war industry fully developed and deployed the Aegis Ballistic Missile Defense System. Once free from the INF Treaty, the U.S. war industry was able to develop and deploy intermediate-range missiles. The day after D.C. formally withdrew from the INF Treaty, Secretary of War Mark Esper (former Raytheon vice president) said he was in favor of deploying ground-based missiles to the Far East.[58] Within a few weeks of withdrawing from the INF Treaty, the Pentagon and war industry had tested an intermediate-range missile.[59] Raytheon had developed the payload, and Lockheed Martin was in charge of command & control and the launcher assembly, a lieutenant colonel in Pentagon public affairs informed me. Weaponry reaching well beyond 350 miles (approximately 563 kilometers) will be "industry standard," according to Lieutenant General Eric Smith, commander of Marine Corps Combat Development Command.[60]

U.S. war corporations are also developing hypersonic missiles.

Hypersonic is anything that can fly five-times the speed of sound or faster. Hypersonics are fast *and* maneuverable. Two prototypes stand out in the U.S. arsenal right now: a "tactical boost glide" prototype, which is launched from a regular missile (itself launched from an aircraft) to fly through the atmosphere towards the target; another prototype, the "hypersonic air-breathing weapon concept," uses a scramjet (an engine, without a traditional turbine, that compresses air and combusts it to power the projectile) to fly horizontally towards the target. Potential targets of a hypersonic missile include apartment complexes, trains, bridges, tunnels, humans, military bases, radar installations, airports, seaports, aircraft carriers, and utilities. Hypersonic missiles can carry nuclear warheads, but first industry will put conventional warheads onboard. Promise.

Hypersonics increase the chance of war. Militaries around the world will put their forces on lengthy, taxing periods of high alert in order to try to recognize and track any incoming hypersonic missiles. But hypersonics are very difficult to track. Hypersonics are so fast that military and government leaders have a compressed time to react or even to make the simplest decision. It is a recipe for disaster.

Great power competition fuels the development of hypersonics. D.C.'s establishment media channel great power competition when justifying industry's development of hypersonics: "After repeated warnings that Russia and China have each developed a hypersonic missile that could punch through U.S. missile defenses, the U.S. Air Force says it will spend an estimated $1 billion to develop one of its own."[61] When pressed on specifics, industry personalities cite Chinese short-range hypersonic glide vehicle tests and claims from Russian President Vladimir Putin about Russian hypersonic missile capability. A major corporate persona, Michael Griffin, has been leading the charge on hypersonics, using a classic Cold War trick: pretending the enemy is leaps and bounds ahead of the U.S.[62]

Michael Griffin is the Under Secretary of War for Research and Engineering. His corporate roots touch Johns Hopkins University Applied Physics Lab, CIA's In-Q-Tel, and Orbital ATK.[63] He is the recipient of the Missile Defense Agency's Ronald Reagan Award. (He was chief technology officer for the Strategic Defense Initiative under the Reagan administration.) In his current capacity as Under Secretary, Griffin commands an immediate budget of around $20 billion. Using the passive voice, *Aviation International News* notes, "There has been a major push in the U.S. for the past couple of years for offensive and defensive hypersonic weapons development, including the awarding of more than $3 billion in contracts to major defense contractors Raytheon and Lockheed Martin."[64] Industry executives love hypersonics because there are no international agreements pertaining to hypersonic missile development or use—the ideal incubator for a corporate product of war.

Cost is no issue. Hundreds of millions of dollars across the War Department have been spent just developing the missiles' composite ceramics that can withstand the high temperatures produced at hypersonic speeds. One test flight of a hypersonic vehicle can cost up to $100 million, according to *The New York Times*.[65] On 23 September 2016, Lockheed Martin was allocated over $171 million to work on the hypersonic air-breathing weapon concept with DARPA. On 31 October 2016, Raytheon was allocated over $174 million for the same project. (The Pentagon dropped over $2 billion into hypersonics prior to 2018.) In 2018, the Pentagon gave Lockheed Martin more than $1.4 billion for hypersonic prototypes to be launched by Air Force aircraft. By June 2019, an industry team was ready with a prototype featuring Northrop Grumman's 3D-printed engine and Raytheon's air vehicle.[66] By July 2019, Lockheed Martin's hypersonics business had a value of around $3.5 billion.[67] The FY2020 war budget had around $3 billion allocated publicly towards hypersonics.

Republican and Democratic presidential administrations have promoted hypersonic research and development with equal vigor. Congress does its part by keeping the money torrential and by passing a law in 2018 demanding that the Pentagon has a hypersonic missile in service by autumn 2022. All sides in the military-industrial-congressional triangle are in sync.

As we saw with many other newfangled weapons, developing offensive weaponry allows industry to then market defensive products to address the ramifications of targeted countries' efforts to respond. To this end, Raytheon is currently working to track and disable hypersonics from low-earth orbit. Industry is putting complementary infrastructure in place. The Space Development Agency, created by corporation-men like Mike Griffin and Pat Shanahan, has many tasks, one of which is developing and deploying sensors in low-earth orbit to track incoming hypersonic missiles and facilitate the Pentagon's strike. Initial development of other command and control technology will cost billions.

It would be far safer to remove nuclear weapons from hair-trigger alert and start peace negotiations. But there's no money in peace. As of April 2019, the MIC is no longer disclosing the size of its nuclear stockpile, at last count roughly 3,800 warheads. More arms do not equal more power; a small portion of the U.S. nuclear arsenal could destroy all life on Earth dozens and dozens of times over.[68] Even limited nuclear war would end human life on Earth.[69] These weapons are unusable. Yet nuclear war is only a matter of time under the current system. Even Paul Nitze, the coldest Cold Warrior and father of NSC 68 (one of the principal government documents abetting the post-WWII entrenchment of the U.S. war industry) came to realize the danger of nuclear weapons.[70]

Writer Richard Krushnic and Professor Jonathan Alan King summarize our circumstances:

> Imagine for a moment a genuine absurdity: somewhere in the United States, the highly profitable operations of a set of corporations were based on the possibility that sooner or later your neighborhood would be destroyed and you and all your neighbors annihilated.[71]

The nations of the world have spoken. In December 2016, they voted in the United Nations General Assembly to begin the process of banning nuclear weapons. The General Assembly adopted the Treaty on Prohibition of Nuclear Weapons on 7 July 2017. The International Campaign to Abolish Nuclear Weapons won the 2017 Nobel Peace Prize. The U.S. war industry is *the* obstacle to achieving a world without nuclear weapons.

ENDNOTES

1 "DOD Identified Army Casualty." *U.S. Department of Defense*. Release No. NR-174-19. 1 July 2019.

2 For Plutonium pollution, see Kate Brown's *Plutopia* (New York: Oxford University Press, 2013). To paraphrase author Alan Weisman (*The World Without Us*. New York: Picador, 2007, p. 262, *passim*): Depleted uranium has a very dense form. Its half-life is 4.5 billion years. There are at least a half-million tons of this substance in the U.S. Different types of nuclear waste contamination span the Waste Isolation Pilot Plant in southeast New Mexico, Los Alamos National Lab in northern New Mexico, Hanford Nuclear Reservation in Washington state, Rocky Flats near Denver International

Airport in Colorado, the Savannah River Site Defense Waste Processing Facility in South Carolina, and other locations. Los Alamos is a good example of nuclear pollution. During 1946-57, Los Alamos dumped thousands of gallons per day in the New Mexican desert, an area now known as "Acid Canyon," one of the most contaminated places on Earth. Staci Matlock covered this pollution in "TRINITY: 70 Years Later—'Los Alamos will never be clean'" (*The Santa Fe New Mexican*, 13 July 2015).

3 Schlosser, Eric. *Command and Control: Nuclear Weapons, the Damascus Accident, and the Illusion of Safety*. New York: Penguin Press, 2013, p. 327. Schlosser was referencing a study by Sandia Labs.

4 Burns, Robert. "AP Exclusive: U.S. nuclear inspection results now concealed." *Associated Press*. 3 July 2017.

5 An authority on nuclear weaponry, speaking in Helen Young's documentary *The Nuns, The Priests, and The Bombs* (2018), put total U.S. spending on nuclear weapons since 1943 at roughly $10 trillion. *The New York Times* on 1 July 1998 ("U.S. Nuclear Arms' Cost Put at $5.48 Trillion") cited a study putting total spending on nuclear weapons since 1940 at roughly $5.48 trillion. These numbers are consistent given rates of nuclear-related weapons production, war spending, and inflation. The International Campaign to Abolish Nuclear Weapons indicates that U.S. spending on nuclear weaponry during one year, 2011, was $61.3 billion. See <www.icanw.org/the-facts/catastrophic-harm/a-diversion-of-public-resources/>. That's roughly $6,992,927 per hour.

6 The last bits of the national labs were finally and fully corporatized in 2006. Lawrence Livermore National Lab is run by BWX Technologies, Battelle, Bechtel, and AECOM. The University of California is part of this team. Battelle, the University of California, and the University of Texas A&M run Los Alamos National Lab, NM. Other corporations involved in Los Alamos' activities include Huntington Ingalls (naval nuclear power), Fluor (management and expertise), Longenecker & Associates (environmental management and technical help), Merrick & Co. (architecture and engineering), and two lesser-known corporations, the nuclear-materials firm TechSource and Strategic Management Solutions, which focuses on facility operations. Fluor runs the Savannah River site in SC with Huntington Ingalls and Honeywell. A portion of what the corporatized labs work on is the U.S. government's nuclear "stockpile stewardship" program, which uses supercomputers—including *Sierra*, the second-fastest computer on the planet as of this writing, and *El Capitán*, the intended successor to *Sierra*—to model nuclear explosions and simulate how nuclear triggers and other internal mechanisms operate. See "The new supercomputer behind the U.S. nuclear arsenal." *Verge Science*. 20 November 2018: <www.youtube.com/watch?v=PS_PlorW6pM>.

7 The international campaign known as *Move the Nuclear Weapons Money* <nuclearweaponsmoney.org> provides more information about the corporations involved in producing nuclear weapons. Though the site lists 17 corporations, the number is now down to 16 because Northrop Grumman has acquired Orbital ATK.

8 Schwarz, Jon. "How to dismantle the absurd profitability of nuclear weapons." *The Intercept*. 4 May 2019. "Producing Mass Destruction: Private companies and the nuclear weapon industry." *PAX*. May 2019: <www.dontbankonthebomb.com>.

9 A few examples of recent nuclear-related construction include building a support facility at the TA-55 secure area of Los Alamos National Lab, NM; building a chemical metallurgy research building, TA-46 at Los Alamos; building the National Nuclear Security Administration Albuquerque Complex in NM. Relevant contracts issued 15 Feb, 24 April, 21 June 2018.

10 Axe, David. "The U.S. Military Has a New Facility for Overseeing Nuclear War." *Vice*. 10 July 2018.

11 *New York Times*' William Broad and David Sanger ("U.S. Ramping Up Major Renewal in Nuclear Arms," 21 September 2014) on recent upgrades: (1) $150 million for National Criticality Experiments Research Center; (2) billions at Los Alamos National Lab; (3) roughly $700 million for a plant in Kansas City, MO; (4) millions for Lawrence Livermore National Lab; (5) $100 million for a new weapons testing complex at Sandia National Lab; (6) $145 million for the Pantex Plant, TX; (7) a massive new complex planned for the Y-12 complex at Oak Ridge, TN. "We're glad to have the thousands of jobs," Sen. Lamar Alexander (R-TN) said, reciting industry talking points.

12 Many war corporations profit from Trident II production: Aerojet Rocketdyne (propulsion systems), BAE Systems (engineering, integration, and R&D), Boeing (navigation technology), Draper Labs and MIT (guidance systems), General Dynamics (missile tubes for the submarines that launch the Trident II), L3 (flight test instruments), Moog (parts and controls), Northrop Grumman (rocket motor and underwater launcher), Peraton (reentry systems), Southern Research Institute (thermal protection materials), SPA Inc. (studies & engineering), Teradyne (testers), Textron (re-entry vehicles). Industry is able to profit at every turn. On 4 Nov 2015, the Navy contracted Northrop Grumman to manufacture ballast closures, firing unit test simulators, and other goods "in support of the New Strategic Arms Reduction Treaty." Even in arms reduction the industry profits! Industry also regularly charges to address or monitor obsolescence (e.g. 29 June 2018).

13 Terri Quinn, Department Head for Computing, LLNL, exemplifies such equivocating in "The new supercomputer behind the U.S. nuclear arsenal" (*Verge Science*. 20 November 2018: <www.youtube.com/watch?v=PS_PlorW6pM>, 6:15): "What we do is we answer questions for the Department of Energy."

14 Corporations working on Aegis include Boeing, Honeywell, and Northrop Grumman. Draper Labs, Johns Hopkins University, and MIT's Lincoln Lab play roles. Contracts to Lockheed Martin for Aegis goods and services include 2014 (20 Aug, 3 Sept, 24 Sept, 25 Sept, 1 Dec), 2015 (2 June, 1 Dec), 2016 (27 July, 31 Oct), 2017 (27 Mar, 8 Nov), 2018 (25 June, 13 Aug). Over $806,300,000 were allocated on these thirteen contracts, I calculate.

15 For example, Conley & Associates (Newport News, VA) sells maintenance & sustainment of Aegis technology, vessels, and platforms, and Teledyne Wireless (Rancho Cordova, CA) sells repair & manufacture of traveling wave tubes used in Aegis. Communications & Power Industries manufactures and repairs microwave tubes installed in the fire control system aboard warships using Aegis weapon systems. The U.S. Navy, Australia, Japan, and South Korea purchase such technology. Global Research & Technology Corp. (Camarillo, CA) sells testing and evaluation services for Naval Air Warfare Center Weapons Division "Aegis Externally Directed Team Leader and Weapons Test & Evaluation Division," per 13 Sept 2018 contract.

16 Lockheed Martin's corporate literature, for example, is rife with claims of threats. One test "demonstrated the integrated capabilities of the Aegis Weapon System and how it has *continually evolved to counter advanced threats*. As a proven world leader in systems integration and development of air and missile defense systems and technologies, Lockheed Martin delivers high-quality missile defense solutions that protect citizens, critical assets and deployed forces from *current and future threats*" (emphasis mine), as seen in "Latest Aegis Combat System Is Successful Against Medium Range Threats Ballistic Missiles" (*Lockheed Martin*, 30 August 2017). MDA contracts reflect the ways in which the War Dept. has avidly lapped up industry's stoking of institutionalized fear: Together, Boeing, Raytheon, and Lockheed Martin come up with ways to "destroy several objects within a threat complex by considering advanced sensor, divert and attitude control and communication concepts." Issued 11 and 13 Aug 2015. On 31 Jan 2018, Boeing was allocated over $6.5 billion to work on "development, integration, testing and deployment of ground systems software builds to address emerging threats" for GMD. On 3 Aug 2016, Parsons sold services (technical, engineering, advisory)

and management so MDA can be "adaptable and responsive to intelligence based threats and to defend the homeland, regional interests, allies, and deployed forces against ballistic missile threats." Profiting as a team, Lockheed Martin, Northrop Grumman, and Raytheon sold on 10 July 2018 up to $4.1 billion of "autonomous acquisition and persistent precision tracking and discrimination to optimize the defensive capability of the ballistic missile defense system and counter evolving threats."

17 General Atomics' San Diego, California, branch refines missile tracking technology for MDA. If you're using a drone to track an ICBM or a laser on a drone to disable an ICBM in its launch phase, then your drone needs to be close to the enemy's ICBM launch site. The chances are slim that your drone will be in the right place at the right time, even slimmer when you consider that an enemy will not launch an ICBM when your drones are lingering in the vicinity.

18 "Poland to acquire PATRIOT defense system." *Raytheon*. Published 26 March 2018. Last updated 1 October 2018: <www.raytheon.com/news/feature/poland-signs-loa-for-patriot>.

19 Macias, Amanda. "A rare look inside the heavily guarded compound where Lockheed Martin builds the THAAD missile." *CNBC*. 6 August 2019.

20 "By combining Northrop Grumman's 50-year experience and success on the nation's Minuteman ICBM program with Boeing's heritage GMD leadership, we provide the optimum mix of integrated development and sustainment capabilities for a system that demands nothing less," quoted in "Boeing and Northrop Grumman GMD Team Receives Contract from U.S. Missile Defense Agency." (*Boeing Mediaroom*, 30 December 2011). "The Boeing-led team currently operates and sustains the deployed GMD weapon system while developing and testing new technologies to provide increased reliability and to meet evolving customer needs and requirements." L. David Montague (former president of a Lockheed missile division and co-chair of a panel critiquing certain GMD) said exorbitant bonuses paid to Boeing while its product was consistently failing tests and underperforming suggest that MDA is a "rogue organization" in need of strict supervision. See Willman, David. "A flawed missile defense system generates $2 billion in bonuses for Boeing." *LA Times*. 2 September 2016.

21 Issued 17 Sept 2018. "This will support the development, implementation, sustainment and assessment of human resources processes, procedures, plans and policies to support MDA workforce."

22 Ground-based radars are located in AK, CA, MA, Greenland, and northeast England. Additional corporate oversight takes place in Colorado Springs. Corporations, principally GE and Raytheon, manufactured the radars. As of this writing, InDyne, Summit Technical Solutions, and Harris Corp. operate and maintain them. Harris has sold collection & analysis, operational safety, engineering, field service teams, hardware repair, improving missile detection, keeping licenses and subscriptions up to date, mission assurance, resolving obsolescence, upgrading software, spares, administering operations, and managing the system. Harris has also been known to charge for "suitability and effectiveness." Boeing & Raytheon produced sea-based X-band radar, which TOTE Services (Jacksonville, FL) operates and maintains. Great Eastern Group (Fort Lauderdale, FL) has worked on X-band logistics in Dutch Harbor, AK. Gryphon Technologies (Huntsville) works on communications. Raytheon sells logistics, engineering, "product improvement," SME, cybersecurity, and modeling & simulation. The *LA Times* (5 April 2015) highlighted X-band and other costly flops. At least 5 contracts directly pertaining to the X-Band radar have been issued since that *LA Times* investigative report came out. Funds allocated to corporate X-band operations exceeded $115,506,000 (9,922,000 + 57,675,000 + 1,252,000 + 35,600,000 + 11,057,000). Contracts: 30 Sept 2015, 15 June 2017, 27 Oct 2017, 1 Nov 2017, 15 Aug 2018. Harris: 2017 (3 March, 19 April), 2018 (27, 30 April).

23 "The painful history" of GMD—which "has cost $123 billion since 2002"—"now stands at nine successful tests out of 18 since 1999, exactly 50 percent," says Sydney Freedberg (*Breaking Defense*, 30 May 2017). As of 2019, 20 operational missile interceptors reside at Vandenberg AFB,

CA, and Fort Greely, AK. Assuming for a second that North Korea had the technology and intent to reach the mainland U.S., it would never launch a single missile; it would launch multiple to assure success. MDA's tests do not account for that. MDA plans for 64 ground-based interceptors, says Jen Judson (*Defense News*, 25 March 2019).

24 At least 6 contract announcements issued from summer 2015 through spring 2017 allocated over $200,280,000 to this "Multi-Object Kill Vehicle." Contracts: 11 Aug 2015 Raytheon $9.7 million (M), Lockheed Martin $9.68M; 13 Aug 2015 Boeing $9.8M; 9 March 2017 Lockheed Martin $53M; 3 April 2017 Raytheon $59.6M; 12 May 2017 Boeing $58.5M.

25 The Air Force Lt. Gen. in charge of MDA issued a two-fold fib: "This test demonstrates that we have a capable, credible deterrent against a very real threat," as quoted in Broad and Sanger (*The New York Times*, 25 March 2019). No. The "deterrent" was not capable. And, no, the threat was not that real. It is always inflated.

26 Broad and Sanger (*The New York Times*, 25 March 2019) report: In the past, MDA "has been accused of exaggerating its 'kills' in order to quiet critics who say a 50 percent successful interception rate is far from satisfactory... The [March 2019] test was not announced beforehand and the statement on the outcome was released late in the day, which seemed to suggest that the test had encountered problems. The statement also introduced a note of hesitancy. 'Initial indications show the test met requirements,' it said. 'Program officials will continue to evaluate system performance based upon telemetry and other data obtained during the test.'"

27 For example, after a GMD test in May 2017, CSIS, which receives a lot of war industry funding, applauded: "Today's intercept means that hit-to-kill deniers are going to have an even harder time contending that homeland missile defense doesn't work," cited in Freedberg (*Breaking Defense*, 30 May 2017). See also Thomas Karako's "The GMD Intercept: What Does It Mean?" *CSIS*. 30 May 2017.

28 Corporate interests at Vandenberg have included Booz Allen Hamilton cyber security & IT; CACI maintaining & operating the satellite control network; Cherokee Nation BOSS; Indyne launch control; Kratos helping track communications satellites; L.C. Wright pampering and doing legwork for admirals, generals, and senior civilians; MacAulay-Brown business support, strategic advice, and corporate analysis; ManTech administering special access programs and compartmented activities; Millennium Engineering & Integration certifying the corporate provision of vehicles that launch satellites into orbit (like United Launch Alliance's multi-billion dollar Vulcan rocket under development); and Parsons advisors, engineering, and site operations. Data Computer Corp. of America (Ellicott City, MD) has run communications infrastructure. RG Next, the General Dynamics and Raytheon JV, runs and maintains launch & test range systems. Strategic Alliance Business Group plans and programs facility use, administers safety functions, and oversees facility sustainment. ULS (Boeing / Lockheed Martin JV) works on vehicles that launch satellites into orbit. Relevant contracts: 2017 (23 May, 2 Aug, 15 Aug, 27 Sept, 4 Oct, 27 Nov, 29 Dec), 2018 (30 Jan, 22 Feb, 9 March, 12 April, 18 April, 31 Aug, 18 Sept, 20 Sept, 26 Sept, 27 Sept). I dropped from this collection random units using Vandenberg infrastructure (like corporations helping Navy units run target practice). I also excluded construction firms repairing launch structures or building NRO facilities.

29 Truestone has run fiber-optic cables to the site. Torch Technologies has run MDA testing there. Parsons and RGNext have kept the facilities up and running. Relevant contracts: 22 Sept 2016, 23 May 2017, 13 June 2018, 4 Sept 2018, 28 Aug 2019. Construction firms are crawling all over the place. San Juan Construction (Montrose, CO) is restoring a pier (28 July 2016).

30 Swenson, Kyle. "The U.S. put nuclear waste under a dome on a Pacific island. Now it's cracking open." *Washington Post*. 20 May 2019. Abella, et al. "Background gamma radiation and soil activity measurements in the northern Marshall Islands." *Proceedings of the National Academy of*

Sciences. July 2019. Amos, Jonathan. "Seafloor scar of Bikini A-bomb test still visible." *BBC News.* 10 December 2019. Rust, Susanne. "How the U.S. betrayed the Marshall Islands, kindling the next nuclear disaster." *LA Times.* 10 November 2019.

31 Tyson and Lang. *Accessory to War,* p. 402.

32 Willman, David. "A flawed missile defense system generates $2 billion in bonuses for Boeing." 2 September 2016.

33 For a military take, see Jim Garamone. "Wake Island Embodies Reality of America as Pacific Power." *DMA.* 3 February 2018.

34 In NAVFAC Pacific, Cape Environmental Management (Honolulu, HI) has tackled environmental remediation at various locations, Engineering Concepts (Honolulu, HI) has been in charge of environmental investigations, permit applications, and environmental studies, Helber Hastert & Fee Planners (Honolulu, HI) has prepared documents, including National Environmental Policy Act documents, Element Environmental (Aiea, HI) has worked on Superfund sites, and Cardno GS and AECOM as a JV have drafted NEPA and environmental documents. Multiple corporations have operated in the Northern Mariana Islands. This is just a handful of overall activity. Relevant contracts include 20 July 2016, 18 Sept 2017, 31 March 2016, 28 July 2016, 31 Jan 2017, 25 March 2016, 6 Sept 2017, 27 April 2018, 29 July 2016.

35 Mehta, Aaron. "Pentagon reveals fate of money paid to industry after missile defense program was canceled." *Defense News.* 4 September 2019.

36 McLeary, Paul. "Pentagon Issues Classified RFP for New Missile Interceptor." *Breaking Defense.* 6 September 2019. In parallel to the $1.088B, $4.1B was allocated on 22 March 2019 to a team (Boeing, Northrop Grumman, Raytheon) and subcontractors for expanding GMD. The work was to accelerate establishment of dozens of additional silos and interceptors. The work emphasized industry staples: sale of "state-of-the-art" technology, cyber, and addressing "emerging threats." *The New York Times* (Broad & Sanger, 25 March 2019) cited at least $300 billion sunk in one decade on missile defense, as tallied by Stephen Schwartz of the *Bulletin of the Atomic Scientists.*

37 Ferdinando, Lisa. "Work Helps to Inaugurate Ballistic Missile Defense Site in Romania." *Defense Media Activity.* 12 May 2016.

38 Prof. Stephen F. Cohen ("Who Will Stop the U.S.-Russia Arms Race?" *The Real News Network.* 25 March 2018) comments on the likelihood that the Aegis site at Deveselu is actually targeting Iran: "It's disinformation. It's American propaganda." Cohen informs us that Russia protested when D.C. left the ABM Treaty in 2002. "We told Russia, 'why are you worried? It has nothing to do with Russia. This is all about Iran,' and, quote, 'rogue states,' unidentified. Russia said, 'OK, in that case let's build it together. We actually have better radar facilities than you have. We'll build it, we'll manage it together.'" D.C. systematically refused every attempt Russian made to join in the creation of a missile defense system. Even the publication *War On the Rocks* conceded in 2018, "The facts are clear: None of the missiles Iran has under development come close to being able to hit the United States. Nor can they reach much of Europe beyond its southeastern corner" (Elleman & Fitzpatrick, 5 March 2018). Rational, thorough, non-ideological analyses of Iran's capabilities can be found at Costello, Ryan. "Think Again: Iran's Missile Program." *NIAC.* February 2018: <www.niacouncil.org/wp-content/uploads/2018/02/Think-Again-Iran-Missile-Program.pdf>; and "The Real Facts on the Iran Nuclear Deal." *The Center for Arms Control and Non-Proliferation.* 31 August 2015: <armscontrolcenter.org/wp-content/uploads/2015/08/8-31-The-real-facts-on-the-Iran-nuclear-deal.pdf>.

39 To see the full list CNAS donors, visit <www.cnas.org/support-cnas/cnas-supporters>.

40 A major purchaser of the PATRIOT missile system, Romania is becoming one of the U.S. war industry's favorite customers in Eastern Europe. To the Romanian government, Armtec sold

countermeasure flares, Pyrotechnic Specialties sold impulse cartridges used for activating flares, Colt sold M4 carbines, Raytheon sold short- and long-range air-to-air missiles, and Leidos sold mission planning computer programs. Relevant contracts: 2015 (21 May, 25 Sept), 2016 (9 May, 26 May, 13 June, 1 July, 28 July, 9 Sept, 8 Dec, 20 Dec), 2017 (31 March, 13 April). Other FMS to Romania: 2016 (18 Feb, 21 June, 31 Aug, 1 Sept).

41 "Northrop Grumman's Todorov on $9.2B Orbital ATK Acquisition, Missile-Defense Space, Evolving Threats." *Defense & Aerospace Report*. 6 August 2018: <www.youtube.com/watch?v=gnADkxrX5tI>, (2:30).

42 Daniel B. Poneman, the deputy secretary of energy and former principal at the international capitalist advisory firm known as The Scowcroft Group, said, "The whole design of the modernization enables us to make reductions." Quoted in Broad and Sanger (*The New York Times*, 21 September 2014). The war industry knows that simultaneous increases in nuclear infrastructure allows for a huge ramp-up / expansion in the nuclear arsenal—after a bit of lobbying and campaign funding, of course. Though the Obama Administration shunned diplomacy in many cases, it did push for the Senate to ratify the New START Treaty. Industry disapproved of such measures and pushed its Congress for more funding.

43 Jon Kyl (R-AZ), for example, received campaign contributions from a variety of entities that work in and profit from the nuclear war industry, including Bechtel Group, Raytheon, Blackstone Group, KKR & Co., Citigroup, and dark money PACs. Adam Schiff (D-CA) is also in favor of "modernizing" U.S. nuclear weaponry and supporting infrastructure. War corporations are his top campaign contributors. Think tanks that receive substantial funding from the war industry and that advocate for modernization include Brookings, CNAS, and CSIS. Brookings' 7 June 2019 panel "Falling apart? The politics of New START and strategic modernization" was in favor of modernization. CNAS' 14 June 2019 National Security Conference was in favor of modernization. (Gold Sponsors of the conference—giving $50,000 or more—could receive such perks as CEO participation in a CNAS panel and private discussion with the think tank's chief.) CSIS' ongoing Project on Nuclear Issues favors modernization.

44 The Congressional Budget Office estimated the cost to revamp the U.S. nuclear weapon infrastructure at $1.2 trillion from 2017 through 2046. Former senior policy advisor in the Dept. of Energy, Rober Alvarez, asserts (*Washington Spectator*, 20 December 2017) that the true figure is roughly $1.74 trillion, because the total cost needs to include nuclear waste management and environmental restoration. (NNSA's estimates of the price of nuclear weapons typically do not factor in important costs associated with decommissioning weaponry, disposing of nuclear waste, and providing healthcare to workers.) Ten years of modernizing and maintaining D.C.'s nuclear arsenal is expected to cost nearly half a trillion dollars, according to the CBO ("Projected Costs of U.S. Nuclear Forces, 2019 to 2028," January 2019). See also Mehta, Aaron. "Here's how many billions the U.S. will spend on nuclear weapons over the next decade." *Defense News*. 24 January 2019.

45 Broad and Sanger. "U.S. Ramping Up Major Renewal in Nuclear Arms." 21 September 2014.

46 The increase is roughly $61 billion. McCarthy, Tom. "Does the U.S. really need a huge boost in military spending?" *The Guardian*. 9 February 2018. Gilbert, David. "The Pentagon's spending increase is more than Russia's entire military budget." *VICE News*. 27 March 2018. "Trump to increase military budget above China, Russia." *Al Jazeera*. 10 February 2018.

47 "Nuclear Posture Review." *U.S. Department of Defense*. February 2018, p. XIII.

48 Borger, Julian. "Intelligence chief contradicts Trump on North Korea and Iran." *The Guardian*. 29 January 2019.

"North Korea nuclear: U.S. intelligence report says regime to keep weapons." *BBC News*. 30 January 2019.

49 The "B61-12s could each cost as much as twice their weight in gold," journalist John LaForge reports ("The New Nuclear Weapons: $1.74 Trillion for H-bomb Profiteers and Fake Cleanups." *Counterpunch*. March/April 2018). Contracts range from $127.6 million allocated to Boeing on 26 April 2019 to $18.4 million allocated to Peerless Technologies on 8 March 2019.

50 Andreasen, Steve. "Let's get our nuclear weapons out of Turkey." *LA Times*. 11 August 2016.

51 Trevithick, Joseph. "B-2 Flies First 'End-To-End' Tests with New Nuclear Bomb Amid Growing Cost Concerns." *The Drive / The War Zone*. 2 July 2018. "At the current price of gold at the time of writing, each one of the B61-12s could actually be worth nearly twice as much per pound." Trevithick goes on to suggest that the money could be better spent on other weapons of war.

52 The GAO notes: "independent cost estimates historically are higher than programs' cost estimates because the team conducting the independent estimate is more objective and less prone to accept optimistic assumptions." Quoted in "B61-12 NUCLEAR BOMB: Cost Estimate for Life Extension Incorporated Best Practices, and Steps Being Taken to Manage Remaining Program Risks." *U.S. Government Accountability Office Report to the Committee on Armed Services, U.S. Senate*. May 2018. Indeed, capacitor problem soon increased the B61-12 price by $600-700 million, per *Defense News*, 25 September 2019.

53 Kristensen, Hans M., Matthew McKinzie, Theodore A. Postol. "How U.S. nuclear force modernization is undermining strategic stability: The burst-height compensating super-fuze." *Bulletin of the Atomic Scientists*. 1 March 2017.

54 BAE Systems (Rockville, MD) received contracts (6 July, 9 Sept 2016), largely administrative (e.g. acquisition program documentation, advisory & assistance services, assessment of alternative ICBM Guidance Sets [MGS] concepts, business & financial management, data management & data rights, demonstration/validation of MGS tech, integration, logistics planning, performance evaluation, program risk management, quality assurance, requirements analysis, schedule management, strategic planning, systems engineering, technical and trade studies) to get the ball rolling on "ground based strategic deterrent." Valerie Insinna of *Defense News* reported on 17 June 2019, "In August 2017, the service awarded a $349 million contract to Boeing and $328 million to Northrop to mature their designs and reduce risk, cutting Lockheed Martin from the competition. It is unclear how much the program will ultimately cost." The Pentagon "previously estimated its price tag as anywhere from $85 billion to $100 billion," but the "newest estimate, produced in June, has not been disclosed." In July 2019, Boeing withdrew from the ground based strategic deterrent competition, leaving Northrop Grumman as the lone corporation vying to build the next generation of land-based intercontinental ballistic missiles.

55 For example, NATO is in the process of building a massive storage depot for war matériel in Poland. Paid for with NATO Security Investment Program, construction of the $260 million facility in Powidz entails razing up to roughly forty acres of trees. Sprenger, Sabastian. "NATO foots bill for massive U.S. combat depot in Poland." *Defense News*. 28 March 2019.

56 "The treaty ended a crisis of the 1980s that had come to be seen as a hair-trigger for a nuclear war." USSR "had deployed a missile in Europe called the SS-20, capable of carrying three nuclear warheads. The United States had deployed cruise and Pershing II missiles. All had the capability of reaching targets in as little as 10 minutes. The Soviets were particularly fearful of a strike that could obliterate them before they could retaliate, further raising the possibility of a mistake or misunderstanding that could lead to an unspeakable outcome," reported Gladstone (*The New York Times*, 8 November 2018).

57 "INF nuclear treaty: U.S. pulls out of Cold War-era pact with Russia." *BBC News*. 2 August 2019. Look at the *Times'* wording: "But the real action is likely to be in Asia. The Pentagon has already been developing nuclear weapons to match, and counter, what the Chinese have deployed. Completing that effort would take years. Until then, officials said the United States is preparing to modify existing weapons, including its non-nuclear Tomahawk missiles, and is likely to deploy them in Guam, where the military maintains a large base and they would face little political opposition" (David Sanger, 1 February 2019).

58 Gibbons-Neff, Thomas. "Pentagon Chief in Favor of Deploying U.S. Missiles to Asia." *The New York Times*. 3 August 2019.

"'Now that we have withdrawn, the Department of Defense will fully pursue the development of these ground-launched conventional missiles as a prudent response to Russia's actions and as part of the Joint Force's broader portfolio of conventional strike options,' Secretary Esper said," reported Deb Reichmann (*AP*, 2 August 2019). Raytheon and Lockheed Martin were already working on munition delivery devices that surpass the 500-km limit imposed by the INF Treaty, I note.

59 "INF nuclear treaty: U.S. tests medium-range cruise missile." *BBC News*. 20 August 2019.

60 "USMC's Smith on commandant Berger's guidance, Pacific & Autonomous Systems Priorities." *Defense & Aerospace Report*. 25 August 2019: <www.youtube.com/watch?v=Tn09-7BdFP4>, (13:18).

61 Gregg, Aaron. "Air Force awards massive hypersonic-weapon contract to Lockheed Martin." *Washington Post*. 18 April 2018.

62 In Dec 2018, Griffin "warned that other countries are moving faster in that arena [hypersonics] than the U.S. 'In the last year, China has tested more hypersonic weapons than we have in a decade,' Griffin said. 'We've got to fix that.'" See Jerry Siebenmark "U.S. Defense Contractors See Hypersonic Ramp-up," (*Aviation International News*, 24 May 2019). When sowing fear of a U.S. incapable of producing enough hypersonic missiles, Griffin alleged: "Our adversaries have clearly found ways to make them affordable. China has these things now *by the thousands*" (emphasis mine). Quoted in Judson, Jen. "Hypersonics by the dozens: U.S. industry faces manufacturing challenge." *Defense News*. 8 August 2019. Griffin's warnings must be seen against historical precedent: the MIC's hype of a "bomber gap" and "missile gap" during the 1950s. A lesser-known example of costly products justified by pointing at Moscow is MIT, the U.S. Air Force, and war corporations teaming up to develop and produce the SAGE radar system, which, according to one of its main engineers, never worked as promised. It cost billions of dollars, though. "Cold War Radar System a Trillion Dollar Fraud—Lester Earnest on RAI (1/4)." *The Real News Network*. 24 December 2018.

63 Griffin was president of In-Q-Tel, a CIA venture capital firm. He was also executive VP at Orbital ATK (Northrop Grumman acquired it in 2017), which manufactured rocket engines and munitions. Just before joining the Pentagon, he was CEO of Schafer Corp., which does a lot of DARPA business. He now oversees DARPA as Under Secretary for Research & Engineering.

64 Siebenmark, Jerry. "U.S. Defense Contractors See Hypersonic Ramp-up." *Aviation International News*. 24 May 2019.

65 Smith, R. Jeffrey. "Hypersonic Missiles Are Unstoppable. And They're Starting a New Global Arms Race." *The New York Times Magazine*. 19 June 2019.

66 Insinna, Valerie. "Northrop to build 3D-printed scramjet engine for Raytheon hypersonic weapon." *Defense News*. 18 June 2019.

67 Censer, Marjorie. "Lockheed says value of hypersonic contracts now totals more than $3.5 billion." *Inside Defense*. 23 July 2019.

68 Seymour Melman explains U.S. nuclear weapons: "multiples of overkill"—"humanly, militarily, scientifically a perfectly preposterous idea." See "Special Interdisciplinary Panel—Barriers

to Disarmament." *Towards Preventing Nuclear Omnicide*. St. Louis: First International Conference of the International Philosophers for the Prevention of Nuclear Omnicide, 1 May 1986.

69 Mills, Michael J., Owen B. Toon, et al. "Multidecadal global cooling and unprecedented ozone loss following a regional nuclear conflict." *Earth's Future*. 2.4 (2014): 161-176. Pausata, Francesco S.R. "Climate effects of a hypothetical regional nuclear war: Sensitivity to emission duration and particle composition." *Earth's Future*. 4.11 (2016): 498-511.

70 Nitze, Paul H. "A Threat Mostly to Ourselves." *The New York Times*. 28 October 1999. <https://www.nytimes.com/1999/10/28/opinion/a-threat-mostly-to-ourselves.html>.

71 "Privatizing the Apocalypse: How Nuclear Weapons Companies Commandeer Your Tax Dollars." *TomDispatch*. 22 September 2015.

10

Remotely Piloted Vehicles and Space Assets

UNMANNED AERIAL VEHICLES

One of the war industry's favorite products is the remotely piloted vehicle, also known as unmanned aerial vehicle (UAV) or "drone."[1] Drones can perform the following tasks: watching from above ("surveilling"), launching ordnance against a ground or air target, "painting the target" with a laser so that ordnance from another aircraft or ship can strike it. This technology distances the MIC and the U.S. public from the tangible and visceral effects of war. Drones offer a suitable form of warfare for image-conscious corporate entities.

Drones come in all makes, models, and sizes.[2]

The big drones include:
- General Atomics MQ-9 Reaper (*often armed with missiles*)
- General Atomics MQ-1 Predator (*retired; formerly used by CIA and the U.S. Air Force*)
- General Atomics MQ-1C (*an upgraded Predator for the U.S. Army*)
- Northrop Grumman RQ-4 Global Hawk (*flies higher than the MQ-9*)
- Northrop Grumman MQ-4C Triton (*similar to RQ-4, and often used to observe open ocean*)

The small drones include:
- AeroVironment Switchblade and Raven
- Boeing (Insitu) ScanEagle
- Boeing (Insitu) RQ-21A Blackjack
- Northrop Grumman MQ-8C Fire Scout (*a Textron helicopter*)
- Textron (AAI) RQ-7 Shadow

Big war corporations win altogether in the drone game.

Different war corporations profit together on the same contract. For example, these corporations—PAE, Constellis' Academi division, Boeing's Insitu, and Textron's AAI—have worked under the same contract to provide drones, maintenance, and technical support to the U.S. government worldwide.[3] Here too, multiple corporations coming together to benefit from one transaction happens regularly: four selling management for the Navy's Program Executive Office for Unmanned Systems; seven selling long- and medium-range drones; and six selling expertise developing drones that work together, autonomously, in areas where GPS is not working or is jammed.[4] All for one, and one for all!

War corporations also profit together by producing goods and services for one another's platforms. Take the General Atomics MQ-9. General Atomics makes the drone's body. Honeywell makes the engine. Boeing, Lockheed Martin, and Raytheon make the bombs and missiles. L3 makes the training system and sells depot maintenance, and Raytheon makes the targeting sensor and the radar warning receiver. Many corporations sell goods and services for the MQ-9.[5] It is worth noting that General Atomics drones don't just show up on bases in Afghanistan, Iraq, Djibouti, and elsewhere. They're transported in cargo aircraft, like the Lockheed Martin C-130. When one war corporation wins, they all win.

This tally doesn't include all of the war corporations that work on the satellites that relay communications between the drone and the U.S. Air Force back in the United States, which controls many large drones operating overseas. Corporate equipment, which is located on Ramstein Air Base in Germany, reportedly aids in the relay of these signals to and from Middle East warzones.[6] (Senior German politicians, including the chancellor, feign ignorance on this matter.) Corporate interests intersect in the drone sector like fine needlepoint.[7] Many corporations profit from the Pentagon's drone-binge (though given the industry role in pushing for increased use of drones, one might call it a force-feeding).

The military and congressional sides of the MIC triangle do their parts. The former Textron official now in charge of Pentagon acquisition, Ellen Lord, set up The Trusted Capital Marketplace, wherein the War Department pairs private funding with rising war corporations. This ensures investment in the war industry is plentiful in years to come. Lord first steered that Marketplace toward corporations that make small drones. Congress' 2018 NDAA required the establishment of such a Marketplace.

Great power competition warrants drone deployments encroaching upon Russia and China. Northrop Grumman RQ-4 Global Hawks fly over the Black Sea and South China Sea, for example. General Atomics MQ-9 Reaper drones, operated by the U.S. Air Force, are now at Mirosławiec Air Base, Poland. U.S. mercenaries ("contractors") play a major role in the drone program on Mirosławiec. You know Lockheed Martin's Aegis weapon system is located in Deveselu, Romania. Well, General Atomics MQ-9 drones also operate out of Campia Turzii, a five-hour bus ride north of Deveselu. Meanwhile, U.S. corporations are designing underwater weapons systems, operating IT infrastructure, and administering matériel in Bulgaria.⁸ In summer 2019, Bulgaria's Council of Ministers approved agreements to purchase roughly $1.3 billion of Lockheed Martin fighter jets and equipment.⁹ In autumn 2018 and 2019, the MQ-9 took part in military exercises in Ukraine, part of the latest U.S. thrust in Russia's orbit. Industry sales and military deployments overlap again.

IN YOUR FACE (Fairs, Air Shows, Conferences, Exhibits)

Corporations have many opportunities to market and sell goods and services to the War Department and governments around the world. Corporate displays (fairs, air shows, conferences, exhibits) remind us of the promotional nature of industry.

The Defense Security Cooperation Agency (DSCA), the government agency in charge of facilitating the sale of U.S. weaponry to other countries, is working with D.C. to change the Conventional Arms Trade (CAT) policy, so industry can sell *armed* drones to some of the Gulf countries—absolutist regimes like Bahrain, Qatar, Saudi Arabia, and the UAE. This was seen clearly at the most recent International Defence Exhibition & Conference (IDEX) held in the Emirate of Abu Dhabi, located along the southern elbow of the Persian Gulf.¹⁰ Every major and minor U.S. war corporation with metal in the drone game was present at IDEX 2019, from AAR Mobility Systems to Vertex Aerospace. (Vertex, a former division of L3, was sold recently to American Industrial Partners). Billions of dollars of deals were penned. More money is up for grabs if these drones could be armed, so industry cited great power competition: blame Chinese arms merchants to justify increased sales, including potentially armed drones, to Gulf regimes. China has encroached on the territory of U.S. war corporations by selling drones to Gulf governments. Journalist Natasha Turak quoted the international market area director of a drone manufacturer AeroVironment: "The Chinese are definitely a threat."¹¹ Turak reported that the executive's "colleagues attested to the lengthy U.S. government process for approving even non-lethal drone exports, which they described as a hindrance to international business,"¹² putting more pressure on DSCA to expedite sales. IDEX is one of dozens of displays (arms fairs, air shows, conferences, exhibits, and symposia) that the war industry puts on every year. All such displays are designed by industry to boost profits.

Fairs. Look at Eurosatory, an arms fair that is held every two years in Paris. Under tight security, international VIPs, war industry salespeople, uniformed military personnel, and government officials schmooze, talk shop, and peruse goods and "solutions." Salespeople are personable, knowledgeable, smooth, and charismatic. They are performers. They share laughs, commiserate, provide insight, and establish a friendship or two. The layout is bewildering, like a good casino. The customer (typically a high-ranking military officer or government official) must wander, shop, and sample.

Air shows. The average Joe or the passing onlooker sees planes perform tricks in the sky. Profiteers see an opportunity to sell, sell, sell. War corporations sponsor international air shows and use them to sit down with delegations from dozens of countries. The executive in charge of Raytheon International explains his presence at the 2018 U.K. Farnborough International Air Show: "During the course of the last couple of days we've had well over 400 meetings with over thirty delegations from thirty-two different countries."[13] The Bahrain International Air Show (BIAS), held in part at Al-Sakhir Air Base in the tiny island country, is "commercially-focused" and "seeks to give aerospace businesses a personalized experience, offering access to high-level delegations within the aerospace community all within a dedicated arena."[14] Established in 2010 in Bahrain, which is ruled by the unelected Al-Khalifa regime, BIAS "is renowned for its world-class facilities providing an opportunity to meet with industry peers and customers and participate in the civil and military delegations programme."[15] Naturally, there is a propaganda aspect to air shows.[16]

Conferences. War corporations sponsor conferences to bring together contracting officials, political operatives, and salespeople under one roof. Journalists Dana Priest and William Arkin sum up the essence when describing one particular conference: Vendors "paid for access to some of the people who decide what services and gadgets to buy for troops."[17] Conferences often focus on a specific or burgeoning sector of the war industry. CyberCon 2018, for example, was held at the Ritz-Carlton in Pentagon City and brought to you by ManTech, Raytheon, and KPMG. You know ManTech and Raytheon, both among the top sellers of IT services and cyber goods to the military, the Department of Homeland Security, and other armed bureaucracies. KPMG sells financial services to the Pentagon and war corporations. (Pressure groups' annual meetings are also effective face-to-face networking events.[18])

Exhibits. London's Defense & Security Equipment International (DSEI) is a massive arms fair masquerading as an "exhibit." Sponsored in 2019 by General Dynamics and the U.K.'s BAE Systems, DSEI is a monster. Spanning pavilion after pavilion, the 2019 event featured five "zones"—aerospace, land, sea, security, and a holistic "joint" zone (tackling communication, medical, and innovation). The corporations behind DSEI are proud of the exhibit's "international business opportunities," in which more than 2,750 "global VIPs" from nearly one hundred nations ink deals while perusing the latest war goods and services.

Symposia are different. Symposia are networking events. The Space & Missile Defense Symposium, for example, takes place annually in Huntsville, Alabama. Sponsored by various war corporations, the SMD Symposium attracts academics, uniformed military officials, corporate representatives, and friendly media. There are plenty of showcases. Panels promote industry solutions to any problem or challenge. Fora are comparable to symposia. The 2019 Reagan National Defense Forum in Simi Valley, California, is a strong example. War corporations sponsored the invite-only event. Prominent congresspeople were on the steering committee and in attendance. All speakers were MIC elites, current and former. They promoted fear, pretexts, high military budgets, and worldwide military and intelligence operations. Corporate media moderated.

VARIATIONS ON A THEME

Small drones instruct us about industry's reach and arms proliferation.

AeroVironment is a war corporation with facilities in southern California. AeroVironment's *kamikaze* attack drone, Switchblade, sells well.[19] Grunts can carry the Switchblade in a backpack, set it airborne within minutes, and guide it to hover above the target until they decide to send it in for the kill. AeroVironment's RQ-20B Puma and the RQ-11 Raven are other strong sellers. The Puma and Raven are both hand-launched, fixed-wing drones. AeroVironment has sold to the brutal Egyptian regime and such European nations as Estonia, Norway and the Ukraine.[20] Great power competition demands sales to Eastern Europe, as DSCA director Lieutenant General Charles Hooper made clear on his 4 June 2019 visit to the Brookings Institution.[21]

Textron's AAI division manufactures the popular RQ-7 Shadow, a smallish drone that can be launched from a pneumatic catapult towed on a trailer. Textron sells a variety of goods and services related to the Shadow. Work takes place in the U.S. (corporate facilities in Hunt Valley, MD, and Fort Huachuca, AZ) and such warzones as Afghanistan and Iraq. Foreign customers have included Canberra, Rome, and Stockholm. Other corporations profit via Textron's Shadow.[22] Big drones or small, profit for all.

Kratos is a war corporation that has seen impressive growth in recent years. It has sold a variety of goods and services to the U.S. military, including rocket motors, command & control systems for satellite operations, and devices for target practice. An aerial target that mimics an incoming cruise missile is one of its best-selling products. Kratos is also working on a drone (the "Valkyrie") that works like a wingman, accompanying a manned fighter pilot into battle.

Kratos introduces us to "swarming" drones. Industry is currently pushing drones that swarm a target. DARPA's Gremlins is one such program: tiny drones are dropped from an aircraft, go do their mission, and then are picked up by a Lockheed Martin C-130 cargo plane. Corporations visualize Gremlins as interconnected air-bots that work together to overwhelm the enemy. Gremlins ought to be able to organize themselves in the heat of battle and make some decisions without human input. War corporations develop every single part of the Gremlins program.[23] Kratos fabricates the air vehicles. Its work takes place across the country, including corporate facilities and War Department airspace in Alabama, Arizona, California, Michigan, Nevada, New York, and Washington. Swarming programs are becoming more and more popular.[24] Capitalists market swarming drones as "low-cost," "revolutionary," and benefiting mankind through civilian applications, like search and rescue.

When pushed on the necessity to ban drone weaponry before it proliferates, the war industry resorts to tropes: "progress cannot be stopped" or "if we don't do it, the Russians and Chinese will be leaders in this field." The spiral is always upwards toward profit and conflict. The proliferation of drones now allows war corporations to cash in on developing technology to stop all these drones (technology known as "counter-UAS"). Counter-UAS technology stops drones by jamming or hacking the incoming vehicle or shooting projectiles at it. Black Dart, centered around U.S. Navy infrastructure at Point Mugu, California, is the Pentagon's main contribution to developing and testing corporate counter-UAS technologies. Many U.S. and allied war corporations sell counter-UAS goods and services.[25] Governments worldwide are stepping up counter-UAS purchases. At an arms fair in London, one Raytheon vice president used regrettable language to sum up the counter-UAS sector: "It's exploded: Counter-unmanned aircraft systems is the in-vogue discussion on weapon space and solution set at every trade show we've been to. It's a nonstop revolving door of interested customers in our solutions."[26]

Patterns of industry behavior echo across time. The war industry pushed for ballistic missiles, then pushed for anti-ballistic missiles. The war industry pushed for GPS-guided missiles, then pushed for new surface-to-air missile batteries with advanced radar to destroy the precision missiles. It pushed for cyber tools and weapons, then pushed for cyber defenses once those tools and weapons became ubiquitous. Corporations follow this pattern today with drone technology, developing technology that disables and takes down drones (now that everyone from nation-states to formal militias to gangs have drones). War corporations proliferated drones, and are now profiting from disabling such weaponry. Profit in, profit out.

Drones are not just flying around in the sky. Unmanned undersea vehicles (UUVs) roam the oceans. Industry knows the deep blue sea too offers room for profitable drone warfare. The Chief of Naval Operations and Navy admirals have an institutional and financial incentive to go along for the UUV ride. In summer 2018, the U.S. Navy took UUVs to the next level, inking a contract with about two-dozen war corporations for UUV R&D. Signatories included major corporations (General Dynamics, Northrop Grumman, Lockheed Martin), academic organizations (Draper Lab, Southwest Research Institute, Woods Hole Oceanographic Institute), and information technology powerhouses (L3 and SAIC). This contract suffused UUV research and development throughout industry. From that point on, selling UUV goods and services was as humdrum as selling any other sector of war. Boeing's Orca Extra Large UUV is a frontrunner right now in the UUV sector. UUVs present a growing market.[27] The Pentagon is a piggish kingpin, and the war industry is an artful, tyrannical restaurateur cooking up an endless buffet.

A domestic construction boom has accompanied the industry's push for, and the Pentagon's investment in, unmanned vehicles. In less than twelve months, drone-related construction involved expanding drone facilities at Marine Corps Air Station Cherry Point, mid-coast North Carolina; building mission control facilities for Northrop Grumman drones at Naval Air Station Jacksonville, Florida, and Naval Air Station Whidbey Island, Washington; building hangars for drones at Naval Station Mayport, Florida, and Fort Wainwright, Alaska; and working on a variety of projects at the major drone hubs of Creech Air Force Base and Nellis Air Force Base, Nevada.[28] Construction associated with General Atomics drones has inundated National Guard units (Arizona's Air National Guard 214th Reconnaissance Group, Arkansas' Air National Guard 188th Wing, and New York's Air National Guard 174th Attack Wing). Construction at these Guard sites is ongoing and includes operations and intel production facilities.

The War Department and CIA have built up drone facilities overseas, particularly on the African continent (e.g. Djibouti, Ethiopia, Kenya, Niger, and the Seychelles). Most drone operations in Djibouti have been transferred from Camp Lemonnier to Chabelley Airfield to avoid problems with drone crashes.[29] (Some say that local air traffic controllers were protesting the foreign military presence by not giving U.S. drones the go-ahead to land until they were very low on fuel.) The war industry and the Pentagon claim drone infrastructure in Niger, in addition to U.S. military bases in southern Italy, helps hunt Islamists in Libya. Concordantly, drone infrastructure in east Africa and Saudi Arabia helps hunt Islamists in Somalia and Yemen. Drone infrastructure in Afghanistan assists in the hunt for Islamists in Pakistan and patrols Afghanistan's border with Iran. Excuses abound.

DEATH TOLL

President George W. Bush normalized D.C.'s use of drones to kill black and brown people in distant lands. President Barack H. Obama escalated this form of murder.[30] The General Atomics MQ-1 Predator was the favored instrument during the early years of the Bush administration. The General Atomics MQ-9 Reaper gradually took over this role, assuming the pole position by the end of the Obama administration.[31] The U.S. Air Force basically runs CIA's drone program[32]—a program built purchasing goods and services from the war industry.

D.C. vowed it would only use drones to kill someone when it wasn't feasible to capture the person. In order to be able to strike often, D.C.'s legal experts redefined the meaning of feasibility. D.C. promised it would only target people who posed an "imminent threat" to the United States. But victims of drone strikes were just going about their day—thousands of miles away.[33] So what did D.C. do? It redefined the meaning of imminence![34]

The bodies stacked up. By early 2013, D.C. had killed five thousand people via drone strike, according to some estimates.[35] Sometimes, after an initial drone strike, U.S. drone pilots and sensor operators would wait for first responders and concerned crowds to arrive and then launch another missile. (This is the same tactic some suicide bombers have used across the Middle East: wait for first responders and then detonate a second explosive, killing more innocents.) At the time of this writing, D.C. had used drones to kill over 8,000 people.[36]

MIC members and corporate media applaud. Military-intelligence are using "persistent surveillance" to "strike known terrorists," they say. The Pentagon has "successfully removed a high-value target from the theater," they say. All sides of the military-industrial-congressional triangle play a crucial role convincing the U.S. public that the operations are necessary, accurate, and precise. They only kill the "bad guys." Operations are nothing of the sort. In a "signature strike," CIA and the U.S. military target humans based on their behavior,[37] not any conclusive information that indicates an individual is about to harm U.S. civilians in a terrorist attack. Historian Eric Hobsbawm reminded us, "The greatest cruelties of our century have been the impersonal cruelties of remote decision, of system and routine, especially when they could be justified as regrettably operational necessities."[38] His words can apply to drones or D.C.'s operations as a whole. Hobsbawm was talking about the twentieth century. Horrifically, the twenty-first has been no better.

ONE SEASON

One season of drone sales illuminates the nature of industrial war. While many of us in the northern hemisphere were baking in the heat during June-August 2018, the U.S. war industry was selling drones and related technology (receipts topping $3,509,000,000, by my count). Yes, 3.5 *billion*.

Corporate operations. Three corporations that own *and operate* drones for the U.S. military overseas sold such services in summer 2018: General Atomics,

Textron AAI, and Boeing. The Pentagon credited General Atomics' hands-on contribution as "surge support" in Afghanistan, but that is disingenuous, since corporations pressure Congress and the military to increase the scope of war. Textron AAI's work was specifically for protecting military facilities, and Boeing's—the unarmed ScanEagle drone—was for special operations. These corporations are not just selling products to the U.S. Armed Forces. They make millions selling and often *operating* drones, further increasing the corporate takeover of what was once an inherently governmental job: waging war.[39]

Loyalty. Though headquartered in Virginia, California, and other parts of the United States, war corporations have no loyalty to the nation. They are loyal to the almighty dollar, Euro, riyal, or any currency that comes their way. Boeing's main drone division, Insitu, manufactures and assembles its products along the Columbia River in the Pacific Northwest. Two of its bestselling small drones are the Blackjack and the ScanEagle. On 29 June, Boeing sold ScanEagle drones to Lebanon, and on 21 August sold Blackjack equipment to Poland. On 26 July, AeroVironment sold communications devices to Norway for use with its drones. On 24 July, Boeing sold ScanEagle systems and spares, which the Pentagon is giving to Afghanistan's military. The U.S. occupation of Afghanistan is approaching its twentieth year—two decades of profiteering.

The "jobs" ploy. The industry's drone sector provides opportunity to create and market new weaponry, all the while pretending such weaponry is good for jobs. Boeing's MQ-25 Stingray is a good example of this. On 30 August, Boeing sealed a deal (worth up to $805 million) to provide the War Department with four MQ-25 drones, which are capable of flying from aircraft carriers. Like any proficient war corporation, Boeing spreads production across congressional districts. The MQ-25 Stingray is worked on in Missouri, Indiana, Iowa, Florida, California, and overseas locations. The claim that the "defense" industry brings jobs is a stale public relations ploy. It hides a truth worth repeating: Spending on healthcare, education, or clean energy creates more jobs than spending on war.[40]

Academia. The longer the wars last, the more academic institutions are corrupted. Here, too. On 14 August, George Mason University received over $60 million to help the Air Force Research Lab improve hardware and software that connect and synchronize small drones.[41]

Schemes. By now you're familiar with the General Atomics MQ-9, the Pentagon's workhorse. When there's a U.S. drone strike, the MQ-9 is the likely culprit. War corporations are constantly selling upgrades and supplementary drone services to the War Department.[42] No consumer would ever pay for mandatory software upgrades on their 2018 automobile immediately after driving it off the lot, yet this sort of slick salesmanship is commonplace in the war machine. Such treachery reveals industry's supremacy within the military-industrial-congressional triangle.

Cooperation. Raytheon produces many aircraft sensors in McKinney, Texas, including electro-optical, infrared (EO/IR) devices that go on the underside of other corporation's drones. These devices are the "eyes" of the drone. Very expensive eyes. Raytheon sold plenty of EO/IR work throughout the summer.[43] The day before U.S. Independence Day, the British corporation Rolls-Royce sold the Pentagon $420 million of maintenance and repair on Northrop Grumman MQ-4C's engines. Any platform (a ship, an aircraft, or a land vehicle) is an opportunity, for which war corporations sell goods and services.

While the Pentagon spends billions of dollars on drones, students struggle with mounting debt, children go hungry, the natural world suffers the sixth great extinction, and the nation writhes under stagnant wages, mental illness, and a lack of universal healthcare. *Drone-related* sales during summer 2018—totaling over $3.5 billion by my count—show how profitable this sector of war really is. And this sector is expected to grow with a new, profit-friendly drone export policy.[44]

This is not enough for the MIC's top tier. Bill Greenwalt has worked as U.S. Deputy Under Secretary of War for Industrial Policy, director of federal acquisition at Lockheed Martin, and staffer at the Senate Armed Services Committee. If anyone embodies the military-industrial-congressional triangle, it's Bill—he has worked in each side. Bill now cites great power competition to further loosen the rules governing weapon exports.[45]

As of March 2019, the Executive Branch no longer required the Office of the Director of National Intelligence to release summaries of CIA drone strikes, including the numbers of civilians killed, outside of declared warzones.[46] This new executive order changed nothing, I argue, because ODNI had been releasing clearly falsified numbers.[47] The new executive order still required the War Department to report on civilian casualties, though these tallies too have been suspiciously low.

SPACE: THE FINAL PROFITEER

Drones observe Earth and its peoples from relatively close by. A General Atomics MQ-9 can fly as high as 50,000 feet (15,240 meters), a Northrop Grumman RQ-4 up to 60,000 feet (18,288 meters). Satellites orbit at higher altitudes, cover a wider territory, and stay aloft for much longer durations. The use of U.S. satellites in the planning and execution of military operations became commonplace in the 1980s, particularly during U.S. aggression against both Iran and Iraq in the First Gulf War (1980-88), the Israeli attack against Iraq in June 1981, the 1983 U.S. invasion of Grenada, the 1989 U.S. invasion of Panamá, and repeated U.S. attacks against Libya in the Gulf of Sidra. The U.S. Armed Forces are now completely dependent upon satellites. The U.S. Air Force operates 77 satellites "vital to national security."[48] Parsing corporate activity vis-à-vis the space sector shines light on the militarization of what ought to be a peaceful realm.

The militarization of space has been in the works for decades.[49] Space is one of many sectors in which war corporations cooperate.[50] Today, efforts to militarize space take place mostly in California (Los Angeles Air Force Base and the surrounding El Segundo portion of the city; and Vandenberg AFB in Santa Barbara County, located at the elbow of the California coast, a speedy two-hour drive northwest of Los Angeles); Colorado (Buckley AFB east of Denver in Aurora, Peterson AFB in Colorado Springs, and Schriever AFB east of Colorado Springs); and Florida (Cape Canaveral and Patrick AFB, co-located halfway up the state's Atlantic coastline). The U.S. Air Force and the National Reconnaissance Office (NRO) launch satellites from Vandenberg and Cape Canaveral.

Headquartered in Chantilly, Virginia, NRO manufactures and launches satellites that snoop on planet Earth. Its satellites can reportedly aid electronic eavesdropping, map the earth, and measure the signatures that electronic installations and humans give off. To these ends, it works with other intelligence organizations, like the National Geospatial-Intelligence Agency (NGA) and CIA. Actually, I misspoke. NRO *does not* manufacture or launch satellites. War corporations do all of that *for* NRO. NRO is one of the most corporatized intelligence organizations. War corporations design, manufacture, launch, maintain, and upgrade reconnaissance satellites. In practice, NRO is a corporate entity—run mostly by corporations, for corporate profit—managing "innovative overhead intelligence systems for national security."[51]

The space launch sites used by the U.S. Air Force and NRO are always getting upgraded. Recent construction projects include an NRO facility at Vandenberg AFB; a wharf at Cape Canaveral; and a hangar at Patrick AFB.[52]

The big four—Boeing, Lockheed Martin, Northrop Grumman, Raytheon—hog most design, development, and deployment of space-based technology.

Global navigation satellite systems (GNSS), upon which people rely in their daily doings, are corporate. The most famous GNSS is the global positioning system, or GPS. Large corporations like Boeing, Honeywell, and Lockheed Martin sell GPS provision and sustainment.[53] Over budget and behind schedule, Raytheon is in charge of developing the new ground control system for GPS.[54]

Boeing has run satellites and ground technology that track human-made junk orbiting Earth and has run military communication satellites. **Lockheed Martin's** space products are ubiquitous. The corporation develops, markets, and sells satellites for communications, tracking other satellites and space junk, ground and air navigation, and warning about missile launches. There are instances where the corporation hypes the threat, manufactures the resulting satellite, launches the satellite, runs the ground stations monitoring the satellite, operates the satellite, and maintains the satellite. A sequence like this is hard to beat when it comes to profitability. Lockheed Martin has also run operations at North American Aerospace Defense Command (NORAD) at Cheyenne Mountain, just outside of Colorado Springs. NORAD is a U.S.-Canadian organization focusing on governing U.S.-Canada airspace. Lockheed Martin has deep relationships with other allied nations' intelligence organizations that are developing space-based technology, especially South Korean Defense Intelligence Command and British Defense Intelligence. As the go-to corporation, Lockheed Martin works with the National Aeronautics & Space Administration, NASA,[55] garnering good press for seemingly benign activity in the process. In addition to a huge presence at Air Force space locations, Lockheed Martin's corporate space facilities cover Sunnyvale, California, and Littleton, Colorado, south of Denver. **Northrop Grumman's** space products include satellites for monitoring weather, missile launches and tracking, and nuclear detonations; satellites for communication and navigation; lasers; and rocket engines. **Raytheon** prides itself on having a foot in all parts of the space program;[56] Raytheon specializes in creating and selling the electronics and software underpinning space systems. Its products include radar, satellite communications, and navigation. All four of the aforementioned corporations work on lucrative, highly classified satellite projects, which are kept out of the public domain. This was a basic overview of the biggest corporations profiting from the space sector.

In addition to the fleet in its possession, the War Department purchases worldwide satellite communications services from such corporations as Artel LLC, SES Government Solutions, Inmarsat, and Iridium.

Militarization of space requires getting military satellites into orbit.

The Evolved Expendable Launch Vehicle (EELV) is the overall program through which the U.S. Air Force and the National Reconnaissance Office launch products into space. EELV is "expendable" because it is used only once—the consummate consumable. A joint venture between Lockheed Martin and Boeing known as United Launch Services (ULS) produces launch vehicles (e.g. Delta IV, Atlas V, and new prototypes) to get satellites to orbit. The primary locations of ULS' corporate activity should be familiar to you: Centennial and Littleton in Colorado, Vandenberg Air Force Base, and Cape Canaveral Air Station.[57]

ULS doesn't just sell launch vehicles. It sells all sorts of associated provisions.[58]

ULS had a monopoly on launching military payloads within the EELV program until Elon Musk's SpaceX entered the arena during fiscal years 2016-17.[59] Amazon CEO Jeff Bezos soon followed. On 10 October 2018, Bezos' Blue Origin

LLC cut a $500 million deal to develop a prototype within the EELV program. Rocket propulsion is Aerojet Rocketdyne's bread and butter. With production spread across the country,[60] the corporation's rockets propel everything from the portable Stinger surface-to-air missile[61] to the upper stage of ULS' Atlas V launch vehicle. Northrop Grumman sells solid rocket motors and booster segments (in addition to working on an upper stage engine for Bezos' Blue Origin).[62]

The congressional side of the military-industrial-congressional triangle plays its role well. Section 1604 of fiscal year 2015 National Defense Authorization Act abetted U.S. space profiteering while demonizing Moscow. Section 1604 "requires the development of a next-generation rocket propulsion system that will transition away from the use of non-allied space launch engines to a domestic alternative," according to contract announcements.[63] In other words, the U.S. Congress demands that by the year 2022 the U.S. Air Force and NRO stop relying on Russian RD-180 engines, which presently power the Atlas V launch vehicle out of Earth's atmosphere. New launch vehicles with homegrown rockets are in the works: ULS' Vulcan, Northrop Grumman's OmegA, and Blue Origin's New Glenn. These corporations are free to sell their launch services to commercial customers if the Pentagon does not select them to replace the Russians' RD-180. Anti-Russia frenzy is good for war industry sales, including big-ticket items like rocket engines.

Corporations run the ranges where launch vehicles take flight. This comes in the form of "launch support services" (most tasks that help with the launch) and "range support services" (the general tasks that keep the range running and operational). The Western Range is comprised of Vandenberg Air Force Base and atolls in the Pacific Ocean. The Eastern Range is comprised of Patrick Air Force Base and Cape Canaveral Air Force Station (the duo halfway up Florida's east coast), and Ascension Auxiliary Air Field. Ascension Island is located about halfway between South America and Africa in the middle of the Atlantic Ocean. Historian Daniel Immerwahr describes the island as "one of the most unappetizing landing spots on the map: jagged with rocks, waterless and far from everything... Yet in early 1942 the U.S. Army engineers had arrived, and within three months they had blasted off the island's top and built a long landing strip, followed by barracks, a mess hall, and machine shops—everything needed to refresh the planes [carrying cargo and personnel fighting World War II] and send them onward." Today, the war corporations and the U.S. Air Force on the island play a key role in tracking missiles and rockets launching from Florida. The U.K. is nominally in charge of Ascension.[64]

The Space & Missile Systems Center (SMC) at Los Angeles Air Force Base is the focal point in the Air Force through which corporations sell satellite constellations and militarize space. Corporations practically run SMC's six main directorates.⁶⁵ The Aerospace Corp. runs SMC overall. The Aerospace Corp. sells these operations as "general life cycle systems engineering and integration support for the national space community."⁶⁶ War industry mercenaries greatly outnumber uniformed military personnel within SMC directorates.⁶⁷ The focus of directorates differs, the color of the money doesn't. No matter the job, corporations are in the lead. Mantech, which makes money selling products and contractor personnel to NSA, sells to the Air Force space program. Goods and services include security for SMC, specifically Sensitive Compartmented Information and special access programs.⁶⁸ Johns Hopkins University Applied Physics Lab is very close with SMC.⁶⁹ Corporations have taken charge of SMC financial and acquisition plans.⁷⁰ SMC's vast IT and computer infrastructure is corporate.⁷¹ From highly-classified projects to financials and IT, corporations flood the space and expand.

Harris Corp. has assumed space jobs of all sizes, to the point where it is now the backbone of a lot of ground-based space monitoring.⁷²

Guam is one of the overseas locations—two others are Thule Air Base in Greenland and Diego Garcia in the Indian Ocean—where Harris is operating and maintaining the Air Force Satellite Control Network. (The Pentagon's only base north of the Arctic Circle, Thule is home to an airfield, a deep-water port, and powerful radar aimed at Russia's northern coast.) The U.S. military destroyed Guam when wresting it from the Japanese during World War II. In retaking Guam from the Japanese, the U.S. Armed Forces destroyed Guam's capital with bombs and artillery. Every major structure suffered damage or destruction.⁷³

Shortly after the hostilities ended and D.C. decided to keep Guam as a colony, a U.S. cargo plane landed from Australia. Tree snakes had hitched a ride in the plane's wheel wells. Within three decades the tree snakes had caused more than half of Guam's bird species to go extinct.⁷⁴ U.S. militarism took it from there, devastating the island's environment. U.S. military facilities and infrastructure have wrecked pristine land and encroached upon the Guam National Wildlife Refuge, while Corporate America has run environmental studies and administered rudiments of the decision-making processes regarding military activities on Guam.⁷⁵ Many corporations build and maintain U.S. military infrastructure in the Pacific, with a focus on facilities on Guam.⁷⁶

Like Puerto Ricans, the indigenous Chamorro people on Guam have U.S. citizenship but not total rights. The Chamorro people were not allowed to speak Chamoru in government buildings and schools,⁷⁷ just as Puerto Ricans were not allowed to speak Spanish in schools during the U.S. occupation, post Spanish American War. Puerto Rico and Guam share another difficulty: the War Department and the VA do not provide adequate medical facilities or staff in these colonies, so veterans of all ages and genders must fly to mainland U.S. or Hawai'i, respectively, to get the medical care they need.

U.S. military installations—including Andersen Air Force Base and Naval Base Guam—hog more than one quarter of Guam. Poverty on the island is higher than on mainland USA. Guam and the Chamorro people are fertile recruiting territory for the U.S. War Department, which uses significant financial incentives including signing bonuses to induce people to enlist. Expensive war goods like the Boeing B-1 bomber, the Northrop Grumman B-2 bomber, the Boeing B-52 bomber, the Northrop Grumman MQ-4C drone, and Lockheed Martin cargo planes pollute the air and clog military bases and skies above. Other adverse impacts from the military presence include noise pollution, military housing allowances sending housing prices upward, and sexual crimes.[78]

A variety of corporations sustains the U.S. military presence around the greater Marianas Islands, including running the Guam Range, where the U.S. Air Force trains, often using polluting ordnance, and running BOSS at Naval Base Guam and Naval Support Activity Andersen (surrounded by penury).[79] Corporate America is building more infrastructure that will house and support an increased Marine Corps presence on Guam.[80] Humans across the Northern Marianas islands are aware of and pushing back against this and against the Pentagon's plans to use two islands, Pågan and Tinian, for target practice using industry ordnance (mortars, rockets, bombs, missiles).[81]

Corporatization of space will not let up any time soon. The war industry is constantly seeking out new avenues for profit. For example, Advanced Technology International (ATI) has been allocated roughly $500 million since 2017 to run the Space Enterprise Consortium. The purpose of this Consortium is described by the Alexandria-based *Space News*:

> When the Missile Defense Agency needed design concepts for a space-based sensor layer, it relied on a relatively new Air Force-funded organization to get the money into contractors [*sic*] hands faster than it could have done itself. Since it was stood up a year ago, the Air Force-led Space Enterprise Consortium has seen rapid growth in industry participation and in funding. The consortium has roughly 200 members that include small and large businesses, nonprofit organizations and academic research institutions that compete for contracts, typically for designs of new concepts or advanced prototypes.[82]

The Space Enterprise Consortium is basically a way for industry to obtain government funding and sell space goods and services rapidly.

Conflicts of interest occur regularly in the space sector. For example, McKinsey & Co. implements the Space Acquisition Transformation Plan, which is primarily run out of Los Angeles Air Force Base. McKinsey & Co., a regular seller to the War Department, is in charge of implementing this new plan regarding how the Air Force will best acquire corporate-supplied space assets. And the Pentagon official in charge of crafting policies vis-à-vis the war industry is a former partner at McKinsey. He has since been promoted to chief of staff of the acting Secretary of War (the former Boeing executive named Pat Shanahan). McKinsey has not just aided and abetted the U.S. war machine. According to *The New York Times*, McKinsey has worked hard to support despots, authoritarians, and undemocratic regimes worldwide (allies and foes of the war industry alike). McKinsey recently snagged over $15.7 million to support the F-35 "affordability campaign," an MIC initiative designed to present the F-35 Joint Strike Fighter as reasonably-priced, instead of the ultra-expensive, underperforming aircraft it is.[83] You can't make this stuff up.

This has been a stark, though incomplete, outline of the goods and services industry has sold to the federal government for military activities in space. Purportedly acting in the name and interest of the United States, the MIC—the Pentagon, the U.S. war industry, and Capitol Hill—has militarized space more than any nation or combination of nations. Or, as one executive might put it, the "space value chain is an entire suite of capabilities we use to make the world a safer place."[84]

SPACE FORCE

For decades the U.S. war industry has lobbied for greater militarization of space. Major successes, from the standpoint of corporate profit, have included the 1984 establishment of the Strategic Defense Initiative Organization and the 2002 establishment of the Missile Defense Agency. But victories don't stop industry pressure.

The establishment of a new, separate branch of the Armed Forces for space-related systems (and all the additional funding that would come with it) was always a long shot in the minds of war industry executives and lobbyists. The bureaucratic inertia of the Pentagon's rings stood in the way of establishing this branch, now known as Space Force. It was only a matter of time before greed overcame it. It always does in matters of war and peace. The war industry recognized an auspicious administration in the White House, one extra-compliant to the demands of corporate power, and leapt in. The President of the United States soon announced his desires for the creation of a Space Force.

The reaction within D.C. post 2016 was initially mixed, in large part because one faction of the ruling elite had deep antipathy toward anything coming from that White House. Industry artiste Deborah Lee James[85] represented the middle-of-the-road approach initially favored by some D.C. insiders. It took only a few days for Secretary of War James Mattis to get in line.[86] Business as usual—militarizing space—was charging full speed ahead even during the deliberations,[87] while high-ranking officials stepped up the fear-mongering about great powers, Russia and China.[88] By mid-autumn 2018 the U.S. Joint Chiefs of Staff were in favor of establishing a combatant command for space. Industry was giddy because the Pentagon's leadership promised a speedy acquisition process.[89] By December 2018, a decision was made: the new unit, whether called a force or a command, was to reside within the Department of the Air Force.[90] War industry leaders seemed content with this option, because it would give corporations additional funding without greatly altering the existing functionality of Pentagon apparatuses.

Corporate executives and operatives at the National Space Council and its Users' Advisory Group (UAG) worked behind the scenes to shape space policy. The former is comprised mostly of cabinet Secretaries and other high-ranking government officials whose departments and agencies have been largely captured by corporate interests: the Chairman of the Joint Chiefs of Staff, the Director of National Intelligence, the Secretary of Homeland Security, et al. Sources report that the war industry members on the National Space Council heavily influenced the Council's direction. War industry executives powered the UAG.[91] The establishment of a Space Development Agency—to focus on integrating the Pentagon's technological demands and the industry's wants—offered even more opportunity for profiteers. It didn't matter that existing unified combatant commands, like U.S. Strategic Command, already wielded significant space assets. The war industry thrives from the sale of redundant goods and services across agencies, departments, and commands. And with Space Force/Command expected to cost at least $800 million to get up and running,[92] there would be plenty of money to go around. As of March 2019, the expected cost of the unit had skyrocketed.[93] One month later, the Pentagon was pitching Space Force and Space Development Agency to U.S. Congress and using the ever-present great power "threat" to do so.[94] On 22 May 2019, the Senate Armed Services Committee approved of Space Force. The plan would take Air Force Space Command and inject it with more corporate steroids.

Cue the 2019 Missile Defense Review, which hyped up the traditional array of "threats"—Russia & China and Iran & North Korea, the "great powers" and "rogue states," respectively—in order to justify "strengthening" and "expanding" missile defense,[95] including spending an ungodly amount of money on layers of low-orbit satellites. While mentioning war corporations' *products*, like the SM-6, the writers of the Missile Defense Review were careful to not mention war corporations' *names*. Corporate personnel operating inside the Office of the Secretary of War helped craft the Missile Defense Review. They worked in concert with

Mike Griffin, the Under Secretary for War. Griffin is a veteran, I remind you. A corporate veteran, that is—a man who has trekked around boardrooms and government halls most of his adult life. *The Guardian* quotes Griffin as saying the proposed missile systems would be "affordable."[96]

Tellingly, the Pentagon *can't even establish* Space Command without Corporate America. So at no point is the need for and development of Space Force an issue which is free of corporate demand for profit and the force of its influence multipliers. On 8 April 2019, LinQuest received a contract "to accomplish the necessary functions to assist the establishment of U.S. Space Command." The new acting Secretary of the Air Force (a former policy analyst in the war industry and a former policy director for the Senate Armed Services Committee) was committed to Space Command and a Space Development Agency.[97] In summer 2019, the U.K. joined the U.S.-led Operation Olympic Defender for space operations against great powers. On 29 August 2019, the Pentagon formally established Space Command (SPACECOM) as the eleventh unified combatant command. The House and Senate Armed Services Committees—whose members industry targets with lobbyists, massive amounts of campaign financing, and think tank narratives—soon upgraded SPACECOM: In December 2019, the leaders of these Committees agreed in a bipartisan fashion to authorize Space Force as a military branch existing within the Department of the Air Force. (The arrangement is similar to how the Marine Corps is technically part of the U.S. Navy.) They formalized this in the fiscal year 2020 National Defense Authorization Act.

I anticipate that Space Force will gain institutional and financial momentum and then leave the Air Force bureaucracy, becoming a fully independent branch of the military. And then, the sky is no limit.

ENDNOTES

1 "Drones" is their popular denomination, though the Pentagon typically uses the term "drone" when referring specifically to remotely-controlled airborne targets used in training sorties. Much of the early development and refining of U.S. drone technology occurred in the skies over Palestine and the Balkans in the 1990s. Textron's RQ-7 drone is based on an Israeli model. The airframe that became the General Atomics MQ-1 drone was initially designed by an Israeli (Abroham Karem) and refined during the October War of 1973, according to journalist Yasha Levine ("Billionaire Brothers Behind America's Predator Drones." *Alternet.* 24 April 2013). As of this writing, there are more U.S. military trainees in the pipeline to fly drones than to fly manned aircraft. Worldwide, the drone business—military and civilian—is worth $127B and growing, cited in Hoggins and Bernal "How the $127bn drone industry will change the way we live" (*The Telegraph,* 19 September 2019).

2 Military and industry have created different categories of drone, such as *medium altitude, long-endurance* (MALE). My analysis simplifies this and just divides industry's drones into two categories: big and small. Smaller drones are often directed using controllers similar to or derived from popular video game consoles, closing a cycle that started with the Pentagon using video games

as recruitment tools. Highly-classified projects like Lockheed Martin's RQ-170 are not considered in this analysis of big drones because such aircraft do not show up in the Department of War's daily, public contract announcements.

3 On 8 June 2017, the War Dept. issued one such contract ($1.73 billion). Services include trained personnel, equipment, certifications, installation, operation, maintenance, sustainment, spares/product support.

4 Relevant contracts issued 20 March 2018, 11 April 2018, 5 Sept 2018.

5 More corporations provide goods and services for the MQ-9. Battlespace Flight Services (Arlington, VA) sells drone support and maintenance in Afghanistan and at Creech AFB and Nellis AFB, USA. AECOM sells support and expertise for MQ-9 operations centers, including overseas operations based out of Ramstein AB, Germany, and Kadena AB, Japan. Fiber Dynamics (Wichita, KS) sells landing gear struts that use AGY (Aiken, SC) materials. Honeywell and General Atomics work together to produce a radar system giving the drone a better chance of avoiding mid-flight collisions. CAE USA (Tampa, FL), Crew Training International (Memphis, TN), and The Rockhill Group (Molino, FL) have sold training services and curricula for MQ-9 aircrew from California (March Air Reserve Base) to New York (Hancock Air National Guard Base) and in between (Creech AFB, NV, and Holloman AFB, NM). General Atomics sells fuel tanks that can be added to each wing to extend the drone's time in air. L3's Predator Mission Aircrew Training System was originally designed for the MQ-1 Predator, hence the name. The system, PMATS, has been updated and tweaked to train MQ-9 Reaper sensor operators and pilots. After selling its sensor-based targeting system known as MTS-B to the Pentagon, Raytheon then sells additional turrets, engineering support, warehouse support, high-def electronic units, program management, unit spares, tech data maintenance, depot maintenance, software maintenance, containers, configuration management, support equipment, and other services for the MTS-B. Good examples are contracts from 18 Dec 2014 and 18 Dec 2015.

6 "U.S. Ramstein Base Key in Drone Attacks." *Der Spiegel.* 22 April 2015. "Even if the pilots are sitting at Air Force bases" in the U.S., "and even if the targets are located on the Horn of Africa or the Arab Peninsula, USAFE headquarters at Ramstein is almost always involved," *Der Spiegel* reports. "Ramstein carries the signal to tell the drone what to do… Without Ramstein, drones could not function, at least not as they do now," says one of *Der Spiegel's* U.S. sources. Ramstein's location is crucial: "No satellite circling the Earth has the ability to send a signal from Pakistan to the United States directly. The distance is too far and the curvature of the earth too great." Using two satellites would slow down the connection too much. The U.S.-Germany connection is critical: "… every time a drone pilot in Creech begins his mission, he first logs into the Air and Space Operation Center (AOC) in Ramstein" where hundreds of troops "monitor the air space over Europe and Africa… Once a connection has been established between the drone pilots in Nevada and AOC in Ramstein, the commands are rerouted from the German base to a satellite. From space they are then transmitted to the drones." The AOC in Ramstein is used by many corporate desk mercenaries in addition to uniformed troops.

7 Other examples include Leidos navigation and positioning technology for Textron's RQ-7; Curtiss-Wright mission computers and Intel processors powering Northrop Grumman's MQ-5B; and Raytheon software in Northrop Grumman's MQ-8.

8 Siminski, Jacek. "Almost Unnoticed, U.S. Air Force Begins MQ-9 Reaper Drone Operations out of Poland." *The Aviationist.* 30 May 2018. Insinna, Valerie. "MQ-9 Reaper drones in Romania? It could happen soon." *Defense News.* 27 August 2018. Rempfer, Kyle. "Air Force MQ-9 Reaper drones based in Poland are now fully operational." *Air Force Times.* 5 March 2019. Rempfer put the cost of one aircraft hangar in Campia Turzii at $950 million. EPS Corp. (Tinton Falls, NJ) sells technical expertise to develop and test underwater weapons, including on the Black Sea coast of Bulgaria. Other

EPS work in USA (New Jersey), Montenegro, and Italy. Relevant contracts: 9 Feb 2017, 15 Feb 2018, 13 Feb 2019, 31 May 2017, 26 July 2016.

9 Adamowski, Jaroslaw. "Bulgaria approves draft deals to buy F-16s in record defense procurement." *Defense News*. 10 July 2019.

10 Abu Dhabi is a major staging ground for arms fairs, air shows, and other displays. For example, it hosts UMEX, "the only event in the Middle East dedicated for drones, robotics, components, and unmanned systems," per <www.umexabudhabi.ae>. With funding from the Emirate of Abu Dhabi, transnational capital, and international event trade bodies, the Abu Dhabi National Exhibitions Company Group organizes both IDEX and UMEX.

11 "Pentagon is scrambling as China 'sells the hell out of' armed drones to U.S. allies." *CNBC*. 21 February 2019.

12 "Pentagon is scrambling as China 'sells the hell out of' armed drones to U.S. allies." *CNBC*.

13 "Raytheon's Harris on Global Product Demand, International Sales, Partnerships." *Defense & Aerospace Report*. 2 August 2018: <www.youtube.com/watch?v=phCJaKWZ-pE>, (1:02).

14 "About BIAS." *Bahrain International Air Show 14 > 16 November 2018."* <www.bahraininternationalairshow.com/trade/about-bias>.

15 "About BIAS." *Bahrain International Air Show 14 > 16 November 2018."* Accessed 4 August 2018: <www.bahraininternationalairshow.com/trade/about-bias>.

16 Captain Zoe Kotnik, the first-ever female commander of the U.S. Air Force's F-16 Viper demonstration team, hinted at the allure of airshows: "What I'm looking forward to most is the potential to have an influence on younger generations... I know firsthand how impactful airshows can be and what a difference it makes to young people..." Quoted in Lam, Katherine (*Fox News*, 13 February 2019). See also "Zoe Kotnik: First female F-16 demo commander out after two weeks" (*BBC News*, 12 February 2019). Public events where the crowd demonstrates collective, nationalist support for the Armed Forces (often in the presence of pricy war industry goods, like jet aircraft) are particularly alluring, as testified to in Rushing, Ty. "Doctor on Deployment: Sheldon physician serves Navy in Africa." *N'WestIowa.com*. 4 July 2018.

17 Priest, Dana and William Arkin. "Top Secret America: National Security Inc." *Washington Post*. 20 July 2010. "In mid-May, the national security industry held a black-tie evening funded by the same corporations seeking business from the defense, intelligence and congressional leaders seated at their tables. Such coziness worries other officials who believe the post-9/11 defense-intelligence-corporate relationship has become, as one senior military intelligence officer described it, a 'self-licking ice cream cone.' Another official, a longtime conservative staffer on the Senate Armed Services Committee, described it as 'a living, breathing organism' impossible to control or curtail. 'How much money has been involved is just mind-boggling,' he said. 'We've built such a vast instrument. What are you going to do with this thing?'"

18 For example, all major U.S. war corporations attended the 2017 AUSA Annual Meeting, as made clear in: "Will you join us in 2018?" *2018 AUSA Annual Meeting and Exposition: A Professional Development Forum*, p. 7.

19 Issued 27 Sept 2016, 27 Sept 2017, 29 Sept 2017, 2 Jan 2018, 20 April 2018, 23 March 2018, 29 June 2018, 28 July 2018. Some U.S. Army units refer to Switchblade as a tactical missile, not a remotely piloted vehicle.

20 Issued 14 Sept 2018, 21 Sept 2018, 14 Sept 2015, 16 March 2018. The Russian menace is often invoked in the lead-up to and conclusion of such sales. The RQ-12 WASP was also included in a 26 July 2018 sale to Norway. Other customers include Canada, Germany, the Netherlands, and Portugal.

21 Full conversation with Brookings' Michael O'Hanlon available at Twardowski, Adam. "Advancing U.S. interests through security cooperation." *Brookings Institution.* 11 June 2019.

22 Goods and services that Textron sells for the Shadow include sustainment, performance-based logistics, engineering, memoranda, kits, program management, improvements, spares, technology insertions, technology refreshments, and regular upgrades to the drone's system baseline. Other corporations are profiting. AECOM (URS) runs some testing & training *and* develops some of the tactics for drones. Leidos works on helping the RQ-7 navigate and conduct operations when the GPS system is offline or jammed. L3 produces RQ-7 spares in Salt Lake City, UT. Rockwell Collins provides onboard computer systems. Relevant Textron contracts: 27 Oct 2014, 27 March 2015, 3 April 2015, 22 Jan 2016, 3 Feb 2016, 9 Feb 2016, 23 Sept 2016, 31 Oct 2016, 29 June 2017, 26 Sept 2017, 2 Oct 2017, 27 Oct 2017, and 2018 (21, 24, 25, 28 Sept). See also "Textron Systems Support Solutions Awarded $206 Million For Shadow TUAS Sustainment." *Textron Systems.* 9 January 2017.

23 Dynetics has taken the project lead. Subcontractors: Sierra Nevada Corp. for navigation system; Williams International for engine; Moog for control actuation system; Airborne Systems for parachute recovery system; Systima for C-130 pylon and launch controller hardware; Applied Systems Engineering for flight computer; Sierra Nevada Corp. / Kutta for multi-vehicle control service; and International Air Response for C-130 aircraft and flight test support.

24 Another example of swarming drones is Raytheon (Dulles, VA) low cost UAV swarming technology (LOCUST) prototypes. And with development and production of swarming drones comes new follow-on opportunities for profit: R&D of integrated electronic communications, tracking systems, and onboard defensive capabilities against electronic attacks.

25 Syracuse Research Corp. sells engineering and logistics capacity for developing systems that disable and defeat incoming drones. One system that SRC is working on is called the Low-Slow-Small UAS Integrated Defeat System. Raytheon sells the Coyote drone as a "counter-UAS solution" that slams into enemy drones. Lockheed Martin and Boeing are both developing laser systems to disable incoming drones. CACI Six3 sells counter-UAS technology to the U.S. Navy. Israel Aerospace Industries has many subsidiaries, one of which, ELTA, has a branch in Annapolis Junction, MD, where it sells counter-UAS technology to the Pentagon. The Pentagon has given ELTA a noncompetitive contract, using the excuse that there was a "joint emergent operational need" (a.k.a. we want this quickly). Leonardo DRS, the Italian corporation led by fmr. U.S. Dep. Secretary of War William Lynn, sells counter-UAS technology.

26 Judson, Jen. "Raytheon anticipates international boom in counterdrone sales." *Defense News.* 11 September 2019.

27 Metron (Reston, VA) designs software and creates modular payloads for UUV. Hydroid (Pocasset, MA) sells drones designed to operate in shallow waters. Hadal (Oakland, CA) helps develop large UUV prototypes. Seemann Composites (Gulfport, MS) manufactures materials to construct UUV. Summer 2018 UUV contract issued 30 July, worth up to $794.53M. Other U.S. corporations on the contract: Aerojet Rocketdyne, Alion Science & Technology, AMERICAN Systems, General Atomics, Huntington Ingalls, Hydroid, MOOG, Oceaneering, Raytheon, Rite Solutions, Systems Engineering Associates, Teledyne Brown Engineering, and United Technologies (Hamilton Sundstrand). Industrial components for UUV, like fuel cells, received more bureaucratic backing and financial support after the Pentagon, industry, and the Executive Branch collaborated on a fear-inducing report. More info at Mehta, Aaron. "White House warns of 'domestic extinction' of suppliers in industrial base report— and DOD is ready to help with cash." *Defense News.* 4 October 2018; Peck, Michael. "The Navy's rising tide of UUVs." *C4ISRNet.* 11 December 2015. *Popular Mechanics* reports that the U.S. Navy and industry are planning for unmanned maritime drones to operate ahead of and in concert with Navy warships. *Popular Mechanics* (Kyle Mizokami, 14 March 2019) cites $400 million allocated

to this particular project. A U.S.-led NATO exercise held in Sept 2019 off the coast of Portugal tested networked UUV to hunt enemy submarines.

28 Issued 31 Aug 2016, 27 Sept 2016, 9 Aug 2017, 29 June 2017, 12 April 2017, 22 May 2017.

29 The MIC's glorification of drones overlooks an important fact: drones crash. The General Atomics Grey Eagle and the Textron Shadow have the highest accident rates, according to Jen Judson (*Defense News*, 25 April 2018). Drones have crashed in recent years at Holloman AFB, NM (QF-4 drone used for target practice), the Sierra Nevada mountains (RQ-4), Naval Base Ventura County, CA (MQ-4C), the coast of Spain (RQ-4), and Yemen and Afghanistan (MQ-9). Some in the latter two locations have been shot down, say belligerents opposing D.C.'s designs. In June & August 2019, MQ-9 were likely disabled by Houthi air defenses. Many drones crashed at Camp Lemonnier. In Nov 2019, the U.S. lost a drone of undisclosed make/model over Libya. Crashes have not deterred U.S. reliance on drones as a tool of statecraft.

30 Purkiss, Jessica and Jack Serle. "Obama's Covert Drone War in Numbers: Ten Times More Strikes Than Bush." *The Bureau of Investigative Journalism*. 17 January 2017. For mainstream presentation of legalese, see Bazan, Elizabeth B. "Assassination Ban and E.O. 12333: A Brief Summary." *Congressional Research Service*. Available at <fas.org/irp/crs/RS21037.pdf>.

31 While the Bush administration used open invasion and military occupation, the Obama administration favored drones, special operations forces, and proxy wars. The Trump administration built on such foundations, pursuing all of the above, while conducting more drone strikes in 2 years than the Obama administration conducted in 8 years, according to the *Bureau of Investigative Journalism*, as reported by *BBC News* ("Trump revokes Obama rule on reporting drone strike deaths," 7 March 2019). Observe not just the continuity but the escalation: the Obama administration conducted many more drone strikes than the Bush administration, and the Trump administration conducted more strikes than the Obama administration.

32 A civilian journalist quotes a former General Atomics MQ-1 pilot: "... the lie is that it's always been the air force that has flown those missions... The CIA might be the customer but the air force has always flown it. A CIA label is just an excuse to not have to give up any information. That is all it has ever been." Trevithick, Joseph. "USAF Reveals Details About Some Of Its Most Secretive Drone Units With New Awards." *The Drive / The War Zone*. 13 July 2018.

33 The pilots and sensor operators controlling U.S. drones have struck congregations: weddings, funerals, graduation ceremonies, first responders, markets, houses, etc. See, *inter alia*: Ahmad, Jibran. "Drone attack kills 17 in Pakistan's Waziristan region." *Reuters*. 3 July 2013. Ditz, Jason. "U.S. Drones Attack Afghanistan Funeral, Killing 34 Mourners." *Antiwar.com*. 5 June 2015. Frierdersdorf, Conor. "Drone Attacks at Funerals of People Killed in Drone Strikes." *The Atlantic*. 24 October 2013. Greenwald, Glenn. "U.S. drones targeting rescuers and mourners." *Salon*. 5 February 2012. Greenwald, Glenn. "U.S. drone strikes target rescuers in Pakistan—and the west stays silent." *The Guardian*. 20 August 2012. Michael and al-Zikry. "The hidden toll of American drones in Yemen: Civilian deaths." *AP*. 14 November 2018. "Press briefing notes on Cambodia and Yemen." *UN Human Rights Office of the High Commissioner*. 7 January 2014. "A Wedding That Became a Funeral: U.S. Drone Attack on Marriage Procession in Yemen." *Human Rights Watch*. 19 February 2014. Woods and Yusufzai. "Get the Data: The Return of Double-Tap Drone Strikes." *The Bureau of Investigative Journalism*. 1 August 2013.

34 Many thanks to TV producer Michele Greenstein. On an *RT* newscast ("The Scary Truth About U.S. Drone Policy," 5 December 2018) she did a great job explaining these legal maneuvers. Jeremy Scahill noted on *DemocracyNow*: "The president gives the military a sixty-day window to hunt down and kill these individuals... If the standard is that the people who are being targeted for assassination represent an imminent threat... then why do they have sixty days to do it? Why don't

they need to do it now if it's imminent? Well, that's because they've redefined the term 'imminent' to be so vague as to not even resemble its actual, commonly-understood definition." See "Trump Steps up War on Whistleblowers: Air Force Vet Daniel Hale Arrested For Leaking Drone War Info." *DemocracyNow*. 10 May 2019: <www.youtube.com/watch?v=JAnPGdVPU5Q>, (13:36).

35   5,000 dead according to U.S. Sen. Lindsey Graham. Lennard, Natasha. "Lindsey Graham puts drone deaths at 4,700." *Salon*. 21 February 2013. Zenko, Micah. "How Many Terrorists Have Been Killed by Drones?" *Council on Foreign Relations*. 20 February 2013.

36   8,153-11,650 dead, at least 751-1,609 civilians. Fielding-Smith, Abigail, Jessica Purkiss, et al. "Drone Warfare." *The Bureau of Investigative Journalism*. Accessed 6 December 2018: <www.thebureauinvestigates.com/projects/drone-war>.

37   The rules of "signature strikes" allow armed U.S. bureaucracies to attack people overseas based on patterns of activity deemed suspicious. If, for example, young men of military age enter and exit an area that some unit of U.S. military-intelligence has deemed to be a suspected training camp or possibly home to a militant. And if it seemed these youth carry weapons (as is custom in certain societies), CIA/U.S. military could launch missiles at them. Using "broad definitions to determine who was a 'combatant' and therefore a legitimate target allowed Obama administration officials to claim that the drone strikes in Pakistan had not killed any civilians." Basically, all military-aged males were considered to be the enemy. "Therefore, anyone who was killed in a drone strike there was categorized as a combatant, unless there was explicit intelligence that posthumously proved him to be innocent" (Mazzetti, *The Way of the Knife*, pp. 290-1).

38   Hobsbawm, Eric. *Age of Extremes: The Short Twentieth Century 1914-1991*. London: Abacus, 1994, p. 50.

39   Relevant contracts: 19 June 2018, 7 Aug 2018, 8 Aug 2018 (the latter a continuation of previous noncompetitive deal: 24 June 2016, 19 June 2017). In 2016, General Atomics spent over $1M on campaign contributions and spent over $4M on lobbying. "General Atomics – Profile for 2016 Election Cycle" (*Center for Responsive Politics*, accessed 2 September 2018). This does not include political operations of industry pressure groups to which General Atomics belongs. Chapter Two explains how industry wields influence. The Textron "solution is required to support ISR tasking occurring anytime." Arcturus UAV (Rohnert Park, CA) sells comparable services. One such contract was issued 27 June 2017 to SOCOM. Arcturus' drones can take off and land vertically. Precision Integrated Programs (Newberg, OR, a strong 2-hour bike ride SW of Portland) has sold drone support of USMC activities in Afghanistan. One such contract was issued 14 March 2019.

40   Garrett-Peltier, Heidi. "Job Opportunity Cost of War." *University of Massachusetts Amherst Political Economy Research Institute*. 25 May 2017.

41   In related news, in Oct 2017, George Mason University established the Michael V. Hayden Center for Intelligence, Policy, and International Security. Hayden was director of NSA (1999-2005) and director of CIA (2006-9). Post-military, he has been on many corporate boards. He currently is a principal with The Chertoff Group. He is a CNN national security analyst.

42   On 14 June, General Atomics sold the Pentagon nearly $23 million worth of engineering on MQ-9 radars. On 20 Aug, General Atomics sold $133.9 million worth of new sensors for the MQ-9. On 22 August, General Atomics sold over $11 million worth of engineering on the MQ-1C. Other corporations achieve similar results selling upgrades. At the beginning of June, Northrop Grumman received $61.7 million to "provide operator, maintenance, logistic support and sustainment engineering" in support of its MQ-4C drones "to ensure the aircraft are mission-capable." In straightforward terms, Northrop Grumman got paid to keep doing what it's doing: keeping a costly weapon of war up and running. In mid-July, Northrop Grumman received over $41 million for MQ-4C drones, field service

representatives, and work on training devices. Five days later, Northrop Grumman received $19.3 million for MQ-4C software updates. NG contracts issued 8 June 2018, 13 July 2018, 18 July 2018.

43 On 27 Aug, Raytheon received millions to get the eyes up and running on some of the Navy's MQ-4C drones. Raytheon makes eyes for the General Atomics MQ-9 Reaper as well. These eyes can help the sensor operator target humans, buildings, and vehicles overseas. On 30 July, Raytheon received millions to upgrade some of these eyes in McKinney. On 31 August, Raytheon was allocated over $281M for targeting system turrets, upgrades, and spares. In June, Raytheon received millions for work on the common sensor payload system, an EO/IR device. At the end of August, L3 sold sensors likely used on Textron's Shadow. At the end of June, AeroVironment sold hardware for its Switchblade drone. Issued 26, 27, 29 June; 27 Aug 2018.

44 "U.S. Policy on the Export of Unmanned Aerial Systems." *U.S. Secretary of State*. 19 April 2018.

45 Gould, Joe. "Ex-DOD official offers path to boost defense-industrial cooperation with U.S. allies." *Defense News*. 23 April 2019. Bill's study frames today's great power enemies as a "far more complex" threat than Cold War enemies. Bill is releasing the study through the Atlantic Council, an industry think tank (donors: <www.atlanticcouncil.org/support-the-council/honor-roll-of-contributors>). The Council's board, a veritable compendium of MIC elites, is available at <atlanticcouncil.org/about/board-of-directors>.

46 "Trump revokes Obama rule on reporting drone strike deaths" (*BBC News*, 7 March 2019) used the MIC's phrasing / justification: "Since the 9/11 terror attack, drone strikes have been increasingly used against terror and military targets."

47 In 2013 during John Brennan's confirmation hearing to become director of CIA, Sen. Dianne Feinstein (D-CA) cited government figures that annual civilian casualties as a result of U.S. drone strikes are in the single digits. Journalists, human rights groups, and non-U.S. NGOs regularly report the number of civilian casualties as greatly exceeding U.S. government figures. See Spencer Ackerman ("41 men targeted but 1,147 people killed: U.S. drone strikes—the facts on the ground." *The Guardian*. 24 November 2014); Maggie and al-Zikry ("The hidden toll of American drones in Yemen: Civilian deaths." *AP*. 14 November 2018); and Max Fisher ("Open-source data contradicts Feinstein on 'single-digit' civilian drone deaths." *Washington Post*. 7 February 2013). The Obama-era rule requiring disclosure of such numbers hadn't actually brought any transparency, because CIA and DNI had clearly been falsifying the figures. To paraphrase Air Force veteran Daniel Hale: When pursuing "high-value targets," the War Dept. considers anyone else killed in the drone strike to be an associate of the individual targeted. Are you a male of military age? Then you're a legitimate target. See "Trump Steps up War on Whistleblowers: Air Force Vet Daniel Hale Arrested For Leaking Drone War Info." *DemocracyNow*. 10 May 2019: <www.youtube.com/watch?v=JAnPGdVPU5Q>. Counting civilians as legitimate targets falsifies the numbers.

48 "AF plans to accelerate defendable space with Next Gen OPIR." *Secretary of the Air Force Public Affairs*. 4 May 2018.

49 Early U.S. government policy prioritized military uses of space. The National Security Council during the Eisenhower administration clarified that any use of outer space "whatever purpose it is intended to serve, may have some degree of military or other non-peaceful application." Tyson and Lang (*Accessory to War*, p. 270) reference the National Security Council's Aug 1958 document "Preliminary U.S. Policy on Outer Space," available via <history.state.gov/historicaldocuments>. The JFK and LBJ administrations conceded that ground-based weaponry targeting space assets are *not* considered space weapons in the halls of U.S. military organizations and the war industry. "That's how you weaponize space without weaponizing space," Tyson and Lang remind us (p. 287).

50 Six corporations ("small businesses") came together on 18 Feb 2016 to cooperate on a $504M contract to develop "space, missile defense, and high altitude capabilities." Details explained at "D3I Domain 2 contract awarded." *U.S. Army Public Affairs Office*. 19 February 2016. Eight large corporations came together on 9 Feb 2017 to cooperate on a potential $3.03B contract for R&D of similar and complementary technology. War corporations cooperate regularly on unifying projects.

51 Regarding "largest budget," see "Preparing for the 21st Century: An Appraisal of U.S. Intelligence." *The Commission on the Roles and Capabilities of the United States Intelligence Community*. 1 March 1996. For more on "innovative overhead..." see "Mission." *National Reconnaissance Office*. Accessed 12 February 2019: <www.nro.gov/About-the-NRO/The-National-Reconnaissance-Office/NRO-Vision-Mission-Values/>. Wilson Andrews and Todd Lindeman of the *Washington Post* (29 August 2013) put the NRO budget at an annual $10.3B.

52 Issued 2 Aug 2017, 18 Sept 2017, 19 July 2018. Additional work includes construction and facility sustainment, restoration, and modernization in Colorado Springs, Buckley AFB, Cheyenne Mountain, Fort Carson, F.E. Warren AFB, Peterson AFB, and Schriever AFB. Issued 2 Feb 2016, 17 Jan 2017, 19 Jan 2017, 13 Dec 2017.

53 Boeing sells GPS satellites and technology. Honeywell sells GPS systems to many governments, including the Saudi regime and Apartheid Israel. Lockheed Martin manufactures and sells GPS satellites and software. Northrop Grumman sells GPS technology. PreTalen Ltd. (Dayton, OH) sells goods and services related to GNSS. It often works with the Air Force Research Lab. Some of its R&D focuses on increasing the automation of GNSS. Rockwell Collins and Raytheon sell GPS anti-spoofing technology. United Launch Services (Centennial, CO), which you'll meet momentarily, launches GPS satellites. Sonalysts (Waterford, CT) develops training systems supporting new GPS control systems. Relevant contracts issued 2015 (13 March, 6 Aug), 2016 (2 Feb, 4 Feb, 9 March, 29 March, 16 May, 22 July, 1 Aug, 28 Dec), 2017 (12 July, 9 Aug, 28 Sept, 21 Dec, 22 Dec), 24 May 2018, 26 Feb 2019. Dozens of others, like Mayflower Communications (Bedford, MA), sell GPS components.

54 Erwin, Sandra. "Schedule woes for GPS 3 ground control system far from over, warns GAO." *Space News*. 21 May 2019.

Ellen Lord (former Textron executive, current Under Secretary of War in charge of industry purchases) approved a new baseline for the Raytheon product in Sept. 2018.

55 There is some overlap between the war industry and NASA. For example, on 21 Aug 2018, MEI Technologies (Houston, TX) sold engineering and mission services in support of War Dept. payloads on NASA space vehicles. Lockheed Martin is the lead corporation building NASA's Orion spacecraft, and Sierra Nevada Corp. and Lockheed Martin are building a space plane to resupply the International Space Station.

56 "We understand all the parts of [the entire space value chain] and how they have to interact, so that the data or the information that we flow from one part of the value chain to another is complete and it's efficient."—Robert Curbeam, VP of Raytheon Space Systems ("Innovation Across the Space Domain," 6 April 2016: <www.youtube.com/watch?v=g9fwE7Sf3PU&feature=youtu.be>).

57 Work takes place in Denver, CO; Decatur, AL; Kent, WA; Midland, TX; Jupiter, FL; Los Angeles AFB, CA; and elsewhere.

58 Provisions include auxiliary payload integration, base support, conversion from heritage to common avionics, depreciation, flight termination systems, geosynchronous orbit insertion capabilities, increase of mission resiliency, integration of the space vehicle with the launch vehicle, launch capability, launch infrastructure maintenance and sustainment, launch operations, maintenance commodities, mission assurance, mission integration, mission unique activities, pre-priced contract line items, primary space vehicle mission unique hardware, program management, range operations,

range support, site operations, spaceflight worthiness, systems engineering, tooling, and transportation. Related contracts: 30 Sept 2016, 2017 (31 March, 16 May, 19 May, 29 June, 27 Sept), 2018 (14 March, 11 May, 27 Sept).

59 Space Exploration Technologies (Hawthorne, CA), a.k.a. SpaceX, received 6 contracts from Jan 2016 through the end of fiscal year 2018 (13 Jan 2016, 27 April 2016, 14 March 2017, 19 Oct 2017, 14 March 2018, 21 June 2018). They focused on developing the Raptor rocket propulsion system and launching GPS satellites and an Air Force satellite into orbit.

60 Some of Aerojet Rocketdyne's other projects include creating reusable rocket boosters, unmanned undersea vehicles, and aircraft turbines. Relevant contracts: 2016 (29 Feb, 4 March, 15 June), 17 Nov 2017, 2018 (16 Jan, 22 June, 30 July, 27 Sept). Aerojet Rocketdyne operates with the Air Force Test Center at Edwards AFB and Space & Missile Systems Center at Los Angeles AFB. Work developing booster engine and upper stage engines for EELV takes place across the country: Canoga Park, Sacramento, Los Angeles AFB, CA; Centennial, CO; Huntsville, AL; Stennis Space Center, MS; West Palm Beach, FL. Aerojet Rocketdyne has corporate facilities in Rancho Cordova CA, and Gainesville, VA, too.

61 Relevant Stinger contracts issued 2014 (17 July, 31 July, 26 Sept), 2015 (4 Feb, 31 July, 29 Dec), 28 Dec 2016, 19 Sept 2017, 2018 (25 Jan, 22 June). Aerojet Rocketdyne facilities outside of Camden, AR, make Stinger flight motors. Aerojet Rocketdyne works with the McAlester Army Ammunition Plant, about a two-hour bus ride southeast of Oklahoma City. Lockheed Martin (Marion, MA) makes fuses and warhead bodies for Stinger missiles. Raytheon (Tucson, AZ) makes Stinger missiles, launchers, and parts. In recent years, Raytheon has sold Stingers to India, Italy, Poland, Qatar, South Korea, and Taiwan.

62 Blue Origin contract issued 13 Jan 2016.

63 Issued 13 Jan 2016, 29 Feb 2016.

64 Bit-players like Portico Services have repaired electricity infrastructure at Cape Canaveral. Long Wave (Oklahoma City, OK) sells antenna and maintenance for military operations on Ascension. Raytheon is on Ascension, too. Rhodes+Brito Architects (Orlando, FL) designs and sustains some architecture on the island and at other tracking sites. Description of Ascension during WWII is from Immerwahr's *How To Hide an Empire*, p. 284. RGNext has run the U.S. Air Force's Launch & Test Range System, described in contract announcements as a "complex network of a combination of instrumentation assets," which provides for "launch, testing, and tracking" of military rockets. The corporation has installed infrastructure in the Western Range, replaced frequency monitoring equipment at Vandenberg, engineered infrastructure on Kwajalein Atoll in the Marshall Islands and Huntsville, AL, and set up communications systems at Patrick AFB. Relevant contracts: 6 Nov 2014, 2015 (30 June, 28 Aug, 28 Sept, 5 Oct), 2016 (10 Feb, 24 Aug, 26 Sept, 20 Dec), 2017 (24 Aug, 28 Sept), 2018 (12 April, 29 Aug, 4 Sept, 18 Sept), 22 March 2019. Corporate work on Launch & Test Range System took place at Patrick AFB and Cape Canaveral AFS; Vandenberg AFB; Lompoc, CA; Coco Beach, FL; Pillar Point AFS, which is 20 miles south of San Francisco; Antigua Air Station, Antigua; and Ascension Auxiliary Air Field.

65 At any given time, you have SAIC at Advanced Systems & Development; McKinsey & Co. and Leidos at GPS; Parsons and Lockheed Martin at Launch Enterprise; Boeing, LinQuest, and Northrop Grumman at Military Satellite Communications Systems; LinQuest, SAIC, and Tecolote Research at Remote Sensing; and Boeing, Harris Corp., and LinQuest at Space Superiority Systems. This is just a snapshot. Many corporations overlap in operations and command within SMC. And some of the bigger kids like Lockheed Martin and Raytheon have a presence across the unit.

66 Aerospace Corp.'s work has involved engineering on computer systems, managing integration of sundry space technologies, analyzing & assessing technical performance, performing

"quality control," making sure weaponry and equipment are ready for launch, monitoring launch vehicles and satellite processing, and running orbital operations. It charges for analyzing "user needs," too, saying these services help the government achieve mission objectives.

67 For example, the MILSATCOM Systems Directorate "includes a total force of approximately 150 assigned military, 165 assigned civilians, 317 Federally Funded Research and Development Center contractors, and 320 other contractors."

"Military Satellite Communications Systems Directorate." U.S. Air Force. 4 March 2013: <www.losangeles.af.mil/About-Us/Fact-Sheets/Article/343704/military-satellite-communications-systems-directorate/>.

68 Issued 17 Nov 2016, 9 March 2017, 26 Sept 2018.

69 JHU APL also works with AFRL to develop computer software enhancing the War Dept.'s abilities to dominate space, including the development of satellite navigations systems, electromagnetics, lasers, and small satellites. Relevant contracts include 23 Aug 2016, 10 May 2018, 15 June 2018, 20 Sept 2018.

70 For example, Tecolote Research (Goleta, CA) advises and assists the Space & Missile Systems Center's Remote Sensing Systems Directorate. Areas include finances, acquisition strategies, and general support to the director. Some work at Buckley AFB, and Boulder, CO. Issued 29 Nov 2016, 21 Nov 2017. Related contract issued 11 Dec 2015. Scitor Corp. has sold similar advisory and assistance services. SAIC purchased Scitor in the spring of 2015.

71 Lesser-known operations through SMC include but are not limited to Agile Defense "business development," Artel transponders and networking, and ENSCO systems engineering and integration. ENSCO has sold modeling and engineering support on software designed to collect, process, and analyze space mission data. Colorado Springs corporations like Boecore have run IT services for Army space and missile operations. Data Computer Corp. of America (Ellicott City, MD) has upgraded mission communications (at Vandenberg AFB, Pillar Point AFS, Point Mugu, and Santa Ynez Peak) to internet protocol v6. Valdez International (Colorado Springs) has helped operate and sustain the Air Force Information Network. Elsewhere, Trivec-Avant has upgraded SATCOM antenna systems, and Data Path (Duluth, GA) has sold Wideband Global SATCOM equipment. Relevant contracts 2016 (31 March, 15 April, 6 Oct, 17 Nov), 2017 (22, 28, 30 March; 23 June; 1, 9 Nov).

72 Three examples stand out. Harris has run Distributed Space Command & Control-Dahlgren (DSC2-Dahlgren), which sits at a kink in the Potomac River, an hour-and-a-half drive south of D.C. On a given day, DSC2-Dahlgren is tasking sensors on satellites and keeping an eye on machinery coming out of orbit and reentering Earth's atmosphere. Harris has also run the cloistered National Space Defense Center, Schriever Air Force Base. The NSDC mission is "to ferret out threats to military and spy satellites and take actions to keep American interests safe in orbit," according to the *Associated Press*. Finally, Harris has managed Space Control Depot Support, making sure a lot of space control technologies are up and running and ready for use. Harris' U.S.-based space-work spans many locations, from New Boston Air Force Station in New Hampshire to Colorado Springs to California to Ka'ena Point, Hawai'i. In space monitoring, Harris has sold core sustainment for field service teams, depot and sustainment engineering, development, engineering support, logistics support, management of items and repairables, requirements development modeling & analysis, software and hardware maintenance & upgrades, software development, spares, stock & storage, systems engineering & management, and technical orders support. Relevant contracts: 2017 (31 Jan, 10 March, 2 May, 12 May, 14 Sept), 2018 (31 Jan, 24 April, 28 June, 19 Sept, 28 Sept), 27 Sept 2019. See also Shoaf, SSgt Robert. "21st SW GSU realignment leads to successful space operations" (*614th Air and Space Operations Center Detachment 1*, 4 May 2010) and "National Space Defense Center begins 24-hour operations" (*AP*, 19 February 2018). Information about weather technology is available

in Debra Werner "Harris says its weather sensors fit Air Force budget, schedule" (*Space News*, 19 April 2018). The Ground-Based Electro-Optical Deep Space Surveillance System, or GEODSS, tracks debris and space objects, including geostationary communication satellites. Deep space is roughly 10,000-45,000km in altitude. Satellites in geostationary orbit are in sync with the rotation of the Earth. Harris has kept GEODSS up and running. The Air Force has multiple components providing space situational awareness, and corporations help run them all. GEODSS contracts issued 2 May, 29 Sept 2017. Other relevant contracts: 8 May 2015, 2016 (14 March, 1 April), 2017 (27 April, 2 May, 16 Oct), 2018 (8 Feb, 15 June, 26 Sept).

73   Immerwahr. *How to Hide an Empire*, pp. 202-3. "The war destroyed four-fifths of the island's homes," according to historian Daniel Immerwahr. D.C. then "interned thousands of 'liberated' Guamanians, over their objections, in camps while the navy tore down what remained of the capital to build a military base."

74   Weisman, Alan. *The World Without Us*. New York: Picador, 2007, p. 255.

75   For example, on 31 March 2016, a strong JV between AECOM and TEC Inc. based in Charlottesville, VA, received millions of dollars for architect-engineering services in preparation of National Environmental Policy Act (NEPA) documents and environmental studies within NAVFAC Pacific. An estimated 90% of the work was on Guam. A related task order and modification were issued 28 July 2016 and 31 Jan 2017.

76   Recent activity includes upgrading HVAC at Naval Base Guam; building up infrastructure on Guam, the Northern Marianas, Australia, and Hawaiʻi; building aircraft maintenance/repair facilities and an ordnance operations facility at Andersen AFB, Guam; maintaining the landfill at Andersen; building new hangars at Andersen; building an offload facility for fuel trucks at Andersen; rebuilding Echo Pier on Kwajalein Atoll; demolishing facilities & structures across Guam; upgrading the sewer system at Naval Base Guam; constructing a live-fire training range complex at Northwest Field, Andersen; supporting Navy Housing Condition Assessment programs on Guam; building new dining & training facilities and housing at Andersen; and geotechnical projects across the Pacific. Relevant contracts: 2016 (24 June; 28 July; 10 Aug; 27, 30 Sept), 2017 (31 July; 21, 22, 24 Aug; 6 Nov), 2018 (16 May; 20, 24, 25 Sept), 2019 (17 May; 12, 16, 19 Sept).

77   Immerwahr. *How To Hide an Empire*, p. 319.

78   Journalist Jon Letman interviewed professors Dr. Michael Lujan Bevacqua and Dr. Lisa Natividad and lawyers Julian Aguon and Leevin Camacho. They explain and contextualize the state of affairs. Camacho: "You have this culture on Guam where everyone is very proud of being Chamorro but on the other hand you have this constant exposure to the military and militarization... It's almost part of the narrative on Guam: all these great benefits from being in the military." Aguon: "In many young people's minds the military service is the tried and true road to wealth and well-being and so they quickly get with the program... What's happening now is but one chapter in a long and complicated book about the breaking of a people." Natividad: the U.S. military presence "vampires our best" through military recruiting in Guam's schools. Letman, Jon. "Guam: Where the U.S. Military Is Revered and Reviled." *The Diplomat*. 29 August 2016.

79   Corporations include AT2 LLC (Severn, MD); DZSP 21, a JV featuring Parsons; Landscape Management Systems (Tumon, Guam); and Chugach's Wolf Creek division (Anchorage, AK). Note the state of affairs: victimized peoples (Native Alaskans) indirectly perpetuating the military's victimization of a colony (Guam).

80   This takes place under the Guam Defense Policy Review Initiative (DPRI). Relevant contract issued 4 Oct 2018.

81   Gelardi, Chris and Sophia Perez. "'This Isn't Your Island': Why Northern Mariana Islanders Are Facing Down the U.S. Military." *The Nation*. 12 June 2019. Locals cite many negative effects

of increased military presence: decreased tourism; noxious sounds and smells; amphibious-assault training harming marine life, fishing areas, and seashore; destruction of indigenous heritage.

82 "The consortium provides an acquisition vehicle for everything from spacecraft, launch vehicles and ground systems. If a defense organization needs something developed fast, it can turn to the consortium and get a project completed in months, as opposed to years under the traditional Pentagon procurement process," per Sandra Erwin (*Space News*, 14 October 2018). ANSER owns ATI (Summerville, SC). ANSER is a research organization operating as a not-for-profit corporation. ATI is working with DARPA to develop industry-wide technical standards regarding corporations servicing military and civilian satellites in space. *Space News* describes ATI as specializing in "organizing groups of researchers to tackle technology problems for government agencies." Relevant contracts issued 11 Sept 2018 ($400M) and 2 Nov 2017 ($100M).

83 McKinsey has analyzed the ammunition industrial base and provided consulting services to the U.S. Army. Issued 26 Sept 2014, 1 Sept 2017, 24 July 2018. For more about Eric Chewning, head of the Pentagon's industrial policy office, see Aaron Mehta (*Fifth Domain*, 16 July 2018) and (*Defense News*, 4 October 2018). In *The New York Times*, Bogdanich and Forsythe (15 December 2018) detail McKinsey's work with unsavory regimes and despots. McKinsey has also implemented cumbersome, noncompetitive, costly reorganizations within intel agencies, *Politico* reported (Bertrand and Lippman, 2 July 2019). Work on the F-35 affordability campaign, issued 11 Feb 2019, matures "the current effort through expansion and refinement of existing scope, including strategic sourcing, senior leadership team offsite, and major contract actions." LM has also received funding to pursue F-35 "affordability" and cost reduction initiatives (21 April, 19 May 2017).

84 Robert Curbeam, Vice President of Raytheon Space Systems, spoke in "Innovation Across the Space Domain." *Raytheon*. 6 April 2016: <www.youtube.com/watch?v=g9fwE7Sf3PU&feature=youtu.be>.

85 Deborah Lee James has plenty of MIC experience. She has held multiple Assistant Secretary of War positions, including a stint in charge of Legislative Affairs. After racking up all of this insider knowledge, she became an industry executive, spending years in the top rungs of such war corporations as United Technologies and SAIC. She paused in 2000-1 to re-hone her chops as COO for Business Executives for National Security, the pressure group you encountered in Chapter Two. James left industry to become Secretary of the Air Force towards the end of 2013, a tenure that lasted through 2016, after which she moved to a think tank (CSIS) and industry.

86 The Secretary of War, James Mattis, initially said establishing a Space Force would add more bureaucracy and superfluous costs, according to the *AP* on 3 August 2018. On 7 August, Valerie Insinna ("Mattis supportive of new combatant command for space operations," *Defense News*) reported, "Mattis seems to have reversed course on his previous stance against a Space Force, telling reporters on Tuesday that the Defense Department is supportive of establishing a new combatant command for space. 'We are in complete alignment with the president's concern about protecting our assets in space to contribute to our security to our economy and we're going to have to address it as other countries show a capability to attack those assets.'"

87 On 14 Aug 2018, for example, Lockheed Martin was awarded $2.9B+ to work on "Overhead Persistent Infrared Geosynchronous Earth Orbit Space Vehicles."

88 See, for example, Garamone ("Pence, Shanahan Detail Progress Made in Space Force," 24 October 2018). The *AP* ("Trump wants a Space Force, but Pentagon has different idea," 3 August 2018) duly hyped great power competition to justify greater spending on space weapons: "War in space is not just Hollywood fiction. *The U.S. intelligence agencies reported* earlier this year that Russia and China are pursuing 'nondestructive and destructive' anti-satellite weapons for use during a future war. A related problem that the Pentagon has struggled to address is the sluggish pace of

developing and acquiring satellites" (emphasis mine). The Pentagon "said it is making changes to 'ensure that we are prepared for' potential conflicts in space."

89 Jim Garamone ("Pence, Shanahan Detail Progress Made in Space Force," 24 October 2018) reported that by mid-autumn 2018 the "Joint Chiefs support the stand up of a combatant command for space." Garamone relayed the words of high-ranking Pentagon official (former Boeing executive) Patrick Shanahan: "Speed in leveraging commercial space technology and resources. Speed in escaping red tape. Speed in fielding capabilities sooner. It will reflect our drive to be more effective—effective in maximizing how we are more integrated technically to unlock our ability to be united in our space operations. Effective in creating a solution, and then together—not singularly—leveraging the solutions across the enterprise."

90 Insinna, Valerie. "Trump's new Space Force to reside under Department of the Air Force." *Defense News*. 20 December 2018. Industry would be ensured of institutional staying power and bureaucratic clout of the new beast: The Pentagon was creating a new Air Force Under Secretary for the Space Force *and* a member of the Joint Chiefs unique to the Space Force.

91 Including the CEOs of Boeing, Lockheed Martin, Northrop Grumman, Orbital ATK (now owned by Northrop Grumman), Sierra Nevada, and ULS (the Boeing/Lockheed Martin JV). Others on UAG include the Governor of Alabama (beholden to the enormous influx of cash that war corporations pump into the greater Huntsville-Decatur metropolitan area), and leaders of privatized space transport like Blue Origin and SpaceX.

92 Mehta, Aaron. "Shanahan has identified top pick to lead Space Command." *Defense News*. 29 January 2019.

93 Gruss, Mike and Aaron Mehta. "Space Force to cost $2 billion, include 15,000 personnel in first five years." *Defense News*. 1 March 2019. *Defense News* reports that Air Force Secretary Heather Wilson [yes, Heather Wilson of the consulting firm Heather Wilson & Co., and a woman who allegedly accepted hundreds of thousands of dollars from industry firms that ran national laboratories, including one in her home state of New Mexico] said Space Force could cost $13 billion, while the think tank CSIS downplayed the costs (putting them at a mere $550 million/year), classified spending not factored in.

94 Robert Hood is the Assistant Secretary of War for Legislative Affairs. Hood used to be a vice president at CH2M where was in charge of liaising with Capitol Hill. Hood indicated in spring 2019, "... while members seem to have an understanding of the space threat, the perception is that the Department has not been successful in explaining to them WHY the Space Force is necessary to address that threat." See Mehta and Insinna. "Did the Pentagon do enough to convince Congress it needs a Space Force?" *Defense News*. 11 April 2019.

95 "2019 Missile Defense Review." *Office of the Secretary of Defense*. 17 January 2019.

96 Borger, Julian. "Trump announces huge expansion of U.S. missile defense system." *The Guardian*. 17 January 2019.

97 Insinna, Valerie. "Interim Air Force secretary: I've always supported the Space Force." *Defense News*. 21 June 2019. Acting Secretary Matt Donovan made his comments at the Paris Air Show, an industry gathering sponsored in 2019 by Accenture. A political benefactor and former industry executive Barbara Barrett is in line to become the next Secretary of the Air Force.

11

Two, Three, Many Special Operations

THE STATUS QUO

Special operations forces (SOF) have more training than the average grunt. Each branch of the U.S. Armed Forces has special operations units.[1] U.S. Special Operations Command (SOCOM) is the bureaucratic umbrella overseeing U.S. special operations forces. The Department of War likely has between 7,300 and 8,300 SOF deployed worldwide.[2]

According to *The New York Times,* U.S. Special Operations Forces are "conducting shadow wars against terrorists in Yemen, Libya, Somalia and other hot spots."[3] Reality is not so flattering: U.S. SOF have supported the Saudi regime's destruction of Yemen, contributing to the worst manmade humanitarian crisis on the planet;[4] waged an elective war which helped destroy Libya, which has since become a beehive of warring factions,[5] criminality, and a burgeoning slave trade;[6] and ignored Somali history and local grievances,[7] lumping many Somalis into a rigid category: terrorists inhabiting a failed state. Yemen never was coming under control of the demon-of-the-day, Iran; Libya was never a threat to the U.S.; and the people of Somalia just want a chance to live.

Countries on the receiving end of the U.S. war industry's weaponry could prosper if given the opportunity to function without foreign interference. But a lack of foreign interference would harm the profits of war corporations. Consider Libya from the corporate point of view. Industry's weaponry and instruments were the crux of the 2011 D.C.-led intervention in Libya: missiles, rockets, fighter jets, command & control aircraft, datalinks, bombers, submarines, satellites, small arms, vehicles, radios, IT services, and many other products. Many Libyan civilians perished as a result of War Department operations and war industry ordnance.[8]

U.S. Naval Air Station Sigonella on the eastern end of the Italian island of Sicily was one military installation—an avenue through which industry routed goods and services—that harmed Libya. At NAS Sigonella a joint venture between Valiant and ALCA, based in Kentucky, has run base operations support services, Siemens designed and installed energy infrastructure, and AECOM has run facilities engineering.

Communications equipment blooms at NAS Sigonella. The Lockheed Martin Mobile User Objective System (MUOS) is a military satellite communications system featuring General Dynamics software and Trivec-Avant antennae. The satellites are launched with help from Boeing. Contracts for MUOS have been a regular occurrence in recent years: over $351 million allocated[9] without true competition. Italian government officials and local residents were concerned when the Pentagon established a MUOS ground station near NAS Sigonella. Italians were worried about the station's impact on human health. Without independent or objective oversight, the militarized State Department reported military-industry claims: "MUOS does not threaten the health or well-being of people," but rather "represents an investment."[10] According to State, NAS Sigonella "injects approximately €210 million every year into the local and national economy."[11] This economic card corralled some Italian officials, but many locals are still upset.

Aircraft of all kinds (reconnaissance, refueling, transport, fighter) have operated out of NAS Sigonella.[12] NAS Sigonella also reportedly houses a back-up relay station for drone warfare[13] in case Berlin ever musters the courage to push back against D.C.'s drone operations at Ramstein Air Base.

The above goods and services—a small batch abetting a specific act of, yes, another illegal war,[14] out of one naval air station—are just the tip of the iceberg. The majority of weapons (e.g. cargo aircraft, tankers, reconnaissance aircraft, ground vehicles, small arms & light weaponry, munitions, ordnance, and ordnance disposal) operating through NAS Sigonella were not listed in the above tallies for the sake of brevity.

A Hellfire missile[15] (likely fired from a General Atomics drone) attacked the convoy of the Libyan leader, Muammar al-Qaddafi. Boeing and Lockheed Martin typically manufacture this missile.

Over 7,700 missiles from the U.S. war industry were launched at Libya.[16]

By the time the war industry's War Department was finished, it had destroyed a functional state boasting one of Africa's highest rankings on the United Nations Human Development Index,[17] ruined the people's formal economy, provided space for warlords and zealots to thrive, and pushed north and central Africa into chaos.[18]

Bonus: Since the destruction of the Libyan state in 2011, Libyan territory has become a playground for U.S. weapons of war. Weapons produced by such corporations as Northrop Grumman, Lockheed Martin, Boeing, and Raytheon thrive in the skies and on the ground.[19] And mercenaries (like Frontier Services Group, which was created by Blackwater founder Erik Prince) reportedly operate there.[20] Javelin anti-tank missiles made by Raytheon and Lockheed Martin have shown up, too.[21] Remember this the next time you whiff the winds of war. Remember, too, that U.S. war corporations are lobbying heavily for military intervention in whatever foreign country and have unleashed think tank and media hounds to ensure the narrative circulating D.C. is pro-war, pro-intervention.[22]

SUPERHEROES OR SUPER PROFIT?

Why do special operations forces participate in today's wars?

The enlisted ranks of SOCOM avoid understanding their class interests. They are drawn largely from the lower and lower-middle classes in the U.S., who are largely unaware that the ruling class uses soldiers, sailors, airmen, and Marines as pawns in furtherance of their own interests, not those of America at large. This process works well for the military, as the enlisted ranks self-select; while people who have a strong grasp of history, are aware of D.C.'s misconduct, or grow up with class-consciousness do not typically enlist. Admittedly, some special operations forces simply don't care about the history or the politics behind endless war, or whether it is illegal or immoral: they're just in it for the fight, the camaraderie, and/or the physical test. Many identify as ardent "patriots." This strong sense of traditional patriotism, which industry and the War Department inculcate, obliges SOF to avoid asking questions and to always do what Uncle Sam says, even if, as in the case of U.S. military operations, Uncle Sam is bought by powerful corporations and lobbies. (True patriotism, on the other hand, involves questioning authority and getting rid of corrupt authorities that harm the people.)

Propaganda glorifying SOF—corporate and governmental—is the icing on the cake. It is irresistible: SOF are the tip of the spear, the best of the best. Thanks to the Pentagon and Hollywood deliberately cultivating images of gallantry, daring, invincibility and, yes, sacrifice, special operations forces are uniquely adored in many parts of U.S. society as real-life superheroes. (This does not prevent them from ending up on the slag heap along with other exhausted weaponry of war.) Meanwhile, SOF, not to mention U.S. society at large, unite against demonized enemies and avoid any critical analysis of the domestic political and financial motivators for global war. Without the glue of war, Americans might just focus their energies on the corruption festering in D.C

Despite the fact that they break down doors, raid homes, and terrorize families at night, SOF are trained to believe—and largely do—that sharing meals, providing light medical care, building some infrastructure (e.g. roads, clinics, schools, wells), and training local armed forces translates into winning hearts and minds and/or legitimizing the government or regime that the Pentagon is trying to prop up. Put simply, SOF think that being kind to the local population, no matter where in the world, results in the locals (alternately seen as primitive or savage) liking you and rewarding you with information. But the locals are far smarter than instructors at the JFK Special Warfare Center & School at Fort Bragg or Naval Special Warfare Command in Coronado will ever concede. Locals know who the bad guys are. Locals know who truly cares and who has arrived in their neighborhood with aims ranging from the unkind to the imperial.

Imperial bumbling is nothing new. U.S. troops fighting an insurgency in the Philippines during 1899-1902 tried to win hearts and minds by building roads and schools and setting up sanitation projects in areas under their control. Outside this ambit, they raided houses and burned villages. But the locals did not cough up the guerillas. "Whatever the reason, it was clear that the U.S. inability to distinguish friend from foe was a serious disadvantage," historian Daniel Immerwahr explains. Immerwahr quotes a colonel who referred to the U.S. Army as a "blind giant—powerful enough to destroy the enemy, but unable to find him."[23]

The U.S. military committed war crimes, including rape and massacre, when suppressing the insurrection. Filipino nationalists, anti-imperialists, men and women drawing inspiration from religion, and average Joes who just want foreign forces out of their country have been fighting in various forms and intensities against the U.S. military presence in the Philippines ever since the 1890s. Filipinos know their history. U.S. troops largely don't.

Shortly after 11 September 2001, the Pentagon deployed special operations forces to the Philippines under the guise of "fighting terror." (Not a single Filipino had anything to do with the 9.11 attacks.[24]) Headquartered at Camp Navarro in Zamboanga in the southwest, the unit was known as Joint Special Operations Task Force–Philippines, or JSOTF-P.[25]

Journalist Mark Mazzetti explains one operation, using approved D.C. jargon:

> In 2006, the American military fired missiles at a suspected terror camp in the jungles of the southern Philippines, based on intelligence that Umar Patek, one of the ringleaders of a 2002 terrorist attack in Bali, was hiding at the camp. The missile strike, which the government of Manila announced publicly as a "Philippine military operation," missed Patek but killed several others. The military was never able to determine how many of them were followers of Umar Patek and how many were women and children.[26]

The U.S. Task Force's components are still active in the area, despite a name change.[27] Conventional U.S. military forces, too, roam the Philippines, especially at Clark Air Base on the island of Luzon.

The government of the Philippines benefits from the presence of U.S. troops because it receives increased funding and technology from D.C. An example of this is the Philippines' National Coastal Watch Center, a unit with a broad mandate combatting terrorism, transnational crime, and secessionist movements. The U.S. government financed and helped build the Center.[28] (Raytheon stuffed the Center with "border security solutions" technology.[29]) Meanwhile, the Philippines' government is more than happy to have U.S. troops and mercenaries help fight pesky insurgencies in the south of the country. Manila knows that the Pentagon will never weigh the grievances of those living in Mindanao, for example, prior to deploying troops across the Pacific.

The war industry benefits from a U.S. troop presence in the Philippines because it gets to sell a variety of products to both the Philippines' Armed Forces and U.S. Armed Forces.

Sales to the Philippines in 2018 included Harris command & control technology, targeting equipment, training services from multiple corporations, Raytheon technology to monitor ocean traffic, ordnance, and Lockheed Martin engineering on anti-aircraft fire control systems.[30] These 2018 sales are continuing a modern legacy.[31] Harris' command and control technology revamped the Armed Forces of the Philippines' ability to communicate and coordinate across the country's dispersed isles.

War corporations profit off U.S. forces in the Philippines, especially after D.C. signed a new Enhanced Defense Cooperation Agreement with Manila in April 2014, expanding and entrenching U.S. military operations in the country. L3 has serviced U.S. Air Force C-12 aircraft. Invasive reconnaissance planes are involved in monitoring the Philippines, particularly the southern third of the country. DynCorp and JJLL have kept U.S. military infrastructure up and running. Coastal Pacific Food Distributors has provided the chow. Leidos provided spare parts for the U.S. Navy, while NASC (Warminster, PA) developed ISR sensors. Leidos sold 3D geospatial products to the U.S. Army for understanding the terrain. Erickson Helicopters provided transportation. Violence-minded Corporate America still has a presence in the Philippines as of this writing. Journalist Joseph Trevithick reports, "special troops help Manila with intel, training and transport." In actuality, U.S. war corporations are the ones supporting or carrying out a lot of that activity.[32]

U.S. military officers' careers benefit from implementing MIC aggression. Several U.S. Army officers have commanded JSOTF-P. Upon arrival, an officer declares, "It's a tremendous honor to be able to join the men and women of this Task Force and to serve alongside our exceptional Filipino partners in the fight against terrorism." After a year or two with the Task Force, the officer springboards into the top ranks of SOCOM's bureaucracy. Bathing in rapid promotion, he is soon a 3-star general. At no point do these officers stand up against war profiteers. Rather, they go along for the ride, benefitting professionally from endless war.

Death toll, notwithstanding. From 2001 through early 2012, at least seventeen U.S. troops died from military operations in the southern Philippines.[33] Many more have been maimed. The Pentagon claims these troops are "advising and assisting" and trying to "secure peace and stability." At least 1,500 Filipinos have died as a direct result of U.S.-backed operations in the Philippines since 2001.

Marawi was hit particularly hard, with over 10,000 people displaced.[34]

Corporate media do their job. Even though U.S. troops were in the Philippines long before the "Islamic State," and U.S. troops remain long after, *The New York Times* reported it thus in December 2018: "American forces also recently played a critical role in helping the Philippine military defeat Islamic State-backed Filipino militants who had occupied the southern city of Marawi." Claims from U.S. government and intelligence officials ran wild through the *Times*' next account, a March 2019 piece hyping the Islamic State's presence in the Philippines.[35] Through think tank affiliates and media assistants, the U.S. war industry finds more excuses (e.g. "shared values," "building partnerships," "denying extremists sanctuary") so the Pentagon keeps deploying troops and weaponry. The "ISIS" factor hops across geographic regions. Then a destruction bonanza follows.

SOF are largely incapable of distinguishing among disgruntled locals, bad guys, insurgents, guerillas, and terrorists. They see populations and history only through the imperial lens, approved SOCOM curricula (a substantial portion now crafted and taught by corporations), standard U.S. history textbooks, and, increasingly, narrow-minded, bellicose talking points emanating from industry think tanks and media partners. U.S. military sergeants once read Marx and Guevara, I note. Now they don't even bother reading the writings of their supposed enemies. They leave it up to political operatives, revolving door officials, think tanks, and war corporations to govern formal military education. Myrer's *Once an Eagle* and Pressfield's *Gates of Fire* circulate in some SOF units, but their respective messages of war profiteering and stoicism bounce off the thick armor of fervent greed (corporate and imperial) inherent to SOF deployments overseas.[36]

State and corporate propaganda portray SOF as culturally sensitive and full of expertise about geography and history. Granted, SOF are indeed a few steps up from the average grunt; they're trained enough to learn bits of a foreign language, to work well under severe stress, and to operate a wide variety of goods produced by U.S. war corporations. But they're not educated to the point where they'd question the orthodoxy of U.S. foreign policy or thoroughly study the history of U.S. imperialism. Nor has their education led them to raise moral issues or question international or even constitutional legality. To do so would lead to a crisis in the ranks, including plummeting morale and desertion. Rear Admiral Edward Winters unintentionally said it best: "We will only be limited by our imaginations."[37] Precisely.

The greatest falsehood of all is *"De Oppresso Liber,"* the creed of Army SF. Special operations forces—whether Army SF, Naval Special Warfare, Air Force special tactics, or MARSOC operators—do not liberate oppressed peoples. Under the guise of promoting "U.S. national security interests," SOF kill peasants; aid and abet undemocratic regimes; train local military forces who often go on to harm democratic or labor movements; assassinate official and unofficial enemies of D.C.; help despotic regimes commit war crimes against innocent civilians, like what Saudi Arabia has done to Yemen; or control unruly populations, as attempted in southeast Asia during the 1960s and 1970s. When facing mission failure, SOF argue that they were never given the time, space, funding, weaponry, or political support to get the job done. Since the 1960s, mostly through sheer violence and immense financial resources, they've murdered, oppressed, and stifled peoples struggling for their freedom and self-determination throughout the world.[38]

PROVISIONING HYPER-ENABLED OPERATORS

SOCOM relies on weaponry, transportation, and infrastructure provided by the four branches of the Armed Forces. Individual branches (Air Force, Navy/USMC, Army) cover the acquisition of some major weapons platforms, such as tiltrotor and cargo aircraft, which SOCOM utilizes. But SOCOM also undertakes contracting activity; it has its own budget (in the eleven-digits[39]) and is able to purchase goods and services unique to special operations. SOCOM is a profitable avenue.

The war industry outfits special operations forces like sporting goods companies outfit Tiger Woods or LeBron James. Small arms & light weaponry, body armor, visual augmentation devices, and munitions bedeck the operator.[40] Contracts for SOF gear can be very expensive. One issued 7 March 2019 to six corporations, including the ever-present Atlantic Diving Supply, cost up to $4 billion. War corporations know what they're doing: special operations forces are vessels for industry goods and services.

SOF are deployed over and over again worldwide.[41] Executives at war corporations love this high operations tempo! They see these deployments as stable moneymaking accounts.

The war industry enjoys smooth, steady business opportunities, which are known as "contracting vehicles" in pentagonese:

- Special Operations Command Wide Mission Support (SWMS) typically involves SOCOM scooping up a few handfuls of corporations, which provide ongoing IT services, logistics, and mission support. SWMS provides so-called subject matter experts, advisers, instructors, business professionals, and financial managers.

- Special Operations Forces Global Logistics Support Services (SOF GLSS) provides SOCOM with a steady stream of logistics, maintenance, and parts. Lockheed Martin runs SOF GLSS right now. The Pentagon claims SOF GLSS cuts costs because it's a one-stop shop for on-demand goods and services. The taxpayer wonders whether allocating $8 billion[42] to a corporation with a history of cost overruns[43] is cost effective.

Industry representatives meet regularly with contracting officers to facilitate contracting processes. Corporations call this "bridging the communications gap between government and industry partners."

Strong, regular contracts for consulting and business operations demonstrate how thorough the corporatization of SOCOM has become.[44]

Instead of "We've got more strip clubs than pubs," Tampa's motto should be "Special Operations—A Growth Industry." War corporations have flocked to Tampa in recent years. The local business community supports this.[45] War corporations pitch all sorts of weaponry, gear, and software to U.S. Special Operations Command, which resides on MacDill Air Force Base, hogging the southern chunk of Tampa.

War corporations with a strong presence in and around Tampa focus on different types of product: watercraft (e.g. Vigor Works craft), ground vehicles (e.g. Battelle and Polaris Defense vehicles), training (e.g. Rockhill Group aircrew instruction), counter-IED (e.g. Sierra Nevada Corp. and Syracuse Research Corp. technology), communications (e.g. L3 satellite communications terminals), and administration & acquisitions (e.g. Jacobs logistics). Other categories of sale include small drones and rotary-wing aircraft. Corporations even run SOCOM's military exercises. On 26 April 2018, the command contracted Wittenberg Weiner Consulting to help run training and exercises. On 30 April 2018, Wittenberg Weiner announced it was on track to becoming the largest "defense contractor" headquartered in Tampa.[46] This company contracts as a certified small business.

The industry sector of "intelligence" services overlaps with special operations. The office of Archimedes Global in Wesley Chapel is a short drive north-northeast of Tampa. It sells intelligence products, as well as public relations, information operations, and security personnel. Archimedes Global exemplifies the corporate provision of "intelligence" services. Its sales have included the services of linguists and analysts of varying caliber, and instructors, technicians, engineers, and advisors. Personnel work on different tasks, including countering-IEDs, supporting face-to-face intelligence gathering, analyzing communications, and servicing equipment. Archimedes' services can be found in many of the MIC's favorite overseas locations, including Djibouti, South Korea, and Germany. Intelligence goods and services sold to SOCOM are too numerous to list here. Carahsoft, Raytheon, L3, and General Technical Systems are some of the main sellers.

The above categorization of industry goods and services sold to SOCOM is a mere soupçon. SOCOM financial transactions are often kept away from public eye. SOCOM personnel can simply classify contracts and operations, shirking genuine public oversight. War corporations, whose employees have the ability to classify information, also suffer no independent critical oversight. Billions are up for grabs. An acquisition chief at SOCOM, James Geurts, qualifies this: "We try to have fifteen to twenty ways to buy something. Velocity is my combat advantage."[47] Colonel John Reim, the man in charge of SOCOM's purchases, prioritizes assured communications and getting the "right information at the right time in the right format to our operators," hence creating and sustaining a "hyper-enabled" operator.[48]

In industry eyes, the hyper-enabled operator is a vessel extra-packed with goods and services.

In order to carry on packing these vessels with more and more goods and services, industry relies on great power competition, neoliberal platitudes, and financial legerdemain. SOCOM's commander describes hyper-enabling: "We need to take the massive amount of data that we swim in, and through man-machine teaming provide the right information with the right slice of bandwidth at the lowest signature possible to enable the operator to sense, make sense, and act."[49] Hyper-enabling the operator can involve pushing new versions of traditional gear (e.g. armor, boots, guns, helmets), but it mostly encompasses fields that offer more profit: biomedical monitoring, communications, computing, cloud, data, human-machine interfaces, real-time social media monitoring, and visual augmentation, as listed by Jim Smith, a SOCOM acquisition leader.[50] Great power competition is factored in. (Smith notes that such on-demand technology is very useful for SOCOM personnel operating in Eastern Europe and the Pacific. Industry is working on the technological hurdles associated with communicating and moving data in areas where Russia or China might push back using electronic warfare.)

The industry drive for hyper-enabled operators has reached many corners of the command: SOCOM has established a task force within its science & technology directorate to push hyper-enabled technologies, bloating the system further; and a recent industry display featured a SOCOM "disrupter event" to solicit new "hyper-enabled" technologies. Colonel Alex MacCalman of SOCOM notes that hyper-enabled operators are nothing less than end-to-end digitization of industry and warfighting.⁵¹ Corporations market this development as reducing the grunts' workload and allowing them to focus on the work at hand (pursuing "high-value targets")—a miniature of the justifications used when forcing neoliberal economic policies upon global populations.

SOCOM uses other transaction authority (OTA) "as it pursues the hyper-enabled operator concept," *National Defense Magazine* reported. "OTAs have become popular contracting mechanisms that help cut through acquisition red tape through authorities granted by Congress."⁵² You've seen OTAs used by Futures Command in Austin, Texas, and the Pentagon's Defense Innovation Unit in Silicon Valley. What the Defense Innovation Unit is to Silicon Valley, SOFWERX is to Tampa. DEFENSEWERX is a 501(c)3 organization; its SOFWERX is an offshoot through which industry and SOCOM collaborate, design, prototype, and build. SOFWERX draws on a network of tens of thousands of personnel from academia, government, and corporations. Hyper-enabled grunts are just supercharged vessels.

SOFIC 2019 AND MARSOF 2030

Every spring, the war industry holds one of its biggest displays in Tampa. At the Special Operations Forces Industry Conference, or SOFIC, war corporations promote their goods and services and network with local military brass, high-ranking Pentagon officials, program executive officers, program managers, and SOCOM acquisition personnel.

From top industry executives to senior SOCOM officers, the U.S. military and industry play from the same profiteering page at SOFIC.⁵³ Sponsored by Bank of America, Booz Allen Hamilton, General Dynamics, HP, Lockheed Martin, SAIC, and others, SOFIC 2019 was emblematic of industry's control. In 2019, over four hundred corporations set up shop in roughly 900 booths to display their goods and services. Over 12,000 people from about forty countries attended. The industry pressure group NDIA put the number at 12,888 attendees. (NDIA co-hosted the event.) Tampa's NBC news affiliate, *WFLA*, put the number at 13,000.⁵⁴ NDIA's senior vice president of meetings and business partnerships was pleased with it all: "2019 SOFIC was a great year for setting the bar for innovation, small business, and connecting USSOCOM industry and the entire SOF community."⁵⁵ The commander of SOCOM acknowledges that SOFIC greatly influences how SOCOM plans for the future and acquires goods and services.⁵⁶

Only men and women with influence in SOCOM's procurement process gave speeches at SOFIC 2019.⁵⁷

War corporations sell a variety of goods and services at SOFIC, though most products at SOFIC 2019 were IT-heavy (e.g. command & control, satellite communications, ISR, simulated training) as opposed to traditional weaponry (guns & ammo).

Industry doctrine steered the show.

In 2018, officers, civilians, and industry personnel affiliated with U.S. Marine Corps Special Operations Command (MARSOC) concluded an eighteen-month study to develop a vision guiding Marine Special Operations Forces (MARSOF). The resulting document, MARSOF 2030, contained four distinct concepts to shape activities, procurement, and warfighting. Traits and descriptors of great power competition (e.g. "powers pursuing regional primacy," "erosion of U.S. military advantage") featured prominently in the MARSOF 2030 document. Here are the MARSOF 2030 concepts, each with its official description, and a description of its appeal to industry.[58]

MARSOF as a Connector. "MARSOC seeks to leverage its command and control architecture to provide a foundation from which U.S. and coalition actors and capabilities can be brought to bear on problems whose solutions require the synergy of military and non-military instruments." (Such corporate language betrays industry's influence on MARSOF 2030.) This concept is all about command & control—the technologies that connect and facilitate coordination among military forces. Yes, unmanned and electronic warfare technologies are part of this. *MARSOF as a Connector* is more than that. It's about doubling-down on command & control technology and forcing it into every corner of Marine Corps special operations. War corporations are looking, via this concept, to push their command & control technologies onto allied governments and militaries, and, moreover, to enhance the SOF-industry presence at every level of decision-making—the battlefield, combatant commands, interagency efforts, and across federal government. All of this is carried out using industry-approved PR terms like "integration," "synchronization," and "hybrid warfare." Military officers eat it up.[59]

Combined Arms for the Connected Arena. "Our units must be able to thoughtfully combine intelligence, information, and cyber operations to affect opponent decision making, influence diverse audiences, and counter false narratives." This concept is all about amplifying information operations, signals intelligence, and offensive & defensive cyber warfare. The relevant corporate goods and services involve collection of information; automated sifting and analysis of this information; disrupting local unfriendly or anti-imperial organizations when they broadcast truths or narratives that SOCOM and war corporations deem unhelpful or contrarian; placing more corporate intelligence analysts across SOCOM echelons; and monitoring all actors involved (U.S. personnel for insider threats and global persons for enemy inclinations). "Furthermore, we must be able to synchronize operations, activities, and actions in the information environment with those across operational domains and, when necessary, fuse cognitive and lethal effects." In other words, blend and coordinate psychological operations, cyber offense, and information gained from mass-monitoring with on-the-ground military maneuvers. *Combined Arms for the Connected Arena* is justified by pointing to key words: "contested environment," "threat narratives," "interconnected domains," and "illicit networks." The profitability will be entrenched from day one: Incessant purchase and integration of electronic gizmos, cyber tools, and IT services are "foundational," and demand cultivation of an institutional ability to combine information ops and advanced technologies. "To achieve this, we must change the manning, training, and equipping of our force."

The Cognitive Operator. "Creating operational and strategic effects in the future operating environment will require a SOF operator with an equal amount of brain to match brawn; foresight in addition to fortitude." This concept is all about reformatting the MARSOC bureaucracy, making it more responsive to industry weight; altering recruiting and retention procedures to attract trainees and retain operators who are excited by the prospect of cutting edge gear, and unquestioning of a corporatized paradigm; thereby allowing industry to develop a whole new generation of training and military precepts. (Cognitive psychologists have been present at SOFIC, sniffing for opportunities.) The war industry knows the average MARSOC grunt isn't the brightest bulb in the shed, so it seizes upon *The Cognitive Operator* to push SOCOM to acquire human/machine interface technologies for front-line units, and to back up the on-the-ground MARSOF with more corporate personnel and informative tools. This stuffing/bundling is marketed as providing MARSOC with "resources" and "solutions," and addressing "threats" while "minimizing open hostilities."

Enterprise Level Agility. "Our cohesive, focused force confers an organizational agility that allows the Command to rapidly reorient the organization to confront new challenges as they emerge." This concept is all about catching what's left, providing industry with a skeleton key through which to access and corporatize any remaining turf, parcel, or scrap of the MARSOC goldmine. "Mere declarations of agility will be insufficient to achieve this vision, MARSOC will have to examine processes, asses emerging requirements, and adapt capabilities across DOTMLPF to achieve a capability that currently resides only in one area of SOF Enterprise." The initialism DOTMLPF is a tribute to the all-encompassing nature of *Enterprise Level Agility*. DOTMLPF stands for doctrine, organization, training, matériel, leadership, personnel, and facilities. Industry covers it all!—from recruitment to retention, from initial training to continuing education, from stateside installations to battlefields overseas.

MARSOC officials relied thoroughly on these four industry-infused concepts when attending SOFIC 2019.[60] Naturally, war corporations played the "our troops" card: Companies are bringing out their "newest products and newest innovation that will help our Special Forces Troops do their mission more effectively to save lives and come home safe," claimed one executive.[61] Industry had Marine Special Operations Command pinned before anyone even stepped into the SOFIC pavilion.

SOF CONSTRUCTION FOR NONSTOP WAR

Military construction is a strong indicator of where the priorities of the MIC lie. Construction pertaining to special operations forces has soared in recent years. Dedicated SOF facilities are being built across the nation, coast to coast.[62]

Coronado is a strip of land right across the bay from San Diego and Chula Vista, California. It is home to Naval Special Warfare Command, including west coast SEAL teams and a lot of Naval Special Warfare training. The NSW presence on Coronado—the area now goes by the name *Naval Special Warfare Coastal Campus*—has undergone a massive physical transformation in recent years. Naval Special Warfare construction projects point to the capacious nature of nonstop war.[63]

Military construction is often against the will of the local people. Naval Special Warfare Command is building a waterfront operations facility on a peninsula in Pearl City, on the island of Oʻahu, Hawaiʻi. The waterfront facility features an athletic center and areas for training and planning, equipment storage, vehicles, and water entry. The peninsula on which construction is taking place is across the bay from the bulk of Joint Base Pearl Harbor-Hickam. Corporate boardrooms and other high-ranking U.S. Navy officials are looking to increase Naval Special Warfare territory and time spent in Hawaiʻi. Training will include greater use of war goods like AeroVironment drones, Boeing and Textron helicopters, Lockheed Martin gunships, Boeing cargo aircraft, and Bell-Boeing tilt-rotor aircraft. A recent environmental assessment obtained by the *Honolulu Star Advertiser* indicated that Naval Special Warfare Command was looking to triple the amount of training time spent in Hawaiʻi, *Defense News* reported.[64] "The environmental assessment said the number of training events on the islands is to increase from 110 annually to 330." As explained earlier, the U.S. Armed Forces helped colonize Hawaiʻi, and many Hawaiian Natives and their descendants justifiably opposed further militarization of the land. The Pentagon and war industry pay the Natives little attention.

Why is there so much construction in SOCOM? The upper echelons of the Pentagon support such military construction because it provides more funding and bureaucratic power. Capitol Hill supports it as well as the "tip of the spear" military units because they bring jobs and money to congressional districts and campaign coffers. No congressperson would dare criticize spending on SOF in the pro-war environment that industry has cultivated in D.C. The U.S. war industry pushes unbridled construction in SOCOM because these facilities and troops end up using industry goods and services. And because some construction firms carrying out military construction (e.g. AECOM, Jacobs) are themselves war corporations, benefitting from laying the military infrastructure and then from the ensuing military training and operations.

SEEKING NEW ENEMIES

MIC elites recognized in the mid-2010s that a war against "terrorism" was losing some flavor and resonance. (Perhaps too many independent media outlets were seeing through the disinformation and the lies?) So war industry think tanks, public relations personnel, and media assets worked to shift the focus toward foes like Russia and China, whose "threat" could justify acquisition of major weapons platforms and increased war spending. Remember, war industry think tanks, like CNAS, were among the primary and initial advocates for industry's great power competition. Brigadier General (ret.) Donald Bolduc contributed to this discourse. Bolduc once commanded U.S. special operations forces in Africa. He is now on numerous boards of directors and holds several advisory positions in Corporate America, one of which is IDS International of Arlington, Virginia.[65] IDS International has sold maintenance and operation of "critical infrastructure and training for combined security transition command Afghanistan," a contract issued 13 January 2015 made clear. IDS International's advisory board is packed with industry executives.[66] Bolduc counsels against bringing the troops home: As the Pentagon dealt with fallout from a few U.S. military casualties in West Africa, Bolduc pledged that "without the presence that we have [in Africa] now, we're just going to" see increased "effectiveness of the violent extremist organizations over time and we are going to lose trust and credibility in this area and destabilize it even further."[67] (A Pentagon study contradicts Bolduc: Increased violence has *accompanied* the U.S. military's presence on the African continent.[68]) Bolduc exemplifies the uncritical complacency seen today in high-ranking military officers which may indicate blatant conflicts of interest. Bolduc (R-NH) is now running for U.S. Senate and leaning heavily on his military credentials.[69]

After roughly two decades of war, wherein the MIC used and abused U.S. special operations forces, causing untold casualties, Capitol Hill is nowhere near bringing these troops home or drawing down the wars. Rather, Capitol Hill is going along with a profitable priority: bringing more conventional troops onto the scene in order to shift the positioning of SOF deployments. Senator Joni Ernst, a member of the Senate Armed Services Committee and recipient of plenty of war industry and Wall Street largess,[70] advocates, "instead of such heavy reliance on Special Forces, we should also be engaging our conventional forces to take over missions when appropriate, as well as turning over operations to capable indigenous forces."[71] (She doesn't mention that those indigenous forces would certainly be trained by U.S. mercenaries or troops and supported by U.S. industry goods.) The conventional U.S. forces set to replace SOF would come from existing infantry and military police units, replenished annually through intense corporate-led recruitment. An assistant secretary of war agreed, assuring the House Armed Services Committee about the "need to look at the line that separates conventional operating forces from SOF and seek to take greater advantage of the 'common capabilities' of our exceptional conventional forces."[72] The then Secretary of War said he anticipated "more general purpose forces being used for some of the missions. In the past, we used only special forces to do it. The general purpose forces can do a lot of that kind of work that you see going on and, in fact, are now."[73] The commander of SOCOM reported to the House Armed Services Committee, "As we focus on today's operations we must be equally focused on required future transformation. SOF must adapt, develop, procure, and field new capabilities in the interest of continuing to be a unique, lethal, and agile part of the Joint Force of tomorrow"[74]—an industry jackpot, whether or not the SOCOM commander realizes it. Bringing conventional troops into former SOF roles frees up the special operators for great power competition and expands the overall corporatized breadth of the U.S. Armed Forces.

The war on terror is going nowhere. It will continue in parallel to great power competition. Industry profits no matter the direction or foe, real or imagined. SOF are not reined in. They're dispersed elsewhere, and conventional U.S. forces fill the void.

ENDNOTES

1 Most SOCOM on-the-ground units are capable of shooting ("direct action"), training others, and rescuing those in need. The Army's SOF, known as special forces (SF) or "green berets," traditionally focus on training military or paramilitary units in other countries ("foreign internal defense"). Navy SEALs are primarily shooters specializing in over-the-berm approaches to enemy territory, though in recent years they've spent most time on dry land. Navy special warfare combatant-craft crewmen (SWCC) are trained to operate fast boats and infiltrate/exfiltrate SEAL teams. Air Force pararescue specialize in rescuing troops in hostile territory. Air Force combat controllers call in airstrikes and help seize airfields. Marines are the newest unit to join SOCOM, though their reconnaissance units have operated on special operations missions for decades. The Marines' units in SOCOM, MARSOC, are now called "Raiders." SOCOM has expanded substantially in recent years. Many in its ranks (e.g. pilots, administrators, PSYOPS, and support personnel) derive great pride in referring to themselves as special operations forces, though they are not shooters. This is a simplified introduction.

2 7,300 cited in Gibbons-Neff and Schmitt "Special Operations Forces in Africa Likely to Face Cuts in Major Military Review" (*The New York Times*, 4 June 2018). 7,785 cited in Karl Rozelsky

"Intro to USSOCOM and SOF AT&L" (*Special Operations Forces Industry Conference*, accessed 23 July 2018). A SOCOM spokesperson put the number at 8,300 in Nick Turse "Commandos Sans Frontières: The Global Growth of U.S. Special Operations Forces" (*TomDispatch*, 17 July 2018). Sandra Erwin (*National Defense*, 6 June 2013) cited 11,000 SOCOM personnel deployed. Exercises SOF are involved in include Cobra Gold in the Asia-Pacific, Eager Lion and Eager Response in the Middle East, Alligator Dagger and Flintlock in Africa, Jackal Stone in Europe, Southern Star in Latin America, among many others. Operations include Exile Hunter, Jukebox Lotus, and Kodiak Hunter. See Turse and Naylor "Revealed: The U.S. military's 36 code-named operations in Africa" (*Yahoo News*, 17 April 2019).

3 Gibbons-Neff and Schmitt. "Special Operations Forces in Africa Likely to Face Cuts in Major Military Review." 4 June 2018.

4 The destruction of Yemen was covered in Chapter Five. Joint Special Operations Command, which is part of SOCOM, has been operating with no congressional oversight in Yemen since at least 2010, per Dana Priest (*Washington Post*, 27 January 2010). Mark Mazzetti (*The Way of the Knife*, p. 229) says SOF have been in Yemen since 2002.

5 Under full pressure from U.S. war corporations and the Hillary Clinton State Department, the Pentagon and NATO launched an elective war, sending in SOCOM during the early going. Journalist Conor Friedersdorf describes Clinton's role in leading the war-drive against Libya: "Using contested intelligence, a powerful adviser urges a president to wage a war of choice against a dictator; makes a bellicose joke when he is killed ['we came, we saw, he died']; declares the operation a success; fails to plan for a power vacuum; and watches Islamists gain power." See "Hillary Defends Her Failed War in Libya" (*The Atlantic*, 14 October 2015). HRC repeated talking points that industry often uses when laying the groundwork for optional war (e.g. the leader to be toppled is a "murderous dictator"). Aside from war profiteering, other Western motivations for intervening in Libya included Qaddafi making moves away from the U.S. dollar toward a gold-backed currency, and the imperial aims of French politicians and the profiteering of French war corporations (many of which work with U.S. war corporations). For factions, see Callum Paton ("Battle for Libya; A guide to the country's factions and militias." *International Business Times*. 15 June 2015) and Maryline Dumas ("Inside Libya: The war for oil." *Middle East Eye*. 17 March 2017).

6 Cascais, Antonio. "Slave trade in Libya: Outrage across Africa." *Deutsche Welle*. 22 November 2017. "Migrants for sale: Slave trade in Libya." *Al Jazeera*. 26 November 2017.

7 Chamseddine, Roqayah. "Imperialism, Intervention, 'War On Terror' Detonate in Mogadishu." *MintPress News*. 27 October 2017. Chamseddine presents a cogent analysis of imperialism and possible local grievances. Nuances might include al-Shabaab taking the environmentally friendly step of banning single-use plastic bags, asserting correctly that the bags "pose a serious threat to the wellbeing of humans and animals alike," as reported in "Somalia's terror group bans 'harmful' plastic bags" (*Middle East Monitor*, 3 July 2018).

8 Chivers and Schmitt. "In Strikes on Libya by NATO, an Unspoken Civilian Toll." *The New York Times*. 17 December 2011. With a major presence in the Mediterranean, the U.S. Sixth Fleet operated the USS *Mount Whitney*, which was built by Huntington Ingalls and contained weaponry and systems from all major war corporations, ranging from Raytheon command & control systems to Dell computers. War corporations had packed USS *Mount Whitney* with high-tech data storage and communication capabilities and the ability to transmit large amounts of data at once. Carrying a crew of around 150 enlisted personnel and a dozen officers, the USS *Mount Whitney* regularly operated out of Italy. Admiral Sam Locklear commanded operations from the USS *Mount Whitney*. ADM Locklear was later tied to the Fat Leonard corruption scandal. Leonard Glenn Francis, a military contractor from Malaysia, bribed U.S. Navy sailors with cash, electronics, the services of sex workers, and expensive

dinners. Francis' firm got many lucrative deals to resupply U.S. Navy ships. The Pentagon cleared ADM Locklear of wrongdoing, the justification for which was largely redacted. The Navy conducted its investigation without transparency. The Pentagon never disclosed the number of people it kicked out of the Navy for taking money or gifts from Fat Leonard. For more information, see *Washington Post* (Whitlock, Craig. "'Fat Leonard' and his prostitutes affected Pentagon's pick to lead Joint Chiefs." 1 April 2018) and the *AP* ("U.S. Navy admiral pleads guilty to lying to investigators in 'Fat Leonard' bribery case," 10 June 2016). After retiring, Locklear paid a visit to his old stomping grounds. "It's such an honor to have someone like him take the time to come back here and talk to not only students here, but to us corps members," said one JROTC participant at Byrnes High School, as reported by Elise Franco ("Retired 4-star Navy admiral offers advice to Byrnes students." *Gatehouse Media*. 13 April 2018). Locklear now sits on corporate boards (Fluor, HALO Maritime Defense Systems) and the think tank CSIS' Southeast Asia Program Advisory Board.

    9 MUOS transmits data, video, and voice messages. In Jan 2015, General Dynamics was tasked to work on the mobile, ground parts of MUOS, like handheld and manpack radios. In April 2015, a JV between Boeing and Lockheed Martin called ULS was tasked with supporting a launch vehicle carrying a payload that included MUOS commodities. Since the majority of this particular funding allocation was designated for the NRO and GPS payloads, I am only considering 10% (of the over $138 million awarded) as applicable to the MUOS project. This contract was nominally competitive, though at the time ULS had near complete dominance of the military's space launch sector—ULS' only rival, Space X, was just coming into the launch business—so this contract was not truly competitive. In Oct 2016 and Nov 2017, Lockheed Martin received funding for MUOS engineering, logistics, and spares. In Dec 2017, Trivec-Avant was tasked with improving some antennae on MUOS assets. In March 2019, LM received more money for MUOS. $351 million came from tallying the allotments of the aforementioned contracts: $13,331,955 + $45,517,301 + $92.8M + $92.9M + 13.8M (10% of $138,041,011), $92.8M.

    10 "MUOS: What It Is, What It's Not." *U.S. Department of State—U.S. Mission Rome*. March 2015.

    11 "MUOS: What It Is, What It's Not." *U.S. Department of State—U.S. Mission Rome*. The Pentagon considered MUOS fully operational in autumn 2019, per *C4ISRNet*'s Nathan Strout (21 October 2019).

    12 General Dynamics C-37 aircraft, for example, can be used for transporting proud flag officers or gathering signals intelligence. Packed with goods, it is a corporation's dream. Deadly war industry products operate out of and transit through NAS Sigonella. A good example is the Lockheed Martin AC-130, featuring Boeing bombs, a General Dynamics rotary cannon, and Northrop Grumman ordnance.

    13 "U.S. Ramstein Base Key in Drone Attacks." *Der Spiegel*. 22 April 2015.

    14 McKinney, Cynthia. *The Illegal War on Libya*. Atlanta, GA: Clarity Press, 2012.

    15 Harding, Thomas. "Col Gaddafi killed: convoy bombed by drone flown by pilot in Las Vegas." *The Telegraph*. 20 October 2011.

    16 Chivers, C.J. and Eric Schmitt. "In Strikes on Libya by NATO, an Unspoken Civilian Toll."

    17 The historian Garikai Chengu said it best: "In 1967 Colonel Gaddafi inherited one of the poorest nations in Africa; by the time he was assassinated, he had transformed Libya into Africa's richest nation. Prior to the U.S.-led bombing campaign in 2011, Libya had the highest Human Development Index, the lowest infant mortality and the highest life expectancy in all of Africa." See "Libya: From Africa's Wealthiest Democracy Under Gaddafi to Terrorist Haven After U.S. Intervention." *Counterpunch*. 20 October 2015. The 2011 UN HDI is available at <www.undp.org/content/undp/en/home/librarypage/hdr/human_developmentreport2011.html>.

18 I paraphrase Max Blumenthal's excellent description in *The Management of Savagery*, p. 155.

19 For example, the U.S. Armed Forces and government agencies using expensive industry goods and services have launched over 550 drone strikes against Libya since 2011, per Nick Turse, et al. "Secret War: the U.S. has conducted 550 drone strikes in Libya since 2011—more than Somalia, Yemen, or Pakistan." *The Intercept*. 20 June 2018.

20 Ayesh, Mohammed. "Mercenaries fighting alongside Haftar in Libya." *Middle East Eye*. 29 April 2019.

21 Declan Walsh, et al. "American Missiles Found in Libyan Rebel Compound." *The New York Times*. 28 June 2019. The *Times* quoted the U.S. State Dept.: "We are aware of these reports and are seeking additional information. We expect all recipients of U.S. origin defense equipment to abide by their end-use obligations." The *Times* later reported that the missiles had been sold to France (Schmitt and Walsh, 9 July 2019).

22 One corporation has lost a bit of business, for the time being. AECOM had been practically running Libya's Housing & Infrastructure Board before the NATO military intervention. For more on AECOM's presence inside Libya, see diplomatic cables available on *WikiLeaks*, <www.wikileaks.org>: "U.S. Companies Win $2 Billion Worth of Infrastructure Contracts as Rewards for Political Relationship" (18 Dec 2007); "Opportunities for U.S. Firms as Libya Invests Billions in National Infrastructure Development" (12 Dec 2008); and "Risky Business? American Construction Firm Enters Joint Venture with GOL" (28 Jan 2009). It will be interesting to see AECOM's posture after the current proxy and civil wars in Libya settle. The post-Libya environment has revealed some interesting gifts. "After Gaddafi fell and rebels sacked Libyan intelligence headquarters, troves of documents were found detailing the close ties between American and Libyan intelligence. There was even a letter to Moussa Koussa from Porter Goss, the former CIA director, thanking the Libyan spymaster for his Christmas gift of fresh oranges" (Mazzetti, *The Way of the Knife*, p. 254).

23 *How To Hide an Empire*, pp. 96-8.

24 The National Commission on Terrorist Attacks Upon the United States (the "9.11 Commission Report") is available online at <www.9-11commission.gov/report/>. It indicates 15 of the 19 hijackers were from Saudi Arabia, 2 were from the UAE, 1 was from Lebanon, and 1 was from Egypt.

25 Most soldiers, sailors, airmen, or Marines assigned to front line special operation units speak their target language very poorly, or not at all. Army Special Forces are traditionally the best at languages among frontline U.S. SOF. Initial Army Special Forces language training is mediocre, rarely lasting more than six months. Passing the U.S. Army's Special Force Qualification Course requires only "elementary proficiency" in a foreign language. ("Elementary proficiency" in the government's ILR scale is writing in simple sentences or fragments, rife with errors in grammar and spelling, and possessing such a weak vocabulary as to only express the most basic needs.) SOCOM grants sporadic opportunity for follow-on language study once a grunt is through the initial training pipeline, but only in the rarest occasions does the grunt acquire anything approaching fluency. And, given today's relentless operations tempo, follow-on language training is almost never thorough or sufficiently rigorous. I estimate that far less than one percent of one percent of frontline SOF shooters can speak their target language with ILR fluency. Rarely does a front-line special operator deployed to the Philippines have even working knowledge of one of the country's 130+ dialects & languages.

26 Mazzetti. *The Way of the Knife*, p. 134.

27 The new name is Pacific Command Augmentation Team – Philippines.

28 "U.S. and Philippines: Building Partner Capacity for Maritime Domain Awareness." *Pacific Command Public Affairs*. 9 June 2015.

29 "Raytheon-designed coastal watch center opens in Philippines." *Raytheon*. 18 May 2015.

30 Relevant 2018 contracts issued 19 Jan, 26 Jan, 14 Sept, 5 Oct. Raytheon missiles sold to the Philippines on 9 Aug 2018 were worth up to $110 million. Targeting equipment must be seen in context of IBM's 2012 sale of surveillance and policing technology to Davao City, Mindanao. Writing in *The Intercept* (20 March 2019), George Joseph described the sale well. D.C. is also sending Hamilton-class cutter ships, built by what is now Huntington Ingalls, to the Philippine military.

31 Select prior sales to the Philippines: 2015 (18 Aug, 23 Sept, 15 Oct, 29 Oct), 2016 (13 Sept, 21 Sept, 29 Sept, 9 May), 2017 (15 Aug, 18 Sept).

32 The 2014 EDCA allows U.S. troops to operate out of Philippine military bases. Bases include Antonio Bautista AB, Basa AB, Fort Magsaysay, Lumbia AB and Mactan-Benito Ebuen AB. See Schogol, Jeff. "Marines to rotate through the Philippines." *Marine Corps Times*. 15 April 2016. *Reuters* (Mogato, Manuel. "U.S.-Philippine pact to highlight Obama's Asia rebalance—minister." 8 April 2014) described the EDCA as U.S. forces using Philippine bases, increasing a presence (especially U.S. Navy presence) in the Philippines. D.C. is sending surveillance aircraft (Lockheed Martin and Boeing), drones, and littoral combat ships (which are made by multiple war corporations, including General Dynamics and Lockheed Martin) to U.S. forces on Philippine bases. J&J work focuses on the Marines, U.S. mercenaries, and U.S. SOF who are the replacements for JSOTF-P. Support ranges from mundane administrative tasks and the provision of cable TV to airfield security, vehicle maintenance, and serving food. Two corporations make up JJLL: J&J Worldwide Services (Austin, TX) and the real estate giant Jones Lang LaSalle (Chicago, IL). According to JJLL <www.jjwws.com/the-republic-of-the-philippines-bos-phase-in>, BOSS takes place at 5 locations in Manila and Zamboanga. Contracts cited regarding U.S. war corporations: 3 Nov 2014, 2015 (10 June, 15 Sept, 20 Oct), 2016 (20 April, 28 June, 30 Aug, 12 Dec, 21 Dec), 2017 (23 Feb, 29 Nov, 21 Dec), 2018 (13 Feb, 28 March, 17 April, 7 June, 30 Aug, 27 Sept, 14 Nov), 21 March 2019. For more details on reconnaissance aircraft and U.S. troops, see "U.S. Spy Planes Help Philippines in Fight Against ISIS-Linked Militants" (*AP*, 10 June 2017); Yeo, Mike. "U.S. aircraft in Philippines in battle against ISIS" (*Defense News*, 10 June 2017); Trevithick, Joseph. "Yes, American Commandos Are Still in The Philippines" (*War is Boring*, 5 November 2014). A 30 March 2018 sale to the Pentagon, which falls under the administrative umbrella of the Defense Threat Reduction Agency WMD Proliferation Prevention Program, is the result of a classic ruse: pretend a country is vulnerable to WMD smuggling and/or WMD development, goading the Pentagon to address the situation militarily. On 20 Sept 2018, Raytheon received more money for this contract.

33 Lee, Darrick B. "U.S. Special Forces, Philippine Service members honor the fallen during 'Wild 42' Memorial Observation." *Joint Special Operations Task Force – Philippines Public Affairs*. 22 February 2012.

34 Over 100,000 people were displaced in the city of Marawi. Much of the city's infrastructure was destroyed or damaged. "Inside the battle-scarred Philippine city of Marawi." *BBC News*. 7 June 2019.

35 Beech and Gutierrez. "How ISIS Is Rising in the Philippines as It Dwindles in the Middle East." 9 March 2019.

36 Messages of stoicism are present in *Gates of Fire*. A school of thought that originated in ancient Athens, stoicism stresses adopting an even temperament, living in the present, and reduction of material possessions, among other principles. Stoicism is an honorable and effective way to live, but is incompatible with the technology- and gizmo-heavy kits that SOF carry, let alone the for-profit, destructive nature of the MIC in general, of which SOF are a part.

37 Ginther, James. "Naval Special Warfare Welcomes Group 10 to Force." *Naval Special Warfare Public Affairs*. 26 May 2011.

38 In Latin America alone, U.S. SOF have helped kill thousands in Colombia, El Salvador, Guatemala, Honduras, Nicaragua, and Panamá. They've supported death squads and dictatorships in Argentina, Bolivia, Brazil, Chile, Paraguay, and Uruguay. U.S. SOF line up against the people of Latin America who demand progressive or democratic reform.

39 SOCOM's 2015 budget was around $10 billion, per Marcus Weisgerber (*Defense One*, 27 January 2015). SOCOM's FY2018 fund balance with U.S. Treasury was $10.18 billion, per "FY 2018 USSOCOM Financial Statement Reporting Package," 30 Sept 2018: <www.socom.mil/Documents/FY2018_USSOCOM_Financial_Statement_Reporting_Package_UNCLASSIFIED.pdf>, p. 1.

40 This includes ammo from Culmen International (Alexandria, VA), Black Hills Ammunition (Rapid City, SD), and Ultra Defense (Tampa, FL); grenades from American Rheinmetall Munitions (Stafford, VA) and Combined Systems (Jamestown, PA); Dillon Aero (Scottsdale, AZ) miniguns; Sig Sauer (Newington, NH) upgrades to carbines; Ensign-Bickford (Simsbury, CT) detonators; Hardwire (Pocomoke City, MD) armor inserts; L3 (Londonberry, NH) aiming lasers & training; and Nammo Talley (Mesa, AZ) light anti-armor weapons. Visual augmentation includes FLIR handheld devices, L3 night vision goggles, and Optics 1 laser range finders. Larger ordnance includes Dynetics small glide munitions and Raytheon missiles. (Ultra Defense has sold to Afghanistan, Burkina Faso, Chad, Congo, Colombia, Djibouti, Iraq, Jordan, Niger, Pakistan, Peru, Romania, Somalia.)

41 Nick Turse ("Commandos Sans Frontières: The Global Growth of U.S. Special Operations Forces," 17 July 2018) explains in *TomDispatch*: In 2017 alone, SOF "deployed to 149 countries—about 75% of the nations on the planet." At the halfway mark of 2018, "America's most elite troops have already carried out missions in 133 countries," according SOCOM's figures. CIA's own special activities division complements SOF in many places. CIA's paramilitary units operate in roughly 134 countries, per Annie Jacobsen, speaking at the bookstore Politics and Prose in Washington, D.C., about her new book *Surprise, Kill, Vanish* (New York: Hatchette Book Group, 2019). Jacobsen's full talk, given 21 May 2019, is available at <www.youtube.com/watch?v=qk5QIIgnWtE>.

42 Issued 11 Aug 2017.

43 Lockheed Martin's F-35 program comes to mind.

44 Examples include Cruz Associates (Yorktown, VA) technical support to SOCOM's Technology Applications Contracting Office; Mayvin Consulting Group (Annandale, VA) business management and program support; and Odyssey Systems Consulting Group (Wakefield, MA) advisory and assistance.

45 The Tampa Hillsborough Economic Development Corporation <tampaedc.com/defense-security> describes the financial incentive: "Locally, a $14 billion military industry has developed around areas such as cybersecurity and information technology, intelligence and analysis, training and simulation, and advanced manufacturing, with nascent opportunities in biotechnology and rehabilitative health." For perspective, the War Dept. awarded more than $13.4 billion in contracts to the state of Maryland in 2016, according to the Maryland Department of Commerce ("Maryland Launches Online Tool To Map State's Defense Spending," 29 March 2017). The commander of SOCOM, 4-star Gen. Raymond Thomas, thanked the Tampa mayor in a 2018 address to industry. See "Watch USSOCOM Commander Thomas' Keynote Address at NDIA's SOFIC 2018." *Defense & Aerospace Report*. 23 May 2018: <www.youtube.com/watch?v=9cXf34xaQ6g>.

46 "Award Sets WWC to Become Largest Defense Contractor Headquartered in Tampa, FL." *In the News*. 30 April 2018.

47 Erwin, Sandra I. "Secretive SOCOM opens up to private sector." *National Defense*. 25 January 2016.

48 "USSOCOM's Reim on Great-Power Competition, Communications Challenges, Acquisition Lessons Learned." *Defense & Aerospace Report*. 26 May 2018: <www.youtube.com/

watch?v=W0qMgJhRUYQ>, (4:00). Col. Reim was relying on great power competition when advocating for the acquisition of goods and services.

49 "Watch USSOCOM Commander Thomas' Keynote Address at NDIA's SOFIC 2018." *Defense & Aerospace Report*. 23 May 2018: <www.youtube.com/watch?v=9cXf34xaQ6g>, (15:48).

50 Tadjdeh, Yasmin. "'Hyper-Enabled Operator' Concept Inches Closer to Reality." *National Defense Magazine*. 3 May 2019. Other related fields include enhanced stand-off identification and characterization; probabilistic applications to speed up decision-making; intuitive mobile apps for data aggregation; social network mapping tools; and tactical communications and navigation. All SOCOM forces (e.g. logisticians, medics, PSYOPS personnel, shooters) can be hyper-enabled, Smith says.

51 Tadjdeh, Yasmin. "'Hyper-Enabled Operator' Concept Inches Closer to Reality."

52 Tadjdeh, Yasmin. "'Hyper-Enabled Operator' Concept Inches Closer to Reality." Noncompetitive "other transaction authority" is detailed in 10 U.S.C. 3719, I note.

53 The senior vice president for meetings and business partnerships at the pressure group NDIA praises SOFIC for giving corporations an environment where they "can have candid conversations and create unique partnerships to meet the needs of the special operator." See Tadjdeh, Yasmin "Annual SOFIC Conference Kicks Off in Tampa" (*National Defense*, 21 May 2018). "For industry participants, SOFIC provides a multitude of significant opportunities for networking, business intelligence, brand promotion and product demonstration. Participants are offered detailed insights and tips on how to do business" with SOCOM "and information on what capabilities are most desired by the community," per "About SOFIC," <www.sofic.org/about-sofic>. The assistant chief of staff for requirements development at Marine Special Operations Command says, "SOFIC is an invaluable forum that brings together our warfighters, capability developers and industry partners to engage in those conversations and scouting efforts that will ultimately hasten innovation." See Kinney, GySgt Lynn "Marine Raiders talk SOF innovation at SOFIC 2019" (*DVIDS*, 22 May 2019). The commander of SOCOM, General Raymond Thomas, affirms that SOFIC's purpose is "to bring together stakeholders" from "military, government, academia, and industry" to "discuss and drive solutions to today's hardest problems and to explore the current and future trends of technology and industry for future challenges." Quoted in the 23 May 2018 episode of the *Defense & Aerospace Report* ("Watch USSOCOM Commander Thomas' Keynote Address at NDIA's SOFIC 2018," <www.youtube.com/watch?v=9cXf34xaQ6g>). "This is an opportunity that we do every year to interface and collaborate with our industry partners, to share what our needs are and to tell the industry our interest so we can all move away from the conference with a clear understanding of how we are going to accelerate SOF innovation," says SOCOM's Colonel Alex MacCalman in Gannon, Meghan "SOFIC showcases future technology, advancements for Special Operations Forces" (*WFLA 8*, 21 May 2019). All military and industry stars are aligned.

54 Gannon, Meghan. "SOFIC showcases future technology, advancements for Special Operations Forces."

55 "New records in exhibitors and attendance among highlights of the 2019 SOFIC." *PR Newswire*. 23 May 2019.

56 Gen. Thomas was in charge of creating the program of objective memorandum, SOCOM's guiding document for the following decade. The memorandum lays out SOCOM's acquisition priorities. This spans aircraft, seaborne vessels, ground vehicles, precision weaponry, cyber tools, IT, and integrated communications. Gen. Thomas affirmed, "Our decisions and discussions today [at SOFIC 2018], the results from forums at SOFIC, will be a major factor in what our forces fight with and what technologies they will use for years to come." See "Watch USSOCOM Commander Thomas' Keynote Address at NDIA's SOFIC 2018." *Defense & Aerospace Report*. 23 May 2018: <www.youtube.com/watch?v=9cXf34xaQ6g>, (11:00).

57 Speakers included heads and directors of SOCOM's Office of Small Business Programs, Acquisition Agility, Directorate of Procurement, Directorate of Logistics, Directorate of Science & Technology, Data, Acquisition Executive; and the heads of Program Executive Offices for Special Operations Force Support Activity, Special Operations Forces Warrior, Services, Maritime, Fixed Wing, Rotary Wing, and C4. Civilian honchos from the Pentagon (all former military officers) made the trip to Tampa: Principal Deputy Secretary of War for Acquisition Enablers; director of the Pentagon's office of small business programs; and Assistant Secretary of War for Special Operations & Low Intensity Conflict.

58 All quotes in the following four concept paragraphs, unless otherwise indicated, were taken from "MARSOF 2030: A Strategic Vision for the Future." *Special Operations Command – United States Marine Corps Forces*. March 2018: <www.marsoc.marines.mil/Portals/31/Documents/MARSOF%202030.pdf?ver=2018-03-29-143631-557>.

59 The guiding document signed by Maj. Gen. Carl Mundy, USMC, admits this concept "will require an ambitious effort to change current authorities and permissions" and "require investments in select regions to cultivate the required partner relationships above the tactical level." MARSOC's team leader for science and technology cited complex battlefields as a reason to acquire new and improved communications and weaponry: "We seek to develop technology that complements our current targeting efforts from stand-off distances... This will consist of systems that are employable across our formations, down to the individual operator," per GySgt Lynn Kinney "Marine Raiders talk SOF innovation at SOFIC 2019" (*DVIDS*, 22 May 2019).

60 Kinney, GySgt Lynn. "Marine Raiders talk SOF innovation at SOFIC 2019." *DVIDS*. 22 May 2019.

61 Quoted in Meghan Gannon (*WFLA 8*, 21 May 2019). The executive was from FLIR.

62 SOF construction projects include a conditioning/rehab center at the Dam Neck Annex, NAS Oceana, VA; facilities, including a "squadron operational facilities complex" and a parachute rigging facility, at Fort Bragg, NC; a training complex at Camp Lejeune, NC; an operations facility at Hunter Army Airfield, GA; expansion of AFSOC at Hurlburt Field, FL; a facility for Air Force pararescue at Patrick AFB; a headquarters and classroom at Fort Campbell, KY; squadron operational facilities at Cannon AFB, NM; a tactical ground mobility training & maintenance facility at NAS Fallon, NV; a facility for 1st Marine Special Operations Support Battalion, Camp Pendleton, CA; and a Desert Warfare Training Center at Camp Billy Machen, north of Brawley, CA, in the shadow of the Chocolate Mountains.

63 Projects include demolishing structures; building a new entry control point; building new SEAL Team operations facilities; building special reconnaissance operations facility (firms included such War Dept. regulars as The Whiting-Turner Contracting and RQ Construction) and a center for strength, conditioning, and rehab; building a training detachment operations facility (includes combat training tank complex, rooms for gear storage, instruction rooms, admin offices, turf field, obstacle course); renovating barracks; and at Silver Strand Training Complex-South, building utilities infrastructure, a mobile communication detachment facility, and logistics support operations facility. Contracts include 22 Oct 2015, 27 Jan 2016, 30 March 2017, 28 Sept 2017, 20 Sept 2016, 26 July 2018, 13 Sept 2018, 10 Aug 2017, 10 Sept 2015, 13 Sept 2018, 30 Sept 2015.

64 Larter. "After years fighting terrorism, the SEALs turn their eyes toward fighting big wars." *Defense News*. 17 January 2019.

65 "Brig. General Donald Bolduc, U.S. Army, Retired." *Spirit of America*. Accessed 24 July 2018: <https://spiritofamerica.org/staff/brigadier-general-donald-bolduc>.

66 "Advisory Board." *IDS International*. Accessed 25 July 2018: <www.idsinternational.net/advisory-board>. Dobriansky was "Distinguished National Security Chair" at the U.S. Naval Academy

and is now operating under Ash Carter (fmr. Secretary of War) and Eric Rosenbach (fmr. chief of staff to Secretary of War) at Harvard's Belfer Center; Flynn was SOCOM Chief of Staff; current managing director of Veracity Worldwide (which sells expertise and advice to war industry and private equity), Handley was British MI6 and then in charge of strategic analysis for London's BAE Systems; Klasky deals with corporate innovation and energy management at General Electric, which makes propulsion systems for a variety of aircraft; pulling on his time working for U.S. Dept. of State's intel wing and administering USAID (which allegedly provides non-official cover for CIA case officers), Kunder leads a consulting firm that sells expertise and services for international development and post-conflict reconstruction; Singer is the war industry's most affable character, whose work aids and abets the MIC; Wood has been COO of U.S. Joint Forces Command, worked for Reagan administration's National Security Council, and helped develop/implement the War Dept.'s war-first reaction to 9.11.

67 Turse, Nick. "Commandos Sans Frontières: The Global Growth of U.S. Special Operations Forces." *TomDispatch*. 17 July 2018.

68 Turse, Nick. "Violence has spiked in Africa since the military founded AFRICOM, Pentagon study finds." *The Intercept*. 29 July 2019.

69 In his campaign video, Bolduc "is introduced via news clips of his mission in Afghanistan shortly after the Sept. 11, 2001, attacks..." DiStaso, John. "Bolduc, announcing U.S. Senate run, calls Shaheen 'part of failed leadership in Congress.'" *WMUR Manchester*. 24 June 2019.

70 "Sen. Joni Ernst – Iowa, Contributors 2013-2018." *Center for Responsive Politics*. Accessed 24 July 2018.

71 Turse, Nick. "Commandos Sans Frontières: The Global Growth of U.S. Special Operations Forces."

72 Turse, Nick. "Commandos Sans Frontières: The Global Growth of U.S. Special Operations Forces."

73 Daniels, Jeff. "Mattis: U.S. forces fighting ISIS shifting focus to more 'stabilizing' role in 2018." *CNBC*. 29 December 2017.

74 "United States Special Operations Command's Efforts to Transform the Force for Future Security Challenges." *U.S. Senate Subcommittee on Emerging Threats and Capabilities*. 11 April 2018.

12

Transitioning

"[W]hen a population is no longer prepared to accept the order given by decision makers, then those persons cease to be decision makers, as decision-making means not only the issuing of commands but the readiness of the population to accept and to implement."

—Professor Seymour Melman[1]

The United States military provides the troops and installations, the war industry provides the goods and services, and Congress provides the funding and legislation that enables the wars. The MIC propagandizes the public, perverts culture, transfers treasure to war corporations, sends our loved ones to wreak destruction and die in foreign lands, and pollutes the air, soil, and water worldwide. War has become permanent because the war industry has captured government and bends it to its ceaseless quest for profits. There will be no escape from interminable wars until this reality is recognized and resisted. It is incumbent upon us all to forge a new society which operates to our benefit, not to our cost. To this end, here are a few suggestions for those working within the system regarding where to go from here. In a democratic assertion of people power, all three sides of the military-industrial-congressional triangle must be addressed simultaneously and thoroughly.

EDUCATION AND ORGANIZING

We must promote peace education in our schools, universities, and political, cultural, and religious organizations, to help the public better understand the MIC, how to undermine it, and why we must. We must teach one another about the true impacts of war, the folly of its glorification, the waste of our resources, and the suffering and neglect of our veterans.

We must resist military recruitment in our schools, communities, and states.

We must propose, elaborate, and compile credible alternatives for industry and foreign policy, useful for antiwar organizing. We must support, join, and fund peace organizations of all stripes and learn from their long experience, their wide range of organizing tactics, and their proposals for winding the warfare state down. They play a foundational role in ending wars.[2]

Not everyone in the antiwar movement will agree on every aspect of how to transition from the warfare state or on future social goals for the United States, but against the MIC the public can form a united front. Targeting the MIC should be the focal point in order to achieve a broad-based movement. This is where our common interest lies. We must take this struggle to the military, the war corporations, government at all levels, all media, Silicon Valley, and research and academic institutions.

It is incumbent upon organizers to study how governments respond to mass movements, and to anticipate and deflect efforts to infiltrate, discredit, and disrupt them. Governments use fear, intimidation, xenophobia, ethnic and gender issues, homophobia, patriotism, slander, derision, personal weaknesses (pride, greed, lust, envy), and other points of leverage to split mass movements apart.

ELECTIONS AND LEGISLATION

Exorbitant military spending should be made an issue in every political election across the country, from local and state races to federal elections, while demonstrating where, locally or nationally, such money could be better spent. The extent of candidate funding from the war industry should be exposed and deplored. We must make those in Congress and those running for it realize that they have more to fear from an antiwar public than to gain from the war industry. It is We, the People, who hold the power to put public officials in office or remove them from it. Candidate commitment to transitioning from endless war must be a plank in every winning campaign—local, state, and federal.

We also need to eliminate corporate personhood and get money out of politics in order to enable the democratic reflection of the people's will.

Creating a functioning economic system that cares for people and the planet is a priority. Local and state laws can prohibit public funds from investment in war corporations. Congress can defund dubious, needless wars once the people have its back. War corporations' profits from goods and services will dry up without military appropriations, forcing them to transition to other products and services—something that corporations are regularly forced to do anyway to address the shifting demands of the domestic and global marketplace.

Implementing congressional term limits and ending gerrymandering will improve democratic institutions.

The legislative reclamation of public radio will allow independent, non-corporate news media to inform the public, deconstructing both the industry's hype of "threats" and the aggressive military doctrine promulgated by the Pentagon. Threats—industry's sustenance—evaporate under the light of peaceful rationality. Anonymity and privacy must underpin human relationship to technology and the enterprises that produce and govern such technology.

Going forward, we must declare in our legal and moral code that the atmosphere is a public trust. We must seek to enshrine *ecocide*—defined as extensive damage, destruction to, or loss of ecosystems—in U.S. and international law as a crime on par with genocide.[3]

DEMOBILIZATION

The Pentagon's total worldwide possessions cover 4,775 sites on roughly 26.9 million acres across 45 countries, according to the FY2018 Base Structure Report.[4] U.S. military installations overseas should be turned over to the respective host countries, with a view to promoting friendlier ties with them.[5] Citizens of those countries must be allowed to decide what to do with the installations. A fraction of the Pentagon's annual military construction funds is sufficient to repatriate or destroy the most sensitive equipment on overseas bases. The annual cost of these overseas installations—around $150 billion[6]—is then freed up to address real human needs stateside, including affordable housing and public infrastructure.

A united, engaged citizenry can compel government to bring the troops home. Immediate transfer of the Overseas Contingency Operations funding to the Department of Veteran Affairs can pay for the initial phases of this transition. Members of the U.S. military are a disciplined workforce which can be retrained to engage in infrastructure repair and development,[7] teaching, and many other occupations which could benefit from their patriotic energies.

Winding down military installations inside the U.S. offers a wonderful opportunity for re-wilding. Designating certain military installations off-limits to all humans allows the natural world to rebound. Such areas as Dare County Range in North Carolina, the Mountain Home Ranges in Idaho, White Sands Missile Range in New Mexico, the Pacific Missile Range in Hawai'i, and the Joint Pacific Alaska Range Complex are a great place to start.

DISOBEDIENCE

U.S. soldiers, sailors, airmen, and Marines mutinied in 1945 when, after World War II, the War Department tried to keep them overseas to man the Pentagon's bases. On Guam, the U.S. troops burned the Secretary of War in effigy. They rose up in such numbers that the War Department couldn't punish them.

"[W]as the army really going to court-martial tens of thousands of its own men? Was it actually going to execute anyone? The uprising had grown so large that this was hard to imagine."[8] The War Department didn't punish the troops. And the troops got their way.

A few decades later, U.S. troops stopped following orders during the Vietnam War. They stayed inside the wire or attacked the officers who ordered them on patrols.[9] This disobedience contributed to ending the war. Today's troops can follow precedent. Why? The troops know intuitively that they are being used as pawns, deployed abroad to benefit corporate profit. Industry executives and officials in both political factions are ultimately responsible for the deaths of U.S. troops and civilians overseas. The terrible but transformative realization among U.S. families—that their loved ones died in vain and that needless war-making has to be stopped—can contribute to the reconfiguration of authority inside the United States. Military veterans, more receptive to the truth, can help those in uniform.

The civilian officials and high-ranking officers in charge of the U.S. Armed Forces have temporary authority. We, the People, hold ultimate power over them. We exercise our rights when limiting the war-making powers of the Pentagon's leadership.

THE DRAFT

If there must be a war—a true war in defense of the United States, and not its empire—all must share the burden. In such circumstances, there is little doubt that the public would support a military draft which would include all income ranges without deferments. This will not make up for the centuries during which the upper class declared wars and the lower and middle classes fought them, but it will help create an even playing field today. Indeed, the fear of the social resistance to a military draft that includes all sectors of the population is one of the reasons that the Pentagon has not instituted it; so paradoxically the draft itself can help to encourage antiwar behavior and lead to a true Department of Defense.

DEMILITARIZING INDUSTRY

The demilitarizing of industry can be brought about from above, from within, and from below.

We didn't always have war corporations. Prior to World War II, state-owned, state-run arsenals manufactured weapons of war according to need, and not with a view to profit. We can return to this. **Nationalizing** the war-related assets of the biggest war corporations is a strong first step in regaining control over war production. Stripping war corporations of their war components will leave them free to concentrate on—and indeed improve, as is much needed—their competitive performance in the purely civilian portions of their businesses. Adapting to changing demand is a challenge that businesses normally face, and many U.S. corporations may have become lax, used to living on the guaranteed military dole.

The federal government is no stranger to planning a shift away from war, Seymour Melman explains:

> From 1943 on, the War Production Board soon followed by the creation of the Committee For Economic Development sponsored post-war planning for the United States. Towns, state governments, companies set up post-war planning officials. That was the title that appeared everywhere. There were vice presidents for post-war planning, assistants to governors for post-war planning. And it was pursued everywhere. In January 1969, one of the last official acts of President Lyndon Johnson was the report—was the economic report of the president—which included a major proposal complete with detailed data and budgeting for a peace dividend for the United States to replace the wartime expenditures in Vietnam.[10]

Alternative Use Committees (staffed with a strong representation of blue-collar workers) can address how to better use, in a non-military manner, the existing industrial facilities across the United States and redesign the enterprise to balance local needs with the demands of the country as a whole. Economic Conversion Finance Banks can hold and divvy out government funding to local and state authorities.[11]

Robust laws and international cooperation can temper capital flight, preventing international financial institutions from removing their money from the United States and investing it elsewhere. Investments in domestic infrastructure can then be incentivized by the kinds of funding and financial offerings which heretofore were available primarily for military investment. Departments of Agriculture, Education, Energy, Interior, Labor, and Transportation can rise as the Department of War falls.

The bulk of the pressure for demilitarizing industry must come from below. But here the issue transcends the military component of industry to address the overall corporate control of the U.S. economy. Huge corporations have become laws unto themselves in all spheres. They promulgate legislation to their benefit, pay sky-high CEO salaries, produce according to short-term profit rather than need, and monopolize the market to the disadvantage of all comers. Whether one supports small and medium-sized private enterprises or worker cooperatives,[12] all sides of the 99% can see that the restructuring of major corporations will lead to the equalizing of social benefits.[13]

Workers, in particular those working for newly-configured cooperatives transitioning away from war, can refuse to support D.C.'s flailing military adventurism. At nominal sacrifice, workers can convert the industrial output of their cooperatives into goods and services benefitting the public and environmental good. For example, a food distributor based in California could refuse to provide food to Naval Support Facility Diego Garcia, Naval Station Guantánamo Bay, and other imperial outposts, focusing instead on the needs of Californians. A factory in Arizona could make aerodynamic composites for space exploration instead of deadly missiles. A shipbuilder in Newport News, Virginia, could focus on facilitating cooperative-to-cooperative or worker-to-worker maritime trade instead of constructing warships. A logistics firm in Colorado Springs that has run military bases could be harnessed to improve affordable housing. A full-service IT and project management firm headquartered in Reston, Virginia, could sprout the rudiments supplementing the retraining of the troops and blue-collar workers who used to produce weapons of war. There are many such opportunities to create meaningful, peaceful work.

Many humble and diligent workers reside within the war industry. These people are just trying to make ends meet, welding, soldering, or buffing, or running the increasingly automated machinery that assembles products of war. They intuitively understand that the executives of war corporations do not care about them. Executives just want compliant labor and are trying to automate most of the workers' jobs anyway. It is critical that Congress and community take care of this working class when converting the war industry to peaceful endeavors. For example, blue-collar workers making armored vehicles in Ohio should receive priority training, financial support, and educational opportunities during the transition. Those wishing to retire should be taken care of with benefit packages comparable to those who retire from the U.S. Armed Forces.

Dismantling the MIC can be a part of the Green New Deal (GND), a legislative initiative to reconstruct U.S. society (agricultural practices, transportation, and industrial activity) by reducing human-made greenhouse gas emissions. Popular with the U.S. public,[14] the GND is particularly helpful in how well it stresses the need to "promote justice and equity by stopping current, preventing future, and repairing historic oppression of indigenous peoples, communities of color, migrant communities, deindustrialized communities, depopulated rural communities, the poor, low-income workers, women, the elderly, the unhoused, people with disabilities, and youth." Accordingly, the GND aims to provide "high-quality education, including higher education" for all, implemented "with a focus on frontline and vulnerable communities" as "full and equal participants." From the GND we learn to ensure "the use of democratic and participatory processes that are inclusive of and led by frontline and vulnerable communities and workers to plan, implement, and administer" the mobilization "at the local level."[15] This is democracy at its finest; Alternative Use Committees can achieve this.[16] Citing midpoint estimates between university professors and a conservative think tank, one mainstream columnist notes that creating "a low-carbon electricity grid, a net-zero transportation system," and upgrades to all existing buildings to energy-efficient standards would cost less than half of the annual military budget.[17] The money is there to change our society. We just need to seize it (and the initiative).

Mid-level jobs (physicists, mathematicians, engineers) within the war industry typically require graduate degrees. These jobs are transferable to the non-militant civilian world. The abilities and knowledge that mid-level workers possess are attractive to organizations that will receive a major funding boost cut from the budget of the War Department: Department of Education devising new curricula, Department of Housing & Urban Development establishing affordable housing, Department of Energy grappling with the energy crisis, Department of Health & Human Services tackling the pollution that capitalist enterprises have left behind, National Aeronautics & Space Administration exploring space, grants and subsidies for organizations focusing on sustainable energy, and National Oceanic & Atmospheric Administration monitoring the oceans and atmosphere.[18]

INTERNATIONAL SOLIDARITY

The military-industrial-congressional triangle insulated itself from U.S. society in order to operate at maximum speed and minimum supervision, diverting the wealth of society toward the interests of the leaders of the MIC. Increasingly people at home and abroad realize, it is everyone against the MIC. The U.S. antiwar movement must ally, online and off, with its counterparts in other countries, worldwide, and in particular where U.S. or U.S.-supported wars are taking place. All are in this together, to do the right thing for their families and future generations. Pushing back against the corporate monopoly on the use of violence requires and offers great opportunity for teamwork and solidarity. Solidarity can form across aggrieved families, from the streets of Colombia to the streets of Yemen to the streets of the United States. Solidarity can form across all those who have been on the receiving end of the corporatized U.S. surveillance state.

Each year, the Pentagon holds military exercises in North and South America, Asia, Africa, and Europe—all over the world. Eagle Resolve is an annual U.S. exercise (featuring Gulf Arab militaries) that focuses on protecting petroleum and military infrastructure, patrolling the Persian Gulf, and interdicting vessels. Hundreds, perhaps thousands, of locals have to assent in order for just one military exercise, such as the multinational exercise Eagle Resolve, to kick off. Locals can push back creatively, from "losing" paperwork to monkeywrenching to blocking access to terrain in their thousands.

European nations can push back against the MIC. Consider U.S. operations at Ramstein Air Base in Germany. The German people can summon courage to use the NATO Status of Forces Agreement to end the U.S. presence.[19] Under enough people pressure, European governments can pass laws banning U.S. weapon storage on European soil.[20]

Antiwar organizations can assist the peoples of dominated nations and U.S. client states in their efforts to kick out D.C.'s troops and war corporations, and reclaim their sovereignty. Expelling D.C.'s military presence is a daunting task, as the struggle for sovereignty has been fought for, for decades in many areas of the world. But as today's desperate workforce becomes more aware how the MIC's endless wars are pushing the U.S. itself toward poverty and degeneration, people power and political awakening offer a hopeful recipe for an alignment of efforts.

PROSECUTIONS

The lieutenant general who helped plan and carry out the destruction of Fallujah (known as the "Second Battle of Fallujah") in November-December of 2004 is a uniformed war criminal. D.C. has plenty of those. But there are also many civilian war criminals in the leadership ranks of war corporations (e.g. "Vice President of Program Management Excellence," "Executive Vice President of Missiles & Fire Control," or "President of Ordnance & Tactical Systems"). Initiating wars of aggression and murder for profit, the defining activities of war corporations, are crimes against peace.

The London Charter provided the Nuremberg Trials' framework for prosecuting the Nazis after World War II. The London Charter defined the charges war criminals face: crimes against humanity (e.g. killing civilians), crimes against peace (e.g. pushing for and starting a war), and war crimes. Crucially, the Nuremberg Trials prosecuted the economic leadership of Nazi Germany, including the leaders of weapons manufacturers.

Many industry elites are psychopaths far removed from the difficulties faced by the public at large. It is important to not write off these psychopaths as "evil." The CEOs of war corporations are not evil. They have excelled in an environment that we have permitted them to foster, a permissible society that idolizes financial accumulation and those at the top of hierarchies. They are our problem. We must own and address this problem. Is your name listed on the "Leadership" tab of a major war corporation's website? Imagine that you can be tried in

Nuremburg-style courts.[21] Restorative justice—community-driven, collaborative, and engaging—awaits war criminals.

REDIRECTING FUNDING

Where do we get all the money to implement such drastic, necessary changes? Redirecting the Pentagon's vast trillion-dollar budget is essential to rebuilding U.S. society. The following pathways direct military funds toward an underfunded civilian need:

- aircraft procurement funds—unemployment benefits easing the transition during blue-collar workers' retraining
- base realignment and closure funds—shutting down military installations overseas
- defense working capital funds—basic income to blue-collar workers most affected by automation, racism, and deindustrialization
- civil construction funds and military construction funds—public housing supplement
- operations and maintenance funds—Medicare for all
- Overseas Contingency Operations funds—education, retraining, and healthcare for the troops
- military research, development, test, and evaluation funds—medical research, pandemic preparedness
- transportation working capital funds and Pentagon reservation maintenance funds—public infrastructure, particularly mass transit

This itemization is just one of many possible redirections.

What would you do with money that used to go toward war? Pay for free college? Clear student debt? Care for humans in poverty? Arrange for compensation (also paid for, in part, by former MIC elites) to the MIC's victims, our siblings, from Colombia to Niger to Afghanistan to Cambodia? Rewild parts of the U.S.? Expand the national park system? Rebuild U.S. diplomacy? Fund libraries? Fund international scientific endeavors?

The opportunities await.

ENDNOTES

1 Melman, Seymour. "Special Interdisciplinary Panel—Barriers to Disarmament." *Towards Preventing Nuclear Omnicide*. St. Louis: First International Conference of the International Philosophers for the Prevention of Nuclear Omnicide, 1 May 1986. Melman's writings are available at <economicreconstruction.org/node/222>.

2 Some organizations engaged in formulating an alternative foreign policy and from which the public can learn about the banes of war and antiwar organizing include the American Friends Service Committee, CODEPINK, Courage to Resist, Food Not Bombs, the Poor People's Campaign, the Quincy Institute, United National Antiwar Coalition, U.S. Peace Council, the War Resisters League, and Women's International League for Peace and Freedom.

3 Kelsey Juliana has advocated for enshrining the atmosphere as a public trust. Polly Higgins has fought very hard for placing ecocide on par with genocide. For more on Juliana, see <www.ourchildrenstrust.org/kelsey>. For more on Higgins, see <pollyhiggins.com/about>.

4 The Base Structure Report (BSR) does not go into great detail about overseas sites smaller than 10 acres or sites valued at less than $10M. Moreover, the BSR does not include certain sites—owned and nominally operated by other countries—out of which the U.S. military operates.

5 Citizens in countries around the world regularly protest the U.S. military's presence on their soil. Notable examples include recent protests in Adana, Turkey; Alice Springs, Australia; Bogotá, Colombia; Dublin, Ireland; Fussa and Okinawa, Japan; Kaiserslautern, Germany; Manila, Republic of the Philippines; Pyeontaek and Jeju Island, South Korea; Souda Bay, Crete, Greece; and Vicenza and Ghedi, Italy. The U.S. public must come to understand: *they don't want us there*, even if their co-opted political elites might.

6 Overseas military installations (e.g. bases, camps, outposts, etc.) cost around $156 billion or more, annually, scholar David Vine indicated in his 2015 book *Base Nation* (New York: Metropolitan Books). David Vine is one of the premier scholars studying the manifestations of U.S. empire overseas. Two years later, in 2017, he offered $150 billion, a "very conservative" estimate as to how much military deployments and overseas installations cost each year. See Vargas, Luke. "The Cost and Benefits of U.S. Military Bases Overseas." *Talk Media News*. 1 May 2017.

7 The American Society of Civil Engineers (ASCE) estimated in its 2016 report, *Failure To Act: Closing the Infrastructure Investment Gap for America's Economic Future*, available at <www.infrastructurereportcard.org>, that the U.S. economy will lose roughly $4 trillion in GDP during 2016-25 if necessary investment in infrastructure is not made. In 2017, ASCE graded U.S. infrastructure a *D+*. In coordination with state and local governments, the federal Works Progress Administration (1935-43) put millions of people to work on building and improving domestic infrastructure. The WPA's annual budget was $1.3-$1.5 billion ($24.5-$28.25 billion in today's dollars). For perspective, a *single* military contract issued on 15 May 2017 for C4ISR programs was valued at up to $37.4 billion. An adjustment in priorities frees plenty of money to fund a new domestic jobs program focusing on infrastructure and sustainable energy. A single Northrop Grumman B-2 bomber costs a little over $2 billion. This is roughly the cost to upgrade Amtrak high-speed trains, according to *Wired* magazine (Aarian Marshall, 26 August 2016). Momentum will build after the public uses $2 billion to upgrade Amtrak instead of purchasing another needless bomber. Another example: Just one aircraft carrier, such as the USS *Gerald Ford*, costs more than $13 billion (not including maintenance and regular upgrades). $13 billion is how much it costs to rebuild New York-to-New Jersey Amtrak infrastructure, according to *Newsweek* (Grace Guarnieri. "Trump Halts $13 Billion Obama Amtrak Plan Despite Calls For Infrastructure Spending in 2018." 31 Dec 2017).

The *Wall Street Journal* on 19 April 2019 (Lauren Weber, "Why Companies Are Failing at Reskilling") cited the Organization for Economic Cooperation & Development when noting that the

United States ranks "second-to-last among 29 developed nations in terms of taxpayer-funded training investment." This would change during demilitarization of industry, and the concordant retraining of the troops and blue-collar industry workers. Public discretionary funding (abundant once War stops hogging roughly 60%) can pay for technical training and higher education for future workers (e.g. current high school) and transitioning war industry workers and enlisted troops. Cooperatives, too, can reinvest profits into worker training, higher salaries, and R&D (whereas corporations presently use profits to pad executives' pockets and buy back stock). Hands-on retraining and education, not just classroom lectures, is preferable. Training can focus on growing opportunities in sustainable energy (geothermal, solar, wind), functioning levees, healthcare, expansion of mass public transit, and affordable, clean water for all. Beware: Dying industries (war, fossil fuels) and politicized union elites will fearmonger about cost and job loss. We must start retraining as soon as possible—in the troops' case, preferably before they leave the military's auspices. (Not all troops need retraining. Some military jobs transfer well to the civilian world. These include aircrew, cargo and freight workers, civil engineer, dental assistant, media and public relations, nursing, IT jobs, paramedic, Seabees, translators, and interpreters.) I advise loosening cumbersome licensing requirements, which mean well but often bring with them loads of red tape, for workers who are retraining out of the war industry. By routing plenty of public funding through community and state colleges we can build upon local groundwork while empowering communities. I recommend utilizing advances in technology to match skills, aptitude, and aspirations with available jobs; utilizing social media to publicize retraining options; and embracing the wide age range of employees exiting the war industry and the enlisted ranks of the Armed Forces. Rolling admission and multiple start dates for programs can trim the lag between unemployment and retraining. By continually refreshing course material, we can match federal jobs programs with the evolving needs of communities. Mandating full acceptance into retraining programs makes sure bureaucrats can't skim only the applicants they deem most likely to succeed. Implementing basic income can cushion the shock as we adjust out of the precarious economy we presently live in and as technology continues to render certain skills obsolete. Automation ought to create more leisure time for the workers, not increase the money flowing to the c-suite. Work must be meaningful, otherwise the former enlisted troops could end up longing for the sense of identity and militant unity that defined their time in the Armed Forces. Priority should go to comprehensive training, safe work conditions, and raising the federal minimum wage. The future can look bright. Remember: a dollar spent on healthcare, education, or sustainable energy creates more jobs than a dollar spent on war (Garrett-Peltier. "Job Opportunity Cost of War," *University of Massachusetts Amherst Political Economy Research Institute*. 25 May 2017).

    8 Historian Daniel Immerwahr explains the uprising in *How To Hide an Empire*, pp. 232-4.

    9 Neale, Jonathan. "People Change: American Soldiers and Marines in Vietnam 1965-73." In M. Gonzalez and H. Barekat (Eds.), *Arms and the People: Popular Movements and the Military from the Paris Commune to the Arab Spring* (pp. 173-192). New York: Pluto Press, 2013. For a thorough analysis of military resistance to the war in Southeast Asia, see Willson, S. Brian. *Don't Thank Me for My Service: My Viet Nam Awakening to the Long History of U.S. Lies*. Atlanta, GA: Clarity Press, 2018, pp. 259-290.

    10 See "War Or A New American Agenda." *National Commission for Economic Conversion*. 20 February 1991: <www.c-span.org/video/?16620-1/war-american-agenda>, (45:17).

    11 Regarding Alternative Use Committees' role in economic conversion, Seymour Melman explains: "And that has to be done close to the point of production, because only the people who are at the point of production are conversant with the capabilities and the limitations of the occupations, the factory space, the means of production, the sources for raw materials, supplies, tooling, components, and the like... You cannot do redesign of production operations by remote... That is not to say that

community groups—headed, say, by mayors—do not have an important role to play" to provide input and to help defray income and stabilize employment (1:24:09). "War Or A New American Agenda." *National Commission for Economic Conversion*. 20 February 1991.

12 Employees can transform small- and medium-sized war corporations into cooperatives. In a cooperative, the workers collectively make the decisions, day-to-day and strategic. There is no board of directors. Decisions are made based on open discussion and a decision-making process that relies on the agreement of the majority or the unanimity of all workers. To the extent that workers want leadership, leaders are elected on rotating basis. Leadership is a duty and responsibility, assumed not for title or prestige. It's okay if you don't maximize profits for bankers or Wall Street. Workers taper the needs of the cooperative to the community. Cooperatives are resilient and adaptive facing adversity.

13 To begin with, government regulators can exercise their trustbusting authority to break up recent mergers and acquisitions in the war industry (e.g. AECOM + URS; Jacobs + CH2M; United Technologies + Rockwell Collins; Raytheon + United Technologies; L3 + Harris).

14 "Memo: U.S. Voters Strongly Support Bold Climate Solutions." *Data For Progress*. 19 March 2019: <www.dataforprogress.org/the-green-new-deal-is-popular>. Relman, Eliza and Walt Hickey. "More than 80% of Americans support almost all of the key ideas in Alexandria Ocasio-Cortez's Green New Deal." *Business Insider*. 14 February 2019. Gustafson, Abel, et al. "The Green New Deal has Strong Bipartisan Support." *Yale Program on Climate Change Communication*. 14 December 2018.

15 GND programs emphasize strengthening unions, featuring jobs that pay family-sustaining wages; stopping "the transfer of jobs and pollution overseas"; building resilient infrastructure, including smart, distributed power grids; collaborating with farmers to reduce agricultural carbon emissions and other pollution; overhauling transportation systems, including investments in high-speed rail and accessible, affordable, clean public transit; upgrading existing buildings to achieve efficient energy & water; afforestation and forest preservation; and providing the public with "(i) high-quality health care; (ii) affordable, safe, and adequate housing; (iii) economic security; and (iv) access to clean water, clean air, healthy and affordable food, and nature." Full GND text available at <cleantechnica.com/2019/02/08/heres-the-full-text-of-congress-green-new-deal-resolution-introduced-by-rep-alexandria-ocasio-cortez/>.

16 Journalist and political analyst Glen Ford informs us: "Black people should see GND as an arena of struggle for self-determination, communal repair, and justice-creation." Ford advises drawing upon the National Black Political Agenda for Self-Determination as guidance in this struggle. The nineteen points contained within this guidance focus on the importance of family, equality, housing, education, healthcare, and other principles which a progressive and inclusive coalition can support. Ford, Glen. "The Black Stake in the Green New Deal." *Black Agenda Report*. 7 March 2019. The National Black Political Agenda for Self-Determination can be viewed at <www.africanamerica.org/topic/national-black-political-agenda-for-self-determination-19-points>.

17 $340 billion annually, over 30 years. "Like the original New Deal, this would be managed capitalism rather than state socialism." Cassidy, John. "The Good News About a Green New Deal." *The New Yorker*. 4 March 2019.

18 Space-lift and satellite technology known to the National Reconnaissance Office can be transferred to NASA and NOAA.

19 Article XIX concerns denunciation. See "Agreement between the Parties to the North Atlantic Treaty regarding the Status of their Forces." *NATO*. 19 June 1951. Available at: <www.nato.int/cps/en/natohq/official_texts_17265.htm>.

20 There is opportunity to leverage nationalism when appealing to European troops. This can involve encouraging European troops to ask themselves: how many of their brethren have died for

D.C.'s endless wars? Other nationalists might ask themselves: how much have D.C.'s wars (with their complicity) contributed to the flood of refugees potentially destabilizing their states?

21 War criminals can be made to fear the courts, particularly international prosecutions which have the capacity to threaten their freedom of movement. In 2001, Henry Kissinger fled France in fear of legal prosecution. A French judge had questions about Kissinger's role in supporting South American military dictatorships during the 1970s. Such regimes disappeared thousands of dissidents and progressives, including several French nationals. See Patrick Bishop "Kissinger shuns summons" (*The Telegraph*, 31 May 2001). In 2009, a British court issued an arrest warrant for Israeli politician Tzipi Livni, who had been accused of war crimes for her role in the Gaza Massacre ("Operation Cast Lead," in Israeli military terminology) of winter 2008-9. Livni cancelled her planned trip to London and stayed away until Israeli authorities and British Zionists succeeded in obtaining automatic immunity for all Israeli government officials who travel on official business to the U.K. See Stuart Winer "Livni dodges war crimes arrest in London" (*Times of Israel*, 15 June 2015).

Index

A

AAR, 10, 101, 178–179, 226–227, 338
academia, 28, 50, 53, 66, 136, 207–229, 254,
    292, 293, 344, 275
    drones, 344
    greater Boston, 207–211
    languages, 214–218
    medical advancements, 212
Accenture, xi, 49, 244, 254, 263
accounting, 1, 50,
    Defense Finance and Accounting Service,
        103–104
    tricks, 182
Advanced Persistent Threats, 138, 209
AECOM, xi, 3, 7, 16, 55–56, 59, 67, 133, 171,
    180, 184, 215, 261, 367, 379
Aegis Weapon System, 21, 167, 226, 317,
    319–320, 324, 337
Aerospace Industries Association (AIA), 51, 66,
    81, 142
Afghanistan, 1–2, 18, 23, 25, 59, 75, 110,
    145, 168, 176, 177, 178, 180, 181,
    185–186, 187, 188, 189, 213, 220,
    221, 258, 294, 296–297, 337, 340,
    342, 344, 379, 397
    Afghan Air Force, 9–10,
    burn pits in, 7–8
    green-on-blue attacks, 313
    modern history, 8–9
    uniforms, 294
Africa Command (AFRICOM), 58, 73, 95,
    106, 176, 179, 182–186, 217,
    222, 256, 258, 286, 289, 291, 342,
    366–368, 379–380
Air Force, United States, 4, 5, 7, 11, 13, 44, 71,
    72, 75, 96, 105, 106, 113, 136–137,
    141, 143–144, 165, 167, 186, 208,
    211, 219–220, 229, 246, 247, 252,
    255, 258, 262, 313, 315, 318, 322,
    324–325, 336–337, 342–343, 370,
    372, 373,
    vis-à-vis space, 346–351, 352–353
Air Force Contract Augmentation Program
    (AFCAP), 14–15, 31, 54, 57
Air Force Research Laboratory (AFRL), 22,
    123, 207, 211, 215–216, 222, 223,
    233, 266, 344, 362
Al-Assad, Bashar, 188
Allen, John, 75, 235
Al-Shabaab, 110, 181–185
Amazon, 48, 257, 347
    cloud services of, 249, 250–252
American Forces Press Service, 72, 282
American Institute of Aeronautics and
    Astronautics (AIAA), 67
AM General, 55, 137, 157, 179, 194, 200
Apartheid Israel (see: *Israel*)
Aramco, 175, 198, 231
Argentina, 166–167
Arizona, 67
    war industry within, 18, 63, 83, 200, 211,
        235, 236, 341, 342, 361, 394
    University of, 211
Army Prepositioned Stock (APS), 181
Army Research Laboratory, 211, 214, 223
artificial intelligence / machine learning, 135,
    154, 211, 220, 230, 233, 234, 249,
    254, 270, 272, 274
assassination, 52, 61, 65, 108–109, 150, 151,
    152, 169, 172, 173, 189, 229, 284,
    293, 299, 342–343, 372, 396
as-Sisi, Abdel Fattah, 110, 170, 222
Association of Old Crows (AOC), 67, 238
Association of the United States Army
    (AUSA), 53, 66, 236, 238, 275, 355
AT&T, 104, 159, 264, 274–275
audit, 78, 103–106, 108, 245
Austin, Texas, 27–29, 113, 375

Australia, 49, 147, 163, 165–166, 171, 180, 200, 262, 349
austerity, 5, 62, 150–151, 166, 214, 228, 291, 292, 293
authority, x, 25, 26, 58, 60, 95, 96, 107, 109, 136, 148, 166, 187, 211, 290, 294, 368, 392
Authorization for Use of Military Force (AUMF), 109, 202
autonomic logistics information system (ALIS), 167

B

Baghdad, 16, 163, 168, 311
Bahrain, 165, 167, 177, 178, 180, 228, 338–339
Baltimore, Maryland, 20, 62–63, 83, 84, 172, 191, 219, 221, 226, 231, 242, 255, 266, 267
ballistic missiles (see also: *nuclear weapons*), 19, 108, 120, 134, 162 165, 208, 236, 262, 271, 314–316, 323, 333, 341
base operations support services (BOSS), 13–18, 19, 94, 117, 153, 295, 350, 384
Bell (see: *Textron*)
Bezos, Jeff, 251, 347–348
bin Salman, Mohammad, 52, 228
bin Zayed, Mohammad, 52
Blackstone Group, 56, 87, 208, 332
boards of directors, x, xi, 47–49, 51, 52, 67, 75, 89, 134, 136, 138, 145, 179, 189, 207, 210, 219, 224, 228, 282, 353, 358, 378–379, 400
boards in government, 68
Boeing, xi, 10, 18, 19, 22, 23, 25, 48, 51, 53, 59, 62, 74, 75, 101, 109, 113, 116, 133, 136–138, 143–147, 165–168, 170, 173, 175, 178, 186, 211, 215, 225, 254, 260, 281–284, 290, 323, 350, 351, 367, 378
 anti-ballistic missiles, 316–319
 contributing to congressional campaigns, 55–56
 drones, 336–337, 342, 344

nuclear weaponry, 315–316, 322
 space, 346–347
bombing, ix, 9–11, 18–20, 23, 33, 69, 72, 74, 113–114, 136, 137, 148, 149, 151, 171, 173–174, 183, 184, 188, 195, 197, 200, 214, 290, 314, 322, 337, 349–350, 382
Booz Allen Hamilton, xi, xiii, 7, 20, 23, 52, 57, 114, 139, 142, 218, 241, 244, 245, 259–260, 253, 330, 375
brain drain, 228–229, 316
Brazil, 281–282, 301
Brennan, John, 70–71, 359
Brookings Institution, 75, 340
Bush, George W., 18, 145–146, 317, 319, 342
Business Executives for National Security (BENS), 67, 210, 364
burn pits, 7–8

C

CACI, xi, 20, 36, 50, 101, 141, 142, 153, 201, 215, 225, 241, 244, 255–259, 263, 320, 356
Cameroon, 95, 180, 182, 203
Camp Arifjan (Kuwait), 180, 181
Camp Lemonnier (Djibouti), 73, 182, 342
cancer, 7–8, 12, 55, 314, 316
Caret, Leanne, 53, 86, 145, 194
Carlyle Group, 56, 75, 81, 101
Carter, Ash, 44, 73, 143, 210, 282, 388
casualties, 1–2, 9, 10–11, 18, 26, 29, 52, 65, 73, 110, 149–150, 174, 179, 181–186, 202, 212, 233, 313, 342–343, 345, 359, 371, 379, 392
 death toll from global wars, 342–343, 345
 see also: *bombing*
Center for American Progress, 51, 87, 91
Center for Strategic and Budgetary Assessments (CSBA), 136
Center for Strategic and International Studies (CSIS), 40, 48, 50, 51, 75, 80, 81, 82, 87, 154, 204, 300, 330, 332, 364, 365, 382

Central Command (CENTCOM), 49, 180, 289
  air transport, 178–179
  operations within, 177
  sales to countries within 176–177
Central Intelligence Agency (CIA), 8–10, 12,
    16–17, 19, 21, 49, 53, 57, 61, 65,
    70–71, 74, 108–110, 136, 149, 209,
    210, 219, 246, 253, 254, 279, 322,
    325, 346
  Amazon cloud services, 250–251
  case officers, 112, 244, 388
  drone strikes, 183–184, 336, 342–343, 345
  Guantánamo Bay, Naval Station, 295
  Somalia presence, 181–182, 184
  torture, 88, 150, 152, 223
Center for a New American Security (CNAS),
    40, 89, 154, 232, 235, 320, 332, 379
China, 71, 75, 118, 134–138, 142, 166, 167, 182,
    212, 220, 261, 279, 298, 317, 322,
    321, 324, 337, 338, 352, 374, 379
Chief Executive Officer (see: *executives*)
Clapper, James, 111, 129, 267, 275
Clinton, Hillary, 36, 210, 301, 381
cloud service (see: *information technology*)
CNN, 71, 115, 129, 132, 174, 275, 358
Cold War, 8, 41, 42, 58–60, 68, 118, 134, 247,
    267, 282, 290, 297, 325, 359
Colombia, 29, 108, 189, 220, 280, 283–286,
    287–288, 297, 395, 397
Congress abetting drone development/
    procurement, 337
Congressional committees, 51, 53, 55–57,
    61, 111, 119, 153, 156, 210, 237,
    247–248, 267, 277, 321, 345, 352,
    379–380
Congressional Budget Office, 75, 136, 332
Congressional Research Service, 15, 117, 187
conscription (see: *draft*)
Consolidated Afloat Network Enterprise
    Services (CANES), 248, 253
construction, 3–7, 16, 19, 32, 39, 41, 94–95,
    115, 118, 131, 133, 137, 156, 178,
    183–184, 200, 215, 247, 291, 313,
    315, 320, 323, 327, 333, 346, 360,
    391, 397
  drones, 342
  intelligence facilities, 246–247, 266–267,
    269,
  jobs, 63, 295, 378–379
  Middle East, 180–181, 199, 304,
  Naval Station Guantánamo Bay, 295–296
  Southern Command, 283, 295–296, 310,
    311,
  special operations, 217, 378–379, 387
  U.S. construction firms in Apartheid Israel,
    171
contractors (see: *mercenaries*)
contract types, 92–93, 99
Conventional Arms Transfer, 110, 204
cooperation, intra-industry, 134–135, 153, 243,
    317, 345, 346
corporate media (see: *media*)
cost-plus, 92–93, 117
counternarcotics (see: *War on Drugs*)
Cross Functional Team (CFT), 27
cyber / cybersecurity, xiii, 49, 63, 119, 134–135,
    141–142, 144, 176, 210, 211, 219,
    224, 234, 236, 237, 239, 242, 246,
    249, 253, 254, 259–261, 267, 269,
    270, 273, 274, 282, 284, 330, 331,
    339, 341, 376–377, 385, 386

D

Dallas, Texas, 20, 22, 83, 146, 220
data links, 23, 134, 145, 239, 261–262, 264,
    268, 274
DDB Chicago Inc., 114
Defense Advanced Research Projects Agency
    (DARPA), 42, 78, 80, 117, 123, 141,
    209–213, 220, 224, 231, 233, 236,
    237, 239, 249, 274, 325, 334, 364
  Gremlins, 340–341
  World Modelers, 213–214
Defense Business Board. 68, 141
Defense Federal Acquisition Regulation
    Supplement (DFARS), 98, 120

Defense Intelligence Agency (DIA), 158, 220, 250, 258, 266–267, 288
   corporatization of, 243–246, 265, 275, 322
   National Media Exploitation Center (NMEC), 184, 246
Defense Media Activity, 72
Defense Policy Board, 51, 68, 141, 235
Defense Production Act, 178
Defense Security Cooperation Agency (DSCA), 40, 49, 67, 77, 104, 161, 164–165, 187, 191, 205, 236, 281, 338, 340
Defense Threat Reduction Agency, 123, 139, 141, 266, 384
Defense Video and Imagery Distribution System (DVIDS), 72–73, 89
Deloitte & Touche LLP, 86, 104, 122, 123, 231, 244, 245
depleted uranium, 12, 38, 172, 185, 290, 326
Deveselu, Romania, 15, 319–320, 331, 337
Diego Garcia (see: *United Kingdom*)
disability, 100–101, 121
displays (arms fairs, air shows, conferences, exhibits), 66, 338–340, 355, 375
Djibouti, 15, 40, 73, 122, 182, 203, 236, 337, 342, 374, 385
draft, 289, 392
Drake, Thomas, 242, 265
Draper Laboratory, 22, 208, 213, 215, 231, 328, 342
drones, xvi, 13, 15, 18, 22–24, 62, 66, 68, 72, 137, 147, 165, 168, 173, 176, 182, 223, 236, 254, 255, 273, 274, 304, 317, 338
   back-up relay station at NAS Sigonella, 367
   construction pertinent, 337, 342, 378
   crashes, 357
   deaths, 65, 73, 109, 150, 183, 202, 342–343, 345, 383
   great power competition, 337–338
   introduction to, 336–338
   kill list, 109
   legalese, 109–110

   platforms for corporate cooperation, 133, 158, 163, 191, 336–337, 345
   proliferation, 185, 341
   swarming, 340–341
   undersea, 208, 341–342
DRS / Leonardo DRS, xi, 55, 161, 167, 320, 356
Dunford, Joseph, 138
DynCorp, xi, 20, 23, 51, 101, 167, 173, 194, 200, 215, 304, 370

E

ECS Federal, 215, 254
Egypt, xi, 59, 110, 170–171, 176, 180, 222, 340
Einstein, Albert, 46
Eisenhower, Dwight D., xi
Elbit Systems, 23, 63, 171
Elta North America, 171, 356
Ernst & Young LLP, 85, 104, 122, 123, 124
Esper, Mark, 27–28, 135, 324
euphemism, 25, 70, 148, 196
   list of, 149–152
executives, 2, 13, 19, 20, 24, 27, 28, 29, 62, 63, 68–69, 107, 144–145, 175, 179, 224, 242, 247, 253, 258–259, 352, 392, 394
   candid arms merchants, 186–187, 285, 338, 339
   chief executive officer, 49, 52, 53, 58, 62–63, 69, 72, 75, 145, 165, 208, 212, 226, 230, 235, 251, 253, 260, 317, 347, 393
   cyber, view of, 260
   female, 52–54
   in Pentagon leadership, 50–52
   prosecution of criminals, 396–397
   pushing great power competition, 135–136, 141
   solutions, 142–143
   university boards, 207
   view of global warfare, 188–190, 372
Evolved Expendable Launch Vehicle (EELV), xiii, 347–348

F

Federal Acquisition Regulation (FAR), 97–99
Federal Emergency Management Agency (FEMA), 96, 291
Federally Funded Research and Development Center (FFRDC), 224
finances (see: *accounting*)
fixed-price contract, 92–93, 117
Fluor, 13, 43, 48, 56, 159, 215, 291–292, 327, 382
Foreign Intelligence Surveillance Act (FISA), 110
    Foreign Intelligence Surveillance Court, 264
foreign military sales (FMS), 164–190
    case study MQ-4C, 165–166
    Israeli purchases, 169–170, 173
    overview, 164–165
Fors Marsh Group, 114
Fort Gordon, 243, 266, 267, 270
Fort Meade, 73, 171, 225, 241–243, 263, 270
Fort Worth, Texas, 20, 22–23, 63, 171
fossil fuel, xiii, 3–5, 10–12, 14, 17, 50, 59, 73–75, 102, 173, 175, 177–179, 181, 210, 251–252, 259, 264, 277, 292–293, 399
    Silicon Valley exploration of, 251
FOXNEWS, 71, 101
France, 5, 24, 83, 167, 174, 204, 289, 338, 365, 383
fraud, waste and abuse, 30, 105, 108, 182, 242, 292, 294, 315
Futures Command, 27–30, 375
F-35 (*see*: Joint Strike Fighter)

G

Gates, Robert, 49, 143, 219
Gaza, Palestine, 65, 151, 169, 171, 173
General Atomics, 19, 21, 23, 55–56, 72, 109, 113, 165, 185, 336–337, 342–345, 367
General Dynamics, xi, 18, 21–23, 49, 53, 55, 59, 69, 71–72, 97, 104, 133, 137, 147–148, 179–180, 215, 227, 241, 244, 252, 263, 283, 290, 297, 315–316, 320, 323, 339, 342, 367, 375
    contributing to congressional campaigns, 55–56
    support of Saudi regime, 174–175
General Electric, xi, 22, 55–56, 133, 165, 170, 251, 281
    tracking biological processes, 115
Germany, 15, 62, 137, 167, 337, 374, 396
Goldman Sachs, 50, 69
Google, 56, 251, 253–255
great power competition, 134–138, 141–142, 166–167, 182, 210, 220, 249, 258, 261, 279, 298, 314, 319, 322, 324, 337, 338, 340, 345, 352
    effect on special operations, 374, 376, 379–380
GSD&M, 65, 113
Guam, 18, 289, 349–350, 391
Guantánamo Bay, Naval Station (NSGB), 179, 246, 295–296, 298, 394

H

Hacking for Defense (H4D), 221
Hagel, Chuck, 143, 282, 285, 303
Hanscom Air Force Base, 208–209
Harris Corp., xi, 20, 60, 137, 141, 167, 192, 194, 225, 241, 244, 263, 266, 275, 306, 320, 349, 361, 362, 370, 400
    contributing to congressional campaigns, 55–56, 273
Harvard University, 75, 80, 209–210, 219, 221, 228, 232, 240, 305, 388
    Belfer Center, 80, 219, 232, 388
Hawaiʻi, 5, 15, 102, 318, 349, 363, 391
    colonization/militarization of, 214–215, 234, 275, 378
    war industry within, 215, 242, 243, 362
Heritage Foundation, 75, 77, 91, 136, 154, 300
Haspel, Gina, 53, 70, 88
Hewson, Marillyn, 51–52, 69, 79, 193, 233

Hezbollah, 122, 169, 193, 220, 300
Hill Air Force Base, 236, 313, 322
the Hive, 22–23
Hollywood, California, 60, 73–74, 90, 113, 278, 368
Honduras, 23, 279, 282–283, 287, 300, 301, 303, 306, 310, 385
Honeywell, xi, 23, 25, 30, 48, 86, 118, 191, 192, 194, 201, 273, 274, 315, 327, 328, 337, 346, 354, 360
    contributing to congressional campaigns, 55–56
Hooper, Lt. Gen. Charles, 187, 191, 205, 236, 340
House Armed Services Committee, 57, 91, 156, 210, 267, 380
House of Saud (see: *Saudi Arabia*)
Hughes, Langston, 226
Huntington Ingalls, xi, 21, 56, 62, 69, 86, 141, 215, 273, 315–316, 327, 356, 381, 384
Huntsville, Alabama, 19–20, 66, 83, 226, 233, 235, 245, 317, 339, 361, 365
hypersonic weaponry, 135, 220, 223, 321, 324–326

I

improvised explosive device (IED), 94, 157, 213, 224, 256–257
indefinite-delivery/indefinite-quantity (IDIQ), 93, 117
information technology (IT), xiv, 21, 135, 215, 241–264, 342, 385
    cloud, 249–255
    construction, 246
    cost, 243–244
    definition of, 241
    overload, 248–249
    waste, 241–244
In-Q-Tel, 49, 325, 334
intelligence / espionage, ix, 9, 16, 21, 40, 49, 70, 109–112, 139, 154, 172–174, 176, 195, 204, 207, 218, 221, 243–248, 279, 291
    (see also: *Central Intelligence Agency*)
    corporate intelligence products, 23, 36, 43, 50, 57, 60, 117, 143, 145, 180, 184, 196, 215, 216–217, 220, 236, 242, 250–255, 258, 275, 277, 295, 297, 346, 373–374
    counterintelligence, 219, 245, 265
    intelligence community, 209, 252, 266, 267, 322, 345
    sources and methods, 109–110
intelligence surveillance reconnaissance (ISR), 123, 248, 267, 274, 358, 370, 376,
C4ISR, 123, 243, 255–256, 259, 398
Intermediate-Range Nuclear Forces (INF) Treaty, 323–324
International Criminal Court (ICC), 145
International Monetary Fund (IMF), 11, 167
Internet of Battlefield Things (IoBT), 234
investment banks, 31, 51, 55, 59, 68–69, 230, 273, 320
Iraq, 1–2, 7–18, 20, 29, 32, 36, 37, 41, 57, 59, 71, 73, 89, 91, 96, 116, 120, 122, 144, 146, 152, 157, 168, 171, 174, 177, 180, 181, 183, 185, 189, 192, 195, 199, 201, 203, 213, 215, 220, 239, 251, 253, 258, 293, 296, 305, 306, 311, 337, 340, 345, 385
Iran, 10, 59, 71, 74–75, 88, 108, 122, 142, 169, 173, 186, 188–189, 195, 196, 201, 206, 213, 233, 259, 317, 319, 331, 342, 345, 352, 366
    U.S. and Israel harming Iran, 213
Islamic extremism (see: *jihadists*)
Israel, xi, 17, 59, 61, 65, 73, 75, 108, 148, 152, 168–173
    espionage activities, 172
    relation to U.S. war industry, 23, 51, 110, 169–170
    war corporations in the U.S., 15, 63, 171
    weaponry against Palestinians, 173
Ivy League, 209–211

J

Jacobs, xi, 3, 6, 35, 36, 133, 180, 261, 307, 315, 320, 373, 379, 400
James, Deborah Lee, 186, 351, 364
Japan, 24, 40, 43, 82, 84, 104, 156, 165, 167, 181, 192, 234, 239, 259, 262, 266, 275, 328, 349, 354, 398
jihadists, 9, 16, 17, 20, 61, 151, 161, 181, 186, 188–189, 204, 206, 235, 278, 342, 371, 381
jobs, xii, 14, 17, 19, 24, 26, 47, 59–60, 62–64, 100, 136, 186, 282, 290, 295, 317, 344, 378, 394–395
Johns Hopkins University (JHU), 68, 98, 216, 235, 240, 328
    Applied Physics Laboratory, 212, 218–221, 325, 349
Joint Direct Attack Munitions (JDAM), 74, 322
Joint Enterprise Defense Infrastructure (JEDI), 251–252, 270
Joint Hometown News Service, 73
Joint Strike Fighter, 23–24, 43, 49, 57, 62–63, 82–83, 95, 165, 167, 170, 194, 200, 239, 262, 351, 364
joint venture (JV), 44, 85, 133–134, 223, 262, 282, 295, 347, 366, 383
Jordan, 15, 36, 95, 177, 180–181, 192, 199, 201, 203, 236, 239, 262, 304, 385
JPMorgan Chase, 31, 50, 320

K

KBRWyle, xi, 14–15, 115, 117, 159, 171, 180, 201, 320
Kearney & Co., 50, 78, 106, 123, 124
Khashoggi, Jamal, 52, 196
King, Jr., Dr. Martin Luther, 226–227
Klare, Michael, 134, 153
KPMG LLP, 43, 104, 123, 124, 339
Kuwait, 10, 11, 15, 36, 37, 60, 118, 120, 167, 177, 180, 181, 192, 199, 201, 228, 236, 239, 262
Kurds, 188

L

land vehicles, 179–180
language, 92, 148, 164, 234, 235
    corporate provision of language knowledge, 15, 102, 220–221, 215–218, 220, 232
    Defense Language Institute (DLI), 216–217
    poor proficiency, 47, 61, 108, 112, 129, 215, 217–218, 371, 383
Latin America, 59, 87, 186, 197, 231, 258, 274, 277–299, 301, 303, 306, 331, 348, 381, 385, 395
leaks, 250, 282
Leahy Law, 164
Lebanon, 168, 169, 193, 196, 199, 204, 220, 344, 383
legal code, U.S., 80, 88, 107–113, 125, 128–129, 148, 183, 232, 235, 253
legal counsel, 109, 110, 128, 235, 269
Leidos, xi, 2, 23, 69, 80, 86, 116, 120, 123, 142, 158, 180, 213, 244, 263, 266, 273, 275, 295, 332, 354, 356, 361, 370
Libya, U.S. intervention in, 366–268
Lincoln Laboratory, 22, 208–209, 231, 328
Littoral Combat Ship (LCS), 62, 119, 135, 137, 147, 384
lobbying, xiii, 11, 24, 26, 37, 47, 59, 61–70, 76, 86, 91, 104, 107–109, 125, 127, 145, 151, 155, 157, 170, 172, 174–175, 185, 198, 260–261, 286, 295, 316, 321, 332, 351, 353, 368
locations of industry, overview 20–24
Lockheed Martin, xi, 10, 20–25, 28, 32, 41–44, 48–49, 51–52, 59, 62–63, 69, 76, 79, 81, 83–87, 107, 109, 113, 120–123, 126, 133, 137–142, 145, 147, 153, 157–159, 162–163, 165, 167–168, 170, 174–176, 178, 192–194, 198–200, 205, 208, 212, 262, 266, 271, 274, 275, 281, 301, 302, 305, 315–316, 317, 319–320, 322,

324–325, 328, 329, 330, 337–338,
341, 342, 345–347, 350, 356, 360,
361, 364, 365, 367, 370, 382, 384
  contributing to congressional campaigns,
    55–57
  funding STEM, 225–228
  Orlando, 239
  scientific and engineering employment,
    229
  special operations, 373, 375, 378
  (see also: *Joint Strike Fighter*)
Logistics Civil Augmentation Program
    (LOGCAP), 15, 151
London (see: *United Kingdom*)
Lord, Ellen, 53, 135, 187, 337, 360
Los Angeles Air Force Base, 23, 208, 224, 346,
    348, 350
L3, xi, 22, 35, 60, 65, 104, 119, 168, 190, 191,
    192, 194, 203, 213, 244, 253, 263,
    270, 271, 273, 302, 304, 306, 328,
    337, 338, 342, 354, 356, 359, 370,
    373, 374, 385, 400

M

Manning, Chelsea, 209–210, 245
Marshall Islands, 18, 318, 361
Massachusetts Institute of Technology (MIT),
    22, 68, 81, 207–209, 212, 218, 221,
    224, 226, 228, 230, 231, 233, 240,
    293, 328, 344
  Media Lab, 208, 231
Mattis, James, 49, 77, 186, 352, 364
McCain, John, 55, 69, 81, 139
McCarthy, Ryan. 27–28, 49
McKeon, Howard "Buck", 57, 85
media, corporate, 16, 47, 60, 70–75, 86, 89, 91,
    94, 113, 151, 157, 175, 185, 260,
    316, 321, 323, 340, 343, 371
Melman, Seymour, ix, x, 64, 334, 389, 393, 398,
    399
mercenaries, xiii, 2, 8, 14, 16–17, 24, 209, 40,
    73, 104, 108, 122, 127, 137, 144,
    151, 177, 179, 183–185, 189, 203,
206, 217–218, 237, 239, 244, 259,
267, 280, 284, 286, 287, 289, 293,
297, 318, 349, 367, 370, 380
Mexico, 171, 189, 194, 286–287, 296, 301
Meyers, Seth, 73–74
microelectronics, 133, 158, 212, 233, 261,
    263–264
Microsoft, 119, 243, 249, 251–253, 257, 270,
    271
migration, 278, 296, 297
military education, 222
minerals, 9, 33, 35, 185, 205–206, 264, 277
Mine Resistant Ambush Protected (MRAP),
    140, 157, 180
Miscellaneous Obligation Reimbursement
    Document (MORD), 96, 118
Missile Defense Agency (MDA), 48, 141, 223,
    316–321, 325, 350–351
MITRE, 50, 224, 237
MSNBC, 70–71, 80, 89
Muilenburg, Dennis, 145–146
MullenLowe, 114, 130

N

National Academy of Sciences, 222
National Aeronautics and Space Administration
    (NASA), 95, 119, 347, 360, 395
National Defense Authorization Act (NDAA),
    43, 55, 57, 69–70, 81, 95, 260, 290,
    337, 348, 353
National Defense Education Program, 225
National Defense Industrial Association (NDIA),
    2, 52, 53, 54, 66, 70, 138, 142, 161,
    171, 225, 226, 275, 375, 386
National Defense Strategy, 138, 154
National Geospatial-Intelligence Agency
    (NGA), 21, 80, 129, 246, 250, 255,
    266–267, 346
National Public Radio (NPR), 72, 321
National Reconnaissance Office (NRO), 21,
    237, 250, 266, 330, 346–348, 382,
    400

National Security Agency (NSA), 21, 34, 43, 49, 57, 77, 78, 81, 171, 172, 182, 195, 214, 215, 217–218, 221, 231, 242–244, 246, 255, 257, 259, 282, 322, 349, 358
    corporations in the vicinity of, 242–243
    GCHQ relations, 263
    legal underpinnings, 110–111, 128, 129
    mission, 243, 252
    recruitment, 225
    Silicon Valley firms, 250–253, 269
    telecommunications corporations, 264
    Trailblazer, 241–242
    zero day exploits, 261
National Security Resources Board, 68
National Security Technology Accelerator (MD5), 221–222
Native Americans, 101–103
Naval Air Station Sigonella, 366–367
Navistar Defense, 35, 56, 140, 144, 157, 161, 179, 180, 201
neoliberal economic policies, xii, 29, 59–60, 73, 106, 150, 232, 255, 274, 279, 283, 291–294, 308, 375
Niger, 40, 95, 182, 185, 203, 204, 342, 385, 397
Nigeria, 185, 192, 204
Norquist, David, 105–106
North American Aerospace Defense Command (NORAD), 141, 157, 314, 347
North Atlantic Treaty Organization (NATO), 10, 14, 36, 110, 120, 137–138, 155, 161, 165, 167, 228, 232, 240, 262, 281, 284, 305, 314, 322–324, 357, 381, 383, 396, 400
North Korea, 71, 75, 142, 167, 188, 317, 330, 352
Northrop Grumman, xi, 28, 42, 53, 59, 69, 137, 145, 153, 163, 170, 173, 194, 206, 225–226, 236, 239, 240, 259–260, 263, 265, 266, 281, 284, 320, 327, 329, 331, 333, 367
    contributing to congressional campaigns, 55–57
    influence, 48, 141, 231
    leadership, 51, 53, 159, 273, 334, 365
    locations, 20, 22–23, 62, 233, 243
    products, 72, 83, 90, 113–114, 117, 120, 133, 147, 158, 160, 165–166, 191, 192, 197, 205, 213, 236, 253, 271, 275, 305, 315–317, 322–323, 325, 328, 336–337, 342, 345, 350, 354, 358, 359, 360, 361, 382, 398
    space, 346–348
Novakovic, Phebe, 53, 86
nuclear weapons, ix, 25, 41, 80, 129, 134, 135, 138, 208, 224, 259, 261–262, 313–326, 332
    close calls / danger, 314–315
    cost, 30, 315
    laboratories, 107, 315, 322
    modernization, 110, 151, 235–236, 321–326
    triad, 315–316, 323

O

Obama, Barack, xiv, 18, 41, 57, 77, 109, 183, 186, 188, 196, 202, 203, 232, 235, 251, 254, 267, 277, 295–296, 299, 301, 310, 319, 321, 323, 332, 342–343, 357, 358, 359
obsolescence, 146–148, 162, 163, 328, 329
oil (see: *fossil fuel*)
Operation Barkhane, 185
operations and maintenance (O&M) funds, 94, 118, 119, 243, 265, 397
opportunity cost, 295, 298, 345, 397, 399
Oshkosh Defense, 140, 157, 161, 179, 180, 200
other transaction authority, 375, 386
overseas contingency operations (OCO), 30, 43, 55, 94, 149, 182, 270, 391, 397

P

PAE, xi, 10, 23, 35, 36, 59, 123, 133, 159, 203, 244, 263, 336
Pakistan, 1, 8, 29, 41, 126, 128, 161, 168, 171, 176, 177, 180, 187, 192, 199, 200,

201, 203, 205, 239, 262, 297, 310, 321, 342, 354, 357, 358, 385
Palestine, 37, 168, 171–172, 185,
    ethnic cleansing of, 61, 169
    testbed for weaponry, 170, 189, 353
Panetta, Leon, 103, 128, 143, 281–282, 303
PATRIOT missile system, 23, 27, 28–29, 130, 155, 170, 198, 199, 317, 319, 331
patriotism, xii, 3, 25–26, 79, 115, 132, 239, 247, 251, 259, 368, 390–391
Petraeus, David, 128, 132, 183, 210
Philippines, 58, 95, 128, 189, 289, 295, 369–371, 383, 384, 398
    purchases from U.S. industry, 370
plugs, 103, 121
pollution, 1, 3–8, 102, 122, 138, 156, 215, 264, 290, 314, 316, 326–327, 350, 395, 400
Pompeo, Michael, 128, 145, 198, 235
pressure groups, 2, 47, 51–54, 66–69, 129, 142, 161, 171, 210, 225, 226, 237, 268, 275, 320, 339, 364, 375, 386
pretexts, 11, 47, 86, 134–138, 140, 166, 210, 261, 340
PricewaterhouseCoopers (PwC), 43, 104
private equity, 22, 51, 55–56, 62, 68–69, 72, 77, 89, 91, 204, 208, 210, 230, 238, 273, 306, 388
propaganda, 11, 17, 22, 37, 44, 58, 72, 76, 113–116, 130, 139, 150–151, 240, 275, 279, 313, 331, 339, 368, 371
protest, ix, 11, 37, 102, 112, 129, 135, 151, 178, 192, 214–215, 221, 254, 262, 289, 301, 342, 398
psychological operations (PSYOPS), 115, 132, 151, 377, 380, 386
public relations, 6, 10–11, 24, 59, 64, 72, 78, 80, 103, 108, 111, 115, 132, 174–175, 184, 209, 240, 251, 277, 317, 344, 379, 399
Puerto Rico, 18, 35, 54, 84, 108, 144, 160, 280, 289–294, 296, 298, 307–308, 310, 349

Vieques, Puerto Rico, 18, 126, 289–290, 307
Putin, Vladimir, 321, 323, 325
P-8A aircraft, 119, 147, 163, 165–166, 191, 305, 306

Q

Qatar, 16, 53, 161, 165, 167, 177, 180–181, 186, 192, 199, 201, 228, 236, 239, 262, 266, 338, 361

R

Ramstein Air Base, 270, 337, 354, 367, 396
Range Generation Next (RGNext), 134, 330, 361
rape, 2, 108, 182, 286, 369
Raytheon, xi, 13, 18, 21–23, 25–26, 42, 59–60, 62, 66, 67, 74, 81, 84, 107, 122, 125, 126, 137, 140–142, 144, 153, 155, 158, 162, 163, 165, 167, 170, 191–194, 197, 199, 225–228, 248, 271, 273, 290, 302, 304, 315, 319, 329, 330–332, 345–347, 356, 359, 370, 374, 381
    BBN, 22, 218, 233
    contributing to congressional campaigns, 55–56, 81
    executives / leadership, 19, 28, 44, 48, 49, 52, 69, 78, 86, 104, 109, 128, 135, 174, 175, 187, 210, 211, 230, 232, 239, 259, 260, 339, 341
    ordnance, 18, 83, 113, 118, 120, 121, 130, 133, 137, 117, 190, 211, 274, 282, 290, 317, 320, 324–325, 337, 361, 367, 384–385
recruitment and retention, 49, 74, 88, 113–116, 131, 132, 144, 171, 227, 272, 289, 354, 377, 380, 389
remotely piloted vehicles (see: *drones*)
Research Triangle Park, 223–224
revolving door, 49, 341, 345, 371
Romania, 15, 137, 167, 192, 239, 319–320, 332, 337, 385

Roosevelt, Franklin D., 177, 400
ruses, 143–146, 310, 319, 384
Russia, ix, 8–9, 35, 43, 58–59, 69, 71, 75, 81, 83, 86, 134–138, 141–142, 144, 149, 154, 155, 156, 172, 182, 212, 220, 232, 234, 268, 279, 298, 314, 317, 319–322, 323–325, 331, 334, 337–338, 341, 348–349, 352, 355, 364, 374, 379

S

Sahel, 185, 189, 204
SAIC, xi, 10, 20, 23, 24, 36, 50, 53, 59, 79, 140, 157, 167, 180, 199, 214, 237, 239, 241–243, 244, 246, 263, 273, 302, 342, 361, 362, 364, 375
sanctions, 1, 11, 37, 59, 108, 122, 152
Santiago, Sonia, 54, 306
satellites, 13, 19, 20, 21, 118, 134–135, 141, 149, 184, 191, 194, 198, 249, 255, 266, 267, 277, 306, 320, 340, 367, 373
    launch, 133, 253, 330, 346–348
    navigation, 346
    overview of corporate roles, 345–348
    use in recent military attacks, 345–346
Saudi Arabia / the Saudi regime, 16, 52, 78, 108, 167, 173, 177, 196, 201, 206, 209, 228, 236, 240, 262, 342, 383
    domestic unrest, 173
    funding Silicon Valley, 255
    lobbying, 174–175, 198
    purchasing U.S. weaponry, 86, 102, 110, 120, 126, 161, 173, 177, 186, 192, 196, 197, 199, 227, 239, 260, 338, 360
    "Saudization" / war corporations, 175
    Yemen, destruction of, 85, 173–176, 366, 372
schemes industry uses when contracting, 99, 242, 344
science, technology, engineering, and mathematics (STEM), 225–228, 238, 239

Schiff, Adam, 57, 81, 332
secrecy, 171, 247–248, 250, 267, 288, 315
Secretary of State, 87, 145, 173, 210, 235, 301
Secretary of War, 2, 19, 44, 49–51, 53, 73, 75, 88, 128, 136, 142, 143, 160, 169, 174, 210, 219, 244, 253, 266, 281, 285, 321, 324, 351, 352, 364, 380, 388, 391
Section 127e (see: *10 U.S. Code Section 127e*)
Senate Armed Services Committee, 51, 56, 119, 153, 277, 345, 352–353, 355, 379
Sensitive Compartmented Information Facility (SCIF), 246–247, 267
Shanahan, Patrick, 105, 136, 144, 186, 254, 260, 326, 351
Sierra Nevada Corp., 10, 36, 53, 86, 191, 204, 226, 304, 356, 360, 365, 373
signals intelligence (SIGINT), 43, 49, 60, 86, 111, 112, 117, 135, 172, 184, 215, 220, 242, 244, 269, 274, 277, 288, 382
Signals Intelligence Directives (USSID), 110, 128
Silicon Valley
    Defense Digital Service, 254
    Defense Innovation Unit, 375
    MIC elite liaising with, 254
small businesses, 99–101, 120, 121, 123, 158, 204, 274, 373, 375, 387
Smith-Mundt Modernization Act, 72
Snowden, Edward, 129, 196, 244–245, 282
solutions, xiii, 15, 23, 32, 35, 42, 48, 59, 66, 77, 119, 123, 124, 134, 142–146, 150, 159–160, 165, 180, 185, 190, 199, 200, 234, 238, 256–257, 258, 262, 266, 268, 302, 306, 327, 328, 329, 338, 340, 341, 347, 356, 365, 370, 377, 386
Somalia, 41, 109, 128, 180–184, 189, 201, 202, 203, 342, 366, 385
Southern Command (SOUTHCOM), 106, 297, 283–289, 296–298, 300, 301, 303, 306

history, 277–280
mission, 279
partnership, 280–281, 302
South Korea, 31, 104, 156, 166, 181, 192, 201, 246, 262, 328, 361, 374, 398
Space Force, 351–353
Space and Naval Warfare Systems Center, 248
special access programs, 245
special operations (U.S.), xiv, 105, 128, 149, 217, 224, 257, 357, 386
    activities/operations, 2, 108, 126, 179, 181–186, 366, 368–369, 372
    class interests of personnel, 368
    curricula, 305, 371
    equipment/kit, 304, 344, 367, 372–374
    propaganda in support of, 368, 372
    terrorizing families, 184, 368–369
    transitioning to great power competition, 135, 379–380
Special Operations Command (SOCOM), 106, 119, 142, 220, 285–286
    budget, 372
    construction within, 311, 378–379
    contracting vehicles, 372–373
    hyper-enabled operator, 374–375
    Joint Special Operations Command (JSOC), 109
    Joint Special Operations Task Force-Philippines (JSOTF-P), 369–371
    Marine Special Operations Command (MARSOC), 376–378
Special Operations Force Industry Conference (SOFIC), 375–378
special relationship (see: United Kingdom)
SRI International, 213–214, 248
Stanford University, 212–214, 236
State Department, U.S., 16–17, 19, 36, 40, 79, 96, 101, 125, 151, 170, 174, 186, 198, 208, 235, 302, 367, 381
strategy, 124, 132, 138, 210, 220
    industry's strategy, 46–47, 50, 75, 115, 154, 176, 184, 259
    lack of military strategy, 185–186

submarine, 21, 22, 60, 69, 72, 78, 87, 117, 120, 129, 134, 137, 208, 215, 239, 262, 274, 314–316, 321, 323, 328, 357, 366
suicide, 2, 31, 343
supply chains, 24, 33, 49, 62, 102, 117, 213, 233, 302
symposia, 2, 86, 226, 268, 338–340
Syria, 1, 16–18, 20, 29, 109, 140, 170, 188–189, 215

T

Tampa, Florida, 83, 124, 161, 354, 373, 375, 385, 387
taxes / taxation, 1, 3, 11, 20, 27, 30, 31, 63, 77, 93, 101, 107, 113, 124, 150, 165, 198, 208, 235, 242, 269, 278, 287, 292, 293, 320, 373, 399
10 U.S. Code Section 127e, 182, 184
terror / terrorism (see: *War on Terror*)
Texas, colleges and universities, 219, 222, 327
Textron, xi, 13, 19, 22, 23, 53, 60, 89, 133, 135, 139, 142, 166, 187, 192, 194, 203, 205, 213, 230, 273, 303, 304, 328, 336, 337, 340, 344, 353, 354, 356, 357, 358, 359, 360, 378
    Bell, 22, 62, 121, 133, 146–147, 192, 279, 378
think tanks, role of, 10, 74–76
third country nationals (TCN), 14, 38, 122
threats, 118, 136, 152, 165, 219–220, 236, 256, 320, 377
    cyber as a threat, 259–261
    hype of, 16, 42, 48, 49, 58–60, 71, 74–75, 81–82, 88, 137, 138–143, 144, 149, 153, 154, 158, 159, 185, 247, 278, 280, 296–298, 299, 317, 319, 322, 328–329, 330, 338, 343, 347, 352, 366, 379–380 391
    insider threats, 139, 141, 142, 158, 245
Tidd, Adm. Kurt, 277–279, 284, 286, 297–298, 300, 303
"tools they need", 143–145

torture, 78, 88, 109, 150, 152, 173, 178, 182, 189, 195, 223, 232, 309
Trailblazer, 241–242, 247
training, corporate, 115, 177–178
Transportation Command (TRANSCOM), 106, 178–179
Treasury Department, 20, 77, 103, 108, 113, 122, 182, 210, 298, 320, 385
treaties, 98, 110, 120, 170, 284, 289, 316–317, 322, 323–324, 326, 328, 331, 332, 333
Trident II (D5) submarine-launched ballistic missile, 120, 208, 231, 262, 316, 320, 323, 328
Truman, Harry S., 168
Trump, Donald, 18, 89, 109, 143, 176, 186, 277, 319, 323, 357
Tucson, Arizona, 18, 63, 83, 200, 211, 235, 236, 361

U

Ukraine, 81, 155, 161, 189, 338, 340
United Kingdom, 24, 34, 37, 83, 104, 132, 166, 172, 231, 239, 262, 329, 339
    Naval Support Facility Diego Garcia, 18–19, 41, 179, 262, 349, 394
    special relationship with USA, 120, 163, 208, 237, 262–263, 274, 348, 353
United Launch Services / United Launch Alliance, 133, 330, 347–348, 360, 365, 382
United Technologies Corp., xi, 13, 22–23, 59–60, 125, 138, 153, 160, 165, 175, 193, 238, 273, 323, 356, 364, 400
contributing to congressional campaigns, 55–56
University-Affiliated Research Centers (UARC), 224
unmanned aerial vehicles (see: *drones*)
unmanned undersea vehicles (see: *drones*)
USA PATRIOT Act, 107, 112, 130
U.S. Army Corps of Engineers (USACE), 6, 22, 39, 40, 118, 119, 123, 137, 181, 201, 233, 234, 237, 281

USS *Liberty*, 169, 192

V

Vectrus, xv, 15, 48, 104, 144, 180, 201, 241, 320
Veritas Capital, 104
veterans, U.S. military, 25, 61, 233, 289, 359, 391–392
    in corporate posturing, 3, 67, 175, 227
    homeless, 29
    in small businesses, 100–101
    veterans harmed, 2, 7–8, 349, 389
    veteran suicides, 2, 73
ViaSat, 23, 170, 262, 274, 304
Vision 2030, 174–175
V-22 tiltrotor aircraft, 146–147, 192, 273

W

Wahhabism, 16
waivers, 111–112
war crimes, 33, 87, 91, 110, 112, 145, 182, 369, 372, 396, 401
War on Drugs, 29, 59, 95, 277, 287–288
    mirroring War on Terror, 296–297
    terrorizing families, 287
War on Terror, 9, 14, 17, 60–61, 75, 135, 257, 282, 366, 369
    academic support, 61
    counterterrorism funds, 94–95
    eco-terrorism, 150
    lawyers leading U.S. counterterrorism bureaucracies, 107–108
    legalese sustaining, 109
    likelihood of a terrorism, 278–279
    lucrative nature of, 134
    threats / hyping as threats, 139, 185–186, 278, 293, 343, 379
wealth / wealth gap, x, 20, 27, 29, 35, 72, 77, 114, 125, 291, 297–298, 363, 395
    of industrial nodes, 21–24
Wilson, Heather, 54, 219, 365
Work, Robert, 235, 254, 320

Y

Yale University, 210, 228
Yemen, 29, 52, 65, 108, 189, 311, 342, 366, 395
    Saudi-led destruction of, 173–176,
        188–189, 372

Z

Zionism, xiii, 11, 60–61, 82, 168–173, 176, 210,
        292, 300, 401

CPSIA information can be obtained
at www.ICGtesting.com
Printed in the USA
FSHW012042250221
78946FS